SUPRANATIONAL CRIMINOLOGY:
TOWARDS A CRIMINOLOGY OF INTERNATIONAL CRIMES

SERIES SUPRANATIONAL CRIMINAL LAW: CAPITA SELECTA, Volume 6

Published in the series:
1. *Supranational Criminal Law: a System Sui Generis*, ROELOF HAVEMAN, OLGA KAVRAN and JULIAN NICHOLLS (eds.)
2. *Double Jeopardy Without Parameters: Re-characterization in International Criminal Law*, OLAOLUWA OLUSANYA
3. *Harmonization of Criminal Law in Europe*, ERLING JOHANNES HUSABØ and ASBJØRN STRANDBAKKEN (eds.)
4. *Sentencing and Sanctioning in Supranational Criminal Law*, ROELOF HAVEMAN and OLAOLUWA OLUSANYA (eds.)
5. *Application of International Humanitarian and Human Rights Law to the Armed Conflicts of the Sudan: Complementary or Mutually Exclusive Regimes?*, MOHAMED ABDELSALAM BABIKER

Editors:
Dr. Roelof H. Haveman (editor in chief)
Dr. Paul J.A. De Hert (European Law)
Dr. Alette Smeulers (International Criminal Law and Criminology)

MAASTRICHT SERIES IN HUMAN RIGHTS, Volume 7

Published in the series:
1. INEKE BOEREFIJN, FONS COOMANS, JENNY GOLDSCHMIDT, RIKKI HOLTMAAT and RIA WOLLESWINKEL (eds.), *Temporary Special Measures – Accelerating de facto Equality of Women under Article 4 (1) UN Convention on the Elimination of All Forms of Discrimination against Women*
2. FONS COOMANS and MENNO T. KAMMINGA (eds.), *Extraterritorial Application of Human Rights Treaties*
3. KOEN DE FEYTER and FELIPE GÓMEZ ISA (eds.), *Privatisation and Human Rights in the Age of Globalisation*
4. INGRID WESTENDORP and RIA WOLLESWINKEL (eds.), *Violence in the Domestic Sphere*
5. FONS COOMANS (ed.), *Justiciability of Economic and Social Rights*
6. JAN C.M. WILLEMS (ed.), *Developmental and Autonomy Rights of Children: Empowering Children, Caregivers and Communities. 2nd revised edition*

The *Maastricht Centre for Human Rights* supervises research in the field of human rights conducted at Maastricht University's Faculty of Law. This research is interdisciplinary, with a particular focus on public international law, criminal law and social sciences. The titles in the Series contribute to a better understanding of different aspects of human rights *sensu lato*.

SUPRANATIONAL CRIMINOLOGY: TOWARDS A CRIMINOLOGY OF INTERNATIONAL CRIMES

Alette SMEULERS and Roelof HAVEMAN (eds.)

intersentia

Antwerp – Oxford – Portland

Distribution for the UK:
Hart Publishing Ltd.
16C Worcester Place
Oxford OX1 2JW
UK
Tel: +44 1865 51 75 30
Fax: +44 1865 51 07 10

Distribution for the USA and Canada:
International Specialized Book Services
920 NE 58th Ave Suite 300
Portland, OR 97213
USA
Tel: +1 800 944 6190 (toll free)
Tel: +1 503 287 3093
Fax: +1 503 280 8832
Email: info@isbs.com

Distribution for Switzerland and
Germany:
Schulthess Verlag
Zwingliplatz 2
CH-8022 Zürich
Switzerland
Tel: +41 1 251 93 36
Fax: +41 1 261 63 94

Distribution for other countries:
Intersentia Publishers
Groenstraat 31
BE-2640 Mortsel
Belgium
Tel: +32 3 680 15 50
Fax: +32 3 658 71 21

This research project was financed by the Netherlands Organisation for Scientific Research (NWO – Veni Vernieuwingsimpuls), the Faculty of Law of the VU University Amsterdam and the Maastricht Centre for Human Rights.

Netherlands Organisation for Scientific Research

 Maastricht Centre for Human Rights

vrije Universiteit amsterdam

Supranational Criminology: Towards a Criminology of International Crimes
Alette Smeulers and Roelof Haveman (eds.)

© 2008 Intersentia
Antwerp – Oxford – Portland
http://www.intersentia.com

ISBN 978-90-5095-791-5
D/2008/7849/41
NUR 825

TABLE OF CONTENTS

III.   TOWARDS AN INTEGRATIVE STUDY OF INTERNATIONAL CRIMES AND STATE-CORPORATE CRIMINALITY: A RECIPROCAL APPROACH TO GROSS HUMAN RIGHTS VIOLATIONS

PART II.   MEASURE AND MAP INTERNATIONAL CRIMES: RESEARCH METHODOLOGY

IV.   MISSING PIECES. SOME THOUGHTS ON THE METHODOLOGY OF THE EMPIRICAL STUDY OF INTERNATIONAL CRIMES AND OTHER GROSS HUMAN RIGHTS VIOLATIONS

V. THE UNACCOUNTABLE GENOCIDE. A CASE STUDY OF THE ROLES OF THE U.S. STATE DEPARTMENT AND U.S. GOVERNMENT ACCOUNTABILITY OFFICE IN CALCULATING THE DARFUR DEATH TOLL

PART III. INVESTIGATE THE CAUSES OF INTERNATIONAL CRIMES

VI. GENOCIDE, WAR CRIMES AND CRIMES AGAINST HUMANITY IN CENTRAL AFRICA: A CRIMINOLOGICAL EXPLORATION

IX. DESTRUCTIVE BELIEFS: GENOCIDE AND THE ROLE OF IDEOLOGY

Alex ALVAREZ... 213

X. PERPETRATORS OF INTERNATIONAL CRIMES: TOWARDS A TYPOLOGY

Alette SMEULERS 233

PREFACE

The last few decades have witnessed an unprecedented reorientation of international criminal law. For long, international criminal law was perceived to deal mainly with piracy and war crimes. But today, after the creation of international criminal tribunals and with the benefit of the jurisprudence of these tribunals, the normative reach of combating international criminality has enormously expanded. This is particularly illustrated by the spelling out of the scope and nature of crimes against humanity in the Rome Statute of the International Criminal Court and concomitant practice of international tribunals, for instance as regards the international criminalisation of rape as a crime against humanity. At the same time international crimes are not only addressed to by norms and instruments of international criminal justice, focusing on the criminal responsibility of perpetrators, but also human rights instruments are treating international crimes as gross violations of human rights entailing state responsibility. Thus, the Convention against Torture and Other Cruel, Inhuman or Degrading Treatment or Punishment has established a system of universal jurisdiction over the crime of torture requiring international cooperation and judicial assistance between State Parties.

It must also be noted that international law and practice as evident in the current status of international humanitarian law and international human rights law, is increasingly taking the human factor into account, as a pressing collective and individual concern. Already in earlier years, instruments and procedures were developed to prevent and combat policies and practices that constitute gross violations of human rights falling within the category of international crimes, but such instruments and procedures did not implicate responsible leaders and executioners who were shielded by rules and practices of immunity and impunity. Neither did the victims of these policies and practices receive the attention, the acknowledgement and the care due to them. Their fate and their interests, as individual persons, as families and as communities were largely ignored. It is only in recent years that the international community, increasingly aware that lasting peace and sustainable development must be based on the requirements of restorative justice and retributive justice, is more engaged in efforts to mete out criminal justice to perpetrators of international crimes and to afford reparations to victims of gross violations of human rights and serious violations of international humanitarian law. The human person is moving in international law from anonymity to identity, from invisibility to visibility, from object to subject, as a person invested with rights and responsibilities.

The present book seeks to bring in various ways international crimes within the realm and reach of criminology and appears to reinforce the trend just outlined of treating international crimes as acts and omissions where *people* are abusers and *people* are sufferers. Who are the persons who commit international crimes or allow these crimes to happen? What are their motivations? Under what conditions are they committing these crimes? What is the role of the state, the autocratic state, the militarised state and the failed state? Are religious and ethnic factors playing a role as well as racist attitudes and behaviour? What is the involvement of non-state actors such as transnational corporations or terrorist and other criminal gangs and groups? These are questions which also beset the minds of policy and law makers at national and international levels in their efforts to prevent and combat international crimes and in developing strategic plans to that effect. Similar questions are in the minds of national and international adjudicators who are called upon to render justice. Concerned sectors of civil society, defending human rights including the rights of women and children, are also seeking answers to these questions. The present book shows a variety of approaches and is to be welcomed as a constructive undertaking to raise a series of pertinent questions relating to international crimes and to discuss them from a criminological perspective. The book assumes that criminologists do not have a monopoly in providing full and final answers to the questions raised. At the same time it also proves that criminology can render an important contribution in outlining and defining the ramifications of international crimes and that in this respect a great deal of intensive work is still to be done.

Theo van Boven

I. CRIMINOLOGY IN A STATE OF DENIAL – TOWARDS A CRIMINOLOGY OF INTERNATIONAL CRIMES: SUPRANATIONAL CRIMINOLOGY[1]

Roelof HAVEMAN and Alette SMEULERS

1.   INTRODUCTION

International crimes, such as war crimes, crimes against humanity and genocide, are extreme forms of violence. The fight against these crimes is high on the international political agenda. Exemplary are the efforts to bring peace to northern Uganda in a peace accord between the Lords Resistance Army (LRA) of Joseph Kony and the Ugandan government. This is not amazing, considering the high number of people being killed and the extreme damage caused. In case a situation is qualified as a threat to international peace and security the UN Security Council, on the basis of Chapter VII of the UN Charter, has the power to intervene by military means, breaching the otherwise absolute right to national sovereignty of states. One anxiously seeks ways also on other levels to prevent these kinds of extreme violence. Repression after the crimes – by punishing offenders – also has a high priority on the international political agenda. Crimes against humanity, genocide and war crimes have been made punishable by many international conventions. The offenders are considered *hostes humani generis*: enemies of all humankind. By many it is considered important to prosecute and try these offenders, in order to counter impunity. Criminologists however have hardly studied war crimes, crimes against humanity and genocide. That is remarkable. The tribunals of Nuremberg and Tokyo after World War II marked the birth of an international criminal law superseding individual states, and especially since the end of the Cold War supranational criminal law has gained momentum. Examples of this rapid development are the establishment of the International Criminal Tribunal for the former Yugoslavia (ICTY) in 1993, a year later followed by a similar tribunal for Rwanda (ICTR) and the establishment of a couple of

---

[1]   This article is partly based upon two articles previously published in Dutch by the respective authors in 2005 and 2006 (Haveman 2005, Smeulers 2006) in which they strongly argue for the development of supranational criminology as a separate specialisation within criminology.

internationalised tribunals during the following years. The establishment of the International Criminal Court (ICC) in 1998 and its becoming effective four years later has been an important milestone in this development. In particular the ICC has major implications, not the least on a national level, as State Parties to the treaty have to criminalise war crimes, crimes against humanity and genocide in their domestic laws.

One would expect that criminologists closely follow this development by studying the crimes and all related aspects, as they do with respect to crimes on a national level. But the contrary is true. It is difficult to understand the reason for this inertia. Criminology is the field of science that studies criminality in all its manifestations. These crimes have been criminalised as 'domestic crimes' in many countries already for decades. The possibility to try these crimes on a supranational level since the early nineties of the 20th century is a confirmation of the serious nature of these crimes. It is therefore hard to see why the most extreme forms of criminality, namely war crimes, crimes against humanity and genocide – the latter often being called the 'crime of crimes' – are not studied by criminologists. In our opinion it is important that the study of these crimes grows into a separate and fully fledged specialisation within criminology. By studying this form of criminality from a criminological perspective using its theoretical framework and research methodology, and by integrating all the research done in other disciplines, like history, political science, sociology, psychology and many other sciences, criminology might contribute to the prevention of these kinds of extreme violence. Given the huge numbers of victims it is worth giving it a try.

2.   THE HARVEST OF A CENTURY

Reading criminological publications of the past century one has to conclude that criminologists have written very little on war crimes, crimes against humanity and genocide. This is not to say that these crimes are new and were not committed until recently. On the contrary: the 20th century has been a very violent era in this respect. Many disciplines have realised this and have acted correspondingly. In particular since the fall of the Iron Curtain in 1989 a new branch of criminal law has developed at a very fast pace: supranational criminal law (Haveman et al. 2003). And much has been published about war crimes, crimes against humanity and genocide, about the situations in which these crimes take place, about possible interventions to prevent or stop these crimes from being committed, and about the efficacy of these interventions. These publications however have all been written in the field of criminal law, public international law, psychology, history, sociology, journalism, polemology and political science, in short, in many scientific domains, but remarkably little has been published by criminologists.

It is interesting to note that many of these publications could be called criminological, albeit that they have not been written by authors who label themselves as criminologists, nor have these publications been published in criminological journals or used by criminologists. Some best selling examples from the abundance of such literature are the following: *Eichmann in Jerusalem* by Hannah Arendt (1963); *Ordinary men* by Christopher Browning (1992); books that describe the process which in the end led to a genocide and its aftermath, such as Presser's *Ondergang* [Downfall] (1965), Mamdani's history of the Rwandan genocide (2001), Klemperer's diaries (1995) and his book on the language of the Third Reich (1975), Stover & Weinstein's *My Neighbor, My Enemy* (2004); many biographies that try to explain the character of the 'leaders', such as Kershaw's biography of Hitler (1998, 2000), and Overy's *Interrogations* (2001); journalistic books about offenders (Hatzfeld 2005), child soldiers (Dongala 2003), and stories of a genocide, such as Gourevitch's *We wish to inform you that tomorrow we will be killed with our families* (1998). Another example: the discipline of what has become known as *transitional justice* has led to many publications on the aftermath of conflict situations, for instance about truth and reconciliation commissions (Hayner 1994; Krog 1999).

Compared to the wealth of publications on war crimes, crimes against humanity and genocide in other scientific domains, the number of specific criminological publications is disappointing. Yacoubian (2000) for instance analysed publications during the years 1990–1998 in 13 'prestigious periodicals devoted to the discipline of criminology' and presentations at the 'annual meetings of the American Society of Criminology (ASC) and the Academy of Criminal Justice Sciences (ACJS)'. Of more than 12,000 papers presented during that period at the ASC conferences only twelve (0.001%) dealt with genocide; only six out of 7,000 (again 0.001%) papers presented at the ACJS conferences were about genocide; only 1 of the 3,000 articles in periodicals dealt with genocide. A substantive part of the criminological literature on crimes against humanity, war crimes and genocide consists of difficult to find conference papers. Several scholars have argued strongly in favour of criminology paying more attention to crimes against humanity (Schwendiger & Schwendiger 1970; Chambliss 1989; Cohen 1993, 2001; Laufer 1999; Day and Vandiver 2000; Friedrichs 2000a; Hogg 2002; Drumbl 2003–2004; Roberts & McMillan 2003; Bijleveld 2005; Fijnaut 2005; Woolford 2006), which is a strong indication that this does not happen sufficiently. Others apply criminological theories to the supranational penal practice, in particular genocide (Sherman 2000; Drumbl 2000, 2002; Alvarez 1999; Day & Vandiver 2000; Afflitto 2000; Yacoubian 1997, 2000, 2003). Without doubt this enumeration of criminological publications is far from complete. The conclusion however that there is little attention for crimes against humanity, war crimes and genocide within criminology is not too daring.

3.   PROS, CONS AND DENIAL

If indeed it is true that criminology shows no interest in war crimes, crimes against humanity and genocide, in the situations in which these acts take place and in effective interventions, the questions loom: why this inertia? Are there arguments that speak for the development of a supranational criminology? If yes, why have they been neglected?

A first explanation for criminological inertia might be that supranational criminal law as a separate field of penal law is relatively young, and has grown into maturity only since the establishment of the *ad hoc* international criminal tribunals in the early nineties. The crimes were qualified as such within international law but rarely implemented in national law. International criminal law was furthermore seldom effectively enforced. Criminologists often define crime as human behaviour that has been *criminalised by the legislator* (Kaiser 1988; Van Dijk et al. 2002). Another definition defines crime as *deviant* behaviour (Sutherland 1947; Jäger 1989, 7). These definitions become problematic when interpreted in a restrictive manner, for instance when 'legislator' refers to the *national* legislator or 'deviant' behaviour only entails behaviour that has been labelled as such by the *national* state. In these restrictive interpretations the state determines what is punishable, hence what has to be considered as crime. War crimes, crimes against humanity and genocide are outside the scope of such a definition, as it is mainly the international community that criminalises these kinds of behaviour and labels them as such in treaties and conventions.[2] Although many of these treaties urge states to embody these provisions into their national legislation, many states have not done so until recently, and if they did so before, have not enforced the provisions. This is one of the reasons that these crimes fell outside the scope of the definition of crime, used by criminologists to define their research area.

This has changed dramatically with the establishment of many *ad hoc* international(ised) courts and tribunals since the early nineties; the domain of international criminal law that deals with these crimes has grown rapidly. Within the past decade supranational criminal law has expanded enormously and at an

---

[2]   Provisions on these types of crime can be found in treaties which address states as to what kind and type of behaviour and conduct is acceptable. The Hague Conventions (1917) and the Geneva Conventions (1948) proscribe legitimate behaviour in times of war, international human rights treaties such as the International Covenant on Civil and Political Rights (1966) and regional treaties such as the European Convention on Human Rights (1950), the American Convention on Human Rights (1969), and the African Charter on Human and Peoples Rights proscribe what behaviour and conduct is expected from states in peace time. These treaties entail provisions that provide that states may not torture or kill. Provisions which actually state that the individual perpetrators can and should be held accountable can be found in treaties like the Geneva Conventions (1948) and its two Additional Protocols (1977), the Genocide Convention (1948) and the Torture Convention (1984).

extremely fast pace. Except for the ICTY, the ICTR and the International Criminal Court (ICC) a handful of internationalised tribunals have been established, such as in Sierra Leone, Kosovo, East-Timor and Cambodia (Ambos and Othman 2003; Romano et al. 2004). During the same ten years the discussion on the phenomenon of truth and reconciliation commissions has gained momentum, with the South African Truth and Reconciliation Commission an impressive example (e.g. Sarkin 2004b; Krog 1999). The ancient 'national' concept of crime has been superseded by a new crime concept embracing international developments. There is no reason why this development should not be reflected in the field of study of criminology. Hence, there is no longer any reason to exclude certain forms of crime: whether it is violence, murder, genocide, theft, the dumping of outdated medicines or chemical waste in the third world, crimes against humanity, rape, the illegal exploitation of natural resources in Africa or war crimes; all this belongs to the domain of criminology.

A second explanation why criminology has not studied this type of criminality so far is that war crimes, crimes against humanity and genocide are often committed with some involvement of states. War crimes can only be committed during a violent and armed conflict and hence during a period of systematic and structural violence; crimes against humanity are by definition part of widespread and large scale violations, just like genocide which is a crime committed with the explicit intent to destroy a particular group in whole or in part. These kinds of crimes can hardly be committed by one individual alone, but require a collective of people. Within legal science international crimes are therefore described as forms of structural criminality or system criminality. The majority of these crimes are committed at the instigation of the state or are sanctioned and condoned by the state or by state officials, either or not in the exercise of their function. The fact that states are suddenly the perpetrators and no longer merely the authorities who try to prevent and punish crime, turns the theoretical framework of criminologists upside down and gives it a complete new dimension. To conventional mainstream criminology 'state crime' might seem like a *contradictio in terminis.*

'State crime' can be defined as 'state organisational deviance involving the violation of human rights' (Green & Ward 2004, 2). This term makes the involvement of states in crime explicit. The criminological concept of state crime overlaps, although not entirely, the legal concept of international crimes. On the one hand state crime covers more: not all forms of state crime qualify as international crimes.[3] On the other hand not all international crimes are forms of state crime, as for instance also rebel armies and terrorist groups can commit international crimes. In many cases however international crimes are committed

---

[3]   International crimes are the crimes which can be prosecuted by all states within the international community on the basis of the universality principle and can be prosecuted by the ICC: war crimes, crimes against humanity and genocide.

by the state and hence can be labelled state crimes. This implies a fundamentally different starting point when studying this type of criminality: no longer is the state the instance to formulate the normative framework on right and wrong and to act accordingly by prosecuting and trying offenders of these norms, as with ordinary crimes; the state now is the offender itself, for which an international penal framework has been developed. This means that the nature of the crimes and the context in which they are committed are completely different from the nature and context of ordinary crimes.

These two factors – notably that the state is often the offender and that the violated normative framework is the international framework – turn the study of this behaviour completely upside down. This is true for the role of the state, the type of crime committed and the type of perpetrators. If a regime itself turns criminal by for example committing genocide then the perpetrators who physically commit the crime can no longer be said to commit an 'act of deviance' but rather an 'act of obedience', or as defined more appropriately by Kelman and Hamilton (1989), the perpetrator commits a 'crime of obedience'. If the state is very powerful and repressive the consequence may be that law-abiding citizens, conformists and passive followers, become involved in international crimes. Adolf Eichmann is often considered the typical obedient bureaucrat who merely took responsibility towards his superiors and to obeying their orders instead of taking responsibility for the overall outcome of the policies he was executing and coordinating (in his case the transportation of the Jews to the concentration camps and thus their extermination). Such a mentality is not uncommon in modern bureaucracies; quite the contrary, modernity and modern bureaucracies promote this type of functional and technical responsibility (Cf. Bauman 1989). Modernity breeds the armchair perpetrator and exposed the – what Hannah Arendt (1963) called – banality of evil.

Regimes which turn evil such as Nazi Germany are characterised by an *Umwertung aller Werten*, the inversion of right and wrong, of normal and abnormal, and the fact that many individuals willingly and without taking further responsibility themselves, without further thinking about the consequences, become loyal executors of the state implied policy which might be the extermination of an undesired group and thus genocide. Studying violence of a state and genocide is consequently not per definition any longer centred on deviant behaviour by individuals within a state, but at least as much around the question how state violence and genocide could have become the norm within a state. The questions which need to be asked in order to understand state crime and international crimes are new and different compared to the questions to be posed when studying ordinary, common crime.

In other words: we have to study all those individuals who keep the criminal and malignant system moving. The most important question is thus not why they show *deviant* behaviour, but why they *obey and conform* themselves and do not revolt. When studying people who committed war crimes, crimes against humanity and genocide we quickly come to the conclusion that these offenders are neither deviant, nor sick or mentally disturbed, but on the contrary conformists to the extreme. For a discipline like criminology in which one is used to looking for defects or risk factors that explain why a certain individual behaves deviantly, this means an entirely different way of reasoning. It means that an entirely different starting point has to be chosen when studying international crimes compared to cases in which ordinary crimes are studied. This may very well be one of the main reasons for why this 'big evil' has been kept outside the scope of the classical theoretical traditions within criminology.

A third explanation, which follows from the abovementioned, is that the issue of crimes against humanity and genocide might be too complex and too difficult to grasp. Whoever really tries to understand the background of the conflicts in for instance Rwanda, the Sudan or former Yugoslavia is easily discouraged by the complexity of it (Babiker 2007; Bijleveld & Haveman 2005). However, isn't it exactly the task of criminologists to analyse and explain at first sight unexplainable and complex problems? As also on a domestic level criminologists have taken up the task of studying the causes of crime and to search for ways to prevent crime from being committed. This is exactly the challenge for *supranational* criminology.

On the other hand it may be true that traditional research methods are only to a limited extent usable in situations in which crimes against humanity take place. Quoting Yacoubian (2000, 14):

> 'Field research presents physical dangers that make the standard problems of the method pale in comparison; survey research is abstruse because it would be difficult to obtain anything but availability samples; experiments are inappropriate; and the use of unobtrusive measures is severely hampered by, first, access to official records, and second, language barriers. These issues are further confounded by the need for a researcher to obtain at least a reasonable familiarity with the history and the culture of the area under study. The time needed to do so is unreasonable for academics, particularly those that have not yet earned tenure.'

If this is true, and to a certain extent it may very well be, it rather seems to be a reason to develop new research methods and techniques, appropriate to study this field of crime. Moreover one may ask why this argument apparently does not apply to all those other disciplines which have focused on war crimes, crimes against humanity and genocide. After all, not every study needs field work. The application in theory of existing criminological knowledge on the supranational level, next to and together with other disciplines, may lead to new insights. Wouldn't it be a great challenge to apply the social control theory and theories regarding moral panic or blaming and shaming to the supranational level? The criminologist, traditionally equipped with a wide and varied arsenal of research methods and techniques, may contribute substantially to the knowledge of international crimes by performing comparing analyses and developing typologies that give a better insight into the diversity of situations which lead to massive violence and a variety of other international crimes (Jonassohn & Björnson, 1998). Criminology itself can gain new insights from this because current theories can be tested and adopted, and new ones will be developed.

Some consider it problematic that the criminologist in doing so enters the realm of the political scientist. This should not be an obstacle however. Embracing the part of political science that deals with these forms of crime can only be enriching for criminology as a science. In particular we think here of knowledge of political power relations in a state, of core concepts such as political power, violence and force, as well as of development of theories on how a democratic regime can transform into a repressive state. A study into the functions of repression and the nature of dictatorships and totalitarian regimes is indispensable for the study of crimes against humanity and genocide in particular. Also the discipline of polemology is important in this respect. It may not always be clear where political science ends and criminology starts. However, comparable problems have emerged and have been surmounted with respect to psychology and sociology. It therefore must also be possible with respect to political sciences.

Could it be then – a fourth explanation – that because so many others in other disciplines are already writing about these crimes that criminologists think that there is nothing to add for them? This is possible. But isn't criminology in fact the combination of all those other disciplines, giving it its own flavour? Criminology, which by definition is an inter or multidisciplinary science, may fulfil an important role on the supranational level. Criminologists may be the intermediary discipline between psychologists, historians, sociologists, criminal lawyers, polemologists, conflict managers and all those others who study wars and genocides. Criminology then serves as the great interdisciplinary mediator, bringing together insights of other disciplines that already for a long time have studied situations in which atrocities take place, each with its own objectives. Without doubt this field of research is quite complex, and it may be difficult to decide where to start, but isn't this exactly one of the main factors that could make supranational criminology so challenging?

Yet another explanation for the lack of interest of criminology in war crimes, crimes against humanity and genocide may be that they are committed too far away from home to attract the attention of American and European criminologists, who are already completely preoccupied with national – and directly felt – crimes, and who gather their necessary contacts amongst practitioners (including 'criminals') nearby (Yacoubian 2000). Against this explanation is that the distance between researchers and practitioners has considerably been bridged by the establishment of international tribunals in Europe, Asia and Africa. Large scale conflict situations all over the world are broadly covered by the media on a daily basis. Last but not least some of these kinds of crimes are committed by nationals of many Western countries, for instance during peace keeping operations elsewhere in the world. Related to this is the argument that the societies in which war crimes, crimes against humanity or genocide take place often find themselves in a bad state, with scientists – if any – having no means to do proper research themselves. This creates some kind of moral obligation for scientists elsewhere in the world to choose this field of criminology as their focus, trying to find possibilities to prevent new atrocities from happening. Further, these international crimes are not ordinary crimes, but crimes that, due to their nature and the scale on which they are committed, have far reaching consequences for the victims, for the societies in which they are committed and for the world as a whole. The 20th century has seen an estimated 191 million victims of international crimes (WHO 2002). They warrant our attention.

Is lack of money the reason for the criminological inertia? Should governments be more active in financially stimulating these kinds of studies? Without doubt this is important, but can it explain the almost total lack of research in this field?

It seems as if there is no real convincing argument for criminology to exclude crimes against humanity, genocide and war crimes from their field of study, except maybe for the normative framework-argument. This argument might have been valid although we should not ignore the fact that such a framework has already existed for a longer period than one is inclined to remember: already sixty years ago, after the Second World War, international tribunals were established to try war criminals – in Tokyo and Nuremburg – and also on a domestic level many war criminals have been prosecuted and tried. Since the establishment of the two international tribunals in the early nineties this argument has definitely lost its value.

Maybe the reason mentioned by criminologist Stanley Cohen (2001) is the most plausible, that is 'denial':

> '[P]eople, organizations, governments or whole societies are presented with information that is too disturbing, threatening or anomalous to be fully absorbed or openly acknowledged. The information is therefore somehow repressed, disavowed, pushed aside or reinterpreted. Or else the information 'registers' well enough, but its implications – cognitive, emotional or moral – are evaded, neutralized or rationalized away',

as reads the first sentence in his book *States of Denial*. When confronted with extraordinary evil people tend to close their eyes. Criminologists are just like ordinary people. They may nevertheless not shy away from the conclusions of their own research, never mind how impenetrable these crimes are and how discomforting the findings. Hilberg, the famous holocaust historian, remarked: 'Wouldn't you be happier if I had been able to show you that all the perpetrators are crazy?' (Bauman 1989, 83). We definitely would, yes. Instinctively we may try to hide ourselves behind an incriminating finger raised at the offenders as the bad culprits, rather than looking at ourselves. This may be exactly the reason that studies like the one by Goldhagen (1997), spreading the message that it was 'them' instead of 'us', are more popular than studies by Browning (1992), messaging that 'it might very well be us'. Just as people often respond with denial to atrocities or blame the victims, they respond with similar 'states of denial' to the implications of studies into these atrocities, as Cohen remarks (1993, 2001). Understanding that in particular circumstances all of us are capable of torture and genocide is threatening and disastrous for our self-esteem. Hence we prefer to deny this. According to Cohen (1993), this structural denial of human suffering and the nature of the offender have had repercussions in criminology. If this is true, we have to face the truth and break out of this state of denial.

As already has become apparent there is no reason why criminologists *should not* study war crimes, crimes against humanity and genocide, besides there are many reasons why they *should*. Apart from those already mentioned above, several important ones can be added. The most important one is that criminology has a lot to offer. By placing the current state of the art within a criminological framework and by using criminological research tools and methodology, new venues of research can be tackled with greater insight. Of all scientists criminologists are those with specialised knowledge of crime, criminality and criminals: this knowledge comes in very handy when trying to understand how societies become violent and engage in collective violence, how organisations that under ordinary circumstances are law-abiding turn to crime and how ordinary law-abiding citizens can be transformed into perpetrators. Not only can our knowledge of these types of criminality be enhanced enormously but criminology itself can benefit from focusing more on this type of criminality, precisely because this type of criminality is so different from ordinary crime. The role of the state is different and the perpetrators are different, hence research on this type of criminality can be an important test case for many traditional theories on crime. Criminologists should study the way in which criminological theories apply to international crimes, and study the way in which criminological research methods and techniques can be used in cases of international crimes. As Yacoubian (2000, 14) has already explained (see the citation above), it speaks for itself that not all current research methods can be used in cases of international crimes. With respect to criminological theories it has to be studied whether and, if so, to what extent they are valid regarding international crimes.

International crimes have been studied by many scholars from various disciplines. However, although these studies have produced many clarifying and sometimes revolutionary ideas and insights, it often suffers from being too haphazard and without any coordination. The result is a catalogue of case studies from which it is difficult to draw lessons for future research. By being sort of an interdisciplinary umbrella science, criminology could promote the interconnectivity between various studies within different disciplines, by stimulating the development of new theories, binding various case studies together and trying to find new theories or adapting existing theories. Criminology has good credentials to become the necessary integrating factor between various disciplines that currently study situations in which war crimes, crimes against humanity or genocide are committed. Criminology could, for instance, re-study case studies on genocide, such as the holocaust, the genocides in Cambodia during the seventies (Kiernan 1996) and Rwanda in 1994 (Prunier 1997). Until now the focus in those studies has been on the unique aspects and causes of the situations under study. Of course this is necessary but there is a lack of a scientific approach which focuses more on common features of the cases, and asks and answers questions such as: which groups run the greatest risk to be victims of genocide? Are there common phases in the genesis of a genocide and if so, how can they be detected?[4]

Criminology can furthermore give an important impetus to the development of international criminal law. To give just one example: one may question as to whether the concept of individual criminal responsibility, as used in domestic criminal systems with respect to ordinary crimes, can be used also in cases of crimes that can be seen as expressions of systematic or structural criminality and are committed by states. Within this perspective the crimes are seen as collective crimes, with a small upper layer who have the criminal intention, but may be far away from those who physically commit the crimes. The latter group kills, rapes and plunders, but can they be held criminally responsible on the basis of their individual responsibility if they commit the crimes in a situation in which human right violations have been normalised? Without the criminal intent (*mens rea*) a certain act (*actus reus*) cannot be considered a crime, the offender therefore not a criminal. It may be questioned to what extent these basic principles of criminal law – individual criminal responsibility, but also for instance the role of defences (a.o. duress, mental incapability), the function of punishment (a.o. deterrence,

---

[4]   Cf. the 'Indicators of Systematic and Massive Patterns of Racial Discrimination' that may lead to violent conflict and genocide: Committee on the Elimination of Racial Discrimination, 67th session, CERD/C/67/Misc. 8, 19 August 2005.

prevention) – are applicable in cases of war crimes, crimes against humanity and genocide. Do these basic criminal principles correspond with the social reality of the situations in which these crimes are committed and can they therefore explain anything about the offenders? What is the relationship between the 'big machine' and the individual cogs? The development of a typology of offenders, based upon role, rank and motive could explain more about the offenders and tell more about the 'criminal' element in their behaviour. Empirical research examining the current case law of the international courts and tribunals on their compatibility with the social reality of international crimes could give an impetus to the development of a more just and realistic concept of individual criminal responsibility of offenders of war crimes, crimes against humanity and genocide.

Furthermore it is crucial that the fast growing group of criminal lawyers who work in the supranational criminal law field – as scientists or practitioners – learn more about the complexities of their work, and realise that laws and regulations are only a small part of social reality. Roberts & McMillan (2003) were among the first to stress in detail and convincingly the importance of 'criminology in international criminal justice':

'Legal scholars and social scientists must become aware of the international dimensions of their research and scholarship; and international lawyers must be open to alternative approaches, methodologies and perspectives. All must embrace new forms of collaboration'.

A development comparable to the domestic level, where criminal law is 'guided' by criminological insights, is lacking on the supranational level. Concepts used on the supranational level are taken from the national level. The nature of international crimes and the context in which they are committed however is entirely different from the nature and context of domestic crimes.

The last argument for the development of a strong supranational criminology deserves more attention. From a moral point of view we consider that everything possible has to be done to prevent war crimes, crimes against humanity and genocide from happening in the future. Hence it is crucial that we gain more knowledge on effective interventions. Supranational criminology can substantially add to this knowledge, as criminologists are trained to study the causes and to think about the best and most effective means of prevention. On the basis of all knowledge already acquired through sociological, psychological and historical research, it is possible to do fundamental and structural research on the prevention of these crimes in the future. If we know the groups that are most vulnerable to becoming victims of large scale violence like genocide and the reasons for this vulnerability, it may become possible to develop strategies to strengthen their ability to fight against this. If we know why bystanders, both individuals and states, stay inactive upon seeing atrocities happening, we possibly may develop strategies to intervene in an effective manner. If we know more about the offenders and why they commit their crimes, we may develop mechanisms to prevent them from becoming war criminals and the like. If we know what exactly turns a specific situation into an 'atrocity producing situation' we may be able to prevent those situations from developing in the future.

4. TENTATIVE DEMARCATION OF THE FIELD OF STUDY OF SUPRANATIONAL CRIMINOLOGY

The field of study of supranational criminology comprises war crimes, crimes against humanity and genocide, as well as the supranational penal system in which these crimes are prosecuted and tried. Moreover supranational criminology should cover similar behaviour that has not yet been criminalised as such. And supranational criminology should study mechanisms to deal with this behaviour, including the crimes, other than the supranational penal system.

To start with the crimes, these are all part of large scale, widespread or systematic situations. In terms of the ICC Statute[5]:

- War crimes, which in broad lines are the violations of the law of the war, '*in particular when committed as part of a plan or policy or as a part of a large scale commission of such crimes*';[6]
- Crimes against humanity, entailing acts such as killing, deportation and rape, but only '*when committed as part of a widespread or systematic attack directed against any civilian population*';[7]
- Genocide, that is acts such as murder or measures to prevent births, but only when '*committed with intent to destroy, in whole or in part, a national, ethnical, racial or religious group, as such*'.[8]

The behaviour underlying these acts is considered criminal in national legislation but the crimes are not labelled as war crimes, crimes against humanity or acts of genocide and thus do not focus on the particularities of these crimes, namely the large scale or systematic way in which they are committed. The systematic, planned and large scale killing, raping or abuse of (groups of) people, either or not with the intent to destroy them as a group, is what gives these crimes their special character. It has to be stressed that it is not the border crossing aspect that

---

5   Different instruments know different definitions of the groups of crimes; we have opted for the
     ICC definitions as the latest in a row, reflecting the state of the current art.
6   ICC Statute Art. 8
7   ICC Statute Art. 7
8   ICC Statute Art. 6. The term genocide stems from Lemkin 1944.

makes these crimes international crimes. On the contrary: a substantive part of war crimes, crimes against humanity and acts of genocide are committed in internal armed conflicts, without any border crossing whatsoever. This is different for crimes such as trafficking in drugs, weapons or human beings for which the border crossing aspect is more common, and hence by some are referred to as *transnational* crimes rather than as *international* crimes. It is the large scale, widespread and systematic nature of war crimes, crimes against humanity and genocide and their severe and endangering effects that make them a special form of criminality. The crimes are acts against humanity as a whole; the offenders are considered *hostes humani generis*, enemies of humankind in general. As it has been laid down in the ICC Statute: these are 'unimaginable atrocities that deeply shock the conscience of humanity'. It supersedes the interest of individuals and individual states; it is therefore supranational. That is what makes the prosecution of these crimes considered to be of global interest.

Regarding the behaviour that is the object of study, an exclusive focus on criminalised behaviour would be too restrictive. As the focus in 'regular' criminology is not restricted to behaviour that has officially been criminalised, but also includes behaviour that has not yet been criminalised but might as well be – behaviour similar to formally criminalised behaviour – supranational criminology should not restrict itself to the official discourse on what is crime, but also on which behaviour can and should be considered an international crime. Terrorist acts, for instance, have not yet been criminalised all over the world as a separate category of crimes, but in certain aspects these crimes are quite similar to war crimes, crimes against humanity or genocide and can in some cases already qualify as such. An example of a different kind: Africans often point to the fact that there is a 'northern' bias in the definition of crimes against humanity. What about the fact that a substantive part of the world – Africa and Asia – does not have access to effective and in the Western industrialised world, readily available and widely distributed HIV/Aids medicines? Why is it not considered a crime against humanity that these medicines are kept too expensive for developing countries to buy and distribute and thus cause many unnecessary deaths? Why is the destruction of nature (and culture?) as a result of, for instance, oil winning not considered a crime against humanity? Why are 'offenders' restricted to natural persons, is criminal responsibility restricted to individual responsibility, and is it impossible to prosecute and try corporations, such as oil companies or weapons factories?

It is not only the special character of the acts under scrutiny that makes these crimes supranational and in a class of their own, also the penal system that deals with these criminalised acts is supranational and *sui generis*. In particular the International Criminal Court (ICC) has the ambition to grow into a global –

supranational – criminal court. The ICC functions on a supranational level. The State Parties to the ICC Treaty have shared part of their sovereignty with the ICC. It is not the penal system of individual states nor the penal system governing interstate cooperation – which traditionally is called (horizontal) international criminal law: mutual assistance, extradition – that deals with these international crimes, but a penal system on a supranational level, in force for 'the' world in general (albeit for the time being only for the little more than 100 states that have ratified the treaty), and directly applicable to all citizens in that part of the world without any involvement of the national judiciary. There are supranational prosecutors and supranational judges who together prosecute and try suspects, though without a supranational police force. The legal basis of their actions is a supranational criminal code and a supranational code of criminal procedure: the ICC Statute and Rules of Procedure and Evidence. This law is a *sui generis* combination of inquisitorial and adversarial penal systems, of common and civil law, of public international law, international human rights law and criminal law. It is moreover a system that functions on a global level comprising many (legal) cultures rather than in a relatively simple monoculture, as domestic penal systems do (Haveman et al. 2003).

What has been said with regard to the behaviour to be studied, notably that supranational criminology should not be restricted to formally criminalised acts but also cover behaviour similar to formally criminalised behaviour, pertains to the responses to this behaviour as well. A single penal focus would be too restrictive. Broadening one's scope to non-penal approaches could be very interesting. Those non-penal approaches may be partly similar to national alternatives for a penal approach – ADR, for instance – but will be quite different in many aspects at the same time. The nature of the crimes and the circumstances in which they are committed as well as the situation after atrocities have been committed ask for different solutions. There is no supranational police force or social services that exist on a domestic level. In quite a few situations the state has collapsed to a certain degree. This may mean that structural interventions are required rather than punishing or otherwise correcting individuals. In this regard a recently and still growing discipline is interesting to look at: notably what over the past ten years has become known as *transitional justice* and *post-conflict justice*. In the transitional justice discourse a broad spectrum is presented of interventions and responses to atrocities that have been committed by a former regime, differing from situation to situation and expressly not restricted to a penal approach. Five strategies are distinguished,[9] subsequently focusing on individual responsibility (e.g. criminal law, but also 'mixed forms, such as Rwandan *gacaca* and the hybrid courts in Uganda), truth finding (e.g. truth commissions),

---

[9]   See, e.g. the Report of the Secretary-General to the Security Council, *The rule of law and transitional justice in conflict and post-conflict societies*, S/2004/616, 23 August 2004, para 8.

compensation (damages and memorials) (Rombouts 2004), institutional reforms (civil service, judiciary and corporations), and reconciliation (reconciliation commissions and peace education) (Salomon & Nevo 2000).

Summarising, a tentative demarcation shows that the field of study of supranational criminology entails war crimes, crimes against humanity and genocide, behaviour that shows affinity with these crimes, the causes and the situations in which they are committed, as well as possible interventions and their effectiveness; the interventions comprise penal systems – domestic, internationalised and supranational – in which the crimes are prosecuted and tried, as well as non-penal interventions. Research on the supranational criminological field can be summarised as comprising the following groups of issues:

- Defining and conceptualising the respective international crimes;
- Quantifying and mapping of these forms of crime;
- Searching for theories and ideas that may explain and model these forms of crime;
- Analysing and making an inventory of the ways to conduct post-conflict justice;
- Developing preventive and repressive strategies to fight these forms of crime.

5.   OUTLINE OF THE BOOK

The aim of this book is to put supranational criminology, the criminology of international crimes, firmly on the criminological agenda. In the final paragraphs of this chapter we will briefly set out some of the main issues discussed by the contributors to the volume and we will place their contributions within a broader framework. The chapters have been structured alongside the abovementioned issues although an extra part is included in order to give victimology the place it deserves on the criminological agenda. Invited scholars have set out to describe the state of art, present current research and set out lines for future research. It should be read as a start of a more encompassing research agenda of supranational criminology in practice.

5.1. DEFINING AND CONCEPTUALISING INTERNATIONAL CRIMES

The first part of the book is dedicated to the important task of defining and conceptualising state crime. International crimes have not been systematically studied within criminology, but state crime is a well known concept. William Chambliss was one of the first scholars to draw attention to this important and often neglected area of research which focused on the crimes of the powerful. Chambliss devoted his presidential address to the American Society of Criminology in 1988 to *state-organised crime* which he defined as 'acts defined by law as criminal and committed by state officials in the pursuit of their job as representatives of the state' (Chambliss 1989, 184). The concept of state crime has been further conceptualised by authors such as Barak (1991), Friedrichs (1998), Ross (1995 and 1998), Kauzlarich and Kramer (1998), Green and Ward (2004), Friedrichs and Rothe (2006) and in Germany by Jäger (1989) under the heading of *Makrokriminalität*. Most, if not all of these scholars, fall within the tradition of critical criminology. Unfortunately state crime and the systematic study of international crimes is still not a major subject within mainstream criminology.

Other social scientists, like historians, political scientists, sociologists and psychologists, have produced several classical works on, especially, genocide (Kuper 1981; Fein 1990, 1992). New concepts, such as *politicide* and *democide*, which are related to genocide, have been developed (Harff and Gurr 1987; Rummel 1994). Particularly the Holocaust on the Jews during the Second World War has been studied by many scholars. Genocide studies are a growing discipline. Other international crimes such as torture, mass rape and ethnic cleansing have received far less attention within the academic world. The majority of publications on these topics are legal in nature rather than sociological and criminological. One of the major tasks of supranational criminology is to integrate these academic traditions and bring them together to thus repair 'the fundamental historical neglect of criminology' (Friedrichs 2000a).

In the first part of the book Friedrichs and Barak stress the importance of putting the criminology of international crimes on the criminological agenda. Friedrichs notes that this mission is 'an impossibly ambitious project albeit an important one.' Barak stresses virtually the same point by calling for a supranational criminology at this 'historical juncture which is characterised by a process of globalisation and a clash of civilisations'. Both scholars stress that criminologists need to 'think outside the scope of conventional criminological boxes.' In his contribution Friedrichs clarifies the terminological confusion within criminology. One of the major points he addresses is that social harm would represent a key point of departure for supranational criminology. Friedrichs furthermore enumerates the relevant issues within the field of supranational criminology by defining and describing concepts like sovereignty, universal jurisdiction, nationalism, legitimacy, human rights, transitional justice, cosmopolitanism and sustainability. In the third chapter Barak stresses the need to focus on international citizenry and the global community. Many transgressions are committed by nation states and state-corporate alliances and these need to be studied. Barak stresses the important point that not only acts of commission but also acts of omission should be studied as well as the market policies of globalisation that result in the denial of fundamental human rights to whole groups of people.

5.2. QUANTIFYING AND MAPPING CRIMES

The second part of the book focuses on methodological issues. The essence of science is to present conclusions which are based on sound methods and conducted in an unbiased manner. A new field of supranational criminology consequently needs to use methodologically sound tools to conduct research. In the past, especially political scientists or organisations such as the Stockholm International Peace Research Institute, have tried to measure and map the number of armed conflicts in the world and to discover statistically relevant relations between, for example, arms trade and conflicts or have used data on trade, refugee flow, the number of minority groups, etc. This research is important in finding relations between various variables and the incidence of war crimes, crimes against humanity and genocide (Harff 2003). Scholars like Rummel (1994) and Balint (1996a and 1996b) have tried to measure the total number of victims of armed conflicts and international crimes. Recently however more and more detailed studies have been conducted and published on quantifying the damage within a particular conflict (Hagan et al. 2005; Coghlan et al. 2006; Ball et al. 1999, 2002; Ball and Asher 2002; Bijleveld and Morssinkhof 2006). The potential importance of conclusions based on this type of research not only from a scientific point of view but also from a political point of view is paramount. Correct data or otherwise reliable estimates on the number of victims are crucial and will make it possible to identify trends and will not only help us to better understand the causes but will also make it possible to conclude whether or not a specific situation is a genocide.

In her contribution, Bijleveld focuses on the methodology of the empirical study of international crimes. She contends that measuring the incidence of crime is one of the four main domains of criminology and is crucial if the field of supranational criminology wants to develop into a mature field of science which is taken seriously. Bijleveld stresses the importance of methodological sound research but also warns that there are particular methodological complications in estimating the number of victims: the doubly-dark number, the lack of baseline data, the survivor bias in victim surveys, the security issues, the underreporting of some crimes (especially rape). Bijleveld concludes that researchers have to accept some uncertainty and should respect the need to gauge their findings against other studies. This is the only way to constantly refine the research methodology.

The Darfur crisis and more specifically calculating the death toll thereof is the central focus of Hagan's contribution entitled, 'The unaccountable genocide'. Political issues and aims can influence death toll estimates. A remarkable point in relation to the Darfur crisis is that the U.S. government had already qualified this crisis as genocide, but later seemed to retract this. Qualifying a crisis as genocide has political ramifications (Power 2001, 2002). Labelling a conflict as genocide not only legitimises an international intervention, it even obliges the international community to intervene. Hagan discusses the various methodologies used to estimate death tolls and concludes that 'the State Department has inappropriately applied concepts and methods from a population health paradigm, while ignoring the relevancy of a crime victimisation approach.' Like Bijleveld, Hagan calls for a sound methodological approach based on expertise from criminologists specialised in crime victimisation approaches to calculate the data.

5.3. THE AETIOLOGY OF INTERNATIONAL CRIMES

The next few chapters, in part III of the book, focus on the causes of international crimes. The authors have tried to look at this type of criminality from a criminological perspective. In their contribution, Rothe and Mullins examine the aetiology behind war crimes, crimes against humanity and genocide in, especially, Central Africa by using a typically criminological framework in which the basic modalities of crime are studied, namely: motivation, opportunity, constraints and enactment patterns. In contrast to mainstream criminology they use four different levels of analysis: international, macro, meso and micro. Among other things they conclude that an unstable global economy can have a detrimental effect on states and that global forces can enhance criminogenic factors.

The central argument in Cunneen's contribution is that 'many contemporary states are built on crimes committed against colonised and enslaved peoples'. Colonial practice and policy must be placed in the context of state crime, as the structural breaches of human rights must be considered a form of state crime. In his chapter Cunneen is particularly focused on the indigenous peoples of Australia, Canada and the US who were excluded when these countries became liberal democracies. Examples of such violations are deprivation of liberty, deprivation of parental rights, abuses of power and violation of international human rights standards, forced labour and governmental fraud. Racism was institutionalised. 'Definitions of state crime clearly need to be able to incorporate these types of crime [as they are] some of the most profound injustices perpetrated within the boundaries of liberal democracies.'

In the next chapter Huisman tackles the role of corporations and their representatives as perpetrators of or accomplices to international crimes. In the first part of the chapter Huisman conceptualises corporate crime, state-corporate crime and international crime. In the second part he states that the involvement of corporations with international crimes can be studied from the perspective of corporate crime. According to Huisman the globalisation of business has criminogenic aspects: they offer illegal opportunities, create motives to use these opportunities (easy profit) and make it possible for offenders to get away with it. There is a discrepancy in the fact that it is beyond dispute that corporations have a moral and legal responsibility to respect human rights but that corporate liability is not yet an accepted phenomenon within international criminal law.

Alvarez describes why a genocidal ideology is a crucial feature of genocide. Belief systems profoundly influence our personal identities as human beings and our perceptions of the world around us. The ideology is the intellectual framework of beliefs that provides purpose and meaning for the destruction of a population. Perpetrators kill because they perceive it as just and moral to do so. In general, ideologies have a basic structure consisting of membership, activities, goals, a set of norms and values, position and group relations and resources. Ideologies are strongly influenced by nationalistic, historical, scientific and religious precepts and are clearly influenced by culture. A genocidal ideology does not grow overnight. It builds on existing stereotypical images of a specific minority group. Nationalism, past-victimisation, dehumanisation, an absolutist worldview, utopianism and the tendency to scapegoat a certain group are recurrent themes in ideologies which enable genocide.

In the next chapter the focus is on the perpetrators. Smeulers concludes that despite the horrendous nature of crimes such as war crimes, crimes against humanity and genocide, the perpetrators of these crimes are usually ordinary people who act within extraordinary circumstances. Within these extraordinary circumstances people get caught up in a malignant system and are transformed into perpetrators. Ten types of perpetrators who all play their own specific role within a destructive state apparatus are distinguished. International crimes can only be explained by understanding the unanimous accord in which these perpetrators act. The ten types are the criminal mastermind, the careerist, the fanatic, the devoted warrior, the profiteer, the professional, the conformist, the follower, the criminal/sadist and the compromised perpetrator. All these types of perpetrators are indispensable 'lethal cogs' (Alvarez 2001).

The two final chapters in this part of the book critically analyse the American War on Terror. In her chapter on the sociology of torture Martha Huggins contends that the prisoner abuse in Iraq, Afghanistan and Guantanamo Bay could have been predicted. Torture is a socio-organisational dynamic which is nurtured and sustained by definable elements that promote, hide and justify it. Crucial components are mislabelling torture, employing ideologies which support and promote it and legal means to justify it. Torture is then elevated to the organizational level: multiple actors including perpetrators and facilitators interact within a hierarchical division of labour through organisational and insularity and secrecy while encouraging and rewarding competition. The consequences thereof are impunity. Only on rare occasions are a few allegedly rotten apples prosecuted 'leaving the larger torture system and its powerful facilitators essentially intact.'

A more philosophical approach to the American War on Terror is taken by Michael Welch in the next chapter. Welch compares America's policies in the War on Terror with Foucault's exploration of power and punishment by making many references to historical developments. Targeting specific groups as unlawful combatants and having them stand trial before military courts rather than civilian courts set the stage for a series of crucial political and military decisions that reconfigure the economy of the power of punishment in the War on Terror. Welch compares these trends with the monarchical power in the classic age and the evolution from penal reform to counter-law. Because the militarised trials undermine due process and the rights to a fair trial, they leave detainees like those at Guantanamo Bay in a legal black hole.

5.4. THE RESPONSE TO CRIME

In the fourth part of the book the focus is on the various responses to international crimes. Jennifer Balint addresses the problem that the law possesses insufficient tools to address international or state crime. International crimes are different from ordinary crimes because they are committed 'in the name of the state' and carried out within the framework of the institutions of the state often as a resultant of political manipulation. The two main problems are that the particular dimensions of international crime are inadequately addressed through legal processes and that the law lacks specificity. Balint gives an overview of approaches which have been taken to address international crime and concludes that the predominant means have been war crimes trials in which individuals were held accountable. Despite the efforts of international tribunals to address the criminality of organisations the dominant approach has failed to conceptualise international crime as acts perpetrated by institutions of the state and thus fails to recognise the structural and historical dimensions. According to Balint, addressing state crime requires the unravelling of the institutional responsibility of the state and civil institutions, and providing for the possibility of institutional transformation and restoration.

Stephan Parmentier, Kris Vanspauwen and Elmar Weitekamp argue that restorative justice mechanisms may offer a more balanced approach towards the victims and perpetrators of mass violence than retributive justice. The strength of (international) criminal justice mechanisms and other retributive justice mechanisms lies in the establishment of factual truth and criminal responsibility in a limited number of individual cases but shows shortcomings in relation to establishing any collective truth or in achieving reconciliation. The authors argue that a restorative justice approach could very well complement retributive justice mechanisms. Restorative justice views crime as a violation of people and relations rather than as a violation of the law. In their paper the authors present the so-called TARR model which represents the building blocks of post-conflict justice: Truth – Accountability – Reconciliation – Reparation. The four key principles, being personalism, reparation, reintegration and participation, can offer a meaningful answer to the needs of a society in transit. In situations of mass violence the authors argue the two models should be converged.

The chapter by Roelof Haveman is an in-depth analysis of the *gacaca* system in Rwanda. In the genocide in Rwanda 800,000 people were killed and 800,000 citizens were turned into direct suspects or offenders. It was a sheer impossibility to try these suspects in regular courts and after a pilot phase which started in 2002, the *gacaca* system officially started in January 2005 and now has tried the vast majority of suspects. From a legal perspective the *gacaca* is often criticised, for instance as it does not meet the western standards of fair trial: suspects are tried *in absentia*, witnesses, judges and suspects are threatened, and every citizen is obliged to take part in *gacaca*, to give just some examples of criticisms, often leading to a total denouncement of the phenomenon. According to Haveman we have to consider the *gacaca* from a combined legal, historical, psychological, sociological and political perspective. *Gacaca* is a social process, a psychological phenomenon and a cultural phenomenon with historic roots. Doing justice to a phenomenon such as *gacaca* to deal with great numbers of individual perpetrators means that we have to step outside our well known theoretical dogmas.

The last chapter in this part of the book, by Uwe Ewald, takes an entirely different approach as it focuses on reason and truth within international criminal justice and more in particular on the international criminal tribunals. Ewald discusses how evidence is structured and constructed within international crimes in order to arrive at the judicial truth which is proclaimed by the judgments. The manner in which evidence is structured 'provides a key to understanding those sophisticated 'internal' and 'external' factors and mechanisms of evidence and 'truth' production. Ewald shows how historical paradigms change international evidence production.

5.5. VICTIMOLOGY

The fifth part of the book is dedicated to the victims. Kauzlarich concludes that although states are the most destructive agents of misery and oppression across the globe, criminology has contributed very little to the understanding of these crimes and their victims. Traditional victimology research has heavily investigated victim-offender relationships, but little research of this type has been conducted on victims of war and state crime. Supranational criminology should forge a new path of understanding of the world's most profound instances of violence and should take a fiercely humanistic approach to the people who die or are otherwise hurt by the state. Yet victims suffer enormous psychological and existential damage by living in conditions of war, oppression and genocide. According to Kauzlarich, genuine supranational criminology should include a reference to international human rights law and should study suffering across the globe compassionately and with a sharp eye on prevention, control and victim healing. In its focus on victims it should take both direct and indirect harm into account.

5.6. PREVENTIVE STRATEGIES

The focus of the next chapter is on the role of the international community. Fred Grünfeld takes a political science and international relations approach and focuses on the state and the international community as bystanders to international crimes. According to Grünfeld the third parties are the focal point for the prevention of gross human rights violations, because the perpetrator is unwilling and the victim is unable to prevent or stop the atrocities. The bystander can be defined as the third party that will not act or that will not attempt to act in solidarity with the victims of gross human rights violations. The role of the bystander is crucial because the perpetrator will act in response to the behaviour of others. Not acting therefore will transform the bystander into a collaborator. Grünfeld shows that the genocides in Rwanda and Srebrenica might have been prevented if timely action had been taken. In both situations warnings from different sources with clear, very serious signals of the worsening situation were not adequately processed by the UN or not shared with the troops on the ground, which were supposed to protect the safe haven. Grünfeld concludes his chapter by proposing ten guidelines for preventative strategies.

6.   CONCLUSION

War crimes, crimes against humanity and genocide have for long been almost totally neglected by the science that studies crimes, the situation in which these crimes take place, possible interventions to stop these crimes from being committed and the efficacy of the interventions: criminology. Criminology lives in a state of denial when it comes to these large scale, widespread and systematic committed atrocities. This book tries to face the truth and to break out of this state of denial. Supranational criminology – or the criminology of international crimes – entails the study of war crimes, crimes against humanity and genocide, behaviour that shows affinity for these crimes, the causes and the situations in which they are committed, as well as possible interventions and their effectiveness. The interventions comprise penal systems – domestic, internationalised, supranational – in which the crimes are prosecuted and tried, as well as non-penal interventions. Defining and conceptualising the respective international crimes; quantifying and mapping of these forms of crime; searching for theories and ideas that may explain and model these forms of crime; analysing and making an inventory of the ways to conduct post-conflict justice; and developing preventive and repressive strategies to fight these forms of crime. All these topics together form the object of supranational criminological research. In the final chapter of this book some of the most important findings will be summarised and an agenda for future research will be set out, giving special attention to the importance of this type of research for the developing field of international criminal law.

PART I
DEFINE AND CONCEPTUALIZE
INTERNATIONAL CRIMES
AND STATE CRIME

II. TOWARDS A CRIMINOLOGY OF INTERNATIONAL CRIMES: PRODUCING A CONCEPTUAL AND CONTEXTUAL FRAMEWORK

David O. Friedrichs[1]

1. INTRODUCTION: CRIMINOLOGY POST-MAASTRICHT

In 1999 the late Ian Taylor (1999a) published an article entitled 'Criminology post-Maastricht.' Taylor was concerned with identifying the challenges confronting critical criminologists in the 'new Europe' that emerged out of the Maastricht Treaty for the European Union. Taylor was surely correct that the post-Maastricht Europe was a new context that would impact on the meaning of citizenship, the nature of employment patterns, and the forms of social control and justice, in ways that would significantly intersect with the concerns of criminologists. During the same year Taylor (1999b) published his last book, *Crime in Context: A Critical Criminology of Market Society*, that offered a broader critique of criminology within the evolving context of a 'market society.' While Taylor identified a range of transitions characteristic of our contemporary era, the emergence of a 'market society' and related 'market culture' was taken to be the dominant form of transition.

A gathering of criminologists in the old city of Maastricht in April 2007 was also concerned with promoting an adaptation of their field to a fundamental historical neglect of international crimes within the context of our evolving social order. A 'market society' – or a global economy profoundly driven by a 'neo-

1   Parts of this article were originally drafted while I was serving as Visiting Professor of Law at Flinders University in Adelaide, Australia. I appreciate the support of the law school, as well as a faculty research grant and funding provided with my appointment as Distinguished University Fellow by my home institution, the University of Scranton. This article served as a basis for the author's opening presentation at the Expert Meeting on International Crimes at Maastricht University, 12–14 April, 2007. It complements a related article, 'Transnational Crime and Global Criminology: Definitional, Typological and Contextual Conundrums,' originally presented at the Prato Transnational Crime Roundtable in Prato, Italy, 28–30 June, 2006. That article is to be published in a forthcoming issue of *Social Justice*.

liberal' or corporatist agenda – is one important part of this context, but only one. Criminologists affiliated in some way with the 'supranational criminology' agenda also want to promote a 'criminology post-Maastricht,' although with a different focus from that adopted by Taylor. In this case the call for redirection is focused upon broad, evolving global transformations rather than the more limited societal changes resulting from the 'new Europe' that emerged out of the Maastricht Treaty.[2]

2.   CRIMINOLOGY IN TRANSITION

The contours of the criminological enterprise inevitably change over time. At the outset of the 19th century, for example, we have the English Magistrate Patrick Colquhoun (1800), in his *A Treatise on the Police of the Metropolis*, surveying the many forms of conventional crime plaguing the London of his time, some of the reasons for such offences and the justice system remedies. At the outset of the 20th century, we have August Drahms (1900), in his *The Criminal*, also surveying the various forms of conventional criminality, but in this case informed by a Lombrosian biological determinism that was quite typical of the criminal anthropology of that period. At the outset of the 21st century, criminology has become a vast and multi-faceted enterprise, with an especially broad range of substantive foci, theories and methods, but conventional forms of crime and their control remain the dominant concerns. We can speculate on the future direction of the field of criminology during the course of the new century. One can state with some confidence that the contours of the field will be significantly transformed during the course of this century. But it seems worthwhile to differentiate between the direction that 21st century criminology is likely to take and the direction that it should take.

If one holds the conviction that those who will live out their lives during the course of the new century will contend with immense challenges, then the urgency of promoting a criminology that addresses these challenges in some form becomes quite imperative. These challenges include the question of whether human beings will be able to maintain a sustainable environment, surviving catastrophic climatic changes, destruction of diverse species and ocean life, new infectious disease pandemics and pathogens, extreme destitution in developing countries, unstoppable global migrations, economic and political crises and collapses, escalating international terrorism, large scale inter-group and nationalistic wars, the proliferation of weapons of mass destruction and nuclear apocalypse (Martin

---

[2]   This article draws mainly upon the relevant American literature, rather than the European literature, in part on the assumption that many other contributors to this book will discuss that literature quite thoroughly.

2006). And these challenges all too often encompass at their core large scale crimes of powerful political and private sector entities.

If criminology as a field of academic endeavour survives the present century it seems quite certain that attention to the whole range of 'conventional' forms of crime, and their control, will be one part of the work of this field. A principal objection to the character of contemporary criminology, however, is one of proportionality. An 'inverse' hypothesis of criminological concerns can be posited: that is, there is an inverse relationship between the level of harm caused by some human (individual or organisational) activity and the level of criminological concern. Those who have now called for a supranational, international, transnational or global criminology are at a minimum calling for a fundamental realignment of criminological concerns, and for far more attention proportionally to the large scale forms of harm as opposed to the more conventional smaller scale forms of harm characterised as conventional crime.

What will the status of supranational, international, transnational or global criminological concerns be at the outset of the 22nd century? Hypothetically, there are several alternative scenarios. Supranational concerns could inform the dominant framework and focus of criminology; they could have parity with conventional, domestic concerns or they could remain marginal to the mainstream of the discipline. Of course other scenarios are possible, including that criminology as a discipline will have evaporated, and that contemporary criminological concerns will have been absorbed piecemeal into other trans-disciplinary paradigms. The present alternatives, then, seem to be between criminologists maintaining a criminological identity and framework while engaging with disciplines and concerns transcending traditional criminological parameters, and criminologists abandoning their disciplinary identification, simply becoming part of an interdisciplinary endeavour addressing international crime issues. Within critical criminology, there is some division on these options. I basically favour the former option, on the pragmatic grounds that those who come from a criminology background are more likely to have some impact if this option is embraced as opposed to the alternative. If critical criminologists abandon criminology as a discipline, its conventional crime and crime control focus is simply likely to become reinforced.

Criminology has been largely retrospective or present-focused, explaining crime and its control in the past and the present. A 'prospective' or 'anticipatory' supranational criminology ideally identifies emerging conditions conducive to fostering increases in supranational forms of crime, and identifies as well optimal policies and practices that prevent, deter or at least limit such crime. Some criminologists bemoan the relative neglect of criminological research by public policy makers (Smith 2006). Although this neglect can be explained in different ways, there is often a fundamental disconnect between both the outlook and the agenda of policy makers and politicians, and those who produce criminological research. Even mainstream criminology produces much research at odds with political objectives, although a significant proportion of such research has been supportive of these objectives. Criminology as a discipline has been criticised, by those on the left, as serving the interests of the state (Hillyard, Sims, Tombs & Whyte 2004). From a progressive vantage point, then, an immense conundrum for a supranational criminology is this: How would such a criminological endeavour avoid being co-opted by the state to serve its own purposes, and in doing so become complicit in the expansion of state power and oppression?

The establishment of a supranational criminology that realises a fundamental impact both in the realm of scholarship and policy confronts some immense challenges. But if one adopts the position stated earlier, that potential supranational crimes of the future collectively pose a devastating threat to human existence and in the extreme case to the survival of the species, then it would seem that criminological engagement with international crime and its control is quite imperative.[3]

3. INTERNATIONAL CRIME AND SUPRANATIONAL CRIMINOLOGY: TERMINOLOGICAL CONFUSION

Criminologists who address international and transnational forms of crime and the control of such crime have adopted different terms for the criminological enterprise with which they are engaged. This generates a certain level of confusion. Accordingly, some clarification of the optimal meaning of different branches of

---

[3]   Those who advocate a shift of criminological attention to supranational, international, transnational and global crime and justice concerns should anticipate reservations about or objections to such a shift. In purely practical terms, criminologists researching international crime and justice face formidable challenges relative to researching conventional forms of crime and justice, including: the lesser availability of funding; travel, language and cross-cultural communication issues; and the greater complexity, ultimately, of the phenomena in question. The dissenting position is that criminologists do not have the professional competence to address the relevant phenomena on a sophisticated level, and at best simply become 'commentators' in relation to international crime and justice. Further, criminologists addressing international crime and justice may inspire resentment from those (e.g. international politics scholars) who believe that such criminologists are infringing upon their turf. And if such criminologists encourage graduate students in the field to follow their lead, do they put these students in circumstances less likely to lead to academic employment and tenure? Consequently, critics could claim that a shift toward international crime and criminal justice promotes diminished respect for criminology as a discipline, and for criminologists. It might lead to criminological resources being deflected from traditional areas of criminological inquiry where a measurable impact is possible. In the worst case scenario of such a shift, supranational criminology has no measurable impact on either the scholarly understanding of international crime and justice, nor on the prevention, deterrence or control of such crime.

such criminological inquiry would seem worthwhile. I will here simply define these related or interrelated criminological enterprises quite concisely: *A comparative criminology* addresses the nature of the crime problem and the form and character of criminal justice systems in countries around the world; *A transnational criminology* is focused principally upon transnational or cross-border forms of crime, and endeavours on various levels to control and respond effectively to such crime; *A global criminology* is best applied to the study of the evolving context within which crime and criminal justice now exists; and *An international criminology* focuses on international crime – or crime that is specifically recognised widely across nations as crime against humanity – and international law, as well as the institutions of international law. In my understanding, the newly introduced term *supranational criminology* adopted by European criminologists, based especially in the Netherlands, corresponds most closely with an international criminology.[4]

Admittedly, there is considerable overlap between the forms and foci of the different non-traditional branches of criminology just identified, and these terms have been applied quite interchangeably. Some questions that arise in this context are as follows: Can one move toward a resolution of this terminological confusion? Can one achieve some consensus on the optimal use of such terminology? What is the interrelationship of the key foci of these different forms of emergent branches of criminology? Can 'canonical' works within each of the criminological branches delineated here be identified, and does such an exercise bring commonalities and differences between them into sharper focus? In many of the growing number of surveys of different forms of transnational and international crime there is often some lack of coherence in the ordering of the topics subsumed under that heading, e.g. terrorism, organised crime, sex trafficking, crimes of states and so forth. Is there a logical ordering for this range of activities? Is the transnational element proportionally equivalent for all these forms of crime? Can this be reliably measured? Does it make a difference in terms of analysis?

4. CRIME, SOCIAL HARM AND SUPRANATIONAL CRIMINOLOGY

The appropriate meaning of the key term 'crime,' and its relationship to the notion of social harm (Henry & Lanier 2001), obviously represents one key point of

---

[4]   I have addressed the distinctions between these 'criminologies' in somewhat more detail in 'Transnational Crime and Global Criminology: Definitional, Typological, and Contextual Conundrums,' *Social Justice* (forthcoming).

departure for a supranational criminology.[5] The promotion of a 'social harm' approach embraces this notion as a more appropriate focus of concern and interest than crime in the conventional sense (Hillyard, Pantazis, Tombs & Gordon 2004; Pemberton 2004). Criminologists who identify with the supranational criminology project should also engage themselves in the work of 'social harm' criminologists, with obvious intersecting points of interest. But how broadly does one stretch the notion of social harm to intersect in relation to 'crime', in some sense? Some criminologists and social philosophers (Gordon, 2004; Pogge, 2005) have characterised poverty as the world's largest source of social harm, a function of historical crimes by Western developed nations, complicit in millions of preventable deaths and an ongoing massive crime against humanity. If one accepts such claims, worldwide poverty is encompassed within the framework of a supranational criminology. But such a diffuse conception of crime has the cost that it deflects attention and resources from more narrowly defined forms of international crime, and creates an overwhelming, unfocused criminological perspective. Any such costs of these more diffuse conceptual frameworks have to be evaluated in relation to the benefits. A second issue that arises in relation to the 'social harm' project is an evaluation of the costs and benefits of literally abandoning criminology, possibly in favour of zemiology, the study of harm itself. Finally, to the extent that the 'social harm' approach is associated with the abandonment of even a pretence of objectivity and neutrality, as opposed to direct advocacy on behalf of those identified as the socially harmed, the costs and benefits of such a stance must also be weighed.

5. A PROVISIONAL GENEALOGY FOR A SUPRANATIONAL CRIMINOLOGY

It may be a useful exercise to engage in a genealogy of criminological concerns. What is the 'ancestry' of emerging criminological specialties or lines of inquiry? Historical approaches in the field of criminology most typically focus upon the development of theories, criminological personalities or criminological institutions. Much less attention has been directed to the emergence of different substantive interests.

A criminology of international crime that focuses on crimes of powerful entities (including states) in the context of a global framework surely has its seminal roots in the famous initiative of Edwin H. Sutherland (1940) in his 1939 American Sociological Society Presidential Address. His call for attention to

---

[5] I have elsewhere – in collaboration with David Kauzlarich – set forth my understanding of the optimal approach to defining the term crime (Kauzlarich and Friedrichs 2005).

white collar crime challenged the almost exclusive criminological focus upon conventional forms of crime that was the norm up to that time and remained the case for some time afterwards. Sutherland's book (1949), *White Collar Crime*, addressed the crimes of major American corporations, and in this regard also extended the scope of criminological inquiry from individuals and gangs to organisations, and from predominantly local entities to national entities.

It took several decades before white collar crime scholarship achieved some real momentum, sometime in the 1970s. Sutherland's original conception of white collar crime was restricted to private sector activity, however, and principally of corporations. Some of the surveys of white collar crime that began to appear by the early 1980s embraced a more inclusive conception of crimes of the powerful, to include the crimes of public officials (Simon 2006). In the late 1980s, most specifically with William Chambliss's (1989) 1988 American Society of Criminology presidential address, we get the more formal emergence of attention to what he labelled state-organised crime or crimes of states. Stanley Cohen's (2001) work, exemplified by his *States of Denial*, called for criminological attention to violations of human rights. Surely these initiatives both encompass and provide a point of departure for the various emerging lines of inquiry now being pursued within the framework of transnational, international, supranational or global criminology. Obviously some other strains of criminological inquiry have contributed as well, especially comparative criminology and the criminology of organised crime. To a limited extent, a criminology of international crimes may draw upon the criminological investigation of professional crime. On the other hand, mainstream criminological exploration of conventional forms of crime and juvenile delinquency and traditional forms of criminal justice does not contribute in a measurable way to this lineage.

Within the context of the sparse and concise genealogy outlined above, some basic questions arise. Which variables impede, and which promote, the growth of a particular field of inquiry? Why was the emergence of a criminology of white collar crime so limited until the 1970s? What kinds of factors would contribute to a more rapid development of a criminology of international crime or supranational criminology? Joachim Savelsberg and Sarah Flood (2004) have shown that shifts in criminological concerns occur as a function of cohort effects (formative experiences of a generation of criminologists), period effects and changes in institutional environment, including the availability of research funding. Accordingly, some optimal confluence of such factors will surely play a central role in the extent to which criminologists collectively embrace a supranational criminology and their key concerns.

6. A CRIMINOLOGY OF GENOCIDE, WAR AND HUMANITARIAN INTERVENTION

By any measure, a criminology of genocide and a criminology of war are two key strains of a criminology of international crime or supranational criminology. Humanitarian intervention, as a response to alleged crimes of states and as a controversial form of pre-emptive or preventive warfare, is a major issue within international affairs. I offer here a few observations on these matters. First, in recent years a number of criminologists have called for a *criminology of genocide* (Day and Vandiver 2000; Hagan, Rymond-Richmond & Parker 2005; Morrison 2004). Indisputably genocide has been neglected by criminologists historically.[6] Here I will simply identify and comment upon some issues raised by Andrew Woolford (2006) in his call for a *critical* criminology of genocide. Specifically, according to Woolford, such a criminology needs to be reflexive and non-redemptive, undisciplined and critical, and responsible. He expresses concern about an alleged failure of criminology as a discipline – in relation to genocide – to reflect on its 'taken for granted' assumptions, uncritical acceptance of legal categories, and complicity in the constitution of objects of study; its tendency to 'essentialise' both offenders and victims of genocide, and to fully acknowledge the socially constructed character of the concept of genocide itself; its tendency to apply narrowly framed etiological theories to complex politico-historical circumstances; its application of 'naïve positivism' and quantification to genocide; its focus on deaths emanating out of genocide to the neglect of other crimes (e.g. rapes) that occur in relation to genocide; its focus on states and state actors as perpetrators of genocide to the neglect of significant non-state actors (e.g. militias and warlords); its adoption of a neutral or objective stance; its territorial claims for criminology in relation to the study of genocide and privileging of benefits to criminology as a discipline through engagement with genocide; and its relative neglect of the work of criminologists in countries directly affected by genocide. Woolford (2006, 103) concludes with an ambitious call to 'reorder our discipline and society in a manner that helps to make genocide unthinkable.' I do not happen to fully agree with Woolford's reading of the work of criminologists – including myself – who have addressed genocide as a criminological phenomenon. I do think his critique is worth serious attention, insofar as criminological engagement with genocide is complex on many different levels. A supranational criminology of genocide as a crime has to establish the right balance between reflexive concerns and substantive analysis, uniquely criminological and multi-disciplinary dimensions, and between broad scholarly credibility or legitimacy and promoting moral commitments or mobilisation against genocide.

---

[6]   I have elsewhere identified some reasons for this neglect (Friedrichs, 2000a).

The specific call for a *criminology of war* is also quite recent and might be said to parallel the call for a criminology of genocide (Hagan and Greer 2002; Jamieson 1998; Kramer & Michalowski 2005b). War and acts committed in the context of war can be shown to intersect in many different ways with both the theoretical concerns and the empirical findings of criminology (Jamieson 1998). In 'Making War Criminal' John Hagan and Scott Greer (2002) have drawn upon the work of criminologists Sheldon Glueck and Austin Turk to advance our understanding of how crimes of war come to be criminalised. Ronald C. Kramer and Raymond J. Michalowski (2005b) have applied an integrated model of organisational deviance to the case of the pre-emptive invasion of and occupation of Iraq by the United States (and allies), which they characterise as a case of state crime. In terms of scale, nuclear war may represent the ultimate crime that threatens us during the 21st century, but with isolated exceptions nuclear war and related nuclear issues have been almost wholly neglected by criminologists to date. David Kauzlarich and Ronald C. Kramer's (1998) *Crimes of the American Nuclear State* is a pioneering exception to this proposition. In *State Crime* Penny Green and Tony Ward (2004) have addressed war crime as a criminological phenomenon within the context of a broader consideration of the whole range of crimes of states.

On the one hand, a sophisticated criminology of war must concern itself with the literature on many of the macro-level phenomena identified in this article. On the other hand, criminologists can potentially make unique contributions to the understanding of war by delineating both parallels and differences between war as crime (and crimes committed within the context of war), and the whole range of other forms of crime, from conventional crime to white collar crime.

Finally, much recent scholarly attention has been devoted to *humanitarian intervention*. Such interventions increased significantly during the 1990s (Malmvig 2007; Molier 2006). The NATO attack on the former Yugoslavia during this period was one central focus of controversy and the invocation of humanitarian rationales for the U.S. invasion of Iraq inspired much criticism. Indeed, the Iraq misadventure may well have compromised the capacity for urgent and meritorious humanitarian interventions in other countries, going forward (Molier, 2006). But commentators are divided on the long-term impact of this military initiative as well as the wider 'war' on terrorism on future humanitarian interventions.

In one sense humanitarian interventions can be characterised as an ultimate form of supranational policing in a globalised world, and in light of ever-expanding globalisation it seems quite certain that both calls for and critiques of humanitarian intervention will intensify during the course of the 21st century. Clearly, humanitarian interventions are undertaken when the interests of powerful states are threatened or compromised in some way, and rogue states are seen as sponsoring terrorism in some form; they are not undertaken solely in response to violations of human rights, no matter how severe. Helle Malmvig

(2007) has argued that the enduring conflict between traditional notions of state sovereignty (and state interests) and the interventionist privileging of human sovereignty (or the universal human rights of individuals) can be resolved by promoting a new conception of state sovereignty that recognises the importance of respecting human rights and humanitarian values being in the interest of states within the international order of today.

When humanitarian interventions have been undertaken, their legality in relation to international law has been challenged, as have both the true motivations of those who instigate the interventions and the specifically harmful consequences of these interventions. On the other side, the failure to initiate effective humanitarian interventions – famously, in the case of the Rwanda genocide and more recently in the case of ongoing genocidal activity in Darfur – has inspired harsh criticism from human rights advocates and movements. David Kennedy (2004) in *The Dark Sides of Virtue: Reassessing International Humanitarianism* has produced a highly visible challenge to those who have promoted humanitarian interventions (specifically on humanitarian grounds) to be more honest and realistic about the costs and consequences of humanitarian interventions. This critique has itself been challenged – for example, on its treatment of the human rights movement as a monolithic entity (Charlesworth 2002; Gaston 2005) – but what is quite certain is that this debate will continue. And in light of all that is at stake in humanitarian interventions, it is a debate that needs to be attended to with the utmost seriousness and attention.

Criminologists should be uniquely qualified to compare the supranational form of policing involved in humanitarian interventions with more conventional forms of policing that criminologists have thoroughly studied. Critical criminology in particular has a long tradition of exploring and exposing the 'dark side' of policing, and activity carried out in the name of policing that has had demonstrably harmful consequences. More broadly, then, criminologists should be able to contribute to the understanding of how policing activity intersects with or fosters other forms of criminal activity.

7. SUPRANATIONAL CRIMINOLOGY AND RELATED CONCERNS

The establishment of a supranational criminology is in some respects an impossibly ambitious project. A truly sophisticated supranational criminology must concern itself with a wide range of phenomena, with many of these phenomena addressed by a vast literature. I believe it is useful to identify the whole range of enduring and emerging concepts and 'global concerns' that intersect with those of a supranational criminology. A number of such concerns have been addressed earlier; the list of further such concerns could be extended considerably. A supranational criminology, for example, should incorporate *a criminology of crimes of the state*, a *criminology of state-corporate crime*, a *criminology of crimes of globalisation* (i.e. crimes of international financial institutions), a *criminology of crimes of international high finance* (e.g. investment banks), a *criminology of crimes of transnational corporations*, and a *victimology of international crimes*. These large topics have been addressed elsewhere, by myself and others.[7] I will also, for parallel reasons, refrain from addressing two other central components of a supranational criminology: *international law* and *international tribunals*. Rather, I here identify and briefly comment upon a finite and selective number of other concepts and concerns that are components of a supranational criminology and that have captured my own interest. These concepts and concerns might be regarded as elements of a prospective, comprehensive mapping of the terrain of a supranational criminology. The construction of such a mapping – ideally, as comprehensive as possible – would allow those working on projects within the scope of supranational criminology to first, consider which of these pieces are and are not relevant to their own particular project, and second, consider how their particular project is related to other projects. Of course each of the concepts or concerns identified here, as well as those discussed earlier, encompasses a large (and sometimes overwhelmingly large) literature. What follows is obviously provisional and limited, in the extreme, but ideally offers one point of departure for further exploration.

Some concepts that have not been a significant part of the vocabulary of criminology traditionally are important in relation to an emerging supranational criminology. *Sovereignty* is one such concept. Although this term has different meanings, in this context the state's exclusive control over the territory bounded by the state's borders is central. The term 'jurisdiction' is part of conventional criminal justice discourse and parallels that of sovereignty in certain respects. Obviously, the controversial concept of *universal jurisdiction* will be of central interest to students of supranational crime (O'Keefe 2004). In a world of increasing globalisation and transnational crimes sovereignty, jurisdictional claims become increasingly problematic or irrelevant (Sands 2005, 15–16). Sovereignty claims are often an illusion in terms of their traditional meaning. They are increasingly invoked to justify various forms of state-organised law-breaking. Criminologists must attend to sovereignty and jurisdictional issues as they intersect with international crime and its control.

Nationalism is also a concept little addressed within criminology traditionally. Nationalism – in this context putting one's own nation's interests first – has a long and problematic history (Calhoun 1998; Spencer and Wollmann 2002). In one view, nationalism is a form of socio-pathology within the context of a world of

---

7   For example, see Friedrichs, 1998; Rothe and Friedrichs, 2006

weapons of mass destruction. Criminology as a field has studied individual and gang pathologies quite extensively. Which principles can be applied to the pathologies of nations? Significant points of intersection exist between issues of nationalism and international crime and criminal justice. Nationalistic tendencies promote or deter international crime. How is nationalism directly complicit in some forms of international crime? Does international crime and the promotion of international criminal justice contribute to a resurgence of nationalism?

The concept of *legitimacy* refers to an order of authority perceived to be valid and deserving of compliance. This concept has been an important one in macro-level analyses within sociology and political science, and as an aspect of law-related scholarship, but not within criminology. Legitimacy is complicated in a globalised, postmodern world (Clark 2005; D'Aspremont 2006; Franck 2006). Legitimacy claims become increasingly problematic and contested as one moves from the local to the global. For example, on what specific grounds are the legitimacy claims of international tribunals based? What are the consequences for their effectiveness if legitimacy is largely withheld from such institutions? How do globalisation and emerging postmodern tendencies foster legitimacy crises domestically? How do legitimacy crises create conditions conducive to promoting certain forms of international crime?

The topic of *human rights* has, of course, inspired an immense literature. Obviously human rights concerns intersect in fundamental ways with the issues addressed by a supranational criminology. The concerns of international law scholars focused upon human rights are of special relevance (Bagaric and Morss 2006; Buergenthal 2006; Donoo 2006). Elizabeth Stanley (2006) is among those who have issued a specific call for a criminology of human rights.[8] Within the present context special attention has to be paid to claims that human rights discourse has been co-opted by neo-liberal interests to advance their own agenda of economic exploitation, that international financial institutions embrace a 'market friendly' version of human rights, and human rights can be viewed as a hegemonic Western construct, at odds in certain respects with conceptions of human rights associated with the 'Third World' (Evans 2005, 128; Rajagopal 2006, 768–770). Whether or not one adopts such provocative claims, students of international crime are well-advised to approach the vast realm of human rights with critical caution.[9] Criminologists, in particular, are well-positioned to address how conceptions of human rights come to be integrated with conceptions of crime and its control, and how such conceptions are resisted.

---

[8]   See also Mark Drumbl's (2003) parallel call for a 'Criminology of International Crime.'

[9]   Tony Evans (2005), in *The Politics of Human Rights: A Global Perspective*, provides us with a concise but exceptionally lucid critique of the status of human rights in the world today.

The whole matter of *transitional justice* is also critically interconnected with the supranational criminology project (Bohl 2006; Roht-Arriaza and Mariezcurrena 2006). Transitional justice – encompassing the transition from authoritarian to essentially democratic political systems, and the process of addressing crimes and injustices of past regimes – is now the topic of considerable literature (Hayner 2002; Minow 1998; Teitel 2000). A comparative survey of and evaluation of major historical cases of transitional justice in the recent era – with South Africa and Iraq as just two cases – should enrich our understanding of both optimal and failed forms of such justice. In particular, criminologists should be especially well-qualified to address the role of criminal justice institutions in this process.

The recent era has also witnessed a significant rise in interest in *cosmopolitanism*. The term 'cosmopolitan' has been invoked in different ways. The notion of a cosmopolitan outlook especially relevant to a supranational criminology is one that views humans as part of a world community with allegiances to all human beings, transcending particularistic attachments, and takes into account the impact of globalisation on local and national issues (Appiah 2006; Delanty 2006). A 'cosmopolitan turn' or a social science methodology incorporating the fundamental premises of a cosmopolitan outlook, comes out of this (Beck & Sznaider 2006). In this 'methodological cosmopolitanism' the conventional parameters of social science methodology are transcended, and 'the dualities of the global and the local, the national and the international, us and them, have dissolved and merged together in new forms that require conceptual and empirical analysis' (Beck & Szaider 2006). Accordingly, the initiatives being undertaken in relation to methodological cosmopolitanism would appear to be of special interest to those committed to a supranational criminology.

Interest in *sustainability* has expanded greatly in recent years. As a concise definition of sustainability, we have the following: '[T]he effort to frame social and economic policy so as to preserve with minimum disturbance earth's bounty – its resources, inhabitants and environments – for the benefit of both present and future generations' (Rhodes 2006, B24). Sustainability science is an inherently interdisciplinary enterprise exploring the interaction of natural and social systems or combining environmental with social sciences, with a view toward contributing positively to a sustainable environment. This endeavour has a strong environmental orientation, and sustainability initiatives are especially focused upon everyday practices of waste disposal and energy conservation to contribute to a long-term sustainable environment. But environmental sustainability raises some fundamental issues for international law and jurisprudence (Gillroy 2006). Within criminology itself, an emerging 'green criminology' – focusing upon environmental crimes – intersects most directly with the concerns of the sustainability movement (Beirne and South 2006). But if a relative absence of violence and chaos is also a central element of a sustainable environment, then concerns of the sustainability movement and a supranational criminology intersect at other points. Furthermore, the impact of the work of those who pursue supranational criminology projects is that much greater to the extent that such work can be connected with mainstream movements and the 'sustainability movement' is framed in such a way that it has especially broad appeal.

8.   ON CONTEXT: GLOBALISATION, A POSTMODERN WORLD AND THE AMERICAN EMPIRE

Crime and its control can only be coherently studied and understood within a particular context. Traditionally crime and its control have been addressed within the following contexts: first, a locality, state or nation; second, a traditional or modern society; third, a Western framework; and fourth, a historical era, most recently that of the 'Cold War'. This is hardly a comprehensive delineation of the relevant context within which crime and its control have been addressed, but surely it encompasses principal dimensions of such contexts. Admittedly, much criminological analysis does not specifically address context, but it is then a 'taken-for-granted' or unstated dimension of the analysis at hand.

A supranational criminology has to address the very fundamental matter of *globalisation*, insofar as going forward the importance of this phenomena as the larger context within which international crime and its control occurs is sure to intensify. The literature on globalisation is now vast.[10] By any criteria, increasing global interconnectedness and interdependency is central. A supranational criminology must adopt a characterisation of globalisation most relevant to understanding international crime and its control. Especially relevant dimensions of globalisation would seem to include: first, the growing global dominance and reach of neo-liberalism and a free-market, capitalist system that disproportionately benefits wealthy and powerful organisations and individuals; second, the increasing vulnerability of indigenous people with a traditional way of life to the forces of globalised capitalism; third, the growing influence and impact of transnational corporations and international financial institutions and the related, relative decline in the power of local or state-based institutions; and fourth, the non-democratic operation of transnational corporations and international financial institutions, taking the form of 'globalisation from above' instead of 'globalisation from below.'

---

[10]   See Friedrichs 2007b for a more detailed characterisation of globalisation. See Pankaj Ghemawat 2007 for one statement of the case that contemporary claims regarding globalisation are overblown.

It is no less important to engage in the emerging *postmodern* dimensions of our social environment. The transformation of typically modern attributes of our society in a postmodern direction is occurring at an accelerating pace. Our communities are fragmented, complex and increasingly 'virtual.' Western, developed societies are at the centre of a global community, simultaneously transmitting and receiving materials and ideas in and from other societies. Conventional forms of bureaucracy are giving way to more flexible, adaptable 'adhocracies', with constant changing of institutional arrangements and roles to fit specific situations. The computer has rapidly been replacing industrial machinery at the core of our technological existence. Mass communication is evolving with almost lightening speed into a form of interactive communication, as exemplified by cable television and the internet. Growing 'fluidity' is taking place in residence and career, with people moving back and forth between different residential locations and in and out of different careers. All of these changes impact on the character of international crime and its control. Of course such changes co-exist with enduring modern and traditional attributes of society. Accordingly, students of international crime must attend to the proportional relationship between traditional, modern and postmodern attributes of the social order, as a fundamental dimension of the context within which international crime and its control occurs.

Clearly, the *post-Cold War* political environment is a significant contextual element of our world and more recently the *post-9/11 world* as well. It is still arguably too early to assess the extent to which responses to 9/11 will endure over time. Here I will limit myself to one aspect of the American response, as it has broad ramifications for international crime and its control. The term *American Empire* has been invoked with reference to a resurgent form of nationalism on the part of the United States, which intensified in the wake of 9/11 (Ferguson 2004; Johnson 2004; Mann 2004). The George W. Bush administration is now widely viewed as promoting a new form of imperialism centred on American dominance of the world. In an alternative view, *American hegemony* more accurately captures present circumstances than does the term 'empire' (Rajagopal 2006, 771). By any measure criminology has been shaped historically within the context of *Western hegemony*, and disproportionately by American dominance. But whether we are currently witnessing an American empire or hegemony, a central defining feature of international relations is surely involved.[11] President Bush himself is regarded by many citizens of the world and many Americans as well, as a 'war criminal' complicit in the most serious international crimes (Campbell 2006; Holtzman 2006).[12] Of course the opposing view holds that only America, as the world's sole

---

[11] For an argument that American hegemony is in decline, see Immanuel Wallerstein (2006).

[12] The crimes of American presidents have been largely neglected by criminologists (see Friedrichs 2000b).

surviving superpower, can effectively provide global policing in response to criminal states and international terrorists and can promote democracy internationally. For students of international crime, then, the American case brings into especially sharp relief the complexities of disentangling global policing and global state criminality. Whether it is either possible or desirable to separate ideological commitments from objective analysis when it comes to such questions is a matter of enduring debate.

Altogether, the political, economic and cultural influence of and challenges to the dominance of the United States, especially from developing countries, will constitute a core dimension of the context within which international crime and its control must be understood.[13]

2. THE GLOBAL JUSTICE MOVEMENT AND SUPRANATIONAL CRIME

An expanding dialogue on a broad range of global justice issues is increasingly evident today (Brock and Mollenhoff 2005). International crime is surely among the most visible of these issues. The challenges of controlling international forms of crime are obviously immense and the role of governmental entities in doing so is immensely problematic. In one view, then, the best hope for any such control resides with the collective activity of private parties or concerned citizens. The so-called anti-globalisation movement that has erupted in the recent era has challenged in a fundamental way the 'top down' claim that neo-liberal economic policies are both universally beneficial and inevitable (Cavanagh 2002). The term 'global justice movement' seems preferable to the term anti-globalisation movement, insofar as the latter term has a powerfully negative character, and the true essence of this movement is a widely diffused demand that global policies promote justice for ordinary people, rather than favouring powerful organisations and privileged classes. The World Social Forum, established in 2001, is an especially significant product of the global justice movement, providing a highly visible meeting ground for the wide diversity of constituent social groups opposed to top-down neo-liberal global policies (Fisher and Ponniah 2003). Some topics addressed by the World Social Forum, of special relevance to the phenomena of international crime, include a call for the adoption of the precautionary principle (i.e. acting against anticipated harm), broader extension of human rights, reparations for historical crimes against indigenous peoples (and for the unconditional autonomy of presently existing indigenous peoples), the privileging

---

[13]   Many books have been published recently that attempt to characterise the present political, economic and cultural global context. I find Richard Falk's (2004) *The Declining World Order* especially persuasive.

of the common good over private profits, the promotion of ecological sustainability and the dismantlement or radical reform of the international financial institutions. The global justice movement in all its manifestations is rooted in a post-Enlightenment recognition of the capacity for self-governance and the power of the people to withdraw legitimisation from the existing system of governance (Langman 2005, 43). The present global justice movement is made up of a broad diversity of different constituencies, including labour unionists, peace activists, environmentalists, feminists and indigenous peoples. Clearly, these constituencies do not all have the same agenda – indeed, in some cases their agendas may be in conflict – and it is obviously a mistake to assume that 'popular' constituencies necessarily have progressive agendas. Without having illusions, then, about both the dangers and the limitations of a global justice movement, its potential to effectively challenge many major forms of international crime should be taken seriously. What lessons can be derived from studies of the impact of past social movements on local, state and federal criminal justice policy that might be applied to an understanding of the potential of such movements to have an impact on international criminal justice policies?

Students of international crime must engage themselves in the work of those who have been investigating the new forms of social movements arising in an increasingly 'borderless world' (McDonald 2006). The 'new transnational activism' incorporates social activists with enduring domestic concerns, but also an increasing focus on global issues (Tarrow 2005). Accordingly, the resulting social movements have both traditional and new dimensions. One of the defining new attributes of the emerging social movements is that computer technology and the internet play a central role in communication and mobilisation, and as Lauren Langman (2005, 46) argues, traditional social movement theories cannot account for some fundamental aspects of these more flexible and democratic new social movements. The work of Manuel Castells (1997), on the 'network society,' is accordingly identified as providing a fundamental point of departure for addressing emerging global social movements – and 'cyber activism' – in relation to responses to international crime.

10. INTERNATIONAL CRIME AND GLOBAL GOVERNANCE

The question of global governance is certain to become progressively more urgent and more widely discussed during the course of the 21st century, and it is quite imperative that students of international crime and law engage themselves in the evolving transnational discussion on this question. The key terms here – including 'global' and 'governance' – are invoked in different ways, with popular writers tending to equate global governance with 'government' whereas academics and international practitioners tend to equate it with complex public and private structures and processes (Dingworth & Pattberg 2006, 187). Global governance is not synonymous with international relations, since the latter tends to be restricted to relations between sovereign states while global governance encompasses non-state actors (Dingworth & Pattberg 2006, 191). At a minimum, then, global governance can serve as a 'heuristic device' capturing (or describing) the ongoing, accelerating transformation of the international system.

For many centuries, philosophers and jurists have speculated on the necessary conditions for achieving enduring peace and justice between nations (Hoffman 2003; Murphy 1999). Recognition of the interdependence of a globalised world has accelerated greatly in the post-Cold War era and especially since 9/11 (Barnett & Duvall 2003; Esty 2006). On the one hand, the notion of global governance in the form of a centralised entity that in some fundamental sense governs the entire world, strikes many commentators as a utopian fantasy (as a positive development) and a frightening nightmare (if actually realised). A 'world government' is profoundly problematic for those on both the conservative and the progressive ends of the ideological spectrum. For conservatives, the concession of national sovereignty is especially objectionable; for progressives, the notion of such a concentration of power is especially objectionable. But global governance in contemporary discourse transcends simplistic notions of world government.[14]

For some commentators, the basic form of global governance has remained unchanged over the past half century or so and remains a matter of dominance by a small number of global states (Kuper 2004). For other commentators, transnational global governance is already here. Anne-Marie Slaughter (2004) has argued that the complex global web of 'government networks' linking officials in different nations who cooperatively oversee and enforce international agreements constitutes a form of global governance. Some other specific manifestations of global governance include: the intergovernmental understandings of G-8 and the World Economic Forum; international humanitarian law; *ad hoc* trans-governmental collaborations (e.g. the Nuclear Suppliers Group); transnational policing; trans-local bodies (e.g. the World Organization of United Cities); interregional constitutions; private global regulatory agencies (e.g. the International Accounting Standards Bureau); and aboriginal initiatives (Barnett & Duvall 2003). As two commentators observe, 'Networks constitute the new social morphology of our societies (...)' (Coleman &

---

[14] The United Nations is widely regarded as the closest thing we have to an institution of global governance. But of course it remains highly controversial and during the course of its history has had a very mixed record in response to international crimes (Judt 2007; Kennedy 2006; Totten 2005). A supranational criminology should evaluate both the potential and the limitations of the UN in response to international crime, going forward.

Wayland, 2006). Networks, in this reading, provide the basis of an emerging 'global civil society'. But such a society is hardly constituted only of progressive organisations, and is more likely to be characterised by conflict and violence than by rational, cooperative relations.

Sanjeev Khagram (2006) persuasively argues that some forms of authentic global governance for the future are at least hypothetically possible and are in principle preferable to the current state of global disorder, which is likely to intensify in the future in the absence of the adoption of an effective form of global governance. For those sceptical of the broad notion of global governance, Khagram (2006, 98) reminds us that at one time some 300,000 political units existed in the world, whereas today only 200 countries constitute the principal political units. The 'sovereign state' model so much taken for granted today is historically relatively recent and has many demonstrable limitations (Khagram 2006, 106–110). Today we have in the world everything from super-states to failed states. Clearly, however, the historical trend has inexorably moved toward consolidation of political units. Authentic global governance, of course, represents the ultimate consolidation. After noting that what he labels multilaterism/polyarchic interstatism – democratic cooperation between functioning, formally equal sovereign states – is the most widely embraced model for global governance today, Khagram (2006, 110) observes that this model was not even on the agenda (or clearly envisioned) at the beginning of the 20th century, when imperial and colonial rule was dominant. Accordingly, we should not suffer from the illusion that we can easily envision the form of global governance some one hundred years from now, at the outset of the 22nd century. Khagram then identifies and evaluates alternative (not necessarily mutually exclusive) models, including, grassroots globalism: the radical decentralisation of authoritative relations with self-governing local communities and with multinational corporations eliminated as primary modes of production and distribution, replaced by socialist/solidaristic/ ecologically embedded economies; multiple cooperative regionalisms: regional collectives of states and societies bound together by interregional organisations as well as multiple cooperative regionalisms; world state: a more or less democratically constituted and governed entity, with the Universal Declaration of Human Rights as a foundational document, and either a planetary military-security establishment or a completely demilitarised world; networked governance: either a trans-governmental network of state governmental and bureaucratic actors or in a multi-stakeholder variant, networks of state and non-state actors in various sectors of society; and institutional heterarchy: a world of multiple types, forms and levels of authoritative political organisations and units, with both independent and interdependent actors on various levels of government engaged.

Andrew Kuper (2004) calls for a global-federative scheme comprising multiple levels of territorially nested jurisdictions. He observes that some tasks of government – including the regulation of the global environment – are better administered by non-territorial entities. Accordingly, international regulatory bodies are needed, and should include representatives of NGOs (non-governmental organisations) and IGOs. International institutions of global governance should include advocacy agencies that canvass and prioritise the concerns of citizens, and bring them before the international policy-making organisations; and accountability agencies, that educate and inform citizens of what governments are doing. In a parallel vein, Simon Canely (2006) calls for the establishment of international institutions as an essential (if hardly flawless) element of a global political framework responsive to the whole range of global injustices in the world today. Such institutions, in his view, should possess transparency, equality and impartial enforcement mechanisms as properties.

Each of the foregoing models or 'architecture' for world governance incorporates higher levels of transparency, participation and accountability than is true of the hierarchical, bureaucratic and technocratic forms of global decision-making dominant today (Khagram 2006, 112). The future form of global governance, whatever form it takes, is likely to include both the formalisation of existing transnational networks as well as the development of new forms of cosmopolitan citizenship and institutional heterarchy (Khagram 2006, 110). A global civil society, for example, is one important dimension of evolving global governance. The notion of 'civil society' itself is a very old one, going back at least to the classic Greek philosophers, and as John Ehrenberg (1999) has shown, different conceptions of this term have been adopted over a period of some two thousand years. At a minimum, it is most commonly invoked today to refer to those public, voluntary associations – neither part of the purely private realm of the family, nor part of the purely public realm of the state – that play a key role in social life. A global civil society, in one view, can serve as an antidote to the activities of predatory states and unregulated markets (Barnett & Duvall 2003). It is important to bear in mind, of course, that transnational advocacy is not necessarily progressive, that many formalised transnational civil society organisations are oriented toward technical, scientific and professional matters, and that the forms of non-state actors engaged in transnational issues include for-profit companies, business associations, ethnic communities and religious groups as well as organised criminals and terrorists (Khagram 2006, 104–105). Ideally, a global criminology can play a constructive role in all of this by working out the complex nature of the evolving relationship between transnational capitalism and international or transnational crime, the likely implications of the different models for international or transnational crime and its control, and the optimal model in terms of the broad promotion of global justice.

11. IN CONCLUSION: AN AGENDA FOR A SUPRANATIONAL CRIMINOLOGY

First, an emerging criminology of international crime should attempt to arrive at some consensus on defining itself coherently. It should identify the parameters of expanded criminological concerns within the context of globalisation. It should address the definition of the crime issue anew within this context. It should attend to defining the key terms associated with an emerging supranational criminology clearly and cogently. It should develop a coherent typology of transnational, international and global crime, and of the institutions of control of such crime.

A supranational criminology needs to address systematically the formidable methodological issues that arise in relation to studying international crime. It should adopt a credible 'world order' framework within which international and transnational forms of crime and their control can be analysed. It should identify optimal strategies for promoting a broader awareness within the discipline of the need to adopt a global framework. It should identify viable and useful empirical projects that can advance the understanding of international and transnational crime and their control. It should also identify optimal strategies for securing funding and support for such projects. It should identify the major policy issues that now arise in relation to international and transnational crime and their control, and the optimal resolution of these issues. Finally, it should delineate the relationship of an emerging supranational criminology to a range of disciplines – including international law and comparative politics – that address some of the same concerns.

III. TOWARDS AN INTEGRATIVE STUDY OF INTERNATIONAL CRIMES AND STATE-CORPORATE CRIMINALITY: A RECIPROCAL APPROACH TO GROSS HUMAN RIGHTS VIOLATIONS

Gregg BARAK[1]

1. INTRODUCTION

As we inaugurate a supranational criminology that we hope will become a new criminology that develops and expands its influence over time in the world of 'gross human rights violations', we should aspire to become not only a multi-disciplinarian and comparative field of investigation and study, but we should also give careful examination to the historical record. As a new field of criminology, regardless of what other past and present criminologies have or have not done epistemologically and methodologically, a supranational criminology should be, at the same time, both 'backward looking' and 'forward looking' so as to be able to best define our praxis in the present. It should also be about the intellectual enterprise of linking or integrating *what has been done* with *what could be done*, not only for the purposes of 'justice' and 'closure' with or without impunity and perhaps with both, but from the perspective of helping to establish standards for measuring the gravity of ordinary and extraordinary crimes against humanity and for creating remedies and strategies of accountability, restoration, and recovery (locally and globally) for perpetrators, victims, and bystanders of such gross human rights violations as sexual torture, war crimes or genocide.

---

[1] The author wishes to thank Dawn Rothe and Alette Smeulers for their comments on an earlier draft. For the final version of this chapter, I would like to thank all the participants at the Maastricht Expert Meeting for their papers/chapters/presentations/discussions.

2. POLITICAL ECONOMY AND NATION-STATE NEUTRALITY

For more than three decades national economies have become 'increasingly integrated into, and subordinated to global markets for money and commodities, under the aegis of transnational corporations, monetarist policies, and neoliberal ideology' (Turner 2003, 5). 'Globalisation,' as this process has come to be labelled, has been

> *'driven by the quest by private corporate and financial capital to escape effective regulation and taxation by states, to exploit cheaper, often unwaged forms of labour, and to realize greater efficiency and cost-effectiveness from transnational forms of corporate organizations such as sourcing networks and vertical integration of productive and distributive operations.'* (Ibid.)

These 'processes of globalisation' or the recently emerging global markets have established new concrete interconnections among the declining hegemonies of the advanced industrial centres, bringing about in its wake a reorganisation of 'corporate driven' societies increasingly based on international or transnational relationships, accelerated not only by an age of information and instant communication, but also by the decentralisation of capital away from the 'core' nation-states and toward the 'peripheral' nation-states, primarily into the countries of Southeast Asia.

Nevertheless, the state and its complex apparatuses, organisations, and interests are not withering away any time soon. On the contrary, whether these states are part of the core or periphery, they are adjusting their neo-liberal policies at home and abroad to the demands of global capital or to the structural relations of imperialist domination and expansionism. At the same time, many nation-states are adjusting their hegemonic and religious ideologies to the 'clash of civilizations' or to the so-called cultural clashes of East and West, where societies belonging to the former are alleged to have 'negative culture and pre-modernity' and the latter societies are alleged to have 'values and modernity' marking them as 'superior,' entitling them to 'call the shots' as it were (Huntington 1997). Similarly, 'the accumulation and expansion of capital, and the preservation and extension of its conditions of existence, remain the major determinants of domestic and international state activities in societies with capitalist economies' (Pearce 2003, xi).

Theoretically and practically, to ignore these global realities of state and capitalist development, at this historical juncture, when we are trying to establish a new field of inquiry, *supranational criminology,* dedicated to the study of the political and economic power relations of *gross human rights violations* or to the international, state, and/or state-corporate actions or inactions responsible for the establishment of such crimes as slavery, genocide, ethnic cleansing, or political imprisonment and torture that have been outlawed by international law, is not only the equivalent of not having our own separate and independent scientific agenda or problematic, but, speaking symptomatically, it also potentially represents another offshoot of the criminological enterprise that becomes: subservient to sundry state apparatuses, subordinate to neo-liberal policy research agendas of state-capitalist control and regulation, and servants of the bureaucratic customs of 'administrative' criminology and 'actuarial' justice. Similarly, not to examine these egregious structures responsible for these 'criminal systems of oppression and exploitation' in relationship to the emergence and development of an international criminal court and the concept of international criminal justice would be the same as conventional criminology not examining the emergence and development of the administration of domestic criminal law in relation to both street and suite crime. Finally, both angles of investigation are essential for a fully integrated study of the dialectics of social structure and collective agency, whether we are discussing the establishment or enforcement of rights or the ignoring of such crimes against humanity as torture and genocide. A case in point, for example, regarding international justice would be to explain why the war crimes tribunal in The Hague and the International Court of Justice did, in fact, suppress the full military archives in deference to the state and rule that Serbia was not guilty of the crime of genocide.

Traditionally, harms or 'crimes' and 'violence' have referred to either legitimate or illegitimate acts within nation-states and are subject to domestic norms, laws, and order internally defined or they have referred to legitimate or illegitimate acts between nation-states and are subject to international norms, laws, and order externally defined. In an age of global crime/violence, however, harms are transnationally invented and/or reinvented as their new forms of 'crime' and 'violence' represent reconfigured social relations or acts involving perpetrators and victims located in, or operating through, more than one country, and typically these are not subject to internal or external controls or regulation. In the absence of such definitions and controls, many transnational, global, international, and supranational criminologists, human rights activists, and other concerned citizens and groups are struggling with this lack, with its multitude of harms and dangers, and with strategies for developing global norms, laws, and a transnational order based on the recognition of universal human rights and social justice for all peoples.

Moreover, during the current phase of globalisation, involving disorganisation and reorganisation, the changing situation worldwide is one in which there is increasing crime and violence of various kinds within, between, and across nation-states. The latter forms of crime and violence, for example, *trafficking in human beings*, are typically classified as both international and transnational crimes, and they are increasingly based on the fragmentation of former political units, the polarisation of peoples vertically and horizontally, and the intensification of indigenousness more generally in developing as well as developed countries (Barak 2000; Sassen 2003; Ghezzi and Mingione 2003). Often left out of the conceptualisations of 'domestic' crimes against the state and of 'global' crimes against the hegemonic international political and economic order, are the transgressions committed by states and by state-corporate alliances, in violation of their own criminal and civil laws as well as various forms of international law (Chambliss 1989; Perdue 1989; Barak 1991b; Kramer 1992; Tunnell 1993; Kauzlarich and Kramer 1998; Ross 2000c; Donnelly 2003; Tombs and Whyte 2003; Michalowski and Kramer 2006; Rothe and Mullins 2006a), which provide inseparable and reciprocal relations with virtually all forms of crimes, national or international (Barak 2007). As the social anthropologist, Jonathan Friedman (2003, xiv) explains about the relationship between globalisation and violence:

'In order to understand the processes involved it is necessary to take seriously the systemic changes occurring in the global political economy that have produced major shifts in forms of control over resources, the relation between capital and states and in the transformation of the conditions of livelihood and labor. The global transformation of capital accumulation is articulated to major reconfigurations of political power in the world, to major dislocations of population, to the disintegration of microsocial forms of life for many, and to the intensification of both everyday domestic, local, and regional violence.'

Hence, in an age of globalisation, an integrated study of international crimes and state-corporate criminality should immerse itself in 'the relation between world processes, the distribution of conditions of social existence, and the way people in such conditions create and configure their worlds, whether they are the worlds of investment bankers or of the marginalized and "flexible"' other (Friedman 2003, xiv). More specifically, the study of an integrated or reciprocal approach to international crimes and state-corporate criminality should be inclusive not only of the entire range of violations involving both violators and victims that are sanctioned or prohibited in law, but it should also include those acts of legally sanctioned state repression as well as state omission and market policies of globalisation that result in the denial of fundamental human rights to whole groups of people, whether or not these 'harms' are defined, by national, or international humanitarian law (e.g. crimes against humanity), international human rights, or even when, for example the unprotected behaviour of the sexuality of gay men, lesbians, and members of other sexual minorities, is outlawed and subject to the full extent of the penal law.

In the context of an evolving list of 'universal' human rights over the past 300 years, more specifically the past half of century, we are still a far cry from having

eliminated the right to discriminate as exemplified by the case of sexual minorities
in virtually all societies (Donnelly 2003). In other words, even though Article 2 of
the Universal Declaration of Human Rights guarantees the right to protection
against discrimination, the current interpretation of existing international human
rights law does not extend protection to all victims of systematic discrimination.
As the Article states, 'Everyone is entitled to all rights and freedoms set forth in
this Declaration, without distinction of any kind, such as race, colour, sex,
language, religion, political or other opinion, national or social origin, property,
birth or other status.' However, this statement is highly exaggerated for a number
of reasons, perhaps the most contradictory being that everyone is not entitled to
all human rights without distinctions of any kind. 'States are not prohibited from
taking into account *any* status differences. Individuals are entitled only to
protection against *invidious* discrimination, discrimination that tends to ill will
or causes unjustifiable harm' (Donnelly 2003, 225, emphasis in the original).
Hence, the inclusive right to full non-discrimination does not exist as of now. In
fact, in many nation-states the intimate behaviour and loving relationships of
sexual minorities are still prohibited in law, subject to an array of official, quasi-
official, and private violence, and these violators of various sexual taboos also find
themselves suffering under substantial civil disabilities. As Jack Donnelly (2003,
229) argues:

> 'Sexual minorities are not merely people who engage in "deviant" sexual behaviour – for
> example, fetishists of various types – or even those who adopt "deviant" (sexual)
> identities (e.g., "swingers"). They are those despised and targeted by "mainstream"
> society because of their sexuality, victims of systematic denials of rights because of their
> sexuality (and, in most cases, for transgressing gender roles). Like victims of racism,
> sexism, and religious persecution, they are human beings who have been identified by
> dominant social groups as somehow less than fully human, and thus not entitled to the
> same rights as "normal" people, the "rest of us."'

Indeed, over the past several decades remarkable strides have been made towards
the development of a global collective consciousness based on principles and
values of human rights. Most members of the international or global community
today, think in terms of the Universal Declaration of Human Rights. Nonetheless,
as history teaches us the moral phenomenon of internationalism or universalism
that the world is witnessing did not materialise 'out of whole cloth'. It evolved over
time, solidifying only during the latter half of the 20th century, as it became part
of a universal discourse. At the same time, the reification of such a consciousness
is far from being realised in terms of the *realpolitik* of international relations and/
or criminological scholarship (Rothe and Mullins 2006c).

Additionally, an internationally expanded and globalised 'humanistic'
definition of crime and social justice speaks to both the traditional legal-retributive

approaches to law and order and to the newer or alternative social-world community approaches to inequality and repressive justice such as restorative, accountability, or *Gacaca* forms of 'popular' justice; the former more conducive to practices of adversarialism and war making, the latter more conducive to practices of mutualism and peacemaking (Barak 2005). A humanistic as opposed to a state-legal or even international definition of crime and justice also recognises that killing people are always morally problematic even though at the same time, 'the moral and sociological questions are [often] confused by uncritical acceptance of the definition of murder by either states or organized religions' (Pearce 2003, xiii-xiv). The point, of course, is that a supranational criminology should not be morally and legally neutral nor should it align itself with any one nation-state legal system; rather, it should always situate the state in the 'eye of the problematic' and align itself, if you will, with the international citizenry or global community. Otherwise, a supranational criminology risks the likelihood of intellectual servitude to various nation-states as the 'untheorized claims to neutrality implicitly endorse extant ideologies' and the established political and economic arrangements (Ibid, xiv).

Similarly, it should be underscored that the various atrocities that the world has witnessed over the past century, whether officially or unofficially acknowledged, should not be tolerated by a supranational criminology. As such these state and international violations represent profound issues of social control and social reform that cannot afford to be avoided in general and in terms of the harms that they cause their victims in particular. As Rothe and Mullins (2006a, 17) write about these dialectical relations in terms of their integrated theory of state crimes and the ICC:

> 'At the international level, existing relations based on specific conditions create broad social forces that can act as constraints against a state's intended policy. This can include NGOs, other nation-states, and inter-governmental organizations such as the UN. Moreover, there are the broader global economic forces that can produce or constrain competition and goal attainment. The larger international culture or ethos can also produce an environment wherein a set of objectives can be replaced with covert or overt activities by a state. Presently, controls at the international level can occur by means of economic or political sanctions or threat of military actions; at the same time, these mechanisms often fail to act as controls for other nation-states due to lack of consistent application (...). Alternatively, international law may hold more power. As street crime research has shown, social location and position strongly influences deterrence (...). Those actors most likely to be involved in state crime would seem to be those who are most influenceable by law. This observation forms the foundation of our arguments here focused on the ability of the ICC to eliminate impunity and engender a deterrent value of certain inter-national laws.'

Finally, Rothe and Mullins recognise the inefficacy of the UN's Security Council,
for example, to sanction states endlessly. But 'without formal mechanisms to
enforce those sanctions, there is nothing to compel compliance, thus providing
further opportunity for state criminogenic behaviors' (Ibid.). They also underscore
the social tardiness of the actions of the international community when they note
that the 'most egregious of crimes, those which the ICC has been designed to
prosecute, such controls have historically done little to deter; typically, they come
into play long after criminal actions are over and the viability and integrity of the
state which has committed them has been compromised' (Ibid.).

The rest of this chapter will be divided up into three parts and a conclusion of
sorts. The first part provides a taxonomy of the full range of international crimes
as well as state crimes. The second part provides an integrative framework for
studying both international crime and state criminality. The third part provides a
view of international and state criminality from the perspective of peacemaking,
non-violence, and social change, helping to locate supranational criminology in
the centre of the ongoing struggle for universal human rights and against
imperialist integrations or market empires.

3. A CRITICAL TAXONOMY OF INTERNATIONAL CRIMES AND STATE CRIMINALITY

In terms of a 'supranational criminology,' a critical taxonomy of international
crimes and state criminality should begin with the 'legal' and it should end with
the 'social.' For illustrative purposes, 'does racially motivated, lethally destructive,
state supported, and militarily unjustified violence constitute genocide?' (Hagan,
Rymond-Richmond and Parker 2005, 526). Well, the legal and social scientific
answers to this question may be the same or they may differ as well as change over
time. For example, in the case of research on the Darfur region of Sudan, Hagan,
Rymond-Richmond and Parker have argued that the answers to the questions of
genocide, legal and social, should coincide. However, 'the United States, the
United Nations, the African Union, Amnesty International and Human Rights
Watch differ on whether and why the atrocities occurring in Darfur are best
defined as a genocide, a crime against humanity, or ethnic cleansing' (Ibid, 528).
More specifically, the UN Commission of Inquiry on Darfur 'explicitly concluded
that genocide did not occur, and that war crimes and crimes against humanity
did, in the course of the government's efforts at counterinsurgency' (Ibid, 553).

From this example, a supranational criminology needs to recognise that while
all genocides by definition are crimes against humanity, not all crimes against
humanity rise to the symbolic significance of genocide because of different legal,
social, and political interpretations of what constitutes extraordinary crimes

against humanity. More generally, a supranational criminology needs to recognise that the labels of international and state crime not only carry different political and economic meanings and as such have different social consequences, including pathways to recovery and recourses to justice, but such legal categories have not as yet recognised state-corporate criminality, nationally or internationally. Finally, a supranational criminology needs to incorporate an integrative and dynamic perspective on the reciprocal interactions of the patterned relations of interpersonal, institutional, and structural crime as these are informed by the social, cultural, ideological, and material relations of production.

Like my 'reciprocal theory of violence and nonviolence' argues, as the interpersonal, institutional, and structural levels of violence or non-violence converge in time and space, then at least three things occur: First, the severity or intensity of violence or non-violence swells in magnitude. Second, the incidents of violence and non-violence become more or less prevalent. Third, the distinguishing factors of the spheres of interpersonal, institutional, and structural violence and non-violence become less distinct (Barak 2006). The same types of dynamics are at work in the presence and absence of international and state-corporate crime. Typically, however, just as most conventional analyses of crime or violence, integrated or non-integrated, remain confined to one level of analysis; the same limitations can apply to the study of supranational criminology. In the same vein, when introducing their integrated model of state crime Rothe and Mullins (2006a, 9) note: 'Traditional criminological inquiry into the epistemological and etiological factors of crime and crime control has, for the most part, produced theories addressing one specific level of analysis.' They go on to make the case for an integrated, multilevel, and inclusive analysis of state crime because of the 'complexities in time-space, history, culture, politics, ideology, and economics' (Ibid.).

Situated within this reciprocal approach to international crimes and state crimes, allow me to proceed with my representation of a critical taxonomy of these harmful exchanges between individuals and states alike. According to the practice of law, *international crime* refers to acts such as to violations of international public law. This body of law includes charters, treaties, resolutions, and customary laws, inclusive of those crimes defined by the statutes of the International Criminal Tribunals and the ICC. More specifically, at this point in time, since the crimes against the peace/crimes of aggression have not as yet been defined by the general assembly, only the first three types of violations of international criminal law listed below are actually applied, for example by the legal jurisdiction of the ICC:

- Crimes against humanity
- War crimes

– Genocide
– Crimes against the peace (aka 'crimes of aggression').

International crimes are often thought of as 'transnational' crimes, but legalistically, they are 'ordinary' crimes that can be prosecuted locally, even though cross-border in nature. Moreover, these criminal violations do not qualify for prosecution by international criminal tribunals. These violations include:

– Smuggling
– Trafficking in human beings
– Arms trafficking
– Drug trafficking
– Money laundering.

One might conclude, therefore, that these criminal violations can be catered to by conventional criminology and need not be of any concern to a supranational criminology. And, while this may be true, it is also the case that these crimes are increasingly influenced by and involved with the transnational global relations of these gross human rights violations. In any event, as I argue below, at least one exception in terms of priorities should be given to the transnational crime of trafficking in human beings.

State criminality refers to 'acts of commission' or 'acts of omission'; the former in violation of national criminal or civil laws as well as international laws, the latter as official or unofficial social and institutional policies that result in the denial and/or repression of fundamental human rights to whole groups of people. Moreover, those crimes currently prosecutable by the ICC 'all fall under the rubric of what criminologists refer to as state crime: internationally defined unlawful actions committed by nation-states, typically to advance the social, economic, ideological, or political interests of the state or those in control of the state' (Rothe and Mullins 2006a, 1).

Let us briefly define and/or characterise each of these categories of illegal and legal harms. First, we turn to those crimes that are against international criminal law, and to that autonomous branch of law and the courts or tribunals set up to adjudicate cases in which persons have incurred international criminal responsibility. These crimes, created by treaty and convention, may be prosecuted before international courts and tribunals, but questions of jurisdictional prosecution of persons, natural or fictitious, in the municipal or federal courts of the nation-state in which the arrest is made are subject to a variety of legal distinctions.

For example, because the United States does not abdicate its sovereignty or recognise the primacy of international law (monism), for any international criminal law to be relevant, it must be incorporated directly into the U.S. criminal law through Congressional legislation. Thus, to meet its obligations under international agreements, the United States has enacted statues covering genocide, war crimes, torture, piracy, slavery, and trafficking in women and children. On the other hand, the Canadian Crimes Against Humanity and War Crimes Act, S.C. 2000, incorporates customary international law, including the following as domestic crimes: genocide, crimes against humanity, war crimes, breach of responsibility by a military commander or a superior civilian or otherwise, offences against the administration of justice of the ICC, and possession or laundering of proceeds derived from these crimes. More generally, under s51 of the International Criminal Court Act 2001, the ICC has complimentary jurisdiction to prosecute where states do not prosecute (unable or unwilling), if the state where the crime occurred or the state where the perpetrators are from are both signatories and ratifiers of the Rome statute.

More particularly, in international law 'crimes against humanity' refer to acts of murderous persecution against a body of people whose harm is superior to the harm of all other criminal offences. The post World War II International Military Tribunal and the Nuremberg articles defined crimes against humanity as: murder, extermination, enslavement, deportation and other inhumane acts committed against a civilian population, before or during the war; or persecutions on political, racial or religious grounds in execution of, or in connection with any crime within the jurisdiction of the Tribunal, whether or not in violation of the domestic law of the country where perpetrated. According to Article II of the Genocide Convention, any of the following acts committed with intent to destroy, in whole or in part, a national, ethnical, racial or religious group involving such behaviours as:

- killing members of the group,
- causing serious bodily or mental harm to members of the group,
- deliberately inflicting on the groups conditions of life calculated to bring about its physical destruction in whole or in part,
- imposing measures intended to prevent births within the group,
- forcibly transferring children of the group to another group (Hagan et al. 2005, 528).

More recently, the Treaty for the 'Rome Statute' of the International Criminal Court established in The Hague in 2002 follows the principle of complimentary. During the process of negotiations, 1996–1998, the issue of universal jurisdiction was a significant stumbling block for several states (e.g. China, U.S., and Israel). As with many, if not most, processes of lawmaking, compromises occurred and the Court failed to attain universal jurisdiction. The closest thing approaching

universal jurisdictional powers lies with the ability of the Security Council to
forward a case to the Court regardless of whether or not that state had ratified the
Treaty. Nevertheless, the ICC has authority over genocide, crimes against
humanity, war crimes, and crimes of aggression. For the purpose of the Statute,
crimes against humanity include any of the following acts when 'committed as
part of a widespread or systematic attaché directed against any civilian population,
with knowledge of the attack':

- Murder;
- Extermination;
- Enslavement;
- Deportation or forcible transfer of population;
- Imprisonment or other severe deprivation of physical liberty in violation of
  fundamental rules of international law;
- Torture;
- Rape, sexual slavery, enforced prostitution, forced pregnancy, enforced
  sterilisation, or any other form of sexual violence in comparable gravity;
- Persecution against any identifiable group or collectivity on political, racial,
  national, ethnic, cultural, religious, gender, or other grounds that are
  universally recognised as impermissible under international law, in connection
  with any act referred to in this paragraph or any crime within the jurisdiction
  of the Court;
- Enforced disappearance of persons;
- The crime of apartheid;
- Other inhumane acts of a similar character internationally causing great
  suffering, or serious injury to body or to mental or physical health (Rome
  Statute 1998: Article 7).

Similarly, 'crimes against the peace' though seldom referenced today were first
incorporated into the Nuremberg Principles and subsequently included in the
United Nations Charter. In international law, a crime against the peace 'consists
of starting or waging a war against the territorial integrity, political independence
or sovereignty of a state, or in violation of international treaties, bilateral
agreements or (legally binding) assurances' (Wikipedia). The acts are also referred
to as 'crimes of aggression' when they use armed force with the intent to deprive
a state of any part of its territory, permanent population, constitutionally
independent government, ability to conduct relations with other nation-states, or
with the intent to overthrow the government of a state or to impede its freedom to
act unhindered. In the hierarchy of international law, crimes against the peace
theoretically trump virtually all other international crimes, except when such
aggression is engaged through the United Nations with the aim of repressing

genocide, crimes against humanity, war crimes, slavery, torture, and/or piracy. Regretfully, while the ICC incorporates crimes of aggression, it was left undefined until a future time when such definitional jurisdiction could be agreed upon by member states.

Finally, 'war crimes' in international law refer to those punishable criminal offences that violate the laws of war and involve an inter-state conflict by any person or persons, military or civilian. War crimes not only refer to violations of international humanitarian law and to the established protections of the laws of war, but also include failures to adhere to norms of procedure and rules of battle. These acts may include mistreatment of prisoners of war or civilians, and are subject to the ICC. War crimes are sometimes part of instances of mass murder and genocide, and can overlap with those crimes under international humanitarian law described as crimes against humanity, but are not technically labelled as 'state crimes' although they may occur simultaneously.

Next, we turn our attention to 'transnational crimes' such as smuggling, trafficking in human beings, arms trafficking, drug trafficking, and money laundering. Although cross-border in nature, these 'ordinary' crimes can be prosecuted by individual states. However, as I noted above, I believe that a case can be made for including trafficking in human beings within the domain of supranational criminology proper along with international and state criminality. To put it simply, trafficking in human beings differs from the other transnational crimes, even that of people smuggling. The latter receive illegal entry into a country for a fee, and are free to go as they wish after arriving. The former are subjected to an equivalent of modern day slavery. Trafficking in human beings is also likely to involve physical force, fraud, deception, or other forms of coercion or intimidation to obtain, recruit, harbour, and transport people. As for the definitions of these crimes, they are as follows:

- Smuggling is illegal transport, in particular across a border. Taxes are avoided; or the goods themselves are illegal; or people are transported to a place where they are not allowed to be.
- Trafficking in human beings is the criminal commercial trade ('smuggling') of human beings, who are subjected to involuntary acts such as begging, sexual exploitation (e.g., prostitution and forced marriage), or unfree labour (e.g., involuntary servitude or working in a sweatshops.
- Arms trafficking encompasses the illicit trade usually, but not always, in small arms, involving 'the exchange of weapons for money, drugs, and other commodities that crosses national borders and spans the globe' often representing the weapons of choice in the majority of today's regional conflicts and by many terrorist groups operating around the world today (Stohl 2005, 1).

- Drug trafficking refers to the illegal trading of illegal drugs within the underground international economy whose activity may also consists of the production and distribution of illegal psychoactive substances.
- Money laundering, 'the metaphorical 'cleansing of money' with regards to appearances in law, is the practice of engaging in specific financial transactions in order to conceal the identity, source and/or destination of money and is a main operation of underground economy'.

Before turning to state crimes, it is worth underscoring that money laundering has come along way since the days of Prohibition in the United States and the conviction of Al Capone in 1931 for tax evasion. Historically, the term 'money laundering' was applied exclusively to financial transactions related to organised crime. Today, government regulators, such as the U.S. Office of the Comptroller of the Currency, have expanded its application 'to encompass any financial transaction which generates an asset or a value as the result of an illegal act, which may involve actions such as tax evasion or false accounting'.

Lastly, we turn our attention to *state crimes*. In addition to the 'crimes of commission' or to the nation-state violations of domestic criminal and civil laws, as well as various forms of international law, there are the 'crimes of omission' or the nation-state-corporate harms 'committed by government agencies or caused by public policies' that 'create additional groupings of victims and forms of victimization that are traditionally overlooked or downplayed: victims of social, political, and economic injustice; victims of racial, sexual, and cultural discrimination; and victims of abuse of political and/or economic power' (Barak 1991a, 4; Arat-Koc 2005; Gosnine 2005; Razack 2005). These state crimes may also derive from occupational positioning or political motivations. For example, 'occupational' state crimes are usually identified with and committed by individuals employed by the government who take advantage of their positions to engage in crime for personal and/or monetary gain. Unlike political state crimes, these crimes are not motivated by a desire to maintain the status quo or to resist or facilitate change, and they are not engaged in by agents working from the top down (Barak 1991a).

In their hybrid state-corporate formations, these state-facilitated crimes of business commission and governmental omission, for example, should also include the estimated 15,000 young boys who were enslaved in the Ivory Coast in 2001, a place where nearly half of all the world's cocoa beans – chocolate's essential ingredient – is still produced. On small farms in this part of the world, young boys pick cocoa beans from dusk to dawn. Traffickers, or '*locateurs*,' as they are called, approach young boys offering toys and good-paying jobs. The boys are then sold to unscrupulous growers, who force them to work long hours harvesting. These growers are also known to beat their child labourers with branches, bicycle chains, and other objects. The cocoa beans are then sold to 'silent conspirators,' the chocolate industry, represented in the United States by Hershey and M & M/ Mars. These twenty-first century forms of child slavery persist because of other conspirators as well, including federal contracts and taxpayer subsidies for the cocoa and chocolate industry, led by the Chocolate Manufacturers Association, have often succeeded in defeating protectionist legislation outlawing any dealings with these forms of child slavery (Working for Change 2001). The lack of social and legal controls, in short, allows these types of gross human rights violations and oppressive forms of exploitation to persist as globally normative for some, but certainly not all, nation-states.

4. SUPRANATIONAL CRIMINOLOGY: AN INTEGRATIVE PERSPECTIVE

The study of international crimes and state criminality is by definition a politically charged enterprise involving, among other things, the study of power, ideology, law, and justice – domestic, international, and global. As was noted in the introduction, the study of international crimes and state crimes cannot be separated from the processes and, therefore, study of a global political economy. Moreover, the dialectical relationships of the nation-state and its agents and representatives as both 'protectors' and 'violators' of international and state criminality, require that a supranational criminology incorporate as fundamental to its study and analysis not only the dynamic relations of a privatising capitalist state, but also a praxis of research and activist intervention that strives to shape a global or universal agenda over that of a transnational state-corporate agenda.

Studying these social, political, and criminal relations necessitates that criminologists and others develop conceptual frameworks of international and state criminality that are not only inclusive of the 'socio-legal' as described in the previous section, but that are also capable of aiding our understanding and evaluation of the 'gravity' or relative harms and injuries caused by an array of criminal behaviours and/or neoliberal policies of nation-states, North and South, East and West. There is also a need to examine the evolving international criminal apparatus for policing and adjudicating international and state criminality. In addition, an integrative perspective to international and state crimes calls for an interdisciplinary and comparative approach to the study of the overlapping interpersonal, institutional, and structural harms and violations as well as the responses to these gross human rights violations, capable of constructing both a comprehensive etiology that incorporates the full range of the social and behavioural sciences as well as the humanities and a thoughtful recourse toward

helping to maximise or universalise human rights in both discourse and
practice.

An integrative or 'holistic' approach to international social relations and
problems is not exactly a new concept. Holistic thinking of this kind was
characteristic of the 19th century whether one is discussing Durkheim, Weber or
Marx. In the post WW-II period, the pre-globalisation goal of the UNESCO
project was to pursue a holistic and rational understanding of interpersonal and
international conflicts. While this project did not succeed, some argue that its
time has passed; others, however, argue that its time is only still emerging and,
therefore, could come to fruition somewhere down the road. Whatever happens
historically from this point forward in the study of international crimes and state
crimes, the age of globalism, post-modernism, and fragmentism holds open the
possibility for an integrative spirit of social science activism, despite the rather
conciliatory stance toward state capital espoused by those advocates of the Third
Way such as social theorist Anthony Giddens (2000) or former U.S. President Bill
Clinton.

Much of the text and subtext of our discussion and examination of international
crimes and state crimes is inescapably about the dialectical processes involved in
the integration 'versus' disintegration of the world's populations: including the
feasibilities, obstacles, and contradictions of these relations. In its original
depictions, during the 1950s and 1960s, the social science integrative approach
linked predatory crime and violence primarily to two sources: conflict and crisis.
In the former model, they were viewed as a product of wilful agency or as situated
persons. Their acts, in other words, were calculating, instrumental, and involved
adversarial strategies of game theory. In the latter model, these crimes were a
manifestation of what was in some ways a dysfunctional bureaucracy or
pathological failure of the system itself, where individuals reacted according to
their positions in the social order. The problem back then, in a nutshell, was
viewed as a part of the modernisation project of progress and reform, and how not
only to integrate the actors into the system as a way of reducing conflict, but also
how to reform the system's institutional failures so as to avoid crisis.

In the globalised and post-modern neo-liberal world of the contemporary
corporate-state complex, the study of predatory crime and interpersonal violence
in general and of non-state terrorist acts in particular dwarfs the attention and
resources given to the study of the 'crimes of the powerful' (e.g., corporate, state),
be they national or international violators. At the same time as there is this relative
indifference to these state-corporate violations, the case of the United States and
Abu Ghraib prison in Iraq or the one holding 'enemy combatants' of the U.S. at
Guantanomo Bay, Cuba, come immediately to mind, there is also a resignation of
sorts to the growing problems of international crime and the violations of
universal human rights as 'given', subject to finding the best policies of 'what

works' and 'what doesn't' in the effort to 'control' and 'regulate' rather than 'reduce' or 'eradicate' these problems. These types of criminal 'omissions' and narrow conceptualisations are typically not challenged by administrative criminologists and other social scientists in service to the state who are dependent for their research on funding from 'neoliberal' state-corporate sources with their own agendas to contract for. In fact, as Tombs and Whyte (2003, 262–263) explain:

> 'The greatest challenge faced by those who wish to conduct research which presents an alternative to the neo-liberal view of the world may not necessarily be an intellectual one. After all, much of the theoretical justification both for the primacy of the market and for the strident pro-business stance of contemporary Western states is based upon updated versions of eighteenth and nineteenth century liberal economic and social theory – hence the "neo" bit. It is not difficult to challenge intellectually these variants of primitive and reductionist economism, whether the rational choice theorists in criminology or the 'trickle down' ideologues of classical economics. Much more difficult is breaking down the new common sense, the conventional wisdom of neo-liberalism, that has accumulated momentum in recent years—and most centrally, the idea that "There is no Alternative" (TINA) to the global expansion of a neo-liberal capitalism. Confronting this mantra has become a necessary part of conducting critical research.'

Part of confronting the mantra involves bringing back into the analysis of crime in general and of international and state crime in particular, the relations of 'class conflict' and a Marxist political economy. Reflective of a reciprocal and dialectical approach to the base and superstructure, a 'political economy' as an organising framework or as a general approach to interdisciplinary study has a powerful logic, transgressing the disciplinary straightjackets of politics, economics, and international relations, and at the same time, requiring analyses of the way in which ideas about what constitutes crime and justice have emerged, in contrast to the a-historical character of much of what currently passes for criminology and sociology. Once more from Tombs and Whyte (2003, 263),

> political economy is crucial in that its integrated historical and international character forces us to recognize that there are always alternatives – things are, have been, and can be different. Marxist political economy shares these features, but is specifically organized around concepts and ideas that have greater (not, as is claimed, less or even no) relevance today than when first forged in the adolescent stage of capitalist development. The labor theory of value and the theory of surplus value, the necessarily antagonistic relationship between classes, and the inherent tendency of capitalism to expand destructively while at the same time reproducing the contradictions upon which it is founded, are all crucial tools for understanding and engaging with the trajectories of the world around us.

Of course this is no less true for the study of international crime and state criminality. Yet, while we still have predatory crime and violence as conflict and crisis, we now also have increasingly violence as semi-autonomous, 'purely' destructive or self-destructive acts, ends in themselves. Whereas previously instrumentally organised violence was the predominant form of violence, and pathological or periodic crises in institutions due to non or mal-integration was viewed as 'causing' personal violence, there are now, in addition, forms of individual and group violence characteristic or expressive of the structurally and cultural deteriorating relations of early 21st century neo-liberal capitalism as it moves back-and-forth or between the preglobal world order of nation-states and into the new global world order of transnational corporate laissez-faire market states (Barak 2003; Derber 1998).

Clearly, there has been a diversification, not to mention an intensification of the levels of predatory crime and violence worldwide. In the post-modern world of state social science, the view seems to be less optimistic about the possibilities of integrating the actors into the system than it is about repressing marginality, opposition, and resistance, and of resigning itself to a perpetual system of inequality and privilege with its 'systemic' crimes in 'high' and 'low' places. That is to say that the majority of contemporary schools of violence seem to share a common pessimism:

> 'that the world is increasingly a stage without actors and attracted uniquely by the law of the jungle constituted by the market, chaos, or clash of identities and cultures, much more than by relationships that are negotiated involving a minimum of mutual recognition'. (Wieviorka 2003, 116)

This defeatist, cynical, and acquiescent social science of inequality, injustice, and state violence, needs to be challenged by a critical approach that recognises that there are small yet growing worldwide efforts aimed at peacemaking and mutualism, for instance, and that these global social movements and the changing nature of crime and violence all need to be analysed in terms of both 'free-market' globalisation and empire (Korten 2006).

Despite these intellectual shortcomings, I would argue that whether one ascribes to a 'clash of cultures' perspective, a 'unipolar' perspective with the United States as the only superpower or empire state, a 'multipolar' perspective involving not just the USA, but other political, economic, and social groupings and organisations, a highly 'fragmented' perspective with the risk of generalised violence, destruction, and/or annihilation, or a neoliberal 'third way' hybridisation of Keynesian and post-Keynesian economic policies – all of which are indicative of a new paradigm of the study of global crime and violence – that students and critical scholars of international and state crimes need to now, more than ever, analyse these phenomena in its theoretical and applied totality, both in the spirit of the older UNESCO project and in the spirit of the newer human rights and social justice agendas, ensnared by or in dialogue with an integrated political economy of advanced capitalism.

Not even a preliminary discussion of an integrated study of international crimes and state crimes, such as this one, would be near complete without some discussion of the availability of access to offenders and sites of offending and/or the appropriate methods to employ in the pursuit of a supranational criminology. Like the relative absence of the study of corporate and state crime from academic criminology and beyond, the study of a supranational criminology, especially as a newly emerging field of study, is subject to a dearth of relevant work and experience to draw upon as methodological resources. In other words, methods to date for researching international and state crimes are vastly underdeveloped, and wanting. Interestingly, in a related discussion of 'scrutinising the powerful,' Tombs and Whyte (2003, 7–8) comment:

> *'There are no examples of texts organized around a sustained concern for methodological issues raised in the processes of "researching the powerful", either within criminology or indeed across social science. Neither is this vacuum in methodological work confined to Britain or Europe: it is a global phenomenon. At the same time, within criminology, but also across the broad spectrum of the social sciences, work which addresses questions of method and methodology is proliferating (...)'*

One could certainly say the same thing about the study of international crimes and state crimes, as the perpetrators of these offences are primarily powerful people, groups, organisations, and networks. Similarly, access to these relatively powerful offenders and their sites of offending are difficult at best, and contrast somewhat sharply with access to at least some of the victims of these crimes. Of course, methods of generating data on international crimes is certainly easier than generating data on state crimes, especially since much of the latter remains part of the 'dark figures' of crime. In fact, there are a few official cross-national crime data sets with their usual problems of reliability and validity such as Interpol or the European Sourcebook, an International Crime Victimization Survey (ICVS), and the UN's Survey of Crime Trends and Operations of Criminal Justice, not to mention the reports of various NGOs and other non-profit organisations such as Amnesty International, the UN Human Rights Commission, or the Human Rights Committee established in 1966 to monitor compliance with the International Covenant on Civil and Political Rights, which is binding.

Incomplete data on international crime and state crime, official or unofficial, is certainly better than no data, but at the same time, an understanding of the nature of these crimes, in addition to the quantitative numbers, calls for the development of an international 'cultural criminology' derivative of qualitative, ethnographic, and/or historical investigations. These types of hybrid or integrated studies can facilitate making the crucial connections between the specific changes, fluctuations, and patterns in international crimes and state criminality and the general relations of advanced capitalism and its corresponding policies of contributing to or reducing these harms in the light of the proverbial 'what works' and 'what doesn't work' (Barak 2001). A few studies come to my mind that exemplify the kinds of research that I believe are fundamental to a supranational criminology. First, there is Rothe and Mullins' (2006a) examination of global social control, the ICC, and its response to the war crimes and crimes against humanity within the Democratic Republic of the Congo. Second, there are those studies by John Hagan and his colleagues, one addressing the prosecution of the crimes of war in the Balkans (2003) and the other examining the crimes of genocide in Darfur (Hagan et al. 2005). In fact, insights from these investigations into the control or regulation of international and state criminality are reflected in the thinking underpinning this essay.

It is also important, once again, to underscore the importance of specifically addressing and examining the state-corporate crimes of, for example, profiteering and racketeering over no-bid contracts for supplying mercenaries and reconstruction teams by the likes of Halliburton or Bechtel. These state-facilitated 'crimes of war' benefit generally from un-prosecuted illegal wars in Iraq and Afghanistan. These business and governmental interactions benefit particularly as they are also part and parcel of an infrastructure where private contractors assist states in getting away with torture and murder as they claim 'plausible deniability' as part of their defence that the government did not specifically order the crimes in question. As Michalowski and Kramer (2006, 9) underscore: these state-corporate relations create 'a political culture and organizational framework that ultimately [leads] to heinous acts that would not have occurred without that culture and those frameworks.' Until these cultures and frameworks or criminogenic conditions are recognised socially and addressed legally, these crimes of gross human rights violations will remain *beyond incrimination*, not to mention the lesser, ordinary crimes of war, in Iraq alone, accounting for hundreds of thousands of malnourished children, a collapsing health care system unable to address preventable diseases, and the displacement of more than four million people forced to flee their homes over a four year period (Editorial in the *New York Times*, April 22, 2007: 'Iraq's Desperate Exodus').

Finally, it is these types of integrated pictures or analyses of international and state crimes and the varied responses to them that bring greater understanding of the nature of these harms and their control. At the same time, these types of study like that of the budding, and hopefully, burgeoning field of supranational criminology, will not only bring heightened attention to these offences, pressuring academic bodies, governments, and other organisations to bring their actions into conformity with the universal declaration of human rights, but in the process research agendas of this kind will also help to further legitimate an expanding sense of an international community and of human rights worldwide.

5. PEACEMAKING, NON-VIOLENCE AND SOCIAL CHANGE

There is a tendency in peace studies and non-violent circles to discuss international conflict and power relations primarily in terms of social groups and material interests. It should be noted, however, that these social, political, and economic interests for addressing issues of international, state, and state-corporate crime are also psychological. Many of these psychic interests, which tend to be personal and even subconscious in nature, are experienced as unresolved 'conflicts and desires' in a Freudian sense. In other words, these personal-political conflicts or desires are often as, or more, emotional than they are material. Accordingly, in the name of peace and justice we often see patterns of both violence and injustice rationalised away for some kind of greater 'defensive' good (Barak 2003; Donnelly 2003).

Furthermore, models of non-violence primarily reveal themselves in two contexts: first, as alternative or competing visions to the traditionally limited paradigmatic view of adversarialism, hierarchy, and inequality; and second, as expressive of the more recent emergent paradigm of mutualism, love, and equality. Each of these paradigmatic models for viewing human nature provides plenty of meaning and orientation to the world. In the adversarial model, human interaction 'is based on conflicts of interests, wars, and the opposition of people to each other and to nature'; in the mutuality model by contrast, 'cooperation, caring, nurturing, and loving' are viewed 'as equally viable ways of organizing relationships of humans to each other and to nature' (Fellman 1998, 5). Historically, the adversarial model has been dominant and the mutuality model has been the subordinate or alternative model. In the 21st century, however, it is quite likely that in the expanding spirit for universal human rights that mutualism will also grow in both its attractiveness and attainability as it becomes more familiar and more routine in global affairs.

I do not mean to suggest that in any way short of the dialectics of materialism that there is some kind of natural or linear progression or evolution from adversarialism to mutualism or from violent to non-violent relationships either between people or nation-states. Nor am I suggesting that these competing cultural and mental states of being are exclusive of the other or that they do not coexist in time and space. On the contrary, my argument elsewhere has been that both have existed in some kind of social, political, and ideological relation to each other for thousands of years (Barak 2003). Hence, I argue here that both paradigms need to be taken seriously by a supranational criminology as each expresses the often contradictory interaction of self and society or of character and social structure, and these apply to the full range of ordinary and extraordinary crimes of violence.

The struggle to develop a fuller and richer mutualism as a challenge not only to reign in and control our adversarial tendencies, but also as a means of resisting those international crimes and state criminality more particularly, involves individuals, families, communities, tribes, nation-states, and, ultimately, the planet, all working together to alter traditional as well as international patterns of social interaction. These struggles against the hegemony of neo-liberal policies of global market economies or against the older feudalistic-authoritarian, anti-democratic regimes, and in the name of social justice and human rights, or for the creation of more equitable, peaceful, and non-violent alternatives to revenge, retribution, and repressive justice, are not about negating competitiveness, conflict, capitalism, or religion per se, but rather, these are about reducing as much as possible the systematically destructive and counterproductive aspects of these social and institutionalised arrangements with respect to the etiologies of both international and state criminality. In a few words, this struggle for 'social justice' is ultimately about dismantling state-corporate systems of oppression and exploitation that are at the roots of most, if not, all forms of gross human rights violations.

What I am calling for amounts to a radical departure from mainstream social science and the neo-liberal agenda of state-regulated or influenced criminology in general. In other words, I am advocating a supranational criminology that aligns itself with international and transnational rather than with nationalistic or nation-state points of view and with those social organisations and movements trying to serve the more 'collective' and interdependent interests of the larger global community. To make this type of 'leap of faith' transition from a statecraft dominated point of view to a worldcraft shared point of view is to take a stance more likely to adopt non-violent than violent approaches to social conflict.

Historically, each of the non-violent struggles for justice that had succeeded in the latter half of the 20th century, such as the American civil rights movement to outlaw segregation and discrimination, the movement to upend the apartheid structure in South Africa, or the movement to oust the Communist Party and establish a new governmental structure in Poland, have also served to delegitimate the adversarial fallacies that only violence can overcome violence and that those battles with the greatest stakes have to be settled by force of arms. In other words, there are other less destructive pathways to regime change that do not intensify or escalate divisions between peoples. These social actions and non-violent movements against state criminality and the violation of universal human rights share in common with all models of non-violence and peacemaking, whether addressing interpersonal, institutional, or structural levels of conflict and violence, a belief in the spirit, theory, and practice of mutualism over the spirit, theory, and practice of adversarialism (Barak 2003).

More specifically, when it comes to peacemaking and non-violent policy considerations, there have been national and international efforts to mobilise people in the struggle for human rights and social justice. These social movements have been both domestic and global, and from an international perspective, they have included such diverse bodies as the United Nations, regional organisations of nation-states such as the Organization of African Unity, the Organization of American States, or the European Union, intergovernmental organisations (IGOs), nongovernmental organisations (NGOs), transnational organisations (TNOs), and even multinational corporations (MNCs). In still a very limited sense, these types of organisations alone and especially in tandem have furthered efforts in peacekeeping, third-party mediation, global debating, regionalism, international law, and more, all of which contributes to an expanding and universalising discourse of human rights and social justice.

Early into the 21st century, these types of policymaking and peacemaking efforts are seriously taking up the challenges of adversarialism, mutualism, and even world governance. As Barash and Webel (2002, 371) have written in their soon to be a classic textbook on the subject, Peace and Conflict Studies:

> "Although their record has not been perfect, there is much to applaud in the activities of international organizations. Some of these – notably the United Nations—promote human planetary betterment in numerous ways, including but not limited to the keeping of negative peace, that is, the prevention or termination of war. They also represent a partial step in the progression from individualism through nationalism to globalism, a transition that may well be essential if we are ever to give peace a realistic chance. As such, international organizations can be seen as possible halfway houses toward the establishment and solidification of international law, and perhaps even world government."

At the international level, this means that students of supranational criminology or nation-states can also choose to package their repressed anger and hostility, and indulge in wars with enemy combatants, or they can choose to adopt peaceful strategies of cognitive interaction, altruistic humanism, and compassionate negotiation. For example, as an alternative to waging war in Afghanistan and Iraq, the USA could have declared Al Qaeda and its terrorist conspirators 'mass murderers' for their actions of 9/11. Their terrorist actions did not have to necessitate an escalation of violence in the name of a 'war on terrorism.' In other words, there already are criminal laws against terrorism both domestically and internationally. These crimes don't require going to war against nation-states, even when they harbour such perpetrators, particularly when doing so involves 'pre-emptive' first strikes that are in violation of international law. Thus, these terrorist acts should have been fundamentally treated as international crimes against humanity, and these terrorists could have been pursued as wanted outlaws rather than as military or enemy combatants (Barak 2005).

Such an approach to 9/11 would have helped to differentiate associated peoples, Islamic and non-Islamic, who happen to reside in countries where terrorists have been recruited and trained, from terrorists themselves. In the process of engaging in a more traditional retributive form of justice and pursuit of these criminals, vis-à-vis the 'rule of law' rather than the 'rule of force,' the USA could have helped to isolate rather than to spread the 'extremist' behaviour in the name of some kind of radical fundamentalism. At the same time, the U.S. itself would not have also committed a variety of war crimes and crimes against humanity, in addition to the more fundamental crimes against the peace. In short, as a criminal or human rights matter and not a matter of war making, the U.S. would have avoided the occupation of two countries in the centre of the Arab and Islamic world, and inadvertently assisted with the spreading of both bin Ladenism in general and sectarian violence in particular, as part of an expanding and reciprocal spiralling of acts of terrorism and counter-terrorism.

6. CONCLUSION

The type of integrative and reciprocal praxis described in this chapter as well as its vision for a supranational criminology of international and state-corporate criminality relies on a fundamental appreciation that gross human rights violations is ultimately an expression of the political economy of inequality and repression that operates through, between, and within the intersections of governments and businesses. Hence, in the real world of capital and geopolitical conflict and power, bringing about both the expansion of what constitutes gross human rights violations, or what reaches the level of gravity necessary to release the socio-political mechanisms and/or international legal procedures in place for confronting these crimes against humanity when they reach some kind of relative moral-objective status of 'extraordinary' rather than 'ordinary' crimes, as well as what constitutes those political-economic realities necessary to facilitate both the global development of economic democracies and the global development of the legal controls and regulations of systems of oppression and exploitation as a means of or for preventing gross human rights violations in the first place, requires a worldwide multilateralism, a shared consciousness of identity and ethics based on a global social contract, and a willingness of states to be able to give up some aspects of their sovereignty to allow for a *realpolitik* of internationalism.

At the same time, with respect to an emerging supranational criminological endeavour only in its infancy, there is much work and study to be conducted. Still fundamental to its development are the needs to articulate the key methodological, theoretical, and applied parameters capable of exercising social justice in the pursuit of challenging international and state criminality as well as facilitating the means for controlling these crimes against humanity. All of the political, economic, ideological, social, and legal changes and adaptations required will, of course, takes years of struggle. That struggle, however, should not only be waged in the socially constructed juridical worlds of 'bourgeois' law and order, but also more fundamentally in the politically and economically constructed worlds of 'universal' law and order.

The reciprocal political-economic model to studying global relations and supranational criminology called for here has been grounded in a Gramscian analysis of democratic social science and dialectical materialism. Thus, it is geared towards the development of mixed social economies within the framework of 'fair' rather than 'free' economies of global capitalism. Stated differently, an 'extant international community founded on core principles of universal rights and justice is the best hope that disempowered and marginalized populations have to counteract the currently prevailing forces of ever increasing domination of Western capital and of US imperial ambitions' (Rothe and Mullins 2006c, 26). From an historical perspective, both of these types of global social movements are conducive for the development and expansion of international law and, ultimately, very long range, for the establishment of some kind of world parliament or global government that regulates the 'laissez-fare' neo-liberal market for the benefit of the global masses. Specifically, these social movements are in struggle against or resistance to the dominant neo-liberal policies of laissez-faire capitalism and privatisation, responsible for such escalating global issues as poverty, inequality, and social conflict, the 'fuel' for the transnationalisation of crime and crime control.

In closing off this conceptualisation of international and state crime, I see a partisan, integrative, and reciprocal approach to the study of gross human rights violations and the linkage of this scholarly activity, with those groups and organisations independently involved in the movement for universal human rights and against crimes against humanity, as absolutely essential to the successful deployment of a supranational criminology. In other words, only by evolving a global criminology dedicated to eradicating as many of the 'causes' of international and state-corporate crime as possible and to establishing as many 'protections' from all types of social harm and human exploitation, will a supranational criminology survive and develop as a viable alternative to nation-state criminologies.

PART II
MEASURE AND MAP
INTERNATIONAL CRIMES:
RESEARCH METHODOLOGY

IV. MISSING PIECES

Some Thoughts on the Methodology of the Empirical Study of International Crimes and Other Gross Human Rights Violations

Catrien BIJLEVELD

1. INTRODUCTION

International crimes, among which can be classified acts such as crimes against humanity, war crimes and genocide and other gross human rights violations (GHRV), are a relatively understudied topic in criminology. Yacoubian (2000), in a much-cited example, calculated that less than 1% of all presentations at American criminology conferences until then dealt with genocide and gross human rights violations. The reason for this relative disinterest cannot be quantitative: approximately 191 million people lost their lives to collective violence in the 20th century (WHO 2002), more than half of whom were civilians. Nor can this disinterest be due to qualitative insignificance: in fact, genocide is often described as the most heinous of all crimes, the ultimate offence or the Big Evil. In a more juridical vein, as Van Zyl Smit (2004) phrased it: genocide is aggravated murder. International crimes are the criminal pendant of some of the most severe GHRV. GHRV therefore are sometimes comprehensively labelled international crimes, although there is no perfect overlap between the two categories. We will employ the two terminologies interchangeably here.

While until recently this general criminological disinterest was only perceived as striking in some criminological niches and related circles, respected and mainstream criminologists have if not embraced, at least recognised the topic as relevant for criminology. This implies, if the study of international crimes is to become a regular one within criminology, that, just like for other objects of study, we would want to study four domains. These concur with fairly universally accepted notions of what are the relevant objects of study within criminology. These are:

1. the study of the incidence of crime;
2. the study of explanations for criminality, the aetiology of offending;

the reactions to crime;
  victims or victimology.

study of the incidence of crime, would then fall studies that assess the inciue.. e of conflicts or outbreaks of violence, and of the number of offences committed. Also, studies that attempt to describe rather than quantify only international crimes would fall under this header. This would be studies that explain the background to conflicts, the outbreak and development of crimes committed, in time and space, and studies that describe the nature and the context of the crimes. Under 1, one should perhaps also place studies that attempt to gauge the damage of international crimes. Under 2, the study of the aetiology of crime, would fall studies at macro, meso as well as micro-level. Macro studies would attempt to explain the eruption of conflicts from state or macro-level factors such as the totalitarianism of regimes, the extent to which there are trade relations with many other nations, from the (non-)intervention of international organisations or from international relations and trade interests, etc. Micro studies would be geared towards perpetrators. Meso-studies would be focused on levels responsible for the commission of such crimes that fall between the micro and state level, such as businesses. Under 3 would fall studies on, for instance, the perceived effectiveness and fairness of responses to such crimes, such as international tribunals, truth commissions, etc. The study of victims, under 4, would imply the study of the extent of victimisation (partially overlapping with some of the topics under 1) characteristics of the victims, relations between offender(s) and victim(s), and the effects of victimisation.

In this chapter, an attempt will be made to outline the methodology needed for, and particular to, the study of international offending. The author reasons from the assumption that international crimes must become a regular topic within criminology. Secondly, the author assumes that international crimes can only become a respected and relevant topic if it is studied properly, that is, through the appropriate methodology. As will be argued below, because of its specific nature and context, many international crimes need tailored methodologies. As such, this chapter will detail those methodologies that can be considered particular for this area of study. As will be shown below, not all methodology is particular: many regular criminological research methods and techniques can also be used fruitfully. Also, many particular methodologies are in fact adapted versions of existing methodologies from other disciplines (mainly biology and epidemiology) or are common sense extensions of run-of-the-mill methodologies. In discussing methodologies, this chapter will focus most on quantitative methodologies for assessing victimisation, as this author deems that those must and have been most particularly geared to the study of international crimes.

This chapter will first in section 2 give a number of reasons why international crimes should be studied within the context of criminological research and theorising. Next, in section 3 it will give a number of reasons why studying international crimes in a supranational criminology is a less straightforward endeavour than studying 'ordinary' crimes in a national setting. In section 4, a number of examples will be given of particular difficulties and methodologies that are employed in the study of international crimes. The chapter ends with section 5, in which recommendations are given and a tentative research agenda is set.

2.   FOR STUDYING INTERNATIONAL CRIMES

Let us reiterate first why international crimes should be studied. There are several ways to respond to this question. Looking at the tabulations presented by for instance Harff (2003; Table 1), one sees immediately how the estimates of the number of victims of some of the worst incidents of international crime carry a very wide margin. For instance, the number of victims from the genocide in Rwanda is estimated at between 500,000 and 1,000,000; mortality due to the conflict in Pakistan in 1971 varies by a factor 3, between one and three million. Estimates of the death toll from the conflict in Congo between 1964 and the beginning of 1965 even vary by a factor 10. Apparently, one could say, a lot is unclear and remains to be studied. Employing a different perspective, one could say that as international crimes entail criminality, and that as criminology studies criminality, international crimes are *a priori* included and special arguments would be needed to exclude them. A third argument of convenience is that, as international criminal law and its application has seen such a tempestuous development, this should not go unaccompanied by an auxiliary, supportive body of criminological literature (viz. Roberts & McMillan 2003).

More substantively, one could argue that international crimes must be studied as already indicated above because they are at the tail-end of the spectrum of severity of offending (Van Zyl Smit 2004). Particularly genocide, but also other kinds of gross human rights violations, are amongst the most serious crimes. A criminology that would disregard these acts would skip an important part of its study object. Also, one could argue that there is reason to suspect that international crimes are responsible for the bulk of unnatural deaths worldwide (Leitenberg 2006). However, there is as yet not enough evidence to sustain this as a fact and this is exactly why more research would be needed here too; Leitenberg himself states: '(…) the first point regarding data on deaths in wars and conflicts (is): such figures at times display enormous variance' (cf. Leitenberg 2006, 3). With such enormous margins, the figures become at best a mere statistic (cf. the famous quote by – reportedly – Stalin). What is worse is that with such margins the figures run the serious risk of becoming trivial. Policy makers, the media and academicians may simply resort to stating that casualties are 'large'. While this in itself is not a problem, as long as belief in the seriousness of the conflict under scrutiny is not undermined, the wide margins also make it much easier for perpetrators to hide behind this uncertainty and discard estimates as 'overstatements', 'imprecise' and the like.

It is only realistic to acknowledge that – paradoxically – the sheer magnitude of the scale of the abuses studied in the study of gross human rights violations makes exact determination of casualties less relevant. Whether 500,000 or 510,000 people were killed as a result of a conflict makes little difference in our appreciation of the happenings, and will also have little effect on sentences meted out – if meted out. So why at all attempt to assess as exactly as possible the scale of offending and the number of casualties?

Precise measurement is important, however, as examples below will detail, also and perhaps most importantly because exact measurement of the nature and scale of offending is a precondition to identify patterns in the happenings, to show spatial and temporal variations, and to link offences to offenders. Establishing and devising ways to uncover the pattern may also be useful for linking offences to perpetrators and thus making more effective prosecution possible (Ball & Asher 2002). Obtaining as detailed as possible victim reports on the nature of the offences, remarks made by perpetrators during assaults and the spatial distribution of attacks, may also shed light on offender intent, notably of crucial importance in prosecution for genocide. Understanding the perpetrators is of crucial importance to criminological theorising itself. A number of studies have shown that quite a number of perpetrators are average, normal citizens. This is a perplexing finding and one that topples a sizeable chunk of criminological theorising. While criminologists study perpetrators' personal characteristics to explain their behaviour, and in doing so deploy theories overwhelmingly emphasising personal deviance, by contrast apparently ordinary, law-abiding and well-adjusted citizens under certain circumstances commit the grossest acts (Arendt 1963).

Thus, in order to be able to describe what happened, in order to tell the story of the offences, we first must have measured them well. Only then can we be reasonably confident about patterns in the violations and about the conclusions we might want to draw (Ball, Kobrak & Spirer 1999; Brysk 1994). Reasoned conversely, how can we explain phenomena that we do not measure well?

In addition, as some examples below will show, detailed study of the conflicts is also necessary to link the immediate consequences to the less direct ones. Oftentimes, the conflicts that fall under the umbrella of international crimes or other gross human rights violations, comprise not only direct killings, rape, looting and infrastructural destruction, but have much longer term consequences, with often a manifold higher death toll. For Congo it was estimated that mortality due to preventable causes such as malnutrition and infectious diseases was many times the so-called 'direct mortality'. As Jonassohn and Björnson (1998) argued and illustrated by various examples, famine and other preventable disasters are often used by governments as a cheap and efficient way to get rid of certain segments of the population (De Waal 2002; Prunier 2005). To establish this pattern it is necessary to document and understand the patterns of gross human rights violations, as well as to be able to assess in what ways the scale of the damage could have been mitigated and can be mitigated in similar circumstances in the future.

This latter assessment is also important from a different policy perspective. It is often assumed that in for instance sub-Saharan Africa, preventable diseases like malaria, measles and malnutrition, exacerbated by environmental degradation, are the 'big killers'. If we were able to give all citizens access to health services and have widespread inoculation campaigns, mortality would be greatly reduced is the idea. While that is undoubtedly true, it is important to assess whether gross human rights violations are not bigger killers. Put differently it would be important to gauge mortality risk from various causes: disease and environmental disasters, against 'international violence' (including violence-induced or government orchestrated famines and breakdown of health services).

Lastly, there is in a sense a moral obligation for criminology to study international crimes. In many countries in which such violations have taken place there has been an almost complete breaking down of academic independence and research facilities. Many scholars have left the country or have been killed. It is thus – parallel to the international nature of the offences at stake – also a universal research issue. Putting it differently and bluntly, Western scholars cannot be bystanders and continue to study their own national issues and particular hang ups. Sibo van Ruller, a Dutch historical criminologist, remarked snidely on the fact that the topic of the first criminological conference in the Netherlands after WWII, in a country in which 70% of all the residing Jews and 90% of the Jews in Amsterdam had been deported and killed, was 'bike theft' (1999).

Summarising, we conclude that criminology cannot but study international crimes. The arguments are that there is no argument not to study them. Accurate information is necessary to be able to describe the course of happenings during the conflicts and therefore also to be able to understand what happened. Describing what happened, in as much detail as possible, will also document for survivors, victims and future generations what happened (viz. the Truth and similar Commissions of, e.g. South Africa, Timor-Leste, Guatemala). The study of international crimes and their consequences can also aid the assessment of the impact of prevention, of aid and of measures to alleviate suffering and counter international offending as compared to other policy measures.

Thus, studying international crimes in as detailed a manner as possible is necessary and may be useful for various purposes, not all of them academic.

3. PARTICULARITIES AND A RESEARCH METHODOLOGY FOR INTERNATIONAL CRIMES

What then are the particularities of the study of international crimes that would make it necessary to devote an entire chapter to the topic? We give a probably not exhaustive overview of methodological issues in the study of gross human rights violations.

3.1. THE DOUBLY-DARK NUMBER

A first and foremost complication in studying international crimes is that we are in a sense faced with a doubly-dark figure. In 'ordinary', national, criminology, if we want to study the incidence of certain crimes defined as such under national law, our research is encumbered with the so-called dark number. Police-recorded offences are only a fraction of all real offending and in all likelihood also not a representative fraction. This means that for studying the true incidence of crime and victimisation, victim studies are generally considered a better tool. Victim studies shed only a partial light on offender characteristics, and are generally not considered very useful for studying very rare or grave offences such as rape and – understandably – homicide. They have their own problems, such as recall problems, telescoping and selective underreporting. Anonymous perpetrator studies ('self-report studies') are considered a valid tool to assess offender characteristics.

Thus, in the study of national crime there is a dark number, but there is an organisational structure attempting to collect offence information, and a criminal justice system that – however imperfectly at times – attempts to bring offenders to justice, and records offender, offence and victim information in court files. In the study of international crimes, it is not only offenders who attempt to stay out of the machinery of the criminal justice system, but it is the state itself that actively frustrates the registration of events. Brysk (1994) recounts how in Argentina there was a massive destruction of records. Many instances for many countries have been documented of witnesses to gross human rights violations disappearing or being killed, and of attempts to hide the evidence of killings and other acts. Thus, the criminologist is faced with a doubly-dark number.

3.2.   BASELINE DATA[1]

In principle, it would be possible to check for numbers and identities of disappeared or killed persons by checking against census data. However, many countries in which gross human rights violations take place do not have proper census information. In many instances (Rwanda, Sudan) previous censuses were – although this is contested – in all likelihood flawed and/or tampered with, in the sense that the ethnic group that became victimised in the subsequent gross human rights violations was undercounted. It is reported that the Tutsi in Rwanda were undercounted in the census (and perhaps self-undercounted as many Tutsi reported themselves as Hutu to avoid discrimination). Also, the southern Sudanese population and that of the Nuba mountains in Sudan have been undercounted in successive censuses. The situation is not always so bleak, however. Croes and Tammes (2004) used the extensive Dutch municipal records among others in their landmark study on the survival chances of the Jews in the Netherlands. In prewar Yugoslavia there was a fairly good municipal registration. Verwimp (2004) used data on the respondents in a pre-genocide survey in Kibuye province in Rwanda, and could in doing so fairly accurately for this province assess mortality.

3.3.   VICTIM SURVEYS

Obviously, given that for studying gross human rights violations police data is probably unfeasible, one could resort to victim surveys. These have indeed been used extensively for estimating mortality (see, e.g. for Congo Coghlan et al. 2006; for Sudan, see Depoortere et al. 2004; for Guatemala, see Ball, Kobrak & Spirer 1999; for Timor-Leste, see Silva & Ball 2006; there are many other examples). When many of the population (in particular entire families) have however perished or left the country altogether, victim surveys have their own particular problems. There is then what is called 'survivor bias'. When many (entire families or clusters) have died, victim surveys underestimate mortality. When the survivors are different from those who were killed, there will in addition be bias in the characteristics measured.

For financial reasons, mortality surveys often employ a cluster sampling design. Research has shown that it is important to include a sufficiently large number of clusters, as fatalities tend to be clustered and estimates may become unstable or biased towards the high end. The Burnham study (2006) that estimated

---

[1]   Baseline data, a term originally from epidemiology, is data against which to set data from an unusual situation, such as mortality after conflict, disease after floods, etc. In this example, baseline data is thus the population size before the outbreak of the conflict or the atrocities.

an excess mortality of over 600,000 in Iraq was criticised, *inter alia*, for not employing sufficient numbers of clusters (Guha-Sapir, Degomme & Pedersen 2007).

3.4. SECURITY ISSUES

Even without such issues it is often difficult, especially when conflicts are ongoing (Darfur) or have recently been terminated (Congo, Sierra Leone) to get access to victims. Many will be internally displaced persons (IDPs) or refugees in neighbouring countries. There is obviously no sampling frame and it will be hard to draw a representative sample. Victim surveys for Darfur mostly relied on camps that were accessible either in Darfur or Chad, and there has definitely been undersampling of those who fled to relatives in towns, and undersampling in one large camp in southern Darfur. Burnham et al. (2006) in their study on mortality in Iraq report how their interviewers were not equipped with GPS technology for drawing their samples as that was deemed too risky. Security thus affected the sampling design. Security issues affected access to areas and thus the representativeness of victim surveys in Sierra Leone, Congo and Sudan (Darfur). The Benetech group in Palo Alto designed software ('Martus') to store and categorise data on gross human rights violations, which encrypts the data for safety reasons. Data is centrally stored on a server, where it can also be fixed (so that it is later unalterable). Even if the PCs on which the data is entered go missing, data is always retrievable by those who have access to the central server. 'Analyzer' is another example of such software.

3.5. UNDERREPORTING/NON-RESPONSE

Even if conflicts have ended already a while ago (such as in Rwanda), it can be difficult to get victims to speak out. In studying rape victimisation prevalence in Rwanda, Bijleveld & Morssinkhof (2006) report how female victims of rape are extremely reluctant to speak about their victimisation as rape carries an immense stigma in Rwandan society and women are reported not be willing to declare that they have been raped for fear of not being able to ever find a husband. Secondly, many women were raped by men they know or by men who may even still be living in their vicinity. They are apprehensive of speaking out about the rape as they fear reprisals. Thirdly, many survivors are reported to be unwilling to speak about their experiences as they suffer from survivor's guilt. Lastly, many victims or witnesses are reportedly afraid to speak out because they fear being called to testify. Also, some women report that speaking out about their victimisation is not worth the trouble and the risk; they feel let down by the legal system, particularly the ICTR. See also Gingerich & Leaning (2004). Particularly rape is generally – and this is in all likelihood the same outside the context of international crimes – grossly underreported in victim surveys. Infant mortality is often underreported in mortality surveys.

Biased data may be less of a problem when making comparisons within victim groups, for instance comparing the incidence in PTSD in survivors who have and have not witnessed certain events (see, e.g. Dyregrov et al. 2000 on PTSD in Rwandan children and Geltman et al. 2005 on trauma in unaccompanied minors from Sudan).

3.6.   USE OF SECONDARY DATA

In some cases there may already have been extensive data collection efforts to document the atrocities and collect witness statements. Examples are Guatemala, Argentina, Timor-Leste and South Africa. Especially when these have been collected in a universal and well-documented manner, they can very well be used for data analysis and hypothesis testing purposes. In addition, the accumulating evidence from international prosecution of the admittedly mainly big fish in gross human rights violations is a resource for the academic study of perpetrators, state involvement and involvement of organisations, that is as yet untapped.

In many other cases, human rights groups, international NGOs and the state department report on gross human rights violations. While there have been serious doubts on the state department's 'country reports', these seem to have definitely improved in quality and impartiality (Poe, Carey & Vazquez 2001), and converged in content to what Amnesty International reports. Other organisations such as Human Rights Watch[2], Physicians for Human Rights[3], the International Crisis Group[4], etc., all regularly write reports on ongoing conflicts that can also be used for information to conduct analyses on. Such information, while it is often the only thing to essentially 'go on', is less than ideal from a methodological perspective. The information gathered is uncontrollable for reasons of witness protection. Background information on the conflict may be collected from just one or two sources in the country investigated, meaning that the information – while assumedly of high quality – is extremely unreliable from a social science perspective. Reports from various organisations may be tapping from just one or two similar sources, the only available and high quality ones in a country, giving

---

[2]   www.hrw.org.
[3]   www.physiciansforhumanrights.org.
[4]   www.crisisgroup.org.

high congruity but no interrater reliability in the methodological sense. See also Stohl et al. (1986).

Victim organisations have in some cases also drawn up lists of victims and of the events during the gross human rights violations. Verwimp (2004) for instance worked with the data from the victim organisation Ibuka in Rwanda, which, although incomplete, had information on killings, from which certain patterns could be deduced. Such data has also been collected by advocacy and survivors' groups in Argentina. Smith & Walker (2004) give a nice example of a list of documented incidents for Darfur, in which the number of people killed per locality per date are listed, containing a list of Janjaweed camps, with commanders named. The list contains also details on other crimes committed during the scorching and emptying of localities, such as the poisoning of wells and looting of cattle, drawing attention to the property motives of the perpetrators.

3.7. COLLATING INFORMATION FROM OTHER SOURCES

Aid organisations also publish reports on emergency interventions that can be used for arriving at mortality estimates. Guha-Sapir, Degomme & Phelan (2005) used such data to compute mortality estimates for Darfur. Listing under 5 mortality ratios[5] (<5MRs) and crude mortality ratios[6] (CMRs) and leaving aside outliers[7], they showed how, contrary to Hagan et al. (2005) who employed a blanket[8] estimate from multiple victim survey data and had arrived at an estimate of around 400,000, the number of people killed in Darfur by early 2005 since the start of the conflict was around 120,000. Other reasons why the Hagan et al. (2005) estimate was so much higher than the Guha-Sapir et al. estimate is that in the Hagan paper there was some double counting of violent deaths, calculating a crude mortality rate was problematic because the recall period was unclear and because it is to be doubted whether the surveys employed could be generalised to

---

[5]   The under five mortality rate (or <5MR or U5MR) is correspondingly defined as total number of deaths of children under aged 5 per 1,000 live births.

[6]   The crude mortality rate (or CMR), is defined as the total number of deaths per 1,000 live births; see also http://www.cred.be/docs/cedat/definitionforCE-DAT.pdf.

[7]   An outlier is an observation that differs so much from the other observations that it must be assumed to be either a mismeasurement or a typing error, or to represent a situation that is highly atypical. Outliers are mostly removed from the data.

[8]   A 'blanket' estimate is an estimate that is assumed equal for all relevant aspects of the situation under observation. In the Darfur case, mortality estimates just before reaching the camps were used as temporally invariant, and mortality estimates from the south and west of the region were used as geographically invariant. If the intensity of the conflict under study differs in time and for different regions, such blanket estimates are bound to give under or overestimates.

all Darfurians (Guha-Sapir et al. 2005, 10). In the Guha-Sapir et al. study (2005), the number of direct deaths (deaths attributable to violence) was estimated to be a little under one-third. This differs substantially from the number of direct deaths in Congo (estimated at about one in 10; see Coghlan et al. (2006)) and from the number of direct deaths in Iraq (estimated at 92%; see Burnham et al. (2006)). These differences can mean various things. They may be interpreted to show that the conflicts in Iraq and Darfur in Sudan are 'bloodier', whereas mortality in Congo was a more protracted process, in which disruption and destruction of infrastructure and subsequent malnutrition and disease could become the big killers. They may also be interpreted to show that aid was simply more effectively administered to the displaced population in Darfur. They probably also show that in Iraq, where the population has a much better feeding and inoculation status than in either Darfur or Congo, preventable diseases simply had less of a chance to cause so much mortality. In as yet unpublished work, Bijleveld, Mehlbaum & Degomme (forthcoming) show how in southern Sudan, from 1983 to 2003, also only a very small fraction of the more than 2 million deaths were attributable to direct violence. In southern Sudan, the government of Sudan for years systematically closed off the south, bombed hospitals and frustrated aid. The examples show how quantitative data on mortality can thus be a starting point for comparing and interpreting mortality patterns and understanding genocidal policies.

All in all, it should be said that in studying gross human rights violations, the criminologist encounters particular methodological complications. The first of these is the utter lack of (reliable) data. Second is the problem of implementing victim surveys: many have died, many are reluctant to speak out, many victims or particular victims are inaccessible. This is in many cases worsened by a deficient data collection infrastructure, making it difficult to travel, to design an adequate sampling frame and to obtain baseline data. Reports from those associations and individuals who did gain access to the affected population are limited regionally, temporally, are biased towards emergency situations and offer at most a sketchy picture of happenings. In addition, not mentioned yet, in order to be able to judge the sketchy data, it is often necessary to have in-depth knowledge of the conflict at hand, as well as a good network of specialists on the ground who can direct the researcher to valuable but grey or even unpublished reports. Is it therefore impossible to measure gross human rights violations? As the examples already given have shown and those that follow will hopefully show too, this is definitely not the case. Some particular methodologies need to be employed. And one has to be content with special caution and accept working with underestimates.

4.   EXAMPLES

In this section we will give a number of examples of methodologies employed in the empirical study of gross human rights violations. Either these examples regard fairly novel methodologies, methodologies tailored to the particularities of the problem at hand or the straightforward application of existing methodologies. In each case, this author believes that the application is an example of the manner in which rigorous empirical study of international crimes and its victims may shed light on the phenomena under study.

4.1.   USING CAPTURE-RECAPTURE METHODS FOR STUDYING PREVALENCE (NUMBER OF VICTIMS)

Patrick Ball has published extensively on the application of an impressively solid body of fairly novel estimation methods and for tailoring these to the study of gross human right violations. The methods he employed are not novel as such, as they are extensions of capture-recapture methods from biology.

The idea behind these methods can be sketched as follows. Suppose that we are standing in front of a lake and that we want to know how many fish are in that lake. What we do is the following. We catch 10 fish, we tag them and throw the poor animals back into the lake. After a while, we re-catch 10 fish. Suppose that of that second catch, 1 fish has a tag and is therefore part of the first catch. We can then estimate that the lake contains 100 fish. An intuitive way to understand this is by imagining that if we would want to recapture all original 10 tagged fish, we'd need to do another 9 catches and we'd have them all, ending up with a total of 100 fish.

Hence, this method is called capture-recapture. It goes back a long way. Outside biology, animal ecology and other areas, it has been applied in criminology to estimate the size of the illegal populations, to estimate the number of illegal weapon holders and to estimate the number of drunk drivers.

The method works from a number of assumptions. Firstly, it is assumed that the population is closed: no members leave the population between the first and the second catch. Second, it is assumed that capture the second time is independent of capture the first time. Thirdly, it is assumed that each member of the population has an equal chance of capture for a given list. Fourthly, it is assumed that we are able to match those who are caught the first and the second time (there is no 'tag-loss').

Figure 1. Example of capture-recapture method

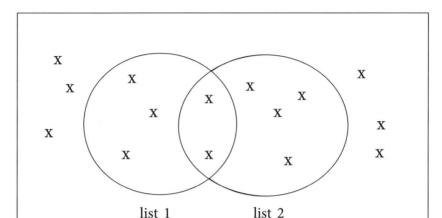

Figure 1 gives an example of the technique. Suppose that we have two lists of people who were killed during a conflict, list 1 and list 2. The number of people on list 1 is 5; we call this number 'A'. The number of people on list 2 is 6; we call this number 'B'. The number of people who appear both on list 1 and list 2 equals 2; we call this number 'M'. Because it is assumed that appearing on list 1 and appearing on list 2 are independent events, the probability to appear on both lists is the product of these two probabilities:

$$\frac{A}{N} \, * \, \frac{B}{N} = \frac{M}{N}$$

with N the unknown size of the population. This can be reworked to show that:

$$\hat{N} = \frac{A * B}{M} = \frac{30}{2} = 15$$

where $\hat{N}$ is the estimated population size.

This means that if we have two lists with names of individuals who were killed during a conflict, we can use the overlap between the two lists to estimate the size of the total population of individuals killed, under the assumptions given above. Of course, to apply this well, we must be sure that the individuals are well-matched. If we fail to match a person who is on list A with the same person on list B, for instance because the name is spelled differently, we overestimate the size of the population, as M then becomes too small. If we over-match, the population size is underestimated. If human rights violations occur in areas where, for instance, no unique spelling of names exists, no surnames are used and people generally do not know their date of birth, matching will be problematic. Next, it may be doubted whether independence between lists is a realistic assumption in the context of human rights violations. Also, one may doubt whether the population is closed: those who flee the country to destinations uncovered by the methods employed, in a sense leave the population. In such cases, when the assumptions are violated, the methods do not estimate the size of the population accurately.

If there are more than two lists, the capture-recapture method is often re-named multiple systems estimation. In that case, more sophisticated models may be used. Ball and his colleagues employed these in several projects, on gross human rights violations in Kosovo, in Guatemala, in Peru, in Timor-Leste (see references below). Ball & Asher (2002) describe how they employed this method to estimate the number of individuals killed in Kosovo between March and June 1999. They had not two, but four lists:

1. A survey carried out by the American Bar Association among approximately 5,000 ethnic Albanian refugees in five different countries (ABA);
2. A list of exhumations carried out on behalf of the ICTY (EXH);
3. A survey of Albanian refugees by Human Rights Watch (HRW);
4. A survey by the Organization for Security and Cooperation in Europe (OSCE).

In each survey, incidents were asked after, and names of people killed and dates of birth were asked. It was also asked from what locality they were, plus details of the date, manner in which the incident had occurred, etc.

Obviously, there may be some difference in how names are spelled in different languages as well as common differences such as between 'Bill' and 'William', which means that linkage of the records in the various lists could not be done automatically, and each and every record had to be checked against records in the other lists. Also, some lists contained duplicates that had to be removed.

Tabulating the overlap between the various lists generated the table (taken from Ball & Asher 2002), that we list as Table 1. Obviously, in this table, the interesting number is the number 'not assessed', in the bottom right corner of the table, the people who appear on none of the four lists. If we can estimate those, we have the total number of people who were killed.

Table 1. List of Victims of Killing Appearing on Several Lists

	ABA	yes	yes	no	no	
	EXH	yes	no	yes	no	
HRW	OSCE					Total
yes	yes	27	32	42	123	
yes	no	18	31	106	306	
no	yes	181	217	228	936	
no	no	177	845	1,131	n.a.	
	Total					4,400

Estimation of this number is done through loglinear modelling,[9] in which the logarithms of the frequencies are estimated through a regression model, just like in analysis of variance, that has main and interaction effects. For this example, the full model would then become:

$$\log(m_{ijkl}) = \quad u + \qquad\qquad\qquad\qquad\qquad\qquad\text{(intercept)}$$
$$u_{1(i)} + u_{2(j)} + u_{3(k)} + u_{4(l)} + \qquad\qquad\text{(main effects)}$$
$$u_{12(ij)} + u_{13(ik)} + u_{14(il)} + u_{23(jk)} + u_{24(jl)} + u_{34(kl)} + \qquad\text{(1st order interaction effects)}$$
$$u_{123(ijk)} + u_{234(jkl)} + u_{124(ijl)} + u_{134(ikl)} + \qquad\text{(2nd order interaction effects)}$$
$$u_{1234(ijkl)} \qquad\qquad\qquad\qquad\qquad\text{(3rd order interaction effects)}$$

In this model, the main effects capture the effect of a certain list. The model is called a full model as it also contains all interaction terms. These interaction terms, such as $u_{13(ik)}$ and $u_{234(jkl)}$ model interaction effects between two resp. three lists.

Now the model given above is not very attractive as it is very complicated. In statistical terms it has the disadvantage that it is so-called 'saturated', that is, the model is built such that it perfectly describes the data, so that there is no estimation. It might thus be better to use a simpler, more parsimonious model. One such model is:

$$\log(m_{ijkl}) = u + u_{1(i)} + u_{2(j)} + u_{3(k)} + u_{4(l)}$$

This model contains only main effects and an intercept term ('u'). Thus, in this model we attempt to estimate the cell frequencies as a function of the various lists that people could appear on, namely (ABA), (EXH), (HRW) or (OSCE). The intercept 'u' is the term that is added just like in regression analysis to make the

---

[9]   On loglinear modelling, regression models, interaction terms, main effects, intercepts and related issues, see, e.g. the classic accessible Knoke & Burke (1980) or from a library the out-of-print but very clear and thorough Tabachnik & Fidell (1989). Parts of Hagenaars (1993) are also useful. Numerous accessible classroom introductions can be googled on the web.

model fit. The intercept 'u' is the number that is inserted to estimate log (m_{ijkl}) when the effects of all lists have been taken into account. This means that the intercept is the most interesting term here: the intercept, being independent of any list but a general additive term, tells us how many people remained unmeasured on all lists. This is exactly the number we are looking for.

Evaluating various models according to how well they were able to predict the data, relative to how simple (or parsimonious) they are, Ball & Asher (2002) chose a model in which a total mortality of 10,356 was estimated. This total number is the sum of all victims who appeared on at least one list (and thus have at least one of the parameters $u_{1(i)}$, $u_{2(j)}$, $u_{3(k)}$ or $u_{4(l)}$ and one or more relevant interaction terms unequal to zero) plus the estimated intercept, which may be viewed as the number who do not appear on any list (and who have therefore all other parameters equal to zero).

Ball & Asher's analysis next proceeded by linking the victims who had been identified to a locality where they had died and a time when this had occurred. Next, the authors could draw graphs of the numbers of killings over time, and could show how these related clearly (though not perfectly) to the refugee flow over time. Next, they could match these numbers to both NATO airstrikes and activities of the Kosovo Liberation Army (KLA). Regressing both refugee flow and numbers killed on both the KLA and activities and their lagged versions, they were able to show that the data did not show any association between NATO activities and the dependent variables. The data did however show an association between lagged KLA activities and refugee flow. The results hold when including region as an explanatory variable.

This principle of data analysis has now been applied several times. A prerequisite is that there are lists with unique identifiers (full names, dates of birth and places of birth) of victims. In some countries this may not be the case. Of course, application is not straightforward and requires a lot of painstaking data cleaning in order to be able to match well. Also, in a large number of cases, lists contain entries that are defined as groups, so that no unique individual identification is provided. These entries are quite numerous. Ball et al. (2002) describe how they also matched such groups across lists. It may be the case that the phenomena under study differ across region or over time. In that case, some kind of stratification in the modelling may be necessary. Carrying out analyses per region may, however, cause numbers to dwindle and may make estimates more unstable.

4.2. INTEGRATING MESO AND MICRO PERSPECTIVES THROUGH MULTILEVEL ANALYSIS

Croes and Tammes (2003) investigated survival chances of the Jews in the Netherlands in World War II. Using archival records, they investigated the, until then, fairly commonly held assumption that, as a municipality had a higher percentage of Catholic inhabitants, Jews' survival chances were lower. This assumption had been based on the finding that during the war, Catholics had been identified as most strongly opposed to the Jews. Croes and Tammes had collected data from various sources and at various levels. For individual Jews, they knew among others the nationality of the person, gender and age. For each municipality, they knew whether the mayor was collaborating with the German occupier, how many police officers collaborated with the Germans, how many inhabitants voted for the NSB, what percentage of Jews were Christian, how many were 'full' or 'partial' Jews and mortality dates as deportations began. Where the personal characteristics constituted a first layer, the municipal characteristics constituted a second layer. In a third layer, the researchers coded the *'Sicherheitsdienst'* area under which the municipality fell, and the *'Sicherheitspolizei'*, the political and criminal police department. Particularly the *Sicherheitspolizei*, which was organised in seven regions over the country, exhibited varying vigour and radicalism in its persecution of Jews. To analyse their data, they used multilevel analysis,[10] a technique that makes optimal statistical use of the fact that the data is layered, within measurements in the lower layers (i.e. individuals) nested within higher layers (i.e. municipalities).

The analyses showed many interesting things. Firstly they showed that Jews of non-Dutch and non-German nationality had higher survival chances, as had older Jews. Secondly, they showed that as the percentage of collaborating police officers increased, survival chances decreased. Contrary to expectation, survival chances in municipalities with a higher percentage of Catholics were higher. Survival chances in municipalities with a higher percentage of Christian Jews were also higher.

Particularly this latter finding is interesting as it shows the strength and added value of the multi-level analysis, over regular analyses. One would expect that the increased survival chances in such municipalities, where Jews were more often Christian, were due to the fact that Jews in these municipalities were more assimilated and would stand out less. While this turned out to be indeed partially the case, further – qualitative – inspection of the data showed that the effect was not only micro, but clearly meso as well: in municipalities where Jews were more often Christian there was a more intricate linkage and closer ties between the

---

[10]   An accessible introduction to multilevel analysis is Kreft & De Leeuw (1998).

Jewish and the Christian communities. Jews in such municipalities had greater access to non-Jewish inhabitants, who could aid them to find a hiding place, false ID, etc.

Collating information from various sources

Guha-Sapir, Degomme and Phelan (2005) combined information from various surveys in Darfur to estimate indirect and direct mortality. Mortality was estimated using two different methods. The first method consisted of an analysis of 17 surveys providing data on non-violence related deaths and violence-related deaths. The surveys were conducted during the period April 2004 – January 2005. Because of the recall period, the covered period was September 2003 – January 2005. The surveys were conducted by several organisations, such as the World Food Programme, Médecins Sans Frontières (MSF), Epicentre World Relief, etc.

The method Guha-Sapir et al. applied essentially amounted to the following. They used the information from the various surveys to compute separate trends, using non-linear regression[11] in mortality for the various affected regions. As opposed to using a blanket estimate (i.e. a mortality estimate that is stable over the entire period of the conflict and across regions) they thus produced a differentiated and nuanced estimate, which captured differences in intensity of the conflict for each region.

After removing one particular survey that had a very different mortality estimate, and by interpolating and extrapolating from the existing nearest data for a number of periods for which no data was available, the researchers arrived at a total number of 134,000 deaths. From this number they subtracted the number of expected deaths and found a total number of 118,142 excess deaths, including a 10% addition for refugees in Chad. Of these 118,142 approximately 35,000 were estimated to have been violence-related. The authors acknowledge that as there were no surveys concerning the outbreaks of violence in south Darfur, the possibly higher level of violence in this region was not taken into account.

A second method the authors employed consisted of an analysis that used all available information to estimate *ranges* of mortality rate by region and month throughout the three districts of Darfur and based on developments during the conflicts. Besides mortality rate estimations, the researchers included secondary factors, such as arrival in camps and nutrition levels in their calculations.

Applying all this data, high and low CMRs were calculated, representing a worst and best-case scenario. For the worst-case scenario, in all cases missing information was imputed with the worst possible estimates from existing sources. If there was conflicting data available, the higher CMR was used. For the best-

---

[11] A special kind of regression where the regression line is allowed to assume a different shape from that of the straight line

case scenario, in all cases missing information was imputed with the best possible estimate from existing sources. In case of conflicting data, the lower CMR was used.

The generally accepted mortality rate for sub-Saharan populations of 0.5 per 10,000 a day was subtracted from the total number of deaths, producing the excess number of deaths that may be considered attributable to the conflict. This method led to a range of 63,000–146,000 excess deaths from March 2003 until January 2005. This method however did not make a distinction between violence and non-violence related deaths.

In their report the researchers discuss the limitations of their method (p. 38–41). Firstly they state that the variability in mortality in different regions during different periods is not totally captured by their methods, even though the best-case and worst-case methods do this. On the other hand, the worst case method may overestimate mortality, and the best-case method may underestimate it. Secondly, they state that because of limited recall periods, mortality may have been underestimated. Thirdly, registration of IDPs could have lagged, resulting in underestimation. However, even with a 20% underestimate this would add not more than 18,000 excess deaths to the end result. Fourthly, there may have been an overestimate as registration in camps is the way to food rations. Lastly, they state that the samples employed may have suffered from survivor bias.

The authors make a final point on the baselines that they employed. Of course, their estimated number of excess deaths depends on the mortality rate for sub-Saharan baseline mortality used; for method 1 they employed the UNICEF CMR of 0.3 and for method 2 the sub-Saharan CMR of 0.5. These different baselines affect the estimates, but failing to include a baseline may easily cause an inflation totalling tens of thousands of deaths.

This issue is also something for which the Burnham et al. (2006) paper on excess mortality in Iraq was criticised: the authors here reportedly used a baseline that was unrealistically low, giving them an inflated number of excess deaths. Guha-Sapir and van Panhuis (2003) discussed how important it is to study mortality not in an isolated fashion, but to always related (post-)conflict mortality to levels before the conflict. Their study shows that often increased mortality during or after a conflict can be directly related to a pre-existing fragility of the population. Also, their analyses showed how the effects of conflicts may be completely opposite to what one might expect: mortality in Kabul during the peak of the conflict was much decreased as compared to levels before its eruption. Just before the conflict erupted, the situation in Kabul was very bleak, but as the conflict started, there was also a massive in-pouring of aid, with greatly reduced mortality. This shows how important it is to gauge estimates.

Correcting for survivor bias

In their study on mortality in Timor-Leste, Silva and Ball (2006) attempt to correct for survivor bias. Their surveys go back a long way and record the number of deaths. From that survey they can estimate the Crude Death Rate[12] (CDR) for Timor-Leste for the years 1971–2004, having population estimates and estimates of the number of people killed. However, the survey estimates suffer from survivor bias.

The authors next attempt to correct these survey estimates and to gauge them against other available information. First they attempt to correct the survey data. Their reasoning is that if they had a reliable, objective number for the CDR in any year, say 1971, they could estimate the extent of underreporting in their survey for that year due to survivor bias. However, East Timor has no reliable census data. Luckily, the US Bureau of the Census for East Timor has data from 1990–2004. Before then, there was no census data available that could be used, and any other existing data was too dubious to be useful. The authors instead used the Indonesian government's claim that for all Indonesia mortality decreased by a similar degree of 45% between 1971 and 1990. This was then used by the authors, starting from 2004, to coarsely extrapolate the CDR in 1971. Obviously this method is unreliable, but no other data was available. From the difference between the estimated CDR and the measured CDR the authors computed a memory fraction, which they subsequently used to correct the survey estimates.

5.   DISCUSSION AND A RESEARCH AGENDA

Studying gross human rights violations empirically can be done with some adaptation of existing methodologies. There will always remain more uncertainty than when studying regular 'national' crimes. Researchers must not only learn to live with that but also to safeguard themselves as much as possible from this uncertainty. Firstly, this can be done by applying run-of-the-mill requirements sensibly, such as attempting to investigate representative populations, and attempting to estimate and correct for bias. Secondly, there will be much more than in other areas of criminological study, the need to gauge findings against other existing information. It may also be feasible to gauge findings against expert knowledge, for instance by employing a Delphi group or some such method.[13]

---

[12]   The crude death rate is the number of deaths per 1,000 population during a certain period, usually per 1,000 population at the mid-point of that period.

[13]   In a Delphi method a group of experts is asked to answer one or more questions. In the first instance, each expert is asked for his opinion. Next, all experts are confronted with the other experts' opinions and are given the opportunity to revise their judgment. The procedure is stopped when consensus is reached or after some pre-set criterion. A focus group is a less

Researchers have at times reported ranges of their estimates to capture the uncertainty. This has advantages and disadvantages. One advantage is the reader can inspect the degree of uncertainty. The disadvantage is that, as ranges become very wide, they also become meaningless. It may then be better to work from reasonable assumptions, derive an estimate with a smaller range, and simply publish and stick to the lower range. There will probably always be underreporting and underestimation, and given that, it may be good to work with estimates that may be considered the bottom line.

Victim surveys have been effectively employed, though often under conditions of insecurity and with their particular estimation biases. Quite a number of macro-level studies (less reported upon here) have surveyed country level indicators and attempted to explain factors associated with the outbreak and resolution of conflicts. While there is mostly a relative oversimplification of all the dynamics that lead to conflicts and conflict resolution, they have nevertheless provided some important insights.

Many studies have focused on mortality. This is understandable, as this is the gravest offence, and is relatively easily studied as it is clearly distinguishable and leaves traces. However, lesser offences have been relatively understudied. One of these is rape and there are indications that rape may be particularly hard to investigate using regular methods. Also, property offences in the context of or as part of international crimes have been understudied. Methodologies to study these should be invested in.

Lastly, there has been a striking scarcity of recent perpetrator studies. Obviously, studying perpetrators is difficult. Apart from Alette Smeulers' work (this volume) the various tribunals should provide fodder enough for criminologists wanting to detail the big time offenders' lives. But what about the current small fish? Those who actually have blood on their hands? Who are they? Are they all law-abiding citizens? It seems that, particularly for the 'lesser' offences for which prosecution seldom takes place by itself, such as rape, a self-report study seems doable.

Lastly, this author believes that methodologies to assess the damage and gauge it should be developed. That includes the economic damage of international crimes.

---

strictly organised variety, in which a group of experts is asked to arrive at consensus on a number of questions.

V. THE UNACCOUNTABLE GENOCIDE

A Case Study of the Roles of the U.S. State Department and U.S. Government Accountability Office in Calculating the Darfur Death Toll

John HAGAN

1. GENOCIDE ACCOUNTABILITY

Gerald Prunier (2005) calls Darfur 'the ambiguous genocide'. A key source of ambiguity about this genocide derives from the failure of U.S. government agencies to meaningfully hold the Government of Sudan accountable for the death toll in Darfur. More specifically, I argue that the U.S. State Department and the U.S. Government Accountability Office have been key sources of low and uncertain estimates of the scale of mortality in Darfur.

The State Department has vacillated in its public policies about Darfur in a way that we characterize as flip flopping. To do so, the State Department has inappropriately applied concepts and methods from a population health paradigm, while ignoring the relevancy of a crime victimization approach. Subsequently, the U.S. Government Accountability Office [GAO] became more concerned about high than low estimates, including an especially low estimate announced by a deputy secretary of the U.S. State Department during a highly publicized visit to Khartoum in 2005. The effect of the low State Department death estimate announced with an official state visit to Sudan's capital was to reduce public certainty about mass atrocities in Darfur. The effect of increasing this uncertainty was to decrease the public sense of urgency about stopping this genocide and holding its architects accountable. A review of Darfur mortality by the GAO further intensified this uncertainty, which it was presumably intended to reduce.

While the GAO is often known for its dispassionate critiques of government policies and programs, it has also been criticized for it susceptibility to intra-governmental pressures. The New York Times columnist, Paul Krugman, recently reported on the perceived need within the GAO to leak a report on the civilian death toll in Iraq to avoid its conclusions being changed. In this context, Krugman (2007) wrote:

'*What about civilian casualties? The Pentagon says they're down, but it has neither released its numbers nor explained how they're calculated. According to a draft report from the Government Accountability Office, which was leaked to the press because officials were afraid the office would be pressured into changing the report's conclusions, U.S. government agencies 'differ' on whether sectarian violence has been reduced.*'

A subsequent *New York Times* article on the presentation of the GAO report on Iraq to Congress confirmed the pre-leak fears by observing that it was 'notably rosier than the draft version' (Herszenhorn 2007). We will see a possibly related set of issues involving the GAO's treatment of a low but poorly substantiated U.S. State Department estimate of the Darfur death toll. However, before we get to the role of the GAO, we must first provide an overview of Darfur death toll estimates and their origins in two alternative social science research paradigms

2.   'COMPLEX HUMANITARIAN EMERGENCIES' AND THE POPULATION HEALTH PARADIGM

Since the early 1990s and the end of the cold war, the concept of a 'complex humanitarian emergency' (Waldman & Martone 1999) has often been used by population health researchers to refer to coerced circumstances of forced migration and mortality in many parts of the world. These emergencies include situations in which efforts to drastically restructure a state, society, or social group have led to civil conflict or international war, resulting in the violent death of large civilian populations and in their substantial displacement to detrimental living conditions – typically to overflowing and inadequately resourced camps – that in turn become breeding grounds for disease, dehydration, starvation, malnutrition, and other sources of excessive deaths (Keely, Reed & Waldman 2001). We first identify key features of these emergencies and then consider how the absence of legal and criminological considerations from the population health paradigm can lead to misleading accounts and bias the estimation and understanding of genocidal victimization.

Although there is debate about the matter (UBC Report 2007), there is substantial evidence that humanitarian emergencies have become worse over the last century, perhaps especially since the end of the cold war, with a particularly lethal increase in direct violence between racial, ethnic and religious groups (Noji & Toole 1997). A finding of particular importance is that civilians have increased as a proportion of all war casualties from about 14 percent in World War I, to 67 percent in World War II, to 90 percent by the end of the 20th century (Levi & Sidel 1967; Noji 1997). Between 1989 and 1999, the number of complex humanitarian emergencies in the world identified by health researchers doubled from 14 to 30 (Natsios 1997), and the last third of the 20th century saw a near doubling of humanitarian refugees in the world (Keely, Reed & Waldman 2001; Waldman and Martone 1999).

The identification of humanitarian emergencies as 'complex' reflects from the outset the concerns of public health researchers about the political complications of initiating and sustaining humanitarian relief and assistance (Toole and Waldman 1990). The first concern reflects the priority these researchers attach to the work of relief agencies in improving the chances that refugees can survive emergency conditions in the face of the 'complex social, political, and economic issues' that confront them (Toole and Waldman 1990, 3300). The second concern reflects the desire to neutrally if not euphemistically understand the contexts and arrangements that relief programs adapt to as 'by nature complex' (Toole and Waldman 1990, 3301). The third concern reflects the concern that relief agencies nonetheless can and should not ignore 'complex and political' arguments about providing equal medical services to communities where refugee camps are located (Toole and Waldman 1990, 3301).

The hard and intrusive political realities of the complex humanitarian emergencies just described led health researchers such as Toole and Waldman to call in the post-cold war period on the international community to adopt a policy that recognized and acted on the need to intervene at early stages in 'the evolution of complex disasters involving civil war, human rights abuses, food shortages, and mass displacement' (Toole and Waldman 1993, 600–605). A crucial element of Toole and Waldman's health initiated agenda was their recognition that once health oriented practitioners achieved access to a humanitarian emergency situation and began to prevent excess mortality, they could also begin to play a role in empirically documenting the unfolding course of the emergency as well as its distribution and magnitude (Toole and Waldman 1993, 605).

Mortality – which is also of obvious interest to scholars who study crime victimization, international criminal law and a criminology of human rights and war crimes – is the most common dimension used to trace and assess the course of complex humanitarian emergencies. The related study of famines has identified a paradigmatic sequence of mortality and related problems marked by the onset of the crisis, followed by its rise to a peak, by the arrival of emergency assistance, and by a hopefully rapid if belated stabilization (Burkholder and Toole 1995). Crude mortality rates (CMRs) are calculated to assess the occurrence of deaths for the population affected by the emergency and its duration.

CMRs are usually calculated as deaths per 10,000 population per day to allow comparisons across settings and situations. These rates are classically expected to rise and fall across the stages noted above, tracing an inverted U-shaped curve of mortality that is negatively skewed by the slower pace of onset, followed by a peak and faster rate of decline in deaths. At least this is the expectation for 'standard' rural famines, and the forced migration and mortality at the end of the 20th century in Kosovo, the southern most province in the Republic of Serbia, further exemplified this pattern, as we describe below (Spiegel and Salama 1998–1999).

A CMR of 1.0 was identified by the U.S. State Department in the mid-1980s as a useful threshold of elevated mortality in complex humanitarian emergencies (Bureau of Refugee Programs 1985). This 1.0 level is two to three times the level of mortality that is regarded as expected or normal in sub-Saharan Africa, and this criterion was adopted in 1992 for public health purposes by the Centers of Disease Control [CDC]. At the same time, the CDC recommended a program of response in which a rapid health assessment would use sample survey methods to establish a baseline mortality rate in a setting, followed by the implementation of a health information system to collect ongoing health data, including mortality (Center for Disease and Control 1992). These developments were spearheaded by epidemiological trained health researchers and have provided an increasingly important picture of the mortality and morbidity surrounding humanitarian emergencies. If criminologists had been involved in these developments, they might have focused more specific attention on identifying criminal sources and responsibility for mortality in these emergency situations. However, criminologists did not become involved in this work during the early post-cold war period.

The primary goal of the population health research on complex humanitarian emergencies has been support for the provision of relief (food, medicine, and shelter) for conflict-affected populations suffering elevated mortality levels. The goal of this research is more often to prospectively plan and provide relief than to retrospectively assign criminal responsibility. Organizations, such as the CDC, have been largely concerned with gathering data as a means to prevent further death, sometimes if not often neglecting the need to assess mortality resulting from state-led criminal violence and deaths of civilians that occur before they assume refugee status. Yet we have also already seen that this epidemiologically and demographically guided research can provide insight into the patterning of politically instigated violence, which is characteristically revealed to be highly contingent on the people involved and the places where these humanitarian emergencies occur (Timmaeus & Jasseh 2004).

Perhaps most importantly, this research reveals that internal and external politics, including the reaction (or lack thereof) by the international community, can radically alter the form and scale of humanitarian and human rights emergencies. For example, in the Democratic Republic of the Congo, mortality rates have not significantly improved from an average of .7 deaths per 10,000 population per day since 2002, and these rates are 75 percent higher in conflict-prone regions of this country (International Rescue Committee 2004). Overall, less developed countries have higher CMRs and are more vulnerable to upward variations from baseline rates than developed countries, making their humanitarian and human rights emergencies quantitatively and qualitatively distinct. In Zaire in 1994, CMRs for Rwandan refugees reached levels as high as 35 deaths per 10,000 population per day (Goma Epidemilogical Group 1995).

Again, although not specifically designed to do so, this body of research further reveals that the population most at risk varies with the nature of the specific roots of the conflict. In the Congo, infants and children under age five have had the most highly elevated mortality rates (International Rescue Committee 2004). In contrast, the elderly were most at risk during the siege of Sarajevo (Watson, Kulenovic & Vespa 1993–1994). In the Srebrenica massacre, military-age males were most at risk of death (Rohde 1997). Women everywhere seem most at risk of rape during politically instigated violence within and between nations, even though, as the Abu Ghraib prison scandal illustrated, sexual assaults against males are probably also everywhere undercounted.

The health research literature on complex humanitarian emergencies is increasingly organized around interpersonal age-sex dimensions and the global North-South divide of development. These are clearly powerful contingencies that shape the form and scale of humanitarian emergencies. We still lack comprehensive data on the age-sex composition of elevated mortality in these emergencies, and this kind of data and analysis needs to be better connected to our understanding of the North-South dynamic of development that slowly but increasingly is the focus of thought and attention in the post-cold war world (Rogers and Copeland 1993).

Despite the social and political dimensions of human rights emergencies and war crimes, epidemiologically and demographically trained health researchers are inclined to focus mainly on health outcomes, whereas criminologists prioritize issues of political and ultimately legal responsibility. Criminology and law can bring further attention to the understanding of war and human rights crimes that a population health approach neglects. A common sequence in these emergencies involves the onset of violent attacks, the flight of the resulting victims, followed by ensuing health problems, all of which contribute to mortality. The key point is that 'the root cause of most complex humanitarian emergencies is that governments and other combatants use violence and deprivation to seek solutions to political problems' (Keely, Reed & Waldman 2001, 12).

The challenge is simultaneously to keep in mind the cumulative and multiplicative effects of violence, flight, and displacement to concentrated encampments, and the political state and non-state origins of the disastrous consequences. From a criminological as well as methodological perspective, it is insufficient to concentrate on health outcomes of these emergencies without simultaneously acknowledging their political and state origins. When the health and crime perspectives are juxtaposed, important socio-legal issues become apparent. For example, treatment of the 'missing' and of 'excess as distinct from normal and expected mortality' and, even more fundamentally, the substitution of the concept of 'complex humanitarian emergency' for 'war and human rights crimes' raise major questions about our understanding of this subject matter.

It is useful to begin with the treatment of the missing in the calculation of CMRs from population-based surveys, which was introduced above as a central concept and method of the health approach. The calculation of CMRs involves dividing (a) the number of household members reported as deceased for a specified period by (b) the estimated size of the sampled population (with the number of respondents multiplied by average household size) and (c) multiplying the dividend by 10,000. The denominator in this calculation is designed to represent the population at risk of death.

The convention in the health literature on complex humanitarian emergencies is to include in this denominator the sum of the sampled population and one half of the reported dead, missing, and absent from this population, assuming that the latter on average were at risk of death for half of this survey period. Yet health surveys of these emergencies conventionally do not include consideration of the missing in the numerator of observed deaths, instead essentially treating these persons as missing data. Often, if not usually, the missing persons in these surveys have disappeared in the chaos of the emergency and are feared or presumed dead by family members and human rights groups. However, the focus in health studies is typically on deaths that can be directly identified as resulting from disease and nutritional or other specified causes, and the missing are therefore omitted from consideration (See for example World Health Organization 2004).

At times, those who study complex humanitarian emergencies add a further category for injuries and violence to these analyses. However, this inclusion of injuries and violence often covers a restricted recall period of risk or the period while in displacement or refugee camps. Violence that results in deaths and disappearances that precede flights to camps are often treated as of secondary importance or ignored and, like the missing, often are simply overlooked. Rather than focus on assigning criminal responsibility for deaths that precede flight to camps, the health focus is typically on saving the lives of those who survive long enough to get to the camps. Our point is that from a criminological perspective, acknowledging and analyzing those who die and become missing before, as well as while in displacement and refugee camps, is important for the purposes of assigning legal responsibility and understanding the root causes of underlying conflicts.

The concept of excess mortality raises a related set of concerns. Analyses of complex humanitarian emergencies often construct a baseline estimate of mortality by identifying an expected mortality rate for the population of interest and at risk, assuming the absence of the risk. The idea is to estimate those who would have been expected to have died during more normal circumstances. This often can be difficult to do, because circumstances in settings like sub-Saharan

Africa seem so seldom to be 'normal.' In this sense, the task is to construct a 'counterfactual' estimate of the 'normal' mortality. This expected or normal mortality is then subtracted from the level of mortality observed during the period of the humanitarian emergency. The difference between the 'expected' and 'observed' mortality is deemed excessive mortality and is used by health researchers as a means of determining the extent and duration of the emergency.

From a criminological perspective, this approach is problematic. Consider the following. An individual or group of individuals in actuarial terms may be expected to die for health reasons within a given period, but during this period of time dies as a result of a criminal human rights violation, for example, being criminally displaced from his or her home. Dying in one's normal place of residence or work is one thing, but dying in a displacement or refugee camp is quite another. This is no longer 'expected' or 'normal'. The implication is that although designating such deaths as expected or normal may be quite useful for some analytic purposes, including charting the timing and scale of a humanitarian emergency, it is misleading for other purposes, including the legal documentation of the form and extent of human rights crimes and war crimes.

The problems considered for illustrative purposes here – the neglect of missing persons, the failure to consider pre-displacement or refugee camp violence, and the treatment of excess mortality – anticipate a broader problem with the concept of complex humanitarian emergencies. This concept, while helpful in encouraging the creation of population and public health based methods for the study of these disasters, can also have the unhelpful effect of blunting and obscuring the meaning of much that is observed to be happening in such emergencies.

Often as a part of working with affected nations, within and alongside the United Nations, humanitarian organizations seek nonthreatening and unobtrusive methods for addressing human rights abuses. Even threatening nomenclature can result in being denied access to settings and people in dire need of humanitarian assistance. The problem, of course, is that the same states and groups that create these emergencies also restrict access to their victims. Insistence on a criminological perspective has the potential to serve as a counterweight to this problem, but first it is important to appreciate how great this problem can be.

3.   THE HUMANITARIAN STRATEGIC EMBRACE

The humanitarian dilemma posed by efforts to divert and co-opt research on human rights abuses is a challenging practical issue that is provocatively depicted in Alex de Waal's book on *Famine Crimes: Politics and the Disaster Relief Industry in Africa* (1997). De Waal argues that what he calls 'Humanitarian International,' the complex of NGOs and relief agencies that respond to humanitarian emergencies, often find themselves engaged in a compromised strategic embrace with states that commit the human rights abuses and war crimes whose consequences they seek to alleviate.[1] Accessing and treating the urgent and deadly consequences of these emergencies can obscure if not obstruct efforts to identify and hold their instigators responsible. This observation is particularly apt in Darfur, a setting that as we will see highlights differences in health and criminological perspectives.

The tension that the contradiction between health and crime priorities generates in the politics of the United Nations broke into brief public view when the British House of Commons International Development Committee received testimony in early 2005 from Mukkesh Kapila, the former United Nations Resident and Humanitarian Coordinator for Sudan.[2] Kapila was the highest in-country UN official dealing with the response to the unfolding violence against African villagers in the Darfur region of Sudan in February 2003. This was the period of onset in the violent attacks and killings in these villages. More than six months later, in October of 2003, Kapila asked that the violence in Darfur be referred the International Criminal Court. As noted previously, this referral did not take place until the United States finally agreed to abstain in the UN Security Council and allowed this referral to go forward in early 2005.

Kapila, who had previously served the UN in the Rwandan genocide, was determined that similar events would not be repeated in Darfur. Yet in March 2004 Kapila was removed from Darfur, with the killing still near its peak. The killing was still in progress in early 2005 when Kapila testified to the British parliamentary committee that the death toll was large and still rising because 'fundamentally the issue was that the Sudan government refused to allow us access when we needed it most' (Ibid., at EV 50). Yet this summary comment only scratches the surface of Kapila's account, which goes on to painfully highlight the conflicted nature of the UN's work with the Sudanese government in response to the killing and resulting health problems in Darfur.

When Kapila was asked how effectively the humanitarian and human rights – or health and crime – parts of the Sudan mission worked together in Darfur, he responded that these were actually competing efforts, that 'we had a real struggle to overcome,' that a 'culture of distrust' existed, and that it was a challenge to 'create one UN approach' (Ibid, at EV 52). He explained that political crises are typically categorized as 'humanitarian problems' and that those in charge of aid operations are 'burdened with the task of doing something about it and when they inevitably fail the blame is put on the humanitarians' (Ibid, at EV 50).

---

[1] A backdrop to these arguments is set in De Waal (1985).
[2] House of Commons International Development Committee, Darfur, Sudan: The Responsibility to Protect, Fifth Report of the Session 2004–2005, Vol. II, Oral and Written Evidence, 2005, London, Station Office Limited.

The point here is that if the government instigates the attacks and killings that lead to displacement into camps where many more victims die of disease and malnutrition, the same government can then also conveniently claim that the fault lies with the humanitarian response rather than with the government. At the same time, the rush to meet the humanitarian need for health and nutritional assistance can compete with and produce compromised efforts to highlight the human rights abuses leading to these humanitarian needs. Kapila clearly saw the violence as ethnic cleansing, a form of genocide. Yet he reported that the response from the international community fit into the Sudan government's strategy of demanding that he and his staff work harder to find humanitarian solutions.

Kapila particularly emphasized another side of this dilemma that involved a competition for scarce resources, saying

> 'this happens in organizations that are funded in a way which is reliant on what sort of image you can present and so on. That means that we had $100 million available for food aid but we had only $1 million available for human rights' (Ibid, at EV 52).

Still, his conclusion was that

> 'even if twice the money came in from the world (...) the arguments would have been the same,' and that the real problem was 'the systematic obstruction by the Sudanese government of humanitarian access.'[3]

Kapila's testimony starkly highlights how difficult the relationship is between responding to health and crime issues in humanitarian emergencies. The U.S. State Department and the U.S. Government Accountability Office were implicated in this complicated relationship as they became involved in investigations of genocidal victimization in Darfur. At first, the State Department countered the 'humanitarian embrace' by launching its own victimization survey with refugees from Darfur who received sanctuary across the border with UN assistance in Chad.

4.   THE ATROCITIES DOCUMENTATION SURVEY

In September of 2004, the U.S. State Department published an eight page report whose chillingly cogent tables, charts, maps and pictures spoke volumes in Documenting Atrocities in Darfur. The report was based on survey interviews in 1136 refugee households in Chad. The Atrocities Documentation Survey [ADS] on which the report was based enumerated thousands of deaths and many more

---

3   Ibid., at p. EV 50.

rapes and atrocities that the respondents personally had seen or heard about before fleeing from attacks on their farms and villages over the previous year and a half in Darfur. Secretary of State Colin Powell made headlines when he summarized results from this survey for the UN Security Council and the U.S. Congress as evidence of a racially targeted and militarily unjustified Sudanese sponsored genocide in Darfur.

The release of Powell's testimony by the State Department was followed minutes later by a separate White House statement from President Bush which again built on the ADS and concluded 'genocide has taken place in Darfur.' This was the first time an American President had rebuked a sovereign nation by invoking the Genocide Convention, and certainly the first time that a crime victimization survey had played a support role in the formation of U.S. foreign policy. This victimization survey recorded a level of criminal detail that no health survey could provide. The resulting report outlined the criminology of a genocide.

Colin Powell and the State Department were motivated in the summer of 2004 by horrific news stories of attacks and killings in Darfur, and by the further fact that Congress had already passed a unanimous condemnation of genocide in Darfur. The Administration wanted to reassert a leadership position on this foreign policy issue by providing systematic evidence of the seriousness of the war and human rights crimes that were reportedly taking place.

The challenge was daunting. It included developing the survey instrument, recruiting interviewers and interpreters, planning the logistics of conducting surveys in 19 locations in eastern Chad that were unreachable by normal roads, designing a sampling plan, moving the research team in and out of the survey locations, and organizing the coding and analyzing of over one thousand interviews. Several hundred of the interviews were conducted for Powell's use in his appearance before the UN Security Council in July, and the full survey of 1136 households in Chad was completed with a preliminary analysis for the brief *Documenting Atrocities* report that accompanied Powell's Congressional testimony in early September.

The field interviews were conducted in July and August of 2004 by two groups working for two week periods each with 15 interviewers that included area experts, social scientists, lawyers and police investigators. A protocol was developed for the survey that mixed the closed-ended format of a crime victimization survey with the semi-structured format of legal witness statements. The interviewers worked with interpreters in ten camps and nine settlements across the West Darfur border in Chad. The sampling was systematic. Interviewers randomly selected a starting point in each camp or settlement and then from within this designated sector selected every tenth dwelling unit for interview. All the adults living in the unit were listed on the survey instrument and one adult from the household was randomly chosen for a private interview, resulting in the final 1,136 sampled households.

Up to 20 incidents were coded for each household interview, with detailed information collected about the nature of the crimes. The legally oriented interviewers were intent on collecting responses to their survey questions with sufficient detail to support potential courtroom claims. The *Documenting Atrocities* report of the survey used univariate descriptive statistics and formed the background for Secretary of State Powell's testimony on September 9, 2004 to the U.S. Senate Foreign Relations Committee that genocide was occurring in Darfur.

We used the ADS data to develop a preliminary estimate cited by Save Darfur of 400,000 deaths. However, the ADS was not the only source of data about the conflict in Darfur available during this period. Probably the best known data on this conflict at the time came from survey work conducted by the World Health Organization [WHO] in the internal displacement camps inside Darfur. Since there is no census or hospital data for Darfur from which to otherwise calculate mortality, the breadth of the WHO survey work is important. However, the differences between the ADS and WHO survey contributions also reflect the important distinctions between the crime and health research paradigms. While the ADS design represents a cutting edge example of the use of the crime victimization approach – with its emphasis on incident based reporting of a wide range of different kinds of criminal events before and in the refugee camps – the WHO survey represents an application of the health research approach to complex humanitarian emergencies – with its parallel emphasis on mortality linked to disease and nutritional problems inside the displacement camps.

Important survey work has also been reported by the French human rights group, Medecins Sans Frontieres [MSF], from surveys conducted in the state of West Darfur. Although the MSF survey work was limited to a smaller number of camps in West Darfur, this initiative represents a unique attempt to combine attention to pre-camp and in-camp experiences, including attention to mortality in both settings. This research will become important in a newer and alternative estimation approach discussed below. First it is important to learn more about the findings of the WHO and ADS studies.

5. EARLY FINDINGS FROM THE WORLD HEALTH ORGANIZATION SURVEYS

As we have noted, organizations such as the World Health Organization, the World Food Program, and the Center for Disease Control and Prevention – especially in a setting such as Darfur – are understandingly more preoccupied with the immediate and ongoing challenges of disease and malnutrition than they are with the past violence that leads displaced persons to flee to camps in the first place. This is a key reason why Powell's State Department and its ambassador on war crimes needed a crime victimization survey and initiated the ADS.

At about the same time as the ADS, during the late summer of 2004, the WHO was conducting surveys of mortality and other health and nutrition issues with the Sudanese Ministry of Health [henceforth referred to as the WHO/SMH survey] across a large number of camps inside the three states of Darfur. This work produced estimates of crude mortality rates [CMRs] of the kind introduced in the previous chapter. Thus a WHO retrospective survey for two summer months of 2004 produced a CMR of 2.14 for the states of North and West Darfur (South Darfur was less fully surveyed). Recall that this is a level or mortality from four to seven times normal or expected levels in sub-Saharan Africa.

It is significant to add some further detail about what this CMR calculated by the WHO includes. This CMR is a meaningful estimate of mortality following displacement due to health problems in the camps, with some added deaths resulting from forays outside the camps during this period to collect firewood or other necessities of life in the camps. Few of the deaths included in the calculation of this CMR could have been due to violent attacks prior to displacement. We will say more about this below. Unfortunately, as we also note further below, the latter point was not well understood at the time, and still is not widely understood today. Of course, for criminological purposes, it is essential to have information on the violent deaths resulting from attacks.

The survey work of WHO also became the source of an influential seven month estimate that 70,000 Darfurian refugees had died in just seven months of 2004, with the deaths again coming almost entirely from malnutrition and disease (Nabarro 2004). This estimate was announced personally by David Nabarro, a middle-aged British 'public health bureaucrat' who describes himself as wanting to come across as 'honest, accurate, down-to-earth, someone who can translate complex facts in a way that makes emotional sense to those receiving them' (McNeil 2006).

Nabarro concluded from the WHO surveys that deaths were occurring in Darfur at the rate of from about 5,000 to 10,000 persons per month. This estimate required going beyond the original retrospective survey by linking the CMRs with separate estimates of the larger population at risk in Darfur. The latter population was estimated from counts of displaced persons in the camps and reported in UN reports known as Humanitarian Profiles. This count of the population at risk can be used along with the CMR, expressed as the number of deaths per 10,000 population per day, to estimate a monthly death toll. Obviously both the CMR and the internal displaced camp population will vary from month to month. However, in the 2004 summer months covered by the WHO survey, the death toll was probably near its peak, and the emphasis was on trying to gauge this emergency level of mortality.

In March of 2005 a UN emergency relief coordinator, Jan Egeland, had just returned from a fact finding trip to Darfur. Egeland is an intrepid investigator of humanitarian emergencies and regularly spoke for the UN from many of the most desperate spots on the globe. He was pressed now by the UN press corps to provide an updated estimate of the death toll in Darfur. At first he enigmatically responded that it was impossible to estimate the death toll because 'it is where we are not that there are attacks'. Then when he was asked to comment on the outdated 70,000 estimate, he responded by saying 'Is it three times that? Is it five times that? I don't know but it is several times the number of 70,000 that have died altogether' (Leopold 2005).

Several days later, Egeland obviously had concluded that the imprecision of his earlier answer was unsatisfactory. In a new response to the press, he extrapolated from the UN's WHO survey by multiplying Nabarro's 10,000 per month figure by 18 months instead of seven. The official UN estimate thus jumped to 180,000 (Reuters 2005). Although this latter estimate was based on no further data collection or analysis, other than simply multiplying the 10,000 monthly estimate by 18 months, Egeland's estimate began to consolidate an early media appraisal of the scale of the genocide in Darfur. While it is doubtful that deaths remained at a constant peak level of 10,000 per month in Darfur for 18 months, there on the other hand were reasons to think the peak monthly death toll was actually higher than 10,000 per month.

6.   A GATHERING CONSENSUS

The projection of 180,000 deaths from the WHO survey work was at the lower end of a collection of estimates receiving attention in the media at the beginning of 2005. In February 2005 a British physician, Jan Coebergh, noted the absence of violent deaths from the WHO survey and, drawing some simple inferences from the ADS, estimated in an article in *Parliamentary Brief* that the true death toll was nearer 300,000 (Coebergh 2005). The scale of this estimate echoed the American activist-scholar Eric Reeves of Smith College who had been posting on the internet similarly large estimates based on parallel assumptions for some time (Reeves 2005). Eric Reeves soon updated his work in a *Boston Globe* op ed piece, projecting a death toll of 400,000. The importance of Coebergh and Reeves' estimates is that they made explicit that their higher projections involved adding deaths resulting from violence recorded in the ADS work to the deaths mainly following from disease and malnutrition in the WHO survey. These estimates were attempts to bridge the crime and health paradigms.

At almost the same time, in conjunction with the Coalition of International Justice [CIJ], we issued a press release detailing an estimate based on a combination of the WHO and ADS surveys. The estimate involved going back through each of the 1136 ADS surveys and retracing all of the steps necessary to make this projection clearly and completely transparent. We concluded that as many as 350,000 persons might have died, and that nearly 400,000 persons were likely either missing or dead in Darfur. The *New York Times* and *Washington Post* now began reporting with some frequency an estimate of 300,000 deaths. Kofi Annan seemly endorsed the higher assessment when he indicated in a *New York Times* op ed piece that 300,000 'or more' Darfurians were thought to have died (Annan 2005). In April 2005, Marc Lacey cited our nearly 400,000 dead and missing figure for the first time in the *New York Times* (Lacey 2005). A consensus was emerging that hundreds of thousands had died, with the estimates now ranging from 180,000 to 400,000 deaths.

7.   THE CONSENSUS BREAKS

In the early spring of 2005, Assistant Secretary Robert Zoellick, the Deputy to the new Secretary of State, Condoleezza Rice, paid a personal visit to Darfur. Zoellick described himself as a mixture of an economist and a diplomat with an 'accountancy past' that included service in the U.S. Treasury as well as State Departments. He later left the Bush Administration to join the Wall Street investment firm, Goldman Sachs, and today is President of the World Bank (Brinkley 2005). Condoleezza Rice spoke to the press before his departure to Sudan to emphasize the importance she attached to the trip. So the press was attentive when Zoellick's visit produced a revised and highly unexpectedly upbeat assessment of events in Darfur.

In a press conference held in Khartoum with the first Vice President of Sudan, Ali Uthman Muhammad Taha, Zoellick startled reporters by declining to reaffirm Powell's earlier determination that a genocide had occurred in Darfur. When he was asked about the characterization of the conflict in Darfur as genocide, he answered that he did not want to 'debate terminology'. He went on to dispute the then prevailing consensus estimates of deaths that we have seen were all in the hundreds of thousands. Zoellick instead reported a new State Department estimate that as few as 60,000 and at most 146,000 'excess' deaths had occurred in Darfur. The State Department subsequently posted a new report on its web site, *Sudan: Death Toll in Darfur*, explaining that 'violent deaths were widespread in the early stages of this conflict, but a successful, albeit delayed, humanitarian response and a moderate 2004 rainy season combined to suppress mortality rates by curtailing infectious disease outbreaks and substantial disruption of aid deliveries' (US Department of State 2004, 1).

The State Department report was brief and did not report the sources or details about the surveys it used, as we note further below. When questions were raised about the incompleteness of the State Department report, it became apparent that much of the work on it was done in collaboration and by outsourcing with the Centre for Research on the Epidemiology of Disasters [CRED], a research program located within the School of Public Health of the *Université Catholique de Louvain* in Belgium. This organization produced two reports respectively in May and December of 2005 titled 'Darfur: Counting the Deaths (Method 1)' and 'Darfur: Counting the Deaths (2).' There is much overlap between the State Department report and the CRED reports, including the joint participation of a State Department employee, Mark Phelan, and State Department funding. Both the State and CRED reports draw heavily from the population health paradigm.

For example, prominent concern about the estimation of 'excess' deaths was a sign that the new State Department estimate and following CRED estimates were tilted toward the public health side of the disciplinary divide that we have emphasized, while simultaneously stepping away from its own victimization methodology. The more explicit sign of this shift was that the State Department had now chosen to exclude the results from its own ADS survey in its new estimate. This was a unique indication of the extent to which the new estimate was framed in the health paradigm of 'complex humanitarian emergencies' rather than the war crimes context of genocide. The new estimates drew heavily on the WHO surveys and were based on the troubling assumption that the kind of survey work done by the WHO comprehensively measured the scale of mortality occurring in Darfur.

Yet it was already clear from public statements by the WHO's David Nabarro (discussed further below) that its survey was a partial picture of the death toll, since by the evidence of Nabarro's own carefully framed remarks, the WHO survey did not take into account those killed in the attacks on the Darfur villages that had provoked the flight to the displacement and refugee camps in the first place. It may also be noteworthy, as we also explain further below, that the Zoellick visit came just a week after the United Nations had given the names of 51 persons identified by the UN's Commission of Inquiry on Darfur to the International Criminal Court (ICC) for possible prosecution (Hoge 2005). The list of suspects was known to include high ranking Sudanese government officials, perhaps even including Zoellick's Vice Presidential host at the press conference in Khartoum. This provides some background context to the press conference which Zoellick held with the Sudanese Vice President, where he announced the new estimate that as few as 63,000 and at most 146,000 'excess' persons were now believed to have perished in Darfur.

The immediate response to Zoellick's announcement of the State Department's new estimate was shock. The *American Prospect*'s Mark Goldberg called the State Department visit to Sudan 'Zoellick's Appeasement Tour' (Goldberg 2005). John Prendergrast, speaking for the International Crisis Group, summarized feelings in much of the NGO community, saying 'for Zoellick to float 60,000 as a low end number is negligent criminally'. He added that 'it's a deliberate effort by the Bush administration to downplay the severity of the crisis in order to reduce the urgency of an additional response. I find that to be disingenuous and perhaps murderous' (Pleming 2005). Prendergrast, who served as a National Security Council official in the Clinton Administration, also indicated a motivation for the low estimate, saying 'we have not taken adequate measures given the enormity of the crimes because we don't want to directly confront Sudan when it is cooperating on terrorism'.

Nonetheless, the State Department's new estimate had an apparently intended effect on major media news outlets. Whereas these sources previously were regularly reporting *hundreds of thousands* of deaths in Darfur, the widely reported death toll now shrunk to *tens of thousands*. Major mainstream news services – including Reuters, United Press International, and the British Broadcasting Service – now included the tens of thousands framing of the conflict as a stock phrase in their new stories, a practice that would continue for more than a year following. A picture soon began to emerge of why the State Department's Robert Zoellick had shifted its framing of the conflict in Darfur, and it supported Prendergrast's speculation about the Bush Administration's war on terrorism.

8.   THE OSAMA BIN LADEN CONNECTION

Within a week of Zoellick's return to Washington, the *Los Angeles Times* reported that just prior to Zoellick offering his new mortality assessment in Khartoum, the CIA had provided a jet to bring the Sudanese government intelligence chief, Major General Salah Abdallah Gosh, to Washington. The purpose of the visit was apparently to elicit information in the war on terror. The *L.A. Times* quoted State Department sources as attesting to the importance of Sudanese cooperation. These sources highlighted Sudan's role in the early 1990s in providing sanctuary to Osama Bin Laden and a base for Al Qaeda operations. Sudan's General Gosh now was quoted as saying 'we have a strong partnership with the CIA'. Gosh had been an official 'minder' of Bin Laden during his time in Darfur (Silverstein 2005).

The *New York Times* reported that the CIA flew Gosh from Khartoum to Baltimore-Washington International Airport on April 17, returning him to Khartoum on April 22, making Gosh's trip coincide with Zoellick's stay in Sudan

(Shane 2005). The *Los Angeles Times* reported Gosh met in Washington with CIA officials on April 21 and 22. Zoellick arrived in Sudan on April 14 and his low mortality estimate was reported in the *Washington Post* on April 22. As chief of Sudan's intelligence and security service, observers have frequently charged that Gosh directed or at least knew of the role of the Sudanese military in the attacks on Darfur villages. Gosh's name is prominently positioned in the Sudanese government chain of command described in the following chapter. A follow-up *L.A. Times* story indicated that the Justice and State Departments were at odds over Gosh's Washington visit, with some in Justice suggesting that the trip should have more appropriately been an opportunity to detain a suspected war criminal (Silverstein 2005b). Gosh met during the visit with Porter Goss, the Bush Administration C.I.A. chief who later resigned amidst allegations and prosecutions of bribes and government contracts.

The suggestion that Sudan's General Gosh is a suspected war criminal is not new, and responsibility for his protective treatment extends beyond the United States. Alex de Waal writes that 'the real power in Khartoum is not President Bashir, who is a pious, tough soldier, but a cabal of security officers who have run both the Sudanese Islamist movement and the Sudanese state as a private but collegial enterprise for the last 15 years (…). And the members of this cabal are serial war criminals' (See De Waal 2004; Flint & De Waal 2005). General Gosh, as Sudan's national security chief, was cited by Congress in 2004 as having played a key role in orchestrating the Darfur genocide (Katz 2005).

Yet the Bush administration saw Gosh as potentially useful in its war on terrorism and in May 2004 had removed Sudan from its list of countries not cooperating in counterterrorism. The trip for Gosh to Washington by private CIA chartered jet during Deputy Secretary Zoellick's trip to Khartoum seemed intended to reward his past cooperation in providing information and to encourage the possibility of future assistance. The *Los Angeles Times* has continued to report on the links between the CIA and Sudan's security service, called the Mukhabarat, noting that 'Gosh has not returned to Washington since, but a former official said that "there are liaison visits every day" between the CIA and the Mukhabarat' (Miller & Meyer 2007). The U.S. State Department recently issued a report calling Sudan a 'strong partner in the war on terror'.

It seems likely that the reduced mortality estimate in Darfur and the temporarily suspended references to genocide were part of the cooperative strategy. President Bush did not mention the genocide in Darfur for a period of more than four months in 2005. In May 2005, the columnist Nicholas Kristof wrote that, 'today marks Day 141 of Mr. Bush's silence on the genocide, for he hasn't let the word Darfur slip past his lips publically since January 10 (even that was a passing reference with no condemnation)' (Kristof 2005).This is the period that the State Department reduced its Darfur mortality estimate and brought Sudan's General

Gosh to Washington. The nonpartisan Congressional Research Service indicates that although Gosh and other Sudanese officials played 'key roles in directing (…) attacks against civilians,' the administration was 'concerned that going after these individuals could disrupt cooperation on counter-terrorism' (Silverstein 2005). This was actually a return to a recurring policy dating at least to the first Bush Administration when it is also reported that 'Washington bureaucrats turned a blind eye towards the policy of the authorities in Khartoum, mainly in the hope of securing their support for American goals in the Middle East' (Burton 1991).

Gosh's visit to Washington apparently reaped benefits both for Sudan and for himself. Sudan subsequently was allowed to enter into a $530,000 public relations contract with a Washington based lobbying firm, C/L International. The public relations aspect of this contract seems to parallel the role of the European Sudanese Public Affairs Council that brought the complaint against Save Darfur discussed as the outset of this article. In the U.S., such activity was in violation of Executive Order 13067 which prohibits American companies and citizens from doing business with Sudan (CRS 2006, 11). Congress forced an end to this deal in February 2006. Still, Sudanese Foreign Minister Mustafa Osman Ismail was also allowed to meet with Secretary Rice in Washington and was promised a review of economic sanctions, while Deputy Secretary Zoellick attended Sudan's presidential inauguration.

Most important, however, is the issue of General Gosh and his success in evading personal sanctions. It is reported that Gosh is ranked number two on the widely leaked UN list of senior Sudanese officials blamed for allowing if not directing the ethnic cleansing in Darfur by the janjaweed militias he is accused of controlling. Nonetheless, Gosh also was able to visit London and meet with British officials (Beaumont 2006). One year after Gosh's visit to Washington and Zoellick's announcement of his low estimate in Khartoum, the UN belatedly imposed sanctions on four men for Darfur war crimes, but the most highly ranked and only government official was a Sudanese Air Force officer (Hoge 2006). A senior State Department official, Donald Steinberg, explained that our interests 'cut on the side of not offending the regime in Khartoum'. The Bush administration pushed to keep Gosh off the list (Katz 2006, 25).

9. STATE'S NEW VIEW OF DEATH IN DARFUR

To alter its perspective and reframe the killing in Darfur, the State Department had to reorganize its survey research by shifting attention away from its own Bureau of Democracy, Human Rights and Labor and Bureau of Intelligence and Research. These two bureaus had worked together to produce the State Department/ CIJ survey of Darfur refugees in Chad and the earlier noted report, *Documenting*

Atrocities in Darfur. The State Department shifted its focus by outsourcing a reanalysis to the research group in Belgium noted above. Working with a new liaison person, Mark Phelan, and with funding from State's Bureau of Population, Refugees and Migration, and using surveys done outside the Department, the Belgian group reported the background details of the new low estimate that Deputy Secretary Zoellick had announced more than a month earlier in Khartoum. Again, this report does not provide the full details on the primary source surveys it relied upon (Guha-Sapir & Degomme with Phelan 2005).

On the Sunday following his Khartoum announcement, the *Washington Post* had reproached Zoellick about the validity of his mortality estimate in an editorial titled 'Darfur's Real Death Toll'. The *Post* insisted that 'the 60,000 number that Mr. Zoellick cited as low-but-possible is actually low-and-impossible' and concluded that 'next time he should cite better numbers'. The editorial cited the more than 400,000 State Department/CIJ estimate of deaths to make its point (Washington Post 2005).

Zoellick (2005) took the unusual step of responding with a letter of protest to the *Post* in which he defended his actions and referred by implication to parallel disputes involving charges that Administration officials invented and stretched intelligence, in this case scientific surveys, to support policy preferences. The description of the population based survey mortality estimates as 'intelligence' was unusual, but perhaps understandable when viewed in conjunction with the Washington visit of the Sudanese security and intelligence minister, General Gosh. Zoellick (2005) protested in his letter that,

> '*I did not invent intelligence or stretch it. I did not recommend that the analysts change their assessment. I did indicate that estimates varied widely and that many were higher. Our estimate was based on more than 30 health and mortality surveys by public health professionals, and it was corroborated by a World Health Organization research center.*'

To support Zoellick's claim, the State Department (2005) had previously posted on its web site the earlier, very brief report with uncited sources, *Sudan: Death Toll in Darfur*.

The corroborative role of the WHO affiliated research center is more fully revealed in the outsourced report from the Belgian group introduced above, but here the WHO's own characterization of this and the later Belgian 'multiple survey' analysis is notable. A late May 2005 protocol from WHO concluded that 'even if, overall, the findings of these surveys are consistent in showing broad spatial and time trends, they cannot be directly compared or combined in a meta-analysis due to differences in the study populations or methods utilized.' A follow-up *Washington Post* article quoted a 'senior State Department official' as saying that the report was 'less scientific than you would think' (Kessler 2005).

The public health specialist newly involved from the State Department, Mark Phelan, has an extensive background of research experience in public health and nutrition surveys.

Why was the State Department now relying on a review involving a health and nutrition expert and based on uncited sources that reported results substantively at odds with its earlier report issued under Colin Powell? What were the unreferenced sources and what could they tell us about death in Darfur during this continuing lethal conflict? How could scientific studies of such a lethal and protracted conflict produce such different conclusions? What can this experience tell us about the place of criminology in science and diplomacy? And what was the role of the Government Accountability Office in assessing the results of these events? The answers to these questions may not definitively tell us whether outsourced scientific research in this episode was, to use Zoellick's words, 'invented or stretched intelligence', but the answers do help to reveal the ways in which scientific research can flip-flop in response to demands of diplomacy, in this case involving a denial of the deaths of many Darfurians.

10. RE-EXAMINING THE SURVEYS

The answers again involve the health and crime perspectives applied in surveying the events in Darfur. The tension between these approaches is apparent from the outset of the outsourced CRED report. In a broadside against the State Department's ADS work from the previous summer (i.e., the survey that was the foundation of Colin Powell's testimony about genocide to the UN and U.S. Congress), the CRED report complains that 'these interviews (...) were not designed in any way to function as a mortality survey nor was there an overall systematic sampling methodology used that could make it representative of the roughly 200,000 refugees that fled to eastern Chad, much less of the entire 2.4 million people affected of Darfur' (Guha-Sapiri et al. 2005, 7). Yet the survey applied a probability sampling methodology we described above (based on a random one in 10 household selection in all 19 identified Chad camps and settlements) and that is explicitly described in the State Department's own *Documenting Atrocities in Darfur* publication.[4] To the extent the CRED sampling argument had force, it was an argument about sample selection bias involving the refugees over-representation of victimization in areas close to the Chad border. Yet there is much evidence in accounts of the Darfur conflict that similar methods of attack and victimization occurred across all three Darfur states, and the

---

4   Department of State Publication 11182, *o.c.*, 5–7.

approximately the same numbers of persons (about one million each) were displaced in each of these states.

Why was the CRED so focused on sampling issues? The answer at least partly involves the criminal victimization (as contrasted with public health) approach followed in the earlier State Department/CIJ work. Despite the common social and political causes of the health and crime dimensions of such humanitarian emergencies, we have noted that epidemiologists and demographers are inclined to focus mainly on the health outcomes,[5] whereas criminologists prioritize issues of legal responsibility (Hagan & Greer 2002). As we have noted, a common sequence in these emergencies involves the onset of violent attacks, the flight of the resulting victims, and ensuing health problems that all contribute to mortality. The challenge is to simultaneously keep in mind the cumulative and multiplicative effects of violence, flight, and displacement to concentrated encampments, and the political state and non-state origins of these disastrous consequences (Hagan, Schoenfeld & Palloni 2006). Surely the substantive issue of including measurement of pre- and post-camp deaths involving violence as well as disease and malnutrition dwarf plausible concerns about sample selection bias. Furthermore, we addressed the issue of potential sample selection bias with supportive results by using only internal Sudan displacement camp surveys in an alternative estimate described below.

Meanwhile, we originally were concerned that the WHO survey work underestimated mortality in Darfur by ignoring almost all of the pre-camp killing that led survivors to flee to the camps. Yet we also were concerned when we undertook our own combined estimation that the ADS work could exaggerate Darfur mortality due to the pre-camp violence by including multiple family members' overlapping reports of the same killings. Stephanie Frease of the Coalition for International Justice had acknowledged this point by noting in an early report of the ADS results that 'refugees included extended family– such as uncles and cousins– in their answers' (Associated Press 2005).

To address this problem, we further examined each of these 1136 surveys from the ADS to establish that during the 17-month period covered, 360 persons *specifically identified as husbands, wives, sons and daughters* were reported as dead or missing and presumed dead. Unless there was a specific reference in the original interview to the death involving a nuclear family member, the death was not included in the 360 total. This requirement of explicit nuclear family membership was invoked to eliminate overlapping, duplicate reports of deaths by extended family members. The count of 360 dead or missing persons formed the basis for the calculation of a CMR of 1.2 deaths per 10,000 people per day, or more than 98,000 persons presumed dead for the first 18 months of the conflict. Note

---

5   See, for example, World Health Organization, *Darfur: One Year On, WHO's Work to Save Lives and Reduce Suffering.*

that this figure exceeds by more than 50 percent the low estimate reported by Zoellick, even though it does not cover the full period of the conflict and does not include deaths from malnutrition and sickness in the camps, which was the focus of the WHO survey cited above. How could there be such a large disparity on such a fundamental matter of life and death?

From a criminological perspective, the key lies in the difference between the Powell State Department's criminal victimization survey methodology and the studies done for health focused organizations in Darfur. Recall that while Powell wanted to testify on the basis of reliable evidence about the genocidal killing that led Darfurians to flee their villages and seek refuge in camps, the public health organizations worked with a different purpose. These organizations subsequently needed to work with and for those living in the camps to stop them from dying of starvation and disease. Population surveys of mortality, morbidity and nutrition are undertaken by these public health organizations to establish the health risks posed in camp settings by starvation and disease. As we have emphasized, these organizations- such as the World Health Organization, the World Food Program, and the Center for Disease Control and Prevention- are more concerned with these immediate and ongoing risks than they are with the past violence that leads refugees to camps. This is why Powell needed his own victimization survey to substantiate his Congressional testimony about genocide.

The survey work was undertaken by the State Department through the Coalition for International Justice in the Chad refugee camps because the Sudanese government would not allow this kind of violence based investigation to be broadly undertaken within its national borders. Instead, as noted in the previous chapter, the Sudanese government wanted to blame the deaths in Darfur on problems of health and nutrition that the international health organizations had failed to overcome and control.[6] The State Department therefore adopted its own alternative victimization survey methodology. Since the refugees in the Chad camps had fled from Darfur, they could provide through their retrospective accounts a window on the violence in the homes and villages they left behind. This kind of indirect estimation approach is increasingly used by demographers, for example, to inquire through surveys of North Koreans who take refuge across the border in China about their family history of nutrition and health problems, including those among siblings remaining behind the closed North Korean boundary (Robinson et al 1999).

---

[6] On this point, see especially the testimony of Mukkesh Kapila, the former United Nations Resident and Humanitarian Coordinator for Sudan, to the House of Commons International Development Committee. Darfur, Sudan: The Responsibility to Protect. Fifth Report of Session 2004–05. Vol. II: Oral and Written Evidence. London: Station. Off.Ltd.http://www.publications.parliament.uk/pa/cm200405/cmselect/cmintdev/67/6711.pdf.

Parallel differences between crime and health surveys are reflected in much of the respective research of other organizations undertaken in studies that have produced distinctively different death estimates for Darfur. Much of the resulting confusion and debate in the case of Darfur goes back to the WHO mortality survey noted early in this chapter as the source of the seven month estimate of 70,000 deaths. We noted that this survey was conducted at about the same time as the State Department/CIJ survey in Chad, in late summer of 2004; but the WHO survey was done inside Darfur and jointly conducted with the Sudanese Ministry of Health [henceforth WHO/SMH], as a health rather than a legally oriented crime victimization survey.

The different foci of the State Department/CIJ and WHO/SMH studies can be seen as complimentary, but the confusion of their separate criminal law and health purposes has led in the State Department's recent reports to the flip flop in conclusions. David Nabarro of WHO attempted to forestall this outcome in October of 2004 when he posted his report of the seven month 70,000 death estimate. He explicitly stated that 'these projections have not sought to detail deaths due to violent incidents within Darfur communities' (Nabarro 2004). The CNN coverage of Nabarro's press conference took note of this in indicating that 'the figure does not take into account deaths from direct violence in the conflict-torn region' (Nabarro 2004).

This would seem to be a clearly understood statement about the WHO/SMH survey, but as recently as February 23 2005 the British Secretary of State, Hilary Benn, testified to the Parliamentary International Development Committee that 'it is my best information that the WHO estimate for the period March to October (...) 2004 did include deaths from injuries and from violence'.[7] Later in the same hearing the Member of Parliament who raised the issue reported that 'I am since told that the Committee has been advised by the WHO that that 70,000 does not include deaths due to the violence from which people have fled, which is obviously the vast bulk of the violence, it includes only that violence which has come about through fights over the distribution and allocation of food within the IDP camps'.[8] Secretary Benn wrote further to the Committee on 14 March 2005 to clarify her view with regard to the WHO/SMH survey that 'it is not possible to calculate with confidence the number of deaths directly related to the conflict'.[9] The Committee felt strongly enough on this matter to present in bold print the statement in its final report at the end of March 2005 that 'the only violent deaths which the WHO's estimate includes are those which took place in the camps for Internally

---

7   House of Commons International Development Committee, *o.c.*, Ev 65.

8   Ibid., Ev 70.

9   Official correspondence from Hilary Benn, Secretary of State, to Tony Baldry MP, Chairman, International Development Committee, 14 March 2005. Provided to the author by the secretary to the Committee and on file with author.

Displaced Persons (IDPs) (...). Cited without clear explanation of its limitations, the WHO's estimate is extremely misleading'.[10]

This might seem to have definitively resolved this issue, yet the issue arises again in the late May 2005 report from the Belgian group that provides further insight into Zoellick's low State Department estimate. The Belgian report, co-authored with the State Department's Mark Phelan, now asserted that

> "the WHO mortality survey and the WHO mortality projections have often been confused and misguidedly used interchangeably. This has led some to misinterpret a WHO statement indicating exclusion of violent death from the WHO estimate, as also meaning violent deaths were not included in the WHO mortality surveys" (Guha-Sapiri et al. 2005, 9).

Yet the point earlier made by the WHO's David Nabarro and the British Parliamentary Committee is that the violent deaths picked up in the WHO/SMH survey represented less common violent mortality in and around the camps rather than the widespread deaths from attacks on the villages that led individuals to flee to the camps.

There are several ways to demonstrate this crucial point of difference between the State Department/CIJ and WHO/SMH surveys. First, there are few deaths due to 'injury and violence' reported in the WHO/SMH survey (less than 15% overall), while all of the deaths in the State Department/CIJ survey are directly or indirectly due to violence (in the village attacks or on the journey to the camps). Second, the majority of deaths by violence in the State Department/CIJ survey are of persons between 15 and 49 years of age, while in the WHO/SMH survey the majority of those who died from injury or violence are over 50 years of age, suggesting the latter deaths may include accidents and injuries among the elderly. Third, while the period covered by the WHO/SMH survey was restricted to the prior two months in the summer of 2004, the average person in an IDP camp had been there for six or more months. This last two month restriction of the WHO/SMH survey, which we again emphasize was jointly conducted with Sudanese government consent and cooperation, is a key way in which the study was prevented from providing evidence of the violent origins of the genocide. The need to collect this otherwise unavailable evidence was the specific purpose of the State Department/CIJ survey.

---

[10]   *O.c.*, Vol. I, p. 11.

11.   A COMPLIMENTARY AND COMBINED APPROACH

Viewed more constructively, the division of labour between the pre- and in camp experience in the State Department/CIJ and WHO/SMH surveys between the pre- and in camp experiences makes their results potentially complimentary. The WHO/SMH survey is especially useful in indicating the health and nutrition related deaths in the Darfur IDP camps in the late summer of 2004, while the State Department/CIJ surveys informs us about the violent deaths from attacks leading victims and their families to seek sanctuary in Chad refugee camps for the preceding 17 months. These two different surveys can be brought together to better inform us about mortality due to health *and* violence in Darfur.

Our approach involves doing a simple recalculation with the combined surveys. We noted earlier that a CMR of 2.14 is reported for North and West Darfur in the WHO/SMH survey (with South Darfur less fully surveyed). Given the discussion above, we take this survey as providing a meaningful estimate of mortality following displacement due to causes in and around the camps, but excluding deaths due to violent attacks prior to displacement. To complete the picture of Darfur mortality, we can simply add the WHO/SMH estimate to the State Department/CIJ survey crude mortality rate due to violence and flight, which is 1.2, yielding a combined estimate of 3.34.

We argued in the previous chapter that it is dubious in terms of legal responsibility to accept any of this mortality as 'expected' or 'normal'. Nonetheless, we also noted that it can be useful to make comparisons to prior levels of mortality to provide a sense of the elevated scale of the humanitarian crisis involved. Since the 'normal' mortality rate conventionally is estimated from .35 to .5 (per 10,000 per day) in a sub-Saharan African country with the demographic characteristics of Sudan, it is reasonable to conclude that the rate of violence and health related death in Darfur for the affected period of 2003/4 exceeded expectations by a multiple of six or more. This rate of death is consistent with deaths of up to 15,000 or more Darfurians a month at the peak of the genocide.

It is uncertain how long the monthly death toll persisted at this elevated level, but the overall conflict in Darfur has been ongoing for more than three years. Recall that the WHO projection was 10,000 deaths per month. The 15,000 estimate we have just presented implies that the WHO/SMH estimate was low, but recall also that Jan Egeland of the UN extrapolated this figure over 18 months, a period that is almost certainly longer than the peak in mortality, even if this mortality was prolonged and sustained. In this sense, the WHO projection may have been both too low and too long, with consequences that are to some extent off-setting.

We introduce a final estimation approach in the following section of this chapter that takes into account monthly variation in the mortality. Our calculations to this point suggest that it is much more likely that the Darfur death toll is between 200,000 and 400,000 than between the 63,000 to 146,000 new estimate of Zoelick's State Department. As noted earlier, this amounts to the difference between tens and hundreds of thousands of deaths. The tens of thousands estimate held sway in much of the media for more than a year after the new State Department estimate. So where does the latter low number come from?

12. THE UNACCOUNTABILITY OF THE GOVERNMENT ACCOUNTABILITY OFFICE

The answer involves the other surveys which the CRED group and Mark Phelan of the State Department incorporated to generate the low estimates that led to the lower bound report of 63,000 deaths. European based CRED, the U.S. State Department, and ultimately the U.S. Government Accountability Office made extensive use of health and nutrition surveys. Establishing the extent to which this is the case is difficult because CRED and the State Department do not clearly identify the surveys they use in their estimates. While full referencing and citation of survey sources would seem among the most fundamental of scholarly research norms, the U.S. Government Accountability Office [henceforth, GAO] takes an unusually relaxed view of this norm in its report on the *Darfur Crisis*.

This problem is apparent from the very outset of the GAO's work. In a cover letter submitted to the ranking members of the House and Senate committees that commissioned the GAO review, the authors report the following internally contradictory information about their methods and deliberations:

'To evaluate the estimates, we reviewed and analyzed public information on the estimates and interviewed the estimate authors regarding their studies' data, methods and objectives. We provided this information and summaries of the interviews to a group of 12 experts in epidemiology, demography, statistics, and the Darfur crisis convened in April 2006 in collaboration with the National Academy of Sciences. These experts discussed their review of this information and evaluation of the estimates during an all-day session and also assessed the estimates in a follow-up survey. State's Bureau of Intelligence and Research, which conducted the department's death estimate for Darfur, declined to speak with us or provide additional information, limiting the expert's ability to fully understand State's methods of analysis. However, despite this limitation, the experts were able to discuss State's estimate in detail and assess its accuracy and methodologies.'[11]

---

[11]   U.S. Government Accountability Office, Report to Congressional Requesters, Darfur Crisis: Death Estimates Demonstrate Severity of Crisis, but Their Accuracy Could be Enhanced, November, 2006, GAO-07–24, 2.

It is unclear how the reported refusal of the State Department to provide or discuss missing and omitted information is consistent with the claim that the committee could review State's estimate in 'detail', much less 'in accordance with generally accepted government auditing standards'. Note also that none of the 12 experts is described as having expertise in the crime victimization paradigm.

This situation is not improved when in its following presentation of 'Results in Brief' the GAO report indicates that 'many experts believed that the lower end of State's estimate was too low and found that published documents describing State's estimate lacked sufficient information about its data and methods to allow it to be replicated and verified by external researchers' (o.c., 3). The review later notes that nine of the ten experts rated the lower-end of State's estimate as too low (o.c., 21).

Overall, the GAO review 'did not rate any of the death estimates as having a high level of accuracy and noted that all of the studies had methodological strengths and shortcomings'. The review did observe that 'in reviewing the estimates, we found we were able to replicate Dr. Hagan's entire estimate based on its description in public documents' (o.c., 27). Nonetheless, the experts indicated greatest confidence in the lower estimates of mortality in Darfur, and lower confidence in the higher estimates, including my estimate. The experts ranked the CRED estimate the highest, while giving State's estimate 'slightly lower ratings for accuracy and methodological strengths' (o.c., 3). As noted earlier, the CRED and State estimates were linked, with State funding CRED and the State Department author, Mark Phelan, overlapping on the reports.

It is perhaps not surprising that some of the same basic problems with the State Department estimate reappear in the CRED reports, especially the problem of missing and omitted primary sources and incomplete information about how the CRED estimates were constructed. Thus, 'several experts found shortcomings in the CRED estimates' data and methods and thought that CRED could have provided more information and clarity in its reporting' (o.c., 21–22) and 'several experts believed that better descriptions of the methods used, including information on specific formulations and calculations, could have been provided' (o.c., 23). A page later, the report offers similar observations about the parallel State Department estimate:

> 'Some experts said that several of the mortality surveys used in State's estimate may have had methodological limitations in areas such as survey design, implementation, or accessibility to insecure regions, resulting in unrealistically low mortality rates. These experts believed that such limitations in source data, in addition to other problems – for example, the estimate's lack of clarity regarding how missing populations are accounted for and use of a relatively higher baseline mortality rate – may have pulled down State's estimate, in particular, its lower end.' (o.c., 24)

The GAO review then offers a summary statement that seems in direct contradiction with its opening letter to the House and Senate committees. Thus on the issue of the 'sufficiency of reporting,' the GAO review reports that 'many of the experts found that the published documents containing State's estimate lacked sufficient information to allow them to replicate the estimate and verify the accuracy and reliability of the data and methods' (o.c., 25). Similarly, 'in our review of CRED's first estimate, we were able to replicate it to some degree only after the authors provided a substantial amount of information, such as specific mortality rates and formulas used and citations for source studies, in addition to the information in the published document'.

The authors of the GAO review also offer the startling conclusion, given their high rating of the State estimate, that 'our review of the State estimate also showed that it could not be replicated with the information contained in the report' (o.c., 25). It comes as little surprise, then, that the GAO review underlined in its recommendations that information about sources and methods should be provided in future work. Despite its claim that it could provide detailed assessments of CRED and State's estimates, and its expression of confidence in these estimates, the GAO offered that 'the measure rated most likely to produce the most improvements was ensuring sufficient public documentation of estimates' data and methods to allow replication of the methods, verification of the findings, and confirmation of the estimates' credibility and objectivity'. The inference was that although the experts did not know the sources of State and CRED's estimates or the methods and the calculations performed on them, they still were confident about them.

So what are the primary sources that State and CRED so incompletely report? Probably the most extensively used of these other surveys is a study jointly undertaken by the U.S. Centers for Disease Control and Prevention (CDC) and United Nations World Food Programme (WFP), again in the summer of 2004 and with the co-authorship of Mark Phelan.[12] The title of the aforementioned study, 'Emergency Nutrition Assessment of Crisis Affected Populations, Darfur Region, Sudan,' is significant in relation to the division of labour we have emphasized between crime victimization and health research. Just as the WHO/SMH study was designed to reflect mortality in the displacement camps from health problems, the CDC/WFP survey was designed to reveal nutritional problems.

---

[12] U.S. Centers for Disease Control and Prevention (CDC) and United Nations World Food Programme (WFP). Emergency Nutrition Assessment of Crisis Affected Populations: Darfur Region, Sudan. August-September 2004. The alphabetized contributors to this study are: Rita Bhatia, Curtis Blanton, Muireann Brennan, Cecelia Garzon, Mark Phelan, Leisel Talley, David Sussman, Andrew Thornel Lyman, Tami Zalewski.

Comparison of figures in the CRED report reveals that the low estimate of deaths by Zoellick in Darfur is dependent on this kind of CDC/WFP nutritional survey, which produced low mortality estimates. However, consider the following: the recall period for this survey was only six months (while among those who were in displacement camps the average duration of stay was 7.5 months), the cause of death was not indicated among nearly half of those who were reported dead in this survey (while among all those indicated as dead only 16 percent reported 'violent injury' as the cause), and these deaths were mostly among older respondents.

The point is that the nutritional studies are a source of likely downward bias in determining the low estimates of the genocide in Darfur. There are further reasons to doubt the validity and purposes of Zoellick's low State Department estimates, including a refusal to meaningfully consider missing persons in these estimates. Yet rather than belabour these further divergences in crime victimization and health orientations to the death count, it is more constructive to present a final mortality estimate from Darfur that we designed to bridge the crime and health divide by including measures of both violence and health related deaths.

The following alternative approach was inexplicably not considered, even though it was published as an article co-authored with Alberto Palloni, a recent President of the Population Association of America, in the journal *Science* two months (September 2006) before the GAO report was completed (November 2006). This is the only peer reviewed estimate of Darfur mortality published in a scholarly journal, and *Science* is one of the most highly regarded journals in the world. The GAO insisted that it did not receive this estimate in time for the report, yet it makes reference to the study in the report, and it was received by GAO even before its publication. I suspect that the reasons this estimate was not considered in the review was that it challenged key assumptions of the population health paradigm and posed further questions about the State Department estimate.

One source of evidence for my suspicion about the unwillingness of the GAO to further address its basic population health assumptions involves its unresolved response to the issue of 'normal' and 'excess' mortality. The GAO review leaves this issue this way:

"In addition, the experts debated whether a baseline of any sort was justified for a humanitarian crisis such as Darfur, arguing ethical and philosophical, rather than technical, considerations. About half of the experts said that deaths that would have occurred regardless of the crisis should be subtracted from the death toll attributed to the crisis. However, two experts took a contrary position, arguing that the concept of expected or normal levels of mortality was not appropriate in the presence of genocide or ethnic cleansing because the perpetrators of those crimes against humanity should be considered culpable for all deaths that resulted from the crises they instigated. Using a baseline to estimate mortality would lead to a somewhat smaller excess death toll than

not using a baseline. For example, State's estimate of total deaths ranged from 98,000 to 181,000, minus 35,000 expected deaths; thus, State's estimated 63,000 to 146,000 excess deaths directly resulting from the crisis."[13]

This passage makes clear how important the debatable population health practice of removing 'excess mortality' is to State having a low end estimate of mortality in the tens rather than hundreds of thousands of deaths. The polemical significance of this low estimate is further addressed below.

13.   A NEW AND ALTERNATIVE APPROACH

Because the estimation of the death toll has been such a source of controversy and is widely believed to be central to a genocide charge, we decided to develop an alternative approach to this estimation that did not rely on the State Department ADS work and instead took advantage of a unique study which bridged the concerns of the crime and health perspectives. This study was led by Médecins Sans Frontières (MSF)[14] and published in the journal of medical research *Lancet* in October 2004 (Depoortere et al. 2004). The study was conducted in only five displacement camps in West Darfur between April and June, 2004, with recall periods from one to six months between October and June 2004, probably the period of highest violence in Darfur. In retrospect, the limitation of sites is easy to understand: the Sudanese government would not authorize the scale of sampling required across many sites to representatively study the wide ranging violence in Darfur.

As in the larger WHO/SMH study, MSF found within camp violence accounting for only six to 21 percent of the deaths across the several camps. But the MSF study also asked about the period leading to flight to four of the five camps. Nearly 90 percent of these deaths resulted from violence. In these camps, the village and flight CMRs (5.9–9.5) were much higher than the camp CMRs (1.2–1.3). Heavy rains and worsening camp conditions subsequently increased the camp mortality rates in the WHO/SMH study reported above; and a further camp studied by MSF already had a mortality rate heading into this period of 5.6. Overall, the average mortality rate across the four MSF camps – with pre-camp violence included in three of the camps – was 3.2. Note that this combined rate is approximately the same level of mortality we estimated above with the joined State Department/CIJ and WHO/SMH studies.

Still, we concluded that it would be more persuasive to develop a new and alternative estimate that estimated mortality in Darfur on a month by month

---

[13]   U.S. Government Accountability Office, *o.c.*, 34.
[14]   For a fascinating account of MSF and other French NGOs, see Simeant (2005).

basis and that took advantage of the different time periods included in the MSF camp surveys. The MSF surveys use essentially the same sampling design as the WHO/SMH survey, although the former are limited to five camps in the state of West Darfur, while WHO/SMH surveyed camps in North and South Darfur as well. Both the MSF and WHO/SMH surveys report age-specific CMRs and some information on violence, although we have emphasized that the MSF surveys systematically included pre-camp as well as in-camp mortality. The strongest feature of the WHO surveys is the number of camps included, while the strongest feature of the MSF surveys is the coverage of pre- and in-camp mortality. We combine the MSF and WHO/SMH surveys to draw on the strengths of both in our new estimate. We narrow the focus initially to 19 months of the conflict and the state of West Darfur, and later draw broader conclusions. The risk population for corresponding months is taken from the UN humanitarian profiles of people counted in the internal displacement camps and people surrounding the camps who together constitute what the UN calls 'conflict-affected persons'. We include UN refugee camp counts in Chad to complete the estimate of the population at risk.

Our new estimate involves calculations of direct and indirect monthly estimates of CMRs to better take into account sources of over and under-reporting of deaths. The premise is that if we have two estimations with contrasting upward and downward biases, then we can look for a more realistic estimate of the actual death toll in the space in between these upper and lower bound projections.

The direct estimation method is based on CMRs that are calculated for all age groups in the surveys. Earlier in this chapter we noted our concern that respondents could use extended definitions of their families to include grandparents, uncles, aunts, cousins and even more distant relatives in their reports of deaths. Put differently, these directly reported CMRs for family members of all ages likely are upwardly biased by reports of deaths of extended as well as nuclear family members, because kinship boundaries often expand and become more inclusive in response to war.

The indirect estimation method we use is alternatively based on CMRs that are calculated for only family members under five years of age. We expected that these reports are less likely to include extended family members because respondents are focused in a more narrow way when they are asked about their own children. [On the other hand, there is a different source of survivor bias involved in under-reporting for this age group. These reports are likely downwardly biased by missing children whose entire unrepresented families have died.] Life tables for sub-Saharan Africa are used to estimate the full age distribution of mortality in peacetime, and violence is then reincorporated into the estimate on the basis of the proportion of violence reported in the surveys.

The overall rise and decline in estimated deaths in West Darfur is consistent with the classical pattern of complex humanitarian emergencies discussed in the previous chapter. Perhaps most interestingly, the peak mid-point monthly level of deaths estimated for West Darfur is about 4000. Below we will argue that there is good reason to believe that deaths are distributed approximately evenly across the three Darfur states. If this is so, the estimate is that the death toll in Darfur peaked in early 2004 at about 12,000 per month. Note that this figure is between the 10,000 estimate of WHOSMH and our earlier 15,000 estimate that combined the findings of WHO and ADS. This 12,000 peak monthly death estimate does not include missing persons and is intended to provide a cautious baseline figure.

We can also now say something more specifically about the 19 months that are best surveyed in West Darfur in 2003–4, and then suggest some broader conclusions. When the mid-points between the high and low monthly death estimates are summed over 19 months, the number of deaths is 49,288. When the right tail of this distribution is extended to May 2006 using additional data from a subsequent WHOSMH survey, the death toll is 65,296 in West Darfur alone. This estimate covers 31 months of the conflict that has now been underway more than four years. If a further 20 months of conflict were well estimated, and/or if all or most missing or disappeared persons were presumed dead, the death estimate would be much higher.

Largely as a result of the violence, more than one million individuals are now displaced or affected in West Darfur. About one million people are similarly displaced in each of the adjoining states of North and South Darfur. If the same ratio of death to displacement applies across states, this implies that close to 200,000 deaths have occurred over 31 months in Greater Darfur. This calculation divides the difference between the potential upwards and downward biases of the direct and indirect methods. If the high direct and low indirect bands of estimates are extended across the three states for 31 months, the range is between 170,000 and 255,000 deaths. So it is likely that the number of deaths for this conflict in Greater Darfur is higher than 200,000 individuals. If extended for the further 20 months and to include the missing disappeared, the number is likely between 300,000 and 400,000 deaths.

14. SOME CONCLUSIONS

Our Science article was intended to establish a 'floor' estimate of Darfur deaths that no reputable news source would go below. The State Department's April 2005 estimate of as few as 63,000 deaths had led the major international news organizations, such as Reuters and the BBC, to downgrade their reports to tens of thousands of deaths in Darfur following earlier reports of hundreds of thousands of deaths. In November of 2006, the GAO did not help matters by vaguely concluding that 'many thousands of civilians died in Darfur between February 2003 and August 2005'.[15] This was a number that sounded uncomfortably consistent with Sudan President Al-Bashir's report of 10,000 deaths.

Why the low State Department and GAO estimates? Colin Powell had called Darfur a genocide in September of 2004. However, in April of 2005, the Deputy Secretary of State travelled to Khartoum to announce the State estimate that the death toll could be as low as 63,000. He also refused in the same news conference to use the genocide term or to confirm that a genocide had occurred, even though this was Powell's State Department determination. We have noted that this was the same week in which the *Los Angeles Times* and *New York Times* both reported that a Sudanese security chief, a General Gosh, was flown by private jet to Washington. He met with CIA officials about intelligence in the war on terror.

Some have speculated there was a link between the low Darfur death toll estimate, the refusal to use the term genocide, and the exchange of intelligence. If this is so, it represents an escalation of the politicization of what the population health paradigm treats as 'complex humanitarian emergencies'. We have argued that the assumptions of this paradigm are understandable but also problematic and we argued for the relevance and importance of a parallel crime victimization approach. The consequences of considering an alternative approach are potentially important. Our Science article incorporates this approach and confirms what all responsible news organizations now regularly report: that more than 200,000 have died in genocidal violence in Darfur. This same article stresses that the death toll could be much higher – indeed as high as 400,000. This is in stark contrast with President Al-Bashir's recent downgrading of the toll to 9,000 deaths and his further observation that no rape occurs at all.

---

[15]   U.S. Government Accountability Office, *o.c.*, 41.

PART III
INVESTIGATE THE CAUSES OF
INTERNATIONAL CRIMES

VI. GENOCIDE, WAR CRIMES AND CRIMES AGAINST HUMANITY IN CENTRAL AFRICA: A CRIMINOLOGICAL EXPLORATION

Dawn L. Rothe and Christopher W. Mullins

1. INTRODUCTION

Despite a growing literature on state crimes and generally large numbers of interdisciplinary literature on Holocaust studies, other forms of mass violence have tended to escape the notice of American and European criminologists. Essentially no criminological attention has been given to war crimes, crimes against humanity and other atrocities occurring within Africa during the 1990s and the early years of the 21st century.

As Western criminologists focus their attention on so-called 'retail' street crimes (murder, robbery, theft, etc.), the world has borne witness to the commission of wide-spread atrocities within the continent of Africa, leaving millions dead, millions more displaced, physically and psychological wounded. Despite their visibility and seriousness, criminologists have refused to apply their theories and knowledge to the understanding of such crisis. We find such silence academically and morally problematic.

In this paper we provide an inductive examination of the etiological factors behind the worst forms of state crime: genocide, war crimes and crimes against humanity. Building upon prior work as well as on-going case analyses of incidents under investigation by the International Criminal Court, we provide an overview of basic modalities of these crimes. To do so we begin with a brief review of state crime and extant international laws prohibiting crimes against humanity and war crimes. Then we present a multi-level integrated theory of supranational crimes designed to explain such events. The theory analyses issues of motivation, opportunity, constraint and control at four levels of analysis (e.g., international, macro, meso, micro). As such, we explore motivational, organizational and common enactment elements of such crimes, focusing on central African cases which are currently under the court's investigation (e.g., Uganda, Darfur and the Democratic Republic of Congo) as well as cases within the region that have similar structures and have been tried by *ad hoc* international tribunals (e.g., the Rwandan genocide). Specifically, we address a few of the common elements identified within our integrated theory of supranational crimes: global economics, social disorder (political instability, economic collapse, ethnic tensions and divisiveness), and militias (including their nature and distribution and typical enactment procedures).

2. LITERATURE REVIEW: STATE CRIME, CRIMES OF GLOBALIZATION AND STATE-CORPORATE CRIME STUDIES

Most scholars trace the origins of state crime studies to Chambliss' 1989 ASC presidential address on state-organized crime. Exploring crimes such as piracy and smuggling, Chambliss shows how states can be crucial in the organization and support of activities that violate their own laws and international laws when doing so fulfil their broader political and economic objectives (see Chambliss 1989, 1995). Criminologists, particularly critical criminologists, quickly seized upon the concept, broadening and enriching the field (see Barak 1991b; Green and Ward 2000; Kauzlarich and Kramer 1993; Kramer 1995; Ross 1995; Tunnell 1993). This early work focused not only on crimes tacitly supported or organized by a sovereign polity, but actions committed by nation-states themselves.

Chambliss (1995, 9) again called for resolving the key question at the foundation of the discipline, the definition of crime, so that the discipline could remain viable and vital. He stated,

> "State organized crimes, environmental crimes, crimes against humanity, human rights crimes, and the violations of international treaties increasingly must take center state in criminology (...). Criminologists must define crime as behavior that violates international agreements and principles established in the courts and treaties of international bodies." (Chambliss 1995, 9).

As more case studies and theoretical papers were published, the sub-field began to look at state criminality as actions committed by states which violated domestic, international, or human rights laws (see Barak 1991b; Kauzlarich and Kramer 1998; Kauzlarich, Matthews and Miller 2001; Mullins and Kauzlarich 2000; Ross et al. 1999; Ross 2000) as well as incidents of states or state agencies failing to take actions which they were clearly obligated to address. While definitional debates continue (see Rothe and Friedrichs 2006), the idea of state criminality is firmly entrenched in the field.

Following Chambliss, we contend that the use of international law – customary law, treaties, charters, international humanitarian law, and international human rights law – constitutes the strongest foundation for defining state crime as this framework includes standards such as human rights, social and economic harms, as well as providing a solid legalistic foundation (see Rothe and Friedrichs 2006; Mullins and Rothe 2006; Rothe and Mullins 2006). International criminal law covers individuals as well as states, thus resolving any ongoing reservations of states as actors versus individuals; Jorgensen (2000, 139) suggests, 'all acts which constitute international crimes may in principle entail individual or state responsibility, or both.' Consequentially, we draw upon existing international law in the definition of an act as criminal. To wit:

> *Any action that violates international public law, and/or a states' own domestic law when these actions are committed by individual actors acting on behalf of, or in the name of the state.*

Such a definition is simultaneously parsimonious and accurate. It draws attention not only to the types of crimes which state crime scholars have focused on for the past decade and a half but also to the more wide-spread incidents that emerge in the context of failed and/or weakened states. Our conceptualization of state crime is intrinsically linked to current statutory international public law. This body of law governs the behaviours not only of states and state actors, but also of quasi-military bodies (e.g., militias), transnational organizations and of individuals.

3. AN INTEGRATED THEORY OF SUPRANATIONAL CRIMES

While many mainstream and critically-orientated theories of crime and criminality have relevance to the explanation of state crime, standing alone each contains serious shortcomings. Building upon the early works of Kramer and Michalowski (1990) and Kauzlarich and Kramer (1998), Rothe and Mullins (2006; 2007) present an integrated theory of supranational crimes and state offending that recognizes the inherent complexity of these phenomena. Any given instance of organizational crime is a product of multiple catalysts and forces. To fully elucidate a singular occurrence, one must examine a number of factors at multiple levels of analysis. This model identifies four levels of analysis: the international, the macro-level of the state, the meso-organizational level and the micro-individual level. Such analytical acuity allows a precise pin-pointing of key forces and how they interact within a specific criminal event or context.

Save for recent work on crimes of globalization (see Friedrichs and Friedrichs 2002; Rothe, Muzzatti and Mullins 2006), most organizational criminology has ignored the social forces and incipient social structures occurring within the international realm in favour of focusing on a state itself. Further, when the international arena is taken into account it is done so in a rather simplistic manner resting upon a highly idealized and reified account of globalization (Whyte 2003). State policies are viewed as inevitably market driven as such, the focus is limited to the dynamics of a global and capitalistic economy, most notably, U.S. centred. However, the institutional elements and context of a state, it's economic, political, cultural, and historical environment, is distinct from and often exhibiting forces in contradiction with those elements at the international level. These forces may influence the nature of social forces within a state's macro-level structure, but can also exert their own unique influences. For example, recently, there has been an increasing trend within the international society pushing for the creation and legitimation of international criminal law. Especially since the foundation of the United Nations, and seen most strongly with the codification of the Rome Statute and the creation of the International Criminal Court, the majority of countries are increasingly giving up absolute sovereignty. As the process of globalization continues to expand, imperialistic agendas resurface and are reshaped (e.g., the US and UK's invasion of Iraq) as drives for liberation and democratization and transnational corporations are becoming the norm in global economic relations, examining the international level is essential.

Yet, these forces do not act upon homogeneous social forms. Any given state, and the social structure it represents, will be the product of long-term historical contingencies and forces that necessitate an examination of factors more traditionally referred to as macro-level forces. Broader cultural, political and economic factors in play at a given time and space can to a greater or lesser extent produce a given crime. For example, the cases currently under investigation at the ICC share a similar history of colonial rule. However, such historical conditions did not result in consistent post-independence outcomes. Issues of nations' specific religions, resources, and geographic and/or ethnic divisions were also factors leading up the events under investigation at the court. Thus, ignoring these state level differences fails to holistically address the etiological and structural factors of the given crimes.

Similarly, since these are crimes committed by organizations (states, state agencies, militaries, corporations, etc) one must explore factors at play within the organization itself – a meso-level analytical focus. As corporate crime researchers have shown, some organizations are much more criminogenic than others. As such, the social processes and organizational cultures are essential in understanding state crimes. For example, the Lord's Resistance Army's long-standing opposition to the Ugandan government is the product of post-colonial political forces and the end result of series of coups and counter-coups. Further, the operative ideology of the LRA is religious in nature, replicating the discourse of Alice/Laweka of the Holy Spirit Movement Army. Further, there is an ethnic basis to the LRA, as it is mostly composed of Acholi from the Ankula region. Within the same conflicts, the Ugandan armed forces (the Ugandan People's Defence Forces, UPDF) have also committed vast atrocities; however, many of these are the result of a lack of authority and accountability within the military command hierarchy: most of these crimes represent a form of general thuggery and banditry. In contrast, the Sudanese regime has actively created the Janjaweed militia to carry out massive crimes against humanity. Further, governmental forces aid in the militias atrocities as well as abide by a systematic state policy focusing on continuing the violence and crimes at hand. Thus, while superficially similar, each of these cases exhibits a complexity of meso-level forces.

A separate body of criminological theory emphasizes the influence of social disorder within immediate residential environments as having powerful criminogenic effects. Typically referred to as social disorganization theory (see Shaw and McKay 1942; Bursik and Grasmick 1993), this line of theorizing suggests that when communities possess a diminished capacity to create and enact informal mechanisms of social control (also referred as collective efficacy), crime rates increase due to the lack of community self-organization. Essential a control theory of crime, this work points out that indicators of concentrated disadvantage are largely responsible for the reduction of a community's ability to act collectively. Additionally, European and American criminologists have established that these disorganized social environments also have a pronounced tendency to produce criminal enterprises of varying levels of organizations – be they street gangs, mafia groups, crime syndicates or drug cartels. In the absence of legitimate forms of social organization, illegal organizations – or at least groups who engage in persistent criminal behaviour – proliferate to provide social structures and opportunities absent due to broader conditions of institutional failures. Here, wide-spread social disorganization is most readily apparent in producing militias which we will discuss later in this chapter.

There are also important elements at work on the micro, or individual level that require explanation to fully understand a given case. Perpetrators and the decision-makers in these cases possess agency. They are not automatons blindly responding to socio-political forces, but rather lively social actors who often wield large amounts of social power and institutional authority that can be brought to bear in the commission of a crime. Such a focus is not to deny the context in which the decisions are made, but to acknowledge the role individuals play.[1] Further, an acknowledgement of agency of actors reinforces the notion of accountability for decisions and actions as well in a legal context. In addition to

---

[1] For example, had Pinochet not assumed power in Chile, would the same atrocities have been committed? Would there still have been an anti-Kurd program in Iraq without Saddam Hussein as head of state? Would the US have invaded Iraq had George W. Bush not been President?

separating out four levels of analysis, the integrated theory identifies four specific factors that structure a given organizational crime at each level of analysis: motivation, opportunity, constraint, and control.

Motivation is the constellation of the general and specific drives that lure and entice a given organization and/or organizational actor toward offending. Specific motivating forces can include the enhancement and/or maintenance of political power (e.g., the NRA's criminal endeavours before and after the 1986 coup and the LRA's focused attempts to overthrow the Musevini regime), personal or organizational economic gain (e.g., the Janjaweed), access to resources (e.g., multiple forces within the DRC), religious factors (e.g. the LRA), or can be as simple as revenge (e.g., the Hutu). As an example, the primary motivation of LRA fighters is their belief that their struggle against the NRM is a divine calling that is being directed and guided by God through the prophet Joseph Kony. General motivations, while often linked to specific, can include factors such as political marginalization of a specific group or party (e.g., colonial powers often marginalized a portion of the population, giving specific preferential treatment to one group). In turn, this can result in specific motivating factors including political or economic gain. Further, ethnic divisions that were created by either colonial or post-colonial authorities can lead to specific motivation including revenge and/or the destruction of the reified 'dehumanized other'. Additionally, it must be acknowledged that while we identify general (or modal) motivation factors, there can also be a wide variety of motivations individually within a criminal group (see Smeulers, this volume).

Opportunities are those social interactions where the possibility for a crime to be committed emerges and presents itself to a potential offender (see Felson 1998). For example at the macro-level, being a state strongly enhances the ability to create and capitalize upon criminal opportunity. Even the poorest countries have tremendous amounts of human and financial capital to draw upon for crime commission. Illegal means are often available; the desirability of drawing upon these means will be even more tempting when legal means of accomplishing the goals are absent, blocked, or constrained. Further the inaction of local or international bystanders will also facilitate the generation of opportunity (see Grünfeld, this volume). While this is not to say that legitimate means may also be present, due to the concept of instrumental rationality, it is often the 'by any means necessary' and the least costly in terms of consequences, thus resulting in the choice of illegitimate over legitimate means (Rothe and Mullins 2006). On the meso-level, opportunity for specific actors is affected by the larger organizational culture and/or state structure. As we noted with previous examples, the opportunity for the Janjaweed to commit the crimes against humanity thus far have been provided by the el-Bashir regime's collusion. The opportunity for the LRA to commit atrocities and continue in a 20 year long conflict was largely been created by the direct economic and social support of the Sudanese government as well as their de facto control of the northern hinterlands.

Constraints are those social control elements that stand to make a potential crime either riskier or less profitable; offenders must navigate around them to neutralize their influence. States are often in unique positions to both navigate around extant constraints and/or to neutralize their actions. For example, Sudan was able to navigate around the constraints of NGOs by curtailing their ability to effectively monitor the regime's activities or have access to civilians that provide testimony of the abuses. Additionally, states can neutralize international pressures by placing the events in question as insurgent activity and/or cases of general banditry by militias. When organizations are sponsored by the government, they are effectively freed from potential constraints of the population or foreign involvement.

Controls are a stronger form of constraint that has the ability to stave off or prevent entirely the criminal action or to address such violations as an after-the-fact control. With any type of organizational offending this typically is in the form of formal controls such as international laws or sanctions by international institutions. The most relevant examples of controls with the cases at hand would be the ICC's current cases and arrest warrants issued at this time. While such controls have historically been highly problematic, we contend that this is indeed changing and in the future such controls may prove to be the only form of deterrence for such state and organizational offending (see Rothe and Mullins 2006). For example, the ICC claims that their indictments have simultaneously reduced the violence within Northern Uganda and compelled the LRA back into peace talks (Agirre 2007).[2] Further, such controls can also be locally generated and implemented (e.g., the Gacaca in Rwanda, see Haveman, this volume). Thus, our theory of supranational crimes examines how each of the four factors works at each of the levels of analysis within the case at hand (see Figure).

	Motivation	Opportunity	Constraints	Controls
International	Political interests	Interstate relations	International reactions	International criminal law
	Economic interests	Complimentary Legal systems	Political pressures	Intergovernmental sanctions
	Ideological interests	Transnational Markets	Public opinion	International finance institutions
		Freeport System	NGOs/Social movements	International Criminal Court
			Oversight agencies	
			Interstate relations	

---

[2]   Agirre, X., Personal Communication, 14 April 2007, Maastricht, the Netherlands.

	Motivation	Opportunity	Constraints	Controls
State/ Structural	Political goals/ power	Resource availability	Internal political pressure	Legal sanctions
	Ideological goals	State secrecy	Media scrutiny	Domestic law
	Economic conditions	Ideological tools/ nationalism	Public opinion	
	Status of government legitimacy	Government structure	Social movements	
	Military goals	Media ownership/ censorship	Counter-insurgencies	
	Access to Resources	Propaganda	State legitimacy	
	Cultural Beliefs	Social Disorganization		
Meso	Operative goals	Relationship with state	Internal constraints	Internal controls (e.g., rules)
Organizational/ Community	Institutional Isomorphism	Economic support	Bounded placement	Legal codes
	Leadership pressure	Organizational structure	Economic sanctions	
	Bound rationality	Local social disorganization		
	Reward Structure	Separation of consequences		
Interactional	Social meaning	Social/structural conditions	Personal morality	International and domestic law
	Indoctrination	Group think	Perceived legitimacy of law	Community-level law enforcement
	Economic pressure	Diffusion of responsibility	Local informal controls	
	Ideological pressure	Group membership	Perceived prosecution	
	Religious Beliefs			
	Situational security			
	Obedience to authority			
	Definition of situation			
	Instrumental rationalization			

We now turn to a broad overview of the general social conditions that have produced wide-spread atrocities in Sub-Saharan Africa[3] and the most typical forms and elements these crimes take.

4. THE SOCIAL CONTEXT AND TYPICAL ELEMENTS OF THE CRIMES

Civil wars, genocides, and crimes against humanity do not merely appear; they are produced by a complex intersection of historical, social, political, economic and cultural factors in a specific time and place. To fully understand the etiology of these phenomena, we must thoroughly understand the broader structural contexts out of which they emerge. We must also understand the basic forms which these events take. In this section, we examine the structural commonalities of central African nations that developed into internecine conflicts producing the crimes of interest to this paper. Specifically, we address a few of the common elements identified within our integrated theory of supranational crimes: global economics, social disorder (political instability, economic collapse, ethnic tensions and divisiveness, militias (including their nature and distribution and typical enactment procedures).

4.1. GLOBAL ECONOMICS

As our theory emphasizes the need to examine social forces at the international level, we will begin with an examination of global economic forces. International commodity markets have been less than stable during the past five decades. Post-colonial African economies are fundamentally dependent upon export economies; fluctuations or collapses in specific commodity markets can have drastic effects on national and local economies. Compared to Western, and many Asian, economies, those of central Africa are less diversified, which amplifies the influence of the drop in value of a given product on the economy as a whole. Such circumstances are typically a hold-over result from the colonial period, where dominating powers set up colonial economies to be focused on the exportation of one or two commodities back to the 'motherland'. Political self-determination and international recognition of national sovereignty did nothing to alter existing economic organizations. For many African states, essential participation in international markets required maintenance of the old colonial cash-crop

---

[3]   As the rest of this paper focuses on certain narrow etiological issues, most of our discussions are directed toward factors that produce motivation and opportunity and *reduce* the influence of constraints and controls.

economies. For example, both Rwanda and Cote D'Ivoire suffered substantially due to the collapse of international coffee markets. As the price of coffee beans fell, peasants in the rural areas found their primary source of economic revenue tighten; states received less tax monies from this now debilitated sector of the economy. Such global forces enhance criminogenic factors experienced both by individuals in the poorer areas and the politico-social elites. Additionally, by the 1960s and 1970s these countries found themselves enmeshed in debtor relationships with institutions of international finance – the World Bank Group (WB)[4] and International Monetary Fund (IMF) and the states which head those organizations.

In return for debt reallocation or admission into forgiveness programs, the WB would demand that macro-structural political and economic changes occur within the debtor nations. Often the Bank also required recipient countries to adopt certain political measures, such as policies that would foster 'democracy' which is often a term denoting the opening of state holdings to private ownership or opening the political platform to a multi-party system (e.g., Uganda). This is an instance of international forces generating changes at the macro-level, especially the way in which the World Bank influences the capital structures of debtor nations.

The World Bank Group provides advice and assistance to developing countries on almost every aspect of economic development. Since the mid- to late 1990s, the Bank utilizes the Private Sector Development (PSD) as its strategy to promote privatization in developing countries. All other strategies must be coordinated with the push towards privatization, removal of import tariffs, and the end of subsidized exports. Thus, the World Bank is often criticized for undermining the national sovereignty of recipient countries through its pursuit of economic liberalization. Having a strong political and policy influence on the World Bank's policies of restructuring, the G8 states' priorities are directed toward private ownership policies. Consequentially, economic enterprises funded by the World Bank are often detrimental to the people they are allegedly designed to help. In many cases, they contradict the needs of specific states and the promotion of human rights (Friedrichs and Friedrichs 2002; Rothe et al. 2006).

---

[4]   The World Bank is not a 'bank' in the commonly-used sense of the term. Rather, it is a specialized financial agency, composed of 184 member countries. The World Bank, conceived during WWII, initially helped rebuild Europe after the war. Once its original mission of post-war European reconstruction was finished, the WB turned its lending practices to development issues. While its rhetoric is often focused on human rights, human dignity and infrastructure development, its operational concerns strongly focus on producing returns for investors and spreading the ideology of neo-liberal capitalist markets. Through the 1970s and 1980s, debtor nations were frequently unable to meet repayment demands. Therefore, during the 1980s, the Bank went through an extensive period focused on macroeconomic and debt rescheduling issues.

Like the World Bank, the International Monetary Fund[5] is central in global economic development policies. Many international observers have been questioning the effectiveness of the remedies embodied in IMF-supported adjustment programs – especially those backed by the Enhanced Structural Adjustment Facility (ESAF), established in 1987 through which the IMF provides low-interest loans to poor countries with specific demands that must be followed. These policies are accompanied by specific requirements for the 'borrowing' country (e.g., currency devaluations and peggings, cuts in social programs and spending on civil works, opening state run industries to private, international investment). As noted by the IMF (1999, 1), 'some even described these remedies as part of the problem rather than the solution.' In part, the remedies for countries' economic hardships are ideologically placed in a global capitalistic vacuum that ignores the primacy of citizens' human rights and the overall social, political, and economic health of a nation.

4.2.   SOCIAL DISORDER

Political Instability

Political institutions are essential structural aspects of a society's macro-level conditions and often frame meso-level conditions. In the region of Africa we are examining here, many of these newly formed states entered the world community with underdeveloped and ill-functioning social institutions and patterns of social organization. With indigenous life ways subordinated, and to a large degree lost, during colonization and many aspects of the colonial order dismantled, newly independent peoples were confronted with having to rebuild a meaningful social order from the ground up, often with little to build upon. Political institutions simply have not been stable save under a one-party state that rules often through fear and force. Absolute control provides ample opportunity for the state or state actors to engage in criminal behaviours. Such states[6] often strongly benefit only a

---

5   The International Monetary Fund is also composed of 184 member countries and is headquartered in Washington, D.C. It was established in 1945 to promote international monetary cooperation, to foster economic growth and to provide temporary financial assistance to needy countries. The IMF 'is the central institution of the international monetary system – the system of international payments and exchange rates among national currencies' (IMF 2006). Since the IMF was established, its above stated purposes have remained unchanged, but its operations such as surveillance (a dialogue among its members on the national and international consequences of their economic and financial policies), financial assistance (loans), and technical assistance (structural adjustment policies) have changed throughout its history.
6   The use of the term state may be questioned, as in some cases explored here; the organization which claims statehood only qualifies as such due to international recognition at the UN. Some

portion of the population. The nature and direction of control and stability is typically in the direction desired by the ruling elite. As long as the charismatic leader can control the military and structures of political authority, there is a veneer of stability and order. Yet, by these very policies, the seeds of discontent and insurrection are often sown by the processes that bring temporary stability – providing motivation for opposition groups that can be lured toward criminal behaviours or atrocities if seen as needed. As consequence of the nature of a one-party state, as well as the Western colonial model, many state actors became quickly corrupt, using the states' resources for their personal gain and that of their kin and allies (e.g., Amin and Obote in Uganda, Habyarimana in Rwanda, Bede in Cote D'Ivoire).

The history of central African political conflicts is filled not only with *coups d'état*, but counter-coups designed to remove despots from power. These wars too frequently become international affairs as opposition groups that initially fled the coup found safe haven in neighbouring counties where they may have ethnic or linguistic ties. Given aid, training, arms and frequently supported by the harbouring state's army, the refugee military forces reorganize, plan, and eventually execute an invasion (e.g., Rwandan Tutsi refugees and Museveni and the NRA). Foreign powers often assist these groups directly or indirectly for several reasons (e.g., Sudan's support of the LRA). One, they may be just as apprehensive of the dictator as the refugee army is; if a leader will use systemic violence in all its forms against its own citizens, what promise can be made to satisfy a neighbour that the sovereignty of a shared border will be honoured? Second, due to the arbitrary nature of colonial territorial lines, and their reinforcement in the post-colonial period, the neighbouring power may have strong ethnic or other cultural ties to the refuge population. Such connections often provide encouragement to get involved with a neighbour's internecine struggles.[7] Third, backing an insurgent group if successful can bring territorial or other natural resources or trade access for the abetting party. For example, Rwanda and Uganda both invaded the Democratic Republic of Congo, in part to obtain control over mineral rich areas of the DRC's north-eastern territories (see Rothe and Mullins 2006). Foreign assistance directly enhances opportunity.

As political orders become less and less stable, as well as more and more corrupt, extant constraints and controls on the macro level substantially diminish.

---

would suggest the term 'government' be used instead to indicate the limited and weak nature of the political apparatus. Additionally, the concept of state crime used broadly suggests the omission of militia behaviours within a case wherein the state is also actively engaged in illegal activities. As such, we consider both to be organizational offenders.

7 Such involvements are also different from interventions led by the international political society as the motivation for the intervener is directly for that state's (or that state's elite's) benefit. UNSC and other interventions are more complex with many more factors than self interest occasionally guides participants.

State-level law and law enforcement ceases to operate in any acceptable manner. Rather, it becomes a tool for the actualization of the social elite's interest, often turned toward the investigation and arrest of political opponents rather than basic crime control. Such conditions of impunity not only enhance opportunity for offending but can also provide additional motivation via the alteration of world-view of core actors within a criminal government or regional militia.

Economic Collapse

Economies in this region have been problematic throughout the last half of the 20th century. Underdeveloped and overly controlled by foreign investment, local peoples and institutions have difficult reaping the rewards of even a functional economy. Even where certain economic sectors (be they agrigarian, mineral, or industrial) are healthy, the ability of these revenues to be spread through the entire population is highly problematic. Local areas benefit strongly, but their economic health often stands in contrast to other provinces or regions without such a resource base. Such cases typically can be traced back to colonial authorities' preferential treatment of one geographic area wherein monies and a strong economic foundation were seeded in a regionalized area at the expense of other regions within the country (e.g., Darfur). In other cases, economic collapse can be precipitated by ecological factors including desertification and long periods of drought bringing additional hardships and tensions to bear on an already tumultuous economic situation. Such factors enhance motivation for forming criminogenic groups as well as motivating the commission of atrocities themselves.

When state economies are overly controlled by foreign investors and/or the global market they are reliant upon the decision-making by commodity market leaders or foreign investors. When drastic fluctuations occur or when a commodity is forced to crash for economic gain of those in control of the market, weak economic states find themselves in dire conditions socially and economically. Especially among those individuals living in communities involved in the production of the said commodity, such economic lapses increase both motivation toward criminal behaviour and provide opportunity via the enhanced social disorder created and the illegitimate opportunity structures which frequently emerge. Such was the case with the coffee market crash in Rwanda that further facilitated the instability of the ruling regime and fuelled already tense ethnic divisions. Further, transnational corporations are often directly involved in black-market and/or illegal export and importing of state resources. As Human Rights Watch and the United Nations have reported, numerous transnational corporations have travelled to the Ituri region of the Democratic Republic of Congo to directly negotiate with warlords controlling the mines. From there, agreements are reached to transport the minerals across the border into Uganda, which then exports the minerals typically in the European markets and exchanges. Particularly, these strategies take advantage of the just mentioned Swiss freeport system, which allows for the open and anonymous importation and sale of commodities from around the globe. Such activities exasperate the already tumultuous economic conditions of states.

At the meso, or community level, economic chaos and hardship generate situations of social disorder, which criminologists have long known produce criminal behaviour through their structuring of criminogenic environments (see Shaw & McKay 1942, Bursik & Gramsmick 1988). As economic conditions deteriorate nationally, local communities lose their ability to self-structure and enact informal self-controls. The inability to act collectively not only creates an attitudinal space that can generate criminal values and motivations toward offending, but also the absence of social constraints on behaviour facilitates opportunities for offending by generating impunity.

Ethnic tensions and divisiveness

A central element within these atrocity-producing environments are a set of intense ethnic rivalries and tensions often – at least in the contemporary post-colonial environment – focused on resources access, be it political, social or economic. Despite the way in which these issues are typically covered in the media (e.g., as long standing, pre-colonial disputes – see Western media coverage of Rwanda and Darfur), many of these nations did not begin their post-colonial experiences with deep divisions built along tribal or ethnic lines. While colonizers in many cases (e.g., Rwanda and Burundi) drew arbitrary divisions amongst peoples and reinforced those splits via their political and economic policies, at the moment of liberation these tensions were rarely forefront in the society.

In the period leading up to the civil wars, and the associated crimes, political parties often played up these tensions in order to create a power base both within the governments and within the citizenry (see Rothe and Mullins 2007). Due to long periods of colonial domination, there were few natural lines along which political parties could be formed and fewer pre-existing bases of political power for a party to mobilize. In fact, the most 'natural' divisions leading to party formation in newly democratic states was geographic in nature and rooted in the existing resource base (be those resources mineral, agricultural, or human capitals). While there was some general correspondence between peoples and territories, these early geographic divisions often cut across ethnic lines. The result was a political scene with dozens of parties possessing unarticulated goals, visions and motives. While all wanted a share of the new political power, a lack of general political drives, positions and ideologies produced hosts of parties indistinguishable from each other save by name. Such political hyper-plurality produced more disorganization than organization; many of these new governments were dissolved in *coup d'état* that established one-party states, that while stable often began to exacerbate the increasingly important ethnic divides to cement power (e.g., Rwanda and Cote D'Ivoire). Motivated to maintain power, leaders often began to generate public discourses of racial and ethnic differences and exclusion. Ethnicity became a political tool of opportunity to stabilize a government and as these states weakened under their own weight of corruption inefficiency, ethnicity became a polarizing force dividing the societies as they moved toward violent civil wars.

We see this operating in the Darfur genocide. The major division within the Sudanese society has long been geographic. Those territories, and the people within them, who were closer to the country's capital received more attention and state-assistance. Primarily this manifested as a division between the North – where Khartoum is located – and the South. The long running civil war in the nation is in fact between these regions. This geographic division coincided with varying forms of subsistence and tribal divisions. Such divisions were later used as tools for political power at a time of inter-factional party splits (1968) to create ethnic identities that would compete with each other, thereby weakening the ability of Sudanese populations to unite in their own common interests. The politically-motivated construction of ethnic identities was reinforced by these divisions, as well as the history of marginalization and lack of political representation. Likewise, the social construction of a nationalism based upon Arab unity reinforced the sense of alienation among groups that did not geographically, historically, linguistically, or traditionally identify with an Arab identity. This was further reinforced by the position of the government and their economic and social preference for the Arab solidarity and identity associated with Northern geographic areas and Khartoum. Ethnicity and/or cultural and religious identifications, while initially abstract ideological political categories, become reified into powerful social forces. Such a re-definition of group identity was used to motivate atrocities as well as, especially within Darfur, to cloud the international vision of what was occurring. By casting it as an ethnic conflict along the lines of Rwanda, Yugoslavia, etc. the actual responsibility and centrality of the standing Bashir regime is ignored, thus providing further opportunity and a level of impunity.

Scholars of genocides and other war crimes have long pointed toward the 'otherizing' effects of ethnic polarization and dehumanization as facilitating violence in general and wide-spread lethal violence in particular. Just as colonial powers dehumanized the peoples of Africa to legitimate colonial domination, ethnic groups dehumanized each other facilitating political and economic subordination as well as wanton violence and destruction (e.g., Rwandan Hutus).

Such divisions operate on the micro level to facilitate the wide-spread abuse and slaughter of targeted peoples. In ethnic-otherizing processes the humanity is removed from the targeted group which in turn facilitates and legitimates violence against them. At the meso level, ethnic polarization serves as a bond of solidarity for militia formation and continuation. Simply, it is a symbolic identity which draws recruit and rallies members around a common cause that is *inter alia* violent. At the international level the discourse serves to negate the responsibility of political and social authorities for creating, stimulating and continuing the conflict. Once framed as a tension existing from deep in history or tied to the colonial period of a region, the standing government, which often encourages such tension for its own purposes, can reduce its perceived responsibly and professed ability to control the violence.

4.3. MILITIAS

One of the hallmarks of all of the cases we explore here is the existence of militia groups. These loosely coupled groups of armed men play central roles not only in the social (dis)organization of post-colonial environments but also are central within the war crimes and crimes against humanity committed. Most of the atrocities are committed either by the militias themselves, by government troops in response to perceived or real militia threats, or through collusion between states and militias. Not limited to this geo-political context, militias frequently emerge in highly anomic societies during periods of transition.[8] As social orders shift, certain populations will feel excluded or threatened – in many cases these perceptions are justified by the real conditions on the ground. Militia groups emerge in response to these real and perceived threats.

Nature and distribution

In the wake of post-colonial social and economic disruption, many young men find themselves faced with little in the way to establish an adulthood identity or other forms of social position. With little economic prospects and having typically been raised in a period where ethnic ideological tensions were strong, militias are a place to achieve group membership, economic opportunities, and to actualize an ethnic identity. In terms of individuals joining militias, meso-level conditions

---

[8] For example, during the 1980s and early 1990s, militia groups were central in events and violence throughout Latin America (though media and governmental bodies tended to refer to them as 'rebel' groups or 'insurgents'). Currently, we see the prevalence of militia groups in Afghanistan and, of course, Iraq. Yet, militia groups have also been central political and military players in other Middle Eastern locales as well. Hamas and the PLO began as militia groups and have now become codified as political entities and parties.

of community disorder provide strong micro-level motivations. Young men who find themselves without other social and economic opportunities will gravitate to joining the only real social organization present in their social environment. The criminological literature on street gangs has long established the draw of gangs in the absence of other empowered institutions (see Jankowski 1991; Shelden et al 2004). Militias are merely another form of this phenomenon. With few viable institutional paths to success and survival, and no external social constraints, militias can be seen by community members as the only stable and empowered social grouping within an area. They strengthen individual identity and social membership; the ethnic composition also carries identity meanings and validation for members, which generate motivation and opportunities to engage in criminal militia activities.

Many of the militias – both organizationally and individually – are holdovers from earlier military units. Civil wars and *coup d'états* are not uncommon in the region; when a standing government (and its loyal army elements) are deposed by insurgencies, such soldiers rarely return to the civilian population; they are even less likely to enlist in the new army. Often, they retreat into the country side (or cross into a neighbouring nation), regroup and resurface as a militia group (e.g. when Obote fled Uganda to return years later for a second term as head of state). Such instances produce a cohesive social group all ready bonded by prior military service and the underlying ideologies well established in individuals and groups when they were in power. Simply, this is a group motivated to potentially commit atrocities due to their harbouring of long standing grievances and violent experiences with the current group in power. Further, their 'underground' status and the fact that returning to pre-conflict community life might expose them to legal prosecution or informal retaliation for past behaviour reduces their susceptibility to extant constraints or controls.

Due to recruitment processes, militias exhibit a strong level of social homogeneity, which will intensify the social bonds of members, thus fuelling a collective motivational force. As much criminology within the social learning school (Akers 1977; Sutherland 1939) has suggested, this will strongly facilitate the transmission of criminogenic values and provide a social context whereby even members less inclined toward such excessively brutal behaviour will be egged on by cohorts. As seen in analyses of earlier war crimes (e.g., the socialization of Japanese soldiers to commit atrocities in the Chinese theatre of World War II, see Chang 1997) once attached to a unit engaged in these behaviours, recruits eventually begin to see the actions as normal; they experience the processes of the normalization of deviance.

As new recruits are exposed to the typical militia modus operandi, they become more comfortable and more inured to the commission of atrocities. For example, many of the child soldiers interviewed by Human Rights Watch that were abducted by the Lord's Resistance Army in Uganda reported that early during their confinement, they were forced to enact discipline upon their fellow abductees. As children were forced to march over long distances, those who fell, developed blisters on their feet or otherwise voluntarily or involuntarily delayed the march were beaten, often severely. As often as not, the LRA soldiers forced other abducted children to carry out the beatings (Human Rights Watch 2003a, 2003b). Such experiences begin the process of desensitization and the normalization of deviance. Once they have had to beat their fellows, often kin or age-grade cohorts, then their ability and willingness to use violence against the citizens they will encounter on later raids is increased, or at least their resistance to such actions are reduced (as those who refuse to violently discipline their peers are beaten themselves).

Opportunities for militia members to engage in criminal actions are nigh omnipresent. With little formal law enforcement active within militia dominated regions and many territories uncontested by government troops, para-militaries are allowed to operate with impunity. There is little operative constraint or control. Through their organizational and military technologies, there is not realistic on-the-ground opposition to their depredations on the locals. For all intents and purposes they are the law and have the ability to back up their will with force, which is used routinely to quell resistance in the hinterlands.

Likewise, state-supported militias – i.e., the Janjaweed in the Sudan or former Interahamwe of Rwanda who cooperate with, if they are not directly commanded by state forces – find themselves in a unique position of power and with 'legitimate' opportunities. Due to the overt or covert assistance of the state in which they operate, such groups can act with total impunity and with financial and tactical supports. In a state of economic crisis, resources are crucial. Thus, militias under these conditions are motivated to serve their own self-interests while simultaneously fulfilling state political goals. In the case of the Janjaweed, they were rewarded with tangibles beyond weapons and money. They received countless herds of livestock which provided them with the ability to gain economic status by selling the livestock as well as secured the level of subsistence by having livestock on hand for products and food. Personal gain and empowerment is clearly a strong motivation for those in power (e.g., government officials) or in strategic positions (e.g., members of a militia). Military leaders, both regular and irregular, stand to personally profit politically and economically from their positions. With no formal social control mechanisms to dissuade them, they become the embodiment of law and order in the lands their militias control.

Terror and Thuggary

Militias have come to the international attention for their widespread use of wanton murder in their carrying out military-related activities. The Hutu militias' destruction of massive Tutsi population in Rwanda is a case in point. Reports from the hinterlands that militias control indicate that one of the most frequent crimes the militias perpetrate is simply general thuggery. From petty theft and robbery to assault (sexual and physical), as militias move through villages and the country side they harass and victimize the civilians they come across. Other conditions can result in the militias' use of thuggery, theft, and/or robbery. For example, in Darfur the Sudanese Liberation Army (SLA) insurgents have also been responsible for attacks on civilians, abductions, and endangering humanitarian access. The insurgents, like all civilians that are left in Darfur, were running out of basic necessities including food, medicine, and the fuel required for their continued mobility and military survival. It would be naive to think it likely that under such conditions the insurgents would not resort to illegal activities to feed themselves and to secure what was needed to sustain their campaign against Khartoum's genocidal actions.

Further, governmental agents including the military and police often partake in general banditry, violence, and/or terror for their own self gain as a simple form of opportunistic behaviour. Such has been the case in Uganda where police and army personnel have been accused of raping civilians for their own entertainment to general petty theft of property left behind by the growing Ugandan refugees. The Ugandan army has also been accused by NGOs of pillaging in regions traditionally opposed to President Museveni.

Both militia groups and regimes often explicitly draw upon terror tactics to generate fear and compliance among the civilians – enhancing opportunity and decreasing potential local restraints. In Sierra Leone and Uganda, militias have become infamous for cutting off civilians' arms, hands, lips and tongues as a way to spread fear. For example, victims of the LRA have stated they have been held down while other militia members 'picked up an axe. First he chopped my left hand, then my right. Then he chopped my nose, my ears and my mouth with a knife.' (Ross 2004, 1) As locals resist or try to call for standing governments (or NGOs) to intervene, they become targets for torture and mutilation. NGOs are often targeted for torture and/or death for intervening in the situation. For example, NGO workers were considered to be legitimate military targets by the LRA because of their support for what they called Museveni's 'concentration camps.' Consequentially, they attacked humanitarian food convoys from the World Food Programme (WFP) and threatened the lives of the workers. As is often the case when humanitarian workers are not afforded security, nongovernmental organizations often withdraw leaving remaining victims to fend for themselves. With both locals and NGOs unable to exercise constraints, conditions of impunity are solidified. Additionally, while the practice of dismembering civilians' body parts enhances opportunity via the generation of fear among the population, it is also a component of institutional isomorphism wherein such practices were first introduced by Belgium to generate fear amongst the subordinate population.

Slavery, Forced Labour

Once settled in an occupied territory, militias often organize forced labour programs. Motivated by the need to maintain operations, mandates from their supporting governments and personal greed, most operations have been designed to revitalize a mineral extraction industry that collapsed in the more general political and social disorder of state collapse. As such, forced labour provides the opportunity to advance economically and have political powers. The blood diamonds industry of Sierra Leone and the gold and colton industries in the Ituri region of the Democratic Republic of Congo are excellent cases-in-point. In both cases, militias first moved in and violently established military control of the geography that contained mineral production sites. Once they solidified their control, they turned to pressing the local population into forced servitude to engage in dangerous and low-technology mineral extraction activities. Yet, the simple possession of raw ores does little to enhance the economic or military positions of the militias. To capitalize on these enterprises, they must find foreign markets willing to purchase the illicit commodities. Such buyers are not difficult to find. Neighbouring states and local companies make deals with both standing governments and militias to gain access to natural resources. Once access to the region has been obtained, then it is a not too difficult task to remove the minerals or other valued commodities over a near by border and ship the goods into one of the many freeports – markets where no records concerning the origins of items or accounting of amounts sold are made – like Sweden, where they find major transnationals eager to purchase the materials (e.g., Metalor, Debeers). Many of these larger jewellery dealers or mineral processing companies can easily hide illegally expropriated minerals in their larger stocks. Such conditions remove one of the strongest potential constraints of these behaviours: the willingness of the international market to absorb and buy these commodities. Western countries and their markets facilitate such acts. If these markets and actors within them refused to purchase illegally expropriated resources, the acts would cease.

Child Soldiers

The first set of criminal charges issued by the ICC were allegations of the recruitment of child soldiers by Thomas Dyilo, the leader of one of the Democratic Republic of Congo's strongest militia groups. The DRC is not the only place in Central Africa where the abduction and pressing into service of children has become a central feature of militia life. Sierra Leone and Uganda have also experienced wide-spread use of underage troops. International law makes it illegal to use anyone under the age of 18 as a combat solider, not to mention the use of abducted or coerced soldiers.[9] In these locales, both boys and girls have been kidnapped and forced into service. While mainly assigned to the menial labour required of an armed group, e.g., fetching water, carrying supplies, digging latrines, both males and females receive military training in the basic use of firearms. Additionally, the children are used as the front line of military engagements (e.g., the UPDF and LRA practices using child soldiers). For example, children may be used for direct combat to compensate for the weakened forces of a militia or a regime; they may be forced to walk across a field believed to be mined, to ensure that the adult men do not set one off. In fire fights, the children are often used as a screen to protect the adults from gun fire. By placing the children in the front of a charge (or a defensive line), they will absorb much of the incoming fire.

These troops are viewed by the militia commanders as expendable. This is further seen in the generally brutal treatment the children receive at the hands of their new masters. When on a march, children who are slow, stumble or fall are often beaten until they either get back up and resume the march at the speed desired by the commanders or collapse into unconsciousness (and death). Escaped children who have talked to Amnesty International, Human Rights Watch and representatives of UNICEF have also indicated that they were deprived of food and water. Girls, while initially used as burden bearers and front line combatants, are given to soldiers, typically commanders, as wives. While motivated to use the children as an expendable labour, the potential of females as sexual slaves and/or wives is an additional motivating force for militia leaders.

The motivation to use child soldiers seems especially prevalent in long-term conflicts. Lengthier struggles will reduce the functional size of militias as troops are killed wounded and desert. In the decades long conflicts seen in Uganda and the DRC, the militia will develop difficulties recruiting new members over time, especially if they make a habit of victimizing and terrorizing civilian populations. To fill out the ranks, paramilitaries use abduction and forced service to maintain

---

9   Time will tell if this extant control effectively reduces the prevalence of this practice. As we mentioned earlier, ICC data suggests that their indictments against the LRA have reduced other aspects of their criminal behaviour.

their strength. Children are desirable for a number of reasons. They are much easier to control than adults. Physically smaller and much easier to intimidate, they poise little threat to adult soldiers. Additionally, due to the plasticity of youth, children present the potential to be indoctrinated into the prevailing ideologies within the militia. It is much more likely that a child who hears the officer's propaganda will believe and internalize it as their own worldview, thereby creating a loyal soldier to the cause. In other words, indoctrination is achieved more thoroughly and necessitates less time and effort than oppositional adults may. The constant threat of abduction has created population of 'night commuters,' children who travel into central urban areas every night to sleep to avoid roaming militia groups. Train stations and other public venues become filled with children every evening, who then return to their villages outside of the cities each morning creating additional humanitarian concerns (Human Rights Watch 1997, 2003a, 2003b, 2004, 2006).

Rape

The sexual assault of women within combat zones and occupied territories is one of the dirty not-so-secret elements pervasive within the history of war fare. It has been recorded in essentially every war in human history. The possibility of a single sexual release is a minor motivation, though the taking of a foreign woman as a 'wife' due to military victory was common – this is rapine in the, literally, classical sense of the term. Abduction of women into sexual and domestic servitude was part and parcel of the rights of plunder. With no standing constraints on their behaviour save their officers, the opportunities for such crimes in any combat zone are ubiquitous. As militia commanders have no interest in reducing this behaviour, it is rampant in the conflicts examined here.

In the post-colonial African context, rape has been as pervasive as in any conflict. Militia and regular army routinely rape women and girls once a village is taken; some of them are forced into marriages or held in sexual slavery for months or years at a time. Additionally, due to the high rate of HIV/AIDS in many of these states, the rape serves as a transmission episode and the inevitable death sentence which the disease brings. When looking at the manifestation of rape in association with recent atrocities, we see an intensification of the nature and scope of sexual assaults on female civilian populations. In the former Yugoslavia, Rwanda, Cote D'Ivoire, Uganda, the Democratic Republic of Congo, and the Darfur region of Somalia (to name a precious few) domestic conflict has produced wide-spread rape scenarios that go beyond the individualistic scenario of men satisfying their immediate sexual desires in a forceful demonstration of hyper masculinity.[10] In

---

[10]   Discussions of this highly organized form of mass rape emerge in the aftermath of both Rwanda and the former Yugoslavia. Perusal of journalistic and historical sources documents

such cases, the motivation for rape is that is serves as a tool of terror and of population elimination – a phenomenon we term genocidal rape. We define genocidal rape as a systemically organized military tactic of terror and genocide. Used to (1) generate fear in subdued population, (2) humiliate the population (both men and women), (3) derogation of women (spoilage of identity), (4) create a cohort of mixed-ethnic children to maintain the humiliation/spoilage/domination. Such a use of sexual assault is an orchestrated tactic of warfare.

Fear of rape is a common emotion that all women near or within a combat zone experience; the wide spread existence of this type of assault clearly enhances the stresses and anxieties already experienced by civilians. Genocidal rape capitalizes upon this and elevates assaults to a tactic of terrorism.[11] Another primary motivation for mass rape is the humiliation of male community members. Often men were made to watch as their wives and daughters were assaulted; isolated reports of soldiers forcing men to rape their own daughters have also emerged. Such actions are vivid demonstrations of the new-found powerlessness of men in the combat zone. Having to either actively or passively participate in this process is an assault on the masculinity of husbands and fathers; due to long standing patriarchal value systems, these men and women simultaneously are reduced to nothing via the destruction of their ability to enact enforced gender norms.

Derogation and identity spoilage of the rape victims are another set of key motivators behind genocidal rape events. Again due to strong strains of patriarchy within the cultures, unmarried women who have been raped are typically no longer looked upon as potential wives – the rape has destroyed their marital desirability. Further, they can also in turn be shunned by family members and have nowhere to turn for survival. Such women will either starve or live the rest of their lives in highly marginal social positions (e.g., begging, prostitution, etc). Such conditions are genocidal as they increase the overall death toll related to the genocidal event, even if indirect and down the line. In raw terms, this is the

---

wide spread sexual slavery (e.g., Korean comfort women) but the use of rape as an orchestrated tactic of warfare is generally unknown until recently. *However* this does not mean it was not common before – it just wasn't thoroughly recorded, discussed, or examined. Absence of documentary evidence does not mean an absence of phenomena.

[11]   Some have argued that all rape is a form of terrorism. For example, a radical feminist interpretation sees all sexual assaults as a tool that men (as a category of person) use to control and denigrate women (as a category of person). Indeed, many women world-wide live with the constant threat (and fear) of being raped. We argue that the key difference between this general and diffused condition and the nature of genocide rape lies in intentionality. Simply, men world-wide do not conspire to organize rape events and men (as a category of person) do not tolerate rape because it terrorizes women. The Rwandan rape brigades consciously and purposefully used sexual assault as a tactic of war with the express purpose of creating fear and anxiety.

removal of women from the breeding population and prevents a population from recovering from a genocidal event.

Finally, as seen in the former Yugoslavia, such wide-spread rape often produced a birth cohort of mixed ethnic children. The effects of this are two-fold. First, it provides a long lasting reminder of the humiliation and derogation of the people as whole. The children that survive to birth and into youth are a constant symbol of the genocide experience. Second, as the children and their mothers are often outcasts from their kin groups because of the assaults themselves, this enhances the social disorganization of villages and cities which now bear the burden of either caring for or ignoring this new underclass of community members.

5. CONCLUSION

In this chapter we have provided an overview of the basic core concepts and enactment structures of major on-going atrocity producing events using the presented integrated theory of supranational crimes. By drawing on the multi-level integrated theory of organizational offending, we highlighted key etiological forces and some potential effects of various social control modalities on such heinous events. For example, we addressed how general and specific motivating forces can interact with opportunity at the various levels. Additionally, we attempted to show how historical, economic, social, political, religious, and ethnic identities are directly involved in forming both motivation and opportunity. Admittedly, this work is based on our ongoing research of crimes in the Great Lakes region of Africa. Yet, our goal is not to provide the end-frame discussion of such crimes, but rather a point of departure for future criminological analyses. State crime research must move beyond the self-imposed emphasis on crimes of the powerful states to incorporate those of the post-colonial world.

VII. STATE CRIME, THE COLONIAL QUESTION AND INDIGENOUS PEOPLES

Chris CUNNEEN

1. INTRODUCTION: COLONIALISM AND STATE CRIME

The purpose of this chapter is to consider how our understanding of state crime needs to be mediated through an appreciation of colonial processes. The chapter explores a number of inter-related issues around the question of colonialism, state crime and Indigenous peoples. The historical relationship between Indigenous people and the development of modern nation states raises the problem of the extent to which contemporary liberal democracies like Australia, Canada or the US were founded on processes we would now regard as state crime, and indeed engaged in activities which at the time could have been regarded as unlawful. Further, while there has been considerable literature on transitional justice and processes for reparations in post-conflict societies, this body of scholarship has tended to ignore the extent to which liberal democracies themselves might be considered in need of 'post-conflict' reconciliation and restorative justice. This chapter explores these questions through a discussion of Australia, Canada and the US, although the primary focus is on Australia and its relationship with the continent's Indigenous peoples.

It is well acknowledged that the modern political state has been integral to the commission of genocide and other state crimes. Genocide and modernity have gone hand in hand (Bauman 1989), and the specific modernity of genocide is that the vastness and totality of 'final solutions' could only be pursued by the modern state with its access to significant resources, administrative capacities and law-making functions (Gellately & Kiernan 2003, 4). However, the colonial context adds a further dimension to how we see and understand the connection between the development of the modern political state and the globalised nature of gross violations of human rights and state crime.

It is not the purpose of this chapter to engage with debates around the difficult issues associated with defining state crime. However, several points can be made at the outset. On the one hand, the concept of state crime can help us understand the development of modern political states and their violent and at times genocidal dispossession of Indigenous peoples. The argument here is that modern state building had as a foundational core an important element of criminality against dispossessed Indigenous groups. In other words, state crime is not an incidental or accidental element in the history of the modern state. The colonial context places state crime at the core of the modern state. Thus how we might conceptualise a 'deviant' state is problematised to the extent that many contemporary states were founded and developed on the basis of state crime – however, state crime might be defined in international law, criminal law or as serious human rights violations.

Many contemporary states are built on crimes committed against colonised and enslaved peoples.[1] Indigenous people have been victims of profound historical injustices and abuses of human rights which can be understood in the context of state crimes committed in pursuit of colonial domination. The claims concerning historical injustices and human rights abuses against Indigenous peoples are multilayered. At the highest level is the claim that particular colonial practices against Indigenous peoples constituted genocide. Below genocide are claims of mass murder, racism, ethnocide (or cultural genocide), slavery, forced labour, forced removals and relocations, the denial of property rights, systematic fraud, and the denial of civil and political rights. Over-generalised claims of genocide against Indigenous people in the settler-colonies of North America, New Zealand and Australia have been controversial (Van Krieken 2004). However there is no doubt that genocide is the appropriate description for specific colonial laws and practices at particular times and places (Churchill 1997, Moses 2000). More broadly, the concept of ethnocide or cultural genocide captures the aggressive attempt to 'civilise' Indigenous peoples through a range of state-endorsed laws, policies and practices. The civilising process itself gave rise to specific state crimes such as the unlawful imprisonment and the denial of civil and political rights.

2. GENOCIDE AND MASS MURDER

Extreme violence against Indigenous people can be defined as state crime in a number of ways. At its most systematic, and where there was clear intention to destroy a particular group then the most appropriate description is genocide. Beyond genocide there are countless examples of state-enforced or state-sanctioned mass murder.

---

[1]   The arguments in this chapter are specifically concerned with Indigenous peoples. However the colonial context also resulted in the crimes of slavery and post-slavery racial violence and discrimination.

The crime of genocide has been levelled against colonial regimes in their treatment of Indigenous peoples in Australia and the Americas. In relation to genocide and Native Americans, Ward Churchill has noted the following:

> *"During the four centuries spanning the time between 1492 (...) and 1892 when the U.S. Census Bureau concluded that there were fewer than a quarter million Indigenous people surviving within the country's claimed boundaries, a hemispheric population estimated to have been as great as 125 million was reduced by something over 90 percent. The people had died in their millions of being hacked apart with axes and swords, burned alive and trampled under horses... intentionally starved and frozen to death during a multitude of forced marches and internments, and in an unknown number of instances, deliberately infected with epidemic diseases."* (Churchill 1997, 1)

Intention is a key element of genocide, and much of the recent analysis draws distinctions between the intentional killing of Indigenous people by colonial forces as distinct from the deaths of Indigenous peoples arising from introduced diseases, malnutrition and other factors that may not have demonstrated a necessary intention to destroy (Stannard 1993, xii). Massacres of Indigenous people by colonial state forces occurred across North America and Australia during the colonial period. On both continents, Indigenous men, women and children were murdered. As Stannard has noted in relation to the US,

> *"the European habit of indiscriminately killing women and children when engaged in hostilities with the natives of the Americas was more than an atrocity. It was flatly and intentionally genocidal. For no population can survive if its women and children are destroyed".* (Stannard 1993, 118–119)

There are well documented massacres of Aboriginal people in Australia in the late eighteenth and nineteenth centuries. There was never any doubt at the time that the Indigenous people and the colonisers were indeed at war in parts of south-eastern Australia (Goodall 1996), in Tasmania during the 1820s and early 1830s (Reynolds 1995), and in Queensland during the mid to later half of the nineteenth century (Reynolds 1993). Yet these 'wars' were never declared as such because of the legal ambiguity of the place of Aboriginal people in Australia. It was assumed that Australia was acquired by peaceful settlement, that Aboriginal people had never been in 'possession' of their land, and that when the British claimed sovereignty over Australia in 1788, Aboriginal people became British subjects.

In some cases this 'war' can be seen as genocide. Moses (2000) for example argues that particular campaigns undertaken by Native Police against Indigenous nations in Queensland during the later part of the nineteenth century were genocide – they were clearly undertaken with the intention of physically destroying a whole group of people. In Western Australia authorities spoke of police 'teaching the blacks a lesson' and 'dealing out a fearful punishment' (Cunneen 2001, 50). At particular moments this can be seen as genocide. As late as the end of the nineteenth century senior state officials described events in the terms of a war of extermination. Correspondence between the Western Australian under-secretary and the premier of Western Australia in July 1895 noted, 'There can be no doubt from these frequent [police] reports that a war of extermination in effect is being waged against these unfortunate blacks in the Kimberley district' (quoted in Cunneen 2001, 50).

It is clear that colonial processes meant that the rule of law as a constraint on arbitrary power and state violence, and as a guarantee of equality before the law was suspended in relation to Aboriginal people in Australia. It is what one legal historian has referred to as a 'rubbery attitude to the law' where basic notions of the rule of law could be cast aside (Kercher 1995, 6). Punitive expeditions were ordered, collective punishment was exercised, armed 'pacification' parties were used against Indigenous people, and at various times martial law was declared. Men, women and children were killed. Kercher (1995, 7–9) has noted that if Aboriginal people were indeed British subjects then the official and unofficial killings which took place were mass murders. Even the declaration of martial law did not legitimise the killing of children, or non-combatants, or captives without some form of trial.

There were relatively recent massacres in Australia in the early part of the twentieth century. The last recorded massacre occurred in 1928 in Coniston, Northern Territory when some sixty to seventy Walpiri people were killed over several weeks by a police party. Murray, the officer in charge openly admitted to a policy of shoot to kill. According to a missionary who spoke to survivors of the killings, 'the natives tell me that they simply shot them down like dogs and that they got the little children and hit them on the back of the neck and killed them'. Murray admitted killing 31 people. Other estimates by missionaries put the figure at between 70 and 100 Aboriginal people killed. An Inquiry, headed by a police inspector, was established into the killings. Aboriginal people were refused legal representation. The Inquiry cleared those who were involved (Cunneen 2001, 55).

Despite the view that Aboriginal people were British subjects, the processes of colonisation required a suspension of the rule of law in relation to Indigenous people. Terror was an important tool of the colonial state and was used as an instrument of control. The summary executions and the hanging of corpses in trees, the attacks on tribal groups as a form of collective responsibility, the indiscriminate killing of men and women, adults and children were designed to terrorise and pacify. In other words, the violence was not simply a series of undifferentiated acts. There was a 'culture of terrorism' which sustained the use of violence (Morris 1992). Colonisers could engage in a form of 'redemptive' violence which involved massacring Aboriginal people defined as 'treacherous savages'.

Different treatment on the basis of race became justified. Aboriginal people were still publicly executed in Western Australia long after the practice of public executions had ceased for non-Indigenous people. Violence became accepted as a normal and justifiable way of dealing with Indigenous people. Racial differences were used to justify the use of brutal punishments. For Aboriginal people, floggings and the use of neck and leg chains remained in use until the 1930s. It was not until 1936 that the Northern Territory superintendent of police banned police punitive patrols and the use of violence in interrogations (McGrath 1993, 103–104).

The basic point to be drawn from this is that colonial expansion and the development of the territorial basis for new states like Australia rested on dispossession, and the processes of ensuring dispossession can be properly considered in the context of state crime. While international law may have justified the acquisition of colonies under particular circumstances, neither international nor domestic law justified mass murder.

3.   THE FORCED REMOVAL OF INDIGENOUS CHILDREN

A key component of the colonial process was the 'civilising' mission which involved changing natives from 'savages' to civilised Christians. It was a task that occupied the European empires over several centuries, and continued into the twentieth century in settler states like Australia and North America. The civilising process was often brutal. Native Americans were placed on church missions where the deaths tolls were horrific. While many of these deaths were caused by European-introduced diseases, the conditions on these missions also directly contributed to the large number of deaths. Severe malnutrition resulted from the inadequate diets and long hours of forced labour. Grotesque forms of punishment were used against the rebellious (Stannard 1993, 138).

The civilising process was to be partly accomplished through the removal of Indigenous children from their communities and families. The Canadian residential school policy was based on assimilation – of changing Indigenous peoples from savage to civilised by educating the young away from the influences of their parents and tribes. As Milloy (1999, xv) has noted in the Canadian context, the process was 'violent in its intention to "kill the Indian" in the child for the sake of Christian civilisation. In that way, the system was, even as a concept, abusive'.

In Canada the residential school system lasted from the 1870s to the 1980s. There was a nationwide network of schools operated by the Anglican, Catholic, Presbyterian and United Churches. Thousands of Indian, Inuit and Metis children were to pass through the schools. The system was a church-state partnership with the Department of Indian Affairs providing the funding, setting the standards and exercising legal control over the children who were wards (Milloy 1999).

In Australia Aboriginal children had been forcibly removed from their families by colonisers since the beginning of European occupation of Australia. However by the late nineteenth and early twentieth centuries there developed a systematic and state-sponsored policy of removal which was far more extensive than any previous interventions. In many states of Australia, Aboriginal children were placed in church-run institutions, while in some states like New South Wales the institutions were operated by the state.[2]

The Australian removal policies rested on specific assumptions about race, 'blood' and racial hygiene. Aboriginal people were divided according to the amount of European 'blood' they might possess. Law became fundamental to the categorisation and separation of individuals within racialized boundaries. According to the social Darwinist ideas, so-called 'full blood' Aboriginal people were bound to die out because of their inferiority. However, the concern for the state was the apparently rapidly growing population of 'mixed blood' children. It was these children that became the target of intervention. By permanently removing them from their families and communities it was believed that this group of children would, over generations, eventually be biologically absorbed into the non-Indigenous population. Their Aboriginality would be 'bred' out. Eugenicist arguments required a proactive state to manage, cleanse and maintain the 'white' population. Law provided the foundation through which an administrative edifice would define Indigenous people as 'full blood', 'half caste', 'quarter caste' and so on.

Both the Canadian and the Australia authorities saw the removal process as part of a civilising mission and spiritual duty to uplift the 'natives'. By today's standards the assimilationist 'civilising' process would be condemned as ethnocide or cultural genocide – and properly considered as a state crime. However, there are separate reasons for considering the forced removal of Indigenous children as a state crime on the basis of what was done to these children after they were removed from their families and placed in the care of either the state or church-run institutions. In other words it is not simply a matter of judging the past by the standards of today. In both Australia and Canada, the system was never properly resourced or supervised, and shocking neglect and physical abuse were common. In 1996 the Canadian Royal Commission on Aboriginal Peoples (RCAP 1996) released its final report. As a result the Canadian Government has acknowledged past injustice and apologised to Indigenous peoples, particularly in relation to the effects of the residential school system.

---

2   For a full discussion of the history of removal laws and policies in Australia, see NISATSIC 1997, 25–1490.

4. THE 'STOLEN GENERATIONS' INQUIRY

In Australia the forced removal of Indigenous children has been the subject of a major federal inquiry. The 'Stolen Generations' Inquiry was established by the Australian Government in 1995 after a long battle for recognition of the issue by Indigenous people and their organisations (NISATSIC 1997, 36). The Inquiry estimated that 10 per cent of Indigenous children were removed from their families and communities under state sanctioned policies and removal practices in Australia between 1910 and 1970 (NISATSIC 1997, 18). Today, most Indigenous families continue to be affected in one or more generations by the forcible removal of children during this time (NISATSIC 1997, 37).

The Inquiry found that basic safeguards which protected non-Indigenous families were cast aside when it came to Indigenous children. The main components of the forced removal of Indigenous children which were unlawful were deprivation of liberty, deprivation of parental rights, abuses of power, and breach of guardianship duties. In relation to international human rights the main obligations imposed on Australia and breached by a policy of forced removals were the prohibitions on racial discrimination and genocide. The policy continued to be practiced after Australia had voluntarily subscribed to treaties outlawing both racial discrimination and genocide (NISATSIC 1997). In other words there are very good grounds for considering the policies of Aboriginal child removal as an example of state crime – a crime that was pursued as part of the colonial project of 'civilising' natives.

4.1. DEPRIVATION OF LIBERTY

In regard to deprivation of liberty, the Inquiry found that 'the taking of Indigenous children from their homes by force and their confinement to training homes, orphanages (…) amounted to deprivation of liberty and [unlawful] imprisonment' (NISATSIC 1997, 253). The safeguard of court scrutiny before detention which protected arbitrary removal of non-Indigenous children, was denied Indigenous children. Indigenous children could be removed by the order of a public servant. At the same time the removal of non-Indigenous children required a court order.

4.2. DEPRIVATION OF PARENTAL RIGHTS

In regard to deprivation of parental rights, it was found that in some jurisdictions legislation stripped Indigenous parents of their parental rights and made a Chief

Protector the legal guardian of all Indigenous children. This was contrary to the common law which safeguarded parental rights – a parent could only forfeit their parental rights if a court found misconduct or that state guardianship was in the child's best interest (NISATSIC 1997, 255).

4.3.   ABUSES OF POWER

Although legislation authorised the removal of Indigenous children, some Aboriginal Protectors and Inspectors resorted to kidnapping or trickery to take the children from their parents. There are many examples of children being taken directly from school without their parents' knowledge, or other cases where Indigenous parents were told their children were being taken to school but were then never seen again (NISATSIC 1997, 257). These actions were abuses of power – actions beyond what was authorised by the legislation.

4.4.   BREACH OF DUTY OF CARE AND GUARDIANSHIP DUTIES

Furthermore, Aboriginal Protectors and Protection Boards had a duty of care and protection to those over whom they exercised control. The report identified at least three ways in which guardianship duties and statutory duties were failed with Indigenous children.

Firstly, there was a failure to provide contemporary standards of care for Indigenous children to the same level as non-Indigenous children. Although standards of care for non-Indigenous children were far from satisfactory, Indigenous children experienced appalling standards of care, brutal punishments, cold, hunger, fear and sexual abuse. Standards of care were less than the corresponding levels of care for non-Indigenous children. Secondly, there was a failure to protect Indigenous children from harm, from abuse and exploitation. Many of the children were verbally, physically, emotionally or sexually abused. Thirdly, there was a failure to consult or involve parents in decisions about the child. Many children who were institutionalised were then falsely told their parents were dead. For further discussion of guardianship duties, state obligations and the removal of Aboriginal children see Buti (2004).

4.5. VIOLATION OF INTERNATIONAL HUMAN RIGHTS STANDARDS

According to the inquiry, the main international human rights obligations imposed on Australia and breached by a policy of forced removals were prohibitions on racial discrimination and genocide. The policy of forced removal continued to be practised after Australia had voluntarily subscribed to treaties outlawing both racial discrimination and genocide, which was from the mid 1940s onwards (NISATSIC 1997, 266).

The legislative regimes created for the removal of Indigenous children were different and inferior to those established for non-Indigenous children. They were racially discriminatory and remained in place until 1954 in Western Australia, 1957 in Victoria, 1962 in South Australia, 1964 in Northern Territory and 1965 in Queensland. In addition, Government officials knew they were in breach of international legal obligations (NISATSIC 1997, 270). The Inquiry found that the policy of forcible removal of Indigenous children could be properly called genocide and breached international law.

> "*Official policy and legislation for Indigenous families and children was contrary to accepted legal principle imported into Australia as British common law and, from late 1946, constituted a crime against humanity. It offended accepted standards of the time and was the subject of dissent and resistance. The implementation of the legislation was marked by breaches of fundamental obligations on the part of officials and others to the detriment of vulnerable and dependent children whose parents were powerless to know their whereabouts and protect them from exploitation and abuse*". (NISATSIC 1997, 275)

In summary, the Inquiry found that the policy of forced removal of Indigenous children was contrary to prohibitions on racial discrimination and genocide, and was contrary to accepted legal principle found in the common law. Finally, the removals had led to other forms of criminal victimisation including widespread sexual and physical assault (NISATSIC 1997, 277–278).

There has been considerable argument in Australia as to whether the policy of removal constituted genocide, and if so, did it continue to constitute genocide in the post 1945 period when policies moved towards assimilation (Manne 2001). However, even if one does not accept that the forced removal policies constituted genocide, there are other substantial reasons for regarding the actions as state crime. The finding of genocide was one part of the claim concerning the violation of international human rights standards – the other was racial discrimination. Furthermore, international human rights violations were only one of five legs to a claim of unlawful behaviour: the others being breaches of statutory and common law duties and principles.

5. INSTITUTIONAL RACISM AS A FOUNDATIONAL HARM

As indicated above, racism was a precondition for the colonial genocides and the systematic abuse of human rights of Indigenous peoples in Australia and the Americas. As Stannard (1993, 247) notes, Spanish and Anglo-Americans saw the natives of the Americas as racially inferior beings. Racial discrimination provided an overarching basis to governmental law and policy towards Indigenous people throughout much of the eighteenth, nineteenth and twentieth centuries. The suspension of the rule of law and the use of terror and violence by colonial authorities against Indigenous people was also contextualised and legitimated within racialized constructions of Indigenous people as inferior, lesser human beings. There is no doubt that these racialized constructions changed during the eighteenth, nineteenth and twentieth centuries: in Australia this move was from notions of barbarism to views about a race 'doomed' to extinction. Indeed competing views about race were often prevalent at the same time. However, what is important is that racialized constructions of Indigenous people inevitably facilitated discriminatory intervention. In Australia institutionalised and legalised discrimination reached a peak during the 'protection' period of the twentieth century.

In terms of understanding state crime, the importance of recognising the role of racism is that it provided a foundational logic to many of the harms that subsequently developed. Specific harms like the forced removal of children occurred as a result of racial discrimination. The policies and practices of protection and assimilation were built on assumptions about racial inferiority which justified discriminatory treatment. After the 1940s ideas about cultural assimilation came to the fore and largely replaced ideas about the biological basis to racial inferiority. However, cultural assimilation was still based on a view of the inferiority of the native – now defined more in terms of culture rather than biology. The ultimate goal had not changed: the disappearance of Indigenous people as a distinct group of people. In Australia, cultural assimilation was seen as leading to a form of 'equality' with European Australians. However, this equality was to be one defined on the assumption of the superiority of white Anglo-Australian cultural, economic and political institutions. It was to be the equality of 'sameness': where everyone could participate on a social terrain defined by the coloniser. The goal of equality still authorised racial discrimination. To reach the level of equality the colonial subject required tutelage. They had to be taught and trained to be equal. As a result, there was authorised intensive supervision and surveillance through a range of state agencies including child welfare, health, housing and criminal justice agencies.

6.   FORCED LABOUR AND GOVERNMENT FRAUD

Overwhelmingly, discussions on state crime concentrate on the use of force – and there is clearly a good reason for this given the role of the modern state in the murder of vast numbers of people (Green & Ward 2004, 1). However, crime is also defined by fraud as well as force. A consideration of the colonial process shows how the state was involved in vast fraudulent schemes against Indigenous people who were under the state's care and protection. These include such matters as stolen wages, missing trust monies, and under-award payments for Indigenous workers. There were negligent and, at times corrupt and dishonest practices which lead to the withholding of moneys from Aboriginal wages that had been paid into savings accounts, and trust funds.

Part of the precondition for this fraudulent activity was state control over Indigenous labour which itself amounted to forced labour and bordered on a type of slavery in some cases. Many Aboriginal workers in Western Australia were not paid wages and were primarily remunerated through rations such as flour, tea, tobacco and clothing. As late as the early 1960s Aboriginal workers employed as stockmen were given 'perhaps two shirts and two pairs of trousers a year, working boots, hat, canvas swag, and a couple of blankets (…) no money' (Toussaint 1995, 259). The exploitation of Aboriginal workers in the pastoral industry was often considered as 'unpaid slavery' at the time (Haebich 1992, 150). Australia was clearly in contravention of various International Labour Organisation (ILO) conventions to which it was a party. In 1930 Australia had signed the Forced Labour Convention which generally prohibited forced labour and working for rations.

Kidd (1997 and 2000) conducted extensive research in Queensland on the way corruption and financial abuse by police 'protectors' and other state officials led to diversion of Aboriginal money from trust funds. In December 2006 the Australian Senate Standing Committee on Legal and Constitutional Affairs [hereafter the Standing Committee] released the report of its inquiry into what has become known as Indigenous 'Stolen Wages'. The terms of reference for the inquiry related to Indigenous workers whose paid labour was controlled by government. Throughout the nineteenth and twentieth centuries, various Australian governments put in place legislative and administrative controls over the employment, working conditions and wages of Indigenous workers. These controls allowed for the non-payment of wages to some workers, the underpayment of wages, and the diversion of wages into trust and savings accounts (Standing Committee 2006, 3). The inquiry took a broad view of 'wages' to include wages, savings, entitlements, and other monies due to Indigenous people.

The Standing Committee found that there is

"compelling evidence that governments systematically withheld and mismanaged Indigenous wages and entitlements over decades. In addition, there is evidence of Indigenous people being underpaid or not paid at all for their work. These practices were implemented from the late 19th century onwards and, in some cases, were still in place in the 1980s. Indigenous people have been seriously disadvantaged by these practices across generations". (Standing Committee 2006, 4)

Typically state protection legislation set out controls on Indigenous workers whereby they could only be employed under a permit granted by a protector. Minimum wages were set for Indigenous workers with a permit. For example in Queensland the wage was set at less than one-eight the 'white wage'. Protectors could instruct the employer to pay the wages of the Indigenous worker directly to the protector. Monies held by the protector were to be deposited in the worker's name in a government bank account where accounts of expenditure were to be kept. Some small percentage of the worker's wage could be given to the worker as pocket money, either by the employer or the protector. In Queensland further deductions could be taken from the wages of Indigenous workers to be placed in an Aboriginal Provident Fund (later the Aboriginal Welfare Fund) which was established for the 'relief of natives'.

In the Northern Territory protectors could direct an employer to pay a portion of Aboriginal worker's wages to the protector to be subsequently held in a trust account. However, it was also the case that after 1933 employers of Aboriginal workers could be exempted from paying *any* wages if the protector was satisfied the employer was maintaining the relatives and dependants of the Aboriginal employee.

In New South Wales the focus of control of the Aborigines Protection Board was the apprenticeship (or indenture) of Aboriginal children. The power of the Board to apprentice Aboriginal children 'on such terms and conditions as it may think under the circumstances of the case are desirable' continued until 1969 (Standing Committee 2006, 15). The protection legislation established the wages for Aboriginal apprentices and directed that a small percentage be given as pocket money to the apprentice and the remainder go into a trust account to be paid out to the apprentice at the end of their apprenticeship.

The inquiry found that governments had put in place compulsory regimes for the regulation of Indigenous money, including compulsory contributions to savings and trust fund accounts. However, governments failed to ensure that Indigenous people received the money they were entitled to, and failed to ensure that the savings and trust fund accounts were properly protected from misappropriation and fraud (Standing Committee 2006, 41).

The stolen wages and missing trust funds of Aboriginal peoples was fraud on a vast scale over many decades. The effects of the stolen wages of Indigenous people and subsequent immiseration arising from this exploitation, is fundamental to understanding the contemporary situation of Indigenous people in Australia. While Aboriginal people substantially contributed to the economic development of the nation, they

> *"were subject to a disabling system which denied them proper wages, protection from exploitation and abuse, proper living conditions, and adequate education and training. So while other Australians were able to build financial security and an economic future for their families, Aboriginal workers were hindered by these controls. Aboriginal poverty... today is a direct consequence of this discriminatory treatment".* (Haebich, cited in Standing Committee 2006, 68)

The long term impact of government policy in the realm of financial controls over Indigenous people is probably as great as the impact of the policies of Aboriginal child removal. It also provides a compelling argument for considering systematic government fraud as a state crime, and shows the importance of seeing colonial policy and practice in the context of state crime.

7. LOSS OF CIVIL AND POLITICAL RIGHTS

It was typically the case that settler colonial states put in place restrictions on the civil and political rights exercised by Indigenous peoples. Thus the foundations of liberal democracies were built on various exclusionary measures aimed at the original inhabitants of the land. In Australia the denial of civil and political rights included numerous legislative controls and restrictions on movement, residence, education, health care, employment, voting, worker's compensation, and welfare/social security entitlements. These restrictions continued well into the later part of the twentieth century.

Under British law imported into Australia at the time of colonisation, Indigenous people were regarded as British subjects. However, as the colonies gained self government and eventually federated into the Commonwealth of Australia, Indigenous people were consistently excluded from the enjoyment of citizenship rights. At a national level, the practical denial of Australian citizenship rights was achieved through various parliamentary legislation and administrative practices beginning with the *Commonwealth Franchise Act 1902* which expressly disenfranchised Aboriginal people.

These restrictions were to remain well into the twentieth century. The *Nationality and Citizenship Act 1948* established the legal construct of 'Australian citizen'. So by virtue of being born in Australia, Aboriginal people were automatically entitled to Australian citizenship. However, this citizenship was largely an empty shell without the citizenship rights that other Australians enjoyed. Even after the passage of the *Nationality and Citizenship Act*, Aboriginal people could not vote in Federal elections, or elections in Queensland, the Northern Territory, and Western Australia.

Indigenous 'citizenship' was thus devoid of the substantive rights and privileges associated with citizenship and was inherently discriminatory (Chesterman & Galligan 1997, 3). It was not until 1962 that Commonwealth amendments to electoral laws removed any remaining prohibitions on voting at the federal level. States began to dismantle their discriminatory laws during the same period. Restrictions on Indigenous voting rights in Queensland were not removed until 1965.

The developments which we associate with the rise of modern social welfare-oriented liberal democracies during the course of the twentieth century need to be considered against the backdrop of a range of exclusionary practices which were essentially derived from the colonial experience. For example, Aboriginal people were largely excluded from the right to social security: a number of federal statutes explicitly disqualified Aboriginal people from receiving government entitlements claimable by non-Indigenous Australians. These included:

- The *Invalid and Old-Age Pensions Act 1908* which barred 'aboriginal natives' of Australia and the Pacific from receiving an old-age and/or invalid pension
- The *Maternity Allowance Act 1912* which disqualified 'women who are aboriginal natives of Australia' from receiving the maternity allowance
- The *Child Endowment At 1941* prohibited the payment of the benefit to an 'aboriginal native of Australia' who was nomadic or dependent on Commonwealth or State support
- The *Widows' Pensions Act 1942* which denied the pension to any 'aboriginal native of Australia'.

These discriminatory laws remained in effect until the 1960s, and discriminatory restrictions on eligibility for social security benefits for Aboriginal people were not completely lifted until 1966.

Individual states in Australia also had their own 'protection' legislation. Among other powers this legislation allowed for control over Indigenous movement and residence in a manner that was incompatible with basic freedoms enjoyed by other Australians. Administrators and police could force Aboriginal people to reside on specified reserves. In addition Indigenous people could be moved from camps, or removed from whole districts to another location or moved between reserves and institutions. We noted above that protection legislation also regulated employment. In addition an Aboriginal person could not marry a non-

Aboriginal person without authorization from the Director of the Native Affairs or a specially empowered protector. State legislation which restricted the citizenship rights of Indigenous people living on reserves in Queensland remained in place until the 1980s (Chesterman & Galligan 1997).

The absence of basic civil and political rights for Indigenous people throughout much of the twentieth century represented an abrogation by the state for ensuring fundamental human rights. As we have seen in the discussions relating to stolen wages and the forced removal of children, the abrogation of fundamental rights gave rise to a range of subsequent crimes. However, there is a good argument that these breaches of fundamental rights should be seen as state crimes in themselves. While there has been much debate on the relationship between human rights and state crime, it is imperative that breaches of fundamental human rights such as freedom from racial discrimination should be seen as state crime. If the principle of non-discrimination had been adhered to in relation to Aboriginal people, then the debilitating laws and policies noted above would never have been enacted.

8. AFTER STATE CRIME: THE STRUGGLE FOR RECONCILIATION AND REPARATION

The final section of this chapter is concerned with the issue of reparations for Indigenous people for the harms caused by colonial law, policy and practice. It focuses in particular on the contemporary demand for reparations and compensation by Indigenous people in Australia, but acknowledges that similar demands are being made by Indigenous peoples in other settler societies, including the United States and Canada. There are also parallels with demands by African Americans for reparations for slavery. Indeed, both African American and Indigenous peoples have lessons which can be learned from each other in their respective struggles to deal with historical injustices. Although slavery was different to the dispossession of Aboriginal peoples, both groups were subject to institutionalized racial discrimination and violence, and within nations that defined themselves as liberal democratic societies guided by the rule of law.

As demonstrated in this chapter, many of the harms against Aboriginal peoples relied on law for their legitimacy. Many were essentially aimed at destroying Indigenous cultures. They were cultural harms in the broadest sense: colonial laws, policies and practices which, at various times, sought to assimilate, 'civilize', and Christianise Aboriginal peoples through the establishment of reservations, the denial of basic citizenship rights, the forced removal of children and forced education in residential schools, the banning of language, cultural and spiritual practices, and the imposition of an alien criminal justice system (RCAP 1996; NISATSIC 1997; Tsosie 2004).

Finding a just solution and remedy for historical wrongs is an important part of any discussion on state crime. In relation to Indigenous peoples in Australia, New Zealand and North America there has been much discussion on reconciliation. However, there can be no effective reconciliation without addressing in a meaningful way the wrongs of the past. Thus reconciliation requires a reparations process. Such a process provides both a moral and a legal response to policies and practices that, as a society, we recognize as abhorrent. This is not simply judging the past by the standards of today. As argued in this chapter, many of the practices engaged in by the state were unlawful at the time – such as the fraudulent misappropriation of the wages and trust funds of Indigenous peoples.

8.1.   PRINCIPLES OF REPARATIONS

The process of developing principles and guidelines on the right to reparation for victims of violations of international human rights law has been ongoing for sometime. It is uncontroversial, in international or domestic law, to state that where a right has been violated it should be remedied. However, the questions of 'who' and 'how' with respect to violations of international human rights law have always been difficult and are now being addressed systematically in the international arena. The Van Boven/Bassiouni principles have developed since the then United Nations Sub-Commission on the Prevention of Discrimination and the Protection of Minorities first commissioned Special Rapporteur Van Boven to report on the issue in 1989. In 1998 the Commission on Human Rights appointed Cherif Bassiouni to further revise the principles developed by Van Boven on the right to reparations for victims of gross violations of human rights. It is expected that these principles will be adopted eventually by the United Nations General Assembly.

The Basic Principles and Guidelines on the Right to Remedy and Reparation for Victims of Violations of International Human Rights and Violations of Humanitarian Law contains 29 principles. Broadly, the principles state the obligation to respect, ensure respect for and enforce international human rights and firmly locate the right to afford remedies to victims within the scope of this obligation. The principles aim to identify and provide mechanisms and procedures to implement existing obligations to victims, and in this sense also aim to rationalise a consistent approach to the means by which victims' needs can be addressed. For example, Principle 7 states that statutes of limitations should not unduly restrict the ability of a victim to pursue a claim against a perpetrator – a particular problem which victims of historical injustices such as Indigenous peoples have faced.

Principles 16–25 address the right to adequate, effective and prompt reparation. Ultimate responsibility for reparations lies with states: a state is to provide reparation for its own violations and in the event that another party is responsible and unwilling or unable to meet their obligations to repair, the state should endeavour to provide assistance, including reparations. Successor states shall provide reparations for violations of previous governments. Questions of how to repair are given extensive attention under the headings: restitution, compensation, rehabilitation and satisfaction and guarantees of non-repetition.

Restitution should, whenever possible, restore the victim to the original situation. Restitution can include the restoration of social status, identity, return to one's place of residence, restoration of employment and return of property (Principle 22).

Compensation should be provided for any economically assessable damage: physical or mental harm, including pain, suffering and emotional distress; lost opportunities, including employment, education and social benefits; material damages and loss of earnings; harm to reputation or dignity; and costs required for legal or expert assistance, medicines and medical services, and psychological and social services (Principle 23).

Rehabilitation should include, as appropriate, medical and psychological care as well as legal and social services (Principle 24).

Satisfaction and Guarantees of Non-repetition includes cessation of continuing violations, verification of the facts and full public disclosure of the truth (to the extent that such disclosure does not cause further unnecessary harm to the victim), the search for the whereabouts of the disappeared and for the bodies of those killed, and assistance in the recovery, identifications and reburial of the bodies in accordance with the cultural practices of the families and communities; apology, including public acknowledgement of the facts and acceptance of responsibility; commemorations and tributes to the victims; inclusion of an accurate account of the violations that occurred in educational material at all levels (Principle 25).

Internationally there has been growing acceptance that governments acknowledge and make reparations for the victims of human rights abuses. There has been widespread agreement on the principle of reparations, including a variety of methods of redress; the importance of public acknowledgment of wrong-doing and apology for harm; the importance of participation of victims in the process of acknowledgment; and the acceptance of internationally accepted human rights norms as a basis for reparations. The Van Boven/Bassiouni principles outlined above provide a broad principled framework for reparations. As a practical example of how these principles have been developed into specific recommendations, we return to the issue of the Stolen Generations and the forced removal of Aboriginal children from their families and communities. The main recommendations of the national inquiry broadly followed the requirements of acknowledgment and apology; guarantees against repetition; measures of restitution; measures of rehabilitation; and monetary compensation.

8.2. ACKNOWLEDGMENT AND APOLOGY

The Stolen Generations Inquiry recognised the need to establish the truth about the past as an essential measure of reparation for people who have been victims of gross violations of human rights. The Inquiry was told of the need for acknowledgment of responsibility and apology in many of the submissions from Indigenous organisations and the personal testimonies of individuals who had been forcibly removed from their families.

Various recommendations called for the recording of the testimonies of Indigenous people affected by the forced removal policies, commemoration of the events and apologies from Australian parliaments and other state institutions, such as police forces, which played a key part in the removal (NISATSIC 1997, 285). Like victims of other crimes, people who have been subjected to the gross violation of their human rights want public recognition of the harm they have suffered – they are not necessarily vengeful. Further, it is recognised that commemoration is an important part of the reparation process. Commemoration allows both mourning and the memory to be shared and to be transformed into part of the national consciousness.

8.3. GUARANTEE AGAINST REPETITION

It is widely recognised that guarantees against repetition are an important part of the reparation process. These include such things as democratisation, political reforms, law reform and the need for compulsory educational modules in schools and universities on the particular issue. Some form of guarantee against repetition is a necessary component of international redress for human rights abuses. It is necessary before the process of healing for all parties can begin and the reintegration of the offender back into the community can occur. Such a notion is basically a reassurance to the community that future harmful acts will not occur.

Clearly, such a reassurance is more difficult in cases where the state has been the perpetrator rather than an individual offender. The process is made even more complex and more imperative when there are multiple victims and offenders and the offending behaviour has at some time received legitimacy and support from state institutions.

The Stolen Generations Inquiry recognised the need for guarantees against repetition. Recommendations in three areas deal specifically with this issue. They include developing educational materials. Secondly there was a recommendation that the Government legislate the Genocide Convention for effect in domestic law (NISATSIC 1997, 295). A further political guarantee against repetition is the recognition of the Indigenous right to self-determination. There were several recommendations on the principle and practice of self-determination.

8.4. MEASURES OF RESTITUTION AND REHABILITATION

The purpose of restitution is to re-establish, to the extent possible, the situation that existed prior to the perpetration of gross violations of human rights. The Stolen Generations Inquiry recognised that 'children who were removed have typically lost the use of their languages, been denied cultural knowledge and inclusion, been deprived of opportunities to take on cultural responsibilities and are often unable to assert their native title rights' (NISATSIC 1997, 296). As a result the Inquiry made recommendations concerning the expansion of funding to language, culture and history centres, funding for the recording and teaching of local Indigenous languages, funding for Indigenous community-based family tracing and reunion services and recommendations aimed at the preservation of records, Indigenous access to records, and Indigenous community management over their own records.

Measures for rehabilitation were also an important component of the reparations package. The Stolen Generations Inquiry was made very aware of the long term problems caused by forcible separation and made significant recommendations in relation to mental health care and assistance in parenting and family programs for those who had been removed.

8.5. MONETARY COMPENSATION

Typically, commissions inquiring into human rights abuses recognise that the loss, grief and trauma experienced by those who were abused can never be adequately compensated. However, such inquiries also usually recommend some form of monetary compensation for the harm that has been suffered – particularly as a form of recognition of the responsibility for the causes of that harm. It is common for such commissions to advocate for simple and relaxed procedural principles to be applied in dealing with applications for compensation.

The Stolen Generations Inquiry recognised that the loss, grief and trauma experienced by victims could not be fully compensated. However, the submissions to the Inquiry also demanded some form of monetary compensation for the harm that had been suffered – particularly as a form of recognition of the responsibility for the causes of that harm. The Inquiry recommended the establishment of a National Compensation Fund to provide an alternative to litigation and to ensure consistency in compensation.

9. CONCLUSION

This chapter shows the need to think about state crime in a broader historical context that recognises the long term impact of colonialism. In particular it is an argument about the importance of understanding the origins of liberal democracies within processes of dispossession and exclusion. Contemporary liberal democracies like Australia were built on processes of state crime – defined by a broad range of offences including mass murder, systematic fraud and institutionally racist laws, policies and practices.

Importantly for an understanding of state crime, these laws, policies and practices did not simply disappear after the peak of the colonial enterprise in the nineteenth century. They were firmly entrenched until well into more contemporaneous times. The colonial experience also shows the importance of thinking about state crime in a context that is broader than a concentration on force and violence. Certainly while the most extreme crimes of the state against colonised peoples involved violence, that is not the full extent of the story. The institutionalised laws and policies built on racial discrimination allowed for a range of crime to develop from those involving the forced removal of Aboriginal children to the systematic denial of basic civil and political rights. Definitions of state crime clearly need to be able to incorporate these types of crime if they are to have salience for understanding some of the most profound injustices perpetrated within the boundaries of liberal democracies.

Further the colonial experience shows the need for definitions of state crime that include fraud as well as force. The systematic state fraud against Indigenous people in Australia and north America continues to be a source of demands for compensation and reparation. The long term loss of access to proper wages, social security benefits and the savings of trust funds has had profound effects on the long term ability of Indigenous people to accumulate basic family wealth. The contemporary impoverishment of Indigenous people is a direct result of state law and practice.

Finally, the struggle by Indigenous peoples to receive compensation and reparation for these historical wrongs raises important questions for how we define and mobilise for adequate remedies to state crime. While there has been much written on truth commissions, restorative justice and reparations, most of this work has not dealt with how historical wrongs should be dealt within liberal democracies like Australia or Canada or the US. The Indigenous experience shows that historical wrongs must be confronted within the heartlands of nations that pride themselves on their liberal democratic traditions. Indeed part of the argument of this chapter has been that liberal democracies, at least in some places, were founded on state crime.

VIII. CORPORATIONS AND INTERNATIONAL CRIMES

Wim Huisman

1. INTRODUCTION

The recent interest in criminology of international crime focuses on the responsibility of the state as perpetrator and the individuals who commit the crime or act as culpable bystanders. However, there is empirical evidence to show that corporations and their representatives can also act as perpetrator or accomplice of international crime. Cases of violent conflicts in which international crimes are committed provide some examples of the involvement of corporate actors.

A recent example of the above involved two Dutch businessmen charged with complicity in committing genocide and war crimes. Although acquitted for complicity to genocide, Frans van Anraat, one of the accused, was found guilty of complicity in committing war crimes. He was one of the main suppliers of the chemicals used by Saddam Hussein's regime to produce chemical weapons that killed many Kurdish and Iranian civilians. Despite an appeal, Frans van Anraat received a seventeen-year sentence in jail.[1] Gus Kouwenhoven was the director of the Oriental Timber Company and the Royal Timber Corporation involved in the illegal trade of timber from the tropical rainforests in Liberia. This trade was used to finance the regime of Liberia's former president Charles Taylor in its civil war in Liberia and neighbouring Sierra Leone, during the course of which many gross human rights violations were committed. Today, Charles Taylor faces trial before the Special Court of Sierra Leone for alleged war crimes. Gus Kouwenhoven was acquitted for complicity in committing war crimes but was found guilty of illegal arms trading.[2] The weapons in question were used to arm the corporations' security forces and also, allegedly, Charles Taylor's army. The appeal procedure against Gus Kouwenhoven has not, at the time of writing, been completed.

The role of corporations in gross human rights violations has been extensively studied by NGOs such as Amnesty International, Human Rights Watch and Global Witness. In the field of business ethics there is considerable attention for

---

[1]   Gerechtshof 's Gravenhage, 23 October 2006, LJN BA 6734.
[2]   Rechtbank 's Gravenhage, 7 June 2006, LJN AY 5160.

the moral responsibility of corporations towards human rights. In the field of international law, there is a traditional focus on states as the main perpetrators of international crimes, although there is an emerging interest for the legal accountability of non-state actors for human rights abuses (Alston 2006; Clapham 2006). However, academic interest from empirical disciplines such as criminology is almost non-existent.

The goal of this paper is to explore the role of corporations in international crimes from a criminological point a view. In this paper, the following questions will be addressed: How should the involvement of business corporations be conceptualised in the context of international crime? To what extent is this involvement criminalised? In what way can corporations be involved in international crimes? To what extent do theories on corporate crime offer an appropriate explanation for this involvement? In answering this last question, special attention will be given to the criminogenic aspects of the role of the state and the globalisation of business.

This paper will consist of two parts. The first part examines in what way the corporate involvement in international crime will fit into criminological definitions. The second part will try to explain this involvement by using criminological theory on corporate crime. The benefit of this exercise is hopefully twofold: corporate crime theory which is mainly nationally oriented is tested for its applicability on international crime and corporate crime theory could offer a better understanding of the under-exposed corporate actor in the crimes that constitute a breach of international law.

2. CONCEPTUALISATION

In this paragraph I will discuss three concepts found in the literature that are applicable to the focus of this paper: corporate crime, state-corporate crime and international crime.

2.1. CORPORATE CRIME

The involvement of corporations with international crime could be seen as a form of corporate crime. Corporate crime is usually seen as a form of 'white collar crime'. Sutherland introduced this term at an address to the American Society for Sociology in 1939 and defined it as 'crime committed by a person of respectability and a high social status in the course of his occupation' (Sutherland 1983, 7). An important observation of Sutherland was that the behaviour of persons from the higher social classes – often in the field of business and trade – was not regulated and sanctioned under criminal law, but by administrative and civil law. Sutherland also included the violation of administrative and civil law in the element of 'crime' because these acts apply to the criteria that are generally used to qualify behaviour as crime: the government forbids these acts because they are socially harmful and sanctions them.

A critique of Sutherland's concept of white collar crime is that it does not distinguish between individual and corporate actors or between natural and legal persons, although Sutherland's research focused on the violations of America's largest corporations (Cressey 1989). After Sutherland, criminologists started to differentiate between individual white collar crime and criminal acts that should be attributed to an organisation: organisational crime. Corporate crime is presented as a form of organisational crime (Tonry and Reiss 1993); state crime or governmental crime is presented as white collar crime (Ermann and Lundman 2002). The term state crime is often used for international crimes committed by states or governmental bodies (Ross 2000a; Green and Ward 2004).

In their classic study, Clinard and Yeager define corporate crime as 'any act committed by corporations that is punished by the state, regardless of whether it is punished under administrative, civil or criminal law' (Clinard & Yeager 1980, 16). This definition illustrates that the study of corporate crime usually has a local or national orientation: the acts of corporations that are criminalised by national law. The acts that this paper focuses on might be committed locally but are also punishable under international (criminal) law. However, most corporate crimes are not serious enough to constitute a violation of international law. While corporate crime in general can have disastrous consequences (Mokhiber, 1989; Punch 2000), many empirical studies on corporate crime concern less dramatic regulatory violations (Van de Bunt and Huisman 2007).

2.2. STATE-CORPORATE CRIME

A concept also used to define the phenomenon that this paper is addressing is the concept of state-corporate crime, introduced by Kramer (1990, 1). He defines state-corporate crime in the following way:

> *"State-corporate crime is defined as an illegal or socially injurious social action that is the collective product of the interaction between a business corporation and a State agency engaged in a joint endeavour. These crimes involve the active participation of two or more organizations, at least one of which is private and one of which is public. They are the harmful result of an interorganisational relationship between business and government."*

Using this concept of state-corporate crime, Matthews and Kauzlarich (2000) identified two forms of state-corporate crime: state-initiated and state-facilitated. State-initiated crime occurs when corporations, employed by the government, engage in organisational crime at the instigation of, or with tacit approval of, the government. State-facilitated crime is defined as the failure of government regulatory agencies to restrain deviant business activities, either because of direct collusion between business and government or because they adhere to shared goals the attainment of which would be hampered by aggressive regulation (Kramer and Michalowski 2005, 21).

The premise for the concept of state-corporate crime is that modern states and corporations are profoundly interdependent (Friedrichs 2007a, 145). Most cases of corporate crime are state-initiated or state-facilitated, especially in the broad operationalisation that Matthews and Kauzlarich (2000) and others (e.g. Green and Ward 2004) apply. In almost all serious cases of corporate crime, some sort of opportunity is provided by governmental agencies, for instance because of loopholes in regulation, a lack of enforcement, collusion and corruption (Huisman 2001). As outlined below, this will especially be the case with the involvement of corporations and international crime.

The cases that the publications discuss about state-corporate crime are not always examples of international crime. An illustration is offered by the volume on state-corporate crime by Kramer and Michalowski (2006): it contains chapters on the contribution of the German company I.G. Farben to the death of millions during the Nazi holocaust (Matthews 2006), but also on the disaster of the space shuttle Challenger, the false billing of the U.S. Army by Halliburton (Rothe 2006) and rollover accidents involving Ford Explorers (a type of motor car) which occurred due to unsafe tyres made by Bridgestone-Firestone (Mullins 2006). This last point raises the question: what are international crimes and when can corporations be held liable for committing them?

2.3.   INTERNATIONAL CRIMES

Two conditions seem to be crucial in qualifying behaviour of a category of actors as crime: these actors have to be competent to conduct this behaviour and can be held responsible in some manner for this behaviour. In the context of this paper, this leads to two questions: Can corporations commit the acts that constitute an international crime? And can corporations be held morally responsible or legally liable for constituting these acts?

2.3.1. International crime and international law

Since the1940s, criminology has been debating the definition of its object of study: crime. In his address to the American Society of Sociology on White Collar Crime in 1939, Sutherland operationalised the element of *crime* in his definition of white collar crime not only as the violation of criminal law, but also as the violation of administrative and civil law. In reaction, some scholars have argued that the misdemeanours discussed by Sutherland and his followers do not always satisfy the legal criteria for crime. Furthermore, Tappan argues that only those acts which result in a conviction by a judge can be a topic of criminological research (Tappan 1947). However, critical criminologists argue that criminologists should study the mechanisms that prevent harmful business behaviour from being criminalised by law (Quinny 1973; Box 1983). For this reason, most criminologists do not limit the definition of corporate crime to behaviour that is punishable by criminal law, but also include the violation of administrative and civil regulation of business (Clinard & Yeager 1980; Passas 1990, 158; Blankenship 1993, xiv; Shover and Bryant 1993, 161). The next step would be including socially harmful business behaviour that is not regulated or subject to any sanction at all, as suggested by some critical criminologists (Quinny 1973). In defining white collar crime, this led Nelken (2002) to the question: 'Must we use the law to draw the line?'

The same controversy could arise when trying to define corporate international crime. An argument to follow a legalistic approach is that otherwise it would be very difficult to decide who is to define international crime (Coleman 1987). A more sociological definition (for instance 'serious socially injurious business behaviour') as often found in critical criminology could lead to endless discussions about which acts are serious enough to be considered international crime. This could distract attention from a more empirical approach to the involvement of corporations with international crime.

Additionally, the term international crime refers to international law and it is generally used in this way. 'International' could also mean that national borders are being crossed in committing these offences. However, the UN uses the concept of 'transnational crime' for these kinds of crime (Mueller 2001). International crimes can be committed locally, but they are defined as crime by international law. It might not be the behaviour itself, but it is ultimately the reaction to this behaviour that makes it international.

Consequently if the answer to the question 'Must we use the law to draw the line?' is positive, the next question would appear to be 'Must we use *criminal* law to draw the line?' This last question is not easy to answer because international criminal law is in a process of rapid development. There is no single international criminal code.

One could argue that the 'core' of international crime is found in the Rome Statute of the International Criminal Court. Article 5 of the Statute limits the jurisdiction of the court to the crime of genocide, crimes against humanity, war crimes and crimes of aggression. When can corporate crimes be considered to be so serious that they constitute (complicity in) one of these 'core' crimes? For instance: trading in arms, chemicals and natural resources is in violation of UN Security Council embargoes, thereby rendering these forms of trade illegal. Can this illegal trade during times of armed conflict be viewed as a war crime and thus come within the purview of Article 8 of the ICC Statute? The ICC prosecutor has already indicated that he believes investigation of the financial aspects of the alleged atrocities in the Democratic Republic of Congo will be crucial for the future prevention of crimes and for the prosecution of crimes already committed (Press release of 16 July 2003). During a session on the plundering of Natural Resources and Destruction of the Environment in Times of Armed Conflict (2007 Hague Joint Conference on Contemporary Issues of International Law) the panellists agreed that corporations engaged in such plundering could be committing the war crime of 'pillage'.

Violation of international humanitarian law committed by or with the complicity of corporations is often punishable under national criminal law. A recent survey found that nine of the sixteen countries surveyed have fully incorporated the Rome Statute crimes into their domestic legislation (Ramasastry & Thompson 2006). The number of jurisdictions in which charges for international crimes can be brought against corporations is increasing, as countries ratify the ICC Statute and incorporate its definitions into domestic law. In fact, even some countries that have not ratified the ICC, have nevertheless incorporated the crimes mentioned in the Statute into their legislation, among which is the United States of America.

The UN Security Council has urged states to address violations of UN sanctions regimes that often exist for conflict situations within their national legal orders. This raises the question which national legal order is applicable to harmful business behaviour. A multinational corporation might officially be located at an off shore location while its headquarters is located in Western Europe or the U.S.; it might conduct its harmful business in countries without a legal system regulating business behaviour and a proper judicial system (Gobert and Punch 2003). National legal systems might apply extraterritoriality to cover violation of international criminal law by their own nationals and by those who injure their own nationals. In eleven countries surveyed by Ramasastry and Thompson (2006), international criminal law statutes apply to serious violations committed by their own nationals abroad and also to serious violations committed against their own nationals. Some countries even extend the possibility of prosecuting international crimes throughout the world through the application of the concept of universal jurisdiction, i.e. it applies to all persons who commit a grave breach of international criminal law anywhere in the world.

In addition to the Rome Statute, other sources of international law might also be applicable to harmful corporate behaviour and define it as crime. For instance, the Basel Convention on the Control of Transboundary Movement of Hazardous Waste and their Disposal defines illegal traffic of waste as 'criminal', which can be committed by 'any natural or legal person.'

As can be seen, although international criminal law is still in a process of rapid development, some harmful corporate behaviour might be viewed as a breach of international criminal law (even through violating national legislation) and could therefore qualify as 'crime'. Could the same apply to other violations of international law, such as human rights violations, violating UN trade embargos and environmental violations? There seems to be a slippery slope: illegal trade in conflict situations might be international crime, but why then not the sale of unsafe products such as harmful medicines which kill many people (DES and Dalkon Shield), child labour and international environmental crime? Literature on corporate crime provides many cases in which large numbers of people are killed or seriously injured, human rights are grossly violated and the environment is seriously damaged (Punch 1996), but when are these international crimes?

In short, some corporate behaviour could qualify as in violation of international criminal law, while other acts 'just' constitute a violation of other forms of international law. When we follow the line of Sutherland in the debate on the definition of crime, all corporate acts that represent a violation of international law should be defined as international crime. However, the current state of international law forms a fragmented and diversified patchwork. In combination with the limited possibilities to hold corporations accountable – as will be discussed below – international law offers little systematic guidance for the qualification of harmful business behaviour as violation of international law, let alone as an international crime. More to the point, current international law does not contain a clear overall requirement for states to regulate the business activities of corporations when they are operating abroad and committing acts that do not reach the threshold of the three 'core' international crimes, namely war crimes, crimes against humanity and genocide.

Nevertheless, specific norms for multinational corporations towards human rights and the environment have been developed by the international community or international organisations. For instance, in 1977, the International Labour Organisation (ILO Declaration) adopted a Tripartite Declaration of Principles Concerning Multinational Enterprise and Social Policy which calls upon governments, employers and workers to respect the sovereign rights of states, respect the national laws and regulations and give due consideration to local practices and to respect relevant international standards.[3] The Organisation for Economic Co-operation and Development (OECD) Guidelines for Multinational Enterprises also targets corporations and reiterates that they should respect the human rights standards of those affected by their activities in conformity with the host government's international obligations and commitments.[4] Also, new multi-stakeholder forms of setting norms are emerging in which international organisations like the UN, NGOs and international corporations are taking part. Examples are: the Kimberly Process Certification Scheme, aimed at reducing the trade in conflict diamonds; and the UN Global Compact initiative which aims at bringing companies together with UN agencies, labour and civil society to support universal principles in the areas of human rights, labour standards, the environment and anti-corruption.[5]

Although they are not legally binding in the sense of a Treaty obligation, these human rights norms do have some legal significance or effect as 'soft law' (International Council on Human Rights Policy 2002). They provide standards for judging the moral and social responsibilities of corporations and might prove to be a trial ground for emerging norms that could crystallise into 'hard' international law. Nevertheless, these soft law initiatives have also been met with some scepticism. Critics emphasise that the norms in these soft law schemes tend to be rather vague and lacking in enforcement mechanisms, which 'makes it [the scheme] little more than a public relations exercise, and may in fact act as a veil for corporate irresponsibility' (Richardson 2003). If it is true that international business is embracing these soft law and semi-self regulatory schemes to prevent more demanding and enforceable legislation, then this would be an argument to also include the violation of these norms in the definition of corporate international crime.

2.3.2. Corporate accountability for international crimes

To state that corporations can commit acts that constitute an international crime is one thing; holding the corporation accountable is another. In academic literature three terms are used concerning this issue: accountability, responsibility and liability. I consider accountability a general concept: can corporations in some way be held to their obligations? Responsibility refers to a moral or social duty to give account for the effects of its operations on, for instance, human rights. Liability refers to the legal consequences of this responsibility. Continuing the legal and non-legal approach to international crime, these two ways of holding corporations accountable will be discussed below.

---

[3]   ILO Declaration para 11.2.
[4]   OECD Guidelines, para 11.2.
[5]   See respectively www.kimberlyprocess.com and www.unglobalcompact.org.

Corporate moral responsibility and human rights
While it can be empirically assessed that corporations can have a serious impact on human rights, it is a normative discussion if, and if so to what extent a corporation has a responsibility to observe human rights. Much has been written about the moral responsibilities of corporations towards human rights (Frynas and Pegg 2003; Campbell and Miller 2004). A central question is: what is the normative framework on which the moral responsibility is based. The attribution of responsibility to transnational corporations for human rights requires clarification regarding from where that responsibility arises and the scope of that responsibility. The quest for the foundation of the moral responsibilities of corporations is the *Leitmotiv* of the academic discipline of business ethics, while neo-liberal economic theory holds that the only moral responsibility of corporations is to make profit. This theoretical and normative debate is beyond the scope of this paper. For the purpose of this paper it may be sufficient to clearly establish that the call for moral responsibility of corporations with regard to their impact on human rights is crystallised into the internationally accepted codes of conduct on corporate responsibilities discussed above. Although the enforceability of this 'soft law' is a problem, these codes do provide a basis for the attribution of moral responsibility.

Corporate liability for international crimes
Apart from the question when a certain act can be defined as an international crime, it remains to be seen if a corporation can be held accountable under international criminal law.

Contrary to some national legal systems, international criminal law does not recognise the concept of corporate criminal liability (Gobert and Punch 2003). In contrast to individual businesspeople, corporations cannot be tried as such before the International Criminal Court. More generally, it is unclear whether corporations can be held accountable under international law for human rights violations. International human rights instruments were not designed to hold corporations responsible (Fokwa 2004).

Nevertheless, due to the increased role of non-state actors in the human rights area, the question of corporate responsibility for human rights violations has triggered considerable attention. The Special representative of the Secretary-General on the issue of human rights and transnational corporations and other business enterprises, John Ruggie, observes that corporations are increasingly recognised as participants at the international level, with the capacity to bear some rights and duties under international law.[6] According to De Schutter, it appears to be possible to derive form the standards existing in the international law of human rights certain duties imposed upon legal persons and in particular on multinational

---

6   UN Human Rights Council, A/HRC/4/035, 19 February 2007, para. 20.

enterprises. 'Although the orthodox understanding of international law sees it as imposing enforceable obligations only *directly* on states or (...) on natural persons, the norms codified in the international law of human rights lend themselves to such transposition' (De Schutter 2005, 314). According to the Special representative, 'simple laws probability alone suggests that corporations will be subject to increased liability for international crime in the future'.[7] And the International Council on Human Rights Policy states that 'International law is now evolving to regulate companies, both directly, and indirectly through states' (International Council on Human Rights Policy 2002, 73).

Although international criminal law does not yet recognise criminal liability of artificial or legal persons, many national legal systems do. The study of Ramasastry and Thompson (2006) revealed that it is the prevailing practice to apply criminal responsibility to legal persons among eleven of the sixteen countries surveyed. Since many countries also have integrated the crimes under international criminal law into their own legal systems, this means that a corporation can be held criminally liable and be prosecuted for international crimes under the domestic law of several countries. Some other countries have evaded the principal discussion about the general criminal liability of legal entities and have adopted specific statutes making legal persons liable for certain specific, important crimes. For example, in July 2007 the Corporate Manslaughter and Corporate Homicide Bill was passed by the UK, allowing corporations to be prosecuted for gross negligence leading to the death of employees or members of the public.[8]

When domestic systems do not recognise criminal liability of legal persons, it might be possible for criminal proceedings to be taken against the management of a corporation for organisational crimes when they were aware that criminal offences had taken place and they failed to put a stop to them. Additionally, even when the prosecution of a legal person is possible, there could be other reasons to prosecute only individual managers. For instance, the Dutch prosecutor in the Frans van Anraat and Gus Kouwenhoven cases mentioned above applied the principle of extraterritoriality by prosecuting the accused for their complicity in committing genocide and war crimes because these individual managers were Dutch nationals while their companies were not.

Although occurring more in the sphere of civil law, corporations in the United States have successfully been held directly liable for violations of human rights under the Alien Tort Claims Act (ACTA). An interesting body of jurisprudence has developed since dozens of transnational corporations have been sued under this Act. For example, Texaco was sued for alleged violations of human rights in Ecuador; Coca-Cola in Colombia; Talisman in Sudan; Royal Dutch Shell in

---

[7]   Ibid, para. 27.

[8]   *The Times*, 19 July 2007.

Burma; ExxonMobil in Indonesia; and Fresh Del Monte Produce in Guatemala. In all of these cases, transnational corporations were sued for alleged violations of human rights occurring in conjunction with their operations in developing countries or in places governed by repressive regimes. In some of these cases, the allegations concerned 'hard-core' infringements on human rights, such as mass murder, rape and torture (Shamir 2004, 638). Limiting the scope of ACTA-subject matter jurisdiction over non-state actors to these 'hard-core' violations, the US supreme Court ruled that if a corporation is charged with violating international law on grounds other than slave trading, genocide or war crimes, it cannot be held liable unless the plaintiff establishes that the non-state actor proximately caused the violation by exercising control over a government actor or shows that a corporate defendant acted in the capacity of a state actor (Shamir 2004, 642).

Most of the 40 cases brought against corporations in the United States under the Alien Tort Claims Act have concerned alleged complicity where the actual perpetrators were public or private security forces, other government agents or an armed faction in civil conflicts. According to the Special representative of the Secretary-General on the issue of human rights and transnational corporations and other business enterprises, corporate complicity is an umbrella term for a range of ways in which companies may be liable for their participation in criminal or civil wrongs. 'Few legitimate firms may ever directly commit acts that amount to intentional crimes. But there is greater risk of their facing allegations of "complicity" in such crimes.'[9]

A final question relating to corporate liability for international crimes is what the notion 'complicity' means in this respect. Does it relate to the concept of complicity as used in international criminal law or does it also encompass broader forms of complicity which do not amount to criminal responsibility? A fairly clear standard for individual complicity in committing international crimes has crystallised in international criminal law: aiding and abetting by knowingly providing practical assistance and encouragement or moral support that has a substantial effect on the commission of the crime. Applied to the complicity of corporations, the International Council on Human Rights Policy (2002) distinguishes four different situations in which the charge of 'complicity' is made: 1) a company actively assists, directly or indirectly, in human rights violations committed by others, 2) a company may be part of a joint venture or similar formal partnership with a government, 3) a company benefits from the opportunities or environment created by human rights violations, even if it does not positively assist or cause the perpetrator to commit the violations, and 4) a company is silent/inactive in the face of human rights violations.

---

[9]   Ibid, para. 30.

2.4. DISCUSSION

In this paragraph, three applicable concepts to the phenomena outlined in this paper have been mentioned above. Definitions of the concept of corporate crime, state crime and international crime can be portrayed as three rings which do not completely overlap. The area in which the above definitions of crime overlap is the scope of this paper. The overlap between corporate crime and state crime is covered by the discussed concept of state-corporate crime.

Figure 1

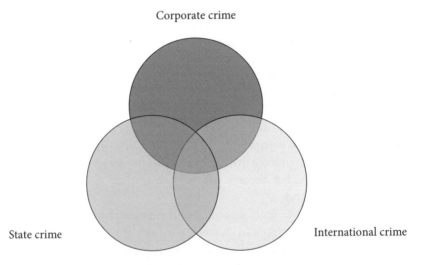

The area in which the three rings overlap is probably of more importance than appears from figure 1. As presumed above, corporations are able to commit or to be complicit in international crimes because domestic regulation and enforcement are lacking; governmental agencies actively facilitate or commit these crimes on behalf of corporate interests.

In defining international crime, three concentric rings can be identified, as shown in figure 2: the core crimes in international criminal law, other violations of international law and non-compliance with soft law. Each of these rings seems to be growing: expanding the scope of corporate responsibilities. Also, an 'inbound' trend might be observed: soft laws crystallise into harder norms the violation of which is increasingly qualified as a 'crime'.

Figure 2

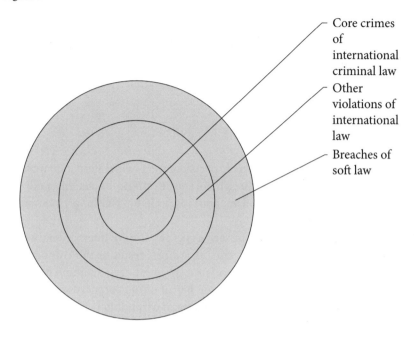

Core crimes of international criminal law

Other violations of international law

Breaches of soft law

In criminology, there is no leading definition of international crime. In general, two traditions of defining crimes can be identified: a legal and a non-legal approach. A choice would depend on the purpose of any analysis: a normative study of criminalisation processes of corporate involvement in international crime would require a non-legal approach, including all three rings, while an empirical analysis of the prevalence of corporate international crime requires a more clear-cut definition based on clearer legal limits.

A review of the literature of state crime and state-corporate crime illustrates the fact that harmful behaviour easily qualifies as crime while it is often difficult to refer to a specific Act or treaty. The normative use of the term crime fits the tradition of critical criminology. However, the moral ambiguities that surround corporate crime in general (Nelken 2002) are intensified due to the lack of an international regulatory framework. This might lead to a polarisation in the debate on the involvement of corporations with international crime. Not restricted by law, critical scholars could easily qualify almost any harmful business behaviour as crime, making it easier to disqualify their opinion as being too radical and anti-business.

However, this does not relieve academic criminology from the obligation to study the phenomena that are excluded by a stricter legal approach. Even more, due to the state of international law, a legal approach in defining international crime does not provide much more clarity and raises a number of questions.

Should we limit ourselves to the 'core' crimes of international criminal law or should we follow Sutherland in including other human rights violations under international law? Additionally, should we include all violations that can be empirically attributed to corporations or should we follow Tappan in limiting ourselves to only those acts for which corporations can legally be held accountable?

3. FORMS OF INVOLVEMENT

Another way to explore the involvement of corporations with international crimes is to study its manifestations. Although not much empirical academic study has been done, investigative journalism and research by NGOs provide many examples.

First of all, corporations could be seen as perpetrators of international crime. In this case, international crime occurs as a direct result of the corporation's business practice. This would be the case when corporate agents commit genocide, crimes against humanity or war crimes on behalf of the corporation. The most notorious example is the contribution of German corporations in the holocaust during the Second World War (Matthews 2006). Executives of the chemical company I.G. Farben were convicted of crimes against humanity after the war. I.G. Farben and other German corporations extensively made use of slave labour and built slave labour camps adjacent to the concentration camps (Borkin 1978; Black 2001). More recent examples of direct perpetration could entail armed security officers of corporations killing or torturing people for corporate interests (Green and Ward 2004).

Usually, however, more indirect forms of involvement of corporations with international crimes are found. A first category is international crime that occurs as a result of direct cooperation between corporations and oppressive regimes. For example, the Anvil Mining Corporation is accused by several human rights organisations of providing logistical support in the form of providing cars and chauffeurs to an army outfit of the Democratic Republic of Congo used in committing a massacre among the villagers of the town of Kilwa. The Dutch prosecutor, in the case mentioned above, suspected Gus Kouwenhoven of providing the helicopter of the Oriental Timber Corporation to forces of President Charles Taylor, which was allegedly used to commit international crimes against villagers in Liberia. According to Human Rights Watch (2003c), foreign oil companies are complicit in the human rights abuses committed by the Sudanese government in forcibly displacing civilians from areas designated for oil extraction. Allegedly, they were not only aware of the killing, bombing and looting of the villages that were located among the oil fields, they also provided logistical support by allowing government forces to use their airstrips and road infrastructure for committing these attacks. A well known ACTA case that might fall under this category was filed in 1996 against Unocal, a giant enterprise engaging in energy resource projects around the world.[10] Plaintiffs argued that Unocal relied on Burmese army units to build a gas pipeline and that the units, with the tacit knowledge of Unocal, resorted to extreme methods of forced labour and forced relocation of villagers in the course of construction (Shamir 2004, 639).

A second, indirect way of corporate involvement occurs when international crimes are committed to pursue corporate interests. There are many examples of police and security forces committing international crimes in the violent suppression of protest against corporate interests. Not insignificantly, corporate interests seem to be the main cause for conflicts in which human rights are abused: for instance banning inhabitants from their land for corporate development and the industrial pollution of the local environment. A well known case is the protest of the Ogoni people in Nigeria against the pollution by oil companies (Green and Ward 2004). Plaintiffs even sued Royal Dutch Shell under the ACTA for conspiring with the Nigerian government against the Ogoni people.[11] The plaintiffs alleged that the Nigerian military – with the knowledge and cooperation of the defendants – arrested and convicted nine members of a Nigerian environmental movement in order to suppress that movement. The arrests, which were part of a widespread intimidation campaign, led to the false conviction and execution of Ken Sero-Wiwa, a Nobel Prize winner and eight other leaders of the Movement of the Survival of the Ogoni People (MOSOP) in 1994 (Shamir 2004, 640). Another example is the violent suppression of peaceful protests against a dam to be built by an Indian subsidiary of Enron Corporation (Human Rights Watch 1999b).

A third example is illegal trade which fuels violent conflicts and contributes to the commission of international crimes. This could take several forms. In the case of Liberia, the concessions paid for the alleged illegal logging of the corporations controlled by the Dutchman Gus Kouwenhoven used to finance the war in which so many atrocities were committed. More directly, corporations may also provide the products (weapons and chemicals) with which international crimes are committed. Besides financing the international crimes of the regime of Charles Taylor, the corporations of Gus Kouwenhoven also allegedly provided the weapons and transport facilities to commit these crimes. The company of another Dutchman, Frans van Anraat, delivered the precursors which where used to produce the poisonous gases that killed thousands of Kurdish and Iranian civilians (Karskens 2007). There are many examples of weapons industries evading international embargoes by providing weapons to governmental forces or rebel groups (Green and Ward, 2004). For instance, Green and Ward (2004)

---

[10]   *Doe et al. v. Unocal Corporation et al.*, 110 F. Supp. 2d 1294 (C.D. Cal. 2000).
[11]   *Wiwa v. Royal Dutch Petroleum Co. et al.*, 226 F. 3d 88 (2nd Cir. 2000).

report that British Aerospace willingly delivered Hawk fighter-bombers to the Indonesian army, apparently aware that these would be used against the civilian population in putting down the uprising against the Indonesian occupation of East Timor in the 1970s. In 1997, the British corporation Sandline International shipped weapons to Sierra Leone in breach of a UN embargo (Whyte 2003).

In general, however, trade corporations may aid dictatorial regimes to stay in power. For instance, various oil companies have allegedly misused the UN *oil-for-food* programme that was supposed to enable the Iraqi government to trade oil for food and medicine for its starving population. The companies made secret deals to profit from this programme and paid kickbacks to Saddam Hussein and his associates.[12]

Finally, even more indirect relations between the activities of corporations and the occurrence of international crimes can be established. For example, corporations may benefit in other ways from violent conflicts in which international crimes are committed. They may benefit from the increase of prices and demand of certain goods and services in situations of conflict and war; they may take advantage of the situation by illegally exploiting natural resources. Another form of involvement is the investment in corporations which make products used to commit international crimes, such as weapons that kill a lot of civilian victims. Following up on the Oslo Declaration on Cluster Munitions of 22–23 February 2007, Belgium became the first country to make it a crime to invest in companies that make cluster bombs. This would prohibit banks from offering credit to cluster bomb makers and from owning shares or bonds in these companies. Recently, financial institutions and investment funds in Belgium, the Netherlands and France announced that they would no longer invest in companies that produce cluster bombs.

The above examples illustrate that corporate involvement in international crime can range from being a direct offender to more indirect relations across a broader range of human rights abuses and other violations of international law. These empirical findings do not answer the normative questions – which forms constitute international crime and to what extent corporations can be held accountable? As outlined in paragraph 2, the delineated definition of international crime determines which of these possible forms of involvement can be seen as corporate international crime.

---

[12]   Preston J. and J. Miller, a Texan is indicted in Iraq oil sales by Hussein aides, *New York Times*, 15 April 2005.

4. EXPLANATIONS

4.1. CORPORATE CRIME THEORY

To what extent are general theories on corporate crime applicable to the involvement of corporations in international crimes? Studies on corporate crime have pointed out the significance of the fact that the crimes are committed in the context of an organisation. Many criminologists argue that corporate crime should be studied in the light of organisational sciences. After all, the findings on 'normal' organisational behaviour could also apply to deviant corporate behaviour. 'Corporate crime is *organisational* crime and explaining it requires an *organisational* level of analysis' (Kramer 1982). These organisational studies show how organisational characteristics or shortcomings can lie at the root of corporate crime. Other studies show how the characteristics of the branch or market, or even unclear regulations and inadequate enforcement can create opportunities for corporate crime.

In criminological literature on corporate crime, several theoretical frameworks for the explanation of corporation crime have been developed (Clinard and Yeager 1980; Box 1983; Coleman 1987; Cohen 1995; Huisman 2001). Most of these models contain three central elements that have to be present for corporate crime to occur: motivation, opportunity and lack of control. Motivation is often found in the culture of competition and corporate strategy. Some criminologists say that the goal of making profit makes corporations inherently criminogenic (Punch 1996). Opportunities are found in the availability of illegal means to achieve corporate goals. A lack of control can be due to inadequate regulatory enforcement or the absence of internal compliance systems.

Shover and Bryant (1993) argue that explanations for organisational crime can be found on several aggregate levels: the micro level of the individual employee or manager, the meso level of the organisation and the macro level of the branch of industry or the political economy. An approach at the macro level involves studying the nature of the branch or market and governmental regulation of that branch. An approach such as this would reveal the extent to which certain characteristics of the institutional environment create – or limit – opportunities for violation. To understand organisational crime committed by transnational corporations, Rothe and Mullins (in this book) add a *supra* macro level of analysis: the international level of the globalising economy.

However, a macro approach to corporate compliance could not explain why – given a certain opportunity structure – some corporations take advantage of these opportunities and others do not. The macro perspective does not explain differences in compliance between corporations in the same branch of industry. To understand these differences, we would have to examine the corporation and its economical, social and administrative environment at the meso and micro level. Ultimately, it is individual managers or employees who take the actions that violate or comply with the law. Although the socio-psychological motives of these employees can be interesting, it is important to realise that their behaviour is determined by the organisational context in which they work. Organisational science shows that the organisation plays a major role in shaping and directing the behaviour of individuals within an organisation (Coleman 2002). Therefore, the focus of most corporate crime studies is on the meso level of the organisation and its direct environment.

Integrative models for understanding corporate crime usually contain the three central elements for the three levels of analysis (Huisman 2001). Kramer and Michalowski (1990) developed such an integrative model for the explanation of state-corporate crime. Their model is based on the proposition that criminal or deviant behaviour at the organisational level results from a coincidence of pressure for goal attainment, availability and perceived attractiveness of illegitimate means, and an absence of effective social control. At the macro level, the element of motivation is 'operationalised' by the culture of competition which puts economic pressure on the meso level of corporations to set ambiguous targets that provide neutralisation on the micro level of managers to violate rules in order to attain these targets. At the macro level, the element of opportunity may provide illegal means to achieve goals, while at the meso level the allocation of means by the internal structure is inadequate relative to an organisation's goals, thereby increasing the likelihood that individual employees will perceive these illegal means as more available or more attractive than legal means to achieve the corporation's goals. The element of the 'operationality' of control means that at the macro level legal, political and social control of corporate behaviour is missing, while at the meso level an internal structure and culture of compliance is failing, resulting in a corporate culture in which the personal morality of individual managers or employees is strongly oriented towards achieving goals and rationalising the use of illegal means to do so, while the direct social control of colleagues sanctions the violation of this informal norm. An important task for the criminology of international crime would be to fill in this model with empirical data specifically for the explanation of the involvement of corporations with international crimes. Such an attempt is beyond the scope of this paper, but some first explorations could be made.

Since most known cases of involvement of corporations with international crime are situated in developing countries and/or during armed conflict, one would expect that opportunity and lack of control are strong explanatory factors. International embargoes lead to a stark increase of prices, armed conflicts lead to an increased demand for weapons and other products used for suppression, and corrupt governments create opportunities to illegally exploit natural resources.

Instead of monitoring corporate behaviour, these regimes are willing to protect corporate interest by force, abusing human rights if necessary. More to the point, while national legal systems in developing countries hardly possess laws regulating business and lack regulatory enforcement, international law and its enforcement do not provide a safety net – yet.

Given the profit motive, one would expect that the opportunities and the lack of control present in developing countries (especially in situations of armed conflict) would automatically result in corporate crime. On the other hand, it could be pondered whether the profit motive is strong enough to get involved in such heinous acts as gross human rights abuses. In the next paragraph the element of motive will be discussed in the context of involvement in international crimes.

In the following paragraphs, two elements will be discussed that seem to be especially relevant for the understanding of corporate involvement in international crimes and which have been touched upon several times in the preceding section. The first is the role that states and governmental agents play in corporate involvement in international crimes. The second element concerns the already mentioned supra macro level of the globalisation of business.

4.2. MOTIVATION AND NEUTRALISATION

Naturally, ample opportunity and lack of control influences the motive of corporations to get involved in actions that might constitute complicity in committing international crime: it also means easy profit. However, as stated above, this *de facto* opportunity structure does not explain why some corporations choose unethical behaviour and others do not. Assuming corporations and their executives are generally strongly committed to the central normative structure, every corporate agent has to cross a moral threshold to be able to violate laws or ethical norms. One could argue that this moral threshold is even higher with a potential international crime. To maintain an identity of being a respectable corporate executive, a corporate offender has to adjust the 'normative lens' through which society would view his behaviour. In their classic study, Sykes and Matza (1957) showed that delinquents adjust this normative lens by using techniques of neutralisation that deny the seriousness of the offence and the blameworthiness of the offender. As Coleman (1987) pointed out so clearly, neutralisation techniques are not only *post hoc* rationalisations of white collar crime, but can also precede rule breaking and thereby morally facilitate non-compliance. 'A rationalisation is not an after–the-fact excuse that someone invents to justify his or her behaviour but an integral part of the actor's motivation for the act' (Coleman 1987, 411). This would lead to the assumption that having neutralisation techniques at one's disposal is a crucial condition for corporate managers to get involved in international crimes. Besides the obvious opportunities and limited control mechanisms, these neutralisation techniques could be an important object of study when doing research on corporations and international crimes.

Coleman constructed a typology of the techniques of neutralisation used by white collar criminals. One of the most common techniques is the denial of harm. According to Coleman, the convicted white collar offender frequently claims that their action did not harm anyone and that they therefore did not do anything wrong. A second neutralisation technique used by white collar offenders is to claim that the laws they are violating are unnecessary or even unjust. Offenders using this rationalisation find support in the influential neo-liberal Chicago school of economics which argues that market systems can only operate at a maximum efficiency when there are no artificial barriers such as government regulation (Friedman 1962; Posner 1976). 'The state has no role except to get out of the way' (Snider 2000, 182). A third neutralisation is that the violation of regulation is necessary to achieve vital economic goals or just to survive. A fourth technique of neutralisation involves transfer of responsibility from the offender to a larger group. The next argument of this 'everybody's doing it' rationalisation is that it is unfair to condemn one violator unless all other violators are condemned as well. The fifth neutralisation method is that a person is not responsible for his behaviour – who therefore cannot qualify as a criminal – when merely conforming to the expectations of others.

In a study on methods which accounts convicted white collar offenders used to justify or excuse their behaviour, Benson (1985 and 1998) identified three general patterns in accounting strategies: accounts oriented toward the offence, accounts toward the offender and accounts toward the denouncer. Accounts that focus on the offence either emphasise the normality and general acceptability of the behaviour ('business as usual') or portray the offence as an aberration, not representative of typical behaviour patterns. When the perpetrator himself is the subject of the account, he will try to show that no matter how the offence is eventually characterised, it is not indicative of his true character. Perpetrators must show that they are ordinary, understandable individuals and separate themselves from their offence and emphasise its unique character. Accounts that aim at the denouncer condemn the condemners. For example, the offender might claim prosecutors are motivated by personal interest rather than a desire to defend social or legal values and that they were singled out for political reasons that had nothing to do with the harmfulness of their behaviour.

Which neutralisation techniques could be expected to be used for reducing the seriousness of corporate involvement in international crimes and the blameworthiness of a corporation?

That would depend, of course, on the type of crime and the form of involvement. Nevertheless, while all techniques used for neutralising corporate crime could be relevant, several might be particularly applicable to corporate involvement in international crime. Corporations active in conflict zones, countries with corrupt governments and countries where widespread human rights violations occur, might say that their actions should be viewed through another normative lens and that the norms and values applicable in developed, Western societies are not suitable for judging their behaviour ('This is Africa'). They might emphasise that their way of operating is 'normal' in the countries and situations in which they are operating – everybody's doing it. They also may point to the fact that legislation regulating business is lacking in these countries, so technically they are not breaking any legal rules. On the other hand, corporate executives that are somehow more directly associated with acts that constitute international crime might emphasise the unusualness of the situation and that they would normally never get involved in this kind of action. In the scarce cases that corporations or corporate representatives are prosecuted for complicity in committing international crimes, the offenders would probably complain about the arbitrary selection of the case and the fact that many corporations commit the same acts without being targeted. Perhaps the most active denouncers of misconduct of international corporations are NGOs, such as Amnesty International, Human Rights Watch and Global Witness. Corporation accounts aimed at these denouncers might attack the selective and politically driven activities of NGOs, whose principal concern may be to maintain a high profile for their particular campaigns and not to ensure that corporations are held equally to account (Muchlinski, 2003). Furthermore, executives of multinational corporations might be able to deny any harm because of the 'time-space-gap' between decisions in the corporate board room and the victimisation of which the cause might eventually be qualified as an international crime. This gap might span continents and many years, not only providing rationalisation but also effectively limiting the attribution of legal causality (Vande Walle 2005).

In the scarce literature on neutralisation in the context of white collar or corporate crime, it is generally assumed that neutralisation techniques are not the result of individuals' unique personalities, but that they are provided by or shaped in the organisational setting in which a corporate agent operates (Shover and Bryant 1993, 158–159; Slapper and Tombs 1999, 119). Benson (1985 and 1998) stresses that neutralisations should not be thought of as solely individual inventions, but they are invented by and in a historical and institutional context. Furthermore, many features of corporate organisation – such as the diffusion of responsibility – facilitate the building of these 'metaphysical escapes' (Benson 1985, 1998).

When neutralisation techniques are crucial for corporate involvement in international crime, also the context in which these techniques evolve is an important object of study. The neutralisation techniques used to justify corporate crime as described in the literature are generally attributed to the culture of competence characteristic for corporate capitalism, the diffusion of responsibility within corporations and criminogenic corporate cultures. To understand the techniques of neutralisation used to justify corporate involvement in international crimes, it is also necessary to study the specific historical, institutional and cultural context in which these are created. Here, we could point at two elements of this context. First, since the moral ambiguity that generally surrounds corporate crime (Nelken 2002) is enhanced by corporate cultures, this will be even more so in the *cultural* context in which international crimes are committed. Doing business in countries where armed conflict roars, corruption is rife and human dignity has little value, might influence the moral standards businessmen apply to evaluate their own actions. Second, techniques of neutralisation might be facilitated by the government. The fact that governments provide ample opportunity due to a lack of business regulation or by showing willingness to suppress any opposition against corporate interests, might also provide techniques of neutralisation for corporations.

4.2. THE ROLE OF THE STATE

According to the integrative theoretical models, corporate crime is likely to occur where there is a failure of social control, combined with opportunity and motivation. Nation states are responsible for exercising control on corporations by regulating business and enforcing these regulations by actively inspecting compliance and sanctioning non-compliance. Corporate involvement in international crime is state-facilitated when this social control is lacking. In paragraph 2 state-facilitated corporate crime was defined as the failure of government regulatory agencies to restrain deviant business activities. This failure might be due to negligence, but it might also be an intentional strategy to attract foreign corporations. According to Matthews and Kauzlarich (2000), corporate crime might also be initiated by the state. State-initiated corporate crime occurs when corporations, employed by the government, engage in organisational crime at the direction or with the tacit approval of the government.

Green and Ward (2004) place both forms of state involvement in corporate crime on a continuum: the degree of state involvement determines when it qualifies as state-initiated. As an example, they describe the case of the Nigerian oil industry as a case of state-initiated crime. The Nigerian state is directly involved in formal joint ventures with oil mining corporations. In protecting the interests of the oil corporations by violently repressing local dissent, atrocities are committed either by state security forces themselves or by private security forces who are trained by state security forces. Furthermore, agencies of criminal justice have been specifically employed by the state to eliminate leaders of protest movements against the oil industry, which led to the execution of Nobel Prize winner Saro-Wiwa and other members of the MOSOP (Green and Ward 2004, 34). The role of states in crimes that are committed in association with the trade of arms may vary from state-facilitated to state-initiated. States may condone or ignore arms transfers to embargoed states but they may also actively promote arms trade, for instance by providing export credits or manufacturing subsidies. Also the exploitation of natural resources might qualify as State-initiated corporate crime when states invite corporations to extract or purchase these resources and help them to circumvent trade embargoes.

The concept of state-corporate crime was developed to study forms of corporate crime in which the state played an integral role. The concept reflects the fulfilment of the mutually agreed objectives of a public agency and a private entity achieved through cooperative illegal activity (Friedrichs 2007a, 147). The study of state-corporate crime rests on the premise that on the one hand, in order to operate, the modern corporation requires a particular legal, economic and political infrastructure which is provided by governments, while on the other hand, governments in capitalist states depend on corporations to supply goods and services, provide an economic base and support government policies (Harper and Israel, 1999). Most cases of corporate crime are state-initiated or state-facilitated. 'A trawl of literature (largely non-criminological) reveals a great many cases where corporations and States have colluded in criminal enterprise for mutual benefit' (Green and Ward 2004, 29). A small group of American criminologists have applied the concept of State-corporate crime to a number of cases that occurred in the United States or involved American corporations.[13] Although these studies have greatly contributed to the understanding of the role of the state in the occurrence of corporate crime, this American focus could create a tendency to generalise from the experience of one country in which crimes of the State are reduced to crimes of the United States (Harper and Israel, 1999). However, the list of corporate crime cases that are state-facilitated of state-initiated can easily be extended by cases from other countries.

For instance, in most cases of corporate crime in the Netherlands, discussed by Van de Bunt and Huisman (2007), Dutch governmental agencies culpably contributed to the occurrence of corporate crime. In Dutch criminology, the concept of 'collusion' was especially applied to enable the understanding of this role of state authorities (Van den Heuvel 1998). A committee of inquiry on the low levels of regulatory compliance in several branches of industry pointed to

---

[13]   Most of these are reprinted in Michalowski and Kramer, 2006.

insufficient motivation on the part of the government to force corporations to comply with the law as one of the causes of non-enforcement (*Commissie bestuursrechtelijke en privaatrechtelijke handhaving,* 1998). This can be traced to the institutionalised tradition of organised cooperation between the Dutch government, employers and labour unions, aimed at reaching agreements rather than conflict, an approach officially labelled the '*Poldermodel*' that was praised by former US President Bill Clinton as an inspiration of his 'Third Way' (Van de Bunt and Huisman 2007). The result is that Dutch government bodies are in many ways dependent on the commitment of corporations to realise their goals. A criminogenic side-effect is an obscure web of shared interests and secret understandings that can be characterised as 'collusion'. The small number of cases of corruption by public authorities in the Netherlands (Huberts and Nelen 2005) may well be related to widespread collusion: it is not even necessary to bribe enforcers and other public authorities in the Netherlands because they are already perfectly willing to keep in mind the interests and views of corporations.

Also, the relationship between a large multinational corporation and a weak government of a developing country may be very different to that between a Federal government department in the United States or any other developed country and its contractors (Harper and Israel 1999). The desire for development through foreign investment often resulted in developing countries ending up dependent on investment by foreign corporations. This dependence might lead a government to sacrifice the environment and the human rights of its population to economic development. This dependence will increase in situations of armed conflict: then the revenues of foreign investment are needed to keep the war effort going. Dependency on foreign investment is also strong in countries with a large financial debt, as is the case in almost all developing countries. According to Barnhizer, 'the debt service obligation almost compels governments to look the other way when foreign and domestic investors offer some hope of increasing economic development and hard currency earnings from foreign trade' (Barnhizer 2001, 146–147).

Further, strong dependence arises in large projects in which a government of a developing country is directly doing business with a large corporation: such as the building of a gas pipe by the military junta in Burma and the US-based electrical corporation Unocal and the Ok Tedi mining project and Australia's largest mining corporation Broken Hill Pty in Papua New Guinea (Harper and Israel 1999). In these cases, governments might even be willing to change the law so that the operations of this specific corporation is not restricted by regulation that would be violated, while the actions of its civilians directed against the corporation might be criminalised, as happened in the Ok Tedi case (Harper and Israel 1999).

The privileged positions of corporations with exclusive contracts or joint ventures with state-organs might also lead to strong personal relationships between corporate executives and politicians or public officials. These personal relationships might further facilitate corporate crime. Allegedly, Liberian president Charles Taylor and Gus Kouwenhoven, director of Liberia's biggest logging companies OTC and RTC had such a relationship. 'Taylor and Mr. Gus were close friends', told the former management-assistant of OTC to a reporter of the Dutch newspaper, *Trouw*. 'They often stayed together here on the complex and played volleyball or went fishing'. The reporter also describes how these logging companies paid large kickbacks to Taylor and his accomplices to obtain logging concessions.[14] Often, these personal relationships go hand in hand with corruption. The desire to generate foreign exchange at an institutional level will coincide with the desire of individual political and corporate elites to gain personal profit. In general, a high level of corruption may facilitate corporate involvement in international crime. Corporations will be able to pay off officials to deflect any unfavourable governmental reactions to their harmful business activities. They may also be able to let governmental forces do the dirty work deemed necessary to protect corporate interests. For example, in Nigeria, a representative of the oil company Chevron was allegedly seen giving money to governmental soldiers, after having shot and killed protesters who had occupied one of Chevron's oil platforms (Green and Ward 2004, 38–39). The countries in which international crimes are frequently committed also score very low on the corruption index of Transparency International (2007).

Not surprisingly, corporate involvement in international crimes occurs in countries with dictatorial political systems. In such a system there is no democratic control of the deals that the regime is making with corporations and the ways in which the government facilitates corporate interest and the destination of the revenues of such cooperation.

The preceding section might create the impression that especially developing countries in the Third World play a guilty role in facilitating or committing international crimes for corporate interests. However, in the case of the involvement in international crimes by transnational corporations, besides the host country, at least one other country can also be facilitating or instigating corporate crime: the country in which the corporation is based, which would not be an offshore island where the corporation is officially registered, but the country in which its headquarters is actually located. Facilitating features can also be attributed to these, most often developed, home countries.

Some countries apply extra-territoriality to their laws and are willing to prosecute nationals for the crimes that they have committed in other countries,

---

14   Arjen van der Ziel, 'Tropisch hout met bloed eraan' (Tropical wood stained with blood), *Trouw*, 3 September 2003.

especially when these are criminalised by international criminal law. However, many other countries show reticence in regulating the acts that their national corporations conduct abroad. For political or economic reasons they might condone the behaviour of their corporate nationals which has harmful effects in other countries. For instance, maintaining a national arms industry may contribute to the political status and independent defence capacity. But upholding this defence industry may decrease inhibitions towards less reputable customers of this industry. Phythian (2000) describes the British government's failure to control arms exports by corporations in Crown dependencies, allowing British corporations to export arms at will, despite embargoes. For example, in 1994 the British Mil-Tec Corporation exported over US$5.5 million worth of arms to the genocidal Hutu regime in Rwanda. In 1997 the British-based company Sandline International shipped arms to Sierra Leone, in breach of a UN embargo but seemingly with the approval of the UK Foreign and Commonwealth Office (Green and Ward 2004, 36; Whyte 2003, 586).

Home states may also more actively support activities of transnational corporations that might result in the commission of international crimes, for example by deregulating or introducing regulations that facilitate rather than restrain, or by frustrating legal actions that are taken against their corporate nationals. For instance, Whyte (2003) argues that the regulation of private military corporations as proposed by the British government will lead to the expansion of a sector in which illegalities and human rights abuses abound and therefore will probably encourage rather than control the incidence of state-corporate crimes. The Canadian government was heavily criticised for trying to intervene in a lawsuit brought against its biggest oil and gas exploration and production company Talisman by the Presbyterian Church of Sudan on behalf of residents of southern Sudan for complicity in committing international crimes.[15]

4.3.   GLOBALISATION

A corporation committing international crimes is not a new phenomenon. Above, the case of I.G. Farben during the Second World War has already been mentioned. And even the Dutch East Indies Company – often cited as being the first multinational corporation in the world – was responsible for the genocide of the entire population of the spice islands' Banda Island in 1621 (Van den Berg 1995).

---

[15]   Larry Neumeister, 'Judge lets Talisman genocide case proceed despite warnings form Canada, U.S.', *The Canadian Press*, 2 August 2007.

However, one could get the impression that the problem of corporate involvement in international crimes is on the rise. Most cases of human rights abuses by corporations reported by NGOs concern multinational corporations. Also, the relation between transnational corporations and human rights is a topic of many academic publications (see for an extensive bibliography, Rumsey 2006).

The rise of transnational corporations and their impact on the economies of states, especially in developing countries, is seen as a result of a process of globalisation. Globalisation as a concept refers both to the compression of the world and the intensification of consciousness of the world as a whole (Robertson 1992). Because of the increasing mobility of people, capital, goods and information, it appears as if the world is getting smaller. As the world is shrinking, both time and space are compressed (Harvey 1989). The world is becoming a 'global village'. Globalisation also means a process of cultural unification, in which Western capitalist culture is seen as dominant and alternative, traditional cultures come under pressure.

Most authors in the field of criminology regard globalisation as a criminogenic development. Gobert and Punch (2003) point out that more and more multinational corporations are shifting the criminogenic and potentially lethal aspects of their business operation to foreign subsidiaries located in developing states. Besides the reason of saving labour costs, Gobert and Punch state that another impetus for locating a subsidiary in a developing country may be the perception that the prospect of civil suits or criminal prosecutions is substantially lower in the developing country than would be the case in the home state of the parent corporation.

Snider (2000) points at the massive growth in the size, power and profitability of the corporate sector. The sales revenue of many large corporations has become bigger than the GDPs of several developed countries, let alone developing countries. Combined with the increased possibilities to escape state regulation as a result of globalisation, this growth in power has created a certain degree of 'sovereignty' of large transnational corporations. 'The sovereign transnational corporation has claimed the right to maximise profits, downsize at will, destroy union and hire the cheapest labour worldwide' (Snider 2000, 189).

According to Passas (1999), globalisation multiplies, intensifies and activates 'criminogenic asymmetries' that lie at the root of corporate crime. Passas defines these asymmetries as 'structural disjunctions, mismatches and inequalities in the spheres of politics, culture, the economy and the law'. These are criminogenic in that they offer illegal opportunities, create motives to use these opportunities and make it possible for offenders to get away with it. For instance, globalisation created the possibility to transport toxic waste to Third World countries where it could be disposed of at a fraction of the cost and without the threat of law enforcement. Illicit opportunities are produced by the fragmentation of enterprises and transactions over more than one country. Price asymmetries create the incentive to move hazardous business activities to other countries. In addition, regulatory asymmetries create the opportunity to cut costs on environmental management and labour conditions while law enforcement asymmetries weaken social controls. Even more, globalisation has fostered 'competitive deregulation'. Competition on global markets has driven corporations to a 'race to the bottom' to find low cost services provided through poor environmental standards, low wages and poor working conditions. As a consequence, large transnational corporations are relocating their production to countries offering more favourable terms (Fokwa, 2004). Developing countries which need regulation to protect their natural resources, the health and safety of its working population and the integrity of its financial system, instead try to attract foreign corporations by regulating less tightly than other countries. Passas emphasises that the illicit opportunities created by globalisation are not counterbalanced by international forms of control of multinational enterprises; here, he sees an important task for international criminal law.

A criminological analysis of globalisation shows that it creates opportunities and motives for multinational corporations to commit crimes and it reduces the possibilities of combating these crimes. The world is small enough for corporations to conduct business on a global level, but it is too big for authorities to expand their control over business. Furthermore, the time-space-compression has created the possibilities for corporations to act globally, but the world is still big enough to hide from the consequences. In her study on corporate crime in the pharmaceutical industry, Vande Walle (2002) discovered that there is still a considerable gap in time and space between the decision in the board room of a Western pharmaceutical company and the women and children that are dying because of illicit testing of medicines in far away countries many years later. So globalisation is providing opportunities to commit corporate crimes, but it is not taking away the neutralisation techniques for corporate managers to take the decisions that in the end will result in serious human rights abuses.

These criminological observations on the harmful effects of the globalisation of transnational business are in line with Marxist inspired literature on the devastating and deteriorating economic realities for most developing countries (Gilpin 1987). In contrast, neo-liberal theory holds that globalisation will lead to economic development and that political and civil rights will expand as countries develop economically (Gilpin 1987). This leads Letner (2004) to ask the question: are transnational corporations 'engines of development' or 'tools of exploitation'? Part of this controversy can be explained by the methodology applied in these two research camps. The former employs corporate and country case studies to illustrate numerous examples of corporations' human rights violations while the latter applies statistical analysis at the national level and finds positive correlations between foreign direct investment and second-generation economic and social rights.

During the last decade, Letner (2004) and others (Meyer 1998; Dunning 1993) have tried to bridge the gap between these to apparently contradictory research traditions. The question they ask is not *if* but *when* are corporations to be regarded as engines for development and when are they to be regarded as tools for exploitation? Two lessons for the study of corporate international crime can be derived from this. First, a combined strategy of statistical analyses and country and corporate-based case studies, is necessary to unravel the complex relationship between corporations and human rights. Second, the impact of transnational corporations on human rights' conditions in the host country and the occurrence of international crimes is likely to be conditional on a number of country, industry and firm-specific variables. For a better understanding of why corporations get involved in international crimes, these variables should be identified in case studies.

Therefore it is necessary not only to study cases in which corporations ended up participating in unethical behaviour. Criminologists tend to look at the *dark side* of man and studying international crime is as dark as it gets. In order to obtain a better insight into the processes that lead to non-compliance, Braithwaite's (1985) study on the coal mining industry shows the usefulness of also studying compliance. Braithwaite tried to determine the organisational differences between coal mining companies that often violated occupational safety and health regulations and those that showed great willingness to comply with regulations. Assuming that not all corporations operating in developing countries and/or countries in armed conflicts are engaged in human rights abuses, and knowing the criminogenic opportunity structures that exist in those countries, it would be very relevant to learn about the restraints that keep these corporations on the right track. By studying their implementation of the concept of corporate social responsibility, we could also learn more about the effectiveness of voluntary instruments like the Guidelines of the Organization for Economic Co-operation and Development (OECD) and the UN Global Compact, as an alternative to international criminal law.

5. CONCLUSION

This paper focused on the involvement of corporations in acts that might constitute an international crime. In the literature on international law, much has recently been written on the moral and legal responsibilities of corporations towards human rights. In criminology, the concept of state-corporate crime captures much of the phenomena discussed in this paper.

However, the overlap of these fields of study, a criminological focus on corporate acts that result in breaches of international law, is rather new. Therefore, this paper is of an explorative nature and raises more questions than it answers on the issues of defining and explaining corporate involvement in international crimes.

When trying to define the object of the study, neither law nor criminology offers much clarity. Criminology offers a choice between legalistic and sociological definitions of crime but in doing so also forces the taking of sides in an ideological debate on the definition of crime. Studying the rapid development of international law applicable to the acts of corporations leaves open the question whether the term crime should only apply to core crimes of international criminal law, other violations of international law or also the non-compliance with the growing body of standards in 'soft law' schemes that address transnational corporations. And although many legal scholars support the notion of moral responsibility of corporations, the attribution of liability for corporate involvement in international crimes is limited to the local level of – an increasing number of – national states.

But even when applying the strictest definition of corporate involvement, the empirical evidence available and discussed in this paper, clearly uncovers corporate involvement in international crime as real. '(...) [P]rima facie, there is a problem: multinationals can take part in alleged violations of human rights' (Muchlinski 2001, 31). Therefore, more empirical research is needed on the prevalence and harm of corporate involvement in international crimes, the setting in which this occurs and the organisational, economical, political and cultural conditions that contribute to this occurrence. This is not only relevant to understand the nature and scale of the problem, but it might also help to solve the conceptual, theoretical and normative problems that surround this phenomenon.

First, studying the various appearances of corporate involvement in international crimes and their prevalence, might contribute to formulate more fitting definitions of corporate international crime. Second, committing or being complicit in committing international crimes can qualify as a species of corporate crime. Criminological theory on corporate crime is useful to understand corporate international crime, but there is also a need for accentuating theories to explain the international crimes of corporations. Corporate crime theories that have mainly been developed in the national context of American business have also proven their applicability for understanding corporate crime in other Western capitalist economies, but have also shown their limitations (Van de Bunt and Huisman 2007). The empirical testing of existing theories might also sharpen these theories for forms of corporate crime in different contexts.

Third, abundant empirical evidence on corporate involvement in acts that constitute a crime under international law might support the conception that corporations should be recognised as perpetrators under international criminal law. This would also reduce the moral ambiguities that surround harmful corporate behaviour. Convincing empirical evidence could even influence the evaluation of the jurisdiction of the International Criminal Court scheduled in 2009 and the expansion of this jurisdiction to acts of legal persons.

The results of research on corporate involvement in international crimes might not only contribute to the acknowledgement of corporate criminal liability, but it might even form an empirical basis for the legal construction of corporate criminal liability in international criminal law. The idea of an empirical basis for the legal construction of corporate criminal liability is already supported by Dutch legal scholars who propose that insights into corporate decision-making derived from criminology and organisational science form a better basis to attribute *mens rea* to corporate criminal liability than the artificial, unsatisfactory construction that has been developed in jurisprudence (Roef and De Roos 1998; De Hullu 2000; Rense 2005). But before such an influence of empirical research on legal debate is justified much research on the involvement of corporations in international crimes has to been done. Such research could start with systematically assessing the business interests that are at stake in armed conflicts and other situations in which gross human rights violations are committed and identifying the corporate actors that are after these interests.

IX. DESTRUCTIVE BELIEFS: GENOCIDE AND THE ROLE OF IDEOLOGY

Alex ALVAREZ

> 'Thus, the primary driving force leading to genocide is not the pathology of individuals organizing and committing the genocide, but the pathology of the ideas guiding them.' (Anzulovic 1999, 4)

1.   INTRODUCTION

Our understanding of genocide has come a long way in recent years. Scholars have increasingly identified many of the various mechanisms and processes that are crucial in providing for the development and implementation of genocides (See for example Alvarez 2001; Jones 2006; Mann 2005). We now realize that, in many ways, genocide appears to be a very contradictory phenomenon. It is both rational and irrational, purposeful yet senseless, sane and insane, all at the same time. This contradictory nature is perhaps best illustrated when we examine the motivations and beliefs that lead to the perpetration of this crime.

On the one hand, genocide typically appears to be motivated by a government deciding that a specific population group must be removed from the national community and then organizing the necessary logistics and resources to accomplish that destructive goal. While the specific context may vary from case to case, this underlying rationality almost always appears to be present. Yet on the other hand, the apparently sane if reprehensible decision to destroy a population and the coherent steps needed to implement that decision often rests, not only on rational and understandable reasons, but also on irrational and emotional perceptions and arguments derived from a number of historic myths, stereotypes, xenophobia, and various other beliefs and attitudes. These affective perceptual elements are often crucial in guiding and shaping the otherwise pragmatic decision making process. We shouldn't be surprised at this. Recent research indicates that emotional elements are an integral part of all reasoning processes (See for example Long & Brecke 2003), or as David Hume once wrote, 'Reason alone can never produce any action or give rise to volition (…). Reason is, and ought to be, the slave of passions, and can never pretend to any other office than to serve and obey them' (Hume 1948, 24–25). In other words, the ostensibly logical and rational thought processes of political leaders who pursue genocidal policies are largely shaped and guided by non-logical and irrational emotions that serve to justify the violence. It is a kind of rational irrationality. This emotive component of genocide is frequently overlooked, yet is nevertheless an important aspect to this crime.

This chapter comprises a brief exploration of the roles that these underlying ideas and beliefs play in facilitating the genocidal process. These belief systems or ideologies, as they are more appropriately known, play a significant role in providing the non-intellectual and non-rational elements necessary for any genocide to take place. In other words, while a government may ostensibly be motivated by clear political, economic, and/or social interests in pursuing genocidal policies, that motivation is generally supported and legitimated by various ideologies that provide the necessary justification for the wholesale killing of men, women, and children from within a targeted victim group. Unfortunately, much of the existing scholarship on genocide either ignores or downplays the role that ideology plays in enabling the violence. One exception to this general rule is found in the work of Ervin Staub who does suggest that ideologies are, 'almost always a part of the genocidal process' (Staub 2003, 353), while another exception is found in the work of the sociologist Helen Fein, whose ideas are worth exploring further.

2. TYPOLOGY OF GENOCIDE

Helen Fein, a leading scholar of genocide, has suggested four primary types of genocide in terms of motivation: Developmental; Despotic; Ideological; and Retributive (Charny 1999). Developmental genocides encompass those in which the targeted groups are seen as an impediment to the colonization or the resource exploitation of a given geographic area. This happens most often against indigenous peoples who have sometimes been perceived as being in the way of progress. In Central and South America, for example, many native peoples have been subjected to genocidal policies as a number of states have attempted to remove them from land found to contain oil, gold, and/or other valuable resources (Churchill 1997; Hitchcock & Twedt 1997; Jones 2006). Despotic genocides, on the other hand, involve situations in which a government uses genocide as a weapon against rivals for political power. Joseph Stalin, for example, worked hard to destroy members of various political, economic, and national groups because they were perceived to be a threat to his consolidation of power (Conquest 1990; Dolot 1985; Rogovin 1998). This included many of his former allies among the Bolsheviks. Dictatorships are invariably concerned with the concentration of power and this particular type of genocide is primarily intended to remove any obstacles to that locus of control. Ideological genocide concerns the attempted destruction of a population because of a system of belief or beliefs. For obvious reasons, this kind of genocide is the most overtly ideological type since they occur because members of a society, especially those in political power, hold true to ideas that encourage them to attempt to eliminate a population. Perhaps the best example of this is the Holocaust in which the Nazis held a number of scientific and medical beliefs about the supposed racial superiority of the Aryan people (Alvarez 2002; Burleigh & Wippermann 1991; Friedlander 1995; Weindling 2000; Weiss 1996). In this world view, the Jews, the Gypsies, and the Slavs were a threat to the genetic purity of the Aryan race and the Nazi answer to this ideological imperative was genocide. Similarly, the genocide in Cambodia during the 1970s is also an example of an ideologically motivated genocide since the Khmer Rouge were attempting to create an idealized and utopian Cambodian state that combined self-sufficiency and ethnic purity. In order to wipe the slate clean and create this new type of society, the regime set about killing anyone who was perceived as a foreign or corrupting influence (Jackson 1989; Kiernan 1996). Last in Fein's typology, are Retributive genocides in which genocide is perpetrated by one group against another to protect or change a hierarchical and stratified political and/or social order. The Rwandan genocide is illustrative of this type of genocide since the violence was initiated by Hutu government extremists intent on preserving power and privilege against the Tutsi minority population who, in the past had enjoyed a dominant position relative to the Hutu majority (Des Forges 1999; Taylor 1999).

Helen Fein's typologies indicate that genocides are perpetrated for understandable reasons. Ultimately, genocide occurs because governmental officials decide that genocide is the preferred method for achieving some goal as suggested by Helen Fein's categories of genocide. While it may appear to be completely unjustified and irrational to outsiders and the larger world community, to those officials advocating the destructive policies of genocide, it makes perfect sense. Unfortunately, however, Fein's typology, as useful as it is, still relegates the role of ideology onto the margins of genocidal activity since it appears to suggest that ideology is only present in one type, at least as far as the primary motivation goes. It is my contention, however, that ideology is a central feature of genocide generally. All genocides have an ideological component that is integral to enabling and facilitating the perpetration of this particular form of group violence. Genocide, in other words, cannot take place without the appropriate ideological support. So what is ideology? What is this necessary prerequisite for genocide? Before proceeding we must first spend a little time defining and discussing this concept.

3.   DEFINING IDEOLOGY

Ideology is a term that was first coined by an 18th century French Enlightenment era philosopher named Antoine Destutt de Tracy who was interested in creating a 'science of ideas' that would allow for the systematic study of ideas and symbols (Love 1991; Vincent 1995). As such it has always been a very broad and ambiguous concept that has been subject to a variety of interpretations and definitions. From Marx who perceived ideology in pejorative terms of class domination, exploitation, and false consciousness to Gramsci's ideas about power and the hegemony of ideas, ideology has meant many things to many theorists and scholars. While there are many different kinds of ideologies that help us make sense of a variety of issues, the form of ideology that is most important for this paper are those which can be called political ideology (Bracher 1982; Mark 1973; Morrice 1996; Schwartzmantel 1998; Watkins 1964). Regardless of the specific kind of political ideology, they are all ultimately about the preservation of certain power differentials and to examine ideology is to study the ways in which meaning serves to establish and sustain relations of domination and subordination.

Generally speaking, however, ideology can best be understood in terms of beliefs and belief systems (van Dijk 1998). Essentially, ideologies are systems of shared beliefs, ideas, and symbols that help us make sense of the world around us. They are the commonly held symbolic forms that provide an intellectual framework of understanding necessary for us to define the world and ourselves as individuals and as groups. In short, we use ideology to tell us who we are. Van Dijk (1998) suggests that ideologies also have a basic structure that consists of:

- Membership: This defines who is a member and what is required for membership.
- Activities: This category concerns what kinds of behaviours are acceptable and expected.
- Goals: This particular element defines what the purpose of the group is in terms of what it hopes to achieve.
- Values/Norms: This relates to what is right and wrong, what can be done and what is prohibited.
- Position and Group Relations: This category delimitates who is our friend and who is our enemy.
- Resources: This last quality relates to the needs and attributes of a particular group (van Dijk 1998, 69–70).

Importantly, this schematic suggests that ideologies provide not only identity, but also meaning and purpose. They define right and wrong and can mobilize populations into action. This means that ideologies are not simply abstract symbols and ideas, but that they also manifest in behaviour. Another way of illustrating this point is suggested by the work of Elinor Scarbrough who divides ideology into two primary components. First are Core Beliefs which are made up of fundamental assumptions about the values, goals, and qualities of a population, and second are Principles of Action which related to the types of behaviours that are acceptable and which are subject to the constraints of the core beliefs (Scarbrough 1984). Ideologies, then, relate to what we believe and how we should act. Obviously, this is only a brief and somewhat superficial overview of a much more complex topic, but it should serve for our purposes.

We should also recognize that all communal life is, to some extent, ideological. Put another way, it is safe to say that ideology pervades all social life. We are, after all, social creatures who live and work within cultures and every culture makes sense of the world through various shared symbols and ideas that give meaning and purpose to life. Culture is the vehicle by which values and attitudes are transmitted, meanings ascribed to a particular group's history and myths, and behaviour dictated. In short, our cultures provide us with the intellectual and behavioural tools necessary to live in and belong to a community and it is within culture that we create our individual and group identities. Newman puts it this way when he writes:

> "The actions of individuals are not simply functions of personality types or psychological predispositions; rather, they are also a reflection of shared cultural expectations. Culture provides us with information about which of these actions are preferred, accepted, disapproved, or unthinkable at a given time." (Newman 1997, 94)

Culture, then, is a part and parcel of all social life and importantly, ideology is an inescapable part of all cultures. Thus, the cultures that human communities create are a primary source of ideology and these belief systems profoundly influence our personal identities as human beings and our perceptions of the world around us. This is the nexus where ideology connects with genocide because genocide requires a framework of beliefs that provides purpose and meaning for the destruction of a population.

To marginalize, disenfranchise, and persecute a group of people requires many citizens to accept the necessity and morality of policies of destruction and this is largely done through the manipulation of belief systems by politicians and others in order to dissimulate, persuade, and mobilize populations in a cause. The evidence indicates that most genocidal perpetrators participate because they have been convinced that their deadly work is a difficult but necessary duty for their race, tribe, ethnic group, and/or nationality (Alvarez 2001; Waller 2002; Weitz 2003). Even though we often think of them as such and describe them as monsters, genocidal killers are not generally motivated by sociopathic needs and desires, but rather because they have accepted ideologies that portray the killing as necessary, just, and moral. There are far too many perpetrators from all walks of life to ever consider that they were all somehow monsters or psychologically different from ordinary folk. Instead, we must accept that those who contribute to the destructive process are generally normal individuals who have come to accept an ideological framework that demands and justifies the elimination of a population. They are ordinary people engaged in extraordinary behaviour that is made possible because they have come to believe in the rightness and necessity of the killing. To use the language of the sociologist Jack Katz, the perpetrators see their work as a form of 'Righteous Slaughter' (Katz 1988). What Katz points out is that the actions of violent offenders are morally shaped. That is, even though they are engaged in destructive behaviour they do so in situations where they feel that what's at stake are 'dimensions of the eternal Good' (Katz 1988, 16). In other words, they are acting, as they perceive it, for noble, legitimate, and justified reasons. Perpetrators of genocide are no different. They are individuals who believe in the rightness and necessity of their actions. One Nazi put it this way, 'The sight of the dead (including women and children) is not very cheering. But we are fighting this war for the survival or non-survival of our people (...). My comrades are literally fighting for the existence of our people' (Klee, Dressen, & Riess 1988, 163), while a Rwandan perpetrator simply said that, 'I defended the members of my tribe against the Tutsi' (Prunier 1995, 247). Clearly, both these individuals felt that they were acting appropriately for just reasons.

It is important to remember that the legitimacy or illegitimacy of any particular act lies not in any intrinsic quality of the act itself, but rather in its definition. Evidence indicates that many perpetrators of crime and violence see themselves as being justified in their actions and often define their acts as a legitimate response to some perceived behavioural or ethical breach on the part of their victim. In this sense, the offender understands his or her violence as a form of social control (Black 1983), and this perception of the crime serves to assist in legitimizing the act not only to the offender but perhaps to others as well (Kennedy 1988; Skogan 1984). Writing about the guards of the concentration camps and the Soviet Gulag, Tzvetan Todorov makes this point when he writes:

> "Guards who committed atrocities never stopped distinguishing between good and evil. Their moral faculty had not withered away. They simply believed that the "atrocity" was in fact a good thing and thus not an atrocity at all – because the state, custodian of the standards of good and evil, told them so. The guards were not deprived of a moral sensibility but provided with a new one". (Todorov 1996, 129)

In other words, those who act violently against others need to feel as if they are acting legitimately and morally and ideology helps create and reinforce these arguments and consequently enables genocide to take place.

Ultimately, this kind of collective political violence requires the transformation of ordinary law abiding citizens into genocidal perpetrators and accomplices. This process can take a bit of time. Keep in mind that genocides don't just happen. It often takes months and even years of prior preparation. Hitler first took power in 1933, but it wasn't until the invasion of Poland in 1939 and especially the invasion of the Soviet Union in 1941 that the mass killing we have come to know as the Holocaust really began (Burleigh 2000). The years between Hitler's assumption of power and the Holocaust was a time when the population of Germany was fed a steady diet of propaganda that served to provide the ideological justification for the persecution and killing that was to come. The same was true in Rwanda, although not quite to the same extent. The killing that erupted in Rwanda in April of 1994 was ostensibly precipitated by the assassination of the president of Rwanda, Juvenal Habyarimana (Gourevitch 1998; Melvern 2004). For a long period of time, however, Hutu extremists had been priming the well of genocide by creating and training militias, broadcasting hate propaganda through the radio, and otherwise preparing the population for the coming violence. Similarly, Serb controlled media outlets suggested that the Bosnian Moslems were planning on attacking and enslaving the Bosnian Serbs. In many ways, this process is about creating and/or refining the ideological consciousness of a group in order to make the persecution and victimization of a group seem appropriate, justified, and even necessary. It is important to note, that these ideas which help mobilize a population are not usually created out of thin air. Instead, genocidally inclined governments and leaders often resurrect and embellish long established ideas about certain minority populations. The Jews of Germany had been among the most assimilated in all of Europe and did not appear to represent a threat. Yet the Nazis were able to tap into a deep vein of anti-Semitic thought that had long been a backdrop to European life. Even though many ordinary citizens may not have been active anti-Semites or may not even have known Jews personally, they certainly were still familiar with the many stereotypical notions of what the Jews were and what crimes and misdeeds they historically had been supposedly responsible for. The Nazis were able to capitalize upon a vast reservoir of hatred that allowed them to successfully portray the Jews as a threat to the safety and racial purity of the German people. Other examples of genocide exhibit the same pattern of targeting historically victimized minority groups such as the Tutsi in Rwanda, the Armenians in Turkey, and the indigenous peoples in North, Central, and South America. In this sense then, ideologies are utilized to mobilize populations into accepting a certain course of action and are therefore an ever-present component of genocide, even in ones that are ostensibly non-ideological.

These ideological justifications often coincide with more practical considerations that can facilitate participation such as outlined by Smeulers in her contribution to this book. She points out that some participants are driven by greed and seek to profit from the persecution while others do so to advance their career. As she rightly points out, individuals rarely act out of a single motivation, but are instead often driven by a variety of factors that work together to help produce genocidal perpetrators. Additionally, these motivations work at both the individual level and the corporate level as illustrated by Huisman in his contribution to this book. As we have established so far, genocides take place for a variety of reasons and can include economic, political, nationalistic, ethnic, and religious motivations. In every case, however, these motivations are intertwined with and buttressed by genocidal ideologies that provide the intellectual scaffolding upon which the genocide is constructed. But how do we know which ideologies are dangerous or potentially genocidal? An examination of the ideological component of historic examples of genocide suggest a number of themes that often appear to play a role in facilitating and enabling genocidal violence. For ease of discussion and narrative clarity I discuss these as separate and discrete categories, yet it is important to point out that they are often closely linked and very much interrelated. In any given example of genocide any number of the themes discussed below may be present and operating and reinforcing each other.

3.1. NATIONALISM

First, ideologies that emphasize difference rather than commonality are particularly dangerous. A good example of this kind of belief system is nationalism which refers to the perception that a group of people are united because they share certain qualities that tie them together as a national community and which sets them apart from people outside of the national body. Of all the ideologies supporting genocide, none is perhaps as pervasive or as pernicious as that of nationalism. More specifically, Michael Ignatieff defines nationalism as follows:

> "As a political doctrine, nationalism is the belief that the world's peoples are divided into nations, and that each of these nations has the right to self-determination, either as self-governing units within existing nation-states or as nation-states of their own.
> As a cultural ideal, nationalism is the claim that while men and women have many identities, it is the nation that provides them with their primary form of belonging".
> (Ignatieff 1993, 5)

In the modern era, it is the nation that has provided one of the most prevalent forms of individual and group identity and has defined who we are. The rise of the nation state involved the transference of loyalties from tangible local entities to much more amorphous and distant collectives which necessitated the development and cultivation of different kinds of loyalties. Whereas one's loyalty was once given to one's tribe, fellow villagers, or a local lord, the nation state required commitment to something greater and more distant and so nationalism was born. As Porter states, 'Nationalism did not create the modern states: rather the modern state stimulated the rise of nationalism' (Porter 1994, 123). Nationalism, in other words, is the belief that diverse people, who may even be geographically scattered, share a common heritage, community, and attributes. Nationalism therefore emphasizes such things as loyalty, affection, and allegiance to the nation. Patriotism, for example, is a product of nationalistic loyalty. Nationalism, then, has been a powerful tool for defining collective identity in the modern era. Unfortunately, it has also often been used as a primary means of differentiating ones own group from those of others. As one commentator eloquently stated, 'While the idea of nationalism may be linked to liberty and universalistic ideals, it also sometimes led to particularism, racism, totalitarianism, and destruction' (Quoted in Volkan 1997, 23).

Nationalism as an ideology is as much about who is not a member of the national community as it is about who is a member. As Therborn writes, 'Since inclusive ideologies define membership in meaningful world and thereby draw a line of demarcation between membership and non-membership, they are also ideologies of exclusion' (Therborn 1980, 25). In and of itself, this is not necessarily a problem. We often differentiate ourselves from others on the basis of various qualities. It does become a problem, however, when those differences are used to persecute others and nationalism has often been taken to indicate that one's own group is not only different, but superior as well. The Nazis, for example believed that the Jews represented a genetic threat to the purity and superiority of the German people. Even though Jews had lived in Germany for a thousand years and even though German Jews were among the most assimilated of all of Europe's Jewish populations, they were still defined as outsiders by German nationalists and Nazis who saw a threat in the very existence of the Jews. These kinds of nationalistic images are often supported by various dehumanizing and derogatory portrayals of the populations that are defined as not belonging to the national community.

Nationalist ideology has also always served to idealize the image of sacrifice, especially in defending the nation against its enemies, both foreign and internal. Genocidal governments have been very successful in harnessing this trait of nationalism. Of this issue, Ignatieff writes, 'Since killing is not to be taken lightly, it must be done for a reason that makes its perpetrator think well of himself. If violence is to be legitimated, it must be in the name of all that is best in a people, and what is better than their love of home?' (Ignatieff 1993, 9). One Argentinean perpetrator put it this way, 'What I did I did for my Fatherland, my faith, and my religion' (Feitlowitz 1998, 196), while a Bosnian Serb asserted that, 'For five hundred years we Serbs have been defending Western civilization against the Turks' (Rieff 1995, 96).These are the words of individuals who feel that their participation was done out of the best of motives; patriotism.

Nationalist ideologies serve to facilitate genocide in another way as well. Intrinsic to ideology is the perception of sovereignty and sovereign immunity which is the belief that modern governments enjoy almost absolute political independence and autonomy. This has meant that governments which have decided to eliminate populations under their political and geographic jurisdiction have historically been able to act with almost complete impunity. Consequently, the international community has been very loath to speak out, let alone intervene in the destructive affairs of other governments. While that unwillingness to speak out has slowly been changing in recent years, the notion of sovereign immunity still predominates and governs the way in which nations relate to each other. If genocide prevention is ever to take place, then, 'the obligation to stop mass murder of innocents must override the rule about not intervening in the affairs of other states' (Robertson 2002, 433).

3.2.   PAST VICTIMIZATION

Second, nationalistic xenophobia is often compounded by a sense of historic suffering and victimization that may serve to justify aggressive action. Ideologies that glorify and mythologize past victimization make it easier to victimize others because it creates and perpetuates a group self image as being a wronged and persecuted people and therefore provides a ready justification for violence directed against those defined as the former victimizer. This theme is often woven into a mythological nationalist ideology that helps to define the history of a people and also to justify violence against a former enemy. Of this process, Herb Hirsch writes, 'Nation-states in particular use, create, or respond to myths about themselves that they wish to perpetuate, and, in turn, the myths are used to justify or rationalize policies that the leadership of the state wishes to pursue' (Hirsch 1995, 26). This is precisely the process whereby memories and images of past victimization are used to justify mass violence in the present. It is a terrible irony of history that many victim groups can themselves become perpetrators. By focusing on past victimization, the violence is transformed from aggressive violence to defensive violence which is much more universally accepted and legitimated. The *génocidaires* are able to define the genocide as a necessary form of self defence perpetrated in protection of nation and family. The case of Serbia is illustrative of this type of destructive ideology. On the 15th of June, 1389 two armies faced each other across a remote plain in the south eastern corner of Europe. The plain was known as Kosovo Polje, the field of Blackbirds. On one side of the field was an Ottoman army and on the other an army composed of various

Serb Princes. The battle was largely inconclusive yet it went down in Serb history as a tremendous defeat that marked the end of a brief period of Serbian independence and ushered in an era of victimization, oppression, and slavery. It hardly seemed to matter that, in fact many Serbs fought on the Ottoman side during that battle, that initial reports suggested a great Ottoman defeat, and that an independent Serbian state lasted intermittently for another 70 years before finally being subsumed by the Ottoman empire. As Tim Judah asserts about the battle, 'Its real, lasting legacy lay in the myths and legends which came to be woven around it, enabling it to shape the nation's historical and national consciousness' (Judah 1997, 30). Over the years, this idea was promulgated in poem, song, and story until it became firmly enshrined in the nationalistic ideological framework of Serbian national identity and culture (Judah 1997). Louis Sell suggests that:

> "All nations shape their image of themselves, at least in part, on myth. For Serbia, the central myth is one of heroic struggle, often against hopeless odds, followed by betrayal and defeat, but also – eventually – rebirth and triumph. Like all national myths, the Serbian picture contains many exaggerations and downright falsehoods". (Sell 2002, 70)

On April 24, 1987, at the site of that ancient battle of Kosovo Polje an obscure communist apparatchik named Slobodan Miloševic prevented police officers from beating a crowd of Serbs and, in so doing, discovered the political advantages of militant nationalism (Sell 2002). He set about recreating himself as the champion of Serbs and was thus able to tap into a deep ideological vein of Serb victimization which he successfully used to help achieve and maintain power and ultimately to mobilize Serb popular opinion and behaviour in service to he violent ethnic cleansing of the early 1990s. Bosnian Serb propaganda constantly played upon the theme of Serb victimization at the hands of the Ottoman Turks in 1389 and by the Croats during World War II which helped legitimate the violence against the Bosnian Moslems and Croats. This was why Serbs engaged in the policies of ethnic cleansing could say things like, 'We defended Europe from Islam six hundred years ago (…). We are defending Europe again (…) from Islamic fundamentalism' (Cigar 1995, p. 65). In short, past notions of victimization, however factually in error they may be, often serve to provide a justification for violence against a group in the present. Ideologies which reinforce such notions of victimization are easily manipulated for genocidal purposes.

3.3. DEHUMANIZATION

Third, we must recognize that ideologies which distance and dehumanize entire populations foster attitudes that make it easier to target and victimize others. In fact, according to Kelman and Hamilton, dehumanization is one of the three most critical preconditions necessary for mass murder to take place (Kelman and Hamilton 1989). This process is also sometimes known as pseudospeciation and refers to the inclination of communities to define their own group as human and other groups as nonhuman (Erikson 1966). In every society, individuals and groups are valued differentially depending upon a number of factors that provide a basis for a calculus of social worth. These variables can include race, ethnicity, gender, and economic status. In truth, some of this is inevitable. The ways in which we tend to differentiate between the in-group and the out-group almost invariably involves some sort of devaluation of those not in the in-group (See Staub 2002). We tend to identify and value those who are most like us and we tend to value less those who are the most different from us and who don't belong to what Helen Fein has termed our, 'Circle of Obligation' (Fein 1993). Certain ideologies, however, take these notions to an extreme degree.

Belief systems that serve to define certain groups as having less worth or value than others are dangerous in the sense that they help make a group more vulnerable to victimization. It is a lot easier to hurt or kill those who are not only different from you, but who are also less than you. The greater the social distance between the victims and the perpetrators, the less difficulty there is in harming them. This is especially true when dehumanizing images are combined with other ideological imperatives that reinforce the need for the violent actions such as xenophobic nationalism.

In many instances of genocide, the ideological framework not only diminishes the social worth of members of a victimized group, but actively defines them as being subhuman or nonhuman. To the Rwandan Hutu, the Tutsis were cockroaches or *inyenzi* and what could be more natural than trying to exterminate insects (Gourevitch 1998). The destruction of an insect not only does not call forth an emotional reaction, but can even be seen as a form of social service since we often tend to perceive insects as carrying disease and being dirty, etc. In very much the same vein, to the Nazis, the Jews were below the Slavic peoples who in turn were ranked below the Aryans. In fact, Jews were not even considered to be human and were often identified in Germany ideological imagery as being animals, demonic, and sometimes even as a form of disease itself (See Alvarez 2001 for a more thorough discussion of this issue).

We even see these kinds of dehumanizing attitudes and images in the way Native Americans have been treated in the violence and genocide inflicted against them in the 18th and 19th centuries (Churchill 1997). In Late November, 1864, to use a notorious example, a large force of cavalry soldiers led by Colonel John Chivington left Denver, Colorado and early on the morning of the 29th ended up on the banks of Sand Creek where a large number of Native Americans, mostly Cheyenne, were camped under a flag of truce in the belief that they were under the protection of the Colorado authorities. With no warning or call for surrender, Chivington's soldiers attacked and killed around 130 Indians, many of them women and children. No prisoners were taken and many of the victims were mutilated after death. Explaining his practice of killing everybody, including children, Chivington reportedly asserted that, 'his policy was to kill and scalp all little and big; that nits made lice' (Hoig 1961; Svaldi 1989). To Chivington and other like him, Native Americans were clearly not human.

In sum, genocide is typically directed against minority groups defined as being different and less than human and it is this perception that assists the killers in making the process of murdering others easier. Historically, then, dehumanization allowed the aggressors to 'strip the victims of their humanity and thus make them seem to stand apart from humanity, which to the perpetrators meant that the ordinary moral norms did not apply to them' (Smeulers 1996, p. 31).

3.4.   SCAPEGOATING

Fourth are those belief systems that scapegoat populations for past and present misfortunes. Scapegoating is an ancient tradition that has been practiced by many cultures around the world. In ancient times a community would symbolically place all of their sins and misdeeds on an animal or a person who would then be ritually cast out into the wilderness or sometimes killed outright (Douglas 1995). In this process of transference the community would be able to start fresh without the wrongdoing of the past haunting it or bringing disfavour from the Gods. In more modern times, the term scapegoating has come to refer to the process whereby innocent individuals and groups are unjustly blamed for the misfortunes and problems of others. People generally like simple and easily understood answers to difficult problems and scapegoating provides this. Of this issue, Douglas asserts:

> 'Where ignorance of the actual causes of distress and harm exists, then human beings inevitably seek for an explanation. It is as if individuals, groups and communities cannot tolerate or live with events that are apparently inexplicable. Thus, when such events occur no relief, no cleansing can take place until some acceptable explanation has been found'. (Douglas 1995, 41)

Unfortunately, life doesn't always provide answers for why things happen or the answer may not be easily understood or emotionally satisfying. Alternatively, it may be that political, military, or religious leaders want to shift responsibility away from themselves or their interests and instead place it on a vulnerable population that can shoulder the blame for mistakes and problems. This is where the role of the scapegoat comes into play.

Perhaps the best example of this process concerns the Nazi portrayal of the Jews as being responsible for Germany's defeat in the First World War, the now infamous Stab in the Back Legend or *Dolch Stoss Legende*. This myth began in November 1919 when Field Marshal Paul von Hindenburg asserted to a government commission that traitors within Germany had engineered her defeat in the war. The army, he asserted, had been stabbed in the back (Edelheit & Edelheit 1994; Fischer 2002; Schivelbusch 2001). These traitorous elements included Jews, Socialists, and Communists. Rather than admit that Germany had been defeated militarily, the country's leaders and many citizens found it easier to accept that certain groups had been responsible. This was an easily accepted lie since the German army had stayed in their trenches until the armistice. During the inter-war years, the Jews were also blamed for the failings of the Weimar government, the collapse of the German economy during the great depression, as well as various other problems. It is important to remember that the Nazis did not invent the scapegoating of Jews, instead they were able to rely on a deep reservoir of European and Christian anti-Semitism that had long blamed the Jews for many historic ills and calamities including the Black Death (Carroll 2001; Prager & Telushkin 1983; Weiss 1996). Scapegoating the Jews provided an easy answer to sometimes complex situations and provided a potent enemy for the national community to rally against and it was these sentiments which the Nazis were able to manipulate and exploit in their quest for power and the creation of a Nazi state.

3.5. ABSOLUTIST WORLDVIEW

Fifth are ideologies that define the world in absolutist terms and see no possibility of compromise and accommodation. Much of the violence perpetrated against the native peoples of North, Central, and South America was motivated in large part by an absolutist Christian belief system that defined the indigenous inhabitants of the new world as heathens and savages who had to convert or die (See for example Cocker 1998; Dickason 1997; Stannard 1992). There was no middle ground that accepted the validity of the native civilizations or their right to exist. The Christian doctrine of that time preached that only Christian civilization was following the true path and other faiths were sinful and posed an affront to God. We find this kind of mindset most often manifested in religious or quasi-religious systems, especially among those who believe in a fundamentalist version of their faith.

Fundamentalism refers to the belief in the literal and absolute truth of the sacred writings of a religion and often encompasses attempts to return that religion to its original practices and principles. All religions modify their rituals, beliefs, and practices in response to social and political changes (Selengut 2003) and fundamentalism tends to reject these changes because they're perceived as moving a religion away from the true path. All religions have an idealized vision of the perfect religious society according to traditions, scriptures, and other holy writings and fundamentalism is intended to bring that vision into reality. Believing in the absolute and infallible truth of their doctrine, fundamentalists acknowledge no moral complexity. The religious scholar Charles Kimball points out that claims of absolute truth such as this are closely linked with violent religious extremism (Kimball 2002). From the point of view of violent religious extremists, there is no ambiguity because all other points of view are wrong and displeasing to God. There is also no room for compromise because that is perceived as a negation of truth. Manichean or dualistic in outlook, fundamentalism divides the world into two easily understood camps; good and evil, right and wrong, light and dark. To the true believer, violence in pursuit of fundamentalist goals is, therefore, perpetrated in defence of God's word and is accordingly sanctified. Those who do not share the same vision of their faith are by definition spiritually and morally inferior and are therefore legitimate victims of righteous violence. From this perspective, the suffering and harm caused can be justified as God's will in bringing about a more moral world (Selengut 2003). It's easy to see why, then, that the European influence on the Native peoples of the Americas was so blatantly destructive.

We see much the same kind of mindset when we examine the actions of various communist dictatorships such as found in Stalin's Soviet Union or in Cambodia under the Khmer Rouge. To the hardcore believers in these regimes, the party was always right and infallible. The Khmer Rouge central party organization was known as Angkar, and according to Alex Hinton, 'Angkar supplanted Buddhism as the new "religion". Like a deity, Angkar (and the revolution it stood for) was depicted in hyperbolic, often superhuman terms, sometimes directly adapted from Buddhism' (Hinton 2005, 128). The world view espoused by Angkar did not tolerate any dissent, opposition, or debate. Rather it preached an uncompromising and absolutist truth that left no room in Cambodian society for those who did not agree or fit in with the vision of a more perfect Cambodian society as espoused by the party. In a similar vein, the official history of the Communist party of the Soviet Union asserts that:

> 'The power of Marxist-Leninist theory lies in the fact that it enables the Party to find the right orientation in any situation, to understand the inner connection of current events, to foresee their course, and to perceive not only how and in what direction they are developing in the present but how and in what direction they are bound to develop in the future'. (quoted in Hoffer 1951, 82)

How different is this position from the doctrine of Papal infallibility? In short, this kind of ideological framework allows no room for differences in thought, appearance, or action. It also encourages a sense of self and group righteousness in pursuit of the absolute truth. Genocidal killers can feel secure in their belief system that dictates the destruction of a population that somehow fell short of the standard for inclusion in the body of the national and/or religious community. Those who know absolute truth with absolute certainty tend not to be among the most tolerant.

3.6. UTOPIANISM

Sixth, are those belief systems which seek to create a utopian future. The word Utopia comes from Thomas More, the English author, lawyer, scholar, and politician who around the year 1516 published a book in Latin that he called *De Optimo Reipublicae Statu deque Nova Insula Utopia*, better known as Utopia. He derived the word from the Greek *Outopia* which means *no place* and the Greek *Eutopia* which means *good place* (Frank & Frank 1979; Mohawk 2000). In this book he described a society that was rationally organized and in which all property was communally held, there were no lawyers and only a few laws because in the absence of conflict they were not needed. Because of the striking nature of this imagery, the term has come to refer to any vision of a perfect and therefore unattainable society. But creating a more perfect society has often involved getting rid of those who don't fit in. As E.V. Kohak so eloquently points out, 'You can't build a utopia without terror, and before long, terror is all that's left' (Quoted in Bracher 1982, 80). Some of the worst human rights abuses occurred in places like the Soviet Union, China, and Cambodia where revolutionary governments decided that in order to fulfil their idealized vision of society they needed to eliminate entire classes of people. The Cambodian Khmer Rouge, for example, took power on April 17, 1975 after a number of years of fighting and immediately began trying to implement their genocidal ideology (Jackson 1989; Short 2004). The Khmer Rouge was a nationalistic group that had been heavily influenced by a number of Leninist and Stalinist philosophical principles. They were also strongly attached to a political philosophy which involved trying to recreate the Angkor Empire of the 9th through 15th centuries, a time when the ethnic Khmer people had ruled much of what is now Cambodia, Thailand, Laos, and Vietnam (Chandler 1992). In their world view, this had been a time of greatness for the Khmer and the Khmer Rouge wanted to recreate this period and reclaim the territory they had once possessed. In order to bring about this revitalized and utopian society, the Khmer Rouge felt it was necessary to start over by wiping out any corrupting influences which included members of the old government and military, the educated classes, ethnic Vietnamese, Chams, and Chinese, as well as numerous other groups that were seen to be a threat to the new social order. Here is how Aaron Beck puts it:

> 'The ideology of the Khmer Rouge called for a complete transformation of society, wiping out any Western influences and converting the country to the purest form of socialism. Individuals were expected to surrender their own freedom of will to that of the collective. The revolutionaries stood for a complete annihilation of modern values, practices, and customs. They sought a revival of ancient glories and purification of the present by emptying out the cities, forcing the corrupt parents to obey their uncorrupted children, and turning their education over to the peasants and workers, who had not been corrupted. Everything inconsistent with the goal was to be wiped out: individualism, personal possessions, families'. (Beck 1999, 190)

Essentially, the Khmer Rouge was in pursuit of a utopian ideal, one that ultimately was unobtainable. The result was a genocide that, in terms of proportion of the population killed, was the most lethal of the 20th century (Rummell 1994). Similarly, the Soviet Union was interested in creating a Socialist workers paradise that was inspirational for many, but which also necessitated, 'thundercrashes of state-directed violence', in order to achieve their perfect society (Weitz 2003, 60). In other words, the massive upheaval and transformation of a society creates tremendous difficulties, resistance, and obstacles from many sources and genocidal violence has often been the preferred tool for overcoming those obstacles and difficulties.

4. CONCLUSIONS

These above discussed ideological themes, then, help provide the rationale, motivations, and justifications necessary for any genocide to take place. As we have seen, ideologies are a necessary part of any genocide because they provide the necessary intellectual framework that motivates and justifies the persecution of the victim group. These beliefs may include a variety of nationalistic, historical, scientific, and religious precepts that validate the violence. The Nazis, for example, held a number of scientific and medical beliefs about the supposed racial superiority of the Aryan people. In their world view, the Jews and the Slavic peoples were a threat to the genetic purity of the Aryan race and when combined with historic and religious anti-Semitism these ideas provided much of the rationale for the industrialized killing of the Holocaust. Similarly, the genocide in Cambodia relied upon a number of ideological imperatives that included certain communist principles united with ethnic Khmer nationalism and these provided the rationale for the Khmer Rouge to attempt to return Cambodia to a historic and mythic time of greatness by killing anyone who was perceived as a foreign and corrupting influence. Genocide, in short, is inextricably ideological. This leads us then to ask how can genocide be prevented, given the pervasiveness and strength of ideological frameworks? While there are many possible strategies for preventing genocide and while any effective system of intervention and prevention must include multiple initiatives at multiple levels, the following recommendations most specifically address the problem of genocidal ideologies.

Nationalistic ideologies, as we've seen, depend upon many myths, fallacies, and prejudices. Genocide prevention techniques, therefore, must also include initiatives intended to educate populations about the uses and misuses of national identity and history, thus making individuals and groups more resistant to the blandishments of nationalistic demagogues. State propaganda must be countered with independent news and media outlets. Genocide depends upon the active participation of the few and the passive acquiescence of the many. The fewer the number of people who have accepted the official discourse around persecution the less ability that government has to enact official and unofficial policies towards genocide. This is especially true in the modern world where mass media are pervasive and powerful instruments for disseminating ideology or as John Thompson writes, 'Today we live in a world in which the extended circulation of symbolic forms play a fundamental and ever-increasing role' (Thompson 1990, 1). It's important to note once more that mass media are an important element in paving the way for much contemporary genocide. The Rwandan genocide of 1994, for example, was preceded by the establishment of a number of radio stations such as *Radio Télévision Libre des Mille Collines* that broadcast hate messages which helped prime the fears and anger of ordinary Hutu against the Tutsi. Once the killing began these same radio stations also helped direct the killers to their victims (Melvern 2004). A similar situation was operating in Bosnia as well. The more that citizens are exposed to counter arguments from a variety of media sources, the less likely it is that genocidally inclined governments will have to ability to mobilize those populations into genocidal action.

In the long term, societies must also be socialized away from the often xenophobic and always divisive fervour of nationalism and difference. Nationalistic value systems and attitudes must be replaced with more international and human rights based ethos that emphasize tolerance and the commonality of human beings rather than their differences. As Herb Hirsch succinctly argues:

'*Since nationalism is the psychological foundation upon which international perceptions are currently constructed, it must be modified by instituting a process of political resocialization from one that emphasizes nationalism to one that emphasizes internationalism and human rights as an overarching ethic*'. (Hirsch 2002, 165)

Nationalism often exalts the 'narcissism of minor difference' and these ethnocentric ideals must be replaced with ones that are more inclusive in orientation. Ervin

Staub reminds us that 'Ideas can be destructive or prepare us for caring and benevolence' (Staub 1989, 282). Perhaps it's time that we started foster the latter and not the former. But this is a long term goal and one which cannot be simply implemented. Cultures, especially long established political cultures, don't just change overnight. This kind of slow moving attitudinal transformation must be accompanied by more direct short term action as well.

Resocialization must be accompanied in the short term with aggressive enforcement of international human rights law through bodies such as the International Criminal Court and the International Court of Justice (See Balint in this volume). This is important not only for the sake of justice, but also because the apprehension, prosecution, and punishment of perpetrators of genocide also serve to help change international and national values and attitudes around genocide, human rights, and sovereignty. We must remember that legal changes often precede and influence attitudinal changes.

There are many other strategies suggested by a multitude of scholars and activists, but ultimately it all comes down to whether or not individuals and groups accept the essentializing ideological messages that justify the persecution of their fellow human beings. Aleksandr Solzhenitsyn, the famous gulag survivor and author put it this way, 'Gradually it was disclosed to me that the line separating good and evil passes not through states, nor between classes, nor between political parties either – but right through every human heart – and through all human hearts' (Solzhenitsyn 1975, 615–616).

X. PERPETRATORS OF INTERNATIONAL CRIMES: TOWARDS A TYPOLOGY

Alette Smeulers[1]

1.   INTRODUCTION

International crimes such as war crimes, crimes against humanity and genocide are extreme forms of collective violence. Lawyers tend to refer to these crimes as structural criminality or system criminality. Criminologists would qualify this type of criminality as state crime, organisational crime or political crime. These types of crime are usually committed in a context of mass violence, on behalf of the state, within a group or by members of a specific governmental or militarised unit or organisation. In some cases thousands of ordinary people get involved. How can this be explained? How can it be explained that large numbers of otherwise ordinary and law-abiding citizens become involved in genocide or other international crimes? The central focus of this chapter will be on the perpetrator of international crimes, not merely on the physical perpetrators but on all those who somehow become involved in the crimes. Perpetrators differ in their motives, the roles they play and the situation within which they operate. The main aim of this chapter is to create a typology of perpetrators in order to better understand the specific role individual perpetrators play in bringing about and preserving a period of collective violence. Telford Taylor, the Public Prosecutor at the Nuremberg trials after the Second World War, said that crimes are committed by individuals, not by abstract entities. By creating a typology of perpetrators this paper aims to give the individuals functioning within these abstract (and destructive) entities a 'human face' and thus provide a tool to enhance the understanding of the interpersonal relationships, the group dynamics and other underlying psycho-sociological mechanisms which can help us comprehend the root causes of international crimes. Such knowledge is a prerequisite to developing effective preventative measures and crucial to administering justice fairly. A typology of perpetrators can furthermore be used as a theoretical framework to attribute individual criminal responsibility and impose fair and just sentences

[1]   This research was conducted with a research grant from the Netherlands Organisation for Scientific Research (NWO – Vernieuwingsimpuls).

which match the actual blameworthiness of the individual perpetrators and which do justice to their individual responsibilities within the collective.

2. ORDINARY PEOPLE WITHIN EXTRAORDINARY CIRCUMSTANCES: SETTING THE CONTEXT

When taking the often cruel, savage and extremely violent nature of most international crimes into account, it is difficult to grasp that the perpetrators are ordinary people rather than psychopaths, sadists or mentally deranged people. Yet, the almost universal outcome of case studies on individual perpetrators or perpetrator groups[2] and general studies on perpetrators of international crimes[3] is that these perpetrators are indeed ordinary people who are not mentally deranged or otherwise disturbed. They are people who do not differ from the very normal and average people who under ordinary circumstances would be law-abiding citizens. There is just one crucial difference: the perpetrators are ordinary people within extraordinary circumstances. Desperate attempts to prove perpetrators of international crimes are mentally deranged, sadistic or psychopathic have failed (see for an overview, Waller (2002, 55–87)). No matter how many people would wish to do so, the behaviour of torturers and 'génocidaires' cannot be explained by merely pointing to possible deficiencies within the individual perpetrators. The fact is that there are simply too many perpetrators: they cannot all be insane. Waller (2002, 69) notes: '(…) not only does the claim of widespread psychopathology among perpetrators contradict the available evidence, but it also contradicts all diagnostic and statistical logic.' The number of violent acts such as murder, torture, mistreatment and rape, committed in a period of collective violence greatly exceeds the crime rates under ordinary circumstances. From this we can conclude that many people, who under ordinary circumstances would not have been involved in this type of violent criminal behaviour, do get involved in committing international crimes. But why and how do these ordinary and otherwise law-abiding people get involved in international crimes?

In order to better understand this phenomenon of the 'law-abiding criminal', first of all, the political, ideological and organisational context in which these

---

[2]   See amongst others Arendt (1964), Sereny (1974, 1995), Steiner (1980), Lifton (1986), Segev (1987), Hilberg (1992), Browning (1992), Heinz (1993), Katz (1993), Crelinsten (1993), Smeulers (1996), Huggins et al. (2002), Haritos-Fatouras (2003), Drakulic (2004), Thys (2004), Hinton (2005) and Hatzfeld (2005).
[3]   See amongst others Kelman and Hamilton (1989), Staub (1989), Bandura (1999), Conroy (2001), Alvarez (2001), Cohen (2001), Waller (2002/2007), Smeulers (2004) and Welzer (2005).

people operate must be analysed: the context of collective violence.[4] On a macro perspective we need to understand what brings about such a period of collective violence. Many scholars have studied the circumstances and preconditions of periods in which international crimes such as war crimes, crimes against humanity and genocide have been committed.[5] It has been shown that periods of political turmoil, rapid changes or difficult living conditions often precede a period of collective violence (Harff 2003). Both revolutions (Melson 1992) and civil wars are often precursor events to genocide (Harff 2003) and other international crimes. A (military) *coup d'état,* a dictatorial regime, a civil war or a war on terror are situations which are often characterised by manifestations of structural or mass violence and international crimes. Although questions on how such periods come about and what the differences between the various situations are, are interesting, these questions are outside the scope of this work. Consequently, the focus will be on the effects such periods mentioned above have on individuals while asking: why do they go along with a situation?

2.1. CONSEQUENCES AND EFFECTS OF A PERIOD OF COLLECTIVE VIOLENCE

Periods of collective violence are often characterised by the mass involvement of people, the progressive use of violence usually towards one specific group who is blamed for the misfortune of the masses and an alleged legitimacy of the violence which is provided by an ideology. Extreme violence and genocide do not start out of the blue. They are the final outcome of a period of escalation in which people get caught up in what Staub (1989) called a continuum of destructiveness. Periods of collective violence often occur in periods of political turmoil or during or after a revolution in which people strive for a better world. Collective violence almost inevitably results in social engineering. The masses aim to get rid of the alleged privileged classes or minorities whom they blame for their misfortune. Ideologies usually serve as motivating forces which at the same time incite and instigate the masses while justifying the violence (see the contribution of Alvarez in this book). Similar mechanisms like the neutralisation techniques as identified by Sykes and Matza (1957) in their work on youth delinquency are used in political discourse in order to rationalise and justify terror and violence. Such ideologies thus function as institutionalised neutralisation techniques. The groups of people

---

4   Cf. Kauzlarich and Kramer (1998, 143) who conclude that organisational crime cannot be explained by relying on psycho-social theories alone.

5   See amongst others Stohl and Lopez (1984), Gupta (2001), Kuper (1981), Fein (1984, 1993), Bauman (1989), Chalk and Jonnasohn (1990), Melson (1992), Horowitz (2002) and Harff (2003).

targeted are often the rich and powerful upper class, the intellectuals, the privileged minorities or those who represent the regime which is about to be or has been overthrown. Especially in cases when masses of people get involved, social resentment is usually a strong driving force. The masses tend to perceive their struggle as a justified war against injustice, unfairness, totalitarian and oppressive regimes and corruption. Perhaps the most remarkable finding is that people who get involved in these types of crime actually seem to believe that what they are doing is the right thing or at least necessary and justified. Waller (2007) for example quotes a perpetrator saying that he did not believe that killing people was right but rather that not doing so was wrong.

When the use of violence is structural and widespread, by definition many civilians get involved. In some cases the violence is institutionalised and the whole state apparatus or even the whole population seems to be involved. If the latter situation is the case, the violence is usually extremely well organised and bureaucratised. Bureaucratisation naturally results in a functional division of labour and is otherwise characterised by a strict chain of command. The result is that within such a malicious system state functionaries and bureaucrats can get involved in genocide by merely sitting behind their desks and filling out forms (Hilberg 1992). Ordinary state functionaries and bureaucrats become 'lethal cogs' (Alvarez 2001, 86). Many others get involved in a more physical manner such as policemen conducting razzia's, camp guards, torturers and executioners.

Looking more closely at the perpetrators who get involved or physically commit international crimes within a state in which these crimes are institutionalised, it becomes apparent that first and foremost, the reason that they commit these crimes is because they think that they have to and that it is for the better good of society. These perpetrators in other words commit crimes of obedience. Crimes of obedience can be defined as acts 'performed in response to orders from authority that are considered illegal or immoral by the international community' (Kelman and Hamilton 1989, 46). For a crime to be qualified as a crime of obedience it is not necessary that the actual crime is committed after a direct order. What is crucial is that the perpetrators believe that the crime is authorised or condoned by the authorities. In other words, a crime qualifies as a crime of obedience when it is supported by the authority structure. It is a crime of obedience when 'perpetrators believe and have reason to believe that the action is authorised, expected, at least tolerated and probably approved by the authorities – that it conforms with official policy and reflects what their superiors would want them to do' (Kelman 2005, 126). This very fact turns the whole analytical framework which underlies criminological theory upside down because mainstream criminology studies people who break the law, people who *do not* live by the rules and people who are *deviant*. But within such a malignant governmental system, military organisation or police unit, it is those who do not break the rules but those who *abide by* the rules who become the perpetrators. When studying perpetrators of international crimes we have to focus on the question why they are *obedient*, why they followed the group, why they *do* live by the (deviant and immoral) rules.

Periods of collective violence usually result in a restructuring of society or social engineering. People however differ in what is at stake for them and in order to make this difference more explicit I have made three categories. The first category consists of the law-abiding citizens who are well adapted, relatively successful and literally law-abiding in the period preceding the period of collective violence. They are not involved in any serious criminal activity and do not have a specific inclination to be involved in crime or violence. This group has a lot to lose with any upcoming changes or the social restructuring of society. They were relatively successful, had good careers, enough wealth and a secure life. A period of collective violence challenges this and not going along with it might result in huge losses.

A second group of people can be qualified as borderliners. They are not involved in any crime but they are less well adapted and not as successful as the first group. To some extent they might feel misfits, unhappy and resentful although this will not always be visible to outsiders nor will it actually materialise in the absence of extraordinary circumstances. In contrast to the first group this group has not much to lose but has much to win: a restructuring of society as a result of a period of collective violence will give them new opportunities and new chances. If they felt lost and unhappy before, they can use the opportunity of the upheaval to feel part of something. Totalitarian mass movements are particularly attractive to individuals from the second group who might fall prey to the political manipulators and become the true believers, the forerunners of the new revolution, the new elite (Hoffer 1951). But also on a very practical level the changes will give these people the chance to achieve wealth, status and make themselves a career: things which had been previously out of reach for them. Thanks to these new opportunities the new situation is appealing to them.

A third group could be described as criminals. These people are for whatever reason already involved in crime under ordinary circumstances and already have a criminal record or are very close to getting one. Some are ordinary criminals; others are sadists and engage in violent behaviour because they enjoy the pain and suffering of others. Some might have sexual or mental deficiencies or are psychopaths and sociopaths. People within this group are often outcasts within society. They however suddenly see new chances to legitimise what they have been doing all along. As long as they stick to a certain ideology and only target a specific group within society they can come to be seen as heroes rather than criminals. The new order can even give them a special status. They can still conduct their activities but now with a legitimate aim.

In conclusion we can say that within a period of collective violence all individuals have to make a choice: they either go along with or they set themselves apart from it.

People are social animals and are naturally influenced by authority, by significant others, by groups and by official state rhetoric. We are raised to obey authorities, raised to behave in conformity to social norms and values, and it appears that we even have a natural tendency to do so. We search for the company of others but at a price: we need to conform to the standards of others and general social norms. It consequently takes guts to set oneself apart and to resist authority or distance oneself from the group. People usually feel very uncomfortable doing so and social-psychological research has shown that people sometimes even change their opinions merely because they seemed to hold opinions which differed from that of the majority of the group. To set oneself apart is difficult and even more difficult when the group starts to use violence and is backed by or even ordered to do so by the state. Probably without being fully aware of the consequences people within the period prior to the collective violence, are confronted with all kinds of small and seemingly insignificant decisions that make them go along with the situation. These same decisions however compromise them into going along with it further and further, and step by step they get more and more deeply involved. Within a period of collective violence, many people slowly progress on a continuum of destructiveness, often without being really aware of it. This process can also be described as a pattern of escalating commitment. People get caught up by it – slowly, but inevitably.

Apart from external pressure there is something else at work here. People generally want to feel good about themselves and when they start to act in a way which is not in line with their own norms and values they feel bad and guilty about themselves. This feeling is called cognitive dissonance (Festinger 1957). A natural reaction to cognitive dissonance is to reduce this nagging feeling by rationalising and justifying their own behaviour. This natural tendency to justify oneself is a crucial defence mechanism which prevents people from turning insane and, if it works efficiently, it ensures that people stay psychologically healthy. This very same natural defence mechanism can however turn into a psychological trap in a period of collective violence. Perpetrators can get caught up and feel imprisoned in their own defence mechanisms. A slow, gradual and progressive hands-on involvement in combination with these natural defence mechanisms make it more and more difficult to stop and get out once people have made the first step. The further the individual progresses on this continuum of destructiveness the more difficult it becomes to escape. This can be illustrated by the Milgram experiment (Milgram 1974). In this experiment Milgram not only showed that people have a natural tendency to obey an authority even if this authority asks them to perform acts which are in clear violation of other norms and values within society, he also showed the danger of getting progressively involved in something. The set up of Milgram's experiment mirrored a continuum of destructiveness. The subjects were to give a slight and acceptable shock to another individual (unknown to them the *victim* was fictitious). In the beginning of the experiment a low 15-volt shock was administered by the subjects, but with each repeated shock the voltage was upgraded by 15 volts. Step by step the subject came closer to absolutely unacceptable shock levels ultimately ending with a shock of 450 volts. This in my view was crucial. Milgram would have never found the same results if he had asked subjects to give the victim a shock of 450 volts right from the start. The reason why the subjects in this experiment did end up giving shock levels of 450 volts was that they got caught up in their own psychological trap. The further they went along with it, the more nervous they got and the more cognitive dissonance they felt. What happened is that the subjects compromised themselves in going along with it. Going along with it in itself was justification for their involvement so far.[6] Reducing the cognitive dissonance by terminating the experiment would have a downside: it would, namely also mean to admit that one had been wrong for quite some time before they took the decision to stop. This for many people is apparently too much. The Milgram experiment illustrates how a continuum of destructiveness works when real crimes are committed. The more people get involved, the more difficult it is to step out to face their own conscience and accept their own mistakes. They get psychologically entrapped. Many people do not start to kill and torture because they hate their victims or perceive killing and torturing them as justifiable but they start to hate their victims and start to believe in the ideology because it justifies the killing and torture in which they have become involved.

During a period of collective violence, ordinary people who adapt to the circumstances by submitting themselves to the social construction of reality in which torturing and killing is turned into something necessary and good, will be transformed into perpetrators (Smeulers 2004). These individuals become entrapped and slowly and gradually change: they start to believe in their own justifications and rationalisations; they start to believe in their own separate reality (Crelinsten 1993, 2003) or escape in what Lifton (1986) called doubling. Doubling is a psychological mechanism which explains how people sometimes adapt to extreme situations by psychologically separating one world, the concentration camp in which they work, from the ordinary world, their home. By means of doubling, perpetrators furthermore separate the role they play in one world from the role they play in the other and can thus be executioner during office hours and a loving father and husband once back at home. Whatever means

---

[6]   This is a well known phenomenon within social-psychology, the foot in the door effect and the escalating commitment. See Baron and Kerr (2003).

are used, people who adapt to a period of collective violence and try to cope with their own roles will be slowly but gradually transformed into perpetrators.

2.2. TOWARDS A TYPOLOGY

Perpetrators of international crimes cannot be understood outside the context in which they operate. This context, a period of collective violence is the foremost reason why they are transformed into perpetrators. Reading hundreds of ego documents (letters, diaries, trial statements, autobiographies and interviews) and biographies of people involved in international crimes made me conclude that there are certain mechanisms and social-psychological processes which cause ordinary and otherwise law-abiding people to be gradually and progressively transformed into perpetrators but I also concluded that the people differ in the way they get involved and the reasons for which they get involved. Some really believe in what they are doing and will use violence in a rational and functional manner whereas others merely seem to take advantage on the situation and use excessive violence. I thus discovered both striking similarities between perpetrators as well as striking differences and realised that those involved in international crimes could be grouped into different types of perpetrators.

In my research I used the same documents used by other scholars and I used their analysis. It turned out however that most studies on perpetrators focus on perpetrators within a specific situation (for example the Rwandan genocide), a specific period (for example the Second World War) or focus on a specific type of perpetrators (for example torturers). In my study I have not restricted myself to a specific situation or period of time; I have not restricted myself to a specific type of perpetrator or group of perpetrators. My aim was to furthermore study all people involved in committing international crimes, no matter whether as leaders, policy makers, bureaucrats or physical perpetrators. My aim was to develop an overarching typology.

In reading the ego documents, biographies and the case law I discovered that people differ in their personal background and why they go along with a situation when a period of collective violence restructures society and seems to set all the norms and values upside down. I discovered that some had a lot to lose and others a lot to win. I discovered that some perpetrators are driven by greed, others by ideology and others by fear. Those driven by fear are not all driven by the same type of fear: some people have been forced to participate by real and actual threats whereas others are driven by fear of rejection of being considered a misfit. I furthermore discovered that the type of role individuals played made a big difference: it is much easier for a bureaucrat to rationalise and justify what he is doing than it will be for a physical perpetrator. The pressure to start to believe in what they are doing is far more extreme for the latter than for the first.

Table 1. Typologies

Gupta (2001)	Smeulers	Mann (2005)	Crelinsten (1993)	Hilberg (1992)	Others
Collective violence	*International crimes*	*ethnic cleansing killer*	*torturer*	*Nazi-Germany*	*case studies*
	Criminal mastermind				Fromm (1973), Post (2004)
Mercenaries (greed)	Profiteer Careerist Criminal/Sadist	materialistic careerist violent	sadist	careerist vulgarians	
True believer (ideology)	Devoted warrior Fanatic	ideological bigoted	zealot	zealots	Hoffer (1951)
Captive participant (fear)	Conformist Follower Compromised Professional	comradely bureaucratic threatened disciplined	professional	bearers of burdens	Fromm (1942) Fromm (1942) Haritos-Fatouras (2003)

In developing my typology I used the work of other scholars who stressed differences between perpetrators. In his study on perpetrators within the Nazi regime, Hillberg (1992) for example concluded that one could distinguish various types of perpetrators and distinguished the careerist, zealots, vulgarians and bearers of burdens. Hillberg clearly did not only take the physical perpetrators into account but also looked at the bureaucrats. Thys (2004) studied perpetrators in international armed conflicts and distinguished the organisers, the specialists and the executors. He focused more on roles rather than on motives to distinguish the types of perpetrators. Post (2004) focused on the leaders and presented full psychological profiles. Several scholars focused on the physical perpetrators like Crelinsten (1993), Kressel (2002) and Huggins et al. (2002) and took the motives and personality of the perpetrators into account. Kressel (2002) distinguished the obedient personality, the uneducated killer and the aggressive killer. Crelinsten (1993) focused on torturers and distinguished the zealot, the professional and the sadist. Huggins et al. (2002) focused their research on Brazilian torturers and murderers under the Brazilian military dictatorship (1964–1985). They found a clear relation between masculinity and the violence used. Huggins et al. distinguish three types of perpetrators: the personalistic cop, the blended personality and the

Table 2. Perpetrator scheme

Types before the period of violence	Consequences and effects of collective violence	Adaptation and transformation process	Types (main motive they are driven by)
Law-abiding citizens			
Well adapted citizens, who would generally not be involved in crime. They are relatively well adjusted and happy.	Collective violence results in a lot of changes and a re-stratification of society. There is enormous pressure to obey and conform. If they do not go along with the situation, passively or actively they might lose everything, become outcasts, make less profit.	They accept the situation and go along with the situation and learn to rationalise and justify what they are doing by redefining certain conventional values. They feel a strong cognitive dissonance and restructure their world and make use of the institutionalised neutralisation techniques.	Careerist (career) Conformist (fear of rejection) Follower (authoritarian) Devoted warrior (devotion) Compromised (direct threat) Professional (internalised threat)
Borderline types			
Less well adapted people who do not feel fully adapted in society, unhappy and resentful – they might be deviant but not real criminals.	A period of collective violence is also a period of social engineering which brings new opportunities and chances. Some suddenly feel part of something important and big.	They have less difficulty in rejecting conventional norms and values because they didn't feel completely happy with them. Some can easily become intoxicated by a charismatic and manipulative political entrepreneur and become true believers	Profiteer (opportunism/ profit) Fanatics (dogmatic ideology)
Criminals/sadists			
Type 1: They are already involved in crime under ordinary circumstances and/ or enjoy pain and suffering from others.	Within a period of structural and systematic violence, violence seems suddenly to be legitimised. What has been criminalised before this period now seems to bring these people honour and glory.	The threshold to commit physical violence is already low and is even lower in this period.	Criminal mastermind (evil) Criminal (personal gain) Sadist (Sexual satisfaction) Fanatics (hatred, resentment)
Type 2: latent type: it would have been likely that they would have got involved ultimately.	Within a period of violence and lack of effective control they get caught up and lose the protective layer of socialisation	The period of collective violence makes them lose their layer of civilisation and act on their so far hidden tendencies	

institutional functionary. Mann (2005, 27–29) focused on the physical perpetrators within periods of ethnic cleansing and distinguished nine types of killers. Gupta (2001) had a broader focus and focused on people who get caught up in a period of collective violence. He distinguished three types of perpetrators: the true believers, the mercenaries and the captive participants. The first type is driven by ideology, the second by greed and the third by fear. Ideology, greed and fear can, according to Gupta (2001), be seen as the three prime motivators which draw people into collective violence. All typologies have been developed on the basis of reading biographies and ego-documents or conducting interviews. All described typologies limit themselves to a specific group of perpetrators and have not been empirically tested yet.

My aim was to create an overarching typology which would be generally applicable and which would emphasise the various roles individuals play and would stress that some types of perpetrators who share a certain psychological make-up take the lead whereas others who share a different psychological make-up just follow the leader or the group. In my overarching typology I have used the other typologies and discovered that they do not contradict each other (see table 1) and that they can be related to the three types of people described in paragraph 2.1, the law-abiding citizens, borderline types and criminals (see table 2). By creating a typology of perpetrators which includes those at the top, the bureaucrats who execute the policies as well as the physical perpetrators, I aimed to point out the differences between the individual perpetrators and to enhance our understanding of how a group of ordinary people turns into a murderous collective. The presented typology can in future research be used as a theoretical framework and tool to study the various roles individuals play within a period of collective violence, to understand the interpersonal relationships and the interaction between the individuals and to analyse group processes and group dynamics.

3. THE TYPES

In the following subparagraphs all the proposed types will be briefly described and the following questions will be answered: what is their role? Why and how did they get involved? What are their main character traits? How predominant is this type? How do they deal with their own involvement? Would this type of perpetrator be likely to get involved in criminality under ordinary circumstances?

3.1. THE CRIMINAL MASTERMIND

In all forms of collective violence there usually is one central leader, the main initiating figure in the criminal conduct who commits or initiates the crimes by his own accord and holds a position of power. This leader is usually the head of state but can also be the head of a specific organisation such as the army or police or a powerful department like the secret service or a terrorist organisation. He is the undisputed powerful leader. These perpetrators are almost exclusively male with strong leadership capabilities, a very manipulative character and often, albeit not always, a hypnotic or charismatic appeal. They are very authoritarian, anti-democratic, extremely vain and arrogant, accept no criticism, believe themselves to be infallible and ultimately come to feel that they have a divine right to rule. They are ruthless, harsh, cruel and merciless and do whatever they deem fit to stay in control. They strive for absolute power and complete control. The stronger their influence the more self-confident they become and the more they believe in their own ideas. These perpetrators can be considered the criminal masterminds.

For some leaders the use of violence is purely instrumental: they are power hungry and rely on force in order to stay in power. Other leaders, however, clearly have an evil and destructive nature: it is their aim to destroy and exterminate. We can consequently distinguish several subtypes of leaders: the strict authoritarian (like Augusto Pinochet), the power hungry careerist (like Slobodan Milosevic), the ruthless dictator (like Saddam Hussein and Josef Stalin), or the charismatic almost divine but utterly destructive leader (like Adolf Hitler) depending on the nature of the regime and the character of the leader.[7] Those who have a strong charismatic or hypnotic appeal might be able to take advantage of a period of political turmoil and social dissatisfaction or resentment by creating a mass movement. Leaders are created and live by the amount of followers they manage to attract. The relationship between the charismatic leader and the follower is often, according to Post (2004, 187–199), essentially a relationship between a *mirror-hungry* leader and *ideal-hungry* followers. The leaders come to the 'psychological rescue' of their followers (Post 2004, 187),[8] although they themselves are sometimes extremely suspicious and paranoid.

Some charismatic leaders deliberately induce receptive states in their followers and thus masterfully manipulate them. In times of extreme hardship otherwise psychologically healthy personalities feel vulnerable and might fall prey to a manipulative leader. Successful leaders can have thousands or even millions of

---

[7] See for a psychological profile of some leaders Post (2004). Jerrold Post worked for many years for the CIA and developed political personality profiles of political leaders to guide the American government when dealing with these leaders.

[8] The charismatic leader attracts individuals who become fanatical followers, see Hoffer (1951) and Fromm (1942) and the following paragraph on the fanatic.

followers who admire them. They can brilliantly attract the attention of the masses and use or even create an ideology which is very attractive and gives the masses all the answers to all the questions. Such leaders are usually narcissists who suffer from megalomania and have an evil and destructive nature (Fromm 1973) which they mask behind their manipulative and sometimes charming appearance. While the criminal mastermind deems himself superior, they need to be worshipped by the (inferior) masses. In some cases a personality cult is created (e.g. in Mao's China). In most cases obedience and loyalty is demanded from the followers and a personal vow to the leader is not uncommon (e.g. in Nazi-Germany). Criminal masterminds fanatically promote a certain ideology but they opportunistically pick and choose the ideology which will bring them to power (e.g. Milosevic, who switched from communism to nationalism). The ideology they ultimately pick is often extreme, nationalistic, undemocratic, intolerant and exclusive but appealing and thus successful. There is always at least one group within society which is excluded: the enemy, the scapegoat. Criminal masterminds know that a common enemy binds people. The enemy can be blamed for all failures and their presence justifies continuous use of violence and ultimate extermination. Criminal masterminds are often driven by hatred and social resentment. They strive for power and control or in some cases for material gain or heroism. As most criminal masterminds are political opportunists they are also skilled survivors and try to escape in time, and only in exceptional cases do they kill themselves (Hitler). When they are caught and brought to trial: they usually reject the legitimacy of the court. They keep seeing themselves as divine and above the law.

Hitler and Stalin are two of the most well documented examples of criminal masterminds in history (Fest 1980; Bullock 1991; Kershaw 1991; Overy 2004). Obviously there are many more criminal masterminds, as for instance Saddam Hussein (Post 2004, 210–238), Pol Pot (Short 2004), Robert Mugabe (Meredith 2002) and Slobodan Milosevic (Post 2004, 172–186) who have been profiled or documented. Compared to all other perpetrators the criminal mastermind stands apart because he will never submit himself to any authority as he perceives himself to be the only and ultimate authority. Criminal masterminds do not commit crimes of obedience; they conspire and initiate these crimes. They plan and order the crimes; they incite and inflame the masses. They are in the true sense of the word criminal masterminds. From a criminological perspective it would be interesting to compare criminal masterminds who commit international crimes with sect leaders like Jim Jones, the self-proclaimed leader of the infamous sect People's Temple and David Koresh, the sect leader of the Branch Davidians. These leaders will very probably have the same characteristics and use the same mechanisms albeit on a smaller scale. Arguably, had the criminal masterminds not have gained political power they would have ended up leading a religious sect or weird organisation, like the one led by Charles Manson.

3.2. THE FANATIC

Some perpetrators are driven by very strong emotions like hatred, contempt and resentment and usually project and direct these feelings onto a particular group which they blame for their misfortune. They look down on the members of this group whom they consider inferior, sometimes even subhuman, not worthy of life. People who turn into this type of perpetrator often will feel resentful to the ruling society or the norms within society and it is likely that they felt themselves to be misfits, not because they believed themselves to have shortcomings but because they deemed society to be unfair or imperfect. Such people can come to commit hate crimes by their own initiative or come to devote themselves absolutely and unconditionally to a fundamentalist ideology or a specific leader who successfully channels their feelings into a fanatical and dogmatic ideology. These people will not easily submit to just anyone. But once they submit themselves to a cause they do everything to achieve their goals and aims. They have an extreme and rigid view. They have no doubts whatsoever and are absolutely convinced of the righteousness of their cause. Whenever they are confronted with proof which would undermine their ideas, they will simply ignore it, convinced that the evidence must have been fabricated. Such people are extremely dedicated to their cause. In extreme cases they are prepared to kill their enemies or are often even prepared to die for their cause. Their fanatical belief resembles a religious zeal and they sometimes feel that they have a mission larger than life. They can come to see the destruction of a certain group or belief system which differs from their own as a holy mission and they will never give up or give in. They would rather die than admit that they might have been wrong. These perpetrators whom I will call fanatics are often very emotional about their cause and therefore difficult to control.

These perpetrators absolutely and fully believe in what they are doing. They are often the instigators who incite others to commit crimes. They can for example become the party demagogue and send hate messages; they can co-conspire with the criminal mastermind and get extremely high positions within the hierarchy. In those cases however they need to be able to show some self-control. Fanatics can also be closely involved in the physical perpetration of the crimes and with their fanatical zeal and hatred take the lead in committing violent and brutal crimes. Violence is not just functional to them, it is more ritualistic and they will often use excessive violence. The followers of a charismatic leader are generally considered the new elite. The forerunners within these new elites are usually fanatics who sincerely believe that they will bring about a better world and they take everything they are told by their leader for granted. Under ordinary circumstances many, albeit not all of these perpetrators, would have been likely to be involved in crimes. The so-called borderliners who suddenly have come to 'see the light' might have become members of a religious sect, turned to religious fanaticism or become involved in terrorism but they would not necessarily have turned to crime. Those driven by strong hate might under ordinary circumstances be involved in hate crimes.

3.3. THE CRIMINAL/SADIST

Many people who are already involved in committing crimes under ordinary circumstances will also get involved in committing international crimes during a period of collective violence. Others might not yet be involved in crimes but have a so far hidden tendency to commit crimes or behave violently and sadistically. What these perpetrators have in common with the criminal mastermind and the fanatic is that the environment in which international crimes are usually committed is not the main or only explanation for their behaviour. These perpetrators would under ordinary circumstances also have been inclined to use violent or illegal methods. They often have a criminal record. These perpetrators take deliberate advantage of the context of mass violence or are deliberately used by others because they will feel fewer inhibitions to use violence and come in handy for the political leaders. It is known that in some cases convicted criminals are deliberately recruited or released from prison in order to do the dirty work, like for example in Darfur (Prunier 2005, 97) or the convicted criminals in Nazi-Germany's concentration camps, the *Kapos*, who although prisoners themselves would be put in charge of the prisoners and as such committed many atrocities.[9] Many criminal organisations operated in the war in the former Yugoslavia. The leader of the infamous Tiger Force, Arkan is an infamous example of a criminal who was already heavily involved in crime before the war and took advantage of the war to go on with his activities (Alvarez 2006, 8).

This type of perpetrator which I call the criminal or sadist is, however, only of limited use to organisations in which obedience, loyalty and discipline are considered important virtues. Criminals and sadists usually lack these characteristics. They are motivated by their own drives rather than by obedience or conformity. It is particularly difficult to control the pathological sadists who derive sexual satisfaction from inflicting pain. Sadists even have difficulty controlling themselves and they will merely go along with the system as long as it is to their advantage. They are never fully committed to a cause, group or leader and will betray the cause whenever it is profitable for them to do so. There are

---

[9]   States sometimes deliberately use criminals in order to be able to put the blame on these individuals in case the atrocities get revealed. Jamieson (2005) reported on this phenomenon as judicial 'othering'.

consequently rather few sadists or otherwise mentally disturbed individuals among the perpetrators.[10] These perpetrators distinguish themselves by using far more violence than requested or necessary to fulfil their task. Almost all case studies show that there are always some perpetrators who go further than others and are clearly driven by violent, sadistic or other sexual impulses (see, e.g. Amnesty International 1977, 32) but this group is always a minority. Todorov (1999, 122) who based his finding on writings of camp survivors concludes that even camp survivors in Nazi-Germany seem to agree that only 5–10% could be called sadists. Although the tendency to commit crime or behave sadistically is already present, the consequences of being in an environment in which violence seems legitimised or at least unchecked can be extreme. See the chilling description of how during the Vietnam War several members of an American unit called 'Tiger Force' committed atrocious crimes by killing innocent people viciously and by collecting their ears as trophies (Sallah and Weiss 2006).

The likelihood that this type of perpetrator would be involved in crime under ordinary circumstances is rather high but it is important to note that the types of crime they would commit under ordinary circumstances might very well be far less extreme than in a context of mass violence. It can also happen that someone is well adapted, showing no signs of any criminal or sadistic tendency but that the brutalisation and lack of control in, for instance, a situation of war results in the emergence of such unknown hidden tendencies. An example thereof was documented by Drakulic (2004) who describes a young Serbian man who had been convicted for minor transgressions before the war. During the war he committed horrendous crimes during an eight-day period killing many people revealing hidden sadistic tendencies.[11] It is however unlikely that without the war he would have become a mass murderer or serial killer. Professionally trained soldiers or policemen can turn out to be sadists while their sadism did not materialize prior to recruitment. War inevitably brutalises people and might thus activate desires which would otherwise have stayed hidden under a layer of socialisation. Some perpetrators are known to have been surprised by the fact that they derived pleasure or even sexual satisfaction from inflicting pain (see, e.g. Arendt 1973, 454).[12]

---

[10] See also Crelinsten (1993: 68), Waller (2002, 69–71), Thyss (2004), Kren and Rappoport (1980, 70), Steiner (1980) and Todorov (1999, 122).

[11] See the case of Jelisic at the ICTY, *Prosecutor vs. Jelisic*, A.Ch. 5 July 2001, case nr. IT-95-10-A in which he was convicted for 13 proven killings but he probably killed maybe even more than one hundred people in an eight-day period.

[12] It is important to note however that many perpetrators are classified as criminals or sadists because they seem to derive pleasure from the pain and humiliation they cause. In many cases nervous laughter and a tough posture are often mistaken for real pleasure.

3.4. THE PROFITEER

Many people are driven by self-interest, opportunism and greed and take advantage of the situation for material gain or other advantages and thus get involved in international crimes in a period of collective violence. These perpetrators do not necessarily strongly believe in the propagated ideology but they embrace it as an efficient tool for gaining power, status or material gain. They use the opportunities that suddenly arise and during a period of collective violence will go further than they would have gone under ordinary circumstances because suddenly everything seems to be allowed and this situation offers them exceptional opportunities. These people are often rather selfish and feel that they have little influence in what happens around them and do not want to take any responsibility for it. They sometimes do have to go through a transformation phase but ultimately accept the different norms and values and come to see torture, rape, murder and even genocide as a fact of life. They might feel briefly horrified when confronted with actual human suffering for the first time but they are opportunists and rationalise and justify what they are doing. These perpetrators resemble the criminal but differ from him in that they under ordinary circumstances would probably not have crossed certain boundaries and commit certain crimes or cruelties whereas the criminals and sadists are far more likely to engage in criminality even under ordinary circumstances. These perpetrators can take up any role. A period of war or mass violence usually opens new possibilities. They can take advantage of the fact that one specific group within society is targeted, for example by taking over their houses or companies, by stealing from them, by blackmailing and extorting them or by making a career which they would otherwise not have been able to do. They might also denounce and betray others for material gain or plunder their homes once the inhabitants have left. These perpetrators can be described as profiteers.

Profiteers need not necessarily be involved in the crimes as such but they support the crimes by keeping quiet and taking advantage. If they are already a part of the system they might, for example, use the situation for an aggressive or sexual outlet and beat or rape their victims or they might start to experiment on their victims who are about to die soon anyway. The profiteer reasons as follows: 'Since these people will die anyway what is wrong with raping, torturing, killing and/or performing medical experiments on them first? What is wrong in taking their property if the victims have been expelled from their homes and will not return?' Some profiteers will commit atrocious crimes out of sheer curiosity and start to conduct experiments which under normal conditions they would not do because these experiments would be considered immoral and criminal. These perpetrators take advantage of the circumstances by crossing borders, which under ordinary circumstances they would probably have never tried to cross.

Others take advantage simply because the opportunity arises and everyone else is doing it, so why shouldn't they?

All periods of mass violence and genocide are marked by the presence of many profiteers. The targeted group is usually an alleged privileged minority and many people will benefit from the elimination of such a group. It is not uncommon that profiteers even kill in order to gain their profit like for example in Rwanda where the alleged privileged Tutsis were targeted. According to Prunier (1995, 231) the Rwandan *Interahamwe* were drafted from the poor and unemployed who could take revenge, do whatever they wanted for free. Hatzfeld (2005) interviewed a group of Rwandan *génocidaires* to whom material gain seemed to be the most important drive to maim and kill the rich Tutsis they resented. Many Nazi doctors who conducted cruel experiments on living people who were to die anyway can also be classified as typical profiteers (Lifton 1986). Three Dutch studies on traitors during the Second World War paint the picture of Dutch citizens who took advantage of the German occupation by denouncing Jews or by betraying people within the resistance in order to gain a small fee of money or a better position within society (Hofman 1981; Meershoek 1999; Van Liempt 2002). Profiteers are furthermore often accomplices and accessories to the actual physical perpetrators. They literally want to make profit and for example do business with cruel and violent regimes by selling weapons or other natural resources to oppressive regimes. Such was the case with two Dutch businessmen, Gus K. and Frans van A. (Karskens 2006) whom were recently convicted by Dutch criminal courts of arms trade and complicity in committing war crimes.[13]

3.5. THE CAREERIST

Many ordinary people are ambitious and driven by an aim to advance their careers and gain power, prestige, a good salary and status. They are usually well adapted and law-abiding citizens who often work hard and do whatever it takes to achieve their goals and aims and to fulfil their dreams: often at great costs to themselves but in many cases also at the expense of others. The re-stratification of society which is usually the aim and the result of a period of collective violence, gives many people an opportunity to advance their career. Particularly to those who did not have a career prior to this period; the events suddenly bring them new and unexpected opportunities. Many people take their chances and use these opportunities to promote themselves, gain a better position, power, influence, prestige or fame and thus get involved in international crimes. Others who were successful prior to the period of collective violence, might have had the choice of either closing their eyes and going along with it or losing everything. Faced with

---

13   See the contribution of Wim Huisman in this book.

this choice many people will decide not to 'stick out their necks' for those who are treated unfairly or badly. They will look away and continue with their jobs as if nothing has happened.[14] These people often do not show hatred or contempt but are merely focused on their own jobs and careers and do not want to endanger these. I will call them the careerists.

Careerists are particularly common when an entire state becomes involved in committing the crimes. Under ordinary circumstances it is extremely unlikely that this type of person gets involved in crime out of their own accord as this might endanger and damage their career.[15] Prior to the rise of a specific leader or a period of collective violence these careerists are often law-abiding citizens but become progressively involved in crimes often because either they are already about to make themselves a career, and simply are not prepared to risk losing their jobs or because they have taken advantage of new opportunities. Ambitious, vain or arrogant people will feel flattered by the ideology which has categorised them as a superior group or elite force. Making themselves a career, having power or ruling over others will give them a sense of power and mastery which flatters their ego. Within an oppressive regime many careerists will rapidly advance to the higher ranks in which they are very useful co-conspirators to the criminal masterminds. They seldom do the dirty work themselves: they plan, organise and delegate in order to keep their own hands clean.

The careerist is related to the profiteer: they both take advantage of the situation and are opportunistic in their way of achieving this aim. The difference between the two is that a careerist is extremely well adapted to the system and consequently rises to a specific position within the regime. Their careers are sometimes closely intertwined with the rise of the criminal system. Whenever careerists realise that it is no longer to their advantage to support a specific regime they will turn their backs on it. The profiteer is usually less well adapted and more individualistic. They do not fully identify themselves with the regime. The phenomenon of people going along with and getting involved in committing crimes in order to further their careers is well known and there are several well documented examples of careerists who rose to important positions within malignant regimes (Sereny 1974; Fest 1987; Knopp 1996; Padfield 2001; Breitman 2004; Drakulic 2004).

---

14 See for example the situation in Nazi-Germany before and during the Second World War as described by Hilberg (1992, 26). According to Hilberg, the old functionaries had to adopt new policies but otherwise continued their work and just stayed in place, not prepared to give up their position. He characterises them as careerists: for some the change of regime meant they had to adapt themselves and for many others who had embarked on a false start it meant new chances.

15 These types of people might however get involved in crime under ordinary circumstances when the organisation or cooperation they are working for gets involved in organisational crime. They would be the typical white collar criminals.

3.6. THE DEVOTED WARRIOR

Most people are law-abiding citizens who under ordinary circumstances obediently do as they are told. Yet in a period of collective violence when the authorities turn criminal, law-abiding citizens can get involved in crimes. Research has shown that many perpetrators of international crimes turn out to be very obedient, loyal and dutiful followers who completely submit themselves to an authority, a leader or an ideology in which they strongly believe. Many people do not feel themselves in a position to make their own judgment and consequently fully devote themselves to an authority they trust. They never question the leader or ideology they follow. This is even more so when they are members of a militarised unit and have gone through a training period[16] – they can easily get involved in international crimes and become perpetrators. They consider obedience, discipline, loyalty and conformity as the most important virtues of a man. Their loyalty and obedience is absolute and unconditional. They have internalised the soldier's code of honour reflecting these virtues in their daily life. They strive for a better and safer world and completely rely on others to tell them how to create such a perfect society. They consider it their job to serve their country, their leader or their superior. They do as they are told and are very eager to do their job well. They have a very strong sense of duty and are very authoritarian. In accomplishing their tasks they often go beyond the call of duty even if this costs them dearly. They are wholeheartedly and uncritically committed and are even prepared to sacrifice themselves for the greater good. To them honour and loyalty are more important than justice. They are the devoted warriors.

These perpetrators are extremely useful functionaries in all organisations. They are the ideal bureaucrats and soldiers: dutiful, law-abiding and reliable. They will not make a fuss: they are decent people, often extremely well adapted to the ruling social context and sometimes even very sophisticated. These are people who will always and absolutely live by the rules. Devoted warriors have a very strong sense of duty and responsibility but they also easily submit themselves to an authority. Under ordinary circumstances this type would never commit crime but their loyalty can be easily abused by malignant authorities. In case of an order which violates their moral code, they will probably push their own feelings aside and focus on their job as they feel bound by their duty to submit themselves to their superiors and do not take responsibility for the overall outcome. Within a malicious system or under the guidance of an evil leader such law-abiding citizens and soldiers can consequently be easily transformed into perpetrators. Devoted warriors do not have an evil character or destructive nature but they can genuinely

---

[16] See on the characteristics of a military organisation and the kind and effects of military training, Dyer (1985), Grossman (1995), Finer (1988), Haritos-Fatouras (1993, 2003), Winslow (1999) and Nadelson (2005).

come to believe that they are doing what is best for their country even if this involves the killing of fellow human beings and children. Devoted warriors are decent men and women who are following the wrong cause. They can accept that torture, murder and even genocide are necessary but they will usually not tolerate corruption or excessive or unnecessary cruelty.

Several examples of devoted warriors have been documented in which it became apparent that they accepted killing human beings but would not accept theft, sexual harassment or unnecessary maltreatment. Kressel (2002) reports that Hoess, camp commander at Auschwitz who can be considered a devoted warrior, shot a guard for abusing a prisoner and Arendt (1964, 109) described how Eichmann who had accepted genocide as a fact of life and even coordinated the extermination of the Jews during the Nazi-Germany era, was horrified when he heard about unnecessary cruelty. To the devoted warrior violence must be functional (Hilberg 1992, 53). The devoted warrior will generally dislike the sadists and fanatics whom they will most likely consider barbarians and they will probably also despise the profiteers whom they will consider unethical. Devoted warriors are driven by ideology and in that sense resemble the fanatic. However, unlike the fanatic, the devoted warrior is a very dutiful person and usually well adapted to the system and thus easy to control. Unlike the fanatic they will totally submit themselves to authority. Within an oppressive system, devoted warriors can be involved as planners and organisers of crimes, supervise these crimes or be otherwise involved in the perpetration of crimes.

The devoted warriors fill the ranks of mass movements and each state apparatus. Their participation in atrocities and international crimes is so intriguing precisely because they are so law-abiding and decent but dedicate themselves to the wrong cause. Due to the fact that they sincerely believe their actions are just and legitimate they will often go beyond the call of duty for their cause and therefore play a crucial role in the perpetration of international crimes. Hannah Arendt's (1964) thesis on the banality of evil is applicable to this type of perpetrator. Adolf Eichmann, the prototype of a devoted bureaucrat committed himself fully and completely to authority and unconditionally accepted both means and cause. He did not give it much thought. This thoughtlessness is a striking yet common and horrifying feature of this type of perpetrator. They are 'terribly and terrifyingly normal' as Arendt (1964, 276) concluded.[17] The devoted warrior has a very typical and intriguing mindset. Many Nazis can be considered devoted warriors (Hoess 1959; Sereny 1974; Welzer 2005) but there are many

---

[17]   The psychologist who examined him at his trial in Jerusalem realised that Eichmann whom everyone considered a monster was 'terribly and terrifyingly' normal and exclaimed: 'more normal, at any rate, than I am after having examined him' (Arendt 1964, 25). See also many others on Eichmann (Mulish 1961; Malkin and Stein 1990; von Lang 1991; Lozowick 2000; Wojak 2001; Cesarani 2004).

other documented examples of devoted warriors in other regimes as well (Rosenberg 1991; Osiel 2001; Payne 2003; Verbitsky 1996; Gobodo-Madikizela 2003). Their psychological make-up is remarkably similar despite the fact that they became involved in the crimes of very different regimes in a very different time period.

3.7. FOLLOWERS AND CONFORMISTS

Many perpetrators have no specific reasons to commit crime, no hatred or resentment no insatiable urge to gain profit but still get involved in crime within a period of collective violence merely because they go along with and follow the current. They don't really think for themselves; they often do not have very strong personalities and certainly do not want to lead or take responsibility. This is especially the case when taking responsibility would mean standing up against the majority and to thus risk exclusion. They are not prepared to 'stick out their necks' and to take such risks. Some of these perpetrators follow a leader or person in command or just follow the hierarchical chain of command: they are very authoritarian. Others are less influenced by authority but are strongly influenced by a group and submit to peer pressure. Both types will seldom act on their own initiative and the groups of which they become a member will determine the path of life they take. It is very likely that they are not always aware of the full consequences of becoming a member of a specific group or blindly following a leader and when they feel entrapped, saying no is simply too late. In this way, they can easily get embroiled in crime. Such perpetrators, who can be called followers and conformists, will do almost anything in their urge not be considered misfits.

Within this type we can distinguish several subtypes: the obedient follower, the naïve follower and the admirer. The naïve follower is not aware of the consequences nor is the admirer. These two subtypes are under the spell of someone they admire strongly or look up to. As a consequence of their idolatry they simply go along with whatever this person says. They feel attracted to a specific person who can, for example, be a member of their group, their platoon leader or the criminal mastermind. They do not realise that their admiration makes them lose their ability to judge the person in an objective manner. They can become involved in physically committing crimes, but they can also play rather minor roles so that they can easily close their eyes to reality and disregard any information as untrustworthy which contradicts what they want to believe. The obedient followers feel comfortable when just following orders and doing as they are told with nobody really bothering them. The obedient follower who works within an organisation simply does as he is told. He does not want to take any responsibility. He accepts things as they are: his position in the hierarchy and the demands for obedience and loyalty. Many obedient followers are rather disciplined and want to perform a good job. The obedient follower is often authoritarian: he accepts orders from someone in a superior position and demands obedience and loyalty from someone in a subordinate position. He does not ask questions on what is right or wrong but simply expects that his superiors know this and expects them to take responsibility for this. An obedient follower is usually very passive and in that sense he can be distinguished from the devoted warrior who usually occupies a higher position on the hierarchical ladder and takes far more initiative. A devoted warrior will go beyond the call of duty, an obedient follower would not. He only takes any action or initiative if he is specifically asked to do so. Obedient followers might feel some empathy for the victims but they take the righteousness of the decision of their superiors for granted. A final point is that in times of crisis, psychologically healthy personalities can feel vulnerable and fall prey to a charismatic leader to whom they submit; they are simply overwhelmed by uncertainty and the security of a group or mass movement with a directive leader makes them feel secure again and is therefore considered psychologically attractive (Post 2004, 195–196).

The conformist does not take any initiative either but simply follows the group and behaves in conformity to the norms dictated within the group. He will never stand up and raise his voice in deviance to what is the general opinion. He submits himself to normative social influence and simply accepts the given social definition of reality. He does not particularly like to be at the centre of attention nor does he aim to take over the role of leader but he follows and goes along with the situation. He does not take any responsibility because the responsibility rests with the leader or the group. He does not feel responsible for his own deeds. The conformist will always seek to express the opinions that are prevalent within the group and if he has other opinions he will not reveal them or will change them. He easily adapts to different situations and can thus be dragged easily into violence and violations. He is afraid of being rejected from the group or to be seen as a coward or an outcast. Sometimes their entire identity depends a lot on their membership of the group. They sometimes feel a strong comradeship and can be very loyal towards their fellow group members. Conformists can play all types of roles. Their role can be rather small and limited but they will often join in the rape, torture or killing of members of the targeted group. It all depends on the groups of which they are a member.

Within the ranks of the accessories there will be a considerable number of followers and conformists. Many of them will have played very small roles, as for example Hitler's secretary who took notes and typed Hitler's speeches. She herself did not commit any crimes nor had any strong feelings about what was going on around her but she was an accessory to the crimes as she played her own yet indispensable role by serving Hitler. She was thrilled by the fact that he had picked her to be his secretary and secretly admired him. She enjoyed being close to so much power and wealth and enjoyed a good life (Junge and Müller 2002).[18] Many functionaries within destructive and oppressive regimes will have had similar small roles and simply went along with the situation. Destructive regimes are built on the silent co-operation of thousands, maybe even millions.

These types of perpetrators can however also become physical perpetrators, especially when they are members of a militarised unit. In his study on Reserve Police Battalion 101, Browning (1992) showed that the reason why many members of this unit accepted the order to kill and execute Jews was that they were afraid of disappointing the others and being considered outcasts, weaklings or cowards, so they went along with it. Many American soldiers of Company C – Charley's Company – which was responsible for the massacre at My Lai during the Vietnam War in which up to five hundred unarmed civilians were killed can be classified as conformists. These trained soldiers were tired and nerve-wracked by the ongoing war. They were sent to My Lai for a 'kill and destroy'-mission of the alleged Viet Cong stronghold there. Upon arrival they only encountered old men, women and children, all unarmed. Yet the order to 'finish them off' was given and almost the whole platoon obeyed this order. They just obeyed, just went along with it, thereby becoming responsible for one of the most atrocious war crimes ever committed by the American army (Bilton and Sim 1992; Kelman and Hamilton 1989).[19] In some cases conformists are outraged by a specific order or policy and yet they do not dare to stand up or defect. In those cases they will go along but try to save some people, try to be a 'good and kind' perpetrator (Lifton 1986; Los 1976). It is known that one soldier at My Lai deliberately shot himself in his foot in order to be able to get out without getting a court martial or probably more importantly, losing face.

Whether followers and conformists will get involved in crime under ordinary circumstances depends very much on the circumstances and the groups they become a member of. Under ordinary circumstances however there are often many more options and alternatives. These people might switch groups in time and are thus less likely to get involved with the wrong groups. However, in an oppressive state or military unit it is much more difficult to defect and the followers and conformists are much more likely to get involved in committing crimes.

---

[18]   Junge realised how naïve she was after the war when she saw the statue of Sophie Scholl who was precisely her age but had opposed Hitler's regime. At that moment she realised that she too should have known better.
[19]   Life magazine revealed the atrocities in an article in 1970.

3.8. THE COMPROMISED PERPETRATOR

Some perpetrators do not commit the crimes out of their own initiative or accord but because they are pressured, forced, coerced or tricked into doing so. They definitely do not agree with the policy and more particularly the crimes but are forced to co-operate. They are usually vulnerable to pressure because they are for example members of or related to members of the targeted groups or because they have a socially underprivileged or vulnerable position, like the unemployed or children. These people co-operate merely because they feel they have no choice or in order to save their lives or the lives of their loved ones. In some cases they co-operate with their persecutors because they are under the impression that if they co-operate they can, to some extent at least, undermine the perpetrators and thus limit the damage and keep the situation in control. In many cases this type of perpetrator plays a minor role as accomplice or accessory but sometimes they become physical perpetrators. In Rwanda during the genocide in 1994 for example, many Hutus who were married to Tutsis were forced to prove their loyalty to the cause by killing other Tutsis. Many did so out of fear that either they themselves or their Tutsi wives would be killed. There are many similar well documented examples from the Second World War. The Jewish Councils for example were forced to co-operate with the Germans in selecting Jews to be sent to the camps. The Councils complied hoping to thus be able to save many lives but by doing so they helped to make the destruction process run smoothly and thus became an unwilling and reluctant accessory to the genocide on their own people (Arendt 1964). These perpetrators can be considered compromised perpetrators.

Many child soldiers can be classified as compromised perpetrators. This is especially obvious when they are abducted and forced but also those who are picked up from the streets where they live in extreme poverty can be considered to be compromised. These children are given shelter, clothes, food, a salary and a better position within society if and only if they join the army or the specific group. They have no means to resist the often armed adults who recruit them. Besides, the alternative is to be shot on the spot or to continue to live in extreme poverty. Most children will take their chances and simply force themselves to adapt and do as they are told. Some child soldiers volunteer but it depends very much on the situation whether the application is really voluntary or whether their vulnerability is abused and they are lured into recruitment (Brett and Specht 2004; Singer 2006; Honwana 2006; Wessells 2006). It is for example known that in Africa many girls are taken as child soldiers and used as sexual slaves for the men. Some of these girls try to become fierce fighters and capture other girls in order to protect themselves from being abused sexually (HRW 2004b, 29–31).

If the story of one of the first defendants who was tried by the Yugoslavian tribunal is genuine he can also be considered a compromised perpetrator. This person was half Croatian half Serb and a reluctant participant in the war (Drakulic 2004, 106–120). When he received the order to execute Muslims from Srebrenica who had been brought to the execution site he complained and initially refused to carry it out. He was however told to either obey the order or to stand in line with the prisoners and be executed himself. Scared and with his wife and young child in mind he reluctantly obeyed the order. He had reason to believe that he would indeed be shot on the spot if he did not comply so he took part in the executions that day and was thus responsible for the killing of about seventy people.[20]

The compromised perpetrator becomes involved in international crimes because coercion, force or threats are used, either explicitly or implicitly. But an initially compromised perpetrator can sadly enough be transformed into a far less reluctant participant. This happened for example to a Dutch Jewish woman who was about to be deported during the Second World War when she was given the opportunity to save her own life by revealing the whereabouts of other Jews. She accepted the offer and got herself into a seemingly never-ending spiral of betrayal. Hundreds of fellow Jews were sent to the concentration camps and certain death as a result of her betrayal (Groen 1994).

3.9.   THE PROFESSIONAL

Some perpetrators are trained torturers or killers. They are members of the military, police, secret service or any other specialised and militarised unit and usually have gone through a specifically designed and sometimes extremely coercive training programme in which recruits are disciplined and learn to accept a very strict hierarchy and are taught to obey all orders unquestioningly.[21] Such training programmes are extremely harsh: the recruits are not only physically exhausted to the point of collapse but are often deprived of primary facilities, continuously humiliated, beaten or otherwise maltreated. During the first months of such a training period they are at the mercy of their superiors and often feel utterly deserted and lost. In the meantime they get desensitised and brutalised. The purpose of the training is to break the recruit's personality and to de-individualise and depersonalise them. Recruits are drilled in order to make them act instinctively, without thinking. They have learned to focus on their jobs and to push all feelings which can obstruct their work aside. Within such extreme, coercive and deliberately designed training programmes recruits are trained to

---

[20]   See the Erdemovic case, ICTY 7 October 1997, *Prosecutor vs. Erdemovic*, case No. IT-96–22-A. The Chamber who convicted and sentenced him was aware of the difficult situation this young man faced. In a close verdict (3–2) he was nevertheless found guilty of war crimes and sentenced to five years' imprisonment. See both the joint separate and the separate and dissenting opinions.

[21]   During WWII the Nazi's called this quite appropriately '*Kadaverdisziplin*'.

arrest people, use violence, maim and kill without mercy (Dyer 1985; Grossman 1995; Haritos-Fatouras 1993, 2003; Nadelson 2005). They have been trained (or actually conditioned) to obey each and every order unquestionably, no matter how extreme and cruel. Initially the recruits within such a training programme will react to clearly visible threats and obey out of fear but during the several months of training (apparently a period of three months is usually enough), they internalise this fear and continue to do their jobs even in the absence of such a clear threat. At this stage they have been successfully transformed into instruments of violence and destruction and they have become professional torturers and killers.[22] After the harsh training period the recruits become professional torturers or killers. Most perpetrators do not particularly enjoy maiming, torturing or killing people but ultimately they can get completely used to violence and violations and come to see their actions as a mere job, as nothing out of the ordinary. Haritos-Fatouras and Gibson (1986), who analysed the methods used at the Greek torture school which operated during the Greek colonels' regime (1967–1974),[23] concluded that 'there is a cruel method in teaching people how to torture. Almost anyone can learn it'.[24]

The only way ordinary people can cope with being coerced into regularly inflicting extreme pain or killing a fellow human being is by emotionally distancing themselves from the pain they cause to their victims and by fully accepting the justification and rationale provided to them by the authority they obey as well as by a mechanism called *doubling* (Lifton 1986). Doubling refers to a psychological state of mind in which people create a separate reality (Crelinsten, 2003) out of the sheer urge to psychologically survive (Smeulers 2004). They accept this separate reality as their professional world in which they live but which is separated from the ordinary world of their private lives (Lifton 1986). These perpetrators have a professional self and a personal or private self. The professional self operates within the professional world in which the individual often wears a uniform and uses nicknames – and the norms and values which apply in this world are in many respects at odds with the norms and values which apply in the ordinary world. Whereas in the ordinary world it is not right to hurt someone, this moral rule does not apply to the dehumanised enemies whom they target in the professional world. To a certain extent the professional resembles the devoted warrior: they both come to see violence as a part of their job. The difference between a professional and a devoted warrior is that the devoted warrior is much more committed to a specific cause than the professional. A professional would

---

[22]   Huggins et al. (2002, 144) note quite correctly that there is a huge difference between the various professions such as torturers and killers. The work of a torturer is 'slow and methodological' whereas killing someone is often a 'quick and spontaneous' act.

[23]   See Amnesty International 1977.

[24]   See also Haritos-Fatouras 2003.

probably have no problem whatsoever in changing sides during a war. To the professional, torture and killing is just a job. To the devoted warrior it is a job with a cause.

A very well documented example of a true professional who has been trained in an extremely coercive training school is provided by Haritos-Fatouras (2003). Haritos-Fatouras describes the training given to the recruits of the military police, the ESA during the Greek colonels' regime (1967–1974). The recruits were forced to go through an extremely coercive training programme in which they were transformed into torturers. Haritos-Fatouras describes how one of the recruits adapted to the coercive system surrounding him and after the initial training period rapidly advanced to the rank of chief prison warden and became a torturer. He was good at his job and at the time proud of it. He could earn several days of leave if he managed to make the prisoners talk and that was what he tried to do. He did not enjoy the violence but ruthlessly used every method, no matter how cruel, in order to achieve his aim of making the prisoners talk and to gather information. In an interview the torturer explained that at the beginning he disliked his job but that he ultimately got used to it. In the end he felt nothing about what he was doing: it was his job, nothing more nothing less, and at the time he thought it was all justified. He did not give it much thought. He was trained to be tough so he was tough. Even several of his victims described him as a professional merely doing his job.[25] In a series of extensive interviews he said that he was transformed into an instrument, a human being without a will of his own who just did as he was told. Only after the fall of the regime did he start to realise what he had been doing. Both the compromised perpetrators and the professional are initially coerced into using force and violence and this is the only reason why they got involved.

4.   HOW DO THE PERPETRATORS LOOK BACK?

Almost all perpetrators of international crimes will perceive their crimes and behaviour as legitimate and justified at the time of committing these crimes. After the fall of the regime and the subsequent return to normality, some perpetrators will have to stand trial and are held responsible for their crimes. Almost all perpetrators who have to stand trial will experience this as utterly unjust. They will feel betrayed. What they did seemed justified and legitimised: the state ordered or condoned their crimes and now they are held responsible and accountable. The devoted warrior, the professional, the conformist and the follower will all feel embittered by the fact that they have to defend themselves

---

[25]   Movie 'Your Neighbours' Son' by Ebbe Preisler in 1982.

once in the dock. They merely followed orders; they submitted themselves to an authority, leader or group. They wanted to do good, sometimes even at great costs to themselves and now suddenly they are held responsible because the authority, the leader or the group they trusted turned out to be untrustworthy. How could they have known? They feel lost and betrayed and expect their former superiors to protect them and take all the blame. But this seldom happens and leaves them exposed. They are angry at the system and the people who turned them into perpetrators. They feel abused and victimised and often end up bitterly accusing their superiors who let them down. Many realise that what they have done is wrong but will keep justifying it to themselves by pointing to the system and transformation process they were forced to go through. Typical excuses given by these perpetrators after they have committed mass atrocities and while standing trial are: 'I had to defend my country', 'I just followed orders' and 'I was merely a small cog in a big machine'.

The careerists too will feel embittered. They had embarked on glorious careers and are now exposed as criminals. This feels to them like an utter disgrace and careerists will probably start to deny any knowledge of the crimes or accept the reality and try to save face and perhaps ultimately their life by simultaneously pointing an accusing finger at their former leader and by acknowledging their limited guilt. Realistic careerists will start to work on a new career. They might show sorrow and remorse but sometimes they might only do so because they know this will earn them respect. In reality it might very well be that the only thing they really feel sorry about are their lost careers and shattered dreams, although in some cases the remorse of a careerist seemed genuine (Drakulic 2004, 181). They will have a strong feeling of bitterness and resentment towards the person they once followed: look what he has dragged me into and now my whole career is shattered. They will probably feel a strong urge to tell their side of the story, a bad luck story in which they have fallen victim to a deceptive leader. It is not uncommon for a careerist to try and reinstate himself by publishing their stories in a book.[26]

Criminal masterminds will try to flee rather than surrender. If they are nevertheless apprehended they will always challenge the legitimacy of the court and deny the court the right to try them. They will try to use the court as a political arena. Fanatics will also not acknowledge the right of a court to hold them accountable. They perceive their own ideology as infallible and each and everyone who dares to question their ideology is perceived as incompetent. Even when in court the fanatics will not give up. They will use each and every opportunity to take the stand and try to convince others of their righteousness. They will seldom do their own defence any good.

---

[26] See for example the books by Karpinski (2005) and Speer (1975).

Criminals and sadists will, on the contrary – unless they are psychopaths – probably be fully aware of the crimes they committed and will consider the fact that they are caught most likely as plain bad luck. They will realise that they were wrong and realise that they have gone too far. For practical reasons they will either simply admit their guilt or take a specific line of defence such as: 'These were the orders I got', 'Everyone did it' or 'I was serving my country'. In the dock it is probably difficult to distinguish them from the devoted warriors, conformists and followers. The compromised perpetrators are also fully aware of the fact that they committed crimes and that things turned out for the worse. They feel guilty about it despite the fact that they know that they had been faced with a devil's choice. They feel genuine remorse and sometimes even feel that they deserve punishment. In the dock a genuine guilty plea is likely.[27]

As long as we take into account that there will be individual differences we might be able to guess what kind of perpetrator someone was by the way he or she defends himself in court. In the dock perpetrators will use all means to defend themselves and some will deliberately lie or misrepresent the facts.[28] Apart from the criminal/sadist and the profiteer who will often and deliberately lie and try to get away with what they have done, it will be nevertheless interesting to listen to the defence arguments of many of these perpetrators. It appears that their misrepresentations of fact are sometimes conscious lies but more often they represent the truth as they perceived it. Many perpetrators did not aim to commit crimes but after the fall of the regime or in the dock suddenly realise that by going along with a situation, taking advantage of the situation and by just doing as they were told, they supported an oppressive regime and committed war crimes, crimes against humanity or genocide. It had all seemed justified and legitimate and now they are held responsible. They feel deceived and horrified and will do anything to sooth their consciences. They suddenly realise that they have been wicked and wrong. More important than deceiving the judges, is arguably their aim to deceive themselves: they desperately want to believe that they cannot be blamed, that they were victims themselves.[29] The lies many perpetrators tell in the dock are not invented excuses but often represent the psychological reality they have created for themselves to cope with the experienced cognitive dissonance (Festinger 1957).

Payne (2003, 163) refers to the lies of perpetrators as 'vital lies' as they keep the image of themselves as a good person intact. The concept of vital lies was developed by Goleman (1984) but fits the line of defence of many perpetrators perfectly.

---

[27] Many other guilty pleas are not genuine but merely accepted in a gamble of taking one's chances in order to get a lighter sentence.

[28] See Payne 2003, for a discussion of the meaning of perpetrators' confessions and Huggins et al., 2002: 196.

[29] See for example Gitta Sereny's (1995) appropriately titled book based on the many interviews she had with Albert Speer, namely *Albert Speer: his battle with truth*.

People aim to justify themselves and want to believe that they are good people. Ordinary people who have committed atrocities will almost inevitably fall into a self-created 'state of denial' (Cohen 2001). Perpetrators who are courageous enough to face the crimes they have committed and accept their own responsibility will often suffer nightmares, nervous breakdowns or a post-traumatic stress disorder. Vernado Simpson, one of the soldiers responsible for the massacre at My Lai during the Vietnam War for example was completely nerve-wracked by the slow and gradual awareness of the devastating truth of what he had done which was triggered by the sad death of his own son (Bilton and Sim 1992, 5–7). He, however, is not the only one. Many perpetrators are known to suffer pangs of conscience (Browning 1989, Alvarez 2001; Huggins et al. 2002, 210; Sallah and Weiss 2006). Ordinary people who have committed horrendous crimes can seldom really cope with the horrors they have brought about. Denial and self-deception will be consciously and unconsciously used in order to psychologically survive this terrible burden.

5. COMMON FEATURES AND CONCLUDING REMARKS

When a social order progresses on a path to collective madness many individuals get involved: some fanatically and willingly, others reluctantly. One of the most remarkable features of a period of collective violence is that many ordinary people end up through circumstances maiming, torturing or killing their fellow human beings. Especially in situations when an entire state becomes involved, many law–abiding citizens become involved in international crimes such as war crimes, crimes against humanity and genocide. As individuals, many of them will not be able to change the course of events but by simply continuing to function – going along – they all play their own small but indispensable role. A criminal mastermind would be powerless without the support of the masses. These masses submit themselves to a collective goal and more importantly submit to a social construction and/or definition of reality in which maiming, torturing and killing a fellow human being becomes a necessity. These masses consequently function within a massive and destructive state apparatus. Many authors have stressed the point that perpetrators of international crimes are ordinary people in extraordinary circumstances. Within conventional criminology, crime is explained by motivation and opportunity and the lack of constraints and control. In criminogenic society the constraints and control are lacking, the norms and values have changed to such an extent that extreme cruelty seems to be nothing out of the ordinary. Due to this situation many people who under ordinary circumstances would probably never have committed any crime, might do so under these circumstances. Extremely violent behaviour such as genocide or torture are no longer recognised or considered as being wrong.

The various perpetrator types described in this chapter can all be easily recognised in an ordinary state apparatus, army or business company, albeit known by different names: the boss, the careerist, the opportunist, the hardworking idealist, the almost invisible but indispensable bureaucrats who do as they are told. Within ordinary circumstances they would not turn to crime. But malicious intent, hatred, fear, greed and abused idealism sometimes create a dangerous mix and may explode in an episode of collective violence. Once this happens many people get involved merely by not actively opposing the orders of the state or not stopping the collective madness. In this manner they inevitably become involved in international crimes. Within an evil system the social context is thrown upside down and in such systems we have to fear those who abide by the law more than those who break the law. All those who believe in state policy, who just do as they are told, who go along with or simply follow the current get involved in mass atrocities. A common feature of all perpetrators is that they submit themselves to the dominant social order and adapt to these extraordinary circumstances and as such get progressively involved in an evil system.

People can be guided by more than one motive. The typology presented here is based on the presumed existence of one predominant motivational factor. Moving forward on a continuum of destructiveness, perpetrators can however sometimes be transformed from one type into another. Followers and conformists can become professionals or devoted warriors or turn into greedy profiteers. A professional can turn out to be a careerist or sadist. Someone who is compromised in co-operating can start to derive pleasure from his position, as for instance many so-called 'Kapos' in Germany's concentration camps.[30] It will largely depend on the type of regime and the ruling ideology to determine what type of perpetrator is predominant. Genocide scholars for example have among others distinguished between ideological genocides and developmental genocides. In the first type of genocide, as was the case in Nazi-Germany, a criminal mastermind supported by a group of loyal careerists and fanatics will lead masses of devoted warriors, followers and conformists, whereas in a developmental genocide an underprivileged minority tries to restructure society and make it fairer. Material and social gain will be the prime motive and the predominant type of perpetrator will be the profiteer. An extremely authoritarian and dictatorial regime like the colonels' regime in Greece (1967–1974) will train a limited number of recruits to become professional torturers and killers. In a war situation, a military unit can

---

[30] In German concentration camps some inmates, usually former convicts or political prisoners were appointed as *Kapos* and had a certain degree of power over the other inmates. Many *Kapos* abused this power.

be easily held under the spell of a fanatic, a criminal, sadist or a profiteer who instigates the crimes in which followers and conformists join.

Scholars have pinpointed many factors which facilitate or cause atrocities such as war crimes, crimes against humanity and genocide and have quite rightly stated that we need to look into many different levels starting with international society. Ultimately, however, it comes down to the individual perpetrator to apply an electric device or to pull the trigger. As public prosecutor Taylor said at the Nuremberg trials: abstract entities do not commit crimes, individuals do. This paper aimed to analyse how and why individuals are transformed into instruments of mass destruction. By creating a typology of perpetrators I aimed to give all these cogs within the machine, the big ones but also the extremely small (but still indispensable) ones a human face.

XI. A SOCIOLOGY OF TORTURE

Martha K. Huggins

1. INTRODUCTION

This chapter has five parts. The first, 'Predicting Torture,' points to my prior research on torturers in Brazil (Huggins et al. 2002), in which I identified conditions that set the stage for and justify systemic state-sanctioned torture. In the second section, 'Torture 101,'[1] I identify the patterned and historically consistent body of research that is foundational for understanding torture as a systemic phenomenon. In preparing for this paper, I assumed that I could locate empirical criminological research on torture in English-language academic and professional publications, and hoped to be guided in further developing my 'Torture 101' model with such information, so I searched the professional and academic criminology sources on-line[2] for scholarship on torture by criminologists. This chapter's third and fourth sections ('Torture and Criminology' and 'Summarizing Results') present the outcomes of that exploration. Having found very little research and scholarship by criminologists on torture, I have set out in the conclusion ('Criminology and Torture'), ways that criminology might study and theorize about torture, which necessarily begins with a resolve to do so.

---

[1]   In many U.S. university curricula, the course designation '101,' as in 'Sociology 101,' points to the introductory nature of the course. Such a course introduces the main paradigms, theories, and research on the subject of the particular discipline. 'Torture 101' suggests what everyone should know for studying torture.

[2]   I researched the English-language publishing on torture (1990–present) by criminologists, hoping to focus particularly on how they approached this subject. One of my greatest challenges was to figure out who among a set of listed authors was or was not a criminologist, defined as a person either trained and working in the discipline in an academic or practice setting, or consistently publishing some articles in professional journals of criminology, and, for academics, also teaching courses in crime, justice, and or deviance. I have left law school faculty and NGO practitioners out of the designation 'criminologist', unless they fit these criteria. For example, legal scholar Paul Chevigny, who taught at the New York University Law School and who has done research for American Watch (Chevigny, 1987), but who also publishes in criminology-oriented journals/books, would be included as a lawyer and law school academic in the 'criminologist' category.

2. PREDICTING TORTURE

As a criminologist of practice, university academic, and long-time researcher with the 'supranational' criminology (www.supranationalcriminology.org) perspective, I had discovered that by synthesizing a wealth of information about the factors that had nurtured and justified 'atrocity' in many different societal and historical contexts – much like Alette Smeulers has done for her contribution to this volume ('Perpetrators of international crimes: towards a typology') – I was able to predict as early as 2002 (Huggins 2002) that torture was carried out at the United States holding facility at Guantanamo Bay, Cuba. I had begun pulling together an academic synthesis for making this prediction long before the infamous photographs of abuses by U.S. personnel against detainees at Central Iraq's Abu Ghraib Prison were shown by CBS Television's '60 Minutes II' on April 28th 2004, and also before the investigative journalism of Abu Ghraib abuse by Seymour M. Hirsch (2004), and legal research and analysis by Special Council for Human Rights Watch, Reed Brody (2004).

Before the journalistic and human rights investigations had been made public, in the first months of 2004 – using a somewhat less fleshed out model of what I had begun to label 'Torture 101' (Huggins 2003) – I wrote editorials warning that torture was very likely to by occurring in Afghanistan and Iraq, as well as at the U.S. prison at Guantanamo Bay. As a criminologist-sociologist who had written about torture and its 'supranational' components in *Political Policing* (1998 and 1999) and in *Violence Workers* (Huggins et al. 2002 and 2006), as well as teaching university courses on torture since 2001,[3] I felt it my professional responsibility to write academically about the conditions fostering and promoting torture. I wondered at the time why other U.S. criminologists were not doing the same. Did the largely national focus of U.S. criminology militate against 'supranational' criminology themes? Did American criminologists see what was going on in Afghanistan and Iraq as subjects for a different academic discipline? Did the human rights components of torture suggest its exclusive relevance for human rights non-governmental organizations? Did the absence of hard data, except as gathered by human rights organizations or by journalists, make the subject seem not amenable to 'objective' criminological research? Did such views consign torture to journalism and human rights organizations, rather than to criminology? These questions motivated me to conduct research into criminological research on torture.

Yet long before that, in Spring 2002, I had submitted an editorial ('Treat prisoners like human beings', 2002), to New York State's *Albany Times Union*

---

[3]   I included a unit on torture in 2001 my Union College 'sociology of deviance' course and have taught an entire course ('Violence Workers') on atrocity and torture since joining the Tulane University faculty in 2003.

newspaper, warning that prisoner conditions at Guantanamo allowed interrogations there to become torture. My model for making this claim was based not on an image of the kinds of people likely to torture, but on the political, social, and cultural facilitating conditions that promote, encourage, and excuse it. After thirty years of sociological research on state violence, including, in 2003, interviews with Brazilian police torturers, I felt confident about the ability of my model to predict such violence in prisons, jails, and interrogation safe houses. Guided by my initial 'Torture 101' model, in early April 2004, I submitted editorials to a number of U.S. newspapers declaring the probability of prisoner mistreatment in Afghanistan and Iraq. The newspaper editors found that my arguments lacked 'sufficient data'. I had asserted that prisoner torture in Iraq, Afghanistan and at Guantanamo could be predicted from decades of research on obedience to authority (Milgram 1974; Zimbardo et al 2000), scholarly research on torture and other violence in Argentina (Payne 2003; Verbitsky 1996), in Brazil (Huggins et al 2002), Cambodia (Chandler 1997), Greece (Haritos-Fatouros 2002); on prisoner mistreatment in pre-WWII Japan (Gold 1996), in Nazi Germany (Lifton 1986; Kater 1989; Smeulers 2004); on the shaping of killers in Poland (Browning 1992), and from research on the normal processes that shape what I label 'violence workers' – U.S. police and death house guards (see Conroy 2001; Henry 2004; Johnson 1997; Toch 1996; Worden 1996).

In my Spring 2004 editorials, I listed ten factors in the U.S. 'war against terror' – particularly in U.S. occupied Middle Eastern war zones and at Guantanamo – that laid a foundation for systemic state-sanctioned torture by U.S. agents. The U.S. Military's[4] Taguba (2004) and Fay (2004) Reports, and the investigative reporting by Seymour Hirsch (2004) and Reed Brody (2004 and 2005) on Abu Ghraib prison torture, would later reveal – much like the older academic research that I had previously synthesized – that torture, as an on-going socio-organizational dynamic, is nurtured and sustained by ten definable elements that promote, hide, and justify it. These ten factors, which are developed below in my 'Torture 101' model, promote and sustain a torture *system* by: (1) labelling torture as something other than what it is; (2) advancing and employing ideologies that support and promote torture; (3) developing ad-hoc legalism to justify torture. Taking these three components as the foundation for *serial* torture, such abuse is elevated to the organizational level – e.g., into (4) a *system* – through the addition of six

---

4   The Taguba Report (5/2004), by Army Major General Anthony Taguba can be located at *http:// news.findlaw.com/cnn/docs/iraq/tagubarpt.html*; see also the investigative report on the Taguba Report and on Taguba himself by Seymour Hirsch in The New York (6/20/2007), Annals of National Security. 'The General's Report: How Antonio Taguba, who investigated the Abu Ghraib scandal, became one of its casualties' (http://www.newyorker.com/ reporting/2007/06/25/070625fa_fact_hersh). For the Fay Report, by Army Major General George Fay, see: 'Executive Summary: Investigation of Intelligence Activities At Abu Ghraib,' 8/25/2004. *(http://fl1.findlaw.com/news.findlaw.com/hdocs/docs/dod/fay82504rpt.pdf)*.

organizational components: (5) multiple actors, including perpetrators – who are in the minority within a torture system – and facilitators – who make up the majority of actors in a torture system; (6) who interact within a hierarchal division of labour that diffuses the visibility of, and responsibility for, torture, (7) through organizational insularity and secrecy, (8) while encouraging and rewarding competition between actors to secure 'the best' information and/or the 'most important' terrorists; (9) and by ignoring torture when it occurs and hiding it from outsiders, (10) which therefore grants on-going implicit and explicit impunity to those who torture, except in those rare cases of public disclosure when a few lower-level actors will be prosecuted as 'bad apples,' leaving the larger torture system and its powerful facilitators essentially intact.

3. TORTURE 101: A CRIMINOLOGICAL MODEL?

3.1. MISLABELLING

The word 'torture' is mislabelled or avoided by perpetrators and responsible officials alike, although those with power have a greater capacity to shape and work to ensure the legitimacy of such euphemistic definitions. Many scholars have demonstrated that torturers use less negative terms to refer to the violence that they carry out (see, for example, Chandler 1997; Crelinsten 1993, Huggins 2003; Payne 2003; Presser 2004; Scully and Marolla 1985). Indeed, the Brazilian torturers I interviewed in 1993, seldom used the word torture, referring to it as 'that type of conduct', 'a conversation with our prisoners', or 'conducting research (…) and looking for data'. They would admit to having carried out such 'lesser excesses' as 'slapping (…) and punching [a prisoner] around a little' or 'hanging [a prisoner] up there'. When torture had gone 'too far', the torturer pointed to his having 'commit[ed] a mistake' or engaged in 'unnecessary excesses' (Huggins et al 2002).

In the case of higher officials, investigations of U.S. 'abuse' of imprisoned Iraqis disclosed a reluctance by United States officials to use the 'T' word, with various U.S. Government-associated actors describing this violence as 'degradation', 'staging', 'mistreatment', 'tough interrogation'. Presumably, these forms of violence – besides being seen as falling well short of torture – can be neatly frozen in time and not devolve into torture. In fact, however, inside a prison and its interrogation chambers – especially during the preliminary 'softening up' interrogation sessions – where, at Abu Ghraib, physical or psychological mistreatment was part of the interrogation process – the 'lesser' forms of violence quickly turn into more serious forms, including torture and killing (see Browning 1992; Haney et al 1977). Violent interactions are not static; violence produces more and usually more serious forms of violence (see Toch 1969, 199; Warden 1996).

3.2. IDEOLOGY

In today's world there is a plethora of ideologies of 'national security'. During the 'Cold War' the war was against 'communists' and fellow-travellers. Torture is nurtured and justified by ideologies that create an ever-expanding category of 'enemy others'. Where 'good' nations are threatened by 'evil-doers', and it is assumed that anyone could be an 'enemy', there can and need be no restrictions on interrogation. Fear, whether or not deliberately instilled,[5] – as with fictions about 'weapons of mass destruction', grants legitimacy to torture. Where a 'threat' is said to operate outside civilized law, a state's response can legitimately follow suit. This was as true during Brazil's military period (1964–1985), as it is for the United States today.

3.3. AD-HOC LEGALISM

As stated above, a torture-enabling culture is fostered and excused by official executive-level decisions that make torture seem legitimate. In 2002, the Bush administration simply declared that detainees were not covered by the U.S. Constitution or international law. Under pressure from the State Department, this ruling was revised to apply only to Guantanamo's 'illegal combatants', a status simply assigned to such detainees by the Bush administration officials rather than by 'military tribunals', as required by the Geneva Convention.

Attempting in Spring 2004 to clarify the Bush administration's position on Iraqi prisoners, then-Secretary of Defense Donald Rumsfeld, explained before the Senate Armed Services Committee that at the Abu Ghraib prison the Geneva Conventions apply to the incarcerated 'in one way or another'. The Conventions apply directly to 'the Prisoners of War, [but] the criminals (…) are handled under a different provision of the Geneva Convention' (NYT 2005, A-6). Rumsfeld failed to identify the legal status of 'battlefield detainees', unless these are the 'criminals' to whom the Defense Secretary referred. The Bush Administration claims to accept application of the Geneva Accords and the UN Convention against Torture – except when it does not, an illustration of what some legal scholars call 'international law a la carte'. Such a flexible legal standard makes prisoners

---

5   For a discussion of how such ideologies are instilled and maintained, see Kelman and Hamilton (1989) on authorization, dehumanization and routinization.

vulnerable to torture, especially when the definition of torture itself shifts according to international, national, and local political pressures.

In fact, the UN Convention against Torture, signed by the U.S. in 1994, defines torture as 'any act that creates severe pain and suffering, whether physical or mental, intentionally inflicted to obtain information, or a confession, or to punish'. Accordingly, Iraqi prisoners were subjected to cruel and unusual treatment and torture when they were:

- held for prolonged periods without formal charges;
- kept without food and water;
- were stripped naked and placed in dark cells;
- held in solitary confinement for sustained periods;
- subjected to psychological terror;
- attacked by dogs;
- burned;
- forced to simulate or perform sex;
- prodded with electric poles;
- subjected to repeated rectal examinations;
- sodomized with light bulbs;
- raped;
- choked until their collapse;
- beaten, sometimes to death.
  (see *NYT* 2004a, A-11)

To maintain that Abu Ghraib prisoners were not tortured must call into question U.S. State Department and CIA lawyers' identifying the conditions under which U.S. interrogators *could avoid* prosecution for having carried out 'rough interrogations'. According to the ad-hoc legal reasoning of Bush administration lawyers:

- Since Guantanamo's 'unlawful combatants' have no status in U.S. Constitutional or in international law, they have no protection against torture.
- Torture by foreign governments – e.g. 'by proxy' – will not implicate the U.S., even though information obtained through torture is passed on to the United States (see Jamieson and McEvoy 2005).
- A torturer is guilty 'only if he acts with the express purpose of inflicting severe pain or suffering on a person within his control.'
- 'The Federal torture statute will not be violated as long as any of the proposed strategies are not specifically intended to cause severe physical or prolonged mental harm.'

– Interrogation that 'simulates torture' may be used as long as such acts stop 'short of serious injury'.
(see *Washington Post*, 6/24/04)

A torture-enabling culture is created and legitimized when lawyers indicate how to skirt international and national laws against torture. Moreover, it provides a façade of legitimacy that the United States Secretary of Defense Donald Rumsfeld was designated to 'sign off' on forms of prisoner interrogation – presumably in Iraq, Afghanistan, and at Guantanamo – considered 'overly stressful'. Like Humpty Dumpty in Lewis Carroll's *Through the Looking Glass*, when Secretary of Defense Rumsfeld certified that torture was not torture, he made this word into what he chose 'it to mean – neither more nor less'.

Abu Ghraib prisoner torture teaches that broad definitional flexibility, backed by the power to make definitions stick, filters down to those carrying out interrogations, creating a favourable climate for torture, albeit often under a different name. Lest the inherently systemic nature of torture be overlooked, the remainder of this analysis places torture within a larger system that includes multiple actors, a division of labour, diffusion of responsibility, competition, secrecy, and impunity. Taking these components of torture systems, one at a time, we begin with the torture system itself.

3.4. SYSTEMIC

Torture is part of a system, not the work of a few 'bad apples'. When torture is systemic, this means that such violence is persistent and widespread, supported by legal and ideological frameworks, incorporated into an official agency with its multiple and intersecting divisions of labour, nurtured and protected by secrecy, and enabled by an absence of any official action against it. In Afghanistan, Iraq, and Guantanamo, torture did not result from chain-of-command failures, in which perpetrators did not follow prisoner treatment regulations. Quite to the contrary, interrogation guidelines were issued at the highest levels of the U.S. government. President Bush was assured that, in the 'war against terror', he had Commander-in-Chief authority to ignore national and international laws applying to torture. Donald Rumsfeld had to approve prisoner treatment. In a 'Gitmoization' of Iraqi prisons, Rumsfeld's top civilian intelligence official, Undersecretary of Defense Steven Cambone, told General Geoffrey Miller, then head of Guantanamo's prison complex, to 'assess' conditions in Iraq, with General Miller recommending that prison guards at Guantanamo help 'set conditions for the successful interrogation' of prisoners. General Miller, who was subsequently placed in charge of Abu Ghraib, must be held accountable for the flood of prisoner testimonies about torture that are coming out of Guantanamo, the prison complex that he had previously directed.

Acting according to the Bush administration's ad-hoc legality, the torturers – whether guards or interrogators – functioned under an explicit chain of command. Torturers' actions were encouraged by rewards for 'softening up' prisoners or for coercing prisoner testimony. Those questioning such violence were held hostage by the possibility of punishment. The normative structure of rewards and punishments at Abu Ghraib Prison created a cultural climate in which no explicit order to torture had to be given (see Haney et al 1977; Huggins et al 2002, Chapter 10; Zimbardo 1970; Zimbardo et al 1973, 2000). Guards and interrogators were shaped by the cultural and social conditions that surrounded them (see Johnson 1997), a sociological truism no less true for service men and women in a war zone than for automobile plant workers or children in a school yard.

3.5. MULTIPLE ACTORS

Systemic torture is fostered and perpetuated by actors and organizations inside and outside the local torture environment. The direct perpetrators of Abu Ghraib torture – some guards and some interrogators, government and private – could not have serially tortured without a range of facilitators who provided organizational, technical, legal, and financial support for their violence. In the immediate torture environment, facilitators included translators, medical doctors (see Bloche and Marks 2005; Kater 1989; Miles 2004; Stover and Nightingale 1985; Thieren 2007), psychologists (Concerned Psychologists 2006), nurses, medics, guards, and dog handlers, among many others. The torture system's higher-up facilitators included heads of state, ministers and ambassadors, lawyers, and chiefs of departments, to name a few. Americas Watch has prepared a brief indicting these powerful facilitators; the American Civil Liberties Union has done the same.

Asking why one person would torture another only addresses a small part of the problem. For example, the factors that cause direct perpetrators to carry out torture may not explain facilitators' enabling it. Seeing atrocity as fostered in various ways by people in differentially situated social positions points to the complexity of atrocity systems and focuses analytical and legal attention on the role of facilitators, rather than just perpetrators, as well as on the political climates that facilitators create in promoting and legitimizing violent social control.

According to this 'Torture 101'-model, facilitators may be more essential to the long-term stability and protection of a torture system than its more visible direct perpetrators. Clearly, torture during Brazil's military period could not have persisted for over twenty years without the active complicity of facilitators. This is as true for the United States today as during Brazil's or Argentina's 'dirty wars'.

3.6. DIVISION OF LABOUR/ DIFFUSION OF RESPONSIBILITY

Our research on Brazilian torturers demonstrated that an important difference between the police who became torturers and those who did not was membership in an elite and/or physically separate and insular police operations or intelligence unit. This important stratum within the larger division of labour of a torture system – a person's task assignment within a police or military system – was the most important predictor of torture. Quite simply, a person could not torture routinely unless associated with an interrogation squad.

In addressing how such specialized violence organizations might shape human conduct, Robert J. Lifton (1986, 425; see also, Huggins et al 2002, Chs. 9 and 10; Jenkins 2000; Morales 1999; Skolnick 1966; Skolnick and Fife 1993) argues that such organizations are 'so structured (...) institutionally that the average person entering (...) will commit or become associated with atrocities.' This suggests that one sphere of responsibility for torture rests on the structure and functioning of such specialized units themselves, which is a product of those who knowingly create these units and place and train people in them.

A division of labour, in which some people directly torture and others facilitate it, helps those not directly involved with torture to define themselves as positively distinct from the torturers. For example, we found among Brazilian police who interfaced with torture teams a tendency to distance themselves physically and organizationally from those they labelled torturers: As one Brazilian policeman asserted, his team would simply arrest suspects and leave them 'to be "officialised" (...). [my squad] just gave interrogators the material to work on.' (Huggins et al 2002) Pointing to the role of superiors in facilitating torture, one Brazilian police official, who had headed both a special intelligence team and a death squad, explained that in his experience torturers are quite likely to come from the ranks of 'more aggressive' policemen: 'If anyone analyzed their psychological profile, it would be obvious that they have a higher tendency for aggressiveness – a very high degree', although, as this police official affirmed, not necessarily for torture. The police official explained that the police who operated 'more physically were noticed' by superiors and placed in 'the most violent police units'. However, in the police official's experience, these men did not automatically become 'good torturers'; their ability to torture emerged through mentoring. In the end, as another Brazilian police official explained, the torturers were 'really exploited by their bosses, by those who [just] want to get the job over quickly' (see Huggins et al. 2002).

The lesson from this and from other research on torture is that such violence does not exist over the long run separate from a larger system that includes facilitators and direct perpetrators. A division of labour among various levels of superiors who knowingly (or even unknowingly) establish and promote torture-facilitating structures and environments, and with the perpetrators who actually carry it out, usually protects the facilitators from exposure by leaving the more visible and considerably less powerful operatives to be punished, as we have seen for Abu Ghraib (Earthtimesorg 2005; Hirsch 2007; Sevastopulo 2005). Moreover, the assembly-line (e.g., highly segmented, task-differentiated) structure of torture systems keeps torture perpetrators from having to recognize the meaning and consequences of their particular role in violence. As one Brazilian torture perpetrator/facilitator told me: 'I never tortured anyone, I just delivered people to the interrogators; I don't know what happened to them after that' (Huggins et al 2002).

3.7. INSULARITY AND SECRECY

Given the steps taken to hide torture, why then did some Abu Ghraib perpetrators take pictures of people being tortured? A Brazilian torturer that I interviewed in 1993 explained that it was 'safe' for him to photograph a man being tortured on the infamous 'Parrot's Perch,' because 'police never talk'. In other words, where actors are answerable only to each other and to the immediate superiors who directly and indirectly permit torture, snapping pictures is very low-risk. Yet, then, why is so much torture carried out at night, as was apparently the case at Abu Ghraib? And why, if the system is organized to hide its unsavoury deeds, do some torturers wear hoods and/or place these on their victims? The social psychological answer (Huggins et al 2002, Conclusion) is that darkness and masks or hoods dehumanize victims and provide anonymity to torturers, this facilitates their carrying out torture. People without eyes and facial expressions can be more easily abused (see Watson 1973; Zimbardo 1970; Zimbardo et al 1973, 2000). By making victims invisible, the torturer has transformed them into non-human 'material' to be worked on – much like the pre-World War II Japanese experimentation teams who called their human guinea pigs, 'stumps of wood' (see Gold 1996; see also, Kater 1989). Such a torturer does not have to see torture victims as human beings or himself as brutalizing them.

The anonymity of prisoners and their vulnerability to torture is compounded when prisoners are held in secret locations as 'ghost detainees.' This practice was authorized for Iraq by Donald Rumsfeld – at the request of then-CIA Director George Tenent. In one case, apparently to assist U.S. military officials in Iraq in hiding seventeen 'high-level' prisoners from International Red Cross inspectors, these detainees were subjected to 'extraordinary rendition'. This practice of sending 'ghost detainees' to another country for imprisonment and interrogation, grew out of the wide-reaching authority assumed by the Bush administration after the September 2001 attacks, in which the CIA was assigned 'the unusually expansive authority' (*NYT*, 3/5/05: A-1) to act without obtaining case-by-case approval from the White House, State, and Justice Departments in transferring suspects to another country to be interrogated (see *Serrano*, 4/25/05). Since September 11, 2001, U.S. agents have secretly transferred as many as 150 detainees to foreign countries that practice torture. The total invisibility of these 'ghost prisoners' to outsiders and the lack of any accountability for their treatment increases these detainees' vulnerability to the 'overly stressful' interrogation techniques that Donald Rumsfeld himself would have to authorize.

3.8. COMPETITION RAGES

Intelligence-system 'speed-up', easily nurtured by a broadly defined preventive war against an expanding category of enemy 'others', encourages competition for intelligence and creates a hospitable climate for torture. As military and civilian intelligence agencies and their agents vie for the 'most' and the 'best' information from and about 'terrorists' – with each of these categories ('best,' 'most,' and 'terrorist') ill-defined and subject to change – torture often results. In military Brazil, what furthered an operative's career or a unit's prestige was capturing the 'most important' subversives, bringing in the 'greatest number' of suspects, or obtaining the 'highest-quality' information. This required above all great speed and secrecy, which very often encouraged the harshest treatment of prisoners during the first hours after a suspect was arrested (see Huggins 1998, Chs. 9, 10).

In Iraq and Afghanistan today, competition between and within U.S. intelligence organizations is further exacerbated where interrogation and guard work are not only conflated, but have been outsourced to private corporations. However, to label the military contract corporations and their employees 'private', of course, disguises these corporations' heavy reliance on Pentagon and CIA funding. Private outsource corporations receive up to 95% of their funds from the U.S. Department of Defense (BW, 11/25/2002). Supported by the CIA and Pentagon, the seemingly private contractees are not really fully 'private' – although, they are routinely labelled such – a fact that makes their interrogators, 'torture proxies' for the U.S. government: These contractees can commit or facilitate torture without immediately implicating the United States, which points to the important role of secrecy and deniability in torture systems.[6]

CACI and Titan, two corporations whose contractees were implicated in Abu Ghraib torture, are ranked 15th and 19th, respectively, among the twenty corporations which together receive half of all Pentagon Information Technology contracts (WT, 5/2/2004). According to Amnesty International's Annual Report for 2006 (AI 2006a)

> "Incidents of torture involving civilian contractors at Abu Ghraib were documented in the US Army's Fay and Taguba reports investigating Abu Ghraib. These reports implicated employees of two companies, CACI International (based in Arlington, VA) and Titan Corp (based in San Diego and recently acquired by L3 Communications). Steve Stefanowicz of CACI reportedly directed the use of dogs at Abu Ghraib, ordered that a prisoner not receive his prescription pain killers, made a male prisoner wear women's underwear, failed to report abuse, and lied to investigators. Daniel Johnson, also employed by CACI, allegedly directed and participated in prisoner abuse and interrogated a prisoner in an "unauthorized stress position," according to descriptions in the Fay report and alleged in a lawsuit brought by the Center for Constitutional Rights. Johnson is the contractor alleged to have directed military personnel Sgts. Ivan Frederick and Charles Graner to torture a detainee during an interrogation. Three Titan employees were accused of abuses in the Fay and Taguba reports, including allegedly raping a male juvenile detainee, making false statements about interrogations, and failing to report detainee abuse."[7]

For private operatives and their corporate sponsors, 'success' is bankable: If interrogation produces abundant information, whether accurate or not, another lucrative government contract is likely to follow. Operating within a contractually defined and brief time period, the contract employee – traditionally unregulated by military, local, or U.S. laws – is relatively unconstrained in how s/he fulfils the contract, as long as the private contract corporation's needs are met. Such needs – especially for those corporations providing intelligence (IT) software for Pentagon and CIA projects – require a constant and abundant flow of intelligence information. Whether or not such information is correct can be relatively less important than its abundance. Where humans and their information are grist for IT software and technology operations and development, torture becomes a research and development 'tool' for securing more military contracts.

---

6   See Isenberg 2004. For a discussion of U.S. private military contractors at Abu Ghraib, see Appendix A of that same report (http://www.basicint.org/pubs/Research/2004PMCapp3.pdf). See also AI 2006.

7   The Fay report refers to the Army investigation and subsequent report on Abu Ghraib by Army Major General George Fay; see FN 4.

3.9.   EVIDENCE IGNORED

Evidence of torture is usually ignored, hidden, denied and lied about. Many torture regimes use press censorship, eliminate legislative and other popular elections, and shut down the judiciary to avoid public knowledge of government-sponsored torture. This was certainly the case during Brazil's military period, however, in the United States, a formal democracy, powerful actors can also dismiss, hide, or, if necessary, lie about interrogators' 'excesses'. For example, when the International Red Cross, Amnesty International and other human rights groups, the family of one American Abu Ghraib guard, and numerous U.S. service personnel, reported prisoner abuse in Iraq and Afghanistan, their charges were ignored, underplayed, dismissed, or hidden by U.S. officials. It took photographic evidence of Abu Ghraib prisoner mistreatment to force serious consideration of U.S. treatment of prisoners in Iraq. In the case of those housed at Guantanamo Bay, prisoners have continually reported abuses there; most of it denied by the Bush administration. Human Rights Watch has recorded prisoner abuse in Afghanistan, where John Walker Lindh, the 'American Taliban', was tortured in 2001 – initially by Afghan allies of the United States and then by U.S. agents. They put Lindh, stretcher-bound, for several days into a windowless, suffocating, casket-like metal container with little food or medical attention. Lindh, a Taliban fighter, could be so treated because, as such, he was adjudged at the time to be an 'enemy combatant', outside U.S. Constitutional and international law protection.

3.10.   IMPUNITY IS WIDESPREAD

Some lower-level torture perpetrators may eventually get public and legal attention for their violence, albeit in terms of explanations and legal arguments that focus on how an actor's individual 'failures' led him/her to torture: the 'bad apple', the 'out of control cop'. When the higher-ups are (infrequently) alleged responsible for torture under their command, the common explanation points to a 'chain of command *failure*', as we have seen for Abu Ghraib. The actions of torture facilitators are seen as a *deviant disruption* of normal organizational arrangements. It adds to the impunity of facilitators – who are in far greater numbers within torture systems than the torture perpetrators – and to the longevity and impunity of the torture system, that when perpetrators and facilitators are 'caught,' the larger political and organizational arrangements that promoted, hid, and excused torture remain intact: Definitions of torture causality that point to the 'exceptionally' *deviant* nature of perpetrators and/or to the 'temporarily broken' status of organizational arrangements, promote impunity.

In contrast to placing torture causality within what criminology would call 'social disorganization' theories, impunity might be reduced by adopting a 'social organizational' approach to understanding torture. The latter perspective, while it has not to my knowledge been specifically employed in most studies of torture, would explore torture as a working component of a larger organizational *system* that includes *perpetrators* and *facilitators*. Researchers would explore how some kinds of political ideologies and ad-hoc legal definitions and certain kinds of system operation all come together to nurture, support, and excuse torture. Seeing torture as a deviant or 'broken' aspect of an otherwise normal system – as some 'bad apple' and 'command confusion' explanations do – limits strategies for eliminating torture to the easily 'fix-able' 'deviant' aspects of a presumably otherwise 'normal' system. This approach, of course, ultimately protects the facilitators, who can then devise new ways of getting around national and international laws against torture, which fosters the system's and its various actors' impunity. New torture perpetrators can always be found, a fact demonstrated by the countries whose once vibrant torture systems have persisted even after their authoritarian or totalitarian periods have ended (AI 2004; for Brazil see AI 2001a). While political leaders and politics change, and the social class, ethnicity, religion, or gender of torture victims may change as well, torture as a form of interrogation, coercion, punishment, and instilling fear remains.

4. TORTURE AND CRIMINOLOGY

4.1. CONDUCTING ON-LINE RESEARCH

Could the research of other criminologists contribute to my 'Torture 101' model? One way to address this is to explore whether criminologists are studying torture and the theoretical models and methods that they have used to study it. I first looked for books or articles on torture by criminologists, on the assumption that criminologists would have studied torture and that one could move from establishing that fact to investigating how criminologists had studied, explained, and modelled torture environments and outcomes. I began by consulting on-line catalogues of two large research libraries at my university: Tulane University's Howard-Tilton and the Medical School Library for their holdings on 'torture'. To see what academic materials on torture would be available to students of criminology, I consulted the web page of the State University of New York at Albany's top-rated School of Criminology (http://library.albany.edu/subject/criminal.htm) and that of the Florida State University College of Criminology and Criminal Justice (http://www.criminology.fsu.edu/p/cjl-main.php). On these web sites was information about the courses these academic programs offered, which I supplemented by a 'Google' search for other academic social science criminology courses. From the two criminal justice programs, I also gained access to on-line academic criminology and criminology-related journals (*Electronic Journal of Sociology, Encyclopedia of crime and Justice, Journal of Criminal Justice Education, Journal of Criminal Justice and Popular Culture, Justice Quarterly, Western Criminological Review*). These web sites also contained links to several professional criminology web sites (International Security Network, National Criminal Justice Research Service, National Institute of Corrections). I also searched the American Society of Criminology's journal, *Criminology,* for its articles on torture.

By triangulating three sets of information – (1) listings on 'torture' in university library catalogues, (2) academic and professional criminal justice journals and of criminal justice organizations; and (3) academic courses on torture – several conclusions could be derived about the role of criminologists in studying torture. These conclusions will be summarized in Part Four, after the findings for each of these sets of sources have been elaborated.

4.2.   TRIANGULATING DATA SOURCES

4.2.1.   *Library catalogues*

The on-line catalogue for Tulane University's Howard Tilton Memorial Library produced 39 references[8] to items (e.g., books or articles) about 'torture'. Only four of these were written by a criminologist.[9] Several others were written by a 'social scientist criminologist', those academic scholars or practitioners from any *social science d*iscipline (including the law) who have conducted research on and/or written about 'torture'.[10] Such a designation does not, of course, mean that such 'social scientist criminologist' authors were criminologists by training or by self- or academic institutional-definition. In any case, the vast majority of references

---

8   In a review of the University of Leiden (Netherlands) catalog, R.II. Haveman located 120 references to the English language word "torture," although he did not indicate the number of these references by criminologists or within the subject-matter of criminology.

9   Huggins, et.al (2002); Crelensten and Schmid (1995); Shaskolsky Sheleff (1987); Newburn and Rock (2006). William Schabas (1996), *The Death Penalty As Cruel Treatment And Torture: Capital Punishment Challenged in the World's Courts,* is an excellent example of a 'legalist' researching in criminology. While there may be many other articles by criminologists or by 'social sciences criminologists,' it was impossible to check each authors name for her/his educational and institutional affiliation. However, visual inspection did not identify other criminologists.

10   I did not include in this analysis criminologists from the physical and/or medical sciences and practice in order to keep my research scope manageable. However, when information derived by scholars and practitioners in this area emerged from a library or Internet search, I did not exclude it from my analysis.

in my on-line search were either (in order of citation), journalists, literary humanists, philosophers, and such humanists as anthropologists, historians, and religionists, as well as area (country) specialists from these or other disciplines. For example, one reference in the Tulane University on-line catalogue was for English Professor, Laura E. Tanner's, *Intimate violence: reading rape and torture in twentieth century fiction (1994)*; another was for historian Kenneth P. Serbin's, *Torture and Justice: Secret dialogues: church-state relations, torture, and social justice in authoritarian Brazil* (2000). Such authors write within the paradigms of their own academic disciplines, not that of criminology.[11]

Knowing that the Tulane University Medical Library had extensive holdings on a number of subjects, some not related directly to medicine, I conducted an on-line search of its catalogue using the designation 'torture'. Two-hundred and fifty-five references were revealed: thirty-nine of these had appeared on the previous Howard-Tilton on-line search. Only four sources from the medical school list had been written by a criminologist.[12] The majority of the medical school holdings on torture were medically oriented and focused on its victims. Beyond that, almost every discipline but criminology was represented among those researching and writing about torture.[13]

Taking both of these catalogue searches together, the findings from my research revealed several additional discoveries about those (as stated, mostly non-criminologists) who have studied torture. First, most non-criminologists writing about torture draw their conclusions from 'qualitative' data, using interviews (Conroy 2001; Serbin 2000), official legal and government documents (Brody 2004 and 2005; Hirsch 2004; Mc Coy 2006; Serbin 2000), 'textual analysis' (Feitlowitz 1999; Tanner 1994), and/or legal deduction and reasoning (Schabas 1996). While qualitative methods have been used in criminological research on a range of subjects, the preferred method among U.S. criminologists has been 'quantitative', which often involves using existing statistics or collecting new ones. Furthermore, founded as it is on Italian and American empiricism, most U.S. criminologist shy away from such emotionally (see Campbell 2001) and/or

---

[11]   I hoped that by refining my search through a new designation, "torture and criminology," I would capture more criminological scholarship on torture, but I got the same outcome: Only 4 books/articles had been written by a criminologist.

[12]   The biggest stumbling block to this research was discovering the academic and institutional affiliation of an author. It is in this area that the greatest number of errors was possible.

[13]   For example, there was Free-lance journalist, Michael Otterman's, *American torture: from the Cold War to Abu Ghraib and beyond(2007)*; Director of the University of California at Berkeley's Human Rights Center (and professor of public health) Eric Stover and physician Elena O. Nightingale's, *The Breaking of bodies and minds: torture, psychiatric abuse, and the health professions (1985)*; Tara McKelvey, a senior editor at the *Prospect Magazine*, and research fellow at the New York University School of Law Center on Law and Security, has authored *Monstering: Inside America's Policy on Secret Interrogations and Torture in the Terror War* (2007) and *One of the Guys: Women as Aggressors and Torturers* (2007); professor of Literature, Marguerite Feitlowitz's, *A lexicon of terror: Argentina and the legacies of torture (1999)*.

politically charged subjects as 'torture,' particularly when associated with highly politicized secret and semi-secret United States socio-political operations. In any case, there has been a long history of criminology failing to even cover police torture inside the United States systematically.

A second discovery from the on-line library research was that those who study torture – whether criminologists or from other academic disciplines – usually explore its use in countries outside their own. For example, my own research for *Violence workers: Torturers and murderers reconstruct Brazilian atrocities* (co-second authors Mika Haritos-Fatouros[14] and Philip Zimbardo 2002) interviewed police who had been torturers during Brazil's military period. Elizabeth Stanley, a criminologist in the United Kingdom, has examined 'Torture and Transitional Justice in Timor Leste' (2005a).[15] Darius Rejali, an American political scientist of Iranian descent on faculty at Reed College (Portland, OR), examined Torture in Iran in, *Torture and Modernity: Self, Society, and State in Modern Iran* (1994). Fida Mohammad, a sociologist/criminologist in New York State, has analyzed 'Torture, Murders, Confessions & Hegemony' in Pakistan (2000).[16] The most obvious exceptions to this pattern are the recent spate of news reports[17] and analyses by U.S. investigative reporters of United States torture at Abu Ghraib Prison in Iraq. However, for the most part, torture seems to appear as something that 'someone else does,' particularly actors in countries outside consolidated formal democracies.[18]

---

[14] Mika Haritos-Fatouros' (2002) ground-breaking work on Greek torturers offers an important exception-- a scholar who studied torturers in her own country.

[15] www.vuw.ac.nz/sacs/staff/stanley.aspx.

[16] http://employees.oneonta.edu/mohammf/CV.html. The excellent Supranational Criminology Website, particularly its 'bibliography' of research on 'supranational criminology' topics (http://www.supranationalcriminology.org/framespage.htm), illustrates the pattern of torture research being conducted on countries outside one's 'home' country.

[17] Over the last fifty years, accounts of torture by U.S. journalists that have made it into the national media have been few and far between. (Indeed, an important research project would be to study how much, and how, torture has been covered by national media outlets. It can be said with relative confidence that, at this time, my own a rough survey of journalistic reports about torture from the 1960s to the present, finds that torture has received relatively little news coverage inside the United States. Most of the time, those who have carried it out – usually actors who are not U.S. nationals, except in the case of some U.S. police – are portrayed as a few 'bad apples' in an otherwise well functioning system. Indeed, torture had been little more than a media 'blip' in the U.S. media until the beginning of the U.S. war in Afghanistan (October 2001) and in Iraq (March, 2003), and the subsequent CBS' '60 Minutes II' graphic photographs of abuse at Abu Ghraib, which became major national and international news, and then the subsequent publication on April 30, 2004, by *The New Yorker Magazine*, of a well-documented report on Abu Ghraib (by Seymour M. Hersh).

[18] I discovered this as well in the search of 'Google' for scholarship on torture.

Martha K. Huggins

4.2.2. Criminal justice journals and organizations

On-line searches for articles on torture in six criminology journals[19] listed on the criminology program web sites for the State University of New York at Albany and for the Florida State University's criminology program, as well as in the journal, *Criminology*, also demonstrated that 'torture' has been little researched and written about at least since the 1990s in English-language *criminology* journals. For the journal *Criminology* (Blackwell-Synergy), between 1969 and 2004, thirty-one references appeared using the search term "torture," most of these treated torture tangentially, as for example the 1990 article by G. Newman and Pietro Marongiu, 'Penological reform and the myth of Beccaria', or the 1977 article by M. J. Lerner, 'The effectiveness of a definite sentence parole program'. Indeed, only two of the articles in the journal *Criminology*, dedicated more than a passing reference to torture. In contrast, a search of all Blackwell-Synergy academic and professional journals (805 such Journals in all, including *Criminology*),[20] turned up 5,624 references to articles on 'torture,' many of these dealing explicitly with torture. These same findings were largely true for *Justice Quarterly*, published by Routledge in partnership with the Academy of Criminal Justice Sciences (ACJS). Among all Routledge journals, for the period 1997–2003 fifty articles turned up using the search term "torture," but none of these was in *Justice Quarterly*. The *Journal of Criminal Justice Education* for the period 2001–2005 had two articles that (from their title) suggest some relevance to the subject of torture.[21] Finally,[22] the *Journal of Criminal Justice and Popular Culture* (JCJPC) (http://www.albany.edu/scj/jcjpc/index.html) had only two references – out of approximately 108 for the period 1999 to 2007 – on torture: One reviewed (Farina 2001–2002) a "museum exhibit" at the Tropicana Hotel in Atlantic City, NJ on *'Torture through the ages'*; the other reviewed (Pugh 2006) a 2005 documentary film, 'Torture: America's Brutal Prisons'.[23]

---

[19] *Electronic Journal of Sociology, Encyclopedia of crime and Justice, Journal of Criminal Justice Education, Journal of Criminal Justice and Popular Culture, Justice Quarterly, Western Criminological Review.*
[20] According to the Blackwell-Synergy web site, the publishing company in 2006 had 805 peer-reviewed journals in print and online formats.
[21] 'Darker than any prison, hotter than any human flame': Punishment, choice, and culpability in *A Clockwork Orange. Illya Lichtenberg, Howard Lune, and Patrick McManimon, Jr. (2004) and* 'Teaching on terrorism: Problems of interdisciplinary integration in introductory level texts.' John Riley (2005).
[22] The *Electronic Journal of Sociology* is listed on the State University at Albany's web site as a resource for criminology students. Of 116 published submissions—articles, editorials—between 1994 and 2006, only one related to torture--tangentially: "The War on Terrorism: The Views of Criminal Justice and Non-Criminal Justice Majors on Terrorism and the Punishment of Terrorists" (Lambert et al. 2005).
[23] Another two articles, each dealing with "war on terror" subjects, may have included torture as a subject, but this could not be determined from the article titles.

Even without covering the other on-line academic criminology sources, it can be said that these support the pattern found in *Criminology, Justice Quarterly*, and the *Journal of Criminal Justice Education*. Such findings were supported by the 'Google' search as well: Like the library on-line research and the search on selected criminology journals, the 'Google' search for articles on torture by criminologists demonstrated that torture has been a minor consideration over the past seventeen years for academic criminology.[24]

Research into the web sites of several professional criminology organizations,[25] turned up a somewhat greater interest in torture. For example, six of the ten articles netted in my search of the National Criminal Justice Reference Service (NCJRS) web site had some relevance for torture: 'Cruelty in control? The stun belt and other electro-shock equipment in law enforcement' (NCJ 1999) and 'Survivors of politically motivated torture: A large, growing, and invisible population of crime victims', (NCJ 1999); 'Making their own rules': Police beatings, rape, and torture of children in Papua New Guinea, (NCJ 2005). The U.S. National Institute of Corrections web site (http://www.nicic.org/?q=torture &site=Library&theme=Library), produced twenty-one references to items about torture – with some of these, however, repeats of prior references. A web site for security professionals, the International Security Network[26] (www.isn.ethz.ch/ about/) – 'a free public service that provides a wide range of high-quality and comprehensive products and resources to encourage the exchange of information among international relations and security professionals worldwide', was relatively rich with references to torture.

4.2.3. Teaching torture

The third component of this analysis is the role of criminal justice academics in teaching about torture, so I examined whether criminal justice curricula contained courses about, or teaching units on, torture. I was alerted early in this examination that torture was not an important part of curricula on criminal justice by Professor Dan Maier-Katkin's statement on his criminology course (cross-listed with religion) syllabus on 'Human Rights and Crimes against Humanity' at Florida State University, that 'genocide, torture, ethnic cleansing (...) have traditionally

---

[24] My own assessment of the indexes of ten top selling U.S. university-level criminology texts also suggested this finding.
[25] International Security Network, National Criminal Justice Research Service, National Institute of Corrections.
[26] 'This organization is based in Zurich, Switzerland, at the Center for Security Studies (CSS) at ETH Zurich (Swiss Federal Institute of Technology Zurich), The ISN has close relationships with leading international partner institutes – research institutes, think tanks, and government and non-governmental organizations. Launched in 1994, the ISN (...) is jointly funded by the Swiss Federal Department of Defense, Civil Protection and Sport (DDPS) and ETH Zurich'.

received *relatively little* [emphasis added] criminological attention.' (see Maier-Katkin, n.d.) At the same time, one of Criminology's founders, Cesare Beccaria, in his 1764 essay, 'On Crimes and Punishments', specifically included torture in his narrative.[27] Beccaria notwithstanding, U.S. criminology has been relatively silent about torture.

I discovered from a 'Google' search that when torture has been covered in criminology teaching, it has been considered among a 'laundry-list' of seemingly similar, although often very dissimilar, subjects. For example, Rutgers University (Piscatawa, New Jersey Campus) offers an elective course for criminal justice majors on 'Political terrorism,' described as an 'analysis of diverse organizations using terror, starvation, torture, and murder for political objectives'. Students at Florida State University were offered two courses that included torture in their subject-matter: 'Human Rights and Crimes against Humanity' (2005) and 'International Human Rights Law & State Crime' (2006). I myself offer a course annually at Tulane University, 'Violence Workers', which covers torture and other crimes against humanity. Thompson Education International – an on-line university that describes itself as 'the world's foremost distance learning network [in Asia]' – offers two courses for its Bachelors Degree in 'Law and Criminology.' One, 'Human Rights', includes a unit on 'the right to be free from torture, inhuman and degrading treatment or punishment and slavery.' A Victoria University (Wellington, New Zealand) course, offered by its Institute of Criminology on 'Liberties, Rights and Justice,' explores 'security and terrorism, slavery and development, immigration and asylum, torture, rape as a weapon of war, 'disappearances' and genocide'.[28]

While a 'Google' search for English-language academic courses on torture is undoubtedly far from inclusive, initial data suggest that such courses are more likely to be offered outside criminology departments and programs than by them. The University of Montana (Missoula, MT) offers an 'inter-session' political science course – an abbreviated course between its two main semesters – on 'The U.S. Response to Terrorism', which examines 'the definition of terrorism, US statutes on terrorism, the detention of material witnesses and enemy combatants, torture and extraordinary renditions, military tribunals, [and] portions of the U.S. Patriot Act (...)'.[29] Another course, 'Crime and Social History', includes a

---

[27] Torture was unacceptable to Beccaria on 'fairness' grounds because it could make 'an innocent man suffer a punishment [that] he did not deserve or could make (...) a weak person more likely to confess to a crime than a strong person, without consideration of guilt.' In a second, 'legalistic,' argument against torture, Beccaria reasoned that 'confessions [derived] from torture should not be valid since an innocent man might confess just to stop torture, and a person [being tortured] might implicate innocent accomplices' just to save himself from torture.

[28] http://www.vuw.ac.nz/sacs/news/docs/IOC30thPubWeb.pdf.

[29] http://www.umt.edu/ce/deo/winter/CourseDescriptions.htm.

unit on 'pre-modernity: mercy, torture, and the Witch-hunts.'[30] A St. Joseph's University (Philadelphia, PA) course on 'The Sociology of Deviance' includes such topics as, 'the Holocaust, state terror and torture, and mental illness (...)'.[31] Several U.S. political science department offerings on 'terrorism' listed 'torture' as one of several sub-topics presumably related to terrorism.[32] Philosophy, which sometimes considers 'torture' within courses on 'The Philosophy of Religion', 'Ethics', and 'Critical Thinking', places this subject on the margins of other course considerations. In a philosophy course on 'Critical Thinking' at the University of Oklahoma, students study 'euthanasia and abortion, the nature and purpose of education, affirmative action, justice and rights, gun control, torture and the death penalty, the existence of God, and other topics of current concern.'[33] In a philosophy offering on 'Problems of Normative Ethics', at the University of California at Davis, students explore 'contemporary debates about the proper moral limits of the state's use of force against other states or individuals.'[34]

Torture has been much more commonly an academic teaching subject in psychology, which has a long tradition of researching and teaching about 'obedience to authority', one of the theoretical foundations for its analyses of torture. Based on laboratory and relatively controlled field experiments, the 'obedience to authority' research has focused primarily on micro-level interactive processes and on the immediate contextual factors that nurture obedience and violence. The Zimbardo Prison Experiment,[35] one of the best-known examples of such studies, has clear relevance to the study of torture. Social psychology has also included victims of torture in its curricular offerings. For example, a Webster University (St. Louis, MO) course on 'Torture, Ethics and Professional Responsibility,' examines 'the various definitions of torture, the international and domestic law concerning torture, the impact of torture on survivors, the effectiveness of torture as a means to obtain information, [and] the role of various professions in torture (...)'.[36]

---

[30] http://www.thomsonworldclass.com.

[31] Saint Joseph's University, Department of Sociology (Philadelphia, PA. (U.S.).

[32] In one departure from the tendency to place 'torture' in a subsidiary curricular position, Darius Rejali offers a Reed College course on 'Torture and Democracy,' which 'examines the interrelationship between torture and democracy, examining the demand for torture and the supply of torture techniques.' http://academic.reed.edu/poli_sci/faculty/rejali/rejali/torture.html.

[33] http://www.ou.edu/cas/ouphil/dept/fall96.html.

[34] philosophy.ucdavis.edu/millstein/phil15syllibus.pdf. It is instructive to note that most courses that include torture as more than a minor subject make use of 'readings packets' that are composed by the faculty member teaching the course, pointing to the need of a reader by criminologists that could fill this void.

[35] www.prisonexp.org. see also H. Kelman "The policy context of torture: A social-psychological analysis." *International Review of the Red Cross*, 3/31,2005. (http://www.icrc.org/Web/eng/siteeng0.nsf/html/review-857-p123).

[36] http://www.webster.edu/~woolflm/torturesyllabus.html.

Another academic discipline that frequently includes torture in its curriculum is law programs. However, such curricula focus primarily on the national and international laws prohibiting torture without analyzing the roots of torture within social organization. Where a curricular focus exists on the latter, it is frequently in courses that combine law and human rights, as for example, at the Harvard University Law School's Human Rights Program, which includes a 'reading group' on 'Torture, Law, and Lawyer'; more commonly, however, in United States law school curricula torture is one of many subjects about atrocities that are included within discussions of international law.

Another important finding from my 'Google' survey was that teaching about torture has tended to 'individualize' and 'pathologize' it, thus stripping torture of its broader organizational, systemic, and political-economic framework. By focusing cross-sectionally (i.e., at one point in time) on those who carry out torture – its perpetrators – and/or on 'torture interactions' within a 'torture chamber' (e.g., between torturers, victims, and facilitator-bystanders), researchers cannot help but come up with explanations for torture that are rooted in individual 'pathology' and/or theories of 'social disorganization that ignore the larger socio-political factors that nurture, hide, and excuse torture.

5. SUMMARIZING FINDINGS

5.1. ON-LINE BOOKS AND JOURNALS, LIBRARY CATALOGUES AND ON-LINE CRIMINOLOGY JOURNALS

(1) Since the 1990s, criminologists have contributed *relatively little* to English-language academic publishing about torture. Indeed, a current academic thesis on torture[37] affirms 'the comparative silence of Criminology in discussing "Torture", particularly in relation to other acts of violence.' (2) Research documenting torture, conducted by research *practitioners* – e.g., human rights organizations and governmental agencies and the social scientists and legalists who work with them – is by far the most represented in on-line library catalogues and on 'Google.' (3) Such human rights *practitioner* research is very *unlikely* to be found – except as a citation within an academic publication – in academic criminology journals. (4) Most *academic research* on torture published in professional academic journals has been carried out by scholars in (ordered according to relative frequency of publication): psychology/human services; health/public health; social sciences (including, area studies, international

---

[37]   Lisa White, lwhite08@qub.ac.uk.

relations, political science, sociology); humanities (literary analysts, historians, philosophers, religion scholars), and legalists. (5) Most academic research on torture has used 'qualitative' methods for data collection, rather than 'quantitative' data collection strategies (see below for definition and examples of each). (6) Torture is usually studied in regions outside the researchers own country and in developing rather than developed, consolidated democracies.

5.2.   ON-LINE CRIMINOLOGY-OF-PRACTICE WEB SITES

The web sites mounted by professional criminologists-of-practice are slightly more likely than the academic publications by English-language publishing criminologists to contain materials about torture, although not necessarily about torture inside the United States.

5.3.   ACADEMIC COURSES

(1) When torture was offered in a university-level academic course it was usually *not offered* by criminology departments. (2) The academic departments/programs most likely to offer a course with a unit on torture were (in relative order of curricular attention): psychology, law, political science, international relations, sociology, and social work. (3) Irrespective of academic discipline, torture as a subject-matter is given brief attention within a larger course. (4) At best, the subject of torture is included within a 'laundry-list' of *seemingly*, although not necessarily, similar subjects. (5) A *common way* of teaching about torture is to root it in the psychology of obedience; *next most common* is to link torture, in an 'essentialist' manner, to certain kinds of 'deviant' politico-social systems or undemocratic practices – 'wars on terror,' 'authoritarian' and 'totalitarian' systems; *least common* is to see torture as a 'normal' *organizational dynamic* that can include some of the above elements and still exist within 'democratic' social systems. (6) Accordingly, torture is usually presented as something carried out by a country other than consolidated democracies.

6.   CONCLUSION: CRIMINOLOGY AND TORTURE

How are criminologists to study torture when there is so little existing criminological scholarship on this important subject? Those interested in studying torture could place their research within a 'human deviance' or 'social disorganization' paradigm. The 'bad apple' and 'chain-of-command failure' explanations would be an example of such a perspective on torture. However, as criminologist and sociologist Albert K. Cohen (1955) might point out, such approaches that rest upon an 'evil-causes-evil' analogy, have limited applicability.

Another theoretical starting point might be for criminologists to research torture from the assumption – as Harvard law Professor Alan Dershowitz does[38] – that all torture is relative: It can be carried out illegitimately by agents of a non-democratic country – particularly when used against those of a democratic one – or it can be employed legitimately by a democratic country in its 'war against terror'. Presumably, the criminologist would seek different causes for each relative case where torture is used – appealing to 'social disorganization' and 'human pathology' explanations when torture is used illegitimately, and 'rational actor' perspectives when torture is used legitimately. Within such a 'torture relativity' perspective, the justification (or not) for torture would seem to turn on 'whose side one is on,' a point made decades ago by sociologist and scholar of deviance, Howard Becker (1967). It was Becker's ethnographic contention that in any social situation there are many different ways of seeing the world; sociological research, in general, and research on deviance, in particular, cannot be effectively carried out without capturing the different points of view and ways of seeing the world. Note that it does not follow from Becker's methodological suggestion that some kinds of torture are inherently morally and socially legitimate while other torture is illegitimate.

The approach I favour is to study torture using what criminology calls a 'social organization' perspective. Such scholarship would envision torture as systemic, resulting from the 'normal' operation of various types of state, bureaucratic, and social organization. The utility of this perspective emerged inductively from interview data for *Violence Workers (2002)*. In explaining the inductively derived findings from that research on Brazilian torturers and their associates, it became clear that there was *no single* criminological or sociological theory for understanding torture. Rather, theories of social organization, of bureaucracy, political organization, career progression, gender (see Huggins et al. 2002), as well as social psychological perspectives and models (Kelman 2005) would have to be fused together to understand torture systems and their diverse actors.

Another insight from criminology and from the sociology of deviance that emerged from *Violence Worker* interview data was that understanding torture requires using a 'sequential' rather than a 'simultaneous'[39] model of causality. As Howard Becker pointed out over forty years ago (Becker 1963), behaviour develops and changes in orderly sequence over time and what can be a cause of behaviour

---

[38]   see http://edition.cnn.com/2003/LAW/03/03/cnna.Dershowitz.
[39]   The latter assumes that all causal factors come together at one point in time to create a certain result.

at one point in time may not be one at another. This was why in our *Violence Worker* research, rather than seeking certain kinds of training as wholly responsible for a policeman's becoming a torturer (impossible in any case since one set of police received no initial training), our research sought to discover the turning points in a policeman's 'career' (Becker 1963) – whether 'status degradation' (Garfinkel 1991) or 'status-amplification' ceremonies – that successively funneled a policeman into a position to carry out 'violence work'. This helps make Lifton's finding from *The Nazi Doctors* somewhat more understandable: A man may enter the police to 'save lives' and to 'protect the law,' but at another point in time this same policeman may be promoted into an interrogation squad – at a time when his country is engaged in a 'war against terror' – with such a promotion placing the policemen in a position ('deviance and opportunity') to carry out *serial* torture (see Huggins et al 2002).

Returning to my 'Torture 101' model, I can conclude with additional insights for a criminology of 'torture-as-social organization.'

- *Treat torture as a system.* 'Bad apple' personality theories are flawed because they: (a) focus primarily on one actor in an atrocity system – the direct perpetrator – and (b) usually at only one point in time. Such frozen-in-time social pathology theories, in turn, (c) personalize and individualize torture, which is in fact actually (d) embedded within a local, national, and (often) international dynamic.
- *Identify torture system actors.* Torture systems contain at least four categories of actors: (a) perpetrators;[40] (b) facilitators;[41] (c) bystanders;[42] and (d) organizational/bureaucratic systems.[43] This is shown very clearly in Smeulers' contribution to this volume, as well as by my own 'Torture 101' model.
- *Remove protection.* By labelling a torture system's direct perpetrators 'atypical,' 'sadistic,' or 'bad apples,' the facilitators behind their actions are protected from punishment, while some perpetrators are the most likely to be punished for their own and the crimes of perpetrators.
- *End system longevity.* The direct perpetrators of torture are the least important elements in a torture system. They can be easily replaced by those who direct

---

[40] These include, torturers, murderers, physical abusers.
[41] Perpetrators include governments officers and their officials; corporations and businesses and their leaders; public prosecutors; justices; lawyers; MDs, psychologists, notaries, and police/military guards who do or do not torture themselves.
[42] For example, those who support police abuses of power in the name of ridding a community of 'undesirables,' 'criminals,' 'gangs,' or who provide respectability for abuses of power.
[43] See, for example, *Violence Workers* (2002), Ch. 7; Robert J. Lifton's *The Nazi Doctors* (1986); Christopher Browning's (1992), Ordinary men: Reserve police battalion 101 and the final solution in Poland.

the system from a position of invisibility. The system will continue without serious interruption, if the perpetrators are the only ones punished.

- *Seek torture's wider causes.* In looking for the 'causes' of torture, researchers must seek its sources using a temporal model (e.g., a sequential model of change [Becker 1956]), and for each 'actor category'. For example, the factors that may cause a person to facilitate atrocity/torture, may not be the same as those that cause a person to directly perpetrate torture. Furthermore, what 'causes' a national and/or international state to foster, facilitate, and justify torture may not be the same as what causes a local actor to perpetrate torture. What causes an international or national corporation to supply torture materials to a country's police, military, and to private contractors, may not have any relationship to why 'bystander communities' support police abuses of power.

- *Eliminate 'evil-causes-evil explanations'.* Torture is rooted in what sociologist Emile Durkheim (1951) called the 'normal' (i.e., routine) aspects of social life. Criminologists will not understand torture if they initially assume that 'bad' people cause 'bad' things. Criminologists must elevate the subject of torture from the 'dysfunctional' to those 'functional' and 'normal' aspects of socio-political life.

XII. MILITARIZING POWER IN THE WAR ON TERROR: UNLAWFUL ENEMY COMBATANTS AND THE MILITARY COMMISSIONS ACT

Michael WELCH

1. INTRODUCTION

Deepening his exploration of power and punishment, Foucault (1977) contends that penality (or penal order) performs functions that extend beyond mere retribution and is enveloped into a broader network of power relations that exist outside the immediate orbit of the penal regime. Indeed, punitive methods should not be accepted as mere consequences of legislation but rather as signposts for emerging social structures and shifting dynamics of power. By taking a critical look at the recent controversy over the unlawful enemy combatants in the war on terror, we are afforded an opportunity to recognize several of Foucault's insights concerning the reach of power. At its most basic level, the unlawful enemy combatant designation is a form of classification that speaks to Foucault's interest in how power gives way to the chores of social sorting: that is, assigning people into socially constructed categories (see Hacking 1986). However, as a point of departure from Foucault's apolitical depiction of power in *Discipline and Punish* as not belonging to any pregiven group or individuals, this chapter sets out to demonstrate that the war on terror is very much a product of how the Bush team has chosen to conduct its counter-terrorism strategy in the wake of September 11. One could argue that another presidential administration might very well have followed a different path of prosecution and punishment; in fact, there has been (and continues to be) sharp dissent even within Bush's inner circle (Cooper and Sanger 2006).

> 'In the aftermath of 9/11, President Bush requested that White House Counsel Alberto Gonzales organize a working group to determine what procedures to use with al Qaeda prisoners once they were tracked down and captured. Gonzales created an interagency task force headed by Pierre-Richard Prosper, a State Department official and expert on war crimes. While some officials in the task force wanted to apply the military justice, Attorney General Ashcroft and his deputy Michael Chertoff, proposed that terrorists be

tried in civilian courts. Gonzales, along with Vice President Cheney, broke the deadlock,
and President Bush issued a military order based on his power as commander-in-chief.'
(Pious 2006, 224)

The decision by President Bush to administer the war on terror by way of military tribunals rather than by criminal courts is notable because it reveals how the president opted to utilize the particular powers of the office. To be clear, Bush issued a military order rather than an executive one.[1] Consequently, the war on terror became militarized in ways that goes beyond literary metaphor, becoming a carefully planned strategy to be housed in the Department of Defense. The military order mandated the establishment of military tribunals according to rules and regulations dictated by the Pentagon's civilian general counsel, William J. Haynes, II, and submitted to Secretary of Defense Donald Rumsfeld for departmental promulgation.[2] Among other things, the new military tribunals depart from past practices since they specifically targeted non-US citizens; previous tribunals never distinguished between citizens and foreign nationals (see Katyal and Tribe 2002).

By initiating a military strategy, Bush's choice of options is especially significant. 'For the first time in American history, the characterization of terrorism as a criminal act to be dealt with by the civilian courts would be superseded by its characterization as an act of war'(Pious 2006, 225). So as to appear that his military order was not unilateral, Bush claimed that Congress provided its support in the joint resolution authorizing the president 'to use all necessary and appropriate force against those nations, organizations, or persons he determines planned, authorized, committed, or aided the terrorist attacks that occurred on September 11, 2001.'[3] Those events set the stage for a series of crucial political and military decisions that reconfigure the economy of the power of punishment in the war on terror. As we shall see, the Bush administration put into motion several unique strategies to detain and prosecute terror suspects, tactics that continue to raise serious questions over their constitutionality and legality under international law (Jinks and Sloss 2004; Kacprowski 2004; Margulies 2004).

That form of militarized prosecution in the war on terror is given close Foucaultian consideration in this chapter. So as to contextualize the formulation of the enemy combatant designation in both historical and theoretical terms, the discussion opens with Foucault's notes on the nature of penal power in the classical age. In due course, the analysis takes into account penal reform in the

---

[1]   'Military order on detention, treatment and the trial of certain non-citizens in the war on terrorism,' 66 Federal Register 57831, 2001.

[2]   'Procedures for trials by military commissions of certain non-United States citizens in the war on terror against terror,' Department of Defense Military Commission Order No. 1, March 21, 2002.

[3]   P.L. 107–40 Sec.2(a), September 18, 2001.

18th century, gradually giving way to counter-law. The phenomenon of counter-law is significant because it undermines criminal law, producing less due process rather than more safeguards against human error, prosecutorial corruption, or a combination of both. At the heart of the examination is militarized penal power emanating from the Military Commissions Act (MCA) of 2006. That legislation and similar militarized tactics in the detaining (indefinitely) and trying unlawful enemy combatants point to key transformations in the redistribution of penal power toward a structure that is highly centralized with the Bush political and military hierarchy (see Welch 2007).

2. MONARCHICAL POWER IN THE CLASSICAL AGE

As a starting point, we extend our view of the history of the present as it pertains to the construction of the unlawful enemy combatant, beginning with a glimpse at the classical age and the nature of monarchical power. Foucault refers to the classical age as the *ancien regime* period in 18th century France when the monarchy wielded absolutist power over people. That form of power, to be sure, was viewed in light of a divinely ordained political theology, relying on revenge and militarism to defend itself against rebellion. During that era:

> '*any crime signified an attack on the sovereign's will. Punishment is thus an act of vengeance, justified by the sovereign's right to make war on his or her enemies and conducted in appropriate warlike terms. In keeping with the military sources of this sovereign power, justice is a manifestation of armed violence, an exercise in terror intended to remind the populace of the unrestrained power behind the law.*' (Garland 1990, 140; see Foucault 1977, 47–48)

The public spectacle, most vividly expressed in brutal executions, provided an elaborate ceremony by which the monarchical power was reaffirmed (Spierenburg 1984). The entire process serves a juridico-political function, implying that the monarchy itself was the real victim and seeks to have its full power restored.

> '*It is a ceremony by which a momentarily injured sovereignty is reconstituted (…). Its aim is not so much to re-establish a balance as to bring into play, as its extreme point, the dissymmetry between the subject who has dared to violate the law and the all-powerful sovereign who displays his strength*'. (Foucault 1977, 48–49)

The excesses inherent in the open spectacle were deliberately used to express the monarchies intrinsic superiority whereby the symbolic and physical strength of the sovereign both figuratively and literally beat down upon the body of the adversary and masters it. Clearly, the ultimate target of punishment was the offender's body, an entity; nevertheless, it is important to stress that the 'public execution did not re-establish justice; it reactivated power' (Foucault 1977, 49). Moreover, the absolute power of the sovereign gained even greater control over the people since the monarchy could exercise the authority to suspend punishment and issue pardons.

The militaristic features of punishment during the classical age also augmented the sheer dominance of the monarchical power. Returning to *Discipline and Punish*:

> *The justice of the king was shown to be an armed justice. The sword that punished the guilty was also the sword that destroyed enemies. A whole military machine surrounded the scaffold: cavalry of the watch, archers, guardsmen, soldiers (…) it was also a reminder that every crime constituted as it were a rebellion against the law that the criminal was the enemy of the prince [crimen majestatis].* (Foucault 1977, 50)

The monarch not only ruled over an armed law but also sat as head of justice (*fons justitae*) and head of war. Punishment, therefore, marked both a battle and a victory, bringing a solemn end to a war. Enhancing further the political theology embodied in the militaristic monarchical power, executions with all their fanfare and drama closed with glorious shouts of 'God save the King'. The public spectacle folded nicely into a series of royal rituals: coronation, entry of the king into a conquered city, and the submission of rebellious subjects (Foucault 1977, 48, 53). Throughout *Discipline and Punish*, Foucault uses the term *supplice* which although it does not have any precise equivalent in the English language is meant to capture the spectacular essence of public torture and executions. In a word, *supplice* characterizes the prevailing trait of the *ancien regime* of penalty (see Foucault 1977: Translator's Note; Cousins and Hussain 1984).

3. FROM PENAL REFORM TO COUNTER-LAW

Discipline and Punish directs critical attention at the emergence of the prison. However, it should not be treated as a historical work per se (Cousins and Hussain 1984; Dreyfus and Rabinow 1983; Garland 1990). Rather, Foucault exhibits a strong fascination with the ways in which the penitentiary came to replace *supplice* as the leading form of punishment (see also Ignatieff 1978; Melossi and Pavarini 1981; Rothman 1971). Whereas the prison did in fact exist under the *ancien regime*, it did not take center stage in the field of penality until reformers pushed to improve the criminal justice system, its procedures, and its institutions, thereby attempting to make the courts fair and punishment more humane. Attacks on corrupt judiciaries and corporal punishment in the later part of the 18th century were led by such thinkers as Cesare Beccaria (1764) and Jeremy Bentham (1970[1789]) who influenced reformers across much of Europe. Over time, *supplice* – most notably the public spectacle – was displaced by confinement, representing a modern approach to crime inviting new theories that, for example, examined the role of environment in criminal behavior.

Still, Foucault does not lose sight of the elements of power as legal reformers redistributed the economy of penality. The judiciary under the *ancien regime* was criticized for its corrupt method of appointments along with a host of external constraints on the trial process, a dysfunction stemming from what Foucault calls 'surplus power' (*surpouvoir*, or super-power) referring to the personal and absolutist power of the sovereign. Since legal offices belonged to the King, he had the latitude to sell them to generate revenue, creating a system driven by market forces rather than judicial competence. Moreover, the monarchy remained a driving influence over the magistrates by issuing orders by fiat; consequently assembling a penal regime riddled by loopholes and vast disparities in sentences from one court to another along with royal pardons that made the system all the more capricious. Penal reformers recognized that power was too asymmetric, leaving the accused enormously disadvantaged in their efforts to be properly and adequately defended. In Foucault's terminology, reformers positioned themselves on two fronts: challenging the 'surplus power' (*surpouvior*) of the monarchy as well as the 'infra-power' of the people 'to indulge in little illegalities without fear of punishment' (Cousins and Hussain 1984, 178). The sovereign had indeed perpetuated both brutal forms of punishment on the one hand while absolving some people from the duty to adhere to certain laws: both of which contributed to a feeling that the entire social order lacked justice and legitimacy.

To penal reformers the answers apparently were clear, revamp the courts and institute more humane forms of punishment: thus injecting a sense of credibility into the system. By doing so, penality would become a linchpin in the functioning of a just society. That new economy of the power to punish also benefited from utilitarian notion of penal calculus from which prison sentences would be assigned according to a highly arithmetic logic: days, months, and years (Foucault 1977). Such standardized quantification throughout the court system not only added to an appearance of fairness (and deterrence) but eventually streamlined a form of prison management that could grant or deduct 'time' for good behavior. The birth of the prison is not necessarily attached to a particular date in history but rather refers to a time when the practice of incarceration became 'self-evident' as the prevailing mode of punishment, leaving behind the scaffold and other barbaric, uncivilized forms of monarchical vengeance (see Foucault 1991).[4]

---

[4]   Foucault (1977, 296–287) does suggest that perhaps Mettray reformatory in France might serve as a good example of the historical birth of prison; however, he still emphasizes its emerging technologies rather than its institutional origin.

From that point in the evolution of penology, scholars often then turn their attention to the prison as an institution operated by newly developed technologies designed to reform convicts into docile and useful members of an increasingly industrialized society and beyond (see Lyon 2006; Mathiesen 1997). With those ideas in mind, it is important to sustain an interest in the broader legal transformations that affect not only the contemporary criminal justice system but also recent developments in the war on terror. With a critical eye on the economy of the power to punish, Foucault offers some particularly insightful notes on shifting legality. Foucault anticipated the suspension of law, referring to that phenomenon as counter-law that operates 'on the underside of the law, a machinery that is both immense and minute, which supports, reinforces, multiplies the asymmetry of power and undermines the limits that are traced around the law' (1977, 222). He goes on to say that law has the potential to invert and 'pass outside itself' whereby counter-law 'becomes the effective and institutional content of the juridical forms' (1977, 223). Counter-law, in essence, emerges as a paradox facing democratic governance.

In his recent work, Richard V. Ericson (2007) attends to counter-law, or laws against law, where it interfaces with neo-liberal political cultures troubled by the prospects of greater risk and uncertainty in late modern society. In an effort to manage and reduce such risk, a precautionary logic leads political actors to adopt extreme security measures to protect society from crime, terrorism, and various threats to national security. Those precautions take the form of specific legal transformations that undermine traditional criminal law and due process (Ashworth 2000, 2003, 2004). Within the context of a risk society, Ericson characterizes counter-law as a type of legal maneuvering in which political authorities strive to gain an advantage in governance by chipping away at long standing safeguards intended to protect persons against unfair and unconstitutional tactics in criminal prosecution. Recent examples of counter-law cited earlier include the convergence of immigration and criminal laws and various provisions contained in the USA Patriot Act (Chang 2002; Welch 2006). Still, it is fitting here to address similar observations on the unlawful enemy combatant designation, especially since it appears to resemble the classical age of monarchical power and recentralization of penality.

4. MILITARIZED PENAL POWER IN THE WAR ON TERROR

Foucault (1977) reminds us that reformers of the 18th century went to great lengths to separate the legislative component of government that enacts laws specifying penalties for certain violations from the judiciary that along with a jury passes judgments and assigns penal sentences. That division of legal labor created a sharp contrast between the classical age of monarchical punishment in which penality was highly centralized and the progressive era of modern criminal justice reform.[5] On a similar plane of thought, the unlawful enemy combatant designation offers evidence of a reversal of reform. Militarized penality in the war on terror imitates the classical age when trials where strictly controlled by sovereign power, reproducing insurmountable asymmetries between the accused and the accuser. Such laws against law is recognized by legal scholars, defense attorneys, and some legislators who voice fierce criticism over the legality of the unlawful enemy combatant designation and the military-style tribunals installed to prosecute them (Amann 2004; Katyal and Tribe 2002).

5. THE MCA: MILITARY COMMISSIONS ACT OF 2006

Over past several years, there have been several conflicting court decisions over the constitutionality of the unlawful enemy combatant designation alongside the treatment, interrogation, and prosecution of those detained. In a definitive decision in 2004 the US Supreme Court ruled on three overlapping cases challenging from the government's authority over enemy combatants, including the use of indefinite detention and refusing them access to federal courts. Declaring that 'a state of war is not a blank check for the president' the High Court ruled that those deemed enemy combatants both in the US and at Guantanamo Bay have the right to contest their detention before a judge or other neutral decision maker (Greenhouse 2004b, A1; see *Hamdi v. Rumsfeld*; *Rasul v. Bush*). In response to the Supreme Court's decision, the White House rerouted its approach by developing a plan and procedure to classify and try terror suspects who could be deemed unlawful enemy combatants. Nevertheless, in 2006 the Supreme Court in *Hamdan v. Rumsfeld* invalidated the system of military commissions Bush had set up for trying terrorism suspects saying that tribunals required Congressional authorization. The court also required that suspects be treated in accordance with a provision of the Geneva Conventions, Common Article 3, which prohibits cruel and inhumane treatment, including 'outrages upon personal dignity.' The Hamdan ruling also raised questions over the legality of the Bush administration's secret CIA detention program while 'making clear that the abusive interrogation techniques used by the CIA violated the United

---

5   Foucault (1977) is often criticized for his treatment of history and political philosophy since he sometimes neglects to mention major works. In this passage, the separation of powers clearly stems from previous analysis by Montesquie and his writings on Trias Politica (see Montesquieu, Baron de, *The Spirit of Laws*, Edinburgh, 1762, originally published 1748).

States' obligations under international law and that CIA operatives could be held criminally liable for such abuses' (Human Rights Watch 2006b, 1).

In response to that ruling, Congress set out to assemble a tribunal system believed to be congruent with decision of the Supreme Court. After months of debate, Congress passed the Military Commissions Act (MCA) of 2006, a measure that Bush swiftly signed into law (Stolberg 2006). Under the revised proceedings, the government – specifically, the executive branch and the military – enjoys numerous built-in advantages in determining whether a suspect fits the classification of unlawful enemy combatant. As we shall demonstrate, the MCA reconfigured and recentralized penal power in the war on terror in ways that gut due process and meaningful judicial oversight; in fact, the MCA created few differences from its predecessor that Bush ordered into effect in November 1, 2001. Likewise, the new law poses serious threats to international human rights by preventing suspects from filing suit via the writ of habeas corpus to challenge the legality of their detention or to raise claims of torture and other abuses (see Swanson 2004). Human rights advocates complain that the MCA tribunal system does not meet the fair trial provisions required by the Geneva Conventions and human rights law (see Kacprowski 2004; Paust 2005).

Given the scope and significance of the MCA, it is important to outline some of its specific features, particularly as they relate to a new economy of penal power. Originally envisioned to dispense battlefield justice, military commissions functioned as criminal courts conducted by the US military and strive to emulate courts-martial. The MCA resembles and also departs from that model by granting the government authorization to prosecute certain non-citizens before a military tribunal.

'The new commissions differ from the old commissions in two important respects: the new commissions' rules provide that defendants cannot be convicted based on evidence that they cannot see or rebut, and that defendants can appeal all convictions to a civilian appellate court.' [6]

'Nonetheless, the MCA contains some of the same troubling provisions included in the old commissions' rules. The relaxed rules on hearsay and evidence obtained through coercion mean that defendants could be convicted based on second-hand summaries of statements obtained through coercive interrogations – without any opportunity for the defendant to confront his accusers. In addition, beyond the procedures and rules of evidence that it explicitly mandates, the new legislation allows the secretary of defense to establish further rules and procedures at odds from their courts-martial equivalent if the Secretary of Defense considers reliance on courts-martial rules and procedures to be "impracticable".' (Human Rights Watch 2006b, 3)

---

[6]   Under the Detainee Treatment Act, passed in December 2005, defendants could only appeal convictions that resulted in a sentence of death or more than 10 years imprisonment.

Under the MCA, the government can try any non-US citizen determined to be an unlawful enemy combatant. Interestingly though, only a handful of detainees at Guantanamo Bay are expected to be tried under the MCA, leaving hundreds others there in a legal black hole: subjected to indefinite detention without charge, stripped of their habeas rights, and without ever being permitted to review the evidence against them. As further evidence of counter-law in the war on terror, the MCA creates military trials against civilians that previously would have been kept under the direction of criminal courts, including terrorism cases. By doing so, it allows the commissions to permit lax rules and procedures that undermine due process and rights to fair trial while being able to sentence the convicted to life imprisonment or even death.

From its origin, the unlawful enemy combatant was a legal construct created solely by the executive branch along with the US Department of Defense that intended to push the legislature and the judiciary to the sidelines as the White House pursues its war on terror. Under the laws of war (international humanitarian law) combatants defined as belonging to an armed force are distinguished from civilians; however, civilians engaging in hostilities also can be treated as combatants and suffer the same consequences: subject to being lawfully attacked and killed as well as captured. The MCA expands the definition of 'combatant' to include those who have 'purposefully and materially' supported hostilities against the US, even if they have not participated in hostilities themselves, thereby recasting civilians as unlawful enemy combatants.

> 'These definitions have essentially been invented by the administration and Congress. They have no basis in international law and undermine one of the most fundamental pillars of the Geneva Conventions – the distinction between combatants, who engage in hostilities and are subject to attack, and non-combatants'. (Human Rights Watch 2006b, 6; O'Connell 2005)

Adding to the highly centralized form of penal power in the war on terror, the MCA strips non-citizens the right to file a claim for habeas corpus to challenge the legality of their detention before an independent court or to seek relief from inhumane conditions of confinement, abuse, and even torture. It is estimated that as many as 200 pending habeas cases brought on behalf of the Guantanamo detainees (and a handful of detainees in Afghanistan) could be summarily dismissed. Court stripping provisions run counter to international law guaranteeing that victims of human rights violations have a right to relief and access to independent courts to contest the legality of their confinement and issue complaints of abuse and torture: the US is obligated to comply with the International Covenant on Civil and Political Rights (ICCPR) and the Convention

Against Torture (CAT).[7] Adding to an emerging culture of impunity within the war on terror, the MAC effectively prevents any person from ever filing claims under the Geneva Conventions in lawsuits against the US or its personnel (Human Rights Watch 2006b).

The new law affords the president the latitude to interpret the 'meaning and application' of the Geneva Conventions, merely reiterating presidential powers to interpret US treaty. Still, the MCA clearly points out that the president's interpretation carries no more weight than any other executive branch regulation, and is subject to being overruled by federal court. Human rights experts, nevertheless, are concerned that the MCA seems to endorse President Bush's view that he has the unreviewable authority to interpret and redefine the terms of the Geneva Conventions (see Jinks and Sloss 2004; Katyal and Tribe 2002). The MCA clearly marks a legal shift from the use of the criminal courts to military tribunals in the war on terror. At the bill signing, Bush was joined by senior members of his war cabinet: Vice President Dick Cheney, Defense Secretary Donald H. Rumsfeld and Gen. Michael V. Hayden, director of the CIA. The new legislation is hailed by key Republican lawmakers who are considered the authors of the MCA, Senators John W. Warner, Lindsey Graham, John McCain, all of whom have close ties to the US armed forces (Stolberg 2006, October 18, E2).

While the MCA obviously was backed by the majorities in the House and Senate, criticism by influential Democrat party leaders has been made public. 'Congress had no justification for suspending the writ of habeas corpus, a core value in American law, in order to avoid judicial review that prevents government abuse,' said Senator Patrick J. Leahy of Vermont, the senior Democrat on the Senate Judiciary Committee (Stolberg 2006, October 18, E2). More than 500 habeas suits are pending in federal court, and Justice Department officials indicated that they would move swiftly to dismiss them under the new law, prompting challenges by civil liberties lawyers, who regard the habeas-stripping provision as unconstitutional. Only days old, the MCA had already spawned one legal contest with many others likely to be filed (Stolberg 2006, E2; see Human Rights Watch 2007; Labaton 2007).[8]

---

[7] International Covenant on Civil and Political Rights (ICCPR), adopted December 16, 1966, G.A. Res. 2200A (XXI), 21 U.N. GAOR Supp. (No. 16) at 52, U.N. Doc. A/6316 (1966), 999 U.N.T.S. 171, entered into force March 23, 1976, art. 9, para. 4.; Convention against Torture and Other Cruel, Inhuman or Degrading Treatment or Punishment (Convention against Torture), adopted December 10, 1984, G.A. res. 39/46, annex, 39 U.N. GAOR Supp. (No. 51) at 197, U.N. Doc. A/39/51 (1984), entered into force June 26, 1987, art. 13, art. 14, para. 1.

[8] The Bush administration claims to have the authority to suspend habeas corpus as constitutional during times of invasion and rebellion, citing President Lincoln's order to suspend of habeas corpus during the Civil War (Ex Parte Merryman 17 Fed. Cas. 144 [C.C.D. M.D. [1861]).

6. RECENTRALIZING THE ECONOMY OF PENAL POWER

While it is true that the humanitarian values of 18th century reformers played a key role in diminishing the use of cruel and barbaric forms of punishment, Foucault (1977) also takes into account another theoretical explanation. In what he observed to have been a dual function of penality, Foucault noted that creating a rational and more certain system of dispensing sentences not only was believed to deter certain kinds of property offenses but also erected limits on the arbitrary power of the monarchy. As Garland puts it: 'Penality was being adapted in to the emerging structures of modernity' (1990,142). The adaptation of penal power to the conditions of late modern society are found in Ericson's (2007) examination of counter-law, or laws against law that enhances more administrative measures of social control while displacing criminal law (see Agamben 2005; Butler 2004). By doing so, counter-law sets out to reduce the types of uncertainties produced by due process and judicial appeals. Many of the tactics used by the Bush team in war on terror mark a recentralization of the economy of penal power that echo previous forms of punishment in the classical age. That apparent reversal ought not be viewed as a historical shift backward; rather, by thinking forward it represents a reconfigured form of penal power in which contemporary political actors seem willing to adopt so as to harness some of the uncertainty of late modern society, with special emphasis on controlling terrorism.

While other scholars are delving into the phenomenon of 'governing through terror', (Mythen and Walklate 2006; see Simon 2006) at this stage of the analysis it is nevertheless important to acknowledge the parallels between counter-law measures in late modern society and absolutist forms of penal power in the classical age. To reiterate, the political theology during the *ancien regime* entitled the divinely-ordained monarchy to interpret any crime as an attack on the sovereign, resulting in an unleashing of military sources with an unrestrained power. While surely expressive in terms of its symbolic value, such militarized forms of vengeance also served instrumental purposes by exacting virtual total control over the accused. Beyond the linguistic metaphor, war and militarization provide legal justification for such tactics as the opening of Guantanamo Bay to hold unlawful enemy combatants. Likewise, recent developments evident in the MCA reinforce – and embolden – the president's authority as political executive and military commander-in-chief, creating a sense that democratic imperatives are being undermined in favor of a more absolutist form of penal power (Katyal and Tribe 2002). It is fitting here to remain mindful of Ericson's (2007) notion of counter-law as it sheds light on the newly administrative types of governance. More to point of this analysis, it also is important to emphasize that the MCA and similar authoritarian tactics in the war on terror demonstrate a more militarized form of counter-law. Militarized laws against law serve clear organizational objectives, for instance the streamlining of the prosecution of terror suspects or simply warehousing them indefinitely without having to bring charges or submit them to a trial. Equally important though, that reshaping of the legal also fortifies penal power in the executive seat of government where the president (and the Secretary of Defense) claims to have the need for greater control and military flexibility in the war on terror.

Much like Ericson's understanding of counter-law that erodes due process and constitutional safeguards while enhancing administrative (civilian) proceedings, the MCA exhibits a militarization effect on the legal sphere, transforming cases of terrorism that previously would have been prosecuted under criminal law into cases for handled by military tribunals. The militarized form of counter-law resembles penal power in the classical age insofar as Bush, the commander-in-chief, refuses to interpret acts of terrorism as the criminal offenses they clearly are. Rather, the President's approach to political violence seems to suggest that terrorism is an attack against the sovereign, in legal parlance 'acts of war (...) under the jurisdiction of the military' (Pious 2006, 223–4). Bush claims to possess the sole discretion (without any judicial review) to designate a person as an unlawful enemy combatant; that charge can be levied against anyone and that person could be detained indefinitely anywhere in the world. Without any established definition of 'international terrorism', or any requirement of 'probable cause', guilt by association rather than concrete acts of hostility could serve as the basis for detention and trial. All judges, prosecutors, and military defense lawyers would be appointed solely by the commander-in-chief. 'In the tribunals the penalties would be set by the president (though he could not change a not guilty verdict) and could include the death penalty, with the penalty being carried out in secret' (Pious 2006, 227). Moreover, the Department of Defense has indicated that it retains the authority to hold indefinitely all those it considered to be dangerous, even those acquitted in their tribunal (Seelye 2005). Many provisions of the MCA and similar militarized tactics in prosecution and detention hark back to the *ancien regime* as described by Foucault:

> '(...) the entire criminal procedure, right up to the sentence, remained a secret: that is to say, opaque, not only to the public but also to the accused himself (...). In the order of criminal justice, knowledge was the absolute privilege of the prosecution'.

> '(...) it was impossible to know the identity of his accusers, impossible to know the nature of evidence, impossible to have a lawyer (...). The secret and written form of the procedure reflects the principles that in criminal matters the establishment of truth was the absolute right and the exclusive power of the sovereign and his judges (...) the king wished to show in this that the "sovereign power" from which the right to punish derived could in no case belong the "multitude".' (Foucault 1977, 35)

Again, the point here is not to argue that enhanced presidential powers in the war on terror, especially by way of a distinctly militarized form of counter-law, is the same as royal power in the classical age. A deeper Foucaultian analysis reveals that while the sovereign went to great lengths to amplify his message of power, most notably in the public spectacle and other ceremonies and rituals, the absolutist form of power couched in contemporary presidential authority is at once firmly pronounced then muted. That type of governance is typical of the way counter-law becomes increasingly administrative by not drawing too much public attention to the manner in which it undermines due process and other democratic checks and balances. Nonetheless, striking similarities exist between prosecutorial tactics in the *ancien regime* and the counter-law measures instituted in the war on terror, prompting us to consider the extent to which the economy of penal power is becoming recentralized within the presidential hierarchy.

7.   CONCLUSION

With echoes of the risk society in the backdrop, the Bush administration says it is justified in establishing the military tribunal system, citing reasons of national emergency. The president claims that displacing the criminal courts with military ones is necessary because sleeper cells of terrorists are poised to infiltrate civilian courts, leaving prosecutors, judges, and jurors vulnerable to physical harm. Since the public nature of criminal courts may threaten to expose intelligence methods, sources, and agents, closed military tribunals also are said to be required to protect national security. To that end, Bush argues that he has the constitutional authority to establish military commissions by fusing his power as commander-in-chief with his oath of office to defend the constitution, citing precedents from Civil War, World War II, and the Korean War. Similar special military tribunals have been instituted in the past, most interestingly the commission convened by President Andrew Johnson to try persons suspected of conspiracy in the assassination of Lincoln. Still, such military tribunals are rare; moreover, with the exception of the Lincoln case, commissions are intended to be used as temporary measures in the absence of regular courts-martial (Fisher 2005; Pious 2006). The war on terror is different from conventional armed conflicts in several ways, in particular its temporal frame in which there is no clear end in sight. Therefore, the MAC and other military tactics are likely to become permanent fixtures in the US government's playbook on counter-terrorism.

Under the *ancien regime*, monarchical authority was contained in the *lettres de cachet*, permitting the king's power to uphold local hierarchies in ways that averted legal accountability (Farge and Foucault 1982). Reminiscent of the classical era, detention as ordered solely by the executive branch of government has become a site for enforcing undemocratic and unaccountable political decisions. Consider the controversy over the harsh treatment and detention of Haitian refugees in Miami in the 1980s and early 1990s. Those practices are characterized by Jonathan Simon as reflecting 'the demands for social order maintenance outside the bounds of democratic decision-making. That was the classic function of royal imprisonment as well (1998, 600). Similar criticisms surfaced in the indefinite detention of Mariel Cubans whereby Judge John Noonan of the US Court of Appeals for the Ninth Circuit, in 1994, ruled that the government's fixation on the dangerousness of the Mariel prisoners constituted a serious threat to democracy. Noonan, too, observed the similarities between monarchical traditions and contemporary detention practices:

> 'The infamous lettres de cachet of the King of France, a device for confining persons on the royal say-so, began as an extraordinary political measure and eventually became a routinized method of preserving order, employed in thousands of cases. As was the case in France, the discretion exercised in imprisoning without trial is in the name of high authority but actually delegated to much lower employees of the government. Our government does limit this easy administrative method of confining person to one small segment of the population. Some evils are too great for any margin to be given them. The practice of administrative imprisoning persons indefinitely is not a process tolerable in use against any person in any corner of our country.' (Berrera-Echararria v. Rison 1994; see Simon 1998, 601; Welch 2002b)

Of course the use of seemingly monarchical – absolutist – power in the war on terror is difficult to overlook given the Bush administration's commitment to counter-law: encompassing such tactics as the unlawful enemy combatant designation, the misuse of immigration law, and torture, all of which proceed with little or no Congressional or judicial oversight (see Bradley and Goldsmith 2005; Chemerinsky 2005; Welch 2006b). Armed with the royal say-so, Bush claims to possess the sole discretion to designate virtually anyone anywhere in the world as an enemy combatant: subjecting that person to a military tribunal likely to spiral down a legal black hole with few, if any, avenues for exit. Human rights advocates have expressed grave concerns over military tribunals that have the potential for creating a new class of 'desaparecidos' (the 'disappeared') who completely vanish from the free world. With an eye on past 'disappearance' campaigns waged by governments in Latin America in the 1970s, international attorneys point to the importance of enforcing the Inter-American Convention on the Forced Disappearance of Persons and the International Covenant on Civil and Political Rights (see Jinks and Sloss 2004; Paust 2005).

The European Union has taken notice of questionable detention practices in the war on terror and has warned member states not to extradite persons to the US if there is a reasonable risk that it will lead to human rights abuses against that individual (see *Chahal v. United Kingdom 1996*). In fact, Spanish government officials in November 2001, indicated to the US that it would refuse to extradite eight men suspected of involvement in the 9/11 attacks without guarantees that their trials would not be transferred from civilian courts (Pious 2006). As this discussion suggests, militarized tactics that contribute to a highly centralized form of penal power go beyond prosecution, figuring also into matters of detention (Amann 2004).

PART IV
DEFINE AND ANALYZE WAYS OF DEALING WITH INTERNATIONAL CRIMES

XIII. DEALING WITH INTERNATIONAL CRIMES: TOWARDS A CONCEPTUAL MODEL OF ACCOUNTABILITY AND JUSTICE[1]

Jennifer BALINT

1. INTRODUCTION

In her Postscript to *Eichmann in Jerusalem*, Hannah Arendt (1963, 186) wrote, 'I held and hold the opinion that this trial had to take place in the interests of justice and nothing else'. She went on to conclude that many aspects of the trial itself demonstrated 'the inadequacy of the prevailing legal system and of current juridical concepts to deal with the facts of administrative massacres organized by the state apparatus' (Arendt 1963, 294). In this she illustrated a central problem in addressing international or state crime. Justice requires the use of law. Yet the law possesses insufficient tools to address this kind of crime. I am not sure that in the meantime much has changed. While we have developed new forms of legal institutions to address crimes committed by the state, most notably the truth commission, we are still grappling with addressing the institutional dimensions of crimes such as genocide. As such, we have not developed new juridical concepts. We are still, largely, putting our hope in individualized legal mechanisms. Our conceptual frameworks are still somewhat limited.

We can identify two sets of problems in how law has in the past, and still today, addresses these kinds of crimes perpetrated by the state. The first is that the particular dimensions of international crime are inadequately addressed through legal processes. By this I mean that the focus is still predominantly on the individual. These are ideological, state driven or state complicit, nation-building exercises. Individuals killing individuals is not what identifies this kind of crime. How to deal with the institutional parameters of international crime is one key

[1] I would like to thank the participants at the Expert-Meeting 'Towards a Criminology of International Crimes' in Maastricht, early 2007, for discussion of this paper; also participants at a seminar in the School of Political Science, Criminology and Sociology at the University of Melbourne where this paper was presented. My thanks too to Nicola Henry for specific comments. For comments on an earlier version of this work, my thanks to John Braithwaite. My appreciation to Nesam McMillan for her research work and valuable comments.

challenge for a criminological paradigm (by institutional parameters I mean both the utilisation and/or establishment of institutions to perpetrate state crime, as well as its structural causes).

The second is that our approach to the use of law in addressing international crime lacks specificity. By this I mean that in our thinking about how law may best address these kinds of crimes we fail to distinguish between different kinds of international crime and what they may require in adequately tackling them. We have no typology of international crime to which we can connect our various legal responses. These two problems are the focus of this chapter.

In taking into account the institutional parameters of international crime, we may find that new juridical concepts are necessary to properly establish accountability and enable restoration/reconstruction. The chapter suggests the concept of civic liability as a framework for institutional responsibility and accountability. Further, in matching our responses more exactly to the type of crime committed, we may find ourselves suggesting a redefining of justice that, in taking into consideration the varying demands of accountability, reconstruction and prevention in the wake of international crime, takes a pluralist approach to encompass its specific structural, institutional, and individual elements.

The chapter begins with a discussion of the particular parameters of international crime, followed by an outline of current approaches to the legal redress of international crime. This is followed by a discussion of distinguishing between and remitting individual and institutional accountability, focused on the notion of civic liability. Next the problem of matching our legal redress to specific kinds of international crime is considered, with a call for an integrated typology of international crime, followed by a discussion of a broader understanding of justice, including social justice, in the wake of conflict.

2.   'IN THE NAME OF THE STATE'. INTERNATIONAL CRIME AND ITS PARAMETERS

Law is increasingly being used to address state crime – repression, human rights violations, genocide. While few such conflicts were addressed through legal means post-World War II (of the estimated one hundred and eighty two conflicts from 1945 to 1996, just twenty-nine – one sixth – had some legal redress), since the 1980s, this ratio has been changing.[2] This includes truth commissions, criminal trials – local and international –, specific legislation such as lustration and compensation legislation, reparations claims, and amnesty legislation. In

---

2   Reanalysis of data, primary sources of which are documented in Balint (1996).

some conflicts, only one legal tool was used – in others there has been a combination.

Since the first South American truth commission in Bolivia in 1982 (this was the second truth commission after Idi Amin's 1971 Ugandan truth commission) – which, while not successful itself, was influential on later and more successful truth commissions – we find that a much higher proportion of conflicts involving state crime have been subject to a post-conflict legal process. Compared to the one sixth addressed post-1945, an estimated half has been the focus of legal redress post-1982. Of the forty-three internal conflicts underway from 1982 to 1996, an estimated twenty-two have been addressed through legal means.

The evidence thus is that law is increasingly being called upon as a tool to address the post-conflict situation. Law is playing an ever-increasing role in the redress of acts involving the perpetration of human rights violations by the state. Since 1996 when I tabulated this data, we can add a host of other legal proceedings: Guatemala, Sierra Leone, East Timor, Iraq.

Does our legal redress, however, address the particular dimensions of these kinds of crimes?

The parameters of international crime are structurally different to those of ordinary domestic or national crime. These are crimes, drawing on the genesis of the international legal concept of crimes against humanity, that are violations of human rights on a *sufficiently savage or systematic scale* (see Goldenberg 1972, 13, and Schwelb 1946). When systematic violations are committed by the state or emerging state, this requires the participation of some if not all of the institutions of the state, necessitating the potential transformation, in whole or in part, of some if not all of these state institutions, and/or the development of institutions by the state or branches of the state for this purpose. We see this in the formation of the *Interahamwe* eighteen months prior to the Rwanda genocide, and its transformation into an armed militia by the ruling post-independence party in Rwanda, the MNRD. Further, what we often see are complicated and complex relationships between perpetrators, victims, bystanders including a particular historical relationship. A change of regime will not necessarily mean the harm has been redressed. That discrimination in the areas of education, training, and government employment against the Tutsi minority in Rwanda effectively ceased with the change of government in 1994, as noted by a US State Department report, is no surprise (Bureau of Democracy, Human Rights, and Labor 2003).

What makes these crimes particular is not necessarily their numbers, but rather their place in the life of a nation: these are crimes committed generally 'in the name of the state' (the existing state or state to be), utilising state or state-like institutions, and committed as part of state or emerging state policy. They are not rape plus murder plus displacement, but crimes committed as a whole package of destruction and displacement of nations, groups and peoples. Of necessity they harness and transform institutions and engage and are rooted in particular ideologies and structural inequalities and histories.

This point of the institutional parameters of such crime is made clear in the context of Rwanda by Alison des Forges and René Lemarchand, both long time scholars of Rwanda. Lemarchand (1995, 8) writes:

> 'The Rwandan genocide is neither reducible to a tribal meltdown rooted in atavistic hatreds nor to a spontaneous outburst of blind fury set off by the shooting down of the presidential plane on April 6, as officials of the Habyarimana regime have repeatedly claimed. However widespread, both views are travesties of reality. What they mask is the political manipulation that lies behind the systematic massacre of civilian populations. Planned annihilation, not the sudden eruption of long-simmering hatreds, is the key to the tragedy in Rwanda'.

Des Forges (1995, 44) notes:

> 'Extremists used its administrative apparatus, its military and its party organizations to carry out a "cottage-industry" genocide that reached out to all levels of the population (...). Those with state power used their authority to force action from those reluctant to kill'.

We see it too in the motivations and structure of the Armenian genocide, described in its wake by the Ottoman Senate president as an 'officially' (*resmen*) sanctioned 'state' crime (*devlet eliyle*) (Dadrian 1994, 10). The later aborted Courts-Martial proceedings acknowledged this: one witness spoke of 'doing government business' (Höss 1992, 220). It is clear that the destruction of the Armenians was a policy of the Turkish state at the time. As Stephan Astourian (1992, 69) notes, the *Aghed* is an essential part of Kemalist Turkey's birth certificate. It was integral to the pan-Turkish ideology of the state, a 'mystical vision of blood and race' which sought a Greater [homogenous] Turkey and was a repudiation of Ottomanism (Astourian 1992, 69). It was carried out by individuals, yet not just any individuals, but soldiers and officers in the Turkish army. As such, it was carried out within the framework of the institutions of the state.

And while Head of State Hitler never signed his name to documents regarding the deportation and extermination of Jews and others, it is known, through knowledge of the command structure of the German state, that such documents had Hitler's implicit approval and that they were carried out in the name of the German state, within the framework of the institutions of the German state, and according to its ideology of National Socialism. The murder of civilians was state policy, and as such, although perpetrated and orchestrated by individuals, constituted an act of state.

An argument for the state (and non-state) institutional parameters of the crime to be recognised is not an argument for the abolition or the tempering of individual responsibility. Tim Mason makes this point clearly in a discussion of the deficiencies of the 'intentionalist' approach to the Nazi regime in comparison with the 'functionalist' approach. Mason (1981, 30) notes:

> 'To argue that the dynamic of Nazi barbarism was primarily institutional and/or economic does not entail any denial that Hitler was a morally responsible political leader who made choices which were inspired by distinctive malevolent intentions – it is only to insist that his will cannot carry the main burden of explanation'.

As Mason (1981, 30) stresses, 'explanation is one thing, responsibility something else'.

3. INDIVIDUALS AND INSTITUTIONS. LEGAL APPROACHES TO INTERNATIONAL CRIME

When international crime has been addressed, what then have been the main approaches? We can characterize them roughly as follows:

Punish as Person not group.

- *Addressing individuals as individuals, yet still in their organizational capacity.* International Criminal Tribunal for Yugoslavia, International Criminal Tribunal for Rwanda.
- *Addressing individuals as individuals who perpetrate crime.* Rwandan national criminal trials.
- *Addressing individuals as members of organizations.* International Military Tribunal at Nuremberg, Turkish Special Military Tribunal, Lustration processes in post communist Eastern Europe, the Dergue military council on trial in Ethiopia (the Dergue trial), some joinder indictments at the International Criminal Tribunal for Rwanda.
- *Addressing the state as the state.* International Court of Justice case: Bosnia and Herzegovina v. Serbia-Montenegro.

And what we see emerging:

- *Addressing institutions and individuals.* South African Truth and Reconciliation Commission, East Timor Commission for Reception, Truth and Reconciliation.
- *Addressing individuals as members of communities.* Rwandan *gacaca*, East Timor *nahe biti* (within truth commission process).

- *Addressing structural dimensions to state crime.* Guatemalan socio-economic accord, East Timor Truth Commission recommendations. We can add here new constitutions, new legislation, new citizenship requirements.

When institutions have been addressed, what has this looked like? Institutional responsibility has been addressed in three main ways:

- *Criminalisation of institutions addressed through collections of individuals.* International Military Tribunal at Nuremberg.
- *Institutions as groups of individuals with a 'common plan'.* International Criminal Tribunal for Rwanda, the 'joint criminal enterprise' of the International Criminal Tribunal for the former Yugoslavia, the 'common purpose' in the Statute of the International Criminal Court, Dergue trial, United States Nuremberg War Crimes Trials.
- *Institutions made up of criminal individuals.* Lustration, denazification.
- *Institutions addressed in a non-criminal manner.* South African Truth and Reconciliation Commission, East Timor Commission for Reception, Truth and Reconciliation.

The individual war crimes trial is the common image of the approach taken to addressing international crime. And largely this is correct. The dominant approach, mostly, has been to address these crimes through putting individuals on trial. However, if we look through our case studies beginning with the Ottoman Courts-Martial at the end of World War I, we can see that quite often there has been some attempt to place these individuals within their organisational role – as Heads of States, as Army commanders, as state officials. In this way, it could be argued, there has been some attempt to get to the institutional state nature of this kind of crime. Slobodan Milosevic was brought to trial as former Head of State – and his charges (for Kosovo, Bosnia-Herzegovina and Croatia) were deliberately joined (see *The Prosecutor v. Slobodan Milosevic*). The first two judgments of the International Criminal Tribunal for Rwanda, the Akayesu (*The Prosecutor v. Jean-Paul Akayesu*) and Kambanda (*The Prosecutor v. Jean Kambanda*) judgments, illustrate clearly the manner in which the Rwandan genocide was perpetrated and locate the crimes committed by these two officials within the wider context of the genocide.

Of course, testimony in the trials to which people with no command responsibility for the genocide were brought (for example the Rwandan national criminal trials) can provide information that sheds further light on the perpetration of the genocide. Yet while an individual judgment may importantly help furnish an account of a particular conflict, the nature of the criminal trial means that any accountability will rest only with the individual – there is no possibility of the allocation of a wider accountability.

At the Ottoman State Special Military Tribunal in the wake of the Armenian genocide (briefly held, then aborted), the institutional dimension can be seen in the defendants being grouped according to their position in the state, and according to the institution to which they belonged. This was explicit recognition of the connection between individuals and the institutions to which they were affiliated and which constituted their identity during this period. Individuals were grouped and put on trial in the following categories: Ministers of the two Wartime Cabinets, Ittihadist Leaders, Central Committee Members, Responsible Secretaries and Delegates, and various local officials.[3] Amongst its findings, the Court found the Cabinet Ministers guilty both of orchestrating the entry of Turkey into World War One, and of committing the genocide of the Armenians.

At the International Military Tribunal at Nuremberg the main group of defendants was linked to a list of organisations and institutions of Nazi Germany, yet still tried as individuals: the indictment of the International Military Tribunal against the twenty four former Nazi officials was directed against them 'Individually and as Members of Any of the Following Groups or Organisations to which They Respectively Belonged (…)' (*Trial of the Major War Criminals* 1947, 27). The idea there was two-fold: both to demonstrate a 'common plan'[4] and to make it a criminal offence to have been a member of organizations declared criminal as a result of the trial – making it easier for subsequent trials. Further, the plan was to find particular organizations to be criminal as such.

The judgment of the International Military Tribunal found the following organizations to be criminal: part of the Leadership Corps of the Nazi party, the Gestapo, the SD, and the SS (*Trial of the Major War Criminals* 1947). These organizations were then banned. The Tribunal found the SA, the Reich Cabinet, and the General Staff and High Command not to be criminal in character. It has been argued that if the Tribunal had found the General Staff and High Command to be criminal, then it would have had to find the equivalent in other countries, namely the Allies' bombing of Dresden for example, criminal as well. As it was, the finding that the Wehrmacht was not a criminal organization created a long lasting public impression both inside and outside Germany (in part never refuted) that the Wehrmacht were not involved in the systematic persecution of Jews and others. The criminalisation of institutions risked authorising the principle of 'collective responsibility' – yet it also resulted in absolving certain institutions –

---

3   For an English translation of the Indictment and Sentence of the main trial, see Kazarian (1971). For information on the trials, see Dadrian (1997).

4   See Minutes from the International Conference on Military Trials, London, July 2, 1945, Justice Jackson explaining the American proposal, which was accepted in the face of Soviet opposition to trying organizations, in 'Related Documents', French (1972).

notably the Wehrmacht – of their responsibility, and putting no onus on them to institute change.

More recently, judgments of the International Criminal Tribunal for the former Yugoslavia have used the concept of 'joint criminal enterprise' (evolving from the 'common plan' at the Nuremberg International Military Tribunal). The Statute of the International Criminal Court (Article 25 (3)(d)) speaks of 'common purpose'. As the Appeals Chamber of the International Criminal Tribunal for the former Yugoslavia in the *Tadić* case noted, '(…) Whoever contributes to the commission of crimes by the group of persons or some members of the group, in execution of a common criminal purpose, may be held to be criminally liable (…)' (*The Prosecutor v. Dusko Tadić*, para 190).[5]

Attempting to establish a 'common plan' can also be seen in the 'joinder' indictments at the International Criminal Tribunal for Rwanda and the Dergue trial in Ethiopia. Indicted as a group, yet judged separately after joint hearings, the idea is that the common crime – for example genocide – has a greater chance to be proven through the illustration of a 'conspiracy' or 'common plan'. Each may not necessarily be accused of the same set of crimes, but potentially a different configuration of crimes. It answers what defence lawyers have argued: that it is impossible for one individual to commit genocide. The 'joinder' approach was anticipated at the onset of both the International Criminal Tribunal for Rwanda and the International Criminal Tribunal for the former Yugoslavia: both sets of *Rules of Procedure and Evidence* made provision for such an approach (see Rules 48 and 49).[6] The MRND (the single party of President Habyarimana, many of whom were the organisers of the genocide) indictment grouped together eight former Rwandan politicians (*The Prosecutor v. Augustin Bizimana et al*). Another joinder focused on four key military leaders (*The Prosecutor v. Théoneste Bagosora et al*). Another indictment was filed for accused from the Butare region (*The Prosecutor v. Pauline Nyiramasuhuko et al*). A further joinder linked three media figures (*The Prosecutor v. Ferdinand Nahimana, Jean-Bosco Barayagwiza and Hassan Ngeze*). The argument made by the Prosecutor's Office of the International Criminal Tribunal for Rwanda was that without a joint indictment, the charge of conspiracy cannot effectively be demonstrated, and that the conspiracy to commit genocide necessarily involves more than one person. As Senior Trial Attorney James Stewart (cited in *Ubutabera* 1998) noted, 'Individual trials are no longer effective; they do not represent the theory of the criminal responsibility of accused'.

---

5   For a useful discussion of the doctrine of joint criminal enterprise, see Powles (2004).
6   Rule 48, ICTY and ICTR: Joinder of Accused. Persons accused of the same or different crimes committed in the course of the same transaction may be jointly charged and tried. Rule 49, ICTY and ICTR: Joinder of Crimes. Two or more crimes may be joined in one indictment if the series of acts committed together form the same transaction, and the said crimes were committed by the same accused.

The important potential of the 'joinder' indictment is a demonstration of the scope of the crime. Joining significant individuals can illustrate the systematic and coherent nature of the killing and dispel the myth of its 'inevitable' nature. In demonstrating the planned nature of the genocide (and other international crimes), its institutional parameters (the executive, the military, and the media, for example, as key players) may be illustrated.

A similar approach to the joining of individuals was taken by the United States military prosecutors in the post-World War Two trials of German war criminals in Nuremberg. The twelve war crimes trials were based around significant associations in Nazi Germany: the Medical Case, the Milch Case, the Justice Case, the Pohl Case, the Flick Case, the I.G. Farben Case, the Hostage Case, the RuSHA Case, the Einsatzgruppen Case, the Krupp Case, the Ministries Case, and the High Command Case (*Trials of War Criminals before the Nuremberg Military Tribunals under Control Council Law No. 10*). The individuals were tried in groups according, in the main, to a central affiliation and association, both state and non-state. Undoubtedly the trials served to prove another point: the penetration of Nazism through all layers of German society. The prosecution of I.G. Farben directors, however, resulted in more than individual accountability: the corporation was broken up into smaller entities, and all its board members were imprisoned.

The process of lustration can be considered a further mechanism that addresses institutional complicity. In the post-communist context lustration has also been termed 'decommunization', and in the Nazi context, 'denazification'. In the post communist context, as Jirina Siklová (1999, 248) notes, it is the process of screening individuals in positions of political or economic influence in order to determine whether they once had ties to the former state security service. It is an attempt both to 'cleanse' institutions and to penalise individuals for belonging to certain organisations, declared criminal. In its practice it includes the removal of certain persons from public positions, as well as the barring of certain persons from holding public office in the future. It has been shown, however, that in its focus on individuals staying in particular office, it has not been effective in either the transformation of these organizations or in the curtailing of individual activities. In regard to the screening laws of the Czech Republic, Siklová (1999, 255) notes that it does not affect high-ranking Communist Party members, or StB (the former state security service) officers for whom spying was a job description. In the Polish case, as illustrated by Maria Los and Andrzej Zybertowicz (2000), former high-ranking Communist Party members do not seek employment in the public sector – rather they have entered the private sector, and form the present *nomenklatura* network of patronage. The South African Truth and Reconciliation Commission chose not to follow a policy of lustration. Desmond Tutu, in his introductory statement, did state, 'It is suggested, however, that when making appointments and recommendations, political parties and the state should take into consideration the disclosures made in the course of the Commission's work' (Truth and Reconciliation Commission of South Africa 1999a, 3).

There has been little conceptualisation of international crime as state crime (the recently concluded International Court of Justice case brought by Bosnia-Herzegovnia against Serbia-Montenegro being an important exception (see *Application of the Convention on the Prevention and Punishment of the Crime of Genocide – Bosnia and Herzegovina v. Serbia and Montenegro*). Nor has there been much attempt to address the structural causes of international crime. While it may be too simplistic to argue that the dominant approach to war crimes trials and international crime in general has been 'putting individuals on trial', we can question the extent to which the dominant approach has indeed been one that conceptualises international crime as acts perpetrated within the framework of a state body, within state policy, and reliant on the institutions of the state to perpetrate it. Most legal approaches have used the institution as a tool of organization in putting individuals on trial, rather than addressing it as such.

We can also question the extent to which these processes recognise the structural and historical dimensions to these kinds of international crime. This is exemplified by the approach taken to World War II crimes in Germany. While international trials were held early on, and an extensive program of local trials held later, and while the Nazi party was outlawed, Germany's citizenship provisions have only relatively recently (January 2000) been changed, with the principle of birth (being born in the country) making individuals eligible, rather than, as was formerly the case, the principle of descent. This I would suggest constitutes a significant change to the body politic in Germany, allowing for the political inclusion and recognition of those who had previously not otherwise been considered properly 'German'. Focusing on the particular institutions and individuals that constituted Nazi Germany, it could be argued, is not sufficient to provide a basis for reconstruction, if we are to consider systematic discrimination suffered by Turkish immigrants. In order to achieve both accountability and reconstruction (a hope for 'never again') the structural dimensions to this crime need to be addressed. Citizenship – or the understanding of who may properly be a citizen – can be considered a key part of this. In the context of redress for the long-standing crime of apartheid in South Africa, Mahmood Mamdani has pointed out that – regardless of the institutional hearings – the focus on individual violations in the Truth Commission process missed the larger structural dimensions of apartheid (the Pass Laws, the forced removals) and the impact of the apartheid policy not just on individuals but on communities (Mamdani 2000). How redress can take into account both the individual, as well as the communal and institutional dimensions when considering the perpetration and impact of these crimes, is a core challenge.

We are seeing the introduction of measures that recognise both individuals and communities – the *gacaca* proceedings in Rwanda purport to be communally based, as were the East Timorese truth commission *nahe biti* reconciliation hearings. Yet, as we have heard from individuals subject to those processes, while these may be one layer of reckoning and accountability, the other of structural change is considered to be of utmost importance. In the context of post-independence East Timor, in a study of community views of the truth commission's community reconciliation process, Lia Kent (2004) found that many victims were frustrated with the lack of attention to continued economic inequalities. As she noted, several victims expressed the view that the deponents are still 'living well' (i.e. prosperously); working in civil service positions, as teachers and for the police; while those who were pro-independence continue to be *aat nafatin* (still living poorly). As one man noted (Kent 2004), 'Economic issues need to be resolved before anything else. We can't just leave the problems of justice but we can't talk about justice if we are hungry'.[7]

We are seeing the introduction of some measures that recognise the structural dimensions to state crime: the South African Truth Commission institutional hearings and subsequent recommendations, the East Timor Truth Commission and subsequent recommendations, the socio-economic accord struck in the wake of the conflict in Guatemala. We can place here also new constitutions, new legislation, new citizenship requirements. The context of these is, however, critical. This is evident if we look at how the Rwandan government has used its 2001 law (Law No 47/2001 of 18/12/2001) punishing any speech or action that promotes discrimination or sectarianism as a tool of intimidation. This law, which may appear to counter the discriminatory propaganda used as a key tool in the 1994 genocide, is now said to be used itself as a means of government repression (Amnesty International 2004).

The decision to investigate some of the key institutions in South Africa under apartheid entailed a recognition of the framework within which such dehumanisation and oppression was possible, the institutional parameters of such crime. It involved a recognition of apartheid as a crime formulated by the state executive, implemented by the state legislature, and complied with by a number of state institutions such as the judiciary, the armed forces and the police,

---

[7]   Lia Kent, PhD candidate in the School of Political Science, Criminology and Sociology at the University of Melbourne, is currently expanding this study to examine the relationship between local, national and international understandings of transitional justice in Timor-Leste.

and a crime which was also supported by a number of non-state institutions (albeit with strong links to the state) such as the Church.

While the bulk of the South African Truth and Reconciliation Commission hearings were individual hearings, the Human Rights Violation Committee also established 'institutional', 'group', and 'special event' hearings. These hearings were designed to illustrate and examine the structure of apartheid – to examine the main state and non-state institutions in apartheid South Africa, to illustrate those groups particularly affected by apartheid or who were not well enough highlighted in the individual hearings, as well as to focus on particular 'special' areas or events, which may be seen as a microcosm of the functioning of the apartheid system and/or which were seen as warranting special attention. The institutions selected were those the Truth and Reconciliation Report termed 'influential sectors of the apartheid society'. These were all sectors, the Report noted, which had 'come under attack for what was seen by some as their complicity with the apartheid system' (Truth and Reconciliation Commission of South Africa 1999b, 2).

The institutions and sectors identified by the Commission, and made the subject of hearings, were the media, business, prisons, the faith community, the legal system, political parties, the armed forces, the State Security Council, and the health sector. All hearings were reported on in the Final Report, and comprehensive recommendations made. The Commission also convened hearings on three areas that they believed warranted special attention: compulsory military service, children and youth, and women. Each of these hearings received attention in the Final Report. In addition, they convened what were termed 'special event' hearings: the Trojan Horse Hearings, the Caprivi Hearings, and the Mandela United Football Club Hearings.

The failure of the Truth and Reconciliation Commission to focus more directly on state institutions was an unfortunate omission. Separate hearings on the police, for example, would have provided stronger and more consistent recommendations for the South African police force, as well as a truthful accounting of their role during the apartheid era. Separate hearings on the secret service would also have been an important contribution. Similarly, although separate hearings were held for the Armed Forces and the State Security Council, these were not recorded separately. Rather, the findings were recorded within a wider discussion of the state in the Final Report. The important role played by these institutions, and the way in which they were harnessed and transformed to apply apartheid policy, as well as how they interpreted it themselves, would seem to warrant separate treatment in order to highlight the integral role these institutions played.

That said, the inclusion of particular groups and institutions within the Truth and Reconciliation Commission truth-finding process is an important model for including institutions, not only individuals, within such a process. It is an attempt to investigate more fully the parameters and the components of state crime, and to establish accountability across the spectrum. The Truth and Reconciliation Commission is one clear, non-criminal, example of institutional inclusion in addressing the crimes committed. Yet the Commission has no inherent power to follow up its own recommendations. Nor is there any regulatory structure to ensure such follow up. Its final recommendations were intended to be taken up by Parliament and the institutions themselves.

Importantly, the institutions harnessed by the state, that make it possible for state crime to be committed, are not always strictly state institutions. They may include religious institutions, the institutions of business, and other institutions of civil society and public governance. Some of these were indeed targeted by the South African Truth and Reconciliation Commission in its institutional hearings (as well as more recently in the hearings of the East Timorese Truth Commission, findings that have not been embraced by the ruling Timorese government – despite being presented to the President at the end of October 2005, who presented it to the Parliament at the end of November 2005, the report is yet to be discussed in Parliament). The role of the Catholic Church in the deeper acceptance and promotion of discrimination against and exclusion of Jews in Germany from 1933 has been explored by many scholars (see, for example, Lewy 1964). Equally, the role of the Dutch Reformed Church in the apartheid era was investigated by the Truth and Reconciliation Commission. So too has the participation of the medical profession, particularly in the Holocaust and the Armenian genocide (see, for example, Dadrian 1986; Lifton 1986; Müller-Hill 1988). With regards to the Catholic Church, some of these issues were explored internally in the wake of the Holocaust, culminating in the apology for the silence of the Catholic Church during the Holocaust given by the Vatican in May 1998.

4. CIVIC LIABILITY. CONSIDERING INSTITUTIONAL ACCOUNTABILITY

As demonstrated by the South African Truth Commission model (and most recently by the East Timor Truth Commission hearings), addressing state crime requires unravelling the institutional responsibility of the state and civil institutions, and providing for the possibility of institutional transformation. We need to determine how institutional accountability may fit in with overall accountability for state crime. Further, we need to work out ways of addressing the *institutional dimensions* of state crime. It is necessary to acknowledge the different components of state crime and seek remedial paths that may encompass these layers. We can allow for a combination of accountabilities – social, political and legal – for which law can establish an important framework. This requires an understanding of the different layers of responsibility, complicity and accountability.

In recognising these different types of responsibility and accountability we must firstly distinguish between – and remit – individual and institutional accountability. Secondly, in considering the particular justice demands of different kinds of international crime, we must reconceptualise our understanding of post-conflict justice. This section will consider the first proposition. The outcome I am suggesting is a distinction between criminal liability (key leaders) and civic liability (key institutions).

The importance of specifically addressing institutions is demonstrated by José Zalaquett, activist and lawyer during the Pinochet regime, who later served on the *Rettig Commission*, the Chilean Commission on Truth and Reconciliation:

> '(...) from an ethical position, the ultimate purpose of dealing systematically with past human rights abuses is to put back in place a moral order that has broken down or has been severely undermined, or to build up a just political order if none existed in historical memory. Building or reconstructing a morally just order entails developing a political culture and setting in place values, institutions and policies that will guard against the repetition of the type of atrocities committed in the past. This has an assertive role in that certain values and institutions are affirmed. It also has a preventive role: one may not be able to ensure that these atrocities will never happen again, but at least one can create a system to act as a bulwark against their recurrence'. (Zalaquett 1995, 45)

It has been suggested that criminalisation of institutions is a risky path. Like lustration, it runs the danger of operating on an assumption of guilt and some level of collective responsibility. The danger too (as we saw in the case of the German Wehrmacht) is that if institutions are not found to be criminal this can lead to the potentially erroneous conclusions that they are in no need of transformation nor bear responsibility for the harm perpetrated. It is, however, important that institutions be addressed. Civic liability is put forward as a way to conceptualise institutional non-individual accountability, a core component of international crime.

Institutions cannot be part of the criminal justice process. They can however be part of a process of *transitional justice*. As such, they can incur what may be termed *civic liability*.

Civic liability derives from the fundamental responsibility owed by state and non-state institutions to the society in which they are located. Civil society depends for its well-being upon a framework of strong institutions. The abrogation of the responsibility of such institutions to the wider civil society through their participation in the perpetration of gross violations of human rights means that they fail in their duty of care and assume a civic liability. Examples of this include the failure of law to give victims the protection they are entitled to within the existing national legal system. It also involves the failure of the United Nations to effectively intervene and to protect. The concept of civic liability is, therefore, a way in which the institutions of the state – and the state itself – may be allocated responsibility. It distinguishes the liability of the institution from the liability of the individual. It is a way of demonstrating that liability for state crime does not lie solely with the individual (adopting the first step of Fisse and Braithwaite's (1993) corporate crime Accountability Model – identifying institutions and organisations as participants in state crime).

Civic liability offers a framework within which an investigation of how such offences were committed and/or supported by these institutions can take place, and secures a process whereby reforms are explored and implemented. It may be possible, and desirable, to put certain key members of the organisation or institution on trial for these crimes: clear cases are key strategists of the executive, the military, and the police, or individuals within other less central institutions such as the church or the medical system for their own participation.

A priest who gives a sermon in Rwanda supporting the killing of Tutsis, bears both personal responsibility and is an agent of institutional responsibility. For the former, criminal liability may be allocated – for the latter civic liability. Institutions which carry out or more indirectly support genocidal policies do bear an important responsibility for state crime. While individuals may come and go, institutions remain through changes of regime. It is therefore crucial that they be addressed as part of a matrix of accountability for state crime. The giving of an apology by a current state leader for crimes committed by previous executives is an example of this.[8]

Civic liability can thus be broken down into three stages: the selection of key members of particular organisations and institutions for individual criminalisation (criminal liability); the transformation of institutions through the assumption of responsibility by institutions for their actions in an active manner; and the external and internal monitoring of this. That is, institutions are not simply held passively responsible under law for the past; they are invited to manifest the virtue of taking active responsibility for a transformed, substantive rights-respecting future.

The term 'civic liability' originates from this duty of institutions, state and non-state, to protect and nurture civil society, a duty failed during the perpetration of state crime. Institutions can fail in both an active and a passive manner: either

---

[8]   See further, Nesam McMillan's work, PhD candidate in the School of Political Science, Criminology and Sociology at the University of Melbourne, on the role of apology and acknowledgment in relation to the Rwandan genocide (part of a wider project on the international response to the genocide).

as a core institution such as the police, the military, and the executive that actively plans and participates in the crime, or possibly a less core institution such as the church or a national association that may be less active, but still supportive in a secondary manner of the crimes committed.

How to acquit this civic liability? Through participation in truth-finding processes such as truth commissions, in which the workings of the institution and its precise role are identified. Through internal transformation, whereby recommendations are implemented. Through using current international human rights frameworks as benchmarks. Through civil compensation whereby institutions remit some type of debt to victim groups. This is not to abrogate their criminal liability, focused on the key individuals in the institutions; rather it is a different level of liability more appropriate to the institution or association and its role in the society. Civic liability is connected to institutional transformation.

Civic liability applies to both state and non-state institutions and organisations. However, whereas with state institutions, transformative practices can be imposed, this is more difficult with non-state institutions which may enjoy a special status or not have any kind of formal relationship with the state (the difference between a private security organisation which needs to be registered with the state, and the church which does not). It is with these non-state institutions that a process of institutional hearings such as that employed by the South African Truth and Reconciliation Commission can be most effective: a state framework for the review of these institutions and their role, and the provision of recommendations for change. The final set of recommendations in the Report of the Commission highlighted the importance of economic justice in achieving a strong and meaningful human rights culture in order to ensure no repetition of the past and called on the business community to implement particular changes. These investigative hearings contain an expectation of transformation.

Civic and criminal liability – institutional and individual – can make a powerful and effective combination. In the case of individual liability, law can reach behind the veil of potential absolution (as a church leader, a doctor, a lawyer) provided by their institution, and identify individuals in these institutions for criminal action. In such a context, in 1999 the Rwandan President Pasteur Bizimungu stated that no Rwandan is above the law. Addressing a reburial ceremony for 20,000 victims in April 1999 in Kibeho, Gikongoro prefecture to mark the fifth anniversary of the genocide, he asked how long the Catholic church would 'continue to ignore accusations by Christians' against Gikongoro's bishop, Augustin Misago. The bishop, who was present at the ceremony, has been accused of involvement in the killings. 'The Rwandan state did not place Bishop Misago above the law and is not afraid of him,' Bizimungu said, according to Rwandan radio. 'We shall only intervene if the church continues to do nothing' (Integrated

Regional Information Network for Central and Eastern Africa 1999). A few days later, the bishop was arrested on genocide charges.

A two-phase accountability process can be identified:

(1) The immediate project of legal remedy. This is the establishment of causation, responsibility, and potential liability. It includes in its approach both the recognition of the parameters of a state crime, and significant addressing of key perpetrators and remedies for victims (thus both 'specific' and 'societal' remedies) for the offences committed, including the establishment of a regulatory framework for institutional reorganisation and transformation.
(2) The ongoing forward-looking project of transformation (societal and institutional) and the assumption of responsibility for redress for what has occurred. This second stage includes an emphasis on broader societal and state reconstruction.

There are clear and necessary links between the projects of immediate legal remedy and societal transformation. Civic liability is one important link between the two phases – establishing a framework for transformation. The concept of civic liability is put forward as a way in which the institutions of the state may be allocated responsibility within law. It is a way of demonstrating that liability for such crime does not lie with the individual only.

A further plank in the project of accountability and societal transformation is matching our legal redress to the specificity of the crimes, connecting the particular causes of crimes to their legal redress, leading to a possible redefining of post-conflict justice. The next section will consider this proposition.

5.   A TYPOLOGY OF INTERNATIONAL CRIME? MATCHING LEGAL REDRESS TO SPECIFIC CRIMES

In thinking about the relationship between international crime and legal redress, it seems important to consider the differences and similarities between the different types of international crimes. One failure I would suggest in our approach to addressing international crime is the lack of specificity in approach. What would seem to me to be important is the development of a typology of international crime that identifies different causes, different structures, different victim groups, different motivations. This is both if justice in terms of strict accountability and any broader reconstruction is to be achieved – goals that are increasingly put forward as central in the wake of state orchestrated harm. While we can identify certain similarities between international crimes, we can also find particular differences, requiring a different matrix of legal redress. Not all genocides are the same, nor all crimes against humanity. A typology of international crime would cut through in a different way the core crimes of genocide, crimes against humanity, and war crimes. The current lack of specificity in what we are addressing means the redress is less effective in terms of accountability, reconstruction and prevention. What we can observe is that there have not really been typologies of international crime developed in the way that there have been typologies of genocide – this would be a useful project for a supranational criminology.

We have part typologies of these crimes. There have, for example, been typologies of genocide: Ward Churchill's (1986) and Israel Charny's (1994, 1999) 'degrees of genocide', and Helen Fein's (1990), Leo Kuper's (1981), Barbara Harff and Ted Gurr's (1988, 1989), and Vahakn Dadrian's (1975, 1976) contextual typologies. These typologies include acts commonly termed 'international crime' – yet give us causal explanations that we do not generally find in, for example, the transitional justice literature.

Harff and Gurr's typology, for example, is important in its distinction between hegemonial and xenophobic genocide,[9] and in their identification of politicide in which the victims are distinguished, they note, not primarily by communal identity but by their political orientation. This becomes important in terms of the extent to which these crimes are systemic, or an isolated case. Raphael Lemkin's (1944) definition of genocide was itself a kind of typology of destruction. R.J. Rummel (1994) proposed the term *democide* to denote killing by governments, demonstrating that there are subsets of state crime. Irving Horowitz (2002) and Pieter Drost (1959a, 1959b) recognized the link to the state.

'State crime' itself has been defined and conceptualised by a number of authors. Connecting the conceptual work done on state terror and state crime to a matrix of international crime more narrowly defined would be a useful exercise in determining accountability and prevention strategies. We can usefully draw on these for a causal typology of a more narrowly defined 'international crime'.

Gregg Barak (1991a, 1994) argues the necessity of focusing on the structural and organisational nature of governmental abuse, drawing a spectrum from proactive state criminality such as the repression of the Chinese demonstrators in Tiannanmen Square in 1989 and the Iran-Contra affair, to crimes of omission in the context of the US such as the denial of sufficient and adequate housing to the homeless and the informal economy and the traditional forms of criminal activity it produces, and the denial of the fundamental right to work for an adequate

---

9   'In the former the primary motive is to subordinate a communal group by killing enough of its members that the survivors have no will or capacity to resist, whereas in the latter ideology calls for the elimination of the offending communal group.' Harff & Gurr (1988, 368).

income. He connects a concern with state criminality to class and social justice worldwide.

Kauzlarich (1995) and Kauzlarich et al's (2001) typology based around victims and types of state crime is another useful starting point. Kauzlarich et al's (2001) finding that victims of state crime are easy targets for repeated victimization is an important finding for our learning on what needs to be taken into account in redressing these crimes. As they note in their discussion of poverty, institutional sexism and racism, institutional and structural change is generally not forthcoming.

Michael Stohl's and George Lopez's (1984) conceptual work on state terror and their distinction between oppression, repression, and terrorism is useful to consider. Lopez's (1984) framework for the classification of government terror in which he identifies and analyses its key factors – the prevailing political climate (in particular the manner of institutionalising state terror), its ideology, its particular character (in particular internal and external support systems) and its outcomes – would be an important contribution to a causal typology. The crossover work of Barbara Harff (1986) on genocide as state terrorism, in which she poses national structural upheaval and the existence of sharp internal cleavages as key factors to compare across genocides is another contribution – particularly in her positing of the question as to why genocide as a policy choice and not repression.

John Torpey's (2001) reparations typology in terms of the sources of reparations claims is another useful starting point. In identifying the different sources of reparations claims (state-sponsored mass killing, wartime incarceration and economic collaboration in World War II, state terrorism and other authoritarian practices, classical European colonisation, internal colonialism and neo-colonialism) Torpey (2001) provides a useful typology of the different state-sponsored international human rights violations that require redress and the different kinds of redress required for each. Some (e.g. typical World War II claims) he suggests require a more 'symbolic' or 'commemorative' response, and others (e.g. colonial crimes) a more 'antisystemic' or 'transformative' response. Whether these crimes take place over a longer or shorter period, necessitating institutional change, is a further question. Elsewhere I have suggested that a combination of these two is often most appropriate: a backward looking and a forward looking set of legal responses (Balint 1996), also that the manner in which these crimes are ended can be significant in terms of what will be most effective (Balint 2001).

There exist significant points of meeting and departure between genocide and other forms of state crime. Most notably, the institutional nature of such crime is an important meeting point. So too is the perpetration of such acts for the broader purposes of state consolidation and state power. A point of dissimilarity, however, is what is intended for the targeted groups – subjugation in the case of apartheid for example, or destruction as in the case of genocide. This distinction throws up different issues again for legal redress and, in particular, reconstruction and reconciliation in the wake of such crime. We can draw further distinctions between crimes 'in the life of a nation' (genocide, apartheid, totalitarianism, some crimes against humanity) and crimes committed in pursuit of conventional war (war crimes). Where war crimes may be served by a trial (and civic liability processes), other crimes perpetrated against a state's own civilians may be better served by a raft of legal processes that address both the crimes as such, and their underlying causes. We saw this happening, for example, in the case of the truth commission process in South Africa that included institutional hearings aimed at transformation of institutions central to the apartheid policy such as the education, health and legal sectors. In Guatemala, this manifested in the drafting of a socio-economic accord which focused on addressing the poverty, discrimination and social and political marginalisation in that country, which the accord recognised as key contributing factors to the conflict. We could further distinguish between crimes in the course of colonisation, and crimes in the course of communism.

All of the types of crimes mentioned above have been termed state – or international – crime. One of the weaknesses of the current dominant approach – and where criminology and socio-legal studies could make a significant contribution – is a lack of specificity in approach to different types of state crime. In addressing international crime, we need to be specific and recognise the differences within crimes (genocide, crimes against humanity, war crimes) in terms of their causes, and their intended aims. We can then figure out redress that will address these crimes in their particularity and as international crimes.

Matching the types and causes of crimes to redress is important not only in establishing true accountability, but also in establishing a preventative foundation for the future. We see this in the case of many state crimes, that these are not necessarily isolated incidents. They are crimes directed at traditionally marginalised groups and thus redress that will endure must address this. Establishing a typology of types and causes of crimes to legal redress is a project that could lead to a redefining of justice. If individual punishment is our only goal, then it probably does not matter. But if we want to fulfil the increasing demands that law does more, that it be an active player in reconciliation, reconstruction and prevention, then it does.

6.   RECONSTRUCTION AND PREVENTION. JUSTICE AS SOCIAL JUSTICE?

If we do take this path of considering the goals of post-conflict justice to be that of both accountability and the bound up together goal of reconstruction and prevention, then it seems necessary to conceptualise justice as multi-faceted. The consequences of putting post-conflict reconstruction on the law agenda would seem to mean that we broaden our understanding of post-conflict justice.

In our thinking about how law may best address these kinds of crimes we have largely failed to distinguish between different kinds of international crime and what they may require to adequately tackle them. In matching our responses more exactly to the type of crime committed we may find ourselves suggesting a redefining of justice to include for example social justice.

The particular relationship between post-conflict legal processes and a broader societal impact has been the subject of some discussion, with suggestions that post-conflict legal processes do not necessarily lead to structural transformation (see, for example, Lambourne 2004; Mamdani 1996). It may be that the transitional justice model is wrongly focused in order to initiate larger and long-lasting change. Kriger (2000), in the context of Zimbabwe, notes the deep socio-economic problems of post-colonial Zimbabwe, in particular land ownership, and how the transitional justice model with its general focus on individual rights does not provide the framework to address this. Land was also seen to be a key cause of the conflict in Rwanda (Bigagaza & Abong et al 2002). Political inclusion and exclusion as a legacy of colonialism was another significant factor at play in Rwanda. In thinking about establishing accountability and initiating reconstruction, in addressing both individual and institutional responsibilities, as well as structural conditions, we may need to be conceptualising justice somewhat differently and in a more pluralist sense to include social justice.

At the South African truth commission institutional hearings into business, various strategies for redress and as a contribution to reconstruction were suggested. These included social responsibility investment programs, support for non-governmental organisations, and improved employment equity programs. They also included proposals such as the cancellation of all apartheid debt, the introduction of a 'wealth tax', and the establishment by business of a reparations fund. As the Report noted, an alarming gap between rich and poor exists in South Africa, one aggravated by the fact that wealth and poverty are very largely defined in racial terms (Truth and Reconciliation Commission of South Africa 1999b, 21–22). The final set of recommendations in the Report of the Commission highlighted the importance of economic justice in achieving a strong and meaningful human rights culture in order to ensure no repetition of the past. Recognising that it is impossible for the public sector alone to find the resources required to expedite the goal of economic justice, it urged the private sector in particular to consider a special initiative in terms of a fund for training, empowerment and opportunities for the disadvantaged and dispossessed in South Africa (Truth and Reconciliation Commission of South Africa 1999c, 349). The Report noted that it does not seek to prescribe one or other strategy, rather recommends that urgent consideration be given by government to harnessing all available resources in the war against poverty. It did recommend a scheme be put into place to enable those who benefited from apartheid policies to contribute towards the alleviation of poverty (Truth and Reconciliation Commission of South Africa 1999c, 349). As such, it urged that consideration be given to the most appropriate ways in which to provide restitution for those who have suffered from the effects of apartheid discrimination. These were listed as: a wealth tax; a once-off levy on corporate and private income; each company listed on the Johannesburg Stock Exchange to make a once-off donation of one percent of its market capitalisation; a retrospective surcharge on corporate profits extending back to a date to be suggested; a surcharge on golden handshakes given to senior public servants since 1990; the suspension of all taxes on land and other material donations to formerly disadvantaged communities (Truth and Reconciliation Commission of South Africa 1999c, 3).

While there is a broader recognition of the necessity of tying social justice concerns to post-conflict reconstruction, the role of law in this has largely not been addressed. Rama Mani (2002) in a study of the meaning of post-conflict justice, notes the complexity of justice needs post-conflict, particularly in low-income societies, and argues that the underlying causes of conflict, the structural and systemic injustices such as political and economic discrimination and inequalities of distribution, have not been addressed by national and international post-conflict practitioners. J.P. Lederach (1999) has identified the importance of socio-economic justice to peace. The search for social justice post-conflict has been a key feature of studies of post-military regime South America (see, for example, Eckstein & Wickham-Crowley 2003).

In considering the dual aims of accountability and reconstruction in the wake of conflict, it seems necessary to conceptualise justice as multi-faceted. We can usefully draw on Rama Mani's three-fold typology of justice, justice as rectificatory (addressing the direct consequences of conflict-perpetrators and victims), legal (establishing rule of law patterns), and distributive (addressing structural and systemic injustices and distributive inequalities). What seems to me critical is that we attempt to more accurately match the particular international crimes to appropriate and specific redress. In recognizing that different crimes (different genocides, different crimes against humanity) may have different causes, we can determine what needs to be addressed – structurally – in the hope of reconstruction and prevention. In creating a typology of international crimes, their causes, and matching these to potential legal (and non- or quasi-legal) redress, we may find ourselves conceptualising justice more broadly, and ultimately, more accurately.

7.   CONCLUSION

If accountability is to be accurate, then it needs to be comprehensive. For reconstruction to succeed – with a hope that the society can prevent further crimes of this nature in the future – then a broader conceptualisation of justice is required. Solely addressing the individuals will not achieve this. For this, we need to identify the particular dimensions of each international crime. This can be different between crimes, and between particular case studies.

We need to develop a framework – that we may consider as legal pluralist – that brings together the many different legal and quasi-legal processes that address these crimes – and consider new ones that address these acts both precisely (leading to reconstruction), and in their entirety (for accountability). Developing the notion of civic liability can help us with the latter; including social justice in the justice spectrum, with the former. Widening the parameters, however, is not incompatible with establishing individual liability. The International Law Commission in its deliberations on this topic explicitly stated that state responsibility should not replace individual responsibility (Spinedi 1989). A kind of collective liability is not what is sought, the 'responsibility of all and hence the responsibility of none' (see Macdonald 1957, 34). Rather, it is to point to the particular characteristics of such crime, and thus to a different remedial path to that ordinarily taken with domestic crimes of individuals or international crimes such as bribery of foreign public officials or drug offences which, while defined as international crimes (see, for example, Bassiouni 1999), are not necessarily crimes of state in a way that genocide and apartheid are.[10] It is a path which asks that we look to the multi-layered components of the crime (individual and institutional) and to remedies which both allocate responsibility and seek the assumption of responsibility, criminal and non-criminal. It is a path which has been suggested and taken with regard to corporate crime (see Fisse and Braithwaite 1993).

These are particular crimes that have been largely left out of mainstream legal or criminological analysis. As 'administrative massacres organized by the state apparatus' they need to be analysed as such – as sui generis yet using our criminological, socio-legal tools to shed light on how best they may be addressed in the interests of bringing to account and preventing further atrocities. We could use the approach 'these are murders, these are rapes, these are kidnappings' yet in so doing we fail to conceptualise these crimes in their entirety. In not recognising

---

10   We could, however, expand this framework to consider the addressing of torture – see the contribution of Huggins in this volume.

that these crimes are 'more than', we miss an important dimension to them, their ideological and institutional nature. The fulfilment of a decree that 'a people should not exist' (Jaspers 1966, 35) (in the case of genocide), or that a people is less than (apartheid) or invisible (in the case of war crimes). The cooption and transformation of state and non-state institutions, the utilisation of a state structure towards these ends.

Both institutions and individuals, according to their placement, role, and activity, bear differing levels of responsibility and potential liability for international and state crime. While addressing the individuals – the key perpetrators and masterminds behind these acts – and the victims and survivors – is critical, in order to fully address these kinds of crimes their institutional dimensions must be recognised. This is both if justice in terms of strict accountability and any broader reconstruction is to be achieved. Individual responsibility and individual justice are not adequate in meeting our goals, either strict accountability or broader reconstruction. We must look simultaneously to the institutional and the individual levels in addressing international crime, and develop a framework in which addressing the institutional dimensions is not an 'add on' but a core part of the enterprise. In so doing we may find that our justice is ultimately more enduring.

XIV. DEALING WITH THE LEGACY OF MASS VIOLENCE: CHANGING LENSES TO RESTORATIVE JUSTICE

Stephan PARMENTIER, Kris VANSPAUWEN and Elmar WEITEKAMP

1. INTRODUCTION

Despite the continuing decline of the number of violent conflicts in recent years, the post-World War II period can be marked as one of the most violent periods in human history (Eriksson and Wallensteen 2004). Contrary to popular belief, the vast majority of these conflicts did not occur between states but can be qualified instead as 'intra-state' conflicts involving gross and massive human rights violations. It is estimated that in the period 1946–1996, 232 armed conflicts have taken place (Balint 1996b), and since the fall of the Berlin wall (1989–2006), 122 conflicts have taken place, 89 of which were intra-state conflicts (Harbom & Wallensteen 2007). Estimating the number of persons killed, as well as the ones stripped of their fundamental rights, is virtually impossible, but several studies consider them to be in the tens of millions (Balint 1996b; Lacina & Gleditsch 2005).

Serious human rights violations of this nature have in many jurisdictions and for a long time amounted to criminal behaviour and have been brought before criminal justice systems at the national level. In the aftermath of the Second World War, and most recently since the entry into force of the Rome Statute of the International Criminal Court in 2002, such human rights violations can be viewed as international crimes, involving genocide, crimes against humanity and war crimes. Moreover, new mechanisms such as truth commissions have seen the light of day to deal with violent conflicts and to provide a forum for the victims (Bassiouni 2002a; Kritz 1995). The emphasis on the development of more victim-oriented mechanisms is a logical continuation of the growing interest in the fate of victims in favour of the victors of conflicts. By some, this profound shift is explained as the progressive consolidation of the democratic model (Todorov 2001). At the same time, criminology and the understanding of crime has gone through the same paradigm shift, since the social criminal as a survivor in poor communities has made room for the suffering victims (Lea 1999).

It should be clear that 'international crimes' as a relatively new concept cannot be seen as simply identical to the older concept of 'state crimes' (Friedrichs 1998; Kauzlarich et al. 2003): on the one hand, state crimes constitute a wider category than international crimes, as they also involve behaviour that is not traditionally regarded as violent, such as instances of treason, espionage or corruption; on the other hand, state crimes are to be seen as narrower than international crimes, as they are committed by institutions or persons entrusted with state powers, while international crimes can also be committed by non-state actors, such as guerrilla groups or private individuals. Whatever the exact conceptual framework, it should be clear that criminology as a scientific discipline has only paid very scant attention to international crimes, the modalities of committing them, the offenders and the victims. This is quite stunning given the high number of violent conflicts involving international crimes, and the devastating consequences of these crimes for victims and communities alike. In our view, this lack of attention can be attributed to at least two elements: one is the difficulty of obtaining reliable information about these crimes, which calls for new and more sophisticated methods of data gathering and data analysis, after but also during violent conflicts; the other reason lies in the controversial context in which international crimes are committed, as they are frequently closely related to power structures in society, and researching them may constitute a threat to powerful groups. It is therefore our conviction that any initiative, such as the present book, to shed more light on international crimes should be welcomed as a crucial and much needed contribution to criminology.

Debates about serious human rights violations and international crimes committed in the past usually start during times of political transition, that is when societies are moving away from a non-democratic regime. At that time, the new political elite are openly confronted with the fundamental question on how to address the heavy burden of their dark past. This question was posed in most countries of Latin America in the 1980s, in all countries of Central and Eastern Europe in the 1990s, and in several countries in Africa and Asia during the last decade. In much of the legal and the social science literature, this is known as the question of 'dealing with the past' (Huyse 1996). We prefer two notions that are broader and more neutral at the same time, and which we will use interchangeably, namely 'transitional justice' on the one hand and 'post-conflict justice' on the other hand. The first concept has for a long time been defined as: 'the study of the choices made and the quality of justice rendered when states are replacing authoritarian regimes by democratic state institutions' (Siegel 1998, 431) and has in recent years been broadened to include: 'the full range of processes and mechanisms associated with a society's attempts to come to terms with a legacy of large-scale past abuses, in order to ensure accountability, serve justice and achieve reconciliation' (United Nations 2004, 4).

It is used here interchangeably with the concept of post-conflict justice, which in fact is often presented as comprising two related meanings, one referring to: 'retributive and restorative justice with respect to human depredations that occur during violent conflicts' (in other words mostly dealing with the past), the other referring to: 'restoring and enhancing justice systems which have failed or become weakened as a result of internal conflicts' (in other words geared towards the future) (Bassiouni 2002a). Although these two notions are not fully identical, and although they are not without conceptual problems, they seem to catch best the kinds of situations and the kinds of problems associated with the commission of international crimes. We have argued in previous publications that new regimes in their pursuit of justice are facing a number of key issues, namely to search for truth about the past, to ensure accountability of the offenders, to provide some form of reparation for the victims, and to promote reconciliation between former enemies (Parmentier 2003; Parmentier & Weitekamp 2007).

It should be clear that in this chapter we are less concerned with the origins of international crimes, however important these may be to clarify our understanding of the root causes that lead to violent conflicts in the first place. Instead, we will look into various ways of dealing with violent crimes and with the consequences of mass violence in a post-conflict situation. Our major aim is to broaden the perspective of dealing with such crimes, from a retributive approach with a prime focus on punishing the offender(s), to a restorative approach with more attention to victims and communities and to building new relationships. Our main argument is not that retributive mechanisms have no place in post-conflict situations, but rather that restorative mechanisms offer an interesting complement to dealing with a legacy of mass violence. Such approach indeed requires 'changing lenses', as aptly put by Howard Zehr in his seminal work on restorative justice for common crimes (Zehr 1991). But any photographer, professional or amateur, knows that different lenses are rarely substitutes for each other but on the contrary complement one another. Likewise we argue that restorative justice theory, as an emerging discourse within the criminological sciences, offers an additional approach towards understanding the victims and the perpetrators of mass violence. Moreover we suggest that it contributes to broadening the object of criminology, by shifting the attention from common crimes to international crimes, often of a political nature (Parmentier and Weitekamp 2007).

This chapter takes the following structure. First, we sketch the dominant approach to dealing with international crimes, namely through retributive justice and specifically through criminal prosecutions, and we list the strengths and weaknesses of such approach in situations of transitional justice or post-conflict justice. Then, we shift gear to introduce some basic principles of restorative justice, and will look at truth commissions as the primary illustration of such approach in dealing with international crimes. Finally, we try to assess the implications of these two paradigms for our understanding of mass violence in post-conflict situations.

2. THE DOMINANT APPROACH: RETRIBUTIVE JUSTICE

The most classical way to deal with international crimes is to punish the perpetrators and to use the criminal justice system for this purpose. This route fits into a retributive justice approach, which according to Ashworth means that 'punishment is justified as the morally appropriate response to crime: those who commit offences deserve punishment, it is claimed, and the amount of punishment should be proportionate to the degree of wrongdoing' (Ashworth 1997). Much more than in the case of common crimes, criminal prosecutions for international crimes may take place at various levels, national and international.

2.1. STRENGTHS AND WEAKNESSES OF RETRIBUTIVE JUSTICE

Calls to bring the presumed offenders to a criminal court usually ring loud after a regime change has taken place, and the old authoritarian leaders have been replaced by a more or less democratic form of government. At that time, the political context tends to be more conducive to the necessary freedom of speech and of action. Moreover, the case of Pinochet has clearly illustrated that such calls for prosecution can be made long after the crimes have taken place (Roht-Arriaza 2005).

The strong points of criminal prosecution for international crimes have been well documented. According to Belgian political scientist Luc Huyse (1998), there are two main arguments in these debates. The first is related to the reconstruction of the moral order, i.e. the general idea that 'justice be done' to satisfy the desire for justice of society as a whole and of specific groups in particular. This moral argument is frequently coupled with a political one, in the sense that prosecution can also strengthen a fragile democracy, by confirming the principle of the 'rule of law' and by thus providing the firm foundation on which to construct a human rights awareness and culture in a country. In such manner, criminal prosecutions serve the role of breaking through the thick walls of impunity and engage countries on the road to accountability (Combating Impunity 2002).

On top of these two arguments that primarily pertain to the issue of the desirability of criminal prosecution, there are also aspects of legality involved. The American legal scholar Diane Orentlicher (1991) has argued in strong terms that there exists 'a duty to prosecute in international human rights law' for serious human rights violations. She has founded her arguments on the various human rights treaties that contain passages to this effect and on the ensuing case law, and has reiterated these arguments in her capacity as expert on impunity for the United Nations (Orentlicher 2005). In general legal terms, criminal prosecutions and convictions have the advantage of establishing a 'legal or judicial truth', that is an account of the acts and the facts that stands beyond doubt for the parties involved as well as for future generations. In the words of the South African Truth and Reconciliation Commission, this truth is mostly 'forensic' or 'factual' (TRC Report 1998), and it is of course focused on individual perpetrators and victims.

In a large number of cases, the calls for criminal prosecution are voiced by the direct victims of the violations or crimes, those who directly suffered from arrests, torture, convictions and other forms of repression. Also their relatives, and their surviving family members, who have witnessed the crimes and have felt their consequences from close by, tend to be staunch defenders of criminal prosecutions. They wish to know what has happened to their loved ones and to see the offenders called to account (Amadiume and An-Na'im 2000). The examples of the *Madres de la Plaza de Mayo* in Argentina (the so-called Crazy Mothers) or the survivors of the Holocaust are telling examples. In other cases, victims conduct their activities with the support of human rights groups and committees, local but also international, such as Amnesty International, Human Rights Watch and the *Fédération Internationale des Droits de l'Homme* (Amnesty International 2001).

It should be noted, however, that criminal prosecution is not without problems or even risks. Huyse (1998) has listed some of these risks. Contradictory as it may sound, criminal prosecutions of perpetrators may also undermine the 'rule of law' of a new state. Some regimes may incur contradictions with the principle of non-retroactivity of criminal law, notably if they wish to prosecute crimes that have been prescribed or that were not punishable under the former regime. Another problem for a new state is to guarantee the independence and the impartiality of the criminal justice system. This is not always easy, because the criminal justice systems may still be populated by the same police officers and judges appointed by the former regime and still adhere to its values. The examples of Germany after the Second World War and South Africa after apartheid (Dyzenhaus 1998) are interesting examples of this problem. But also when the police officers and the judges are new to the system, problems may occur in that they may want to make a clear break with the past by adopting very repressive policies without due diligence for the rights of the accused. The reality of postwar repression in Western European countries has clearly illustrated the possible risks associated with such approach, which can lead to many controversies and tensions in the long run (Huyse & Dhondt 1991). And of course it is problematic to prosecute the offenders in the case of an amnesty rule, that shields them from further legal action, criminal and civil (Roht-Arriaza & Gibson 1998; O'Shea 2002).

Another category of risks is less of a legal, but more of a political nature. Many new democracies are fragile, as the old political and military elites can be resisting and actively opposing the transitional government. Prosecuting well known offenders or even the threat thereof, can provoke the old elites and even seduce them to seize power again. The examples of Chile and Argentina are telling in demonstrating the power of the old elites and the caution with which the new government has proceeded (Orentlicher 1991). Another problem relates to the capacity of the system. In long-term autocratic regimes, only a small minority tends to possess the knowledge and the skills required to govern a country in political and economic terms. To call to account the members of this elite may lead to growing uncertainty about the future of the elite in general, and may even push them to emigrate from the country, a scenario not unknown to countries from Central Europe in the early 1990s and to South Africa in the late 1990s.

Furthermore, there are problems with the logistics of criminal justice systems that are confronted with the legacy of mass violence. In some cases, the sheer numbers of offenders and potential suspects is so large that the system would become completely clogged if (too) many prosecutions were to take place. The example of Rwanda, where 13 years after the genocide still over 100,000 persons are imprisoned speaks for itself, and it has prompted the Rwandan government to look for new solutions and to revive the old conflict resolution model of *gacaca* and to adjust it to dealing with the crimes of genocide (Penal Reform International, 2002; Haveman in this volume).[9] Even in situations which are less extreme, it is unavoidable to be very selective and to only bring some perpetrators to criminal courts. Then tough questions arise, namely whether the prosecutorial agencies should aim at the heads and the planners of the crimes, who have ordered the crimes or were aware of them taking place or whether they should target those who executed the orders and those who assisted them. And what about the so-called bystanders, who did not actively participate in committing the crimes, but nevertheless witnessed them and in some cases may have benefited from the consequences?

Finally, criminal trials by their very nature are mostly focused on the offenders and on the rights of the accused, and pay far less attention to the victims and to the harm inflicted upon them (Zehr 2003). This is the case with ordinary criminal trials and it is by and large the same with international crimes and crimes of mass violence. This is not to say that victims are completely neglected, but that their role in the criminal process is often reduced to that of witnesses or in other ways.

Given the many difficulties associated with criminal prosecution, many choices have to be made. Therefore, it does not come as a surprise that in practice criminal prosecution has often proved more the exception than the standard. Between the aspirations of criminal prosecutions and their reality, there exist many laws and legal regulations, as well as several practical objections.

2.2. THE TRIPTYCH OF CRIMINAL PROSECUTIONS

States are traditionally well equipped to conduct criminal prosecutions against suspects of regular crimes, through the various institutions of their criminal justice systems (notably the police, the Public Prosecutor's Service, the trial courts and the prison system or other measures for the execution of criminal sanctions). As suggested above, however, crimes of mass violence bring with them new challenges (Parmentier and Weitekamp 2007). One of the challenges lies in the political nature of the crimes, meaning that either the intent of the offenders or the object and context of their crimes relate to politics. Another distinctive criterion between common crimes and international crimes lies in the massive numbers of victims of the latter, and sometimes in the large numbers of perpetrators as well. Therefore, criminal justice systems in many countries, particularly if poorly equipped, tend to be reluctant to engage in widespread prosecutions.

While in the past criminal prosecutions for international crimes were limited to the country where the crimes had been committed, the last two decades have witnessed two important shifts in this regard.

The first shift relates to the development of so-called 'universal jurisdiction' legislation in a number of countries. This allows third countries to prosecute and to try international crimes, without the existence of a link between the third country and the place where the crimes have been committed, the nationality of the offender or the nationality of the victim (Amnesty International 2001; Princeton Principles 2001). The main rationale lies in the fact that international crimes are considered so heinous that they do not only affect the victims and the criminal justice system of the country where they took place, but that they also affect humanity as such, for which reason also third countries put their criminal justice system at the disposal of the world community. Such cases of 'pure' universal jurisdiction are in fact rare in today's world, the actual Spanish legislation and the former Belgian legislation (until 2003) being among the exceptions (Andries et al. 1994; Wouters & Panken 2002). In fact, a number of countries – mostly European – have a limited form of universal jurisdiction, and require at least one specific link with the crime in order to prosecute and try it. While welcomed by some as an ethical triumph for humanity (Combating Impunity 2002), recent events in Western Europe suggest that the efforts to establish genuine systems of universal jurisdiction are often subject to the *Realpolitik* of international relations.

The second major shift to respond to mass atrocity lies in the establishment of criminal justice mechanisms at the international level (Bassiouni 1997). The historical forerunners of this tendency were the two international military tribunals of Nuremberg and Tokyo, establishment by the victorious powers of the Second World War to deal with the crimes of the Nazi regime and the Japanese respectively. After a long period of inertia, two *ad hoc* tribunals, for ex-Yugoslavia (ICTY) and for Rwanda (ICTR), were set up by the Security Council of the United Nations in 1993 and 1994 respectively, for a limited period of time and with a limited territorial jurisdiction. They have been followed by the establishment of a permanent International Criminal Court, entering into operation in 2002 and dealing with three main categories of international crimes: genocide, crimes against humanity and war crimes. While the two *ad hoc* tribunals have a primary competence to deal with serious human rights violations, the ICC has a complementary task to prosecute and try international crimes when State Parties are 'unwilling or unable' to do so, thus leaving the prime locus at the national level (Kittichaisaree 2001). These institutions were paralleled by a number of mixed international-national tribunals, for Sierra Leone, East Timor, Kosovo and Cambodia. The rapid development of international criminal justice mechanisms has been heralded by many as the final start of a new era of justice. Others, like Drumbl (2007, 2000), have argued that the practice of punishment by international tribunals is foremost an example of 'legal mimicry' whereby every new institution tries to build on the experience of the previous one, despite the many different crime situations they are facing and despite the often 'confusing, disparate, inconsistent and erratic' sanctions they have applied thus far. He raises very serious questions about the fact that international criminal justice has been strongly imbued with a western conception of justice, which is liberal and legalistic, and may not be the only model to deal with these 'extraordinary' crimes that involve many victims, many perpetrators and a large group of bystanders – and all of these within a political context. Moreover, some mechanisms run the risk of being driven by economic and political motives (Wilson 2001) and lack the credibility to engage in the restoration of broken relationships in society.

3. CHANGING LENSES TO RESTORATIVE JUSTICE

While the revival of the (international) criminal justice is often regarded as the starting point of a new era for justice in the case of mass violence, the preceding section exposed some of the major problems and shortcomings of the retributive approach to post-conflict justice. Moreover, retributive justice objectives will continue to represent only one side of the 'coin of justice'. In this second part, we argue that the road to post-conflict justice requires further steps, that move beyond the limits of retributive justice. By prosecuting and punishing perpetrators of mass violence, many aspects of the phenomenon of mass victimisation – such as its societal, victimological and especially its criminological relevance – are overlooked. To reach some of the key goals of post-conflict justice, namely to prevent the reoccurrence of the violent conflict and to repair the harm that was suffered during the conflict, it is crucial to consider a number of questions that are criminological *par excellence*: what are the causes of mass violence? What were the conditions that made this violent conflict happen? What are the sociological and psychological reasons that could explain people's involvement in committing these atrocities? We will argue that a restorative justice approach to post-conflict situations can offer a more meaningful answer to these questions.

In recent years the field of transitional justice has seen a number of these so-called 'second-best alternatives' to the classic forms of retributive justice and criminal prosecutions. The more than 20 truth commissions that have been established since the last quarter of the 20th century are the best known examples. Without minimising the significance of other countries in this respect, the examples of South Africa, Guatemala, Peru and Sierra Leone can be seen as the most notable cases of truth commissions (Hayner 2001). We also take them as a point of departure for our account on restorative justice mechanisms. It should be noted that the large majority of these non-judicial mechanisms operate at the national level, while a handful is partly composed of international members (Schabas 2005b).

In the following paragraphs, we first have a look at the basic principles of restorative justice, as they have developed in the area of criminology for common crimes. We then look at truth commissions as one form of restorative justice, and try to see how they comply with these main principles when applied to international crimes. Finally, we try to assess the contribution of restorative justice to deal with legacies of mass violence.

3.1. UNDERSTANDING MASS VIOLENCE THROUGH RESTORATIVE JUSTICE

To assert that restorative justice is of growing importance inside and outside the criminal justice system of many countries is nothing less than a truism. Although no commonly accepted definition seems to exist, the literature makes frequent reference to two definitions. Marshall defines restorative justice as 'a process whereby parties with a stake in a specific offence resolve collectively how to deal with the aftermath of the offence and its implications for the future' (Marshall, 1999). Whereas Bazemore and Walgrave are more goal-oriented as they formulate restorative justice as 'every action that is primarily oriented towards doing justice by repairing the harm that has been caused by the crime' (Bazemore and Walgrave, 1999). In our view, more important than to agree on the exact definition of restorative justice is to identify its key principles. Following Roche (2003), we have listed the following:

1. Personalism: crime is a violation of people and their relationships rather than a violation of (criminal) law;
2. Reparation: the primary goal is to repair the harm of the victim rather than to punish the perpetrator;
3. Reintegration: the aim is to finally reintegrate the perpetrator into society rather than to alienate and isolate him/her from society;
4. Participation: the objective is to encourage the involvement of all direct and possibly also indirect stakeholders to deal with the crime collectively.

The bottom line of restorative justice is to view crime as a violation of people and relations, thereby creating an obligation to make things right. This process should be facilitated by bringing victims and offenders together on a voluntary basis, e.g. in victim-offender mediation programmes, and possibly also with the other stakeholders, e.g. in restorative justice conferences. In these forums, room is made for dialogue and for creating an opportunity, with the help of a mediator, to restore the harm done and to reconcile the relation. The international community, personified by the United Nations Economic and Social Council (ECOSOC), has subscribed to this idea by adopting in 2002 a resolution encouraging countries to use *Basic Principles on the Use of Restorative Justice Programmes in Criminal Matters* in developing and implementing restorative justice in their countries (www.restorativejustice.org). It is striking, however, that developments in restorative justice are almost exclusively focused on less serious property crimes and on juvenile crime. There are a limited number of isolated examples of victim-offender programmes for serious interpersonal crimes (Gustafson 1997; Umbreit, Bradshaw & Coates 2003). But thus far very little attention has been paid to restorative justice for crimes of a political nature, sometimes reaching the level of mass violence and mass victimisation (Parmentier 2001).

3.2. TRUTH COMMISSIONS AS POSSIBLE FORMS OF RESTORATIVE MECHANISMS

In the field of transitional justice there are several examples of mechanisms set up in the aftermath of mass violence that display restorative aspects. We argue here that the best examples are truth commissions, although not all truth commissions share exactly the same features and therefore not all live up to the criteria of restorative justice (Hayner 2001; Villa-Vicencio 2000).

According to Hayner (2001), the following elements have to be present to speak of a truth commission: (1) it has to be set up with public (meaning state or government) support, and cannot be the result of private initiatives only; (2) its objective is not to focus on individual cases but to sketch an overall pattern of human rights violations; (3) it finishes its work by a final report that is given publicity; and (4) the report contains recommendations about how to deal with the legacy of a dark past and how to avoid similar conflicts and crimes in the future. From the above follows that a truth commission is quintessentially a non-judicial body, set up for a limited duration, and without the intent to establish the guilt or innocence of individual persons, but more to contribute to a form of conflict settlement between parties and at the level of society.

Such commissions of inquiry are increasingly considered a valuable and complementary practice to civil or criminal courts because of their strong emphasis on truth, reparation and reconciliation (Christie 2001). The restorative dimension is particularly present at two levels: first, at the institutional level of the commission, as it provides a public forum for victims and offenders to voice and share their experiences; and secondly, at the interpersonal level where individual victims and offenders can meet during or after the process of the truth commission with a view to dialogue, personal healing or restoration in the long term. Again, not all truth commissions adhere to the same operational rules, and there it is important to conduct specific case studies to reveal in which way and to which degree truth commissions fulfil their promise of providing restorative justice (Parmentier 2001). The South African Truth and Reconciliation Commission (TRC) provides an interesting example of how such commissions may contribute to restorative justice, in this case through the work of its three separate committees: first, by providing a forum to victims during the public hearings organised throughout the country as part of the Human Rights Violations Committee, which in a limited number of cases have led to an encounter between victims and suspects or representatives of the apartheid regime; second, through actual encounters between offenders applying for amnesty to the Amnesty Committee and therefore being obliged to disclose all the relevant facts, which in some instances led to a dialogue with the victims or survivors; and third, through the recommendations of the Reparation and Rehabilitation Committee, that issued recommendations to the government on matters of reparation and rehabilitation.

Other examples of mechanisms with restorative justice aspects include customary mechanisms, also called community-based mechanisms, such as the *gacaca* tribunals in Rwanda, set up to process the high numbers of alleged perpetrators of genocide in detention, and with the objective to strike a balance between justice and reconciliation (Uvin 2003; Penal Reform International 2002; Haveman in this volume).

4. MASS VIOLENCE AND POST-CONFLICT JUSTICE THROUGH A RESTORATIVE LENS

When it comes to comparing the two approaches mentioned – retributive justice and restorative justice – it is useful to use the same parameters in order to allow the comparability between the two. For this purpose, we have made use of a theoretical framework constructed over the years in which we try to highlight the core elements of any post-conflict justice situation, that is the key issues that the new elites are confronted with and have to address when regimes have moved from authoritarianism to a form of democracy (Parmentier 2003; Parmentier & Weitekamp 2007). The first is how to bring the truth about the past to the forefront and give it some form of credit; the second is how to make sure that the offenders can be called to account for their acts; the third deals with the problem of how to repair the harm done to victims for the crimes of the past; and the fourth relates to the need of reconciling the various communities and sectors of society in order to rebuild a society that constitutes the new democracy. In this section, we will briefly look into the specific consequences of both approaches, retributive and restorative justice, for each key issue. In the case of restorative justice we will highlight this by combining each issue with one of the four key principles listed above.

4.1. SEARCHING FOR TRUTH

Searching for the truth is not an easy exercise, if only for the content of the notion itself. In its interim report of 1998, the South African Truth and Reconciliation Commission (TRC) proved to be very well aware of the complexity and distinguished four notions of truth: (1) factual or forensic truth, meaning the evidence obtained and corroborated through reliable procedures; (2) personal and narrative truth, meaning the many stories that individuals told about their experiences under Apartheid; (3) social or dialogue truth, established through interaction, discussion and debate; and (4) healing and restorative truth, meaning the truth that places facts and their meaning within the context of human relationships (TRC Report 1998; Parlevliet 1998). Every type of truth has its value and its own procedures to reach it.

It is argued here that criminal investigations – whether national, third country or international – will foremost produce and lead to the factual or forensic truth, and that other types of truth are largely outside its legal realm. This is not to say that criminal courts cannot play a role in creating an environment for other types of truth to develop, but it is not their main objective. Moreover, it should also be highlighted that the truth produced by criminal courts is foremost an individual truth, relating to the facts of one or more individual cases presented before the prosecutors and the judges. Furthermore, the adversarial nature of trials are unlikely to achieve a major contribution to explain the causes of mass violence. The truth that is revealed in court trials is a fragmented fact finding process to serve as evidence to prove or refute the guilt, but never intends to bring forward the truth of the conflict as a social phenomenon. Trials do not allow perpetrators or survivors to produce a story that might coincide and lead to the explanation of the causes of the conflict. In our view, transitional justice mechanisms should provide the conditions necessary to also uncover the social truth, that allow perpetrators and survivors to tell their own story and that allow them to gain back the control over their position and their role in the conflict (Christie 1977), and later also their place in the community. Such processes could lead to a better understanding of the causes of the conflict.

When it comes to assessing the contribution of restorative justice to truth seeking we like to emphasise one of the key principles, namely participation. This principle refers to the dimension of empowerment and stresses that those affected by the crime need to regain their sense of autonomy. This can only be achieved when the stakeholders are actively involved in the process. We distinguish two categories of stakeholders: those directly affected by the crime, and those indirectly involved but not emotionally affected. In post-conflict situations it is an enormous task to clarify the different roles and stakeholders that were affected either directly or indirectly, either personally or structurally by a violent past whereby gross violations of human rights were committed by the state on the one hand and by groups of society (e.g. liberation movements, activists, minorities, etc.) on the other hand. Very few people will appear to be not affected at all, so that dealing with mass victimisation in post-conflict situations will seem to be an insurmountable task to fulfil. Overall, restorative justice pays a lot of attention to victims and their needs, but a problem may arise when the group of victims is systematically narrowed. In the process of the South African TRC, for example, many victims could not be taken into account because they were not 'victimised enough' according to the mandate. Only victims of gross human rights violations were defined as victims in the TRC Act. For a huge number of victims there was no feeling of justice at all, notably the victims of structural apartheid (Mamdani 1997) and the victims who suffered from the everyday apartheid policy. A lot of victims felt disappointed and embittered after the proceedings of the TRC (Gibson & Gouws 1999). These victims felt their rights and feelings had been neglected and justice was not gained. In this respect, it is also important to consider the distinction between individual and collective victims, direct and indirect victims, and see to what extent we can broaden the definition of what victims are so that they can all have the place they deserve in the process of transition. In other words, while the process of truth seeking in the TRC has gone far beyond forensic forms of truth in individual cases and has involved narrative and social truth in a collective framework, it has still fallen short of allowing the participation of a wide range of victims of apartheid.

4.2. ENSURING ACCOUNTABILITY OF THE PERPETRATORS

The second issue relates to the possibilities of calling to account those who have committed gross violations of human rights, that sometimes amount to international crimes. In contrast to common understanding, accountability is far from a straightforward reality. One of the main problems relates to the type of offenders to be called to account, the heads and the planners of the violations or those who executed the orders and those who assisted them, and what to do with the 'bystanders' who did not actively participate in committing the crimes but may have benefited from the consequences. On top of that, it should be clear that international crimes only constitute the symptoms of a violent conflict. Dealing with the most serious crimes without dealing with the underlying conflict itself is merely touching the tip of the iceberg.

In the case of retributive justice through criminal prosecutions there is a major difference between national tribunals and some international ones. National tribunals in principle constitute the primary locus to investigate, prosecute and try perpetrators, and international tribunals and courts only come in at a subsidiary level, when states have proven 'unable or unwilling' (wording of the Rome Statute) to act. The same is roughly true under the universal jurisdiction laws of third countries, who tend to be reluctant to engage in investigations and trials unless they see the absence of any retributive action on behalf of the national state. There is only one exception to this rule, namely with the two *ad hoc* tribunals for ex-Yugoslavia and Rwanda that took primacy over the national courts in the respective countries. However, irrespective of the legal basis and the jurisdiction of the court or tribunal, the same problem of who to try poses itself to all. Although it is impossible to draw general conclusions from the work of national and international tribunals thus far, we like to suggest that the decisions on who to try are heavily influenced by the political context in which the tribunals and courts operate: if there is strong political pressure to start criminal investigations and the former elite are not too strong to resist, then prosecutors and judges tend to start quickly with whomever perpetrator they can find to send a visible signal to the country and the world. That is why in some cases high-level politicians are tried first, and in other cases countries first go for low-ranking officials of the former army and the police; also consecutive steps are possible. Whatever the scenario, it is clear that courts and tribunals only try very small numbers of perpetrators of the multiple possibilities at their disposal. In our view, prosecuting and punishing perpetrators and removing them from society is nothing but a symptomatic response to violent conflicts. Violent state conflicts, however, entail many underlying aspects that have dragged a country into a protracted conflict. All state subsystems, including the criminal justice system, are affected by the conflict and have often also a stake in the conflict. The police service, the courts and the correctional service are to be rebuilt. Who is able to hold perpetrators accountable for their wrongdoings if national jurisdictions are not capable of prosecuting the suspects either because the judiciary does not exist anymore, is overthrown or corrupt or because of the insurmountable task to try all the perpetrators? There are many examples where national criminal justice systems have shown little hope in relation to accountability, while international criminal justice systems, and to some degree also third country systems, have provided better tools to hold perpetrators accountable. Finally, it should be highlighted that criminal prosecution, which basically leads to removing the most dangerous perpetrators from society, may be necessary in the short run but is only symptomatic of an intervention in a latent state conflict where violence can easily re-escalate. Prioritising (international) criminal justice is therefore doubtful as the most adequate response to violent state conflicts, and it could be argued that using selective trials before national or international tribunals may be limited to these cases where incapacitation seems to be the only solution to restore the peace in a given society.

A restorative justice approach to accountability is necessarily different, particularly when coupled with the key principle of reintegration. This principle demands from society that it aims to hold perpetrators accountable for their wrongdoings in a supportive way, taking into account all the needed measures to work towards their reintegration into the same society. The merely punitive approach of trials leaves little room for future reintegration, and this same argument applies to states that choose not to face their violent past and decide to live in a permanent state of denial (Cohen 2001) or amnesia. A restorative justice approach to the issue of accountability is intended to cooperate with the perpetrator. It is seen as a collaborative approach to resolving problems, intended to reintegrate rather then to alienate or isolate the perpetrator from his/her society. We argue that providing a high level of support to perpetrators while not minimising the control over the accountability process could provide the most sustainable and durable response to dealing with perpetrators of serious human rights violations. Another aspect going to the heart of reintegration relates to the beneficiaries of international crimes and serious human rights violations. There is a great deal of controversy around the issue of involving the benefiting parties in the process of accountability and reparation. The experiences of the South African TRC on the (lack of) involvement of beneficiaries show the sensitive character of this matter. The amnesty hearings of the TRC focused only on individual perpetrators and the institutional hearings with large sectors of society (e.g. the business, media, medical and legal professions) was purely voluntary. In this way, the structural evil of apartheid as a system was largely downplayed in favour of the misdeeds committed by some individuals. According to some, the beneficiaries of apartheid were let off the hook without being obliged to confront their past in a direct way (Mamdani 2000; Terreblanche 2000).

In general terms, it is clear that uniform and exclusive approaches do not exist in the field of accountability and that every situation leads to an uncharted path (Huyse 2003). Leading scholars in the field of transitional justice are seeing punitive justice as one of the necessary elements in the overall process towards reconciliation (Kritz 1995; Minow 1998; Huyse 2003). Others have proposed a mixed approach that would incorporate (1) trials for notorious murderers and the leaders of genocide or other crimes, (2) community-based reintegrative shaming for all other offenders, (3) a truth commission able to obtain, in some cases perhaps even by compulsion, testimony from national as well as international officials, (4) the creation of an international fund to facilitate compensation for the victims of a conflict, and (5) elite accommodation of government and institutions channelling cross-cutting political cleavages as a prelude to eventual democracy (Drumbl 2000). Further research is needed to ascertain if such mixed approaches constitute a more adequate approach to establish the accountability of perpetrators.

4.3. PROVIDING REPARATION TO THE VICTIMS

Reparation is becoming increasingly important to address, and even undo, the injustices of the past and the last decade has witnessed an enormous increase of the awareness in this regard. According to the UN resolution of 2005 reparation is to be understood as a very wide concept, including restitution of goods, financial compensation, rehabilitation through social and medical measures, symbolic measures and guarantees of non-repetition of the alleged acts. All of these measures can be individual or collective (Bassiouni 2000). While the principle is now firmly established in international law (Sarkin 2004a), many questions remain (Vandeginste 2004b; Du Plessis & Peté 2007). Although it is generally accepted that the beneficiaries of reparation are the victims, it is less clear how far to stretch this category and whether also indirect victims or society as a whole can be included. Another major issue is to know who is the duty-bearer of the reparation measures, in other words who should be held responsible, the new state agencies or the perpetrators themselves, individually or collectively, and what about the bystanders who benefited? Finally, how should the right to reparation be enforced? Through a general government policy or through individual administrative or judicial action?

As the philosophy of retributive justice is to focus on offenders, it is far less concerned with reparations for victims. This is not to say that victims are always left out in the cold, but reparations for victims are by and large a small by-product of criminal trials. This is virtually identical in criminal courts in the country itself and in a third country, and even applies with more force for the two *ad hoc* tribunals that cannot even award reparations at all. The major exception exists for the International Criminal Court, the competence of which is not limited to awarding reparations for the victims who have participated in proceedings before the Court, but also includes awarding reparation measures for other victims of any given situation through the Trust Fund of the ICC (De Greiff & Wierda 2005). These reparation awards are not limited to monetary compensation but may also entail restitution and rehabilitation measures. Other forms of reparation, such as symbolic measures and structural measures to avoid a repetition of the said crimes, largely fall outside the scope of the ICC and of other courts for that matter. Much will depend on the willingness of the ICC to adopt a dynamic stance on reparatory measures, and to fuel the debates about more extensive forms of reparation, not only for the concrete victims at hand but also for similar victims or for similar crimes. If this were not to take shape, the right to reparation for victims of international crimes would remain purely symbolic (Parmentier, 2007).

Apart from preventing conflicts from reoccurring, the restorative justice principle of reparation is a primary goal of transitional justice. For a long time in the debates on transitional justice, reparation was promulgated as a necessary mechanism, but only a few examples have shown a successful outcome. In the years to come, reparation is expected to rise high on the transitional justice agenda. In the context of the South African TRC, reparations were present at various levels (TRC Report 1998): the Reparation and Rehabilitation Committee awarded urgent and interim reparations to those victims who had provided written or oral testimony to the TRC and were in need of medical, psychological or material help; it also recommended to the government to take measures of various nature, including individual reparations, symbolic reparations, legal and administrative matters, community rehabilitation programmes and institutional reforms. It has to be said that the recommendations have not led to the expected results on the part of the government, and many victims have tried to force the government to implement these recommendations by bringing their claims to the collective level of victim support groups, direct lobbying and even court cases. It remains to be seen what the concrete outcomes of such actions will be.

4.4.   PROMOTING RECONCILIATION

The question remains as to how societies that have been conflict-ridden for a long time and have produced numerous victims can regain some form of social cohesion, which is absolutely essential for its future development. The fourth key issue is that of reconciliation, the process that gradually transforms a divided past into a shared future (Bloomfield, Barnes & Huyse 2003). One of the complexities thereof lies in the very notion that has different meanings to different societies. In the terminology of the South African TRC there are four levels of reconciliation: (1) the individual level of coming to terms with a painful truth, e.g. after exhumations and reburials of loved ones; (2) the interpersonal level of specific victims and their perpetrators; (3) the community level, when addressing the internal conflicts inside and between local communities; and (4) the national level, by focusing on the role of the state and non-state institutions (TRC Report 1998). The challenge lies in the conflicting agendas that could stem from the operationalisation of the concept on the different levels. Another challenge relates to the ideological use of the reconciliation discourse. Many commentators suggest that violent conflicts and human rights violations have disrupted a balanced situation that existed in the past, and that reconciliation actually means going back to that past. However, it is very doubtful whether this retrospective approach is relevant in situations of long-lasting divisions in society, e.g. between the indigenous peoples and the new settlers, and where going back to the past would mean a confirmation of long-term inequalities. It may be advisable in such contexts to talk about 'conciliation' and to see it as a call to address the past in order to construct a new future (Bloomfield, Barnes & Huyse 2003).

The situation is fairly straightforward when it comes to assessing retributive justice and criminal prosecutions in this light. Courts and tribunals are simply not set up with the objective to restore relationships between people and to provide reconciliation, and in very few cases actually contribute to it. Only the *ad hoc* tribunal for Rwanda has the explicit task to contribute to national reconciliation, but it remains to be seen how this aim has taken effect, if any. Again, this does not preclude that the activities of criminal courts may produce reconciliatory effects in the long run, e.g. when court proceedings come to be seen as purifying rituals to wash away the sequels of a horrendous past and to allow individuals and collectives to embark upon the long road to (re)conciliation. But the reality is that international criminal justice mechanisms are often perceived as top-down and short-term missions whereby the international community runs the risk of passing over the social, cultural and historical characteristics of the conflict. As victims' concerns are often overlooked and most of the time neglected in the process of dealing with the past, it is almost ironic to believe that criminal justice mechanisms can produce reconciliation.

Looking at reconciliation through the lens of restorative justice also allows one to bring in the key principle of personalism. This principle refers to the social dimension of 'emotional involvement' that enables the conflicting parties to restore broken relationships. Crimes of mass violence are first of all violations of people rather than violations of law. We suggest that truth commissions bear the promise of being a 'fully restorative justice process' if they stress the importance of encounters between victims and offenders and are also able to live up to these expectations (Weitekamp et al. 2006). One of the implications of such encounter is to organise victim-offender dialogue, either as part of the truth commission process or outside its direct ambit. In our view, the key issue of 'encounter' should be included as a new element in future truth commissions. To date, not one truth commission has gone as far as bringing perpetrators and victims together to deal collectively with the aftermath of a violent conflict, with the possible exception of some amnesty hearings in the South African TRC. Action research carried out in the aftermath of the TRC by the South African Centre for the Study of Violence and Reconciliation (CSVR) will reveal whether this principle of encounter is indeed a tool to be taken into account for future truth commissions. In the South African case, and presumably in other post-conflict nations as well, there is quite a lack of information on how, and more importantly, to what extent victims' expectations were effectively met through the TRC process. Very little is known about their backgrounds, their expectations and their motivations (Verdoolaege, 2002). As to the offenders, it is already shown that if they are brought around the table it might help to reverse the process of dehumanisation of the perpetrator (Gobodo-Madikizela 2003; Drakulic 2004). On a more general level, van der Merwe has illustrated how the national plan for reconciliation in post-apartheid South Africa has led to obstruct and to hamper the individual process of reconciliation for many victims (van der Merwe 2001). Finally, it should be noted that there exist many more legitimate responses to mass victimisation after violent state conflict that are culturally and socially appropriate responses attempting to bring people together in some way. One of the examples could be the *gacaca* tribunals in Rwanda (Penal Reform International 2002). Responses could also include a blend of mechanisms that form an integrated response to deal with the past.

Figure 1: TARR Model in relation to restorative justice principles

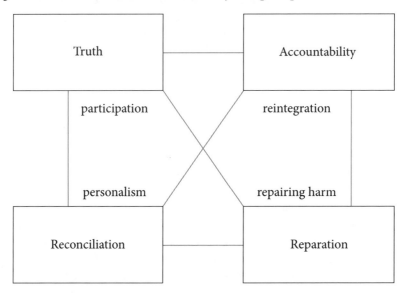

(Source: S. Parmentier and K. Vanspauwen)

The above has demonstrated the strengths and weaknesses of retributive justice approaches for dealing with a legacy of mass violence and international crimes in the context of post-conflict justice. It has also sketched some of the possibilities for restorative justice as illustrated by the work of truth commissions and notably the South African one. This proved important in the light of the many limitations associated with retributive justice and criminal prosecutions for international crimes and in post-conflict situations. First of all, from a normative point of view, we would like to argue that a fully fledged restorative justice approach in combination with limited retributive measures is to be strived for in any post-conflict situation (Findlay & Henham 2005). Moreover, from an analytical viewpoint, we argue that on the road of post-conflict justice it is of great value to explore the new territories of restorative justice practices in dealing with situations of mass violence. Three aspects seem of particular importance, keeping in mind the requirements of effectiveness and legitimacy: (1) a recognition of the complementary character of restorative and retributive mechanisms, each with their specific characteristics and their specific contribution to situations of mass violence; (2) a genuine cooperation between courts and tribunals on the one hand, and truth commissions and other similar mechanisms on the other hand, built on the idea of accountability and reconciliation in the long run; and (3) the development of 'good practices' for restorative mechanisms in dealing with crimes of mass violence. This can take the form of setting up specific programmes of assistance and protection for victims and witnesses, of organising forums where victims and perpetrators can meet, of procedures to follow-up on these encounters, etc. The following Figure 1 highlights the most important principles of restorative justice as they can be matched with the key issues in post-conflict justice.

5. CONCLUSION

In this contribution, we have studied situations of mass violence and mass victimisation, amounting to international crimes, as they emerge in post-conflict situations, that is when regimes have changed from authoritarian rule to democratic forms of government. While the dominant approach to deal with such crimes is the retributive model, mostly by resorting to criminal prosecutions, we have sketched the possibilities and risks of such approach. In our view the strength of (international) criminal justice mechanisms and other retributive justice mechanisms lies in the establishment of factual truth and criminal responsibility in a limited number of individual cases, with the limited possibility of monetary compensation, restitution and rehabilitation for the victims. On the other hand, courts will hardly be able to establish any collective truth for large numbers of perpetrators or any other type of responsibility and it will not be able to provide any symbolic or more structural measures to the victims. And finally, retributive justice mechanisms provide little or no room for reconciliation. This should not come as a surprise. As Drumbl rightly argues in relation to international criminal justice mechanisms (such as the ICC, the ICTY and the ICTR), they 'have been built with little attention to developing a criminology of mass violence or to theorising a sentencing policy for perpetrators of such violence' (Drumbl 2000), and the same can be said for national criminal justice systems.

We have also tackled the question of how to cope with the aftermath of this mass victimisation by gaining a better understanding of the root causes of violent state conflict. In our view, the development of 'best practices' of restorative justice in post-conflict situations is likely to bear the potential to produce the needed research data that could further foster the process of building a criminology of mass violence. The development of a framework, such as the TARR model above is not merely a theoretical typology for the purpose of analysing current transitional justice developments. Each of its constituting concepts and the interconnectedness between some of them are already being discussed in the context of post-conflict case studies (Rotberg & Thompson 2000; Villa-Vicencio & Doxtader 2003; Gibson 2004).

Our study on the importance of applying restorative justice principles to cases of violent state conflict has constituted foremost a theoretical exercise and to validate these presumptions requires further empirical research. Throughout the text we have repeatedly referred to the TRC in South Africa and to the discussions about restorative justice as early as its launch in 1995. Although restorative justice was clearly defined and put forward in the mandate of the TRC, the Commission's success in achieving its restorative objectives was highly debatable and is still questioned today (Villa-Vicencio 2001, 2003). We remain convinced that South Africa has shown to the world that this unique process of a truth commission with restorative aspects has brought about some invaluable steps on the road towards reconciliation. The TRC can be a catalyst for other societies to fully explore the opportunities for maximal restorative justice strategies. At the same time, we argue that future truth commissions should be focused more on the key principles of restorative justice. Referring back to the TARR model we have clearly identified the lessons for the future. First, truth should be related to the need for inclusion, the involvement of all the stakeholders in the conflict; next, accountability should be geared at supporting the perpetrators to take full responsibility while attempting to reintegrate them into society; furthermore, repairing the harm to victims should be the primary objective in any situation and should consist of a wide range of measures; and finally, the truth-seeking process between all stakeholders of a conflict and aimed at repairing the harm for victims should create all the conditions for a meaningful emotional exchange between the parties in the decision-making process on the road to (re-) conciliation.

In sum, we have argued that there is a need for a convergence between restorative justice and retributive justice mechanisms in dealing with situations of mass violence. Retributive justice mechanisms should be prioritised only if this seems necessary to preserve the security of society. But by proposing a purely restorative justice model for successful transitions one will risk jeopardising the restorative potentials that are present in every culture or society that has suffered a violent past (Braithwaite 2002). The sensitivities relating to crimes of mass violence allow us to conclude that a clear-cut approach, while extremely complex, is nothing but desirable.

XV. DOING JUSTICE TO *GACACA*

Roelof HAVEMAN

1.   A *GACACA*

A *gacaca* in Gikondo, a suburb of Kigali.[1] We arrive at around 10 o'clock. The suspects, two women aged between 40 and 50, are already waiting in the hall where the *gacaca* session will take place, guarded by a gendarme with an impressive automatic weapon. Like all prisoners, *génocidaires* and others, the defendants are dressed in pink. They have tried to make their outfits more stylish with gold buttons, puffed sleeves and fitted waists.

Slowly the hall fills up with people from the neighbourhood. After half an hour the nine judges enter the hall. Each wears a sash in the colours of the Rwandan flag. A wooden box is put on the table, with stamps, pencils, forms and other necessities for the proceedings. One after the other they are placed on the table. The session is opened and begins with a minute of silence for the victims of the genocide.

The two women are identified and the indictment is read out. The defendants are accused of killing a neighbour and one of her children in April 1994, at the start of the genocide. It is assumed that no one witnessed the murders, but the bodies of the neighbour and her child were found in the house of one of the suspects. The defendants state that although they were present when the woman was killed, the real murderers were members of the *Interahamwe*, the youth movement that played a crucial role in the genocide. The women say they were unable to prevent the *Interahamwe* from committing the murders, for which they apologise during the *gacaca*. The younger woman looks emotional, her eyes are bleary and when she speaks she looks up at the ceiling. The older woman seems less emotional.

The judges ask questions. The public also participates. A man asks the judges why they have not invited the children of the murdered woman to appear. The judges reply that they tried to do so but learned that most of the victim's children had also been killed. A woman questions the suspects, trying to catch inconsistencies in their stories. A third person wants to know from the woman who initially accused the two suspects of the murder why she had withdrawn her

---

[1]   A *gacaca* attended by the author in September 2005; this is one of the cases that were tried in the pilot phase.

earlier accusation. Community participation is a key aspect of the *gacaca* system. The crimes were committed in this very neighbourhood and the alleged perpetrators still live here, as do the surviving victims and their relatives.

When the judges retire, the hall empties. Only the suspects remain, encircled by some friends, including a woman who just a week before was acquitted by the same *gacaca*. She was released from prison after spending 11 years in pre-trial detention and has returned to live in her old neighbourhood again. The suspects have been detained for over 10 years. If found guilty of genocidal murder, a crime of the second category, they face prison sentences ranging from 20 to 25 years, depending on such factors as whether they have confessed their guilt and shown remorse. They would serve half their sentence in prison and the other half in freedom, performing community service.

The judges decide to put the case on hold in order to set up a judicial inquiry. They want to question a woman who is alleged to have witnessed the actual killings and to collect further facts of the case. Their investigation has to be finalised within one month. The minutes of the proceedings are read out, formally ending the *gacaca* session. Following some comments from the public, the record is amended and signed by the suspects and the witness with fingerprints, and by the judges with written signatures. The judges then take off their sashes and many stay behind for a while to talk about the case.

2.   A RESEARCH QUESTION

Wherever one goes in the country one may see *gacaca:*[2] groups of villagers somewhere on the grass, under trees, with judges behind a table confronting suspects, who are dressed in pink if they are in prison. These are genocide suspects: *génocidaires*. And everywhere in the country one sees billboards with big pictures of *gacaca* in session, urging the population to attend the *gacaca*, under the slogan 'Truth, Justice, Reconciliation': *Inkiko Gacaca; Ukuri – Ubutabera – Ubwiyunge*. Now that the gacaca are running to their completion, the pictures change into pictures promoting 'TIG' – *travaux d'intérêt général* or community service – one of the penalties for *génocidaires*.

Within modern *gacaca* – literally a grassroots lay court system; *gacaca* stems from the Kinyarwandan word for some sort of 'grass' on which traditionally meetings were held – one tries to combine conviction and reconciliation. This combination of, according to some, incompatible goals, together with the magnitude of the crimes and the multitude of victims and suspects (plus relatives)

---

[2]   See for the days of *gacaca* activities all over the country: Programme of Gacaca Sessions' Meetings in Districts and Towns (1 March 2005): http://www.inkiko-gacaca.gov.rw/pdf/ GACACA%20SESSIONS.pdf.

involved, have turned the *gacaca* into one of the most remarkable phenomena of our times. Although not a blueprint for an alternative approach to national and inter/supranational prosecutions and convictions, it may be considered a nation and situation specific example of alternatives for criminal approaches that can be seen in different forms in different places in the world.

Many scholars have commented on the *gacaca* and surrounding circumstances over time, and few in its favour. There may be truth in some or most of the comments, and of course, if comments can be made they should be made. Gacaca are not beyond criticism. Some try to give a well balanced opinion on the *gacaca* (Uvin undated; Cobban 2002; Daly 2002; Vandeginste 2004a; Molenaar 2005). But in many other commentaries something is lacking, in particular in the way facts are evaluated in terms of 'good' and 'bad'. Some base their at times sweeping statements upon the first experiences during the first information phase of the pilot project, others upon expectations before the actual *gacaca* had even started (Sarkin, 2001: quoting many others doing exactly the same and all seeming to agree upon the fact that *gacaca* are a bad idea). Some seem to presuppose that when practice and theory do not meet, practice is wrong and has to change instead of the theory. Others present mere speculations and beliefs as scientific theories. Others again mistake one aspect of the system as *gacaca* as a whole. Sometimes criticism even amounts to some sort of *gacaca*-bashing (Fierens 2005). It seems an unfair way of assessing a unique phenomenon which *gacaca* is; it must be possible to do it differently, to do justice to *gacaca*. The question then is: how does one assess *gacaca*?

In this article I try to raise some questions that have to be dealt with when assessing the phenomenon of *gacaca* – or similar phenomena[3] – from a criminological point of view, as a matter of course without pretending to be complete. Various perspectives on *gacaca* are possible. A legal perspective is the most obvious one for lawyers. Lawyers feel most comfortable when thinking in legal concepts and terms. This is what they are used to doing: labelling acts as crimes, and following penal procedures in order to prosecute and try those accused of having committed these crimes. Apart from a legal system *gacaca* is however much more. 'In essence, gacaca is not a legal practice but a social process', says Molenaar in his study on reconciliation and *gacaca* (Molenaar 2005, 7), and I tend to agree with him. It is a cultural phenomenon with historical roots; it is a psychological phenomenon as part of a complex of ways to overcome the mental aftermath of genocide; it is a political phenomenon, bridging (or widening?) gaps between political opponents or an alleged mechanism for the minority in power to suppress the majority of the population, to give just some examples of ways to approach the *gacaca*. In fact, maybe the least important is to consider the *gacaca*

---

3   Think of e.g. the hybrid system that is in the process of developing in order to deal with the LRA/Lords Resistance Army in Uganda.

as a legal system. An assessment of *gacaca* from a legal point of view is per definition insufficient. *Gacaca* has to be considered from a combined legal, historical, psychological, sociological and political – in short one might say: from a criminological – perspective. Who rejects *gacaca* from one of these separate perspectives has to acknowledge that indeed (s)he rejects or applauds it only from one of these perspectives and therefore does not reject or applaud *gacaca* as a whole. Assessing *gacaca* as an isolated phenomenon, without considering its background, seems impossible. An historical,[4] sociological and political[5] background of the genocide to which the *gacaca* is one of many answers is indispensable for explaining the *gacaca*; it forms part of the *raison d être* of the *gacaca*.

However, within the framework of this chapter it is impossible to describe the whole context in all its aspects. Here I will restrict myself to the most striking – but definitely not by definition the most important – aspects of the context. I start with a description of part of the history of the 1994 genocide in Rwanda, showing the complexity of its causes. Subsequently I will give some numbers of the genocide and the period thereafter, showing the magnitude of the genocide and its aftermath. Thirdly I will give a description of the system of *gacaca*. At least these aspects are crucial to understand some of the background of *gacaca*. In the final paragraph I will give some considerations on how to judge *gacaca*, doing justice to this phenomenon, without wanting to deny its failures. This may be read as an agenda for further research.

3.   A HISTORY OF THE GENOCIDE

Rwanda knows a long history of large scale massacres. The causes seem to depend on the political background of the person who tries to explain it. One aspect is the division between Hutu and Tutsi as two different ethnic groups. This since long existing difference between Hutu and Tutsi became more and more important, and starting already in pre-colonial times was transformed into more outspoken ethnic or racial differences, with the Tutsi as a superior race, allegedly stemming from the horn of Africa (Prunier 2005 [1995], 26–40; Pottier 2002, 110–126). This ethnic differentiation was fixed in 1932 when the Belgian coloniser introduced the 'ethnic' background in identity-cards: since then one was labelled *Wahutu*,

---

[4]   See for a description of the history including e.g. migrations in the region since the 19th century, Pottier (2002, 9–52), called 'Build-up to war and genocide'. For a thorough and well balanced description of the history of *gacaca* in Rwanda, see Molenaar (2005).

[5]   See for the political context, e.g. Sarkin (2001) on the situation up till 2000; very negatively see Oomen (2006).

Watutsi or *Watwa*.[6] What had been more of a fluid and rather complex sociological difference, although becoming more rigid already since the mid-19th century, with, as the official story goes, Tutsi and Hutu in the past having lived peacefully together, was more and more divided. Tutsi were made into the ruling elite, albeit a minority of them; the majority of Tutsi was as powerless and poor as Hutu. Interesting to note regarding this 'ethnification' of Hutu and Tutsi is that at the end of the 20th century it took the ICTR[7] quite some effort to determine that Tutsi were an ethnic group, one of the core elements of the crime of genocide: destroy (in whole or in part) a group on the basis of national, ethnic, religious or racial grounds. The ICTR chose a combination of objective but mainly subjective considerations: was the victim considered to be a Tutsi by the offender and by the victim him or herself (Van den Herik 2005, §III.5.2)? Whatever the lousy scientific background of the 'ethnification' is,[8] if people think it is true, they will act accordingly. And the truth can be manipulated, for instance for political gain. That seems to be exactly what happened.

By the time Rwanda became independent from Belgium in 1962, the differences had been brought to a head. The change of power – in fact the abolition of the monarchy and a redistribution of land ownership – was far from bloodless. Already in 1959 and for years after, many Tutsi fled to neighbouring countries, with another wave in 1972–73 before Habyarimana took power, to come back only after the assumption of power by the RPF/RPA[9] in 1994.[10] Since 1959 until the start of the war in 1990 at least seven mass killings of Tutsi were reported in Rwanda.[11]

---

6   Only shortly before the genocide in 1994 reference to ethnicity was left out of identity cards, beginning in Kigali, as part of the Arusha agreements; this made the holders of neutral cards not less suspect, on the contrary, for who else than Tutsi would like to have a neutral card; one of the mayors of Kigali changed these cards into Hutu-cards as soon as the genocide began. Information from a Rwandan friend: we have however not been able to find confirmation of this.

7   The International Criminal Tribunal for Rwanda, established for the Prosecution of Persons Responsible for Genocide and Other Serious Violations of International Humanitarian Law Committed in the Territory of Rwanda and Rwandan Citizens Responsible for Genocide and other such Violations Committed in the Territory of Neighbouring States, between 1 January 1994 and 31 December 1994.

8   See for a critical review of the discussion on the division Hutu/Tutsi, choosing for political identities rather than cultural or marker-based identities: Mamdani (2001); also Pottier (2002, 110–126).

9   The RPF (Rwandan Patriotic Front) and its army RPA (Rwanda Patriotic Army) were the opposing 'rebel' party that invaded Rwanda on 1 October 1990, starting a war – including political negotiations – with the old Habyarimana regime.

10   By 1964 an estimated 336,000 Tutsi had fled the country to neighbouring countries: Prunier 2005, 1995, 61/62. To give an impression: after the takeover of power in 1994 by the RPF, an alleged 7 to 800,000 people returned from the diaspora to Rwanda.

11   The first mass killing took place in 1959. Since then mass killings are reported to have taken place in 1961 (the year of elections), 1962 (the year of independence), 1963, 1964, 1966–67 and

In October 1990 the Tutsi rebel army, initially under the command of Fred Rwigema, but after his early death replaced by the current president Paul Kagame, invaded Rwanda from Uganda, starting a war against the old regime. Immediately after the invasion, the genocidal climate within Rwanda was intensified. An important role played the so-called *Interahamwe*, the one might say *Hitler-jugend* of the ruling party of then President Habyarimana. This political youth division was formed in 1991, when a multi-party system was introduced under strong international pressure. The purpose of the *Interahamwe* was to bolster President Habyarimana and his party's monopoly on power, although officially it had been abolished. And they did so with great enthusiasm and seemingly unlimited power, not least through the dissemination of the genocidal ideology. The *Interahamwe* roamed the streets in groups, singing that they would put an end to the existence of the Tutsi. The *Interahamwe* determined the truth through violence. White was red if they said so. They robbed people of food and goods as if these were their own legitimate property. It was true street terror by the youth division of the ruling political party of President Habyarimana and it was not stopped by anyone. On the contrary, the written press, of which Kangura is the most well known, published many racist articles denouncing Tutsi in every aspect. In 1990 Kangura published the Hutu Ten Commandments, stating for instance that Hutu should 'stop taking any pity on the Tutsi', and that:

> *'[e]very Hutu should know that a Mututsi woman, wherever she is, works for the interest of her Tutsi ethnic group. As a result we shall consider a traitor any Muhutu who: marries a Tutsi woman, befriends a Tutsi woman, and who employs a Tutsi woman as a secretary or concubine'.*

The national radio – *Radio Rwanda* but more virulent *Radio Télévision Libre de Mille Collines* – incited with much enthusiasm the population to kill Tutsi, before and during the genocide.[12] Tutsi were cockroaches, *Inyenzi*, to be destroyed. Already from the start of the war in 1990 about 8 massacres of Tutsi are reported, amounting to genocide (Schabas 2000).

Therefore, when the genocide started after the airplane of the president was shot down in the air above Kigali on the evening of 6 April 1994 – remains of the plane fell down into his own swimming pool[13] – and the president was killed

---

1973 (the year of the coup d'état by Habyarimana). In neighbouring Burundi on the other hand, mass killings of Hutu were reported, e.g. in 1972.

[12] Hassan Ngeze, the editor of Kangura, and the RTLM responsibles were convicted by the ICTR in 2003 in the so-called Media-case: *Prosecutor v. Ferdinand Nahimana, Jean-Bosco Barayagwiza, Hassan Ngeze*, Case No. ICTR 99–52-T, Judgment and Sentence 3 December 2003.

[13] Up till today it is not clear who was responsible for the downing of the airplane; late 2007 the Rwandan government installed an official commission to investigate this.

together with the president of Burundi and the French crew. This in fact was the culmination of a since long ongoing hate and killing campaign against Tutsi. Hundreds of thousands of Tutsi and moderate Hutu were killed, raped and abused within a period of three months: from 6 April until 17 July, the day the 'rebel' FPR army took power. The stories of survivors are gruesome.[14]

A special aspect of this genocide is that a substantive part of the killing and looting took place within the community in which both victims and offenders were living. It was (and is?) simply known to everybody who was Tutsi and who was not, irrespective of physical features. In case of doubt the identity cards revealed the ethnicity. Different from what one would expect, these communities have not all fallen apart; until this very day still many people – victims, offenders and surviving relatives – live together in the same community; who did what and with respect to who is common knowledge.

The (hi)story of the genocide does not end in July 1994. *Radio Télévision Libre des Mille Collines* had 'warned' the population that they would be killed by the RPF/RPA if they took power and continued spreading panic after the actual takeover. Five million people sought refuge in and outside Rwanda. The violence did not stop directly after the assumption of power; the raping and killing continued until 1998, albeit on a smaller scale, by *Interahamwe* from and within refugee camps and villages along the borders; individual survivors and witnesses were raped, killed and intimidated; schools were attacked, filtering out the Tutsi children.[15]

And this history will certainly continue for generations. Amongst diaspora-Rwandans for instance there are quite some who deny the genocide. The ten Hutu commandments allegedly are still popular amongst certain groups in the diaspora. The theory of a double genocide – not only genocide on Tutsi, but also one on Hutu during and after the Tutsi-genocide – is still going around, notwithstanding facts convincingly denying this theory (Verwimp 2003). Amongst those living in the diaspora are an alleged 40,000 *génocidaires*. Within Rwanda there is a lot of distrust amongst those who fear prosecution before the *gacaca* or state courts, either or not supported by *radio trottoir*, the never-ending rumour machine. Early in 2005 for instance, a rumour spread around that the government had decided to kill all Hutu who one way or another were involved in the genocide. The president – at that very moment on a state-visit to the United States – would have gone to the US to buy an enormous killing machine.[16] Tutsi would wear bracelets that, on

---

14   Shortly after the genocide African Rights published (and a year later amended) the report *Rwanda, Death, Despair and Defiance* (1994, revised ed. 1995, London) which contains a detailed account including hundreds of pages of witness statements.

15   See, e.g. about the first two years after the genocide: African Rights, *Rwanda, Killing the Evidence*, London 1996.

16   The version I personally heard reads that the president had sought political asylum in the US as he was opposed to the killing of Hutu.

the *moment suprême*, would prove that they should be saved. This rumour made thousands of Hutu in the south sell all their belongings and flee to neighbouring Burundi.[17]

4.   SOME NUMBERS OF THE GENOCIDE

The numbers of the Rwandan genocide give a clear image of what happened before, during and after the 100 days between 6 April and 17 July 1994 during which the genocide took place.

The population of Rwanda in 1994 was estimated to be less than 8 million people. Already during the war, before the period we now know as the 1994 Rwandan genocide, mass killings, although on a relatively small scale, are reported. Also RPF-killings are reported. And already by 1993 an estimated 850,000 people had sought refuge, fleeing from the approaching RPF (Prunier 2005 (1995), 175).

During the months of the genocide an estimated 800,000 to one million people were killed – Tutsi and moderate Hutu:[18] 2,000 men and women in a church in Nyange, when the priest ordered the destruction of 'his' church with a caterpillar;[19] 4,000 people on a street in Kigali when they tried to get to a safe place nearby; 5,000 people in a little church in Ntarama; 10,000 people in a church in Nyamata; 20,000 people on the premises of a school and church in Nyarubuye; about 40,000 people at the premises of a school in Murambi, to mention just a few examples. And every time this happened within a few days.

After the official end of the genocide, killings continued, by *Interahamwe* and ex-FAR soldiers.[20] These *Interahamwe* attacks led for instance to 30,000 people being killed in late 1995 to early 1996 in refugee camps in DR-Congo[21] (Prunier 1995 (2005), 381).

Apart from the dead there are the hundreds of thousands of people who witnessed the killings, rapes, etc., amongst whom many were children; many were abused and raped. The *gacaca* courts identified more than 252,913 survivors (41% men, 59% women), including 74,642 orphans, 27,733 widows/widowers and 12,074 persons disabled by the genocide.[22] A survey amongst 3,030 children between 8

---

[17]   With many consequences, like a poor harvest and famine a year later in that region.
[18]   According to the Rwandan government, there were in total 1.074.017 victims in the four years of genocidal ideology, between 1 October 1990 and 31 December 1994, of whom 93.7% were Tutsi; source PRI rapport July-Dec 2001 at 5.
[19]   The priest has been found guilty and sentenced by the ICTR: *Prosecutor v. Athanase Seromba*, ICTR Case No. 2001–66-I; Judgment 13 December 2006.
[20]   The FAR (*Forces Armées Rwandaises*) was the army of the old regime.
[21]   DR-Congo by that time still was called Zaïre.
[22]   Official numbers, see http://www.inkiko-gacaca.gov.rw/pdf/abarokotse%20english.pdf.

and 19 years old a year after the genocide shows that little less than 80% of the children experienced death in their family as a result of the genocide,[23] almost half of whom lost both parents (36% witnessed family members being killed); 61% of the children had at a certain moment been threatened with being killed; 90% at one moment believed they would die; 80% had to hide to protect themselves during the genocide; 16% had to hide under dead bodies; 95% saw or witnessed violence; 70% saw with their own eyes someone being injured or killed; 52% saw many people being killed at the same time; 58% witnessed killing or injuries with machetes; 31% witnessed rape or sexual assault; etc. (Dyregrov et al. 2000; Human Rights Watch 2003a).

Another group of victims, albeit not of genocide, are an estimated 100,000 people – Hutu – that allegedly were killed by the RPF during the genocide and in the years after, partly as individual revenge killings, partly as a deliberate policy, e.g. during the clearance of refugee camps within and outside Rwanda from which *Interahamwe* and ex-FAR soldiers continued to attack the population.[24]

During and after the genocide about 5 million people were displaced, internally and in neighbouring countries. In November 1994, the Goma-region (just across the border between the DR-Congo and Rwanda in the north-west) harboured about 850,000 refugees; about 30,000 of them had died of cholera in the Goma camps during the first month after the end of the genocide (Prunier 2005 [1995], 303–304). Near Bukavu (across the DR-Congo border in the south-east of Rwanda) were about 330,000 refugees; in Tanzania about 570,000 refugees had settled and another 270,000 in Burundi (Prunier 2005 (1995), 374).[25] It took many years to make people return to Rwanda. The UN IRIN[26] for instance reports in November

---

23   Although the research mentions 'war' I assume they do not mean the war from 1990–1994 but that they restrict themselves to the three months of the genocide, considering that one of the interview instructions told the children to 'keep in mind the worst event that occurred to you during the fighting between April and June 1994'; Dyregrov et al. (2000, 7).

24   See, e.g. Prunier (1995 (2005), 356–362), who, in a 10th chapter added in 1997, tries to come to terms with his initial uncritical sympathy for the RPF; see also Desforges (1999, 540–560); Pottier (2002, 76–81 and 160–170) on the well known case of the clearing of Kibeho, April 1995, when thousands of IDP's were killed by the RPA. It might be interesting to study how many soldiers were court martialled for these crimes during and after the genocide; according to an official within the judiciary the dossiers are available to be studied. Human Rights Watch (2000) mentions, referring to the Rwandan Patriotic Army, Department of the Auditorat Militaire, Annex B, Annual Report, 1999, that the military justice system opened files on 843 cases during 1999. It carried out 295 trials, with fifty-eight soldiers acquitted, twenty-eight sentenced to death and 207 sentenced to prison terms ranging from one month to life. It is unclear how many of these cases involved former FAR soldiers charged with genocide, how many concerned RPA soldiers accused of violations of human rights, and how many represent charges of common crime or infractions of military discipline.

25   The numbers for September 1996, so two years later, just before the great exodus, were about 500,000 people less, most of whom had returned during late 1994; Prunier (2000, 373–374).

26   The *UN Department of Humanitarian Affairs, Integrated Regional Information Network, IRIN Emergency updates* give detailed information on refugee movements in the region during the

1996, 2½ years after the genocide, when an 'exodus' of refugees from the DR-Congo and Tanzania into Rwanda and Burundi had started,[27] that during November a total of 473,333 refugees had returned from DR-Congo to Rwanda.[28] The ICRC reported a total of 2,634 unaccompanied minors being identified and registered in Gisenyi on the Rwandan side of the Rwanda-DRC border in the northwest of the country, and being transferred to a transit camp;[29] before the 'exodus', about 20,000 unaccompanied children had been reported in east-DRC.[30] In December 1996 IRIN reported that about 300,000 refugees in Tanzania had left the camps, away from Rwanda, but were stopped by the Tanzanian army and pushed back into Rwanda.[31]

Apart from a substantive part of these refugees due to the genocide having returned to Rwanda, an alleged 7 to 800,000 people came back to Rwanda from the diaspora where they had lived since the first mass killing in the late 50s, 60s and 70s.

In the first years after the genocide many suspects were arrested. By the end of October 1996 a total of 86,200 prisoners were incarcerated in Rwandan detention centres (19) (among them 3,000 women and 2,000 adolescents), an increase of 23,200 people since the beginning of 1996.[32] About 125,000 of those suspects were still incarcerated in 2004, ten years after the genocide, awaiting trial within prisons that were built for less than 20,000 people. In 2003 about 25,000 suspects were released in order to diminish the number of prisoners – for a number of reasons, such as reduction of the costs for the state and international pressure because of the excessive long preventive incarceration. In mid-2005 another 36,000 suspects were released. In early 2007 again 8,000 suspects were released. The information phase of the *gacaca* made clear that over 800,000 persons were suspected of involvement in the genocide. This means that 10% of the current

---

months of November and December 1996.

[27] Prunier (2000, 373–386) gives a thorough description of the complex background of this 'forced' exodus of refugees from DR-Congo, Burundi and Tanzania into Rwanda.

[28] UN Department of Humanitarian Affairs, Integrated Regional Information Network, IRIN Emergency update nr. 56 on the Great Lakes, Document 17 (13 December 1996).

[29] UN Department of Humanitarian Affairs, Integrated Regional Information Network, IRIN Emergency update nr. 35 on Eastern Zaire, Document 32 (21 November 1996). It also reports that UNICEF estimates the number of lone children at that moment much higher, at 4,125, of whom 70–80% were boys.

[30] Ibidem. A communication of the Dutch medical aid organisation Memisa mentions that the Mugunga camp, one of many around Goma, in October 1994 harboured 125,000 persons of whom 21,250 were younger than 5 years old; Van den Bosch (1995).

[31] Ibidem. It also reports that the Ngara camps at that time housed some 490,000 refugees and the Karagwe camps 110,000 people.

[32] Report of the UN Human Rights Field Operation in Rwanda (HRFOR) as mentioned in IRIN Emergency update no. 56.

population has to be tried for their involvement in the genocide or maybe more accurately, 20% of the current adult population.[33]

5. *GACACA*: CRIMINAL LAW AND CRIMINAL PROCEDURE

Although *gacaca* is much more than only a penal system it is first and foremost a system to try those who were involved in the genocide. This paragraph gives an overview of the black letter law concerning the most important characteristics of *gacaca* as a legal system.

5.1. THE ESTABLISHMENT OF *GACACA*

In the late 90s it was estimated that trying all suspects – by that time about 120,000 persons – in regular penal courts would take more than 100 years; considering the speed of the ICTR – 30 to 50 suspects tried in 10 years – it would take the international tribunal 15,000 to 20,000 years to try all the suspects. Amnesty was no option nor were trials before regular courts. During the genocide, a substantive part of the judiciary had been killed or had fled the country.[34] After nationwide deliberations, the *gacaca* were re-invented (Vandeginste 1999). Nationwide more than 12,000 *gacaca* were established, with about 250,000 persons elected as 'judges' (*Inyangamugayo*). *Gacaca* refers to a soft kind of grass/herb – *umucaca* – on which traditionally a community came together to discuss conflicts within or between families or inhabitants on a certain hill (Ntaganda 2003, 48; Molenaar 2005; Reyntjens 1990). How often and regarding which conflicts *gacaca* were still used shortly before its 'reinvention' to try genocide suspects is not entirely clear (Molenaar 2005, 11–21).

The first 'modern' *gacaca* to try genocide cases started with a pilot project in June 2002, with an information phase in 751 *gacaca* courts in 118 (initially 12) sectors and the trial phase starting March 2005. Nationwide the *gacaca* officially

---

33   In 2007 the population amounted to 8,600,000 of whom approximately 50% were under 18 years, i.e. too young to have taken part in the genocide. Considering that 800,000 people had been killed, about 700,000 persons having come back from the diaspora after the genocide (and thus did not take part in the genocide), since 1994 offenders have died and without doubt others are living abroad having fled the country after the genocide, the participation of the adult population in the genocide must have amounted to approximately 25 to 30% of the population in 1994.

34   Judges: 758 before, 244 after the genocide. Prosecutors: 70 before, 12 after the genocide. Information Ministry of Justice of Rwanda: Gacaca Process: achievements, problems and future prospects, at http://www.inkiko-gacaca.gov.rw/En/EnIntroduction.htm. See on the situation up till 1999 regarding trials before regular courts, Vandeginste (1999).

started in January 2005, with an information phase to gather information on victims, suspects, looted property, etc., after which suspects have been categorised; the proper trials started in mid-2006.[35] Extrapolation of the number of suspects 'discovered' during the pilot phase of the *gacaca* led to an estimated 750,000 suspects[36] to be tried all over the country, which number, at the end of the nationwide *gacaca* information phase, turned out to be a rather low estimation: 818,564 suspects are or will be prosecuted for their involvement in the genocide.[37]

The organisation, competence and functioning of *gacaca* courts have been written down in the law.[38] The preamble of this law is clear on what moved the government to create *gacaca*:

> *'Considering the necessity to eradicate forever the culture of impunity in order to achieve justice and reconciliation in Rwanda, and thus to adopt provisions enabling rapid prosecutions and trials of perpetrators and accomplices of genocide, not only with the aim of providing punishment, but also reconstructing the Rwandan Society that had been destroyed by bad leaders who incited the population into exterminating part of the Society',*

and:

> *'Considering the necessity for the Rwandan Society to find by itself, solutions to the genocide problems and its consequences',*[39]

---

[35] Only in Kigali the information phase took more time than expected and was still on its way during 2007; see also National Service of Gacaca Courts, *Report on data collection*, date unknown, to be found at http://www.inkiko-gacaca.gov.rw.

[36] In the pilot phase about 60,000 persons were categorised, of whom about 7,000 were in cat. 1; 35,000 were in cat. 2; and 16,000 were in cat. 3; see for numbers of the pilot phase http://www.inkiko-gacaca.gov.rw/pdf/Achievements.pdf.

[37] See http://www.inkiko-gacaca.gov.rw/pdf/abaregwa%20english.pdf.

[38] Organic Law N° 16/2004 of 19/6/2004 establishing the organisation, competence and functioning of gacaca courts charged with prosecuting and trying the perpetrators of the crime of genocide and other crimes against humanity, committed between 1 October, 1990 and 31 December, 1994; Organic law N° 28/2006 of 27/06/2006 Modifying and complementing Organic Law N° 16/2004 of 19/6/2004 [etc]; Organic Law N°10/2007 of 01/03/2007, modifying and complementing Organic Law N° 16/2004 of 19/6/2004 (...). These three laws together are the revised version of the Organic Law N° 40/2000 of 26/01/2001 setting up 'Gacaca Jurisdictions' and organising prosecutions for offences constituting the crime of genocide or crimes against humanity committed between 1 October, 1990 and 31 December, 1994; Organic Law N° 33/2001 of 22/6/2001 modifying and completing Organic Law N° 40/2000 of 26 January, 2001; which two laws in their turn were an amendment to the Organic Law N° 08/96 of 30/08/1996 on the organisation of prosecutions [in regular courts] for offences constituting the crime of genocide or crimes against humanity committed since 1 October 1990.

[39] This consideration did not appear in the 2000 version of the law. It is an often heard sentence: with the *gacaca* Rwanda shows the world that it can handle its problems itself.

it is decided to adopt this law on *gacaca*, providing for:

> '*penalties allowing convicted persons to amend themselves and to favour their reintegration into the Rwandan Society without jeopardizing the people's normal life*'.

It is interesting to note that since the introduction of the *gacaca* five laws have been passed in parliament, each and everyone refining the whole system, within six years of 2001. This shows the rapid developing character of the *gacaca*, with decision makers trying to cope with problems that turn up during the process or are foreseen already in advance. An example is the introduction in 2007 of the suspended sentence, of which the reason behind it is that the number of persons sentenced to prison is expected to be too high to harbour all of them in the prisons. In late 2007 new discussions started on how to further alleviate the burden of the prisons, for instance regarding the first category cases to be tried by *gacaca* instead of state courts, the sequence of the execution of sanctions – first communal services, then suspended prison part and finally the prison part – and early release of convicted prisoners.

5.2. SUBSTANTIVE CRIMINAL LAW

5.2.1. Genocide and Crimes against Humanity: Three Categories

The crimes covered by the *gacaca* law are crimes against humanity and acts of genocide committed between 1 October 1990 and 31 December 1994, that is starting the day the RPA/RPF invaded Rwanda and the war started. As Rwanda had although ratified the relevant international conventions but not yet provided for sanctions, the basis of prosecution was the penal code.

The crimes have been grouped into three categories.[40] The *first category* is formed by '*les planificateurs, les organisateurs, les incitateurs, les superviseurs et les encadreurs*', that is: those who committed crimes as high ranking officials within religious or state institutions or in militia, or incited to commit crimes, and those who allegedly committed rape and (sexual) torture. This category comprises an estimated 12,000 suspects of whom 10,000 are suspected of sexual torture and rape.[41] The *second category* comprises those who distinguished

---

[40] Art. 11 of Organic Law N° 10/2007 of 01/03/2007. Initially (Art. 51 of Organic Law N° 40/2000 of 26/01/2001) contained four categories. These four categories have been refined and, broadly speaking, by combining the initial 2nd and 3rd categories, been brought back to three categories.

[41] Until Organic Law N° 10/2007 of 01/03/2007 the 1st category entailed also those who distinguished themselves by the zealousness or excessive wickedness with which they took part in the genocide and violators of corpses. As at the end of the information phase of the

themselves by the zealousness or excessive wickedness (*'le zèle (...) ou la méchanceté excessive'*) with which they took part in the genocide, torturers, violators of corpses (*'les actes dégradants sur le cadavre'*), those who 'just' killed someone else, and those who acted with the intention to kill however did not succeed, and other criminal acts against persons without the intention to kill. This category harbours about 400,000 persons. The *third category* is formed by those who committed acts against property. Also this category numbers up to an approximate 400,000 suspects.

All these crimes include the accomplice, i.e. the person who has, 'by any means, provided assistance to commit offences with persons' who committed the said acts themselves.[42] Superiors are criminally responsible for the acts of their subordinates 'if he or she knew or could have known that his or her subordinate was getting ready to commit this act or had done it, and that the superior has not taken necessary and reasonable measures to punish the authors or prevent the mentioned act not to be committed when he or she had the means'.[43]

It is interesting to note that the crimes as such are not crimes against humanity or acts of genocide, although labelled so in the law. After all, to become an act of genocide it has to be established at least that they were committed with the intent to destroy, in whole or in part, a national, ethnical, racial or religious group;[44] to be qualified as a crime against humanity it should be established that the acts were committed as part of a widespread or systematic attack directed against any civilian population, with knowledge of the attack.[45] The (*gacaca*) courts however do not have to establish for each and every suspect again that (s)he committed his or her act as part of a widespread attack or with the intent to destroy an ethnical or racial group.[46] The overarching assumption in the law is that these acts were committed as part of a widespread or systematic attack or with the intent to destroy, in whole or in part, a racial or ethnical group, and therefore constitute acts of genocide and crimes against humanity. They are so to speak symbolically made into acts of genocide and crimes against humanity, without having to prove this. From a legal point of view the crimes to be prosecuted and tried before the *gacaca* are in fact 'ordinary' crimes. I therefore cannot agree with Fierens (2005, 906–908) that the *gacaca* law is retroactive as genocide and crimes against

---

gacaca this category turned out to be too big – about 70–80,000 suspects – to be tried by the regular courts within a reasonable time (as 1st category cases are), the 1st category has been diminished and these two groups have been shifted to the 2nd category.

[42] Art. 53 of Organic Law N° 16/2004 of 19/6/2004.
[43] Ibidem.
[44] The definition of genocide as laid down in the genocide convention and copied by all international instruments afterwards, including the ICC-Statute.
[45] This is the definition of crime against humanity as laid down in the statute of the ICC, Art. 7.
[46] There is probably one exception, i.e. those who committed their crimes as high ranking officials, as the law there speaks about 'those offences', apparently referring to 'the crime of genocide or crimes against humanity' in the chapeau of the article.

humanity were not covered by the law at the time of the committing of the acts.[47]

5.2.2. *Three Punishments*

The law provides for general punishments per category: prison – in custody and suspended,[48] community service[49] and the payment of damages. Initially also the death penalty was possible. In 1998, a total of 22 people were put to death in public execution ceremonies. Since then more than 500 1st category offenders have been convicted to the death penalty, but no one has been executed. The death penalty was finally abolished in Rwanda in 2007.

An important determining factor is whether the suspect/offender has confessed, pleaded guilty, repented and apologised: in that case the punishment is substantially diminished, in order to encourage confessions. For minors who were between 14 and 18 when they committed the crimes, maximum prison sentences are mitigated (in the outline below between square brackets).[50] Children who were younger than 14 years when they committed a crime[51] cannot be prosecuted, but they can be placed in a solidarity camp.[52]

First category offenders incur life imprisonment [young offenders: 10–20 years]; when confessed and repented they face a prison sentence between 20 and 30 years [6½ – 9 years];[53] community service is not possible.[54]

Second category punishments are more differentiated, according to the specific act within this category and again to whether the offender confessed and

---

47 A quick scan shows that the *gacaca* penalties in general are not harsher than the penalties in the Rwandan Criminal Code.

48 Organic Law N° 10/2007 of 01/03/2007 introduced the suspended sentence; the reason behind it is that the number of persons sentenced to prison is expected to be too high to harbour all of them in the prisons.

49 Art. 13 of Organic Law N° 10/2007 of 01/03/2007.

50 Art. 16 of Organic Law N° 10/2007 of 01/03/2007.

51 Art. 79 of Organic Law N° 16/2004 of 19/6/2004. The English text of the law reads: younger than 14 'at the time of the charges against them', which is a different criterion than 'at the time of the events' as mentioned in Art. 78. Reading it other than 'at the time they committed the crime' would create a gap; the French text reads: *'au moment des faits leur reprochés'*.

52 *Ingando* (in Kinyarwanda) are residential camps for groups of about 300 persons (e.g. students), who during a period of 3 weeks to 2 months discuss in particular five themes: analysis of Rwanda's problems, history of Rwanda, political and socioeconomic issues in Rwanda and Africa, rights, obligations and duties and leadership. Also released prisoners undergo *Ingando*.

53 Initially also the death penalty. About 500 people were awaiting the execution of their death sentence, by the time the death penalty was abolished in August 2007.

54 Within the group of confessors a distinction has been made according to the moment the confession is made: before the name was included on the list of perpetrators drawn up by the cell gacaca: 20 to 24 years and after that moment, when the suspect already appears on that list: 25 to 30 years. This distinction already existed for 2nd category cases, but has been introduced with regards to 1st category offenders by Organic Law N° 10/2007 of 01/03/2007.

repented.[55] The zealous murderers, torturers and those who committed dehumanising acts on dead bodies who refuse to confess face a prison sentence ranging from 30 years to life imprisonment [young offenders: 10–15 years].[56] When they confess, the prison sentence ranges from 20 to 29 years [6–7½ years], half of which is commuted into community service, whereas part of the remaining time in prison is commuted into a suspended sentence.[57] For those who 'just' killed someone or had the intention to kill but did not succeed, the sentences are as follows: those who refused to confess face a prison sentence from 15 to 19 years [4½ – 5½ years]; community service is not possible. When they have confessed, the prison sentence ranges between 8 to 14 years [2½ – 5 years], half of which is commuted into community service, whereas part of the remaining time in prison is commuted into a suspended sentence.[58] Lastly, those who committed a crime against persons without any intention of killing them, and who refuse to confess face a prison sentence of 5 to 7 years [2½ – 3½ years], half of which is commuted into community service, whereas 1/6 of the remaining prison sentence is suspended.[59] For those who confessed the sentence ranges from 1 to 4 years [1/2 – 2½ years], half of which is commuted into community service, whereas part of the remaining time in prison is commuted into a suspended sentence.[60] The community service part becomes void when the offender commits another crime, and (s)he shall have to serve the full prison sentence.[61]

As to the *third category*, the law provides that when the offender and the victim have agreed upon an 'amicable settlement', the offender cannot be prosecuted.[62] In the case of prosecution the offender will be sentenced to civil reparation of the

---

[55] Art. 14 of Organic Law N° 10/2007 of 01/03/2007.

[56] Under the previous law (Organic Law N° 16/2004 of 19/6/2004) this was life imprisonment or death, so it has been lowered.

[57] In the group of confessors a distinction has been made according to the moment the confession is made: before the name was included on the list of perpetrators drawn up by the cell gacaca: 20 to 24 years and 1/3 of the remaining prison sentence suspended, and after that moment, when the suspect already appears on that list: 25 to 29 years and 1/6 of the remaining prison sentence suspended.

[58] In the group of confessors a distinction has been made according to the moment the confession is made: before the name was included on the list of perpetrators drawn up by the cell gacaca: 8 to 11 years and 1/3 of the remaining prison sentence suspended, and after that moment, when the suspect already appears on that list: 12 to 14 years and 1/6 of the remaining prison sentence suspended.

[59] In this case half of the prison sentence is not suspended when it regards young offenders.

[60] In the group of confessors a distinction has been made according to the moment the confession is made: before the name was included on the list of perpetrators drawn up by the cell gacaca: 1 to 2 years and 1/3 of the remaining prison sentence suspended, and after that moment, when the suspect already appears on that list: 3 to 4 years and 1/6 of the remaining prison sentence suspended.

[61] Art. 74 of Organic Law N° 16/2004 of 19/6/2004.

[62] Art. 52 of Organic Law N° 16/2004 of 19/6/2004.

damages (s)he has caused,[63] i.e. reparation of the property looted whenever possible, or repayment of the ransacked property or carrying out the work worth the property to be repaired.[64]

Apart from prison and community service, offenders who were 18 years and older when they committed the crimes 'are liable to'[65] the withdrawal of civil rights, perpetual or for the duration of the sentence, i.e. the right to be elected, to become leaders, to serve in the armed forces, to serve in the National Police and other security organs, and to be a teacher, a member of medical staff, a magistrate, a public prosecutor and a judicial council.[66] The rights to be withdrawn and the duration depend on the category and whether the offender has confessed.

5.3. CRIMINAL PROCEDURE

5.3.1. *Three Levels, Three Phases*

First category accused persons are tried before regular penal courts; 'only' second and third category accused persons – the vast majority of all persons accused of genocide and crimes against humanity – are tried by the *gacaca* courts, although by the end of 2007 a proposal reached parliament to have 1st category cases also be tried by the *gacaca*. There are three different levels of *gacaca*: the *gacaca* courts of the cell, the *gacaca* courts of the sector and the *gacaca* courts of appeal.[67] Each *gacaca* court is made up of a General Assembly, a Bench and a Coordination Committee.[68] Apparently there are also *gacaca* established in prisons by prisoners themselves, according to the cells where suspects come from, although not officially; the information gathered there may be used in the official *gacaca*.

The 'general assembly' on the lowest level, that of the cell, consists of all the cell's residents of 18 years and older, at least 200 persons.[69] The general assembly for the sector is composed of all 'judges' of the cell *gacaca* in that sector, together with the sector 'judges' and the 'judges' of the appeals *gacaca*.[70] Each 'bench'

---

[63] Art. 75 of Organic Law N° 16/2004 of 19/6/2004.

[64] Art. 95 of Organic Law N° 16/2004 of 19/6/2004.

[65] I understand that 'are liable to' (in the French text: '*encourent*') means: rights may be withdrawn but not necessarily are.

[66] Art. 15 of Organic Law N° 10/2007 of 01/03/2007. In the previous Organic Law N° 10/2007 of 01/03/2007, Art 76, also the right to vote was withdrawn.

[67] Art. 3 and 4 of Organic Law N° 16/2004 of 19/6/2004 as amended by Art. 1 and 2 of Organic Law N° 28/2006 of 27/6/2006.

[68] Art. 5 of Organic Law N° 16/2004 of 19/6/2004.

[69] Art. 6 of Organic Law N° 16/2004 of 19/6/2004 as amended by Art. 3 of Organic Law N° 28/2006 of 27/6/2006; if the number of 200 persons for the general assembly is not met, this *gacaca* court of the cell has to be merged with another neighbouring *gacaca* court.

[70] Art. 7 of Organic Law N° 16/2004 of 19/6/2004.

consists of seven 'persons of integrity' – the so-called *Inyangamugayo*, see below – and 2 substitutes. They are the lay judges to try the cases before the *gacaca* courts. The members of the bench elect out of their midst the 'coordination committee', that serves as a sort of daily management team.

Three phases can be distinguished in the activities of the *gacaca*. The first phase in particular for the cell *gacaca* is the making of a list of persons who reside in the cell, who resided in the cell before the genocide (and locations they kept shifting to and routes they took), who were killed in the cell of residence or outside, who were victimised[71] and whose property was damaged, and the alleged authors of the offences. This can be done on the basis of confessions, guilty pleas, files forwarded by the public prosecutor, evidence and testimonies and other information. The second phase for the cell *gacaca* is to categorise the suspects in one of the three categories of crimes. On the basis of this categorisation suspects are subsequently tried by the cell *gacaca* (third category), sector *gacaca* (second category) or regular state criminal courts (first category).[72] In order to fulfil these tasks they have various competences, such as to summon any person to appear in a trial, to order and carry out a search, to take temporary protective measures against the property of an accused, and to issue summons to the alleged authors of crimes and order detention or release on parole.[73]

Gacaca meet once a week, if the quorum is present – that is: 5 of the 7 members of the bench and 100 members of the general assembly – and are public except when decided differently.[74] Decisions are made in consensus and if this turns out to be impossible then with an 'absolute majority' of its members.[75] Decisions and deliberations of judges are made in secret and judgments must be motivated,[76] but proceedings are public, except for rape and sexual torture cases. Acts of sexual torture and rape – first category acts – cannot be confessed in public but will all take place behind closed doors. Victims of these acts (or in the case of death or incapacity an interested party) choose one or more members of the seat to submit her complaint, either in words or in writing, or, in case she does not trust the members of the seat, to the public prosecution.[77]

---

[71] A victim is defined as '*anybody killed, hunted to be killed but survived, suffered acts of torture against his or her sexual parts, suffered rape, injured or victim of any other form of harassment, plundered, and whose house and property were destroyed because of his or her ethnic background or opinion against the genocide ideology*'; Art. 34 of Organic Law N° 16/2004 of 19/6/2004.

[72] See the activities as enumerated in Art. 33 and 34 of Organic Law N° 16/2004 of 19/6/2004.

[73] Art. 39 of Organic Law N° 16/2004 of 19/6/2004.

[74] Art. 17 and further of Organic Law N° 16/2004 of 19/6/2004, Art. 23 amended by Art. 5 of Organic Law N° 28/2006 of 27/6/2006.

[75] Art. 24 of Organic Law N° 16/2004 of 19/6/2004.

[76] Art. 21 and 25 of Organic Law N° 16/2004 of 19/6/2004.

[77] Art. 38 of Organic Law N° 16/2004 of 19/6/2004.

5.3.2. Three Remedies

Similar to the ordinary penal system, there are three legal remedies against *gacaca* decisions and sentences: 'opposition', 'appeal' and 'review of judgment'.

Opposition is the remedy against a judgment *in absentia* and is brought before the court that passed judgment at first instance. An opposition is only admissible if the party who was absent pleads a 'serious and legitimate reason' for his absence during the trial. Opposition can be made within 15 calendar days from the day of notification of the judgment passed *in absentia*. Cell, sector and appeals *gacaca* deal with opposition against their own judgments *in absentia*.[78]

Appeal – i.e. a request to a higher court of law to reconsider a decision rendered by a lower court – can be lodged against all decisions of cell *gacaca* – except judgments – and sector *gacaca*, at the sector *gacaca* and appeals *gacaca* respectively. Hence, the sector *gacaca* serve as the appeals court for sentences by the cell *gacaca* on perjury and unlawful pressure and threats on witnesses and judges, and for other decisions in general – not sentences in third category cases – of the cell *gacaca*. The *gacaca* courts of appeal serve as the appeals court for sentences pronounced at first instance by the sector *gacaca* in second category cases. An appeal has to be lodged by the defendant, plaintiff or any other person acting in the interest of justice, within 15 calendar days after the decision or sentence to be appealed against has been pronounced.[79]

Review is possible in cases of contradicting sentences – acquittal and convictions alike – between *gacaca* and ordinary courts, when after a judgment has been passed by a *gacaca* court new evidence turns up contrary to the initial judgment, and thirdly when a person has been given a sentence that is contrary to legal provisions of the charges against him or her. A review can be lodged by the defendant, the plaintiff or any other person acting in the interest of justice.[80]

5.3.3. Hearing and Judgment

The steps to be taken during the proceedings before the *gacaca* courts have been laid down in the law, separate for the cell *gacaca* and the sector and appeals *gacaca*. In broad lines they are as follows.

---

[78] Art. 86–88 of Organic Law N° 16/2004 of 19/6/2004. It seems reasonable to assume that the regular criminal procedural rules apply here, i.e. that this notification must be personal or otherwise within fifteen days from the day when the sentenced person received the notice personally and hence when (s)he becomes aware of the judgment to be opposed against.

[79] Art. 41–43 of Organic Law N° 16/2004 of 19/6/2004, Art. 23 amended by Art. 7–9 of Organic Law N° 28/2006 of 27/6/2006; Art. 89–92 of Organic Law N° 16/2004 of 19/6/2004, Art. 90 amended by Art. 19 of Organic Law N° 28/2006 of 27/6/2006.

[80] Art. 93 of Organic Law N° 16/2004 of 19/6/2004, amended by Art. 20 of Organic Law N° 28/2006 of 27/6/2006.

The cell *gacaca*, only dealing with property crimes, starts with a determination of the damaged property, then linking this to the owners and those accused of having damaged the property, who can present their defence, followed by a response of the owner of the property, upon which the list of property, victims and defendants is adopted. Subsequently the bench explains to the defendants the modalities for granting the compensation by asking each defendant to decide on his or her means and the period of payment, in case of conviction.[81]

The sector and appeals *gacaca* start, in case of a confession, with the identification of the defendants and the plaintiff, and all charges against the defendant are read out loud as well as the minutes of the defendant's confession. Each defendant may comment on the accusation. Then:

> 'any interested person takes the floor to testify in favour or against the defendant and responds to questions put to him or her. Every person taking the floor to testify on which he or she knows or witnessed, takes oath to tell the truth by raising his or her right arm, saying: "I take God as my witness to tell the truth".'

The plaintiff describes all the offences suffered and how they were committed, to which the defendant responds. Then the bench of the *gacaca* establishes a list of the victims and the offences each of them suffered, to which the defendant can respond. The minutes of the hearing are read out loud, and when all agree, the parties to the trial, all who took the floor and the bench put their signatures or fingerprints on the statement of the hearing. Finally the hearing is closed or postponed if deemed necessary to obtain further information.[82] When there is no preceding confession the defendant gets the opportunity to confess during the hearing.[83]

> 'The hearing shall be carried out in calmness. Any person who takes the floor, must be characterized by politeness in speech and behaviour before the persons of integrity, parties, witnesses and the audience at large.
>
> The President of the session can interrupt any person not conforming to the speech taking modality without bawling or rushing him or her in a way or another.
>
> If necessary, the President of the session can give a warning to the troublemakers in the Court, eject or put him or her in detention for a period not exceeding forty eight (48) hours, according to the gravity of the offence. When the committed offence is a criminal

---

[81]   Art. 68 of Organic Law N° 16/2004 of 19/6/2004.
[82]   Art. 64 of Organic Law N° 16/2004 of 19/6/2004.
[83]   Art. 65 of Organic Law N° 16/2004 of 19/6/2004; see Art. 66 in case of a trial *in absentia*.

offence, the Seat forwards the case to the security organs, for prosecution basing on the ordinary laws.[84]

The judgment contains, apart from information on the proceedings and identity of parties, the damaged property that requires reparation and the defendants responsible (cell *gacaca*) or the charges against the defendant (sector and appeals *gacaca*), the facts presented by the parties, the motives of the judgment, and the modalities and period for reparation (cell *gacaca*) or the offence of which the defendant is found guilty and the penalties pronounced (sector and appeals *gacaca*). The judgment is given on the same day of the final hearing or at the subsequent hearing, in public, the date and time of which all present at the hearing are informed.[85]

5.3.4. Confession, Guilty Plea, Repentance, Apology

Confession, guilty plea, repentance and apology play an important part in the *gacaca* proceedings: a special procedure has been introduced in the law, to which every person who has committed one of the three category crimes has recourse. To be accepted as confessions, guilty plea, repentance and apology, the law determines that the defendant must:

1. give a detailed description of the confessed crime, how (s)he carried it out, where and when, witnesses to the fact, the persons victimised, where (s)he threw their dead bodies and the damage caused;
2. reveal the co-authors, accomplices and any other information useful to the exercise of the public action;
3. apologise for the offences that (s)he committed.[86]

The confession, guilty plea, repentance and apology have to be done before the bench of the *gacaca*, the judicial police officer or the public prosecution officer in charge of investigating the case. It shall be done orally during the *gacaca* session or in the form of a written statement (bearing his or her signature or fingerprint). An apology however 'shall be made publicly to the victims in case they are still alive and to Rwandan Society'.[87]

As we have seen already when discussing the penalties, offenders who confessed, pleaded guilty, repented and apologised enjoy a substantive reduction of their sentence. First category offenders however only benefit from it when they

---

[84] Art. 71 of Organic Law N° 16/2004 of 19/6/2004.
[85] Art. 67, 69–70, 83 of Organic Law N° 16/2004 of 19/6/2004.
[86] Art. 54 of Organic Law N° 16/2004 of 19/6/2004.
[87] Art. 59–63 of Organic Law N° 16/2004 of 19/6/2004.

confessed before the moment the cell *gacaca* made up the list of offenders at the end of the information phase, nor do offenders who confess only during the appeals proceedings benefit.[88]

5.4. PARTICIPATIVE LAY JUSTICE

The *gacaca* is a form of participative justice. Every citizen is obliged to take part in the *gacaca*.[89] This is less strange than it seems at first glance when read in conjunction with the duty to testify. Already in the preamble to the law establishing the *gacaca* it is made clear that every Rwandan citizen is obliged to testify on what he or she has seen or knows. The first substantive consideration reads that the crimes were:

> '*publicly committed in the eyes of the population, which thus must recount the facts, disclose the truth and participate in prosecuting and trying the alleged perpetrators*'.

The second one is of the same character:

> '*Considering that testifying on what happened is the obligation of every Rwandan patriotic citizen and that nobody is allowed to refrain from such an obligation whatever reasons it may be*'.[90]

The message is clear: every citizen is obliged to the take part in the *gacaca*, as all having been witnesses to the crimes.

Persons who omit or refuse to testify on what they have seen or know, as well as persons who make a slanderous denunciation, face a prison sentence of three to six months.[91] A similar fate faces those who exert pressure[92] or attempt to do so

---

[88] Art. 55–58 of Organic Law N° 16/2004 of 19/6/2004, Art 58 amended by Art. 12 of Organic Law N° 28/2006 of 27/6/2006.

[89] Art 29 of Organic Law N° 16/2004 of 19/6/2004; the previous Organic Law N° 40/2000 of 26/01/2001 did not contain such a provision.

[90] The preamble of the 2001 law reads: 'Considering that the duty to testify is a moral obligation, nobody has the right to get out of it for whatever reason it may be'.

[91] Art 29 of Organic Law N° 16/2004 of 19/6/2004, doubled in case of a repeated offence. The previous Organic Law N° 40/2000 of 26/01/2001 did contain a similar provision in Art. 32, with a prison sentence of 1 to 3 years maximum.

[92] 'anything aiming at coercing the Seat into doing against its will, translated into actions, words or behaviour threatening the Seat, and clearly meaning that if the latter fails to comply with, some of its members or the entire Seat may face dangerous consequences'.

or threaten[93] a witness or the members of the bench: 3 months to 1 year imprisonment.[94]

The participative aspect of *gacaca* is also demonstrated by the number of persons involved in the *gacaca* as 'judges'. In October 2001 more than 254,000 *Inyangamugayo*, the judges of the *gacaca*, were chosen by the population to fill the benches of about 11,000 *gacaca* courts.[95] This means that together with the suspects, over a million people take part in the *gacaca* in an 'official' capacity, leaving aside the population in general who attend the *gacaca* sessions.

The *Inyangamugayo* are ordinary people from the villages: a report for instance revealed that 92% of the *Inyangamugayo* are farmers of whom 81% earn less than frRw5,000 (approximately €7) per month, which by the way is a reflection of the general situation in Rwanda. *Gacaca* therefore is also a form of lay justice. This is not uncommon for Rwanda. Before 1994 only about 5% of the judges were lawyers.[96]

Together these *Inyangamugayo* form the lay benches of the 11,000 *gacaca* all over the country. Each 'bench' – whether at cell level, sector level or the appeals *gacaca* – consists of seven *Inyangamugayo* and 2 substitutes.[97] The lay judges have to swear an oath before exercising their duties, including that they work for the consolidation of national unity, without any discrimination whatsoever.[98] They cannot judge in a case in which (s)he is one way or another involved, e.g. when the case concerns relatives, good friends or sworn enemies.[99]

According to the law, *Inyangamugayo*, persons of integrity, are persons who have not participated in the genocide, are 'free of the spirit of sectarianism' and from genocide ideology,[100] are of high morals and conduct, truthful, honest and

---

[93] 'words or actions clearly meant to threaten the witnesses or the Seat members for a Gacaca court, aiming at winning acceptance for his or her wish'.

[94] Art. 30–32 of Organic Law N° 16/2004 of 19/6/2004.

[95] See, e.g. Presidential Order N° 12/01 of 26/6/2001 Establishing Modalities for Organizing Elections of Members of 'Gacaca Jurisdictions' Organs.

[96] Compare: in 2006, 95% of the judges were lawyers, not surprisingly all very young. To compare furthermore: before the genocide there was only one faculty of law, producing about 25 lawyers per two years. Moreover, judges were rather marginalised; the main power within the judiciary was with the prosecutors and police.

[97] Art. 8 and 13 of Organic Law N° 16/2004 of 19/6/2004 as amended by Art. 1 and 2 of Organic Law N° 10/2007 of 01/03/2007; before the amendment the number of judges was nine with 5 deputies; initially the bench consisted of 19 people, see Art. 13 of Organic Law N° 40/2000 of 26/01/2001.

[98] Art. 9 of Organic Law N° 16/2004 of 19/6/2004.

[99] Art. 10 of Organic Law N° 16/2004 of 19/6/2004.

[100] 'Ideology of genocide consists in behaviour, a way of speaking, written documents and any other actions meant to wipe out human beings on the basis of their ethnic group, origin, nationality, region, colour of skin, physical traits, sex, language, religion or political opinions'; Art. 3 of Organic Law N° 10/2007 of 01/03/2007.

characterised by a 'spirit of speech sharing'. Government officials, politicians, soldiers, policemen and magistrates cannot be elected as *Inyangamugayo*.[101]

Inyangamugayo can be replaced when for instance they are absent from the sessions of the *gacaca* for three consecutive times without good reason, having been sentenced to imprisonment for at least six months, prompting 'sectarianism' or genocide ideology, or doing 'any act incompatible with the quality of a person of integrity'. Also the bench as a whole can be dissolved, when it makes 'sentimental decisions', lacks 'consensus spirit', is incompetent or behaves incompatibly with *gacaca* court activities.[102] Involvement in genocide has been an important reason for replacement of *Inyangamugayo*. An alleged 40% of them turned out to have been involved in genocidal activities in 1994 themselves.[103]

6. JUDGING *GACACA*

It speaks for itself that *gacaca* can be criticised, both the black letter law and the way it is put into practice. To quote the National Service of Gacaca Courts on problems in practice:[104]

- The genocidal ideology was present almost everywhere in the country and was aimed at jeopardising Gacaca Court activities;
- Endangering the security of genocide survivors, of persons who confessed their crimes and pleaded guilty as well as other witnesses and persons of integrity of Gacaca Courts;
- Destruction of notebooks where collected data was recorded or notebooks were thrown into latrines;
- Persons going into exile allegedly because of Gacaca Courts whereas they actually fled justice;
- Quite a large number of persons were elected as Inyangamugayo who were later on recognised as having committed genocide;

---

[101] Art. 14 and 15 of Organic Law N° 16/2004 of 19/6/2004 as amended by Art. 3 and 4 of Organic Law N° 10/2007 of 01/03/2007.

[102] Art. 16 of Organic Law N° 16/2004 of 19/6/2004 as amended by Art. 4 of Organic Law N° 10/2007 of 01/03/2007; Instructions N° 06/2005 of 20/7/2005 of the executive secretary of the national service of gacaca courts on dismissal of the judge Inyangamugayo from the gacaca court bench, dissolution of a gacaca court bench and replacement of the judges Inyangamugayo.

[103] See, e.g. The New Times, 21–22 December 2005: '*28.000 leaders implicated in genocide*'. This article mentions that since the information gathering started in March 2005, the number of 'leaders' suspected of involvement in the genocide has increased from 688 to 28,477 in December. If I understand this correctly, over 90% of them were *Inyangamugayo*.

[104] National Service of Gacaca Courts, *Report on data collection*, date unknown, to be found at http://www.inkiko-gacaca.gov.rw. See also Kaitesi 2006.

- The large number of officials who committed genocide and who used their positions in a bid to interfere with the smooth running of Gacaca Courts;
- Persons who moved from areas where they used to live during the genocide in an attempt to avoid being made accountable for the crimes they committed there;
- Using Gacaca Courts to intimidate other people in order to traumatise them and this attitude is detrimental to the objective of reconciliatory justice;
- Some leaders of Nyumbakumi who refused to preside over Gacaca Court meetings especially when they knew some top officials and their friends such as tradesmen or other persons were to be prosecuted;
- The fact that some high ranking authorities did not rush to give information so that often information was collected from local communities;
- Collecting information from some specific areas like secondary schools and the National University of Rwanda has often proved extremely difficult;
- Little attention paid to information given by persons who were under age at the time of the genocide.

Many others, in particular international scholars, have commented on the *gacaca* and surrounding circumstances over time, and few in its favour. Criticism entails for instance: modern *gacaca* is only a shadow of its traditional predecessor; there is no fair trial; legal counsel for the accused is prohibited; *gacaca* is restricted to the genocide proper; suspects are provisionally detained for too long a period in overcrowded prisons; the release of provisionally detained prisoners poses security problems for survivors; the judges are not competent to try these cases; judges were involved in the genocide themselves; witnesses are threatened by suspects and suspects are threatened by survivors and neither of them get sufficient protection from the state. Without denying the truth of some or maybe even most of the criticisms, something seems to be wrong in the way these 'facts' are evaluated in terms of 'good' and 'bad'.

Too easily a specific aspect of the *gacaca* that is commented upon as an isolated fact leads to denouncing *gacaca* as a whole. It is important to realise that many similar and other questions can be asked regarding the traditional penal systems – including the international(ised) tribunals and the International Criminal Court – but only very few lead to the conclusion that the system as a whole is useless and should be abolished.[105] This is not to say that a thorough analysis of the *gacaca* – or of the traditional penal system, for that matter – could never lead

---

[105] Lawyers all over the world seem to accept for instance without further proof that the traditional criminal justice systems achieve the goals officially set for them. However, alternatives for these traditional criminal systems, such as truth and reconciliation commissions and *gacaca*, are scrutinised in depth on goal achievement and are often denounced as not sufficiently effective in that respect.

to the conclusion that the whole system should be abolished. But this can only be done after a thorough analysis, having considered the *gacaca* as a phenomenon with many aspects. Such an analysis of the *gacaca* can be done on the level of *gacaca* as a penal system, and in a much wider context as one approach out of many possible approaches when having to respond to atrocities committed in a given society (Longman, 2004: raising many topics for research which makes one realise the futility of one's knowledge).

The way the *gacaca* system is assessed therefore seems unfair; it must be possible to do it differently, to do justice to *gacaca*. In the following I will try to give some other perspectives on *gacaca*, and raise new questions, each and every one of them topics for criminological research. As academic criminological research is my main concern, it is in particular academic publications that I will refer to, rather than reports and press statements of international NGOs.[106]

6.1. TIME AND PLACE SPECIFIC

It is tempting to assess *gacaca* as an isolated phenomenon, apart from time, place and circumstances in which it takes place. Without an eye to the circumstances surrounding the attempts to prosecute and try *génocidaires*, the state is often accused of doing too little too late. It is too easy however to assess what happened for instance ten years ago with the knowledge we have gained in the meantime. Listening to the stories on how the country step by step has been rebuilt after the genocide one realises that the situation then, and therefore the considerations on what to do, were entirely different from nowadays. The old regime deliberately left – or at least tried to leave – a destroyed and empty country for the new government. During the first years a substantive part of the country had to be rebuilt; in the meantime the country was still involved in a regional war. In August 1994 for instance, the Ministry of Justice was heavily damaged, there was no paper or other office equipment, toilets were filled with corpses and salaries were paid in the form of food once a week.[107] The section above dealing with numbers during and after the genocide gives some indication of the total loss of the country. Further it may help to consider the development of Rwanda after the genocide as taking place in periods of two to three years. The first couple of years were focusing

---

[106]   This is not to say that international NGOs are not interesting study objects – on the contrary. It is in particular Amnesty International, Human Rights Watch, Avocats sans Frontières and Penal Reform International that are scrutinising the *gacaca*. Their role as 'one-issue-movements', focusing solely on human rights (and as HRW and AI not being involved in the practice of *gacaca*, commenting entirely from the sideline), however clearly distinguishes them from academic scholars. See also, e.g. De Waal (2003), Cobban (2002), Chakravarty (2007).

[107]   Personal recollection of a friend, coming to Rwanda from DR-Congo in August 1994 to take part in the reconstruction of Rwanda at the Ministry of Justice.

on bringing back safety and security in the country. The second two years ......
etc. This shows the rapid changes in the country, much faster than in stable
societies like in Europe where we are inclined to think in periods of 20 to 30 years.
Societies change. In short: decisions taken at a specific moment have to be
considered as a product of the specific circumstances at a given place and time.

The justice system as well is developing fast. When in 1995 Prunier concluded
his book on the history of the Rwandan genocide with the statement that – apart
from money – justice should come to Rwanda or else 'death would remain a
threatening presence in the political landscape of Rwanda', he probably had every
reason to be sceptical as to whether justice would come in the near future (Prunier
2005 (1995), 355, 388). Thirteen years later the legal landscape has drastically
changed. The influential actors in the justice sector are all determined to create an
independent and impartial judiciary, for instance. I have no reason to doubt their
willingness and ability to succeed. It would be wrong to judge what happens now
in light of the wrongs that happened just after the war. The development of *gacaca*
does not differ from this general picture. *Gacaca* is part of the justice system at
large, and at the moment not the least important one. I would not be amazed if the
practice of *gacaca* as it is at this very moment is quite different from the picture
one had in mind when starting the whole process. Ideological aspects may have
lost their colour; practice will have taken the upperhand. The reported initial
substantive support of the Rwandan population for *gacaca* may have changed
over time.

But not only time, also place should be considered when judging *gacaca* in
Rwanda. As the South African Truth and Reconciliation Commission (TRC) is a
typical product of the situation in South Africa during and after the apartheid
regime, and embedded in the South African culture, the *gacaca* have to be seen as
a typical Rwandan solution, emerging out of Rwandan culture and history.
Similarly, the Ugandan hybrid system to deal with the atrocities committed over
the past decades by the Lords Resistance Army is a typical Ugandan solution. One
may be sceptical about these products of African tradition, and prefer the well
known 'western-traditional' penal approaches, but this neglects that first and
foremost it is the country in which the atrocities took place that has to find a way
out of history, and not western outsiders.

Last but not least, also external circumstances change over time. The decision
to create *gacaca* should be assessed in light of the (geo)political and legal climate
in the years the decision was taken. It is important to note, and again an interesting
topic for research, that it may very well be that the international community, at
the time of thinking on how to respond to the atrocities committed in Rwanda,
was heavily stressing the need to prosecute anybody who allegedly took part in

atrocities. Since at least the 1980s, the 'fight against impunity' was the buzz-word:

> '(...) individuals who commit genocide, crimes against humanity, and war crimes are to be treated as hostis humani generis (an enemy of all humankind). (...) This preclusion [from impunity] extends from the most junior soldier acting under the orders of a superior to the most senior government officials, including diplomats and heads of states' (Bassiouni, 2002b: 257/258).

That it may be impossible or unrealistic to prosecute everybody involved is not often acknowledged (Schabas 2002). It is too unrealistic to be taken seriously to hold on to this dogma, and at the same time to criticise a country that indeed tries to do what the dogma tells it to do for the reason that it cannot live up to all international norms and expectations in an almost impossible situation.[108] It seems more realistic to review the dogma of the obligation to prosecute, but again, if one does so – and some authors apparently have changed their opinion on this matter – it is unfair to criticise the country for having done ten years ago what the world expected it to do at that time.

6.2.   WORK UNDER CONSTRUCTION

Closely related to the point that one should assess *gacaca* in light of the changing times, place and circumstances, is the observation that *gacaca* is a work in progress, or maybe better: under construction. The *gacaca* are an experiment. It is an answer to problems in a situation no country in the world has ever faced. Although based upon tradition, it is applied to a kind of crime committed on a scale for which it never was constructed in ancient times. It is developing each and every day, trying to cope with problems that arise in practice. Examples are the restructuring of categories and the introduction of suspended sentences. It is therefore difficult to assess the *gacaca* as if it has proven its consistency and its robustness, as the traditional penal systems over centuries have.[109] What may be seen as absurd in a traditional, more or less stable and inflexible, penal system, may in the case of *gacaca* be considered a brilliant solution to suddenly arising unexpected problems, such as gaps in the law, multiplication of suspects,

---

[108]   Which, again, changed over time: When the discussion on the *gacaca* began, in the late 90s, the idea was that about 120,000 suspects had to be tried, at that moment imprisoned in jails that were built for only a small part of them. During the *gacaca* information phase it turned out that the number of people to be tried was about 800,000. This number, combined with the character of the crime – genocide as the crime of crimes – and the lack of a well organised justice system, has created a situation for Rwanda unknown in the world.

[109]   Compare in this respect the supranational penal system that also has to be considered as a system under construction.

multiplication of prison sentences. These kinds of changes within the system over a very short time may be criticised as showing the ill-considered character of *gacaca*; it may as well be seen as proof of the flexible nature of the system to respond to challenges in a situation unknown to the world at large. A lot of criticism has been expressed from all corners of society, domestic and foreign. I would not be amazed if those responsible for the *gacaca* in quite some cases already had observed the underlying causes of this criticism and had tried to find a solution long before the criticism arose.

In light of the fact that *gacaca* are a work under construction the relevancy may be questioned of the statement that the current *gacaca* is less than a shadow of its traditional example, as Fierens for instance does (2005: 912/13). Thinking this way is denying that phenomena change according to time and place and circumstances.[110] It seems more fruitful to accept these changes and approach *gacaca* as a hybrid system, combining old influences with new circumstances (Karekezi et al. 2004, 74), rather than reviewing it as if it still were or should be its already long gone traditional forerunner.[111]

Another interesting example of *gacaca* as a work in progress within changing times and circumstances can be seen in the sentences and execution thereof. Since the establishment of the *gacaca* and the first convictions and executions, sentences and the execution thereof have dramatically changed. After 1998 the death penalty has not been executed and was even abolished in 2007; prison sentences are partly made conditional; they will probably even be remitted in the (near) future. This is no sign of arbitrary or inconsequential governmental behaviour, as for instance Kirkby (2006: 109/110) states when discussing the possibility of an amnesty of convicted persons in the future. It is on the contrary a very logical consequence of an historical development. Needs and expectations change. Directly after a war or genocide, the call for strong punishments will be louder than some years later. As in the Netherlands quite a lot of individuals were convicted to death and executed shortly after the second World War, but only a few years later the death penalty was no longer executed, and convicted persons were released before the end of their terms. Exactly the same phenomenon can be seen in Rwanda. This is no weakness but the logical consequence of a changing context. Goals of an approach to atrocities change overtime. The *gacaca* started in strong terms of life sentences and death penalties,[112] but at the end of the day, after everybody has been sentenced

---

110 Cf. Reyntjens 1999 (39/40) who already concludes in 1990 that the *gacaca* have become semi-official and neo-traditional, adapting to modern times.

111 It is another question whether reforming gacaca does not 'destroy' the old and still existing traditional *gacaca* by changing its character in the genocide cases; this however does not regard the functioning of the new *gacaca* as such.

112 Cf. Prunier in 1995 (355) saying of the maybe '100 men who have committed not only a crime against humanity but a sin against the Spirit by locking up a whole nation into the airless sadomasochistic inferno. They have to die.' As for changing opinions cf. also that one of the

and the phase of executing the sentences has been reached, the penalties are in fact much lower than in the initial discourse. Then also more general societal considerations pop up, such as how to deal with all the persons that have been sentenced to prison sentences: is it possible to incarcerate over 100,000 persons in prisons built for only a fraction of that number? Can a country develop upward with the majority of the population living for a very long period of time with at least one member of the family in prison, for whom they have to earn food and without this person contributing to the subsistence of the family? Questions like these, and many others, were less pressing shortly after the genocide took place or at least were over-shadowed by other, at that moment more pressing issues. Release of all prisoners would not have been possible in the years directly following the genocide; it is still controversial but will without doubt happen within some years from now.

6.3.   REALITY VERSUS THEORY

That *gacaca* is a work under construction, changing over time, place and circumstances, also reminds us of the difference between reality and theory. Theories on reconciliation, truth, (transitional) justice and comparable concepts are theories, often very static, as if applicable to all post-conflict situations. Practice may very well be entirely different. Sometimes it seems as if scholars writing on *gacaca* consider theory more important than reality; if the two don't meet, reality should be adapted to theory instead of the other way round. In particular in a field in which so little is known one should be careful not to highlight the theory as the standard for practice. Quite some theories are the results of very interesting philosophical lines of reasoning, but seem to be quite far away from everyday reality. Other theories present mere speculations and beliefs as if they are scientific theories; it may be a very good assignment for students to unveil wrong argumentations. And if at all based upon reality, theory is almost per definition a generalisation of experiences in practice. And after all this goes entirely against the nowadays generally accepted idea that there is no one-size-fits-all approach to post-conflict problems.

Much of what has been written for instance on reconciliation may be interesting from a theoretical point of view but seems very far away from the practice in, for instance, post-genocide Rwanda (much more realistic: Stover & Weinstein

---

reasons for Rwanda voting in the Security Council against the establishment of the ICTR was the impossibility to impose the death penalty; 12 years later Rwanda abolished the death penalty itself.

2004).[113] Theories have to be tested. As Graybill and Lanegran (2004: 4) mention as one of the problems of studying transitional justice:

> *'scholars and practitioners engage in assertions about what these structures [transitional justice institutions] can do but rarely test those assumptions. Common wisdom asserts that truth commissions promote individual healing and reconciliation, which leads to national healing and reconciliation, which in turn provides a bedrock for democracy. But (...) no one has yet proven that truth commissions secure their supposed benefits, such as healing, truth, and national reconciliation. In fact, a few scholars are beginning to conclude that the evidence is decidedly mixed'.*[114]

Another example of an often repeated assumption is that *gacaca* strengthens the ethnic division between Hutu and Tutsi, by labelling all Tutsi as victims – all victims as Tutsi – and all Hutu as perpetrators – all perpetrators as Hutu. Hutu as a group would be identified as perpetrators instead of individualising guilt (Tiemessen 2004, 68). These are mere speculations; evidence is not presented. The stories I hear in practice support the opposite as well (without being scientific proof either of course).

Last but not least, as Daly rightly remarks about justice in the context of responses to the Rwanda genocide: 'Any response Rwanda develops not only must be consistent with principles of justice but also must be pragmatically feasible. Justice that exists only in theory is no justice at all' (Daly 2002, 367).

6.4.   RETHINKING HUMAN RIGHTS

The human rights discussion in fact can also be considered part of the theory versus reality discussion. An important point of critique on *gacaca* regards the 'fact' that the *gacaca* proceedings do not live up to fair trial standards as these have been developed over the years for the traditional penal process. The main points are that there is no right to legal representation, there is no independent and impartial judiciary, confessions play a too important role, and witnesses are obliged to testify.

It would be an interesting topic for a dissertation to rethink the concept of fairness within the context of non-traditional penal approaches such as the *gacaca* in post-conflict situations. Compare what has been said above on rethinking the (international) dogma of the obligation to prosecute or, if this is deemed undesirable, to review all standards of international law as not having been

---

[113]   See also, e.g. Vandeginste (2004a, 7), on how the opinion of the government on reconciliation changed between 1994 and 1998.

[114]   See also, e.g. Longman (2004) on the theories by authors such as Des Forges, Mamdami and Uvin to explain the genocide.

written for these kinds of exceptional situations. I see at least two questions, in line of each other, which can lead to some answers.

The first question is whether one accepts that a post-conflict situation can be so different from ordinary life that rules and principles that have been written for ordinary life do not (fully) apply, that is: in all aspects and unconditionally. Do all ordinary standards apply in a situation in which 10% of the total population is tried for its involvement in a genocide having killed another 10% of the population, including a substantive part of the justice sector actors? The answer is clear for human rights organisations that keep at the sideline, but already becomes more difficult to answer for those human rights organisations that actively take part in finding a 'solution' (Chakravarty 2006). One consideration when trying to answer this question is that in theory we compare *gacaca* with an ideal penal system but that in practice there are very few, if any, jurisdictions that apply all rules and principles on human rights. As Uvin states: we are '(…) rather comparing various practices that are weak and incomplete in the real world' (Uvin, undated: 5).

If one accepts that human rights standards do not always in full and unconditionally apply, the question remains how to determine what then the standard should be to assess whether what is happening in practice is acceptable? Is there a bottom-line? The answer to this could be that we step back from the rules and go back to the principles that underlie a rule such as that 'everybody has the right to legal counsel of his or her own choice'. Human rights principles, the overarching concept of fair trial or due process rules, basically have been developed as safeguards against abuse of power by state organs.[115] The rules moreover seem mainly to have been developed from the principles with a view to relatively formal penal systems. Are all these rules unconditionally applicable to a relatively informal penal system that is based upon broad participation by the population? Wouldn't we be over-dogmatic when doing so, if the underlying principle is met? Taking the right to legal representation for example: in proceedings in which the whole population takes part (or at least is expected and able to) one might say that the role of the defence is taken over by the population. Even stronger: some say that it is not so much the accused as it is the victim who needs legal support in a situation where the majority of the population is on the hand of the perpetrator. Kirkby (2006, 108) states that it may be a conscious 'trade-off between retributive and restorative aims', and that therefore 'criticism should instead focus on the judges' role in both ensuring survivors' expectations are met and facilitating the integration of those confessing to or convicted of crimes back into society' (a similar argumentation is followed by Vandeginste 2004a).

I am almost certain that Rwanda scores very low on international indexes on the rule of law, negatively influenced as it will be by the way *génocidaires* are tried

---

[115] Only recently it has been accepted that human rights can also be invoked when the state did not do enough to protect an individual against another individual.

through *gacaca*; so will for instance Uganda for its choice of a hybrid system in dealing with the atrocities committed by the LRA. But when one accepts that human rights may be reconsidered in a situation such as in Rwanda and Uganda, maybe the conclusion would be justified that on the contrary these countries should rate very high, as at least they seriously try to deal with the perpetrators of genocide in the best possible way considering the circumstances of the country.

6.5. A COMPARATIVE APPROACH

Apart from a difference between practice and reality as such, it should be realised that reality is much more differentiated than often is thought. Judging *gacaca* as a penal system may show this. On the level of *gacaca* as a penal system it is important to use a comparative approach, realising oneself that there are many different forms of penal systems. To stick to the two best known forms of penal systems: the adversarial and inquisitorial systems (sometimes not entirely justifiably equalled to the common and the civil law systems). Interesting in this regard is the observation by Schabas, who attended the first genocide trials before regular courts in Rwanda:

> 'Some of the harsh initial judgments about the shortcomings in the trials were made by lawyers trained in common law jurisdictions, who misunderstood some of the aspects of the "civil law" approach that Rwanda had inherited from Belgium and France. They were shocked, for example, at the relative brevity of the trials, and the reliance on written evidence, and the lack of cross-examination. By contrast, trial observers who came from "civil law" traditions were relatively sanguine and even rather impressed with the proceedings' (Schabas 2005, 886–887).

To give some examples from *gacaca* practice: a trial and conviction *in absentia* may be abhorrent for an adversarial educated lawyer, but is accepted in the inquisitorial process model; the person who rejects this has to acknowledge that (s)he not only rejects *gacaca* but an important part of the world's penal systems. Another one of the criticisms of the *gacaca* regards the duty to testify, as laid down in the law, as we have seen above. Who criticises this should however realise that many criminal codes all over the world provide for a duty to testify for witnesses of crimes. So does the Rwandan Code of Criminal Procedure, threatening the person who does not want to appear or testify with a penalty of one month in prison and/or a fine of FrRw50,000.[116] And as the preamble to the *gacaca* law states: 'the crimes were publicly committed in the eyes of the population,

---

[116]   Law N° 13/2004 of 17/5/2004 relating to the Code of Criminal Procedure, Articles 54–57. FrRw50,000 equals approximately €70.

which thus must recount the facts, disclose the truth and participate' in the prosecution and judging of suspects. This is exactly what can be rather amazing to outsiders: many people participated in the genocide within their own neighbourhoods and afterwards still many people, whether perpetrators, survivors or bystanders, reside in the same neighbourhood as where they lived during the genocide. A general obligation to participate in the *gacaca* is therefore less strange than it seems at first glance.[117] Criticising this aspect of *gacaca* without realising that this is quite common in many jurisdictions in the world is no less than neo-legal-colonialism. It becomes entirely ridiculous when it is linked to *umuganda*, the monthly obligation for the population to perform public services, presented as pre-colonial communal work, which 'the Belgian colonisers and the post-colonial Habyarimana regime exploited (...) to conscript forced labourers for public works projects' (Tiemessen 2004, 69).

A third example regards the role confessions play in the *gacaca* system. It may be interesting to compare the *gacaca* with the guilty plea and plea bargaining tradition within the American criminal system, and to see whether the *gacaca* practice in this respect is more acceptable to American common law lawyers than for civil law trained lawyers in for instance Europe. The same pertains to the role of the judges, the *Inyangamugayo*, who may be compared with the jury in the American adversarial system, for instance in the way they are trained and get instructions on their role in the trial. It may show that these practices are less strange than thought at first hand and maybe also less unfair.

A final example: one of the criticisms on the *gacaca* ventured to me was that 22% of the cases (allegedly) were acquitted, which as such would be firm proof of the unfairness of the *gacaca*. That is an interesting inference. But the question is which presuppositions underlie this statement. At least for an inquisitorial penal system some other conclusions, more favourable to *gacaca*, are possible, which may be (or not) different for an adversarial system. In an average inquisitorial system, with indictments based upon thorough pre-trial investigations, it would mean that either the judges are partial and dependent in favour of the accused or that the pre-trial investigations are not properly performed. In the case of the *gacaca* the latter seems the case; one of the justified criticisms on *gacaca* is that of many accused there are no dossiers speaking against them; apparently – at least that is a more favourite explanation, and I think more logical than the other – the

---

[117] On the other hand this may be true in general; however it does not per definition pertain to for instance Kigali, where many people went to after the genocide, both survivors and perpetrators. It is therefore not amazing that the information phase in Kigali took more time than in rural parts of the country, and that participation in some sectors has been enforced by measures such as giving the population cards that were signed by the authorities when the person had attended a gacaca; not being able to provide this signed card could lead to services not being rendered to the person.

gacaca function as they should do, namely as the necessary filter between accusation and punishment.

6.6. GOALS

Gacaca serve various goals, seemingly more – or at least some other – than traditional penal systems. According to the preamble to the *gacaca* law: eradicating the culture of impunity, achieving justice and reconciliation, accelerating the process, providing punishment, reconstituting society, disclosing the truth, and proving the ability of Rwandan society to find by itself solutions to the genocide problems and its consequences.[118]

A consequence of serving more goals is that one has to take into account all goals if one aims at judging *gacaca* as a whole (Oomen 2006, 174–180). Of course this is not to say that separate goals cannot be studied; an interesting study on one of the goals separately is that on the truth by Ingelaere (2007).[119] One should however realise then that one is only describing part of the phenomenon.

Some do not believe that a penal system like *gacaca* can serve these goals. It is in particular reconciliation that is under fire. Whether this is justified or not remains to be seen, but the sole argument, without any further argumentation, that criminal courts 'rarely enable reconciliation' seems not very convincing (Fierens 2005, 916). Apart from the fact that *gacaca* are in quite some aspects different from ordinary penal systems[120] comparing regular traditional criminal courts having to deal with ordinary criminal cases with a special court such as the *gacaca* dealing with crimes against humanity and genocide in extraordinary circumstances seems quite ineffective. There may be very good reasons to indeed deny regular domestic and international criminal courts a reconciliation function, but important is to see why this is done: an important aspect seems to be the fact

---

[118]   Others, like Oomen (2006, 174 and further), choose goals on a more meta-level, referring to transitional justice scholarship; in fact this comes very close to the goals as mentioned in the preamble of the *gacaca* law.

[119]   Although also in this study there seems to be a remarkable bias, Ingelaere studied 'the truth' in the first phase of *gacaca*, i.e. the information-gathering phase on the basis of which accused were categorised in one of the three categories. He then critically remarks in the final paragraphs of his study that the *gacaca* trial proceedings only establish the forensic truth (at best), however if I understand him correctly, forgetting that this was exactly the aim of the first informative phase of *gacaca*. It is only in the third phase, after the categorisation in the second phase, that the real trials take place, trying to form a more encompassing truth.

[120]   Fierens (2005) is in fact quite confusing in the presumed criminal character of the proceedings: when he deals with reconciliation the *gacaca* are equated with criminal courts who (in general) do not promote reconciliation (at 916), whereas half a page later *gacaca* are denounced as providing not the 'just distance' as criminal proceedings in general do (at 916/17). This shows exactly that it is very tricky to regard *gacaca* as a criminal proceeding, similar to the old traditional criminal systems.

that the victim, who apart from the offender is the most directly involved person in the conflict, is denied almost full access to the proceedings, and whose role is taken over by a representative of the state or even worse, the international community, far away from the community in which the conflict arose. In the ICTR case against Kayishema, one of the witnesses, a woman from Kibuye, a place in the western province of Rwanda, reflects this notion when stating:

> '(...) I kept imagining, "How I wish this trial was taking place in Kibuye!" How I wish I had testified in front of the people of Kibuye whom [Kayisehema] had wronged, and not an audience made up of only foreigners. I felt like walking up to his chair, grabbing him, and bringing him with me to Rwanda' (Cobban 2007, 3).

The traditional criminal justice systems steal the conflict from those directly involved (Christie 1977). It may be interesting to study to what extent *gacaca* in this respect differs from regular traditional courts. But in fact this is very difficult to investigate, as little research is known on the effectiveness of criminal justice systems in general or alternatives such as a truth and reconciliation commission; at the end of the day it seems to boil down to beliefs.

A further problem here is that reconciliation is a very difficult concept to grasp. There are quite a few 'theories' on what reconciliation entails. Whoever expects reconciliation as a direct result of *gacaca* seems to have a somewhat simple idea of reconciliation. Many are the expatriates in Rwanda that, in some sort of surprise, whisper: 'But Hutu and Tutsi still hate each other', aiming to indicate the failure of *gacaca*. I can only fully agree with Molenaar, who states that reconciliation is:

> 'a very long and slow process that is more likely to take generations than decades. Gacaca, which is expected to take some years, only covers an early part of the process and should thus be considered as a point of departure and not the conclusion (...). In second place, gacaca is neither the only requirement for reconciliation nor is it the only event that can influence the process. Even if gacaca became a huge success, achieving reconciliation is not guaranteed' (Molenaar 2005, 141) (see also Parmentier et al. in this volume).

In fact the same can be said about the concepts of forgiveness and justice. These are difficult concepts to grasp; processes that take generations and to which *gacaca* only partly contributes, even if one could call *gacaca* a huge success. 'The problem of justice (...) is not a simple problem of texts and courts. It concerns finding an intermediary between classical justice, the reconstruction of the social fabric, and the prevention of another tragedy, another genocide.'[121]

---

[121] Rwandan president Paul Kagame, then minister of defence, as quoted in Karekezi et al. (2004, 71).

Ending impunity is another goal which is very difficult to prove. History shows that genocide is the result of a systematic development, culminating in the crime of crimes. This implies that it may be possible to explain and prevent genocide in the future by fighting its causes.[122] And this implies that an approach could be assessed in the function of its capability of diminishing structural causes. Impunity for instance is one of the causes and possibly an important one. Mass killings of Tutsi could take place for many years without any consequences for the perpetrators. In light of this and of the discourse at that time on ending impunity, the system of *gacaca*, trying to address as many perpetrators as possible, can be seen as a step forward. But it is important to realise that ending impunity is only one of many developments leading to genocide; in and of itself it will not prevent a new genocide.

Further, goals may change. First, as we have seen above, goals change with the passing of time. But goals may also change in function of different phases in a

---

[122] See the set of indicators 'to detect and prevent at the earliest possible stage developments in racial discrimination that may lead to violent conflict and genocide', of the UN-Committee on the Elimination of Racial Discrimination, *Decision on Follow up Procedure to the Declaration on Prevention of Genocide, Indicators of Systematic and Massive Pattern of Racial Discrimination*, 67th session, CERD/C/67/Misc.8, 19 August 2005. The indicators are: 1. Lack of a legislative framework and institutions to prevent racial discrimination and provide recourse to victims of discrimination; 2. Systematic official denial of the existence of particular distinct groups; 3. The systematic exclusion – in law or in fact – of groups from positions of power, employment in state institutions and key professions such as teachers, judges and police; 4. Compulsory identification against the will of members of particular groups including the use of identity cards indicating ethnicity; 5. Grossly biased versions of historical events in school text books and other education materials as well as celebration of historical events which exacerbate tensions between groups and peoples; 6. Policies of forced removal of children belonging to ethnic minorities with the purpose of complete assimilation; 7. Policies of segregation, direct and indirect, for example separate schools and housing areas; 8. Systematic and widespread use and acceptance of speech or propaganda promoting hatred and/or inciting violence against minority groups, particularly in the media; 9. Grave statements by political leaders/prominent people that express support for affirmation of superiority of a race or an ethnic, dehumanisation and demonisation of minorities, or condone or justify violence against a minority; 10. Violence or severe restrictions targeting minority groups perceived to have traditionally maintained a prominent position, for example as business elites or in political life and state institutions; 11. Serious patterns of individual attacks on members of minorities by private citizens which appear to be principally motivated by the victim's membership of that group; 12. Development and organisation of militia groups and/or extreme political groups based on a racist platform; 13. Significant flow of refugees and internally displaced persons, especially when those concerned belong to specific ethnic or religious groups; 14. Significant disparities in socio-economic indicators evidencing a pattern of serious racial discrimination; 15. Policies aimed at the prevention of delivery of essential services or assistance including obstruction for aid delivery, access to food, water, sanitation or essential medical supplies in certain regions or targeting specific groups.
These indicators have to be assessed against the background of 1. Prior history of genocide or violence against a group; 2. Policy or practice of impunity; 3. Existence of pro-active communities abroad fostering extremism and/or providing arms; 4. Presence of external mitigating factors such as the UN or other recognised invited third parties.

penal process. The aim of criminalising certain behaviour as such in the law will in general be deterrence and setting the norm. The penalties stipulated are general maxima: for crimes against humanity and genocide generally life imprisonment or the death penalty. The goal of sentencing will again be phrased in terms of deterrence, but also in terms of revenging the act committed and showing to what extent in a concrete case the behaviour in question is rejected by society as a symbolic gesture. In many cases sentences will certainly be lower than the general maximum as stipulated in the law. Goals of the execution of a sentence are again different. The deterrent and symbolic functions will be smaller than in the norm-setting and trial phases, and will be more centred on the individual convict, focusing on rehabilitation. As a consequence many convicts will not serve their total sentence (and certainly not the maximum one in the law), but will be released (long) before the end of their term.

Last but not least there may be other – 'hidden' – goals apart from the official ones. Community participation is a key aspect of the *gacaca* system. The crimes were committed in specific neighbourhoods where the alleged perpetrators still live, as do the surviving victims and their relatives. A man who barely escaped the genocide tells me that during the *gacaca* process one can speak up, tell the truth and denounce the involvement of one's neighbours in the genocide. In daily life, he says, you wouldn't call your neighbour to account for his or her role in the genocide; it requires a specific time, place and ritual environment. This is a well known concept also in regular criminal law, but becomes very clear in the *gacaca*, where offenders and victims keep living together in the same communities. This also has consequences for the functions of the *gacaca*, outstretching the old penal functions of a regular court session.

> '(...) gacaca takes away the judicial process from the formal courtrooms, and gives it to the ordinary people in the hills. By doing so, the context in which the judicial process takes place is changed dramatically. One should not underestimate the enormous influence this change of context brings. While lawyers, prosecutors and judges are all trained to restrict themselves to the one event that is at stake in relation to the law, ordinary people are not. You cannot expect them to distinguish gacaca and ordinary life. By bringing justice to the hills, it becomes part of communal life that is larger than only gacaca. One should realise that as a result all events and elements of this life, including age-old disputes between families, will play a role in the judicial process' (Molenaar, 2005: 119).

And *gacaca* have unexpected consequences, not aimed at, as Molenaar argues directly after:

> 'This process also works the other way round. What happens in gacaca has a direct influence on life in the community. Gacaca functions in a community, and in this

community people live in a complicated web of relationships that is shaped by the past and determines people's futures. Since these relations are often familial and/or characterised by mutual dependency, they are extremely important to people and determine for a large part the actions they will take in gacaca' (Molenaar 2005, 119).

It is true, through *gacaca* the judicial process has been integrated into communal life and what the consequences of this will be in terms of 'more tension, reconciliation or both, remains to be seen' (Molenaar 2005, 120). Maybe it is best to conclude that in general one should say that at least for the moment it is very difficult to assess a mechanism such as *gacaca* on the achievement of its goals.[123] To cite Luc Huyse (2007):[124]

'Judging the potential and/or actual performance of TJRM's [traditional justice and reconciliation mechanisms, RHH] also requires sufficient attention for a structural and a temporal aspect of their workings. What do they achieve at the micro level (individual victims and perpetrators), the meso level (clans, communities) and the macro level (national, regional and international)? The temporal dimension refers to the long-term effects. These are extremely difficult questions to answer. We lack even the most basic data to deal with the structural aspect. And all TJRM's are too "young" to be judged on their long-term achievements (...).'

It is less satisfying than one should wish, but from an academic point of view it is better to acknowledge that it is still too early to judge *gacaca* on the basis of its goal-achievement, instead of pretending that we know.

6.7. YOU'RE DAMNED IF YOU DO, YOU'RE DAMNED IF YOU DON'T[125]

For some people nothing seems to be good enough. When prisons are over-populated this leads to substantive criticism, but if prisoners are released in great numbers,[126] this also is fundamentally criticised. The percentage of judges,

---

[123] Which pertains even more to those goals that are introduced by others, such as promoting democracy, see Wierzynska (2004).

[124] Although he expressly states that his paper is not for citation or use outside the context of the meeting at which it was presented as nuances and full references are absent, I fully agree with him that what is quoted above is an important starting point when assessing the performance of what he calls TJRMs/traditional justice and reconciliation mechanisms.

[125] Minister of Justice Tharcisse Karugarama at a conference on the rule of law in The Hague, 26 October 2007.

[126] About 70,000 persons, less than one tenth of the total amount of suspects but a substantive part of those detained, have been released over time. These released suspects follow a 'course' in a 'solidarity camp', in which they get information on the history of Rwanda, the rule of law, human rights, the consequences of the genocidal ideology and those kinds of issues. Afterwards

Inyangamugayo, that had to be replaced for their involvement in the genocide (an alleged 40% of them) for some is proof of a failing system. But it may as well be considered an example of a perfectly working – self-cleaning – system; after all it would be worse had they remained untouched as 'persons of integrity'. Another example: Sarkin (2001, 163–164) criticises – in fact before the *gacaca* were at all established – that 'the more educated, intelligent and potentially more able stratum of society' has been excluded by law to serve as judges in the *gacaca*. This exclusion regards 'heads of government administrations whether centralised or decentralised within the cell level; politically active persons; active military personnel; active members of the national police or the local defence force; career magistrates, unless they are used as legal advisors; members of the managing bodies of political parties, religious sects or non-governmental organisations'. Some pages before in the same publication of Sarkin criticise the 'Tutsisation' of public functions, including the army, police, politics and administrative functions all over the country (151–152). This makes one wonder: what would his conclusion have been if these people had not been excluded from serving as judges?

Sometimes this per definition negative look even turns into conspiracy-like theories, in which every step the government takes proves the theory in practice. The mere establishment of *gacaca*, the hesitation in proceeding with it after the pilot phase, the release of thousands of prisoners from the over-populated prisons, the fact that witnesses and survivors are threatened and the fact that offenders are punished – everything is seen as the function of efforts to 'tighten the control of a minority government' (Oomen 2005, 905–906). I am afraid that had the government done the opposite this would have led to the very same conclusion. Maybe this illustrates the difficulty in finding and implementing a solution to mass atrocities in a country. A win-win solution seems impossible, maybe worse: what to do seems often to be about choosing the best among bad alternatives.

Related to this, last but definitely not least, is the creation of images by governments (sensitising or brainwashing?) but no less by NGOs (as a colleague of mine, professor of human rights, once exclaimed: 'who ever forbade human rights organisations from being positive?') and by the media: what exactly is independent media; what are independent NGOs? The role of language is one of

---

quite a few suspects return to the communities where they originally came from and where they committed their crimes. The ones released are in particular those who were very young during the genocide, those who at the moment of release were very old or ill, and suspects that showed remorse and have confessed. The latter has been commented as being unfair, leaving people who don't have anything to confess as they are innocent in prison. For example the woman, Tutsi, who lost all her family, and whose husband, a Hutu and university lecturer, has been in prison in Butare since 1994, allegedly being a *planificateur*, having returned to Rwanda the day before the genocide began and not having left the country as he wanted to protect his wife; interview 6 March 2007, Kigali.

the interesting aspects in this regard.[127] These are very important actors in creating a perception of what is happening: what people think is true is true in its consequences, as an old and famous sociological dogma goes.

7. EPILOGUE

Many, many other questions can be asked and in practice are, which may not be uncommon in the context of regular crimes but get a special flavour when dealing with genocide. What exactly is reconciliation? Is it really more than a belief? How should confessions be evaluated in a certain culture? What role does the use of language play as an instrument to dehumanise a targeted group and render banal the evil to be done to them. Is it possible to study a traditional approach as an outsider? What is the role of a specific culture? How should one deal with the memory of a genocide? Are *gacaca* more torture than justice for survivors who have to relive their experiences, maybe even without any legal satisfaction? What exactly is the place of survivors? How can one assess the importance of the discovery of many corpses, as a result of *gacaca* hearings, that as a consequence now can get a decent burial? Is it realistic to think in terms of individual offender-ship and individual responsibility in a situation where so many individuals committed such incredible crimes? How should the killing of witnesses, judges and survivors be assessed as a result of their participation in the *gacaca*?[128] And last but definitely not least: what is the truth?

It is difficult to find the truth in Rwanda, as many say. To a large extent this is true, not, as the popular belief goes, because all Rwandans lie, which 'truth' is

---

[127] See, e.g. Klemperer (2000, 1975). Prunier (2005 [1995], 142): 'There was a "rural" banalisation of crime. Killings were umuganda, collective work, chopping up men was "bush clearing" and slaughtering women and children was "pulling out the roots of the bad weeds".' Note that *umuganda*, a still existing phenomenon, is not only collective but also obligatory work; once a month the population takes part in *umuganda*, clearing e.g. roadsides from weeds.

[128] Amnesty International issued a press report in November 2007 urging countries not to extradite suspects to Rwanda; with as one of the reasons that victims and witnesses are not sufficiently protected. This led to many comments, including one of a survivor of the genocide, Yolande Mukagasana, author of several publications, amongst which *La mort ne veut pas de moi* (1998), who in an open letter asked Amnesty International: *'En tout cas, moi je vous demande une chose, c'est de ne plus jamais me suivre sur ma route de lutte contre la mort des hommes par les mains des autres. C'est de ne plus mettre les pieds là où je vais témoigner du génocide tant que la mort ne veut pas de moi. Attendez lorsque je ne serai plus là et faites ce que vous êtes habitués de faire. Ne me poursuivez plus. Tout homme peut tomber, l'essentiel est de pouvoir se relever. Vous aussi, faites votre examen de conscience. Arrêtez de faire la politique destructrice, faite une politique plus humaine.'* It shows among other things the gap between abstract notions of an outsider human rights organisation and the concrete opinions and needs of those directly involved.

---

even taught to children during *éducation civic* classes in secondary school.[129] I do at least not have the impression that Rwandans are bigger liars than other people in the world. However, it is difficult to find the truth because of at least two reasons: the sensitivity of facts and the fast changing situation.

Firstly the truth in Rwanda is extremely sensitive. Every story has several truths. And the consequences of choosing for one truth above another are huge. The situation is still so tense, that every opinion may drive you, *nolens volens*, to the side of one of the parties and make you unreliable for the other side. The chapter Prunier added to his book on the Rwanda Crisis (1997) as a response to criticism of readers and colleagues that he was too positive on the current regime is a perfect example of this. And as Pottier (2002) clearly shows, the truth, like in post-genocide Rwanda, can easily be manipulated for political gain. If ever it is possible to stay neutral as a researcher, it is not the case in Rwanda.

Secondly the situation in Rwanda is changing fast, very fast. Above I have described some examples regarding the *gacaca* and the trial of *génocidaires*. The same seems to be true for the political arena, judicial independence, human rights and other fields in society. This means that 'the' truth in many cases is only the truth for a rather short period of time. This also means that speculations on what will happen in the near future are flourishing, or, *vice versa*, that many statements on what will happen in the (near) future are mere speculations. Added to this are the many speculations on the motives of the ruling elite for certain decisions: the majority of the decisions are allegedly to be directed by negative motivations.[130] In such a situation it seems more productive to look at the facts than speculate about what might be the motive for what is and might be in the future. Doing justice to *gacaca*, or: giving *gacaca* a fair trial, is easier said than done. That is the reality.

---

[129] And is in particular troublesome of course when stated by Rwandans themselves. The ancient Kretenzers are alive again.

[130] An example from a report of Human Rights Watch of 2001 about the establishment of the National Human Rights Commission in Rwanda: 'It is too early to tell whether the Commission will function independently enough to help improve the situation of human rights in Rwanda.' You would say that little can be said then about this Commission and the future. But Human Rights Watch continues: 'Given the strong governmental links of the majority of its members, it *may* prefer to work through personal contacts behind the scenes rather than through public criticism of abuses. While this *may* help resolve individual cases, it will do little towards developing real respect for human rights in Rwanda' [quoted in Sarkin (2001, 155); italics added, RHH]. It *may* be true; it *may* be false. It may be interesting to study the way NGOs comment on what happens in a country and the results of their interventions.

XVI. 'REASON' AND 'TRUTH' IN INTERNATIONAL CRIMINAL JUSTICE – A CRIMINOLOGICAL PERSPECTIVE ON THE CONSTRUCTION OF EVIDENCE IN INTERNATIONAL TRIALS

Uwe Ewald[1]

1. INTRODUCTION: REASON AND EVIDENCE IN INTERNATIONAL CRIMINAL JUSTICE

1.1. WHY SHOULD WE UNDERSTAND INTERNATIONAL EVIDENCE CRIMINOLOGICALLY?

Much has been written from the international law and politics perspective[2] about the emerging system of international criminal justice.[3] However this is just the beginning of a criminological reflection more than sixty years after

---

[1]   The views expressed herein are those of the author alone and do not necessarily reflect the views of the International Tribunal or the United Nations in general. I am indebted to Norman Farrell, Principal Legal Director at the OTP of the ICTY, for his comments and criticism of an earlier draft of this article. I am also grateful for editing assistance and advice by Sarojani Lakhan.

[2]   As evidenced by the continuous production of articles in international law journals such as the Journal of International Criminal Justice or the Criminal Law Forum there is a vast amount of literature reflecting on the legal developments and the case law in international criminal justice. See also Sands (ed.) (2003), Aksar (2004), Kerr (2004), Zifcak (2005), Watkins (2006), Moghalu (2006), Bohlander (ed.) (2007), Mangold (2007).

[3]   The term 'international criminal justice' as used in this chapter follows the understanding, e.g. presented by Scharf: 'The emerging system of international criminal justice is composed of a spectrum of institutions, from purely international courts (such as the International Criminal Court and the *ad hoc* International Criminal Tribunal for the former Yugoslavia (ICTY) and Rwanda (ICTR)), to hybrid international-domestic tribunals (such as the *ad hoc* Court for East Timor, the Special Court for Sierra Leone and the Extraordinary Chambers in the Courts of Cambodia), to purely domestic courts and war crimes commissions. A recent addition to that list, which falls somewhere between hybrid tribunals and domestic courts is the so-called "internationalised domestic tribunal", exemplified by the Bosnian War Crimes Chamber in Sarajevo and the Iraqi High Tribunal in Baghdad' (Scharf 2007, 258–259). Issues such as amnesty laws, truth commissions, extradition or mutual legal assistance, although belonging to the field of international criminal justice, are not considered within this article.

Nuremberg. Although a constant production of books and articles exist which approach international crime[4] and justice from a non-legal, social science perspective,[5] the analysis of the subtle evidentiary processes of reconstructing the material side of international crimes as presented within factual crime theories based on admitted evidence is not yet thoroughly studied. Thus, it comes as no surprise that criminological research on the internal mechanisms of the evidentiary production and the final presentation of factual truth in international criminal justice is still at the beginning (Overy 2001; Salter & Charlesworth 2006).

Official representations of factual 'truth' about international crimes are commonly presented in the light of objectivity and fairness. Against this backdrop, the evidentiary methods applied in international courts and tribunals in reconstructing facts of specific crime bases and their linkage to complex and systematic designs or plans developed by some 'higher-ups' are presented as safeguards of an unbiased approach to the reconstruction of past criminal events (Robinson 2005, 1039). ICTY judgments generally refer to those methods in relation to principles or 'General Considerations regarding the Evaluation of Evidence'.[6] In paragraph 21 of the Brdjanin trial judgment the Trial Chamber states:

> 'Every criminal trial involves two issues: first, that the crimes charged have been committed and, second, that an accused is responsible for those crimes. The object of evidence is to ascertain the truth of the facts with respect to these two issues, in order to enable the Trial Chamber to arrive at a conclusion, because its duty is to decide the issues solely upon the evidence before it.'

On the other hand there is an obvious awareness about limitations to the judicial generation of 'true' statements about the factual reality of crimes.

> 'The unfortunate but obvious fact that, for various reasons, this Tribunal has never had and never will have the opportunity to hear all the persons allegedly most responsible in one procedure creates additional problems. The Trial Chamber is aware that the possibility of divergences from, or even contradictions with, findings in other cases cannot be excluded because they are based on different evidence tendered and admitted (...). The Trial Chamber has endeavoured to come as close as possible to the truth. However, the Chamber is aware that no absolute truth exists.'[7]

---

[4]   The term 'international crime' as used in this chapter refers to serious violations of international humanitarian law and covers in particular the so-called core crimes, also known as Article 5 crimes, referring to Article 5 of the Rome Statute of the ICC, such as war crimes, crimes against humanity and genocide.

[5]   See for references bibliography at www.supranationalcriminology.org.

[6]   See, e.g. Brdjanin trial judgment, para. 20–36.

[7]   Stakic trial judgment, para. 20, 21.

Yet, no assessment exists as to the empirically measurable criteria to determine when the relativity of 'truth' becomes an issue for injustice and unfairness other than concepts like the 'interest of justice' or 'beyond reasonable doubt'. Those issues of unreliability of judicial methods are generally studied, e.g. under the headline of 'miscarriage of justice' (Ginzburg 1999; Nobles 2000; Knoops 2006; Huff & Killias forthcoming) and are furthermore widely evidenced in dissenting opinions of judges and in the appeals proceedings at the ICTY and ICTR where substantial changes in the assessment of the facts of the crimes raise some questions in regard to the reliability of judicial methods of objectively reconstructing the relevant historical reality of international crimes within the tribunal's (in particular prosecution's) internal processes of evidence production.

Hence, there is another well-known 'external' challenge in regard to the objectivity of international prosecution and adjudication and this is the tension between politics and law, power and judiciary. This causes risks for international criminal justice to be selective and biased, in historical as well as current perspectives as just recently stated by Carla Del Ponte (2007a). This issue is widely discussed in the context of universalism, double standard (Weiss, Crahan & Goering 2004, 63, 123) and possible abuse of international law as 'Global Revenge' (Köchler 2003).

Criminological research is needed for a better understanding of both the 'internal' methods of evidence production during international criminal proceedings and the impact of 'external' politics in the evidentiary process in international criminal justice beyond legal discourses on ambivalent evidentiary findings and political disputes and power struggles about the 'right' concept of international justice.

This paper suggests that theory-guided analysis of the manner in which international evidence[8] (May & Wierda 2002; Tochilowsky 2005 and 2006) is constructed provides a key to understanding those sophisticated 'internal' and 'external' factors and mechanisms of evidence and 'truth' production in international criminal justice within a context of global governance. The anatomy of the international evidentiary process as part of a 'regime of truth' (Foucault 1980) will allow the placement of the judicial statements of factual 'truth' (as presented in trial and Appeals Chamber judgments) in the context of their ways of production and thereby shed some light on the 'variety of truth regimes, truth's contingency [which] is dramatically exemplified in transitional context' (Teitel 2000, 72). The general assumption is that there is an underlying, tacit pattern to the diversity of partly ambivalent influential factors determining the international

---

8   The term 'international evidence' is used in this article in a similar way May and Wierda (2002) reflect on evidence in international trials. Hence, it is not meant to draw an artificial line between evidence in national jurisdictions and evidence in international courts.

evidentiary process and aiming at a rationality to facilitate global social control by means of international criminal justice.

The analysis of both the 'internal' methods of evidence production and the impact of 'external' factors on the evidentiary process should also assist in explaining differences in the final construct of war and other international crimes, which may arise between current international courts, e.g. the ICC versus the ICTY or ICTR but also historical diversity in international criminal justice (see section 1.2 of this chapter).

The process of fact finding before international (and hybrid or domestic) courts is multi-layered, framed by Rules of Procedure and Evidence. It is within that framework that 'collected data' on facts of international crimes is presented. The court decides which 'information' is admitted and is called evidence. From this body of evidence findings are made about what happened and whether the person accused is responsible, thus factual findings are presented as 'knowledge' on crimes and individual criminal responsibility. These findings reflect 'judicial understanding' and eventually 'truth', as coined in judgments, in relation to those crimes. The analysis of this process of qualification of factual information over a series of steps which leads to the ultimate conclusion of 'truth' may assist in developing a non-legal understanding of the construction of international crimes. Given that 'understanding' requires concepts (other than 'acquaintance' or 'knowledge' – see Sandwell 1996, 58), and provided that the nature of those analytical processes in international criminal justice does not occur at the judicial surface or can be directly derived from announcements or declarations of those representing the international criminal justice's 'regime of truth'[9] itself but requires a theoretical framework to make sense of the particularities and ambivalences of the evidentiary process (see part 2).

In its empirical part (see section 3) this chapter tries to illustrate part of the actuality of evidence production at the ICTY based on a distinct question: Who provides and selects evidentiary data (with particular emphasis on the role of expert witnesses) finally admitted by Trial Chambers into evidence to constitute the 'judicial truth' of war crimes?

The interpretation of empirical findings against the backdrop of the formerly outlined theoretical framework might shed some light on the political economy of international criminal justice and its role within the wider framework of global governance (section 4).

---

[9]   See for a more detailed explanation of this Foucauldian notion below, point 2.3.

XVI. 'Reason' and 'Truth' in International Criminal Justice

1.2. REASON AND EVIDENCE – HISTORICAL CONTINUITY AND CURRENT DIFFERENCES

Looking back at the Nuremberg trial which has been portrayed as the victory of law over vengeance (Bass 2000; Chesterman 2005, 31), and as 'A Call for Reasoned Justice' (Breyer 1999), it becomes apparent why evidence and its tested presentation at international trial hearings after WWII became the pivotal matter of concern for parties and the court, as Robert H. Jackson stated for his work at the Nuremberg Tribunal (Jackson 1945).

After controversial disputes among Roosevelt, Churchill and Stalin, 'Britain and France were not very enthusiastic about the idea of a trial, but Washington was. The Soviet Union was still for putting the Nazis up against a wall and shooting them' (Downie, Heydecker & Leeb 1962, 79–80). As recently disclosed government documents reveal from the war cabinet's discussions, Churchill strongly opposed the idea of war crimes trials and wanted to execute Hitler in an electric chair and demanded to 'Execute the principal criminals as outlaws' as late as April 1945 (Crossland 2006, 143–144). Finally the delegates of the four victorious powers reached an agreement on 26 June 1945 in London that power should be replaced by legal reasoning in criminal prosecutions of war criminals of the defeated regime. Thus the Nuremberg trial marks the historical milestone where the rule of strength and power (which was free to decide about reactions (or non-reactions) to war crimes or crimes against humanity and genocide) was replaced by the enlightenment principle of law and reason in criminal justice (Bosch 1970, 96). What was proclaimed by Cesare Beccaria (Beccaria [1764] 1995, 34) and Johann Paul Anselm Feuerbach, who coined the principle of *nullum crimen, nulla poena sine praevia lege poenali* (see Ambos 2006, 17–23 on the historical background of this principle going back as far as the 13th century) for modern criminal law centuries ago, finally became true for international law. International crimes and individual liability had to be proven by reliable and tested information on material facts of the crimes, that is by *international evidence*; thus, criminal evidence and reasoning became the crucial cornerstone for the construction of international crimes and the verdict on individual guilt based on it. Consequently, the chief prosecutor in Nuremberg, Robert Jackson, saw his work primarily in collecting evidence[10] to prove the magnitude of crimes and to prevent denial so that future generations would not doubt their historical reality (Jackson 1945, 11; Bernstein 1947; Taylor 1992, 146; Breyer 1999, 40–41).

The generation of evidence at the Nuremberg Tribunal was almost exclusively a matter for the prosecution. All information tendered into evidence was directly generated by the prosecutors and investigators from different sources but mainly

---

[10] 'We must establish incredible events by credible evidence' (Jackson 1945, 5).

from documents created by the defendants.[11] The Nuremberg trials have been portrayed as being mainly based on documentary evidence, that is, written materials authored by the accused themselves or through members of their respective institutions and organisations; eyewitness testimony was marginalised and not considered to be more effective by Jackson.[12] However, in addition to Nazi documents, 'millions of feet of captured moving picture film' and '25,000 captured still photographs' had been examined by the prosecution (Breyer 1999, 41). Footage taken by army units had been shown at trial and was considered 'the presentation of the prosecution's most dramatic evidence of the Nazis' malignancy' (Douglas 1995).

In total, 33 prosecution witnesses and 61 witnesses of the defence gave testimony. Thousands of affidavits were produced to try 21 accused within less than a year. Further affidavits based on interrogation by commissioners provided the basis for six comprehensive reports (Nuremberg Judgment, 1946). What is remarkable for the understanding of international evidence production in contrast to current international courts and tribunals is the clear position of the prosecution and the Nuremberg Tribunal to control the production of evidentiary information based on the sole authority to criminalise and punish crimes according to the IMT-Statute. Consequently, in terms of data, evidence at Nuremberg was almost exclusively presented as primary data produced for the purpose of proving individual criminal responsibility. Later on in the article, it will be shown in more detail that this appears to be one of the most significant differences between evidence presented at Nuremberg and evidence being presented at current international trials.

In contrast – not for statistical comparison but for explorative consideration – the evidentiary context for the ICTY is very different. For 67 accused at the ICTY with completed cases at the Trial Chamber level (per April 2007) more than 4,000 facts and expert witnesses, mainly eyewitnesses, have been heard. More precisely, for 'similar cases'[13] with 45 accused whose characteristics are comparable to the accused at the Nuremberg trial, the average number of prosecution witnesses

---

[11] See Nuremberg Trial Judgment, Trial of Major War Criminals Before the International Military Tribunal, Nuremberg, 14 November 1945 – 1 October 1946, Vol I (1947), 171–341. See also Breyer (1999 [1946]).

[12] 'Jackson in particular favoured the use of captured documentary evidence, material he considered 'harder' and less vulnerable to being discredited by defence attorneys practised in the art of tendentious cross-examination. Prosecution counsel William Donovan's vehement argument that a greater reliance upon eyewitness testimony would have provided the trial with 'an affirmative human aspect' led to his unceremonious removal from the prosecution team after the first week of the trial.' (Douglas 1995, footnote 10, with reference to Taylor 1992, 146–149).

[13] Cases with guilty pleas, single acquittals or referred cases according to Rule 11 bis of the Rules of Procedure and Evidence of the ICTY are not included in this comparison since their characteristics differ significantly from those accused at the Nuremberg trial.

who testified at trial was about 30, another 10 written witness statements were provided per accused and about 500 exhibits were used at trial on average for each of those 45 'similar' accused. The respective numbers for the defence were 20, 5 and 220.[14] As will be shown later in detail (section 3) the sources and originators of evidence and in particular the role of witnesses differ considerably from those of the Nuremberg trial, since '(oral) examination of witnesses is envisaged as the core method of presenting evidence' (Bonomy 2007, 3).

In light of these differences in the production and presentation of evidence at ICTY trials compared to the Nuremberg Tribunal, the question arises whether these differences just represent contingent historical diversity or substantial change in the development of international criminal justice. However, there is a vast diversity of factors which influence the evidentiary process in international trials and in particular the availability of potentially relevant data on factual matters at all times and it requires more in-depth academic research to verify the assumption on historical paradigm changes in international evidence production.

Additionally, there is another contrast. The manner in which prosecutions are conducted and evidence is produced at the ICC, *prima facie* appears quite different from the evidentiary process at the ICTY (Murphy 2006). And indeed there is a different historical context for the emergence and operation of the ICTY and the ICC which might explain part of the difference between the ICTY approach to more comprehensive coverage of international crimes and the more focused and selective prosecution strategy at the ICC. Prosecutor Carla Del Ponte referred to these contextual differences when she compared the time at which she started to lead the prosecutorial process at the ICTY in 1999 with the changed global situation in 2007. Her credo is that with the destruction of the Twin Towers in New York, the vision of a just and democratic world order collapsed and those ambitious criminal prosecutions of international crimes (which emerged in the historical context at the interception of the ICTY) evaporated into thin air (Del Ponte 2007a).

Moreover, while often a rather direct link has been drawn between Nuremberg and The Hague (Ferencz 1999; Sands 2003; McGoldrick 2003; Aksar & Cass 2004; Kerr 2004), there have been in fact three periods where visions and principles of international criminal justice have been formed:

Firstly, from the post-Nuremberg period till the end of the 1980s where basic principles of international criminal law had been established, but 'realpolitik seemed to negate the principles of responsibility and accountability declared at Nuremberg' (Cooper 1999, 11).

---

[14] The number of witnesses and exhibits produced by chambers is rather marginal and has not been included. It should also be noted that the figures presented above are generated from non-standardised information in judgments and transcripts and present only approximations.

Secondly, the sometimes euphorically observed serial collapse of authoritarian states, eventually symbolised by the fall of the Berlin Wall on 11 November, 1989, that produced, what could be called, a 'window of universalistic utopia' where under the headline of 'transitional justice' human rights standards of the western world (De Gaay Fortman 1990; Bleiker 2000; Bell, Nathan & Peleg (Eds.) 2001) should become not only guiding but binding for the rest of the world (Teitel, 2000). Hence, it was the period where the *ad hoc* tribunals and other hybrid courts were created and where the foundations for the ICC and the 'end of impunity' were laid.

Thirdly, 11/9 was followed by 9/11 twelve years later and the 'war of terror' created a roll-back situation where the idea of a universal human rights standard was challenged and undermined by a double standard. Realpolitik once again questioned basic principles of the international rule of law, and the notion of terrorism entered international criminal law in different ways (Boyle 2004; Weiss, Crahan & Goering 2004).

All these historical changes are crucial in explaining the nature of the current organisation of international criminal justice and the production of international evidence due to the simple fact that international criminal justice operates in an international environment. But still, despite all those differences in historical context among for instance the Nuremberg Tribunal, the ICTY and the ICC, I suggest that the dialectics of 'reason' and 'evidence' in international criminal justice as established with the Nuremberg Tribunal and further developed during the proceedings at the ICTY (and other international courts) will remain for current and future international courts. This includes the assumption that the analysis of ICTY experiences could provide useful findings for future international trials.

The understanding of the deeper foundations for the actual meaning of 'reason' and 'evidence' in international justice will finally lead to notions of sovereignty and biopower and the (post-) modern forms of sophisticated techniques of global social control (Passavant & Dean 2004, 166, 206–209) which are significantly linked to discursive strategies based on reason and rationality and integrated into security-related power-and-knowledge techniques.[15]

---

[15] 'Exposure of life to mortal danger is instantiated through different discourses of danger and problematisations of security. To put it in the biopolitical terms… just as there is no single way of recruiting species life into the strategising of power relations - what Foucault called the operation of biopower and biopolitics - there is no single way of exposing life to mortal danger and death. Different problematisations of security and war will depend upon how species life is known and classified, as well as what power/knowledge techniques and political rationalities are employed. This even applies to regimes committed 'in good faith' to the promotion of species life. Nor is this a paradox. It is an effect of the logic of those regimes, a function of their biopolitical generative principles of formation. That said, a further, more threatening, logic is deeply installed in the biopolitics of governance: one that leads to a hyperbolisation of the governmental preoccupation with security.' (Dillon 2004, 78).

2. BASELINES OF A CONCEPTUAL FRAMEWORK: INTERNATIONAL CRIMINAL JUSTICE AS PART OF PUBLIC DISCOURSE – 'TRUTH' AND INTERNATIONAL EVIDENCE

Having shed some light on the pivotal meaning of evidence in international criminal justice and its historical link with the principle of reason (vs. might), emerging after WWII, the following sections will describe baselines of a theoretical framework for this article on how to conceptualise evidence in light of the functioning of international criminal justice. Quite obviously, within the limits of this chapter this attempt can only be preliminary by approaching selected issues which require further elaboration.

2.1. HISTORICAL TRUTH AND EVIDENCE IN INTERNATIONAL CRIMINAL JUSTICE

It cannot be denied that the factual description of international crimes does not qualify as history, yet it is a widely accepted position that judgments on international crimes produce historical records (Expert Report 2005; Tieger & Shin 2005, 4; Alcock 2006). Thus, there is a strong link between the evidentiary narrative on the facts of a crime and historical findings, and therefore lessons from historical science can be useful, for analogy, towards a better understanding of the epistemological difficulties to 'ascertain the truth' during criminal trials in international criminal justice. In 'Defence of History' Richard J. Evans reflects on developments in modern historical science where historical research has either been considered to be an evaluation of objective facts to establish 'objective historical truth' or mainly as a product of historians significantly influenced by their personal view and understanding. While the first refers historical analysis primarily to sources and their credibility, the latter emphasises the historian as the originator of the historical narrative and as the main object to be studied to understand historical statements. Yet, these approaches have been confronted with post-modern discourse theories emerging in the 80s which tend to deny the existence of 'historical truth' and 'objectivity' as such; history is written in the perspective of the presence and the collection of facts is from the outset directed by an *a priori* assumption of the historian. In other words, there is no pre-existing pattern in history and in the end history provides facts in support of all kinds of theories and all it comes down to is the choosing of the 'right' facts. Finally, regardless of the manner of generation, historical knowledge is political knowledge (Evans 1997, see in particular Chapters 1–3).

With respect to the central issue of this chapter, which is the exploration of the nature of international evidence and the practice of the evidentiary procedure in international criminal justice, the dispute in history on the possibility of 'objectivity' and 'truth' in the reconstruction of past events, as reflected by Evans, three key issues can be derived, for analogy, to frame the evidentiary process as a production of a selective historical knowledge about the empirical facts of international crimes.

- Understanding the past – there is a human and societal need for understanding and truth and explaining the past developed throughout modern and post-modern times for the presentation of political and judicial decisions which must present themselves as based on historical understanding. The victory of 'reason' in international criminal justice can be seen as part of this development.
- Ways of reconstructing the past – objective, fact-related truth and relativist originator produced truth, or post-modern deconstruction where discourse creates the meaning of the past, and the question of history comes down to "Whose history?" Apparently, all these perspectives can be observed in the international evidentiary process.
- Political nature of historical knowledge – no matter what method produced historical knowledge it cannot escape its political nature. A closer look at witnesses and exhibits presented as international evidence will show that this is particularly true for the evidentiary process in the international criminal justice system.

It was Nietzsche who once provocatively asked 'Why truth?' (Nietzsche [1888] 2005; Sheridan 1990, 222). Yet, even today the question appears to be a reasonable point of departure for conceptualising international evidence since the linkage between 'evidence' and 'reason' in modern criminal law has to be extended to the issue of 'material truth' (Skinnider 2005). Why? Because the issue of truth is essential for the principal functioning of international criminal justice in terms of peacemaking; former conflict parties as well as third parties to the conflict will only accept judgments from an historical perspective if the statements made about the facts of the crimes are considered to be materially true, that is they reflect facts and relations constituent for the international crime in question. Major violations of material truth (e.g. conviction of the innocent) would lead to denial and recycling of hatred rather than healing (Cohen). Thus despite some discussions on whether the concept of material truth is to be applied in international criminal justice, and the given limitations of criminal proceedings regarding the discovery of historical truth within the framework of the adversarial system as the underlying procedural approach (Bonomy 2007, 350; Hemptinne

2007, 404) the question of whether or not material truth is essential in international criminal justice is ultimately not disputed in principle (Withopf 2005, 80; Cohen 2005, 34).

Hence in the context of constructing international crime, the notion of 'material truth' is the logical consequence of 'reason' in international criminal justice, in other words as long as rationality and 'reason' are required to establish international crimes (even relative), 'material truth' is inevitable to give a judgment the authority of being 'fair', 'just' and 'authoritative'.[16] It is in fact the ultimate claim to be 'true' in regard to the factual issues of alleged crimes that allows judgments and judicial decisions to demand legally binding strength and authority. Therefore 'truth' provides the normative power needed for further law enforcement referring to the former conflicting parties as well as to third parties to the conflict. Hence, 'material truth' is the common ground and universally shared value for all parties involved. As already stated, in view of international judges it is the 'object of evidence (...) to ascertain the truth of the facts' (Brdjanin trial judgment, para. 21). And again, despite differences in the procedural approaches at various international courts there seems to be no significant disagreement about the principle of 'material truth' in international criminal law, and that the 'standards of proof' aim to establish objectively true statements about the facts of a crime. Eventually the answer to Nietzsche's question 'Why truth?' applied to the domain of international criminal justice comes down to the logical need of a last indisputable rational prerequisite to be stated within the judicial judgment and this is that the facts of the crime have happened as an objective historical reality. The rationality of modern criminal law requires proving of the factual existence of the criminal event. If the existence of an international crime cannot be proven by (accepted) evidence, judgments would not have a plausible rationality. It is this plausible rationality which links the fact finding legal process with factual social reality. As a consequence, without a final commitment to the principle of 'material truth', international criminal courts would not be authorised in a context of peacekeeping and global governance. The acceptance of international

---

16   The following has been stated by a Trial Chamber, interestingly under the headline 'The Duty of the Prosecutor': "'Da mihi factum, dabo tibi jus'" – give me (all) the facts and I will present you the applicable law (and a just decision). This wise Roman principle unfortunately is not part of our Rules. However, under the mandate of this *ad hoc* Tribunal the Prosecutor, being part of the Tribunal, is in principle duty bound to present all the evidence available. The fundament of our Tribunal is the Statute based on Chapter VII of the Charter of the United Nations established as a measure to maintain or restore international peace and security. However, there is no peace without justice; there is no justice without truth, meaning the entire truth and nothing but the truth.' Deronjic Trial Chamber judgment, 30 March 2004, para. 6. *See* also Provisional *Verbatim* Record of the 3217th Meeting of the Security Council, 25 May 1993, Statement by the Representative of the United States: 'Truth is the cornerstone of the rule of law, and it will point towards individuals, not peoples, as perpetrators of war crimes. And it is only the truth that can cleanse the ethnic and religious hatreds and begin the healing process'.

judgments is not primarily related to a formal authority of the criminal court but refers to the rationality of the judgment narrative based on indisputable evidence about the facts of crimes which match the collective experience of former conflict parties.

However, it is as often not the announcement of a principle but its reality that decides whether a principle is 'living' or not. Against the backdrop of 'evidence' and 'truth', as discussed here, it means the differentiation between the principle of 'material truth' and the reality of 'judicial truth' (i.e. what is formally presented as 'truth') within the narrative of a judgment. The matter is far more complicated than just referring to the inevitable principle of 'material truth' and the commitment to an 'ascertainment of truth' through an international court and the parties involved in a case. Moreover, as it is true for all principles, they can be broken in the name of the very principle itself.

As the following statement of defence counsel in the context of a dispute about disclosure issues at a pre-trial status conference indicates that there are quite different views on what is 'material' to the 'truth' in a case from the, more often than not, ambivalent perspectives of the parties and the court:

'And I think coming back to your legal tradition, Your Honour, and in the continental system, you would be entitled to the entire file, all of it. You would look at it. And why is that? You certainly don't rely on the Prosecutor to tell you what is material for you to find the truth in the case. *[emphasis – U.E.] Well, the same thing here. I certainly don't want the Prosecutor telling me what he thinks is material in my preparation of my defence, because I may prepare my case slightly differently than he or his colleagues believe that to be.'* (Transcript IT-02–60, p. 84)

In fact, it is the controversy among the actors in the courtroom about the type of evidentiary material to accept to infer the factual 'truth' of a case, which drives and determines international criminal proceedings. It is that the final statement of judicial truth in a case depends quite obviously not only and (at least for some cases) perhaps not primarily, on the available factual information but on the procedure and decision-making of what information is considered to be relevant and admitted into evidence and the rules and practices on how to interpret the admitted evidentiary information. The dispute around that issue is not primarily an effort to determine the best and most reliable methods to 'ascertain the truth' but to achieve quite contradicting objectives expressed in the (mostly) antagonistic case theories of prosecution and defence. Thus, the party-related interest in a particular outcome of a trial – even more so in an adversarial system – tends to override the interest in an 'objective truth' – 'objective' at least in the sense that no interest in reconstructing the past exists other than to establish the reality of the past facts with most objective methods available and to produce unbiased interpretations. Yet, the question arises whether criminal law in general and current evidentiary approaches of international criminal justice in particular, are potentially capable of meeting such a standard of objectivity and of establishing the 'historical record' of serious violations of international humanitarian law (Christie 2004).

There is indication that the announced commitment to 'material truth' is at risk of being rather an ideology than the basis for a common methodology. On the contrary, the practical methods to present evidence aim to persuade the court to accept one of the case theories. At a different level this contradiction is greatly presented by US positions conflicting in themselves, when, on the one hand, the search for truth is declared to be the 'cornerstone of the rule of law' (Provisional Verbatim Record 1993) and on the other, the ICC is doubted as being capable of guaranteeing a fair and just procedure (Gready 2004, 19; Williams 2005). Additionally, the conduct of international criminal trials by an adversarial process 'can be counter-productive (...) [and] is not the best way of getting the truth where detailed exploration and analysis of documentary evidence is required' (Bonomy 2007, 3). Ultimately, the struggle about 'judicial truth' is not necessarily about truth-telling about past crimes, but presenting a version of the 'truth' which persuades the judges in order to get the final approval through a judgment.

Given some reality to these critical thoughts, it would support the assumption that the evidentiary process is not *per se* a 'just' and 'objective' evaluation of objective facts of the crime on the one hand, and failure or miscarriage of justice related to flawed analytical and interpretative methods on the other (although it might appear as such), but mainly a process in which selective information about the facts of the crime is presented and interpreted to support or reject factual case theories, designed to meet party-related interests, aiming to be acknowledged as 'judicial truth'. With some simplification, it can be said that what counts is the control over the production of 'judicial truth' rather than to be as close as possible to the 'material truth' of a case.

All this refers again to the ways of reconstructing the past as discussed earlier with Evans' reflections on historical science. Applied to the issues of international evidence the process of reconstructing the facts of a crime could be interpreted as 'objective', 'originator-related' or 'discursive', and I claim that all three perspectives can help to understand international evidence and the analytical process in international criminal justice. Thus it is quite obvious that an attempt to describe international evidence from a criminological view mainly as a joint enterprise of actors involved in investigation and other criminal proceedings to discover the 'objective historical truth' would be quite naïve. To explain the relationship and finally contradiction between 'material' and 'judicial truth' in international criminal justice in more detail we have to analyse the politico-societal context in which international evidence is produced. The internal evidentiary process reflecting the safeguards to guarantee objectivity and fairness throughout the proceedings which decides whether or not the historical truth arrives as a 'historical record' in the construct of the judicial truth can only be understood if these external influential factors are reflected.

2.2. NEW GLOBAL SECURITY DISCOURSE, HEGEMONIC KNOWLEDGE AND EVIDENCE

In an attempt to consider some major external factors which influence and determine the judicial truth production process within the international criminal justice system, the following section of this chapter deals with the aspect of the institutional framework within which international justice operates. In light of the societal nature of historical knowledge, whether as a 'finding' in historical science or 'historical record' of international crimes in international courts, it becomes apparent that the methods of international evidence production must be placed in the wider context of the politico-societal framework – the new global security discourse.

International evidence and new global security discourse. The evidentiary reconstruction of atrocities is substantially linked to present situations where those past issues of collective violence in armed conflicts are evaluated and defined. Thus the emergence of the current international criminal justice system is related to global politics and governance, in particular to a new global security discourse where, from a critical perspective, 'security is seen to be a function of social construction, integral to successful development and dependent upon the extension of liberal democratic values and respect for human rights' (Dillon, 2004, 80). Literature on global governance in international relations and security studies (Cooper, English & Thakur 2002; Mendes & Mehmet 2003; Larner & Walters 2004) refers to new trends in the definition of global security in particular after September 11, where security is more and more related to 'survival'. Existential security threats are constructed within a discourse and usually linked to extraordinary measures of counter reaction. For the time being, this scenario appears in a constellation where 'survival, priority of action and urgency' (Wæver 2003) determines the basis for a (mainly military and international justice-related) global security design. Wæver describes a 'Dialectics of Security' which identifies main 'sectors', 'referent objects' and 'survival issues' which are all reflected within substantive international criminal law.

Permanent construction of targets for a global security machinery is an ongoing process and amounts to the scenario of a global war situation ('war on terror') with low level conflicts and military police actions and legitimate use of other coercive means, such as political, economic and international justice.

Graph 1. Dialectics of Security (main examples)

Sector	Referent Object	Survival
Societal	Nation	Identity
Political/military	State	Sovereignty
Economic	Firm	No entitlement!
Environmental	'Nature'	Sustainability

(Source: Wæver, 2003)

Although there is no commonly shared definition of 'global governance' and its relation to human security, there is some agreement that 'global governance' does not refer to a 'world government' but rather to an international political process of global structuring and organisation (Wood & Shearing 2007, 63). The process of global governance is mainly based on a network of international and supranational institutions which create a security discourse on social reality on a global scale which provides a topical framework on global security issues. Moreover, in regard to international criminal justice, this mechanism provides evidentiary information to international courts. Consequently, the system of international criminal justice is part of this new network of international and supranational institutions which creates a certain part of this global social reality, and this is the judicial-security segment of the globalisation process. More precisely, international courts are highly dependent on some of the international players as a 'giant without arms and legs', to borrow a metaphor by Antonio Cassese which was used to describe the situation of the ICTY (Cassese 1998, 9).

The nature of that global judicial security process is not yet fully developed (see the interesting position of Burke-White 2006) but there are certainly tendencies which can be observed. Elsewhere, I have tried to capture two contradicting views (Ewald 2006) to be able to approach the international criminal justice system from contrasting perspectives. One perspective follows the UN-concept of 'Responsibility to Protect' (R2P), where the definition and practical determination of a global judicial security problem is linked to the universal principle of gross violation of human rights, while the other, which Hardt and Negri (2000) refer to as interest-related selection and definition of those judicial security issues, that is that gross violations of human rights and mass suffering does not determine *per se* such a judicial security problem for global governance but only if it touches the interests of the 'civilised world'.

Although it is certain that the international criminal justice system is part of the global security scenario and in particular designed to approach threats defined as 'existential' for the 'survival' of humankind, as described as 'Dialectics of security', it is yet too premature to see clearly how the contradiction between those trends, the universalistic suffering-related or selective interest-related approach, reflects in the practical decision-making of the ICC from a historical perspective.

In light of the notion of a 'universal legal culture' (De Gaay Fortman 1990, 243–244) which could be based on commonly shared values across all global cultures, it appears to be possible to develop universal principles as global human rights standards. However, this requires participation vs. discrimination and partnership vs. hegemony where global consent is reached to define global threats to universal human security. Risk perception and threat scenarios would then be balanced and considered to be fair and just throughout different cultures, and overcome the difficulty 'in a non-Western world (...) that the formulation of human rights and the approach toward their implementation may be regarded as Western and alien', even though the values as such are not rejected (De Gaay Fortman 1990, 244; Bell, Nathan & Peleg 2001, 21 with a sceptical view). However, there is a widely shared belief that the new global securitisation policy promoted in the name of 'civilised nations' might end in a deadlock where practical security measures rather repress the conflict than solve it.

In view of some commentators, new frameworks of security and UN peacekeeping are at risk of 'running into the trap of potentially imposing western, universalist hegemonic discourses which may only dampen conflict down rather than solve it in the long run.' Hence these frameworks form the wider global context for international criminal justice. Instead – from this perspective – ending a conflict is more dependent on a 'harmonising' 'regime of truth' about order involving 'voices and interests of all of the actors' (Richmond 2002, 186; see an interesting discussion of these issues in Allen 2006). Others believe that existing approaches in international politics 'still tend to be a-cultural, give rise to the possibility of intervention without consent, based on western models of neo-liberal democratisation and human rights as universally descriptive' (Richmond 2002, 192). And critical questions are raised in regard to the prosecutorial strategy at the ICC. Referring to a supposed lack of will by the 'world community' Haveman claims for the ICC 'that a strict selection has to be made (...) with the danger of (seemingly) political choices' (Haveman 2006, 157).

Against this backdrop the question arises if and how international criminal justice is affected by overt or tacit hegemonic tendencies and whether and how those tendencies can be identified within the evidentiary process (Deacon 2003, 31).[17]

Factors in international politics which tend to produce risks of imposing western hegemonic discourses on non-western realities provide the context in which the above described relationship between 'material' and 'judicial truth' in international criminal justice is defined. Those factors are highly influential in selecting a situation as appropriate for international prosecution as recent examples for prosecution or non-prosecution of alleged human rights violations, e.g. in Darfur, Lebanon, Uganda, Afghanistan or Iraq. After the decision to investigate and prosecute has been made the rules and procedures of the evidentiary process of international trials become crucial in controlling the influence of these risk factors (of politicising judicial decisions) by organising the selective process of admission of evidence as well as the principles of interpretation of the admitted evidence at trial. It is the nature and practice of this process which decides 'how a rights regime creates certain types of subjectivities (victims and perpetrators) and certain types of acts (e.g. common crimes versus crimes against humanity)' (Wilson & Mitchell 2003, 5). Yet, as stated in regard to the United States, there is an 'ideological vacillation between cosmopolitan idealism and unilateral realpolitik' (Fichtelberg 2006, 766).

Rationality-hegemony linkage and international evidence. The ultimate question in regard to any possible bias is whether the evidentiary product of 'judicial truth' on international crimes can claim to be sufficiently 'material', that is reflecting the historical facts of the crime and its context despite a 'skeletonisation' of reality. Yet, there is reason for a critical review since very often participants in armed conflicts find themselves stripped of their subjectivity by evidentiary narratives presented as 'true' crime stories in judgments. And as Judge Bonomy states, referring to the situation in which witnesses from the former Yugoslavia find themselves, in court at The Hague: 'The adversarial process is totally alien to the Balkan culture' (Bonomy 2007, 3). Thus, the position of these witnesses to participate in the 'ascertainment of truth' might be limited.

The risk of a significant disjunction of 'material' and 'judicial truth' in international criminal justice, as described above, through hegemonic discourse is usually disguised by a rationality (and formal legal language) which – from its own perspective – presents facts and inferences in an 'objective' way and meets the formal requirements of a reasoned judgment. Standard formulations to display

---

[17] The importance of this issue also relates directly to the legality and legitimacy of international criminal justice, assuming that '(a) system of "international criminal justice" might be thought to require some consensus on the existence and values of the "international community"' (McGoldrick 2003, 107). And this question appears to be in particular valid for the legal context since 'law skeletonises social narratives, since whatever the law is after, it is not the "whole story"' (Wilson & Mitchell 2003, 5).

and demonstrate compelling rational inferences within judgments are references to the 'beyond reasonable doubt' standard or that no 'reasonable hearing of the facts' could reach a different conclusion. The need to present the factual crime theory of a case in a logical and rationally understandable way and yet as part of a hegemonic discourse can be conceptualised as 'rationality-hegemony linkage'. If international criminal justice is understood as part of an 'official discourse'[18] which in late modernity represents a (new) supra-national legal and administrative rationality (Burton & Carlen 1979) this 'rationality-hegemony linkage' still exists in late modernity[19] and can be applied to the field of international criminal justice and international politics (Carlen, Pratt & Gilligan 2004, 4). This perspective allows one to put the international criminal justice 'internal' points of reference such as the 'end of impunity' or the idea of 'prevention and deterrence' aside, set by those in charge for the functioning of the international criminal justice system, clearly aiming at institutional justification, and to approach the understanding of international criminal justice from an external point of view. With Burton and Carlen we might ask whether the official claims to objectivity, impartiality, fairness and rational analysis indeed lead to some irrefutable version of the 'truth' or whether international criminal justice as other formal bodies should be primarily seen as producers of a legal and administrative rationality in a newly emerging system of global governance. From this perspective, international criminal justice could be understood as a necessary part of political and ideological hegemony (Burton & Carlen 1979, 48) at a supra-national level where legitimisation and representation of 'truth' in international crimes intend to repair crises of international legitimacy and close debates on historical facts of collective conflicts on a global scale. It should be noted that all these reflections serve rather the purpose of hypotheses generation than represent firm assessments of the international criminal justice system.

I suggest that one of the main ways this linkage between rationality and hegemony is reproduced in international criminal justice is the generation of international evidence since evidence provides the knowledge which, as the only

---

[18] According to Burton and Carlen, official discourse is '(...) the systemisation of modes of argument that proclaim the state's legal and administrative rationality' (Burton & Carlen 1979, 48). This definition could be 'translated' for the international discourse on international crimes as 'systematisation of modes of arguments that proclaim the international communities' legal and administrative rationality to prosecute international crimes'. Thus, states committed to the core values of the 'international community' agree in principle on fighting international crimes, in particular genocide and terrorism.

[19] 'It would seem then that this rationality/hegemony linkage may still be important to the legitimacy of the late modern state and its institutions. Indeed, as the impacts of globalisation gather pace, the importance of this linkage assumes supra-national and international dimensions in the management of global markets and contemporary conflicts such as the war on terrorism, the management of social disorder and the conduct of war crimes tribunals.' (Pratt & Gilligan 2004, 4).

available and admitted knowledge at trial, frames the rational definition and inferences finally presented in judgments. Thus, the selection of sources and originators of evidentiary information and ultimately the judicial decision-making on the presentation, admission and rational use of evidence provide the functional context in which the hegemony of normative models is reproduced as 'knowledge' and 'truth' and (selective) criminalisation strategies are conducted.

However, other than at times of the Nuremberg trial, current representations of states within the international community are rather heterogeneous and intertwined with non-governmental organisations; moreover the international public is not merely represented by state authorities since a whole organisational system of civil society and grass root movements have emerged and participated in the discursive enterprise to rationalise social reality, including and in particular gross human rights violations and international crimes. In other words, the function of 'truth'-production in international crime and terrorism to close controversial discourses on past violent conflicts and to proclaim a new (global) legal and administrative rationality based on basic human rights values requires an integration of a multitude of actors who are involved in the production of 'truths'. With respect to the generation of international evidence the loss of state monopoly for top-down production of evidence, as ascertained for the prosecution at the Nuremberg Tribunal, requires the acceptance of multiple originators of evidentiary information to produce acceptable results in the representation of 'truth' where the judicial actors at trial, in particular the prosecutors and finally the judges, operate as (rather powerful) gate keepers in the evidentiary process at different stages of evidentiary knowledge production.

2.3. 'REGIME OF TRUTH' – MODELLING THE OPERATIONAL PRACTICE OF INTERNATIONAL CRIMINAL JUSTICE

The Foucauldian notion of 'regime of truth' (Foucault 1980) can serve as the next step to operationalise the various dimensions of knowledge production through the evidentiary process within international criminal justice (as described before) and to understand the practical details of this process as an outcome of the conduct and decision-making of their actors. However, while some authors state that the 'teleological Grand History of modernisation, progress, liberal democracy, hegemonic leadership and market civilisation amounts to a disciplinary strategy of fixing a global regime of truth within the civilisational assumptions of western man' (Persaud 2002, 58), the use of a 'regime of truth' in this article does not imply *per se* that it can already clearly be stated that such a 'strategy of fixing a global regime of truth' of 'the western man' is the only possible rationale behind the emerging system of international criminal justice. Moreover, the research question pursued in this article is rather to assist in finding out whether strategies of a 'global regime of truth' can be determined by understanding international evidence and the functional mechanism of evidentiary knowledge production in international criminal justice from its internal and external perspective.

With Foucault, it is not the statement of 'truth' as such which decides the functionality, acceptance and effectiveness of definitorial powers, it is the material reality of a societal 'regime of truth' as a whole (Foucault 1980, 131). This 'material reality' is represented by the interactions of international and national players, in particular the network of institutions involved within the global securitisation process, and finally by the organisation of international courts themselves. Applied to the field of criminalising gross human rights violations this 'regime of truth' constitutes the operational practice of international criminal justice. In Foucauldian understanding, 'truth' is produced within the dominant relations of power structures as part of a public discourse. In other words, even 'judicial truth' produced in international courts has to present itself as part of this discourse rather than an authoritative statement of a judicial institution. Hagen and Levi describe this complexity and dependence for the initial period of the ICTY in their analysis of the production of the Milosevic indictment (Hagan & Levi 2004).

This 'regime of truth' as established for the ICTY, embedded in a complex global security discourse, determines the type of disclosure for the construct of 'truth' with the announcement of indictments aiming to be accepted by a wider public. It decides the mechanisms to distinguish 'true' and 'false' statements in support of the 'truth' construct, and the techniques and procedures to generate 'truth'. The judicial 'regime of truth' also defines the status of those who are in charge to determine what is 'true'.

And finally, the 'regime of truth' reacts to public criticism and demand for further explanation, thus representing the discursive nature and socially constituted character of seeking understanding and truth. The general public perception of international judgments and 'judicial truth' as being impartial, fair and objective, politically independent and therefore legitimate depends on the way this 'truth' is discovered, socially generated, processed and finally distributed within the official global security and justice discourse.

While it would go beyond the scope of this chapter to evaluate all the elements described as constitutional for the ICTY 'regime of truth', for the sake of further operationalisation, a core issue of evidence production has been chosen for further consideration. And this is the origination of factual evidence and its processing at different procedural stages of the judicial process. The analysis of the subtle mechanisms of the origination of international evidence enables an understanding of the linkage between the external global security discourse and the internal decision-making on which potentially evidentiary information should be admitted to the judicial discourse within the framework of the judicial proceedings.

The evaluation of the role and impact of institutional and personal originators of evidentiary information goes along with Becker's notion on the importance of the context and circumstances of 'truth' production (Becker, 1967) which ultimately decides the operational functionality and finally the reconstruction of public confidence in power relationships of global governance. Thus, whether the linkage between rationality and hegemony works out depends on the acceptance of 'truth' by social actors. Only if the produced rationality is accepted by a relative majority, international criminal justice in action becomes an effective and permanent factor in the global security scenario.

Moreover, the acceptance depends on the involvement of actors within the field of global security and human rights protection such as the UN or human rights NGOs. As will be shown in section 3 of this chapter there is a great variety of international and national actors originating information later used as evidence at trial and evaluated by the prosecution, defence and finally chambers. It is the post-modern nature of truth production as a highly complex, interactive discourse of a multitude of players participating and sometimes competing over the definition of the final 'judicial truth' about past atrocities which shape the international evidentiary process. Lengthy trials and huge resources are needed to facilitate the conversion of this multi-actor evidentiary knowledge generation into a judicially formed procedure with accepted results.

The role of institutional and personal originators of factual evidence appears to be significant in understanding the structure of evidence and empirical analysis in international criminal justice and therefore the rationality-hegemony linkage as suggested above. Given that the 'regime of truth' in international criminal justice produces evidentiary rationality and reasons to establish individual criminal responsibility on the one hand and hegemony of international community human rights values on the other, the assumption is that the multitude of originators of evidentiary information in concert with the judicial authorities in international justice determine the functioning of judicial reasoning and 'truth' production. Therefore, by generating international evidence, these actors (called originators in this paper) generate the linkage between rationality of 'truth' and hegemony of human rights standards in the enforcement of normative concepts of international crimes on selected cases.

The following section presents first empirical findings[20] regarding the representation of institutional and personal originators of evidentiary information

---

[20] In light of the complexity of the research issue and given the fact that there are no further empirical studies within this particular area of international evidence production and analysis this article can't be more than a first explorative reflection based on a limited case study and summary classification of evidence used at the ICTY. Yet, further research is needed to verify

based on the cases prosecuted at the ICTY up to March 2007. As already stated this article tries to understand the production of international evidence as a key to understanding 'truth' and 'reason' in international criminal justice. Yet, the empirical part can be only explorative and rather illustrative than compellingly inferential in regard to central conceptual issues raised before. Nevertheless, the provided descriptive information gives a first impression on the participation of a variety of institutional and personal actors in the generation of international evidence and allows some quantification of evidence used in cases at the ICTY regarding the origin of evidentiary information.

3. ORIGIN OF EVIDENCE – EXPLORATIVE EMPIRICAL FINDINGS

3.1. EVIDENCE, ANALYSIS AND JUDICIAL REASONING

Before empirical figures on the involvement of institutional and personal originators of evidence[21] within the production of 'judicial truth' are presented, a brief reflection on the role of witnesses and exhibits as the material 'carriers' of evidentiary information should be introduced for a deeper understanding of the significance of 'originators', as defined here, within the international criminal justice 'regime of truth'.

The analytical process of generating evidence in international trials relates to the production of witnesses and exhibits as the only admissible evidentiary entities. Exhibit and witness lists, created by the prosecution and defence, present the entirety of finally selected evidentiary information as a result of a complex investigative-analytical process, provided in support of prosecution and defence case theories, as the only basis for judicial inference on factual crime theories.

---

the findings presented in this article. And most importantly, all figures provided to quantify evidentiary issues do not allow for reliable inferences in regard to the overall proportions of a respective issue at the ICTY since the selected cases do not fully meet the requirements for sampling.

21   'Evidence' refers to raw data, potentially containing evidentiary information, which has been generated through investigation activities or provided by third parties. This excludes OTP work products or translations (only if the translation is the only document in the collection).

Graph 2. Evidence, Analysis and Reasoning

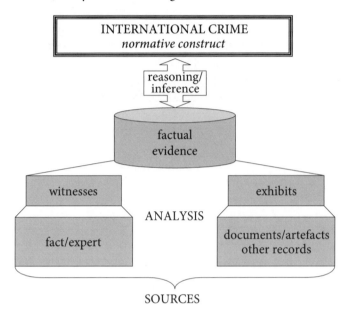

Moreover, the decision as to which evidence to use, decides the involvement of non-judicial actors (as either originators of exhibits, mostly documents, or witnesses or both) in the process of rationalising and reasoning. In preparation of witness and exhibit lists for most of the cases a time and resource-consuming analytical process is conducted, mainly by the prosecution but also by the defence and to some extent by chambers. Applied methods within that analysis of factual information on international crimes and skills of staff involved have a significant impact on the structure and content of the presented evidence.

However, the final evaluation of evidence and inferential processes conducted by Trial and Appeals Chambers during their deliberations are independent from other actors insofar as these actors as originators of exhibits or as witnesses, or judicial actors at trial cannot cross the threshold between the participation in the presentation and discussion of evidence and the ultimate interpretation of this evidence in regard to the individual criminal responsibility of the accused.

The judicial-analytical process occurs during an interactive process mainly under control of the prosecution ('burden of proof'), defence (defence case), Pre-Trial Chambers, Trial and Appeals Chambers at different procedural stages; although the role of the defence is rather reactive to the allegations of the prosecution it has an effective procedural position as a safeguard for fair and just proceedings.

Uwe Ewald

Graph 3

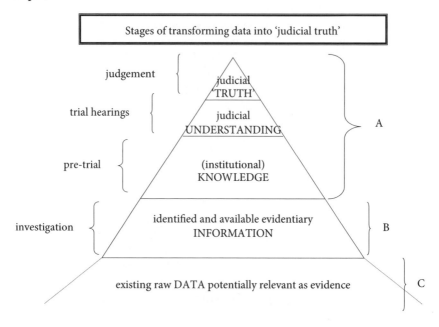

Stages of transforming data into 'judicial truth'

judgement { judicial 'TRUTH'

trial hearings { judicial UNDERSTANDING

} A

pre-trial { (institutional) KNOWLEDGE

investigation { identified and available evidentiary INFORMATION

} B

existing raw DATA potentially relevant as evidence

} C

Throughout this judicial-analytical process, raw data, potentially containing evidentiary information is processed into 'judicial truth' (see graph 3). In light of concepts in data and knowledge management in criminal justice analysis (Kluge, Stein & Licht 2001) different procedural steps can be linked to certain levels of evidentiary knowledge management. In principle, the notion of 'judicial truth' as presented within judgments should indicate that available:

– **raw data** has been analysed and evaluated as
– **information** relevant for cases under investigation which is presented as
– **knowledge**, mainly produced by the prosecution but also by defence teams, referring to facts and relationships presenting the factual crime theory, finally tested and disputed at trial and – in theory – leading to an
– **understanding** of the criminal events based on which individual criminal responsibility can be inferred – presented as
– **'judicial truth'**.

What is important here in understanding the meaning of initial originators of evidentiary information as influential in the rationality-hegemony discourse participating in the construction of the final 'judicial truth' is that they are part of all stages of the proceedings, yet with different degrees of freedom and influence, controlled by judicial actors. While they are strictly judicially controlled and restricted in section A (judgment, trial hearing, pre-trial) by judges, in section B (investigation) by the prosecution (and defence) they appear to have a more influential role in defining or presenting evidentiary material, yet before the investigation starts (section C) they act as stakeholders in their own interest and collect information often not meant to be criminal evidence. The anticipated rationality-hegemony linkage, as assumed to take place within the evidentiary process, occurs during the presentation of evidence at those procedural stages.[22]

3.2. INSTITUTIONAL ORIGINATORS OF (POTENTIAL) EVIDENTIARY INFORMATION

By now the evidentiary collection of the Office of the Prosecutor at the ICTY comprises 'some 7 million pages of documents' (Del Ponte, 2007b). The content and structure of this initial evidentiary material has not yet been the subject of academic research, neither the process in which this raw data has 'entered' the tribunal nor its transformation into admitted evidence and final usage in the reasoning of judgments. Publicly available data on the amount of exhibits which allow the estimation of the basic proportions of this collection in regard to the representation of originators are contained in open trial transcripts and judgments or in the Annual Reports of the ICTY to the Security Council.

The following section attempts to describe basic figures on the organisational structure of institutional originators of evidence used at the ICTY. The descriptive findings presented in Table 1 show the results of an analysis of references to originators of exhibits as recorded in public trial transcripts until March 2007. An availability sample of 2,020 exhibits has been analysed in regard to the institutional originator. Assuming the sample reflects the basic structure of institutional originators of evidentiary information[23] in its entirety, an estimated number of total submissions per institutional originator could hypothetically be determined (see Table 1, column V). Given an estimated total of 580,000 records within the

---

22 The sample size occurred as the result of an indexing process of exhibits in transcripts for cases with at least one convicted person where the originator of the exhibit could be identified. Cases with guilty pleas have not been included insofar as the sample is an availability sample. Consequently, quantifications and inferences are only of an explorative nature and serve the mere purpose to develop a deeper understanding of the multi-actors' involvement in the production of evidence.

23 This hypothetical assumption needs further evaluation. Among others, due to the fact that entire archival collections have been seized by the prosecution it appears that the actual portion of domestic governmental sources is even higher than shown in Table 1 which only refers to evidence used at trial.

evidentiary collection of the OTP, the quantitative dimension of the analytical process in preparation of cases at the ICTY can hypothetically be explored.[24]

The notion of 'institutional originators' of evidentiary information follows principles of organisational concepts in international politics (Coicaud & Heiskanen 2001) which differentiate certain main groups of international actors:

- supranational organisations (e.g. UN and EU),
- international governmental organisations (e.g. OSCE and NATO),
- national governmental organisations,
- international non-governmental organisations,
- national non-governmental organisations,
- academic institutions, and
- the media.

As far as national entities are concerned, it appears to be useful to further distinguish 'foreign' national entities from (not directly involved in the original collective violence) 'domestic' (formerly involved conflict parties).

'Personal originators' of evidentiary information are considered to be witnesses, either as fact witnesses or expert witnesses.

The institutional originators for potentially evidentiary materials have been classified within three main groups of institutions and organisations (see column I in Table 1) as (1) supranational or international (18.1%), (2) foreign (other than involved conflict parties) (28%) and (3) domestic (former conflict parties) (64.2%).

Sub-categories (column II) allow for the differentiation of the institutional origin of potential evidentiary information in more detail. As Table 1 shows, foreign and domestic governmental institutions present by far the main sources of evidentiary information introduced at trial. Yet, domestic governmental institutions from former conflict parties provide more than half of all presented exhibits. Since no distinction has been made here between data collection in the course of OTP investigation and data provided by third parties (e.g. under Rule 70 of the Rules of Procedure and Evidence if not requested by the prosecution) on their own initiative, it is not possible to quantify the portion of evidentiary data as a result of an active approach of institutions and organisations as originator of evidence.

---

[24] Although there will be no new investigations opened at the ICTY it is not possible to quantify the final amount of evidence or numbers of exhibits and witnesses until all proceedings are completed. Thus the figures provided in this paper should not be taken as reliable quantification of evidentiary material at the office of the prosecutor but can only serve explorative purposes and assist further interpretation and hypotheses generation.

Table 1. Institutional originators of potential evidentiary information

I Classification*	II Institutional originator of evidentiary information (sub-categories)	III Absolute figures within availability sample	IV Percentage within availability sample	V Estimated number of total submissions per institutional originator
1	Supranational organisations	199	9.9	57,113
1	IGO	97	4.8	27,839
1	Judiciary/law enforcement (international)	29	1.4	8,323
1	NGO (international)	40	2.0	11,480
2	Governmental institutions (foreign)	179	8.9	51,373
2	Judiciary/law enforcement (foreign)	79	3.9	22,673
2	NGO (foreign)	1	0.05	287
2	Media (foreign)	44	2.2	12,628
2	Academic (foreign)	53	2.6	15,211
2	Private sector (foreign)	1	0.05	287
3	Governmental institutions (domestic)	1,121	55.5	321,727
3	Judiciary/law enforcement (domestic)	89	4.4	25,543
3	NGO (domestic)	61	3.0	17,507
3	Media (domestic)	22	1.1	6,314
3	Academic (domestic)	5	0.2	1,435
	Total:	2,020	100	580,000

(ICTY March 2007)
* 1 = supranational/international, 2 = foreign, 3 = domestic

Already at this level of first descriptive analysis, basic proportions and differences in the participation of various types of institutional originators allow some interpretation in regard to the conceptual assumption of a rationality-hegemony linkage reproduced by the international judicial 'regime of truth'. These proportions indicate that evidence in cases before the ICTY originates from two main institutional domains: the national governmental sources of former conflicting parties (59.9% within the sample) and supranational, international and foreign national (national governments foreign to the former conflicting parties) governmental institutions (28.9% within the sample). Almost nine out of ten institutional originators of potentially evidentiary information are governmental, yet there is a clear quantitative dominance of governments of former conflict parties. Further qualitative and quantitative analysis is needed to characterise the actual impact of different types of evidence dependent on its origin and in regard to particular parts of the factual crime theory.

NGOs comprise the next group with a measurable quantitative portion within the evidence collection of the OTP of about 5% within the sample. Three percent of NGOs operate within the territory of former conflict parties and 2% do so from international NGOs. Whether this finding will remain stable after all data within the evidence collection of the OTP is analysed, remains to be seen. However, it appears to be an interesting preliminary finding that the relative quantitative weight of evidentiary data provided by NGOs is rather small compared to governmental sources (even though the estimated absolute figures show that the contribution is still remarkable and amounts to (estimated) almost 30,000 documents (see column 5, Table 1). This might be a situation particularity related to the conflict in the former Yugoslavia, where functioning governmental structures exist in the former conflict area which respond – despite all differences and at times reluctance – to the requests of the OTP at the ICTY. And eventually a qualitative analysis of materials provided by NGOs will probably show that their impact relates to special issues within the crime theory, and that although the portion of evidence provided by NGOs is comparatively small, NGOs have a significant impact on issues related to victim representation, mainly in the context of crime base and victimisation-related issues.

Another group of institutional originators appears as academic institutions which provide information – 2.4% of all institutional originators within the sample: 2.2% foreign and 0.2% domestic.

And finally, the role of the media as a provider of potential evidence is quite significant although in relative numbers only 3.3% of all institutional originators within the sample have been representatives from the media (2.2% international/ foreign, 1.1% domestic). Journalists are particularly significant as observers who collected information during the conflict, sometimes directly from participants who are later accused.

For both academic institutions as well as the media, which are deeply integrated in their respective intellectual and ideological discourses, it must be assumed that they 'transport' their views and interpretations beyond the factual information they might provide first into the evidence collection and finally into the courtroom. In particular the role of the media has been critically discussed and suspected to form a 'military-media complex' amounting to a 'failure of journalism' and producing double standards (Altheide 2006).

Hence, far more in-depth research is needed to accurately describe and understand the role and possible impact of all these different groups of institutional originators on the construction of the final 'judicial truth'. The 'trajectory' of all pieces of evidence needs to be screened to describe patterns within the evidentiary process which can be attributed and characterised as the influential impact of some originators and to show if those originators and their sources of information are 'behind' different segments of the (judicially 'true') factual crime theory.

From the historical perspective, compared to the situation at the Nuremberg trial (see part 1), the descriptive findings presented above for the ICTY could indicate that the original sources of international evidence have changed quite obviously. This change might not only and not primarily occur as a result of the different nature of the crimes prosecuted and the availability of evidentiary materials, but as a consequence of a substantial change in the 'regime of truth' in international justice and the discursive participation of a variety of different actors and their focus on victims' interests.

3.3. PERSONAL ORIGINATORS: WITNESSES AND 'JUDICIAL TRUTH'

Other than at the Nuremberg trial which – in terms of evidence – was mainly based on documents and documentaries rather than on witness testimony, the trial hearings at the ICTY and apparently other current international and mixed courts rely on the presentation of evidence primarily through witnesses. Although not identical, the structure of witnesses correlates directly with the features of institutional originators since institutions providing evidence will be represented by individual witnesses.

Overview: Following a recent presentation by Wendy Lobwein from the Victim and Witness Unit of the ICTY, during the period 1996–2006, there have been 4,137 witnesses, comprised of 3,861 (93.3%) fact witnesses and 276 (6.7%) expert witnesses, which results in a proportion of 14:1. Based on a semi-automated indexing and text mining procedure using QDA Miner and WordStat (Peladeau, 2005) hits within transcripts, identifying facts and expert witnesses, have been analysed. This resulted in a proportion between fact witnesses and expert witnesses of 76:1 related to the frequency of references in regard to either of the two witness groups during trials.[25] In contrast, the proportion of fact witnesses and expert witnesses (using the same method of text mining) within judgments resulted in a 13:1 proportion.[26] Regardless of whether these figures are confirmed in exactly the same way by more in-depth studies and after the last judgment is rendered at the ICTY, there appears to be no reason to doubt the basic proportions in regard to the relationship between expert witnesses and fact witnesses and

---

[25]   The text-mining procedure identified all hits for witnesses (and not expert witnesses) and expert witnesses (and not witnesses). A random check showed that this method proved to be reliable beyond a 90% level.

[26]   58 judgments were analysed, with 5.191 hits for fact witnesses and 404 hits for expert witnesses.

their different quantitative references at trial hearings in comparison to judgments. The obvious fact of a much higher ratio of references to fact witnesses during trials (in the given estimate almost six times higher) could indicate that the period of trial hearings represent a particular sector in the international criminal justice 'regime of truth' where fact witnesses, who are mostly victims or otherwise personally involved in the former conflict, are deemed relevant to participate in the process of rationalisation of facts of the commission of the crime and the linkage of criminal acts to 'higher ups' by explaining the political and military structure and the functioning of the perpetrating institutional forces.

This (in no way surprising) finding of higher representation of fact witnesses coming from one of the former conflict parties at trial, however, corresponds with the previous finding regarding the institutional originators that almost two-thirds of institutional originators of evidential materials belong to domestic institutions or organisations of the former conflict parties since the stated commitment to the 'ascertainment of truth' requires the establishment of these facts of the crimes and their systematic organisation.

Case Study: The analysis of one of the most complex high leadership cases (so far completed by a Trial Chamber at the ICTY)[27] regarding the representation of fact and expert witnesses provides the following findings.[28]

Out of 146 witnesses (127 prosecution, 19 defence) referred to at trial,[29] 137 or 93.8% were fact witnesses and 9 or 6.2% were expert witnesses (proportion 15:1).[30] This proportion matches the overall relationship reported for the occurrence of all fact witnesses and expert witnesses by Wendy Lobwein. 135 or 92.5% of all witnesses belonged to one of the former conflicting parties, while 11 or 7.5% were international: two from Australia, two from the UK, one from Denmark, one from Kenya (working for the UN) and five from the US. A highly significant

---

[27] *Prosecution vs. Momcilo Krajisnik*, case number IT-00-39.

[28] All figures presented relate to one, although, complex case with a unique feature; thus no generalisations other than hypothetical should be inferred in regard to distributions and relationships of witnesses for all cases.

[29] This case study has been conducted based on references to witnesses within the trial transcripts of the case to describe the role of witnesses throughout different procedural stages. Witnesses, although part of the evidence, but not mentioned in transcripts or judgments have been 'ignored' under the assumption that they cannot have a measurable influence on the evidentiary narratives in both sources. As a consequence the numbers mentioned in this section as 'observed' in transcripts or judgment necessarily deviate from the numbers reported within the judgment as 'presented' at trial: prosecution 93 *viva voce* witnesses and 168 Rule 92 bis witness statements; defence 19 *viva voce* witnesses.

[30] The frequency of references to fact witnesses or expert witnesses has not yet been analysed for this case but it is expected that the number of reference per witness will be higher for experts than for fact witnesses.

correlation[31] exists in the relationship between witnesses differentiated as a witness of fact or expert witness on the one hand and witness origin (domestic, former conflict party vs. international) on the other: fact witnesses came almost exclusively (134, 97.8%) from one of the former conflict parties, while all but one expert witness were internationals. More than one fifth (33 of the 146 witnesses observed at trial = 22.6%) were not directly mentioned within the judgment, including one expert witness.

Findings of a Configuration Frequency Analysis (Lautsch 1995) showed that international witnesses tend to have more trial days than non-international or fact witnesses. A similar indication exists for the number of exhibits tendered through a witness.

The hypothesis which could be generated from these preliminary findings relate to the assumption that (domestic) fact witnesses are mainly linked to crime base and victim-related evidentiary issues and to a lesser degree to inferences of individual criminal responsibility for mid and higher leadership levels (linkage evidence), while evidence given by (mostly international) expert witnesses appears to present a major basis from which 'judicial truth' on the individual responsibility of leadership cases is inferred. Since international criminal justice aims to prosecute those 'most responsible', this could mean that the weight of expert witnesses not belonging to countries and cultures of the former conflict parties but coming from states belonging to 'western civilisation' becomes (relatively speaking) more significant with any procedural stage for the judicial understanding and final construction of 'judicial truth' of international crimes. The question 'Civilisation: Truth or Tool?' as raised by Richard W. Bulliet at the UN workshop on 'What is 'Civilisation'?' (Bulliet 2006) must yet be answered for the involvement of expert witnesses in international criminal trials.

The relevance of this issue finds further support in an analysis of the role of expert witnesses in different types of cases.

Role of expert witnesses in different types of cases: representative cases for three types of perpetrating institutional forces which committed crimes typical for the conflict in the former Yugoslavia have been selected for accused acting within the environment of (a) camps and detention centres, (b) armed forces or (c) political civilian leadership. Examples of these three types of cases[32] have been analysed in regard to the possible 'impact' of expert witnesses (grouped by their belonging to the prosecution or defence) within the reasoning of judgments.

---

[31] A configuration frequency analysis shows significant correlations between witness origin (conflict party or international) and witness group (witness of fact or expert witness).

[32] The cases selected are *Prosecutor v. Kvocka, Kos, Radic, Zigic, Pracac*, case-No IT-98–30/1-T, 2 November 2001; *Prosecutor v. Krajisnik*, IT-00–39-T, 27 September 2006; *Prosecutor v. Kristic*, IT-98–33-T, 2 August 2001.

The heatmap plot[33] shows similarities for both variables based on relative keyword frequencies, keywords representing names of experts. The first variable depicts the simple 'concept of expert witnesses' which forms the groups of experts: defence experts, OTP (hired) external experts, OTP (employed) internal experts; the second variable represents the case types: camp, armed forces, political-civilian leadership. Both variables are hierarchically clustered (see dendograms in Graph 4) regarding their similarity, thus the camp and armed force case are more similar compared to the politician leadership case, likewise, defence and OTP external experts are more similar in contrast to OTP internal experts.

Graph 4. Heatmap of clusters of cases (PIF) and expert witnesses

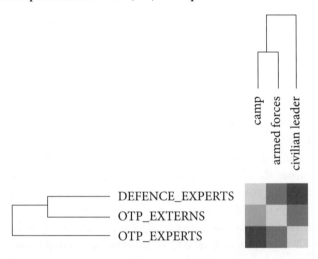

The heatmap plot in WordStat allows for the visualisation of the relationship between the two clusters. Different shades indicate the levels of similarities between clusters of experts and cases. The most significant correlations appear along the diagonal from the left upper field to the right lower field within the heatmap. Based on the objective of this analysis to describe different levels of impact of expert witnesses in relation to different types of cases, measured by relative frequencies of different types of experts (as defined here) the heatmap shows significant differences: defence experts correlate strongly with the camp

---

33   'Heatmap plots are graphic representations of crosstab tables where relative frequencies are represented by different colour brightness or tones and on which a clustering is applied to reorder rows and/or columns (…). When used for text mining, such exploratory data analysis tool facilitates the identification of functional relationships between related keyword and group of values of an independent variable by allowing the perception of cells clumps of relatively high or low frequencies or of outlier values' (Peladeau 2005, 96).

case, OTP external experts with the armed forces case and OTP intern experts (strongest correlation) correlate significantly with the political leadership case.

Based on the fact that the types simultaneously represent different average leadership levels of the accused (camp-related cases: lower and medium; armed forces: medium; and political civilian: higher leadership levels) these findings seemingly support the previous hypothesis that cases with accused at higher leadership levels are more significantly related to expert knowledge introduced by the prosecution mainly through international expert witnesses.

Once again, the presented empirical findings are only valid for the selected cases and do not (yet) allow for reliable generalisation in regard to all cases at the ICTY or even the international criminal justice system and the appearance of expert witnesses in international cases. Therefore, generalising interpretations bear only hypothetical meaning. Yet, just in this hypothetical sense, it could be suggested that the judicial reasoning and inference in international criminal justice beyond issues directly related to the execution of the crimes and large-scale victimisation, might be strongly influenced by legal, political and social concepts as part of 'Western civilisation' given that 'understanding' and 'meaning' of the historical facts of the crimes and the underlying political and military organisation of involved parties relevant to the respective crime theory relies substantially on experts who operate against their cultural and political background of a 'Western civilisation'. If this hypothesis finds material proof in further analysis, the construction of 'judicial truth' in international criminal justice could appear as part of an 'enlargement of the Western historical narrative (...) a means of justifying western rule and domination over other cultures and civilisations' (Pocock 2006, 10) finally even confirming 'reciprocal perceptions of double standards' (Alliance Report, 2006: 13). In any case, even these preliminary and rather illustrative findings strongly indicate that the rationality-hegemony linkage in international criminal justice would find a more differentiated explanation by describing the role of expert knowledge as evidence in international trials.

4.   CONCLUSIONS

It is possible to draw the following general conclusions from the empirical findings that are meant to explore prior assumptions based on an existence of a rationality-hegemony linkage in international criminal justice to legitimise international security politics.

The 'regime of truth' as established and practised at the ICTY is based on a multi-actor approach (see 3.2 and 3.3) rather than a monolithic prosecution-centred concept in generating evidentiary knowledge. There is an active participation of a multitude of actors (stakeholders) from international, governmental and non-governmental institutions and organisations in the provision of information (raw data) related to the facts of the crime and criminal responsibility of suspects.

While international and governmental actors present the main part of potential evidence, in particular, NGOs representing victim interests have a significant impact on information tendered into evidence, indicating a changing role of victims and their participation in international trials, quite contrary to the situation at the Nuremberg trials.

The presentation of evidence and participation of these originators of information at trial and more so its use within judicial reasoning is controlled by the prosecution and finally chambers, and to a lesser extent – on average – by the defence (see results of case study 3.3).

During the trial phase (see 3.3), fact witnesses appear to have more opportunities to present themselves and to provide factual evidentiary information. As expected, they very rarely interfere in the process of interpretation and reasoning based on the provided evidentiary information. Furthermore, the traditional concept of criminal proceedings (adversarial system, cross-examination) confines active participation and representation of witnesses in the inferential judicial process.

Expert witnesses, who in the main part, operate within an international environment, appear to be highly influential in the determination of reasoning and interpretation of criminal responsibility for civilian leadership cases and members of armed forces with the effect that 'western' concepts representing social reality dominate the construction of criminal responsibility and guarantees the hegemony of related values normative frameworks. The international criminal justice 'regime of truth' guarantees that certain sources of data and related interpretations are kept within a certain cultural and political background.

Given the need for objectivity and fairness in conflict resolution as an inevitable element of a peace-making framework in post-conflict societies and in light of the highly discursive and participatory nature of the evidentiary process, the vision of a 'shared regime of truth' (Foucault 1980, 131) might provide some guidance for the truth-finding generation of criminal evidence in international trials which has the potential of providing generic acceptance of judicial reasoning on the facts of the crimes and universal acceptance of the final judicial truth.

PART V
VICTIMOLOGY

XVII. VICTIMISATION AND SUPRANATIONAL CRIMINOLOGY

David Kauzlarich

1.   INTRODUCTION

The volume of injury resulting from state crimes of commission and omission clearly dwarfs the harms caused by street crimes. Whether one crudely considers the number of people killed or otherwise hurt by illegal war and genocide or the state-supported structural inequalities which saturate social life, the state and other forms of politically organised violence are the most destructive agents of misery and oppression across the globe. Consider the following:

–   Genocide in Nazi Germany, Rwanda, Darfur, Albania, Turkey, Ukraine, Cambodia, Bosnia-Herzegovina and other regions have claimed the lives of tens of millions and rendered many more homeless, imprisoned, ill, and psychologically and physically damaged.

–   The United States illegal use of atomic weapons on the people of Japan resulted in 100,000–200,000 immediate deaths, 100,000 more people injured, and hundreds of thousands who subsequently developed cancer and other diseases as a result of nuclear fallout (Gerson 1995; Nagataki, Shibata, Inoue, Yokoyama, Izumi and Shimaoka 1994).

To the raw numbers, one could add volumes of narratives by those directly victimised or witness to violence by states, such as the sorrowful testimony of the Hibakusha in Japan, Holocaust survivors and legions of others around the globe:

'In Spring 1942, my mother, my half-sister, her two children and I were all selected to be taken to Chelmno to be murdered there. My sister could have saved herself, but when they took her two children, she chose to go with them. My mother begged me to escape and hide till the selection of our area of the ghetto was over. "Run in a zigzag," she told me, "and don't stop when they shoot or shout 'Halt!'. I did as she asked and escaped that selection, but my mother, half-sister and her children all perished there' (Roman Halter, Polish Holocaust Survivor, 2007).

'I was there when the perpetrators came to kill my family (...). We couldn't see it happening, but we could hear them screaming (...). I had four sisters who were all killed during the genocide – killed in a terrible way, some of them dumped alive in the latrine (...)' (Freddy Mutanguha, Rwanda genocide survivor, 2007).

It is impossible to overestimate the material and physical loss from these crimes, let alone the hundreds of millions of other injuries sustained by victims of human rights violations and similar forms of oppression. But what has criminology contributed to the understanding of these crimes and their victims? With the exception of a few works, such as those assembled by Ewald & Turkovic (2006), the short answer is 'very little'. Despite growing attention to white collar, corporate and state crime over the last few decades, criminologists are still significantly more interested in retail rather than wholesale crimes and victims. Indeed, the bulk of the work published in academic criminology (including most textbooks and so-called general theories of crime) completely ignores state crime and continues to disproportionately bury itself in traditional street crime.

This chapter represents a small contribution to the new supranational criminology movement, a potential force for re-charting and re-energising the study of wholesale crimes by states across the globe. I begin by discussing the central tenets of critical criminology, its relationship to the study of state crime, and how the new supranational criminology can build upon the work of critical scholars to forge a new path of understanding of the world's most profound instances of violence, neglect and exclusion. Next, I survey some of the major issues in the victimology of state crime including the variety of victims, research on victim needs, and system-level structures and processes related to victims' services. The paper concludes with a re-visitation of the propositions I co-developed some years ago on the victimology of state crime and suggests future paths for theoretical and empirical work in supranational criminology.

2. CRITICAL CRIMINOLOGY, STATE CRIME AND SUPRANATIONAL CRIMINOLOGY

Like Sutherland did so many years ago, critical criminologists have explicitly critiqued the myopia, indifference to suffering and narrow legal positivism of their contemporaries, but these critiques seldom appear in the most prestigious journals in the field nor are they topics which garner much attention at the largest professional criminology conferences. While mainstream criminologists have historically ignored the problems of war and state violence, critical criminologists have studied them for decades. From a humanistic perspective, critical criminology focuses on how inequality and power impact and reflect lawmaking, lawbreaking, victimisation, reactions to crime and social harm. Although critical criminology has become more diverse in recent years, it is rooted in Marxist, feminist, progressive, anarchist and post-modern theoretical traditions (Kauzlarich 2007). As an alternative to mainstream criminology organised around the theme of social justice, critical criminology is specifically concerned with the manners in which structural forces, cultural ideologies and social processes create, sustain and exacerbate social problems such as militarism, racism, sexism, poverty, state and corporate violence, criminal injustice and war (Lynch & Michalowski 2006). Critical criminologists typically maintain that solutions to the problems of crime and injustice are best attained through restorative, democratic and peace-making approaches rather than crime control models that rely on repression, retribution and violence. More fundamentally, critical criminologists call for the restructuring of societies so that the elimination of suffering, inequality, marginalisation and injury in all of their forms are the primary goals of social organisation, not facilitating, accumulating or expanding empire and capital (Tifft & Sullivan 2006).

A hallmark of critical criminology is the critique of the traditional legalistic definition of crime. Such a definition holds that an act is criminal only if it violates domestic criminal law. Alternatively, critical criminological definitions of crime, such as the human rights paradigm advanced by the Schwendingers (1970) many years ago, maintain that crime can be defined as anything that causes social injury, suffering or which violates human rights. Many scholars have since elaborated on the earlier radical definitions of crime (Barak 1991b; Henry & Lanier 2001; Kauzlarich, Mullins & Matthews 2003; Michalowski 1985; Milovanovic & Henry 2001; Tifft & Sullivan 2006, 1980) to include criminological analysis of all forms of oppression and harm, including violence by governments.

Most of those studying state crime are critical criminologists (Barak 1991b; Friedrichs 2000a; Kramer, Michalowski & Kauzlarich 2002; Ross 2000a, 2000c; Rothe & Mullins 2006a) who maintain that domestic criminal law is but one way to define crime, whether committed by the state as an institution or individual actors within their bureaucratic roles. Other ways to define state crimes include references to international human rights laws as codified in the United Nations' Universal Declaration of Human Rights and the Genocide Convention, the laws of war, such as the Geneva Conventions (Kauzlarich, Kramer & Smith 1992), and further, any injury that is demonstrably avoidable and/or unnecessary (Tifft & Sullivan 1980). Moreover, Hillyard & Tombs (2005), and Tifft & Sullivan (2001, 2006) call for the state deferential definition of crime to be replaced by a social harms and/or needs-based definition, which would encapsulate a broad range of physical, financial, economic, emotional, psychological and sexual harms. Wars of aggression are unquestionably represented in these categories. Some radical scholars have gone so far as to argue that criminologists should study the extraction of surplus value and social stratification (Kauzlarich, Mullins & Matthews 2003; Tifft & Sullivan 2006), while others such as Green & Ward (2004, 2000) prefer a narrower definition of state crime that centres on organisational rule-breaking

A genuine supranational criminology, as I conceive it, must grapple with these epistemological and definitional issues as it charts its terrain of inquiry. At the same time, supranational criminology should be a place where suffering across the globe is studied humanistically, compassionately and with a sharp eye on prevention, control and victim healing. The harms should be articulated, publicised (with victim consent if possible), interrogated and subjected to relentless scrutiny. The victims should be supported, tended to and provided every opportunity to pursue healing for themselves, their loved ones and their community. Additionally, supranational criminology should embrace, critique, revise and build upon the decades of critical criminological work, such of which is mentioned above. While there are some other scholarly groups in which human rights violations are studied (the Justice Studies Association and the American Society of Criminology's Division on Critical Criminology, for example) there is no criminological association for the study of state crime or similar types of collective violence. Some colleagues and I have considered starting such an organisation, but material resources and time have limited our ability to do so. Supranational criminology could fill this gap, along with many others.

The lofty goals I have in mind for supranational criminology may be dismissed – even by the sympathetic – as both naïve and tired. After all, critical criminologists have made similar suggestions for decades with regrettably little success. *Yet, the goals of supranational criminology should be high because criminology's voice has been so very low.* Indeed, supranational criminology should be fiercely humanistic because most academics and organisations are not. The majority of scholars remain aloof to the misery and if it is studied, it is with some distance followed by return to a comfortable home or office. Supranational criminology should not follow suit. Instead, it should chart a different course, one that is academic, surely, but one that is not emotionally removed or indifferent to the people who die or are otherwise hurt by states.

More substantively, supranational criminology should indeed examine crimes across state boundaries, but also injury within ethnic, racial, religious, provincial and regional divides in states. Deciding not to study crimes within states would be an error because many are as internally divided as separate states and it is reasonable to assume that similar causal and victimological dynamics are at work. This is evidenced by several large-scale atrocities that occurred in Cambodia and Rwanda, to name a few. Thus, I consider both domestic state crime as well as international conflict throughout this paper. Further, although I focus on the crimes of states, state agents and government agencies in this contribution, mass atrocities are also committed by paramilitary and rebel groups, private security forces and criminal gangs.

3. TYPES OF VICTIMS

Even more than traditional street crime, there is wide range of victims of state crime. Direct harms, for example, can span from property offences to sexual assault and death while indirect suffering can stem from starvation and sickness as a result of economic sanctions and external funding of repressive regimes. By its very nature, state crime is destructive for individuals, but profound affects are also felt by neighbourhoods, communities, and whole ethnic and racial groups (Jaukovic 2002). Social institutions, especially in areas of war and mass conflict, become brittle and often dissolve: schools, hospitals and places of worship can longer provide services to individuals struggling to cope in desperate and painful conditions. Families are divided, people turn up missing, buildings and homes are destroyed, and the basic needs for proper nutrition, clean water and working sewers cannot be met. The individual psychological and emotional damage often becomes the collective pain, and it is difficult for many to maintain hope for healing and restoration (Jaukovic 2002). Even in non-war situations, state sponsored discrimination and oppression, such as the case with South African apartheid, produce pain, anxiety and collective powerlessness. Indeed, political and cultural oppression around the globe is widespread and while this suffering may not receive the kind of media attention that war-torn areas might, the suffering is profound in magnitude.

3.1. DIRECT AND INDIRECT VICTIMS

Sexual assaults, murder, torture, property loss and displacement are among the many types of crimes through which people become direct victims of state crime. Unfortunately, the types and kinds of victims of direct state harm are far too numerous to appropriately discuss here (or perhaps in any document, no matter the size). The gravest of direct harms come about as a result of genocide, injuries associated with mass killings and the emotional, psychological, physical, material and collective structural consequences of war. As indicated in Table 1, Turkovic (2002) sees at least twelve major kinds of direct harm experienced by war victims.

David Kauzlarich

Table 1. Turkovic's (2002, 206) Model of Victims

Direct War Victims	Latent War Victims
Killed	Unemployed
Wounded	Emigrants
Tortured	Drug addicts
Sexually abused	War stress (Dead, Somatic diseases, Insomnia and Depression)
Missing and confined	Human rights violations
Displaced	Personal loss
Refugees	Domestic violence
Property loss	Divorce
PTSD	Organised crime
Landmines	Some conventional crimes
Hostages	
Forced conscription	

Turkovic (2002) not only identifies direct injuries in the context of war but also those which come about indirectly through the chaos, anomie, and psychological and inter-personal damage which accompany such violence. Several empirical studies confirm the ubiquity of these phenomena (Hayner 1992, 2001; Kiza, Rathbgeber & Rohn 2006; Stover 2005). While very helpful in categorising the harms experienced by those in war, Turkovic's model can be expanded to include additional latent and direct harms beyond war such as medical experimentation, sickness and the loss of infrastructure. Regarding the former, for example, in the late 1940s the United States used indigenous populations in the Marshall Islands as guinea pigs in order to gauge the physiological affects of nuclear radiation on the human body. The well known medical experimentations on Jews by the Nazi state are another example. The frequency with which these experiments occur in both domestic and international contexts suggest that they should be identified in a separate category in the future models of victimology.

Further, in order to understand the full range of victims in the context of international crime, we must also be sensitive to how the actions of states and their agents contribute to harm in even more indirect ways, such as through social stratification and structural bodies (e.g. legal and educational systems) which limit the ability of groups and individuals to realise their human potential. In all societies, those with less economic and political status are more likely to suffer harm from state policies which, for example, basic medical care, access to the legal system and educational opportunities on personal or familial income, race, ethnicity, religiosity or gender. Basic human needs such as clean drinking water and working sewers are scarce in many areas of the globe and it is always the disadvantaged who bear the brunt of the suffering. The advantaged, even when facing a form of victimisation, can more easily leave areas of oppression and crisis and have a chance of establishing themselves and their families elsewhere.

These injuries can occur through state sponsored economic terrorism in which sanctions are used as a form of coercion directed toward the civilian population of a target country in order to bring about a desired political or economic change (Dowty 1994; Hass 1998; Hufbauer et al. 1990). The effects of economic sanctions have ranged from moderate discomfort, to the difficulty of the target nation to realise its economic or political goals, to more serious consequences for the population like the spreading of disease, malnutrition and even death (Dowty 1994; Hufbauer et al. 1990). Of course, as is the case in most crimes 'those most likely to suffer from general trade sanctions are the vulnerable: women, children and those heavily dependent on the societal "safety net" provided by international relief agencies' (Cortright & Lopez 1999).

Two examples of the injuries caused by economic terrorism by the United States illustrate the point because both sanctions against Iraq and Cuba have caused considerable and avoidable suffering and death.

The Cuban Democracy Act (CDA) and the Helms-Burton Act in 1996 were major steps in tightening the economic sanctions on Cuba. As the 1997 American Association for World Health (AAWH) has found, the tightening of the economic sanctions in 1992 created health problems for many Cuban citizens in the areas of malnutrition, water quality, and medicines and medical equipment shortages. The AAWH (1997) also found that the outright ban on the sale of American foodstuffs has contributed to serious nutritional deficits, especially among pregnant women. This has led to an increase in low birth-weight babies (AAWH 1997). Additionally, food shortages have led to devastating outbreaks of neuropathy. In terms of water quality, the embargo has severely restricted the access to water treatment chemicals and the parts needed for Cuba's water supply system (AAWH 1997). The decrease in safe drinking water for many Cuban citizens has led to rising incidences of morbidity and mortality rates from water-borne diseases. Finally, because many drugs are developed by U.S. pharmaceutical companies, Cuban physicians have access to less than 50 percent of the new medicines available on the world market (AAWH 1997).

Between the first and second Gulf Wars, the Iraqi people suffered tremendous injury because of state-sponsored sanctions through the auspices of the United Nations against the government of Saddam Hussein. Lack of food and medicine contributed to high infant mortality rates and the inability of Iraqi's to operate schools and hospitals (Alnasrawi 2001). Conservative estimates of the number of Iraqi children who died because of the sanctions start at 100,000, while other estimates place the figure closer to 500,000 (Welch 2002a). Although not a traditional form of warfare, it is clear that economic sanctions can have direct affects on the quality or possibility of life of all (Kauzlarich, Matthews & Miller 2001).

To these unilateral or multilateral state facilitated crimes, we can add external funding by states to support either friendly governments or revolutionary efforts to overthrow unfriendly states. In the 1980s, the U.S. provided at least $4.5 million in assistance to the government of El Salvador to facilitate the repression of the revolutionary group FMLN. In the 1990s, the U.S. provided support to President Habre of Chad, who is likely to go on trial for his political crimes very soon.

The horrors of war and sanctions do not end once the bullets stop flying and the embargos are lifted. Indeed, the enormous psychological and existential damage incurred by those after living in conditions of war, oppression and genocide has been established by several scholars (Ewald 2006; Kiza 2006; Kuterovac, Dyregrov & Stuvland 1994; Saylor 1993; Van Boven 1993). A study of 3,030 child survivors of the Rwandan genocide reveals that the majority of children interviewed go out of their way to avoid thinking or talking about the events (Dyregrov, Gupta, Gjestad & Mukanheli 2000). Some of the specific experiences of these children make these feelings very understandable: ninety percent of the children in the study had to hide to survive at various times, some underneath dead bodies. Similarly high levels of post-traumatic stress are often experienced by soldiers and adult civilians and more often than not, the stress lasts for many years after the trauma (Hashemian, Khoshnood, Desai, Falahati, Kasl & Southwick 2006).

3.2. VICTIMS OF FORCED OBEDIENCE

Civilians and soldiers may be forced to illegally injure others or else face consequences ranging from court martial to death itself. In the Rwandan genocide, civilians were forced to kill others or be killed themselves. Additionally, forced conscription of children is a particularly dreadful form of crime and the practice appears to be growing (Achvarina & Reich 2006; United Nations 2006a). Derluyn, Broekaert, Schuyten & Temmerman (2004) estimate the total number of child soldiers worldwide to be 300,000. Further, the United Nations' Secretary General has identified at least a dozen paramilitary groups (e.g. Liberation Tigers in Sri Lanka; Lord's Resistance Army in Uganda) and states (e.g. Sudan and Congo) which have used children in armed combat. Voluntary adult soldiers are also placed in a position to obey orders that may be illegal and as such may be forced to carry out violence that while approved of by their government is contrary to international law. Therefore, soldiers in illegal wars are put in the position of carrying out actions in the context of general illegality and can therefore be understood to be involuntary/forced agents of crime as well as victims of their states.

One example of this is that while not officially proclaimed by the United Nations, the 2003 invasion and occupation of Iraq violated the most basic tenets of international law. The illegality of the United States' war on Iraq has been thoroughly documented by critical criminologists (Kramer, Michalowski & Rothe 2005; Kramer & Michalowski 2005b). On the most basic level, any war not clearly in self-defence is prohibited by international law. The United Nations' Charter, a principle source of the laws of war, specifies that 'All members shall refrain from the threat or use of force against the territorial integrity or political independence of any state, or in any state in which the United Nations is taking preventive or enforcement action' (United Nations 2006b: Article 2, Chapter 1:4). The only exception to Article 2(4) is found in Article 51 of the Charter: 'Nothing in the present Charter shall impair the inherent right of individual or collective self-defence if an armed attack occurs against a Member of the United Nations, until the Security Council has taken measures necessary to maintain international peace and security' (United Nations 2006b). The intention of this article is to allow a state under direct attack to defend itself. Importantly, however, such a right is limited and only executable when the U.N. Security Council provides an international plan of action (Kramer & Kauzlarich 1999). The Bush administration did half-heartedly attempt to gain the U.N. Security Council's permission to launch a war on Iraq in February 2003 when U.S. Secretary of State Colin Powell presented what is now known to be mostly fictional information on Iraq's apparent possession of weapons of mass destruction and ties to Osama bin Laden, al Qaeda and the September 11, 2001 attacks on the United States. Finding the evidence unconvincing, the U.N. Security Council voted not to support a U.S. attack on Iraq, but this was ignored by the Bush administration and the war commenced shortly thereafter in violation of the most basic principles of international law. While the war could be labelled criminal through a variety of non-legal and humanistic definitions, there is no clearer prohibition of the action than that found in the United Nations Charter. This means that soldiers forced to obey their state's illegal policies in the prosecution of a war are victims of their own government. Along with the millions of Iraqi's either killed, injured or left without basic needs fulfilled, the thousands of American and allied soldiers that have been killed or injured in Iraq should also be understood as victims of state crime. Soldiers and combatants in similar wars and on opposite sides may also be categorised as such (see Young 2006 for an analysis of similarly situated self-traumatised perpetrators).

3.3. VICTIMS OF CRIMES OF OMISSION

While crime events in general are usually thought of as harmful acts, they can also be conceptualised as harmful *failures to act*. Kauzlarich, Mullins & Matthews (2003, 249) categorise such failures as crimes of omission, which 'occur when the state disregards unsafe and dangerous conditions, when it has a clear mandate and responsibility to make a situation or context safe.' This is very similar to Friedrichs' (2004a, 127) concept of state negligence/nonfeasance, in which 'the state fails to prevent a loss of human life, suffering and deprivation that is in its power to prevent.' Most scholars would agree that the appropriate application of these concepts requires that the inaction must relate to an assigned or implied trust or duty of the state. One much publicised example is the series of governmental failures surrounding Hurricane Katrina.

In the days after Hurricane Katrina hit the United States Gulf Coast on Monday, 29 August, 2005, millions of people watched with horror and astonishment as the disaster in New Orleans unfolded. After the hurricane had moved on, the situation quickly began to deteriorate further as the breached levees could do nothing to stop the flow of Lake Pontchartrain into the low-lying areas of the city. Flood levels as high as fifteen feet in some areas left people stranded on rooftops for days. Poor evacuation and relief planning resulted in inhumane conditions and sickness at both the New Orleans Superdome and the Convention Center. Despite some high profile statements by executive political officials, the breach of the levees in New Orleans was in fact foreseen by many, including the U.S. Army Corps of Engineers, the U.S. National Weather Service and the U.S. Department of Homeland Security (Dyson 2006; Grissett 2004; NWS 2005).

Multiple state agents and organisations disregarded warnings of the forthcoming disaster, neglected the levees and inadequately responded after the storm roared into the area. Even the U.S. House of Representatives Select Bipartisan Committee to Investigate the Preparation for and Response to Hurricane Katrina (2006) found considerable governmental negligence surrounding the Katrina Disaster. Its boldly titled report, *A Failure of Initiative*, the committee criticises various governmental agencies and officials that in substance match the victim narratives that a colleague and I collected as part of a study of Katrina survivors (Faust & Kauzlarich 2006).

Although there very well may be more instances of state crimes of omission than commission around the globe, the concept, more than any other type of state crime, is quite contentious. Indeed, questions arise about how state responsibility is to be exactly adjudicated and the extent to which available state knowledge is actionable. Following Green's (2005) research on the Turkish state's complicity by omission in situations of natural disaster, negligent state crime

XVII. Victimisation and Supranational Criminology

should be among the central forms of international crime to be examined in the field of supranational criminology.

There is obviously a vast array of harm and victimisation which result from state crime, as well as the multiple types of actors, agents and organisations which may be directly or indirectly involved in wholesale crime. The crimes can be against individuals, property, communities and states and may cause a range of psychological and emotional trauma that may or may not be reparable (van Boven 1993). Building on the work of Turkovic (2002), Kiza, Rathgeber & Rohne (2006) have clarified the relational aspects of these phenomena on the basis of their impressive study of 1,000 victims of war in 12 different countries (Afghanistan, Bosnia and Herzegovina, Cambodia, Croatia, Congo, Israel, Kosovo, Macedonia, Palestinian Territories, the Philippines and Sudan). They found that most subjects experienced numerous victimisations by non-state group agents as well as state sponsored units and that most offenders acted in groups.

Based on these findings and others, Kiza et al. (2006) expand Turkovic's (2002) model to include more general categories of victimisation, injury and victim offender relationships (see Table 2). Traditional victimological research has heavily investigated victim-offender relationships, but little research of this type has been conducted on victims of war and state crime. This is an especially important area for future research because some instances of violence come directly from executive political officers while others are tacitly supported by internal or external state officials and bodies. Take, for example, the Sudanese government's material support for the widespread violence by the Lord's Resistance Army (LRA) in northern Uganda. While victims of the LRA's brutality, including thousands of kidnapped, raped and tortured children, have suffered immensely, research has shown that victims are surprisingly ambivalent about the LRA because some of the foot soldiers in the organisation were their very own abducted familial relatives (Pham, Vinck, Wierda, Stover & di Giovanni 2005). Victim-offender relationships such as these present a very complicated set of emotions for those harmed and point to yet another reason why victims may be reluctant to fully resist and demand punishment of perpetrators.

In sum, victims of state crime and collective violence may be injured directly or indirectly as a result of explicit actions and policies or those that are tacitly embedded within the contradictions of structural and cultural stratification. Victimisation can also occur as a consequence of the failure of the state to act to eliminate or reduce avoidable suffering, injury and exclusion. In terms of the type of harm incurred, individuals may suffer psychological, physical and material loss. Collectivities such as neighbourhoods, communities, and entire regions and states can suffer disastrous infrastructural effects and destroy their ability to deliver basic human services to the population. Finally, victims may also be those who are involuntarily forced to carry out illegal policies of their states.

Table 2. Forms of War Victimisation (Kiza, Rathgeber & Rohne 2006, 45)

Objective Causes	Individual perception	Victim-Offender Relation
Type I: Loss of income, property, bodily injury, attempted killing, torture and sexual assault	Emotional	Social Proximity: Offender known or unknown
Type II: Displacement and forced displacement	Physical	Organisational affiliation and type: State, non-State, Military and Civilian
Type III: Loss of family members	Economic	Age of offenders and victims

4. VICTIM REDRESS

Victimological research in criminology typically falls into one or more of the following areas: (1) the harm or injury itself, (2) individual perceptions of the gravity and cause of the harm, (3) the appeal to official bodies or agents for reparations, and (4) the extent to which official certification or validation (e.g. from the criminal justice system) comes to fruition (Viano 2000). We know from this research that (a) the risks of victimisation are not borne equally by race, class and gender, (b) previous victimisation is a significant predictor of future victimisation, (c) children witnessing victimisation are more likely to be victimised themselves later in life, (d) victims often do not report their suffering to the police, (e) on the whole, victims are often disappointed with the outcome of police investigations and subsequent court proceedings, and (f) a large minority of victims in some way blame themselves for their injuries (Catalano 2006; Fisher, Daigle & Cullen 2003; Mitchell & Finkelhor 2001).

Popular discourses about victims often dubiously assume that victim healing can be accomplished simply through the formal processing of the offender(s). The logic here is that if the perpetrator is caught, tried, convicted and punished, the victim will be able to somehow regain what she or he has lost. This common-sense belief, however, has been shown to be overly optimistic and quite naïve. As mentioned above, it is well known that the majority of victims of traditional street crime do not use state provided victim services. Part of the reason for this is that victims are unaware of the services offered, but even when they know of the opportunities, they have little faith in their ability to bring about restoration. Indeed, it is well known that as a group, victims report dissatisfaction with traditional criminal court proceedings. Reasons for this include the lack of sympathy and communication from police and prosecutors as well as disappointment with the type and length of criminal sentences. The bureaucratic structure of depositions, interviews and testimony is often alienating for victims and forces them to tell their narratives in a mechanistic fashion. These findings have been repeatedly supported by research on domestic criminal justice processes across the globe (Braithwaite & Yeboah 2004; Catalano 2006; Viano 2000; Wemmers & Cyr 2005). Finally, on a more existential level, victims of serious crimes and their family members are not capable of being 'patched up' like a flat tyre. Serious and sometimes not so serious criminal victimisation can produce life-long physical and emotional debilitation that may never be healed, even with the best intentions and support of friends, family members, communities and state agencies. Indeed, the very proposed panacea to the harm caused by victims (such as testifying in court) can be in and of itself a major form of trauma (Seymour 2000; Lobwein 2006).

As Hayner (2001) and Stover (2005) point out, it is unclear what percentage of the totality of victims of collective violence truly desire to tell their story, and further, whether after publicly speaking of their losses, any healing is furthered. While there are many anecdotal and some empirical reports of victims feeling liberated and on the path to healing because of public story telling, there are just as many reports of victims desiring to bury the memories or feeling much worse after giving public testimony.

More specifically, Hamber, Nageng & O'Malley (2000), Stanley (2005b) and Stover (2005) have found that many of those who testified at the International Criminal Tribunal for the former Yugoslavia (ICTY) and in truth commission proceedings did not feel much catharsis and some in fact experienced anger in the hollowness of the processes and their institutional character. There is a tendency for people to enter into a testimony situation expecting that they will receive significant financial compensation, more fully understand the causes of the crimes, and indeed some wish for the offenders to be clearly identified and punished (David & Yuk-Ping 2005; Laplante & Theidon 2007). Because these outcomes do not occur with regularity, victims understandably become disappointed (Humphrey 2003).

These points are reinforced by a UK study conducted on domestic violence victims (Robinson & Stroshine 2005), as well as a Canadian study on several types of traditional street crime victims. The latter study, by Wemmers & Cyr (2005), found that 'when victims feel that they have been treated fairly, they are more likely to feel able to put their victimisation behind them.' Although a bold claim, it also relates to some of the potential advantages of restorative justice, such as the opportunity for victims to 'tell their story' and communicate the extent of their suffering as a result of victimisation.

Truth commissions and international courts cannot regularly deliver outcomes or structure their proceedings in an expressly victim-centred manner.[1] With

---

[1]   There have been approximately two dozen truth commissions convened over the last several decades. These proceedings have focused on crimes against humanity in several areas of the globe, including Uganda, Chile, Chad, Rwanda, South Africa, Bolivia, Argentina, Uruguay, Zimbabwe, the Philippines, Germany, El Salvador, Ethiopia and other states. The structure

truth commissions, it is often uncertain before and sometimes after a commission completes its investigation whether or not individual offenders will be named, and further, whether trials may be conducted on the basis of the information collected in truth commission proceedings. The record shows that of the several dozen truth commissions convened to date, only four have named the perpetrators. In some instances, complete and wholesale amnesty was given to offenders, as in the case in El Salvador, while the Argentinean truth commission investigation eventually led to criminal trials (Hayner 2001). In the case of South Africa, the Truth and Reconciliation Commission was allowed to offer amnesty on a case by case basis, although the names of offenders were a matter of public record. Indeed, Hamber, Nageng & O'Malley's (2000) study shows that almost all of the South African victims they interviewed felt that granting amnesty to offender is unfair or simply 'wrong'. Victims of the LRA in northern Uganda echo this sentiment in a sense as almost half of those surveyed indicated that, among other things such as restorative justice processes, perpetrators should be held accountable for their crimes and punished (Pham, Vinck, Wierda, Stover & di Giovanni 2005). It must also be understood that truth commissions are principally fact finding units, not a victim services centre. Historically, truth commissions tend to be carried out in places trying to recover from war, massive oppression, and economic and political crisis. The lack of material resources along with the primary business of fact gathering often lead to dissatisfaction and anger. Indeed, those who have been traumatised and then convey their suffering to others in formal proceedings often expect something more concrete to result from their testimony. As one South African witness put it:

> 'I don't think there was any point in me testifying. The TRC promised to help me and I'm still waiting for that help from them and people's perceptions haven't changed about me. As far as I'm concerned, I wasted my time. I'm sure I could have spared myself the pain of talking about my life' (Hamber, Nageng & O'Malley 2000, 28).

Despite the problems victims face before, during and after giving testimony, there are both theoretical and empirical reasons to consider the potential positives. For

---

and results of truth commissions vary, but they do have commonalities: (1) a focus on the past, (2) the focus is on large scale human rights violations over a sustained period of time, (3) they are temporary and result in a final report, and (4) are vested with authority to be able to marshal resources (Hayner 1994, 2006). Truth commissions, then, are quite different than criminal trials and thus victims participating in the processes may receive considerably different treatment.

instance, Chief ICTY prosecutor Carla Del Ponte (2007c) paints a powerful portrait of the importance of victim narratives:

> 'The courtroom testimonies of eyewitnesses are fundamentally important – they tell us about the horrifying conditions of the detention camps, ethnic cleansing campaigns, torture, rape and sexual slavery, mass executions, destruction of property and religious institutions, plunder and looting. Most importantly they tell us about human suffering. They must be told and listened to. They put the picture about the conflicts burdened by ethnic hatred in the right perspective. They tell us what happened in a particular village, town, barrack, and farm. Their personalized stories make us feel how it was to be there – in that particular place at that particular time (...). Those willing to listen will understand that the testimonies of the very modest, not sophisticated people, very ordinary people can bring to understanding of the core issues. As it was, for instance, with many so called crime base witnesses, often very simple farmers from Kosovo, who had to face the late Milosevic in court. There is more in these stories of personal tragedy and suffering than catches the eye at first. They pointedly lead to a conclusion that not only soldiers, policemen or some paramilitaries are responsible for the massive crimes, but also those who were in charge, who fuelled the conflicts using all available official, unofficial and propaganda tools. Those willing to hear will understand from these courtroom accounts that those who ordered and commanded operations and campaigns which led to massive atrocities and suffering – must be held responsible.'

There is some empirical support for this line of reasoning. In a masterful study, Stover (2005) interviewed 87 victim-witnesses who had testified at one of the several ICTY trials. Three-quarters of the people in his sample were Bosnian Muslims, a quarter Croats and five percent were Bosnian Serbs. Stover (2005) found that most victims agreed to testify in order to 'set the record straight', 'speak for the dead' and to better understand why the crimes were committed. The former reasons represent what Stover (2005, 126) calls the 'moral duty to testify' and clearly dwarfed victim interests in what is traditionally known as revenge or just deserts. Based on her extensive practical experience of victims from the former Yugoslavia, Lobwein (2006) also reports that many survivors do this to specifically honour a dead family member, as a gesture of appreciation to their God for their survival or to allow the dead to rest peacefully. Kiza, Rathbgeber & Rohn's (2006) findings underscore this point as half of the war victims they interviewed indicated that international prosecutions should principally be focused on providing a forum for 'victims to tell their stories'. Research in northern Uganda also supports this idea, as the vast majority of those interviewed indicated that they wanted to communicate with other people about their victimisation (Pham, Vinck, Wierda, Stover & di Giovanni 2005). Most victims, it seems, then, place primacy on the opportunity to tell the truth about what happened not only for themselves but also for their communities and people.

Story-telling can help ease the pain. Stover (2005) found that some of his interviewees rejoiced in the collective truth-telling exercise and took solace in the fact that their victimisation – and the victimisation of their friends, families and comrades – could no longer be officially denied. With truth commissions, this outcome can be especially satisfying because most of these proceedings occur in the context of a transitional government, and to that extent, story-telling provides victims with a sense of respect and value, things they did not enjoy under previous regimes (Hayner 1994; Laplante & Theidon 2007; Sooka 2006; Stanley 2005b). A Chilean psychologist who works with war victims illustrates the point:

> 'In Chile, going to the truth commission was like entering into a family: there was a sense of security, a national flag standing on the table, a mandate from the president, and there was this commission saying "We want to hear what you have to say." For over 15 years the state had cast them aside, telling the world that these claims of persons disappearing were all lies. Suddenly, a state commission was ready to listen to their accounts and publicly acknowledge that the disappearances had taken place' (Hayner 2001, 137).

To its credit, the drafters of the 1998 Rome Statute, participants in the Assembly of State Parties meetings, and the current administrative staff leading the International Criminal Court (ICC) both in print and spirit recognise the importance of serving victims of collective violence. The ICC, compared to the ICTY and ICTR, has developed a fairly sophisticated system of providing reparations to victims and their communities (see De Brouwer 2007 and Garkawe 2003 for detailed analyses).

In short, the ICC provides both individuals directly victimised by crime and their communities the opportunity to receive financial compensation. The latter is important to note, as the Court does not limit eligibility for financial reparations only to those harmed by a person convicted of a crime. As Keller (2006, 9–10) explains, also eligible are 'those persons and their families who have suffered physical, psychological and/or material harm as a result of any crime within the jurisdiction of the Court.' What's more, the Court has the authority to provide funds to damaged collectives. In war torn areas such as northern Uganda and Darfur these resources are badly needed not only to increase the likelihood of individual betterment but also for critical infrastructure reconstruction. The philosophy of the ICC in terms of its obligations to victims is laudable, especially because it represents an explicit recognition of the reality of war and atrocity: its consequences extend well beyond individual pain and suffering and cut to the very fabric of human organisation. As Weitekamp & Parmentier (this volume) note, restorative justice approaches to collective violence have great potential to bring about positive change in the wake of even the worst of atrocities and it appears as though the ICC is positioned to execute some of these principles.

Because the ICC is just beginning its work with victims, it is too early to evaluate the impact of the Victims Trust Fund and the propriety of the decision-making leading to the distribution of reparations. Opportunities for research on these matters will shortly appear as the Court moves through its docket over the next few years. In the main, however, the ICC victim services component offers some hope for those who have suffered through extreme circumstances.

5. CONCLUSION

A few years ago, colleagues and I (Kauzlarich, Matthews & Miller 2001) published a paper on the victimology of state crime. Our intent was to make a contribution to the criminological study of state crime by examining the range of victims and circumstances under which people are hurt by both direct and indirect government actions, omissions and policies. We proposed six propositions to guide future theoretical and empirical work on the victimology of state crime:

1. Victims of state crime tend to be among the least socially powerful actors.
2. Victimisers generally fail to recognise and understand the nature, extent and harmfulness of institutional policies. If suffering and harm are acknowledged, it is often neutralised within the context of a sense of 'entitlement'.
3. Victims of state crime are often blamed for their suffering.
4. Victims of state crime must generally rely on their victimiser, an associated institution or civil social movement for redress.
5. Victims of state crime are easy targets for repeated victimisation by the same organisation or institution.
6. The unethical, immoral or illegal state policies and practices, while committed by individuals and groups of individuals, are manifestations of the attempt to achieve organisational, bureaucratic or institutional goals (Kauzlarich, Matthews, & Miller 2001).

Research and theory on victims of state crime and justice system processing of offenders has grown since the publication of the article. Considerable research has been conducted on the structure and process of some formal social control institutions such as the International Criminal Court, various United Nations War Crimes Tribunals and truth commissions (Jamieson & McEvoy 2005; Rothe & Mullins 2006a; Russell 2005; Stanley 2005b; Stover 2005). This is cause for some celebration, as is the apparently growing commitment that the ICC has made to help victims of crime.

The first proposition is obvious and nearly universal in all forms of crime and violence. Whether one considers power in subjective or objective terms, those with the least access to political and economic capital are the mostly likely to bear the brunt of state crime victimisation. This does not always mean that the wealthy or powerful cannot be victimised (e.g. some Tutsis and Cambodians; see Chua (2003) for other examples), but that the chances of victimisation are contextually dependent on current power relationships in a particular society. Second, there is evidence to show that victimisers continue to rely on well formulated techniques of neutralisation (Stanley 2005b). The Bush administration's consistent press to 'stay the course,' and 'protect the world from terrorism' through continuing prosecution of the war on Iraq illustrates the point. Although Americans have grown tired of the hollow rhetoric and quasi-utilitarian justifications, executive branch administrators continue to neutralise the profound harm their policies have caused by appealing to higher loyalties. Third, victims of all forms of crime tend to be blamed for their circumstances. Recent changes brought about by the ICC may temper this phenomenon, although data suggests that there are many Americans who place blame on the excess suffering experienced in the wake of Hurricane Katrina on the victims themselves (Faust & Kauzlarich 2006). The fourth proposition still holds true in many cases, but with the development of the ICC, victims indeed do have the ability to seek reparations from an independent body. Of course, there will be many more victims of state crime than can be served by the ICC, but at least now there is a greater possibility for reparations than in the past. Next, victims are also still at risk of future victimisation, especially in areas such as Darfur where even international security forces have had little impact on the level of violence. Finally, it is becoming clearer that non-state units and groups cause considerable personal and material destruction across the globe. As Kiza et al. (2006) and the United Nations (2006a) report, paramilitary groups and death squads, which indeed do have organisational goals, can present just as great a threat to human well-being than state agencies.

Victims of state crime and other forms of collective violence deserve increasing attention in both practical and academic criminological circles. My hope is that the new supranational criminology movement embraces the study of victims as energetically as it will the study of crime aetiology and distribution. The most obvious opportunity for supranational criminology to contribute to the understanding of victims is through the careful examination of the ICC's new victim services bureau. As the research reviewed throughout this paper shows, victims have different needs and goals. Some simply desire to tell their story, others want to see compensation for themselves and their communities, a few principally want to see the offenders punished and still others only wish to forget the injury. Most have interests, to a greater or lesser extent and at one time or another, in all of the former outcomes and processes. Unpacking these sentiments and evaluating individual and collective victim satisfaction and betterment with future ICC services should be a starting point for developing a humanistic supranational criminology of victims of collective violence. Concurrently, scholars and practitioners should develop a comprehensive catalogue of victim roles, expectations, treatment, functions, reparations and compensation in past and ongoing truth commissions and domestic and international criminal trials. Although there are several important empirical and theoretical accounts of individual proceedings and victim roles (some of which are referenced in this paper, but none of which have been conducted by criminologists), a complete data record does not exist.[2] Such a catalogue would provide the opportunity to systematically gauge the extent to which victims have unique or similar needs by cultural, racial, ethnic, gender, regional and historical dimensions. Collecting and interpreting such data will be an enormous task, but one that is necessary on both academic and humanistic grounds if supranational criminology is to have something meaningful to say about victimology. The past, current and future victims of the worst kinds of crimes committed across the globe deserve nothing less.

---

[2]   The closest approximation, it appears, to a comprehensive narrative on laws and practices relating to victims of collective violence is found in Van Boven's (1993) report to the United Nations. Obviously, things have changed in fourteen years, but this text along with Hayner's (2001, 1994) studies of truth commissions could serve as strong foundations from which to build a comprehensive data catalogue.

PART VI
DEVELOP PREVENTIVE STRATEGIES IN ORDER TO PREVENT INTERNATIONAL CRIMES

XVIII. THE ROLE OF BYSTANDERS IN RWANDA AND SREBRENICA: LESSONS LEARNED

Fred Grünfeld

1.   INTRODUCTION

In my research over the past few years on Rwanda, the results of which were published in the book 'The Failure to Prevent Genocide in Rwanda: The role of Bystanders' (Grünfeld & Huijboom 2007), I focused on why the early warnings of an emerging genocide were not translated into early preventative action. The warnings were well documented by the most authoritative sources and were sent to the leading political civil servants at the UN in New York. I approach the subject from the field of political science and, in particular, international relations. I have scrutinised the communications and the decision-making processes. For this research I have analysed the Inquiry Reports on the Genocide in Rwanda made by the United Nations (UNSG Report Rwanda 1994a), the Belgian Senate (Belgian Senate), the French Parliament (French Parliament 1998), the African Union (OAU) and Human Rights Watch (HRW 1999a). Many scholarly books have been written – and studied for this research – on the role of the UN (Barnett 2002; Melvern 2000), the USA (Power 2002; Shattuck 2003) and France (Lanotte 2007). Moreover supplementary information was obtained from interviews held with decision-makers on the role played by the UN, USA, Belgium and the Netherlands. It is clear that this genocide could have been prevented by third parties. In this chapter I will make use of the conclusions of that research and I will add and compare these with my first results on the Srebenica research.[1] Moreover I will give an insight into the debate on this topic over the last few years at the UN. Possible preventative strategies will be presented at the end of this chapter.

---

[1]   I want to thank Monique Oudt who contributed on Srebrenica during her internship at the Netherlands Human Rights Centre SIM in Utrecht.

2. THE IMPORTANCE OF THE BYSTANDER'S ROLE

Third parties at state and international level are the focal points for the prevention of gross human rights violations, because the perpetrators are unwilling to prevent or stop the atrocities and the victims are unable to do so. This brings us to the conceptualisation of the third party, the bystander. We will look in particular at the relation between the bystander and the victim and the relation between the bystander and the perpetrator.

The atrocity triangle

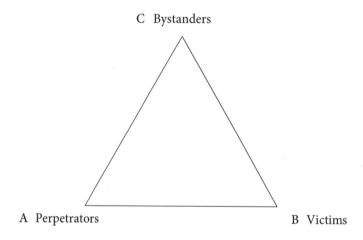

I have developed the following working definition of the bystander: *the third party that will not act or that will not attempt to act in solidarity with the victims of gross human rights violations* (Grünfeld 2000). This means that this bystander will be evaluated afterwards as a collaborator. However, there is an alternative and that is to act or to attempt to act in solidarity with the victims of gross human rights violations. When this occurs, they will be considered afterwards as the rescuers. The threefold distinction of perpetrator, victim and bystander develops afterwards into an elaborated twofold distinction:

1. *Perpetrators and collaborators with the perpetrators;*
2. *Victims and rescuers of the victims.*

A research method that was employed in my previous research (Grünfeld 2003) and on which many models are based for early warnings is one in which the main root causes and immediate causes are investigated and measured by indicators.

These indicators have become more and more developed and, with hindsight, researchers are able to indicate that enough signals were available to constitute a warning. However, in almost all these situations, these early warnings were not translated into early action or any action at all. In short, the main question remains: why did states and international organisations not intervene to stop the escalation? This question takes into account the realisation that early warning—in any form, whether it is simple or very sophisticated—is not enough, because it will not automatically generate the spill over effect from early warning to early action. That is why I have focused on this point: the bridge or gap between early warning and early action. This is also why I analysed the decision-making process before the atrocities took place in order to analyse the lack of prevention.

The role of the bystander is the most decisive factor when the conflict or the human rights violations have reached a stage of repression and coercion. It is the victims, in particular, who are hardly able to resist at that stage and the perpetrators can only be halted in the continuation of their atrocities by the third party. International crimes are the topic of this book which means that we are dealing – in terms of the PIOOM world conflict map – with violent military conflicts (less than 100 deaths in a year) or low intensity conflicts (100–1,000 deaths in a year) or high intensity conflicts (more than 1,000 deaths in the period of one year). Moreover on the PIOOM/Purdue assessment of the terror/repression scale we deal mostly with level 4 situations (targets of the repression – including detention, torture, murder, disappearances, etc. – are the persons belonging to any political opposition) and 5 (situations where the repression has extended to the whole population) [See Appendix I]. In short those situations which are characterised by a combination of violent conflicts and gross human rights violations that do not allow any room for any significant resistance by the victimised target group. In these situations the third party has a crucial role. I would like to emphasise that at an earlier stage (level 2 or 3 where repression and coercion starts after manipulation has taken place) political opposition to the rulers is still possible and in these stages the third party is also important because it can, for instance, support and strengthen the political opposition. In these stages we could say that the international crimes have not yet started but the emerging threat can still be prevented. In this I follow the three main stages in the general discussion on the 'right to protect' (ICISS):

1. Before the atrocities take place, that is the situation of *prevention* and it has been labelled, 'the right to prevent'.
2. During the atrocities, that is the situation of foreign intervention, which has been named, 'the right to act' and is more or less similar to the right to humanitarian *intervention*. Humanitarian Intervention thus refers only to this second stage and not to all three phases of the 'right to protect'.

3. After the atrocities have taken place, that is a situation of *rebuilding* a society and it is called 'the right to rebuild'.

All three stages can be applied to the subject of my contribution on 'developing preventative strategies to prevent international crimes'. The application of the first stage does not need to be elaborated. The second stage is important as well when you define prevention rather broadly and do not limit it to the so-called 'first shot of an armed attack' but also include the prevention of the escalation of the conflict. In my view any activity to stop a deteriorating situation can be viewed as part of the prevention as well.

Very important in this regard is that many atrocities take place in a gradual process and a process in which all aspects of these gross human rights violations – scope, seriousness and frequency – may increase. In many situations the perpetrator is reacting to the behaviour of others. The 'others' are predominantly the third party, the bystander. They may bring a change in the action of the perpetrator depending on whether they oppose or do not react and comply with the perpetrator. Some examples of this behaviour by the perpetrator were seen during the Shoa in Bulgaria and the euthanasia project in Nazi-Germany. In my case studies on Rwanda and Srebrenica I will give some illustrations of this as well. The third 'rebuilding stage' is important in preventing a relapse and the preventative strategies should be orientated towards strengthening the infrastructure and democratisation in society. A well known example of this is the activities of UNICEF which tries to prevent the relapse of child soldiers in many parts of Africa and tries to reintegrate these children who have been both perpetrators and victims at the same time. I will, however, focus on stages one and two in this paper.

3. KNOWLEDGE, IGNORANCE AND INDIFFERENCE

I presuppose that the bystander is aware of the situation in my definition in the previous section of the bystander as the third party that will not act or that will not attempt to act in solidarity with the victims of gross human rights violations. Not helping in these situations is comparable to a person not rescuing someone drowning when he sees a person in difficulty in a lake and when he is a lifesaver. This sort of inaction is an offence under Dutch criminal law. Such a person not responding at the shore of the lake is a 'non-acting' bystander. Two elements have to be realised and added to the supposition; these are:

1. The bystander will oppose the perpetrator by any action he takes to rescue the victim.
2. The bystander may not always directly see the consequences of his action or non-action, but total ignorance is excluded in my definition.

3.1.　INDIFFERENT ONLOOKERS

It is in the interests of the perpetrator that a third party will not obstruct his actions. Moreover the perpetrator is very much aware of the future role of the third party in that society. Because of that role he will behave differently towards those persons. You may compare in this respect the role of Nazi-Germany towards the non-Jewish partners of mixed marriages, the attitude towards the general population of the so-called Aryan people of Flemish, Dutch, Danish and Norwegian origin in comparison to their behaviour towards the population in Eastern Europe. The exclusion of the Jews in Western Europe was implemented differently to their exclusion in Eastern Europe. Although the ultimate aim of exterminating all Jews did not differ and was to be fully implemented everywhere, the perpetrators, in their policies and actions, took the reactions of the other into account in recognising the different roles of the Slavic people and the Germanic people in the future 'Hitler thousand-year empire (Reich)'. The punishment for persons hiding Jews was, for instance, a far less serious crime in the Netherlands (some weeks' imprisonment) in comparison to those hiding Jews in the Ukraine which could result in the killing of the extended family.

The bystander may harm his personal interests by acting in solidarity with the victim. Such harm can take place both at an individual level as well as at a state level or international level. In many situations the refusal or hesitance to take action can be derived from this fear of harming their own national or institutional interests. This will be an important explanatory factor in both the Rwanda and Srebrenica cases.

In short the bystander is not neutral in our definition but may determine the outcome which means that by not taking action he is making the continuation of the atrocities possible. In Elie Wiesel's novel, *The town beyond the wall* published in 1964, he writes his personal story describing the situation in Sighet at the moment when the Jews were gathered at the market place:

> '*It was right here at the old synagogue. Yes, I remember now. At Saturday. The police had herded all the city's Jews into the building. The house of prayer and meditation had become a depot where families were separated and friends said farewell. Last stop before boarding the death train. A memory came to surface so violently that I felt dizzy. The window, the curtains, the face: in the house across the way. A spring day, sunny, the day*

of punishment, day of divorce between good and evil. Here, men and women yoked by misery; there, the face that watched them.

It was then that I saw him. A face in the window across the way. The curtains hid the rest of him; only his head was visible. It was like a balloon. Bald, flat nose, wide empty eyes. A bland face, banal, bored: no passion ruffled it. I watched it for a long time. It was gazing out, reflecting no pity, no pleasure, no shock, not even anger or interest. Impassive, cold, impersonal. The face was indifferent to the spectacle. What? Men are going to die? That's not my fault, is it now? The face is neither Jewish nor anti-Jewish; a simple spectator, that's what it is.

For seven days the great courtyard of the synagogue filled and emptied. He, standing behind the curtains, watched. The police beat women and children; he did not stir. It was no concern of his. He was neither victim nor executioner; a spectator, that's what he was. He wanted to live in peace and quiet' (Wiesel 1995).

The story continues as follows:

'The others, all the others were he. The third in the triangle. Between victims and executioners there is a mysterious bond: they belong to the same universe; one is the negation of the other. The Germans' logic was clear, comprehensible to the victims. Even evil and madness show a stunted intelligence. But this is not true of the Other. The spectator is entirely beyond us. He sees without being seen. He is there but unnoticed. The footlights hide him. He neither applauds nor hisses; his presence is evasive, and commits him less than his absence might. He says neither yes nor no, and not even may be. He says nothing. He is there, but he acts as if he were not. Worse: he acts as if the rest of us were not' (Wiesel 1995).

I concentrated on the role of the bystander in the atrocity triangle and in concordance with Wiesel I did not see the bystander as a neutral third party but as the one who facilitated the genocide in enabling the perpetrator to continue with the atrocities and genocidal acts. I have made the indifference to the fate of the victims part of my definition of the bystander. A bystander is someone who is no longer only a neutral onlooker or passer-by.

3.2. EXCLUDED IGNORANCE

The assumption that the knowledge of the atrocities is available is included in my definition of the bystander. It is in the interest of the perpetrator that the third party is not aware of the atrocities. 34,294 Jews from the Netherlands[2] were, for instance, not murdered in the nearby river Rhine but were transported to the very isolated extermination camp in Poland, Sobibor. When the Nazi's left Sobibor

---

[2] Of the 34,313 Dutch deported Jews to Sobibor, 19 – only two of them have been inside this camp – survived, a survival percentage of 0.05%.

after a revolt in this camp, they attempted to obliterate all traces of their mass murder (Cohen 1985, 22). The third party should not be offended. Knowledge and information on atrocities are kept top secret and when they come out the perpetrators do their utmost to undercut the reliability of the sources. A student from my class has formulated this as follows:

> 'Perpetrators utilize bystander ignorance as a means to perpetuate their atrocities, as such, they strive to maintain this ignorance. For ignorance means inaction and inaction is a free pass for the continuation of human rights violations. When ignorance on behalf of the bystander is not full, and information can be obtained, then the ignorance is more of a choice than it is a fate, and indifference towards the fortune of the victim is the chief factor in maintaining ignorance' (Serbrock 2006).

Seeing ignorance more as a choice than as a fate may have the consequence of preferring to view the start of the genocide in Rwanda as 'just' another civil war – one which the country's inhabitants could and should have sorted out themselves without any moral duty to intervene. Experts who were familiar with Rwandan culture and history sensed that this was not just a civil war, but something far more sinister. However when consulted by staff officers in charge of devising strategic policy plans on the situation they were asked questions such as 'Is it Hutu and Tutsi or Tutu and Hutsi?' This was not ignorance promoted by the perpetrator. It was a chosen ignorance that the bystander could slip into with ease and distance himself from the humans that were suffering and dying. This distance nurtured indifference. The perpetrator didn't even have to lift a finger to maintain the bystander's ignorance that was used to fuel his acts of atrocity. As a consequence the bystander refused to use the term 'genocide'. The term 'chosen ignorance' depicts the bystander in his role of collaborator. The 'chosen ignorance' is essential to understanding the role of the bystander in the post-Cold War period. It is a stronger, more appropriate term for my definition of the bystander than the one used in Stanley Cohen's book *States of Denial*, which is very fruitful in depicting the role of the bystander in the third stage, the aftermath to put it in other words (Cohen 2001). For the first (before, prevention) and second (ongoing, action) stages of atrocities committed nowadays, considering all the information directly available, in particular, to state actors and international actors 'not knowing' can no longer be seen as an excuse for non-action: ignorance is excluded in my definition.

4.   EARLY WARNING

In general, early warnings are always closely related to preventative strategies. The post of 'Special Adviser on Prevention of Genocide' has as its mandate to act as a mechanism of early warning to the Secretary-General and the Security Council of the United Nations. Early warning is coupled with a recommendation to make a decision. Such a decision may involve all kinds of actions or even non-action. Early warning does not exclude a policy recommendation to act forcefully with military means to prevent or stop atrocities. One of the difficult aspects of early warning and so also for the Special Adviser mentioned above is to select the right moment of entry into the

> 'continuum between a dormant situation that could potentially lead to genocide and the escalation of such tensions into large-scale violence or actual genocide. The predicament is that premature engagement in the very early stages could raise concern about interference in matters which are essentially within the domestic jurisdiction of states whereas engagement after the outbreak of large-scale violence or occurrence of genocide would defeat the purpose of a mandate focused on early warning and prevention' (Akhayan 2006, 1050–1051).

Preventative action can be taken in the tension and non-violent stage. In this respect the gathering of information plays a crucial role. This is when Early Warning Systems (EWSs) become important. EWSs have been developed to identify the cause of a conflict, to predict the possibility of an outbreak (when and where) and to propose ways on how to mitigate the situation. From this definition EWSs seem to offer effective means to prevent genocide. Figure no. 1 (Dorn 2002) illustrates the early warning process.

The success of early warning and preventative strategies are difficult to prove or measure because when applied the dreaded situation will not occur, on the other hand being accused of being a so-called 'crying wolf' can easily be made and this accusation will receive a lot of support nowadays since we all know about the non-existence of the weapons of mass destruction in Iraq which was the pretext for the invasion of that country in 2003.

In the two cases presented here – Rwanda and Srebrenica – I will focus in particular on early warnings directed at strengthening the peacekeeping forces. These situations were ones with a UN presence and had UN attention whereas many situations elsewhere are largely overlooked.

Figure 1 (Dorn 2002)

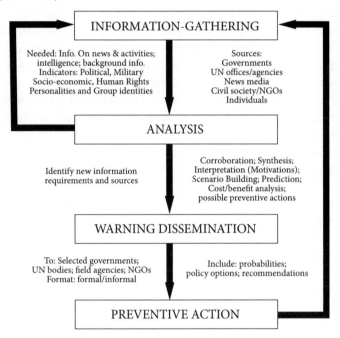

4.1. EARLY WARNING IN RWANDA

The period between 1991 and 1993 were the years in which Hutu extremism laid the foundations for the genocide in 1994. That might have been the right period to intervene. It was only after the Arusha Agreement was concluded in 1993 that the UN involvement with peacekeepers started. Many warnings were made in the years preceding the genocide from divergent sources that gave clear and very strong signals of a worsening situation with the possibility of consequential atrocities (Grünfeld & Huijboom 2007). Various NGOs, such as Amnesty International, Human Rights Watch and also an International Commission of Human Rights Organizations were very clear, concrete and outspoken. The same can be said of the United Nation's Special Rapporteur; he clearly concluded that not politicide but genocide was already taking place in 1993 (Ndiaye). No one paid attention to his very reliable report either inside or outside the United Nations. Moreover ambassadors, ministers and other diplomats from Canada, the United States, France and Belgium also made these serious early warnings public. No one reacted to these outspoken warnings. State and non-state actors informed others, but no action was taken for any prevention. The situation was deteriorating at the end of 1993. No progress was made with the implementation of the peace agreement, and the installation of the transitional government was postponed. The massacre in the neighbouring country Burundi and the continuing and increasing scale of killings in Rwanda worsened the situation. Particularly alarming signals were the elaborated plans to assassinate the political opposition and to provoke unrest in combination with the distribution of weapons. Many early warnings by states and NGOs were made, and these messages were received almost on a daily basis at the Belgian Ministry of Foreign Affairs (Grünfeld & Huijboom 2007, 61–93).

On 11 January, 1994, the UN Force Commander Dallaire sent a cable to the UN headquarters with the alarming information, received by him from a trainer of the *Interahamwe* militia, that Belgian troops were to be provoked, and if these soldiers resorted to force, a number of them were to be killed, thus guaranteeing Belgian withdrawal from Rwanda.[3] The cable continued by saying that the *Interahamwe* had trained 1,700 men in the FAR camps and these were split into groups of 40 throughout Kigali. The informant had been ordered to register all Tutsis in Kigali, which he suspected was to facilitate their extermination. His informant argued that his personnel were able to kill 1,000 Tutsi in 20 minutes. The informant was prepared to identify major arms caches throughout Rwanda, containing at least 135 weapons. Force Commander Dallaire wrote that he intended to take action within 36 hours. However the prompt reply from the top civil servants, Kofi Annan (UN Under Secretary-General and in charge of peacekeeping operations; only three years later in 1997 (until 2006) he became the Secretary-General of the UN) and Hedi Annabi (Head of the Africa Section in the Political Division of the United Nations Department of peacekeeping operations), in New York was that any action by the peacekeepers was prohibited. The request to seize the arms caches was repeated many times by cable and phone but was rejected every time by New York. The top officials decided this themselves without informing the Secretary-General of the United Nations, Boutros Boutros-Ghali (1992–1996) or the UN Security Council. This fax, which contained such a clear warning of the emerging extermination of the Tutsis, should have been shared with both the Security Council and the Secretary-General immediately. This fax should not have been considered simply one of the many alarm signals because speaking of killing 1,000 people every 20 minutes made this fax unique. In hindsight, UN top officials have admitted that the wording of this fax was different to others, acknowledging, 'there are a number of cables that we get of this nature, but not of this magnitude, not with such dire predictions.' Not only the wording of the fax, but also the highly tense political and security situation in Rwanda should have triggered the Secretariat to act. The Secretariat should have interpreted

---

[3]   Fax from Dallaire (UNAMIR/KIGALI) to Baril (DPKO/UN/New York) of January 11, 1994 to be found at: http://www.pbs.org/wgbh/pages/frontline/shows/evil/warning/cable.html.

Dallaire's fax in the light of the pre-existing warnings and intelligence that corresponded with this fax. The explicit and serious warning set out in the fax, together with the highly tense political and security situation in Rwanda, should have led to a far more adequate response from the UN headquarters. Instead, the Security Council was not even informed of this early warning, no decision-making process based upon it could therefore follow and early action to prevent the genocide was precluded (Grünfeld & Huijboom 2007, 95–112). It is important not to concentrate on just one moment in assessing the reaction from New York to the events in Rwanda. It was not only this fax but also the repeated requests based upon the increasing tensions in Rwanda, which were all turned down by the UN political leadership – Riza (Assistant Secretary-General for Peacekeeping operations), Annan and Annabi. They have been condemned in the report of the UN inquiry commission because of their pattern of neglecting all these requests (UNSG Rwanda 1994a, 33–34). Indeed, the continuing refusal of Annan, Riza and Annabi to approve any early action to prevent the atrocities is extremely alarming (Grünfeld & Huijboom 2007, 127–139). The signals from UNAMIR in Rwanda were not ignored, but the early warnings that were received were not translated into any early action, nor were the signals and requests for action forwarded to the UN Security Council. The withholding of this information from the members of the Security Council by the UN bureaucracy precluded any Security Council decision in this field.

The outcome of the inadequate response from New York on the warning fax was that Dallaire and Jacques Roger Booh Booh (the Special Representative of the Secretary-General in Rwanda from November 1993 till May 1994) had to make a *démarche* to President Habyarimana, in which he was informed of the information received and asked to take action within 48 hours. Furthermore, they had to inform the heads of the missions of the United States, Belgium and France and ask them to make a similar *démarche*. This shows that New York fully trusted the President and this line of thinking was in accordance with the expected smooth progress of the peace process. This trust however was not justified. No progress was made in the political negotiations to install a moderate cabinet, whereas extremists gathered more and more influence and destabilised the situation both on the political and security fields in the months preceding the genocide (Grünfeld & Huijboom 2007, 253).

4.2. EARLY WARNING IN SREBRENICA

In the conclusion of the official inquiry report from NIOD (the Netherlands' Institute of War Documentation) to the government of the Netherlands on the Dutch role in Srebrenica it was stated that nothing was known in advance and that the Bosnian Serb aggression took everyone by surprise. Because no early warning was received no preventative action could have been taken and thus the Dutch should not be blamed for having not foreseen the fall of the enclave (NIOD 2002). Wiebes wrote that although there were indications, it seemed that it was not to be expected that an attack was being prepared (Wiebes 2002, 399). He states that the plans for an attack by the Serbs on Srebrenica were made at the last moment and in a short period of time. This did not involve months of preparation, but only a couple of days (ibidem, 404, 405, 409, 410, 431, 440, 441, 444, 445). Neither Dutchbat, nor the Military Intelligence Service (MID) nor the Dutch government in The Hague – confirmed by the former Minister of Defence, Joris Voorhoeve – had any prior knowledge of the attack (Voorhoeve 2007). According to Wiebes (2002, 461) even at an international level no information on an attack was available and thus he concluded in 2002 that 'it is now evident that none of those involved had prior knowledge of the assault. Therefore, the "international community" could not respond in a proper manner.' This report was published in 2002 but since then new information has been revealed which casts many doubts on this version of the story.

The former minister of Defence, Joris Voorhoeve, has now acknowledged that at least two and maybe three states (the USA, the UK and France, FG) were aware in the spring of 1995 of a planned attack by the Bosnian Serbs on the Dutch enclave. He concluded this afterwards, based on information from the Dutch Military Intelligence Service (MID) (Voorhoeve 2005). The foreign intelligence services did not inform their ally Holland (Wiebes 2002, 145) nor did they discuss this information in the Security Council. The impression was that the Security Council did not have the will to do everything that was feasible to keep the safe areas Srebrenica, Zepa and Gorazde. Some members of the Council had already proposed to leave these areas (Voorhoeve 2005). Defending the enclave was – in their view – not the preferred action and thus no measures were taken to strengthen the defence of Srebrenica. Besides they did not even inform the Dutch peacekeepers because that could bring them into an untenable position. The Americans for example wanted – as was told in an interview by the Special Representative of the Secretary General in Bosnia-Herzegovina, Akashi – that the UN troops should leave the vulnerable enclaves in order to launch air attacks, without the risk of the troops being held hostage (Akashi 1998). On 24 May 1995 there was a closed session of the UN Security Council in which the French Lieutenant-General Bernard Janvier (Supreme Commander of UNPROFOR) stated that the UN should give up the eastern enclaves Srebrenica, Zepa and Gorazde (Zumach 1997). In hindsight, Voorhoeve said 'we now can assume that there was a policy – from the government of the US – not to take action against a Serb attack on Srebrenica' (Argos radio broadcast of 5 January 2007). President Clinton's negotiator in Bosnia, Richard Holbrooke, has stated on Sarajevo's television station that US national security adviser Anthony Lake gave him instructions to 'sacrifice' both the territory and the population of Srebrenica and the other Eastern enclaves Zepa and Gorazde (Karadjis 2006). It was confirmed in a recent Dutch radio broadcast that a secret report from the American Ministry of Foreign Affairs was found, which stated that high policy makers in Washington had already decided on 28 May 1995 to 'silently exclude the use of air attacks against the Serbs within the near future.' It also states that both the French President Chirac and the British Prime Minister Major supported the plan, although they did not exclude air strikes totally (Argos 5 January 2007). Others such as Carla del Ponte, Chief Prosecutor at the International Criminal Tribunal for the Former Yugoslavia (Delponte 2006), and researcher Andreas Zumach, studying sources from US and German (BND) Intelligence Services, reaffirm the foreknowledge of the USA (Zumach 1995; Argos 8 August 2003). These Intelligence Services tapped telephone lines between Serbia and Bosnian Serb territory and they heard conversations three weeks before the attack between the Serbian Army Chief of Staff, General Pericic and Bosnian Serb military leader, General Mladic in which they planned the military operation against Srebrenica.

We may conclude that in May when the possibility to prevent the emerging genocide was still possible, the major powers deliberately precluded a preventative action. Moreover these major powers did not share this information at that time with their NATO ally, the Netherlands. The Netherlands together with the Dutch Blue Helmets in Srebrenica were betrayed because the information was withheld from them. Launching air strikes in May, June or early July 1995 could have been a preventative option.

Not only the big Western powers had this information but also the Secretariat of the UN was informed. On 7 March 1995, General Rupert Smith, Lieutenant General Commander of the Bosnia-Herzegovina Command of UNPROFOR in Sarajevo had for instance – after a meeting with Mladic – mentioned the possible attack of the Bosnian Serbs on Srebrenica because Mladic stated that the eastern enclaves nagged him (Parliamentary Report 2003, 130; Argos 29 June 2001; UNSG Report Srebrenica 1994b, 44). The Department of Peacekeeping Operations in New York had observed in spring 2005 on US satellite photos that the Serbs were preparing to launch an attack on Srebrenica. They constructed bunkers, made paths through the woods for the passage of their tanks and strengthened their troops. This statement was confirmed by General Manfred Eisele, who was Assistant Secretary-General for Peacekeeping operations in 1995, and who is convinced that there were early warnings and that DPKO had foreknowledge (Argos 22 December 2006; Argos 5 January 2007). More meetings followed at the beginning of June. The assistant Secretary-General of the UN and head of the peacekeeping organisation in New York made clear that he was aware of the planned attack in March 1995. The option of strengthening the enclave may have been a possibility – although removing tanks from Nordbat II to Dutchbat was not possible because the Scandinavian Parliaments did not agree that their forces could be located in any other Bosnian spot other than Tuzla – but it was not tabled or discussed in the Security Council (Zumach 2002; Argos 5 April 2002). The resemblance is striking to the similar non-action behaviour towards Rwanda one year previous.

Eisele has further stated that the British UN Commander General Rose had frequently informed the DPKO about preparations by the Serbs for a possible attack on the enclave. Reports were presented in New York which clearly showed that Bosnian Serbs wanted to attack the safe areas. Besides, United Nation Military Observers (UNMOs) also reported about preparations in Bratunac, north of the enclave. They confirmed that the Serbs set up bunkers, made paths in the woods for the passage of tanks and strengthened their troops. According to Eisele, non-military officials within the UN systematically ignored the fact that UN troops might have to fight against the Serbs (Argos 5 April 2002, 8 August 2003, 8 July 2005).

Total disclosure of this knowledge – the most important and relevant early warning from the most reliable sources – has not yet been made. However all these indications suggest that taking measures to prevent the collapse of the enclave with a forceful deterrence army was at least a possibility. The argument that Dutchbat collapsed by surprise is perhaps true for the Dutch but not for other major bystanders to the fall of Srebrenica. In some way those bystanders at national and international level – the UK, USA, France and the UN – deliberately made the peacekeepers victim and collaborator at the same time and even in some ways perpetrator.

In the next paragraph we will discuss whether the mandate and the rules of engagement could have transformed the Dutch peacekeepers from idle onlookers to rescuers of the victimised population.

5.   MILITARY STRENGTH AND RULES OF ENGAGEMENT FOR PEACEKEEPERS

The ability of the military to deter or counter attack is related to their military strength, which includes the number of troops they have, the composition of the troops and the material they have at their disposal. The Rules of Engagement (ROE) regulate in which circumstances they are allowed to use what weapons. In other words the possibility to make use of force is to be found in these rules for any peacekeeping operation. The ROE for peacekeeping missions, UN blue-helmets, consists of a number of commands, prohibition rules and directions. The rules tell them at what time and in what manner they can resort to force and from whom they will get the necessary permission to act. These rules have to be made when implementing a mandate. In general it is not the Security Council who draws up the ROE but the Force Commander in co-operation with the commanders of the troop-contributing countries. The Rules of Engagement often give at least two options or standard responses. These ROE regulate under what circumstances weapons may be carried and in what state, how troops should react to hostile action, with or without weapons, and how they should respond in case of self-defence. ROE may also be about the use of force when disarming civilians, paramilitary troops and soldiers, and the control of weapon systems.

5.1.   RWANDA WITH UNAMIR

On 4 August, 1993, the Arusha Peace Accords between the Rwandan government and the RPF were signed. After one year of negotiations and three years of war, the parties agreed upon a power-sharing agreement and made explicit demands for an international force under the responsibility and command of the United Nations. This peacekeeping operation was foreseen as a rather simple operation to implement the agreement and to install the interim government.

The strength of the peacekeeping mission deployed was too weak in all aspects. Four thousand two-hundred and sixty troops were requested by the Rwandan parties concerned and the UN specialists on the reconnaissance mission agreed that at least 5,500 were needed, yet only 2,500 troops were authorised by the Security Council. Because of the feasibility, the Secretariat did not ask the Security Council for the 5,000 blue helmets but limited the number asked for before any debate in the Security Council had taken place (Grünfeld & Huijboom 2007, 50). Again in hindsight, I was told by Beardsley, the deputy Force commander who was engaged in the reconnaissance mission and in preparing the proposal to the Security Council that decreasing the number of troops asked for was the first major mistake. These soldiers were very badly equipped, and only the Belgians were well trained and had good equipment available. However, the Belgians, because of their colonial history and the bad behaviour of the Belgian soldiers, were hated amongst the population. In this way, getting rid of the peacekeepers was thus facilitated and it also contributed to the genocide.

The Arusha Peace Accords asked for a force to guarantee the overall security of the country and assist in the tracking of arms caches. The UN mandate for the peacekeeping force, United Nations Assistance Mission for Rwanda (UNAMIR), only stated that UNAMIR would contribute to the security of the city. Thus, the Security Council devalued the mandate. While the Arusha agreement asked for a force that would *guarantee* the security of the *country*, the force was now limited to the security of *Kigali, inter alia, within a weapons-secure area established by the parties in and around the city.* In addition, the UNAMIR mandate did not provide for the possibility to search for arms, while Arusha had asked for a force that would *assist in the tracking of arms caches* (Grünfeld & Huijboom 2007, 41–42). It was stated in the operational procedures that UNAMIR could be led to organise a search operation with a view to searching for arms, munitions and explosives, but a preliminary authorisation from the headquarters of UNAMIR would be necessary to execute such an operation. This operation would be done in liaison with the *gendarmerie* and the local police and should be carried out with sufficient forces and funds. However, in the rules of engagement, the Force Commander General Roméo Dallaire deliberately included paragraph 17, which widened the scope to make use of military force in cases of crimes against humanity (all available means to prevent any crime against humanity, in original French: *crimes contre l'humanité (...) demanderont moralement et légalement que la Minuar utilise tous les moyens disponibles pour y mettre fin*) (Grünfeld & Huijboom 2007, 44). This paragraph was never approved by New York; in fact, they did not react at all to the proposed rules of engagement, which in the end were never put into practice, because any use of force was prohibited by New York. There could have been some leeway, had the rules been subjected to a broad interpretation, but the rules were interpreted very strictly. In creating the Weapons Secure Area, UNAMIR was restricted to 'helping', 'participating' and 'cooperating with the local authorities'. UNAMIR was not allowed to act alone in dismantling the arms caches, a limitation that would prove to be a great hindrance in carrying out the mandate. One important factor in the failure to prevent genocide in Rwanda was therefore already made in the making of a far weaker mandate, lacking the instruction to allow the use of force that was requested, needed and proposed by the Rwandan parties of the peace agreement.

UNAMIR was hardly able to act and was deliberately provoked. The RPF leader, Paul Kagame, concluded, following an incident on 23 February, that he could no longer count on the peacekeepers for the safety of his Tutsi people (Grünfeld & Huijboom 2007, 120, 125). On the other hand, the mitigating effect of UNAMIR on the violent atmosphere was negated by the top UN officials in New York when they underlined every time that UNAMIR could be withdrawn if Habyarimana did not stop the unrest in the country.

No change of perception

The changing attitude of Habyarimana – coming increasingly under the influence of extremists – was not observed. He was trusted too much. The reaction from New York towards these events in this period was a continuing compulsion to proceed with the peace process; all pressure from New York was placed directly on President Habyarimana. The ultimate threat given by New York to Habyarimana was the possible withdrawal of UNAMIR. All interactions between the Rwandan President and New York were characterised by two aspects. The first aspect was the trust they had in the head of the Rwandan government, holding him accountable for the situation in the country. The second aspect was the trust in the progress of the peace process. Everything was based on both the Arusha agreement and the classic peacekeeping force, UNAMIR, which was the only means of achieving the implementation of the Accords. From this perspective, the UN's reluctance to act is easy to understand. A change of perception, which could have been prompted by all the alarming early warnings, was not brought about.

In this research, the continuing behaviour, as if nothing had changed on the ground since the signing of the peace agreement, is exposed which is obvious from the New York reaction towards the requests from UNAMIR to act. In the three months preceding the genocide, the UNAMIR Commander asked at least six times for a stronger mandate to seize the hidden arms. All these requests were rejected (Grünfeld & Huijboom 2007, 127–130). This would be understandable had the Security Council concluded, for example, that a broadening of the mandate would have endangered the peacekeeping force or the situation in the country. However, this was not the case, because none of these requests and none of these rejections were tabled on the agenda of the Security Council. The members of the Security Council were never informed of these requests from the peacekeeping force, and they had no opportunity to decide whether to act or not. The top officials – Annan, Annabi and Riza, lacking any democratic legitimisation – deliberately kept the members of the Security Council ignorant. We do not know whether the Security Council members would have taken decisions, and, if they had, what kind of decisions these would have been. Instead they missed the opportunity to react to the alarming signals. It is this pattern of negligence by these top UN officials of the very serious warnings from very trustful sources, their own UNAMIR Peacekeeping Force Commander, which is the most horrifying aspect of this period before the genocide. Any preventative strategy to prevent international crimes was predisposed to fail.

The top officials of the United Nations are to blame for their behaviour in not forwarding all these requests – including many Belgian requests for a stronger deterrent force – to the authoritative organ of the United Nations and for making decisions themselves on their own anticipatory expectations of their rejection. Even on 5 April, the day before the plane crash, that triggered the atrocities, when the Security Council had to decide on the prolongation of UNAMIR for another six months (SC Res. 909) the members of the Security Council were not informed by Boutros-Ghali of the deteriorating situation in Rwanda, and not the slightest attention was given to the requests to strengthen and broaden the mandate of the force itself. The prolongation was presented as a routine decision.

Immediately after the plane crash the political adversaries of the extremists were the first to be killed, which meant that the moderate Hutu leaders were also killed during the first few days. These killings can be qualified as a politicide, however, not yet as genocide. It is important to realise this, but the more important and disappointing aspect is again the reaction from New York. Dallaire phoned top UN civil servants, Annan and Riza, five times a day. They always reacted according to the 'organisational process model', as it was a routine decision (Allison 1999). New York prohibited the use of force by UNAMIR every time, even to provide safety to the ministers of the government. During these first days, the Prime Minister and many other moderate governmental officials were killed. Dallaire informed New York of the well-planned and organised terror in Kigali.

The only reaction from Annan, Annabi and Riza to these alarming messages was to keep in close contact with the expatriates and diplomats. From the start, UN headquarters' priority was to save the foreigners in Rwanda and not the Rwandan people. As was predicted months before, on the first day following the plane crash, ten Belgian peacekeepers were deliberately murdered in order to prompt their withdrawal. This was based on a deliberate and well organised plan to kill some peacekeepers. It was carefully designed to bring about a withdrawal of all international interference. In other words, turning the bystanders into direct victims, counting on the world's indifference towards the other victims on the ground precluded any solidarity from the outsiders with the real victims. In these circumstances the perpetrators needed freedom to manoeuvre, and hence no foreign actors were acceptable. The *génocidaires* planned shrewdly and were helped by others outside Rwanda to fulfil their genocidal aims. The important signal was that they were only interested in the safety of their own nationals. A strong military evacuation force made up of British, Italian, French and Belgium soldiers landed at Kigali airport and an American force arrived over land from Burundi to evacuate their countrymen between 8 and 15 April (Grünfeld & Huijboom 2007, 167–178). In these first few days after the plane crash, a politicide took place and not yet genocide. We cannot assess exactly at what date the politicide transformed into genocide, but it must have been in that period. I am not saying that a combination of the evacuation force with the UNAMIR peacekeepers would have been able to stop the chaotic killings. The tragedy is that this option was not considered in any Western capital or at UN headquarters. In my definition at the start of this paper, I wrote that the third party, who will not act or will not attempt to act in solidarity with the victims of gross human rights violations, is the bystander that will afterwards be evaluated as a collaborator. The evacuation force illustrates this role. The *génocidaires* could then conclude that no deterrent force or counter force would obstruct their intentions.

The response of the Security Council and of the Secretary-General to both the start of the genocide and the Belgian withdrawal of its troops came on 21 April, with a total withdrawal of UNAMIR (SC Res. 912) from Rwanda, except 270 men to act as an intermediary between the parties and to facilitate humanitarian relief. It is again remarkable and in line with my findings in this research – as had been demonstrated with the instalment of a force that was far too weak, with the prohibition to seize weapons and use force – that not all possible options were presented by the top civil servants of UN headquarters to the members of the Security Council. Even at the start of the genocide, all attention was still focused on the implementation of the Arusha Peace Accords, though the situation had changed dramatically into a large scale massacre. On 20 April the Secretary-General sent a report to the Security Council in which he now included the option of a massive reinforcement of the troops with an enforcement mandate under Chapter VII. On the evening of 21 April the Security Council voted unanimously for the reduction of the force to 270 persons. The comment of an involved researcher, Barnett, was that with this vote, the SC effectively decided that the 'international community' would not disturb the killers. This was not an unintended consequence and no Security Council member could feign ignorance or argue the fact that he/she was unaware of the implications of this decision. This action was premeditated (Barnett 2002, 127–128).

5.2. SREBRENICA WITH UNPROFOR

The general view was that the Srebrenica peacekeepers were not able and not instructed to defend the safe area. Moreover the classic view of first generation peacekeepers was that they would operate as a buffer between the warring factions and with the consent of all parties concerned and thus no one would start a direct attack on these peacekeepers. With their presence the situation was already safe and would remain stable. Deterrence by presence was the key concept.

The mandate for the United Nations Protection Force (UNPROFOR) was decided in New York at the Security Council. It has changed with regard to the territory, from Croatia (S/RES/743 (1992)) to Bosnia Herzegovina (S/RES/776 (1992)). More important is that this resolution was adopted under Chapter VII (S/RES/770 (1992)), making it a binding decision for encompassing delivery of humanitarian assistance, monitoring the collection of heavy weapons and to supervise exclusion zones (S/RES/ 982 and 987 (1995)). So it was more powerful than in the traditional task of monitoring the ceasefire. In April 1993 the SC decided to protect Srebrenica as a safe area (S/RES/819 (1993)) and later in May 1993 Sarajevo, Tuzla, Gorazde and Bihac were added as safe areas (S/RES/824 (1993)). Bihac was protected by a French battalion, Sarajevo by Egyptian, Ukrainian and two French battalions, Gorazde by a Ukrainian unit, and Tuzla by the Scandinavian battalion Nordbat II. Srebrenica and Zepa were more difficult, as the Canadian battalion deployed in Srebrenica wanted to leave as soon as possible. Eventually, the Dutch battalion Dutchbat was deployed in these two safe areas.

The resolutions were adopted under Chapter VII – i.e. including enforcement measures with the use of force – and the task for UNPROFOR in these areas was to watch over the humanitarian situation in the area, to protect the area and the civilian population, and to demilitarise it. The UNPROFOR mandate with regard to the safe areas was extended in Resolution 836 par. 5 (1993), so UNPROFOR would be able to 'deter attacks against the safe areas, to monitor the ceasefire, to promote the withdrawal of military or paramilitary units other than those of the Government of the Republic of Bosnia and Herzegovina and to occupy some key points on the ground'. Further it would still be engaged in the delivery of humanitarian relief. Resolution 836 par. 9 furthermore ensured UNPROFOR that when acting in self-defence and under Chapter VII of the UN Charter, it could take the necessary peace-enforcement measures, including the use of force. So a military forceful reaction would be allowed when the safe areas were bombarded or when there was an armed incursion into them, or when the freedom of movement of UNPROFOR in or around those areas was deliberately obstructed (Leurdijk 1997, 78; Parliamentary Report 2003, 65–66). The Security Council also decided in resolution 836 par. 10 to allow Member States, 'acting nationally or through regional organisations or arrangements, to take, under its authority, all necessary measures, through the use of air power, in and around the safe areas, to support UNPROFOR'. However robust force was never explicitly mandated to strengthen UNPROFOR and the small group of forces were only lightly armed (Findley 2002, 221–228). The threat of air strikes was needed to completely guarantee the defence of the safe areas (UNSG Report Srebrenica 1994b, 31). The commanders of UNPROFOR saw the mandate as extremely narrow. They interpreted their task strictly as deterring attacks against the safe areas, but not to defend the areas when necessary (Findley 2002, 229–230). Their interpretation was crucial because it was they who chose which rule should be applied and under what circumstances. For instance Rule No. 4 and 5 of the Rules of Engagement are formulated as follows (Berkowitz 1994):

> No. 4: Response to Hostile Act (with Use of Fire)
> Option A: take immediate protection measures, observe and report. Warn the aggressor of intent to use force and demonstrate resolve by appropriate means. Warning shots are authorized. Report action taken. If the hostile act does not cease and life is threatened, Option B can be ordered by the troop commander.
> Option B: On order, Open Fire. Report action taken.
>
> Note: in both Option A and Option B the following maneuvers are authorized (Depending on the situation, orders and reports given by the troop commander):

(1) Withdraw in order to preserve own Force (FG: direct withdrawal when hostile action starts),
(2) Stay in place and defend, or
(3) Move through to escape and preserve own force (FG: not a total withdrawal but temporary escape).

Rule No. 05: Response to Hostile Act (Self-Defence)
Anytime, in self-defence situations, take immediate protection measures and/or return fire without challenging. Report action taken."

The expected behaviour of UNPROFOR is very clearly described in those situations:

General Rules
1. *You have the right to use force in self-defence.*
2. *In all situations you are to use minimum force necessary. FIRE ARMS MUST ONLY BE USED AS A LAST RESORT.*
Challenging
3. *A challenge must be given before opening fire unless:*
    a. to do so would increase the risk of death or grave injury to you or any other person;
    b. you or others in the immediate vicinity are under armed attack.
4. *You are to challenge in English by shouting: " UN! STOP OR I FIRE!" or in Serbo-Croat by shouting: "UJEDINJENE NACIJE! STANI ILI PUCAM!" (utyedinyene natsiye! stani ili putsam).*
Opening Fire
5. *You may only open fire against a person if he/she is committing or about to commit an act LIKELY TO ENDANGER LIFE, AND THERE IS NO OTHER WAY TO STOP THE HOSTILE ACT. Dependent always on the circumstances, stances, the following are some examples of such acts:*
    a. Firing or being about to fire a weapon.
    b. Planting, detonating or throwing an explosive device (including a petrol bomb).
    c. Deliberately driving a vehicle at a person, where there is no other way of stopping him/her.
6. *You may open fire against a person even though the conditions of paragraph 5 are not met if*
    a. He/she attempts to take possession of property or installations you are guarding, or to damage or destroy it; and,
    b. THERE IS NO OTHER WAY OF PREVENTING THIS.

Commanders had two choices when their unit was threatened with regard to applying the ROE: they either held on to the principle of minimum use of force (unlikely to shoot) or they interpreted self-defence strictly (likely to respond to hostile act).

This decision often depended on the attitude and mentality of the unit with respect to the peacekeeping operation and to the conflicting parties, and its assessment of the consequences of its decision for the rest of the mission (NIOD, II.1.3 and 4). Differences in mentality can be seen if you compare the Scandinavian battalion Nordbat II with Dutchbat, which both fell under the command of Sector North East Tuzla. It was up to the Force Commander to decide which option was selected because these Rules of Engagement gave different options for some situations. That made the outcome essentially different for Tuzla under Nordic command and Srebrenica under Dutch command.

5.2.1. Nordbat

From 1993 until the end of 1995, the Scandinavian states sent troops to Bosnia Herzegovina, under the name Nordbat II. They were eventually stationed in the safe area Tuzla, and deployed at Tuzla Airfield. Nordbat II was a Nordic battalion composed of Swedish, Norwegian and Danish troops. It was an armoured infantry battalion, equipped with tanks, APCs and special equipment such as night vision devices. Overall, it included a Danish tank squadron (DANSQN), a Swedish infantry battalion with four companies, and a Norwegian field hospital, Norwegian engineers and a Norwegian helicopter wing (NorAir). This made Nordbat the most heavily armed battalion in Bosnia. The tanks were only added after the Nordic governments, influenced by their parliaments, put pressure on the UN command for better means of protecting their troops (Findley 2002, 142). This deviated from the UN policy, which stated that the troops should be lightly armed. But the Scandinavian governments did not agree with this and demanded that they bring tanks with them, and they stuck to their demand. Criticism was expressed about the heavy armour Nordbat took with it, but Nordbat saw the tanks as a back-up in the bargaining process and as a useful instrument for achieving security. The tanks were also effective in the deliverance of humanitarian aid. Convoys could reach their destinations without problems because tanks drove in front and behind them (Argos 5 April 2002; Findley 2002, 224; Rasmussen 2005).

The mission statement was a tough, robust one: We will shoot back! In Tuzla they were confronted with Bosnian Serb fighters, who attacked them several times. After this, Nordbat came up with an operative plan called 'Bøllebank' which stated that the Danish tank squadron would be put in to counter the attacks (Hansen). Probably the most substantial battle of the Nordbat mission was in 1994 when Danish peacekeepers were shot at by Serb gunners outside Tuzla. On 29 April, 1994 the United Nations observation post 'Tango Two' in the Sapna Finger was shelled by Bosnian Serb artillery and anti-tank weapons. Lt. Col. Lars Moller of Nordbat sent two platoons of Leopard 1A5 tanks to this place. When the Serbs noticed the seven tanks, they began to fire with grenades, antitank missiles, artillery and machine guns. Nordbat first let the Serbs know by standing under light that they were UN tanks and they did not counter the attacks immediately, although the ROE allowed this. However, when the Serbs continued firing, squadron commander Carsten Rasmussen and Colonel Moller gave the order. Both came to the conclusion that for their own survival the tanks had to fire back. Therefore, Moller ordered Nordbat to fire back, destroying five Serb T55 tanks, several artillery pieces, bunkers and an ammunition dump. The Bosnian Serbs reported the loss of nine soldiers but other sources estimated that 150 soldiers of Bosnian Serb origin were killed; there were no casualties on the Scandinavian side. Nordbat showed a tough stance (Rodland 1994; Bodissey 2006; Hansen; Findley 2002, 230; Argos 5 April 2002).

The counterattack was in line with the Rules of Engagement (see above for rule 4) because the Serbs shelled the UN observation post and began to attack the tanks. In normal circumstances, option A of this rule applies, meaning that the troops had to take immediate protection measures, observe and report. They further had to warn the aggressor of intent to use force and demonstrate resolve by appropriate means. Nordbat first showed itself, letting the Serbs know the tanks were UN tanks. But this did not stop the Serbs; in fact they continued firing, directly attacking the tanks. As troop commander, Lt. Col. Moller had the discretion to order open fire (Option B) if the hostile act continued and was life threatening (he did not have to wait for authorisation by a high UN Commander). Moller and Nordbat followed, in general, the ROE in this particular incident. Lt. Col. Moller explains: 'The UN should not bow its head to any of these people. Once you do that, you lose your dignity and, even worse, the other guy will keep walking over you. In the Balkans, you've gotta stand tall' (Bodissey 2006).

5.2.2. Dutchbat

On 2 December, 1993, the location for Dutchbat was announced: Srebrenica and Zepa. Neither the government nor the parliament had discussed the location. Ter Beek accepted the location, since no conditions had been set by the Netherlands (Parliamentary Report 2003, 82–84). The Scandinavians had refused this location. Both the Dutch government and parliament had the feeling that they had to contribute to the peacekeeping operation.

The conduct of Nordbat stood in huge contrast to that of Dutchbat. The Dutch battalion 'Dutchbat' consisted of 550 soldiers of the Airmobile Brigade. Other than Nordbat, it was lightly armed, only equipped with mortars, long-range TOW and anti-tank missiles, and machine gun-equipped APCs, but they did not have tanks. On 25 May 1995 the Bosnian Serbs closed Srebrenica from the outside world. The south of the safe area was the target of another attack on 6 July 1995. First UNPROFOR thought the attack was a small one, but in a few days it became evident that the Bosnian Serbs had another goal, namely to occupy Srebrenica and on 11 July 1995 Srebrenica fell, followed by the horrible massacre of Muslims. Dutchbat left the enclave on 22 July 1995 (Parliamentary Report 2003, 167–168). The UN requested NATO to standby when the Serbs started to attack the enclave. They had a plan to attack 40 Serb artillery positions around the city. The Dutch commander asked at least six times for air support, but only one request was granted. The moment air support was under way, the Dutch Defence Minister Joris Voorhoeve asked Akashi to suspend the attacks, because the Dutch troops were in dangerous positions for air attacks, too close to the Serb gunners (Findley 2002, 250–251). Dutchbat never started a counterattack against the Serbs. The Dutch parliament concluded that the light equipment was an important reason why Dutchbat did not defend; they missed the means and the capacity to do that. The Dutch view was that air support was the only effective weapon (Parliamentary Report 2003, 147–148, 165–166). A former Dutch general, van der Vlis, has stated (NIOD) that logistical problems and the fact that the Serbs would never agree to Dutchbat having tanks, ensured that the Dutch could never have taken tanks to the enclave. They relied more on air support by NATO (Parliamentary Report 2003, 73–74).

Dutchbat did not start a counterattack on its own initiative, and believed they were fully in compliance with the Rules of Engagement for UNPROFOR because it could interpret rule no 4 in its own way – it also authorised the withdrawal and escape of the troops from the area – which was, however, totally different to the Scandinavian interpretation, resulting in the dramatic consequences of genocide for the Srebrenica population.

5.2.3. No change of perception

What can be regarded as remarkable is the lapse of time between the Nordbat counterattack (April 1994) and the fall of Srebrenica (July 1995). The question arises why the Dutch did nothing with the information on the conduct of Nordbat or why the Dutch did not operate as the Scandinavian troops had done. Hadn't they learned anything from this? In my view, the Dutch continued to see the mission as a humanitarian mission with no large peace-enforcement obligations and they therefore stuck to a strict interpretation of the ROE, just as the UN had stated. The purpose of the UN was to keep their impartiality and not to be aggressive, as this would undermine efforts for a peaceful settlement. They did not change their perception of the situation. It had adopted restrictive ROE. Furthermore, confrontation with the Serbs had to be avoided. Nordbat had operated in a different way, but the Dutch did not regard a tougher stance as an option. The UN did not change its strategy after the incident at Sapna Finger by

Nordbat and Dutchbat held on to the traditional peacekeeping behaviour (Findley 2002, 225; Bodissey 2006; Nordland 1994; Parliamentary Report 2003, 63, 69).

No change of mind was made with regard to the intention of the Bosnian Serbs. To confront genocide a change from peacekeeping to enforcement was needed. The use of force was in these circumstances not excluded by the Rules of Engagement as has been demonstrated by Nordbat. In contrast to Nordbat, Dutchbat interpreted the ROE strictly and did not actively defend the safe area. To put forward the idea that if Dutchbat had tanks at their disposal or if the Danish tank squadron had been deployed, the fall of Srebrenica might have been prevented is perhaps not warranted (Argos 5 April 2002 and 12 April 2002). Besides it should be realised – as was explained to me by the Chief of Staff General Couzy – that, particularly, after the successful defence by Nordbat with the use of force by the Danish tanks, the Bosnian Serbs would not, above all their demands, accept the location of other tanks at Srebrenica. The main aspect since the decision of the International Court of Justice on 27 February, 2007 is no longer whether the desired result to prevent genocide was achieved but that 'responsibility is however incurred if the state manifestly failed to take all measures to prevent genocide which were within its power and which might have been contributed to preventing the genocide' (ICJ, par. 430). The obligation to prevent is one of conduct and not one of result. This 'obligation to prevent genocide' of the Genocide convention is not only violated in the opinion of the ICJ when there is certainty that genocide was about to be committed or was under way but 'it is enough that the state was aware, or normally have been aware, of the serious danger that acts of genocide would be committed' (ICJ, par. 432). Serbia and Montenegro was the first state that has been condemned so far for violating the Genocide Convention by not preventing the genocide in Srebrenica.

6. RIGHT TO PROTECT

Some lessons were learned from the genocides in Rwanda and Srebrenica. It was on the day of the memorial ceremonies for Rwanda in 2004 that Annan, the Secretary-General of the United Nations launched his plan for early warning and early action with the following words:

> 'One of the reasons for our failure in Rwanda was that beforehand we did not face the fact that genocide was a real possibility. And once it started, for too long we could not bring ourselves to recognize it, or call it by its name. If we are serious about preventing or stopping genocide in the future, we must not be held back by legalistic arguments about whether a particular atrocity meets the definition of genocide or not. By the time we are certain, it may often be too late to act. We must recognize the signs of approaching or possible genocide, so that we can act in time to avert it' (Annan 2004).

Here he underlines the importance of the changing perception which should have led to the realisation and acknowledgement of genocide at an early stage. An important primary preventative strategy should be perception in time.

Annan realises very well – and maybe more than anyone else at the Secretariat – the need for swift and decisive action when, despite all our efforts, we learn that genocide is happening or about to happen. Too often, even when there is abundant warning, the political will to act is lacking. Such decisive action might be an enforcement action with the use of force. Thus an important preventative strategy is the strengthening of the military forces in cases of genocide and international crimes. Confronted with these gross human rights violations, no neutral peacekeeping forces are suitable any longer. Any military force should take sides against the aggressor/perpetrator in these circumstances and thus should make use of the instruments of Chapter VII of the UN Charter to impose its (UN Security Council) will with an enforcement power.

Annan is asking for guidelines concerning when to act in order to ensure that we have no excuse for ignoring a real danger of genocide when it does arise. His plan has eventually resulted in the following paragraph 139 in the declaration made at the summit of the United Nations in September 2005:

> 'The international community, through the United Nations, also has the responsibility to use appropriate diplomatic, humanitarian and other peaceful means, in accordance with Chapters VI and VIII of the Charter, to help to protect populations from genocide, war crimes, ethnic cleansing and crimes against humanity. In this context, we are prepared to take collective action, in a timely and decisive manner, through the Security Council, in accordance with the Charter, including Chapter VII, on a case-by-case basis and in cooperation with relevant regional organizations as appropriate, should peaceful means be inadequate and national authorities are manifestly failing to protect their populations from genocide, war crimes, ethnic cleansing and crimes against humanity' (UN 2005, 60).

In scrutinising the documents that have led to this summit outcome with the 'right to protect', our conclusion is that the original ideas have been watered down. The original ideas started with the realisation of having to prevent new 'Rwandas' in the future. What started as a duty to protect victims from gross human rights violations by third parties, when their *own state was not able or willing to act* or in cases where the state was itself the main perpetrator of these gross human rights violations, ended in a preparedness to take action when national authorities are *manifestly failing to protect their own population*. The threshold was raised for intervening, and, moreover, this language could be used very well by both supporters of intervention in humanitarian emergencies and those who take an anti-interventionist stance and can legitimise arguments from it (Bellamy 2005).

The final question to be raised in this context is whether the genocide in Rwanda would have been prevented or halted, had 'the responsibility to protect' been in place in 1994. Both decision makers and scholars are rather pessimistic in their answers to this question. On the other hand, the involvement of the Security Council with human rights has increased tremendously. Transparency in the communication has increased and a lack of information as was the case in 1994 is no longer happening if compared to the information available on Darfur today.

The ways for changing minds are, however, more complicated as we have shown in this study where all attention was focused on the implementation of the peace agreement. That is also the main reason why no heavy military means were allowed to be used. However, a neutral peacekeeping force is no longer tenable, when genocide is on the brink of occurring.

It is often said that to prevent or to stop genocide, military means should be available to act when needed. In the 1994 case of Rwanda, I have demonstrated that military means could have been employed and strengthened. The military people that have been interviewed were particularly convinced that with military means, the genocide could have been halted. This was most clearly demonstrated with the evacuation force. Beardsley (Canadian Major assisting Dallaire in UNAMIR) believes that if this evacuation force had stayed, they could have stabilised the situation and the genocide may not have happened. His messages from Rwanda to New York – Beardsley was very familiar with the key players in New York because he had worked in their DPKO department for three months – were not underestimated. Headquarters was just hoping that diplomacy would be the answer and they therefore believed in the no-use-of-force option. In the end, it was this belief among the decision makers in New York in continuing the promotion of the peace agreements and the lack of a shift towards thinking in terms of gross human rights violations, for which other means were needed, which can be seen as a very important factor why the genocide in Rwanda was not prevented. Even so, we have demonstrated that the warnings were clear and reliable and that the means were at their disposal or could have been given to them. Moreover, afterwards all involved regret that no other choices were made in the decision-making to prevent or stop the genocide from 1993–1994. The bystanders at state level and at international level did not act in solidarity with the victims. They did not attempt to rescue the victims by preventing or halting the genocide. Evaluating afterwards, we may conclude that these bystanders turned into collaborators who facilitated the *génocidaires* by not acting against continuing atrocities (Grünfeld & Huijboom 2007, 261). The similarity with Srebrenica is striking. The possibility of air support existed. At least five Dutch requests for air support were made between 5 and 11 July. Only one reached the French General Janvier. In an interview the rapporteur of the UN inquiry commission on Srebrenica, David Harland, told me:

'the Dutch should not be regarded as the guiltiest ones for the fall of Srebrenica. The Serbs are the most to blame and also on the international side, responsibility should be carried by the Council, the UN Secretariat, the UNPROFOR command, meaning General Janvier, and also by General Nicolai about the confusion of the use of air support. Not only did the higher command misread the intentions of the Serbs, but also false and incomplete information was given to the Security Council, to let them think that the situation in Srebrenica was not that atrocious. This was when the fights were already going on' (UNSG Report Srebrenica 1994b, 496).

Again we have to conclude that both the genocide in Rwanda and the genocide in Srebrenica were not prevented and they were also not halted whereas the means to stop them were available. In both situations the development towards an emerging genocide could not be ignored. Many early warnings for both genocides of 1994 and 1995 were made but no action was undertaken to prevent or stop them although instruments to act were not lacking. At the end of the 20th century no bystander at any level can pretend any longer that they did not know or that they were not able to act to prevent these genocides.

7.   GUIDELINES FOR PREVENTIVE STRATEGY

To conclude I would like to formulate ten possible guidelines for preventative strategies:

1. Assess and ascertain the situation and the developments in order to realise at an early moment when changes take place. It is the strategy of changing perception.
2. Early warnings have to be combined with recommendations for policy options. More than one alternative option should be presented to the decision makers.
3. Open transparent communication lines to decision makers are needed. The responsible decision makers with political legitimacy should be able to select and decide.
4. Public opinion is an important factor for any political mobilisation of support. Full access for NGOs to the information is needed.
5. Quantitative, qualitative, governmental and non-governmental information and data are all useful resources. Refinement of early warning mechanisms is not needed.
6. Do not underestimate the perpetrator/aggressor and do not underestimate the power position of the (aggressor/perpetrator) state for any successful strategy.

7. International relations with all influential power positions should be taken into account for any preventative strategy.
8. A preventative strategy within the UN will be more successful – because of less internal and external constraints – than a strategy to implement outside the framework of the UN.
9. Any preventative strategy on international crimes cannot be neutral or impartial.
10. Confronted with international crimes, genocide and in general gross human rights violations, preventative strategies should not to be focused on means to a peaceful settlement but should be adopted under Chapter VII with the possibility to use threats with enforcement powers.

ANNEX 1: SCHEME "HURIVIC," HUMAN RIGHTS VIOLATIONS AND CONFLICT

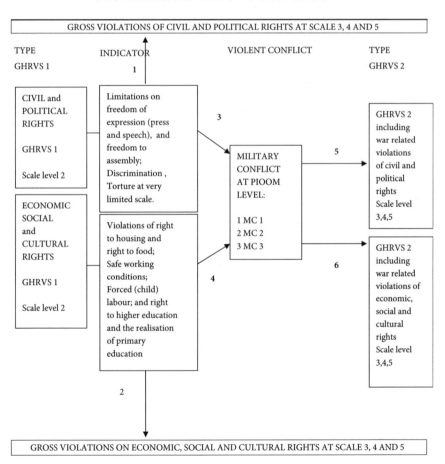

Scale Level 1:   Countries live under a secure rule of law, people are not imprisoned for their views and torture is rare or exceptional. Political murders are extremely rare.

Scale Level 2:   There is a limited amount of imprisonment for non-violent political activity. However, few persons are affected, torture and beatings are exceptional. Political murder is rare.

Scale Level 3:   There is extensive political imprisonment or a recent history of such imprisonment. Executions or political murders and brutality may be common. Unlimited detention, with or without trial, for political views is accepted.

Scale Level 4:   The practices of level 3 are expanded to larger numbers. Murders, disappearances and torture are a common part of life. In spite of its generality, on this level violence affects primarily those who interest themselves in politics or ideas.

Scale Level 5:   The violence of level 4 has been extended to the whole population. The leaders of these societies place no limits on the means or thoroughness with which they pursue personal or ideological goals.

XIX. INTERNATIONAL CRIMES AND CRIMINOLOGY: AN AGENDA FOR FUTURE RESEARCH

Alette SMEULERS and Roelof HAVEMAN

1.   INTRODUCTION

International crimes such as war crimes, crimes against humanity and genocide, require the full attention of criminologists. Criminology cannot and may not ignore these crimes anymore. In the current information age no one can ignore the atrocities which are committed all over the world. We are all bystanders to these atrocities yet criminologists have acted as ignorant and passive bystanders by turning a blind eye and by putting themselves in a deliberate state of denial. Kershaw once wrote: 'The road to Auschwitz was built by hate but paved with indifference.' In his contribution Grünfeld pointed out that in the current information age ignorance can never be a valid excuse and that deliberate passiveness to such atrocities turns bystanders into facilitators of and collaborators to these atrocities. Criminologists may thus no longer turn away on the pretext that these violations are not their business, because as specialists in crime it is their business. Not only for scientific reasons but also for moral ones, because even if there is only a very slight possibility that criminological research can provide possible answers which might make a small difference then it is not only worth trying: it is a moral duty to try. The contributions of all the authors within this book need to be understood as a call to change this attitude of indifference and to firmly put supranational criminology, the criminology of international crimes on the criminological agenda.

The reasons why we should do so are clear and apparent and have been enumerated in many of the contributions. International crimes are forms of widespread, structural and collective violence which not only result in a huge number of victims but they furthermore endanger international peace and security. Criminology can provide both methodologically sound methods and tools and a useful theoretical framework to study international crimes. It must be an intriguing challenge for mainstream criminology to study international crimes precisely because so many otherwise law-abiding citizens get involved in committing atrocious crimes. In studying the aetiology of international crimes, mainstream criminology can test the soundness and validity of its theories and this might give a new impulse to criminology itself. International criminal law has matured over the last decades and criminology should and may not stay behind. In the next few paragraphs we will set an agenda for future research.

2. CONCEPTUAL AND THEORETICAL FRAMEWORK

Supranational criminology should be studied from a clear conceptual and theoretical framework. The first question consequently is: 'what is supranational criminology?', 'What is meant by the criminology of international crimes?' We would suggest that supranational criminology is the criminology of international crimes and should limit itself to studying international crimes in the broad sense of the word. As indicated in the first chapter international crimes are war crimes, crimes against humanity and genocide as defined by the statutes of the international criminal tribunals and the international criminal court but we will not limit ourselves to these crimes. This means that we should study behaviour which has already been categorised as an international crime but also contribute to the scholarly debate on whether or not other forms of behaviour should also qualify as such but to exclude other forms of criminality.

One open question in this regard for instance is: to what extent should supranational criminology also study terrorism and terrorists. It is clear that we can learn a lot from terrorism and that from a criminological point of view it is sensible to study these types of crime in comparison with each other as they can both be considered political crimes: crimes motivated by ideological motives. On the other hand international crimes are often – albeit not always – manifestations of state crime, whereas terrorism usually is not, despite the fact that terrorists are sometimes supported by the government of a third state. The scholars who contributed to the book did not all agree on the question whether or not to include terrorism in the subject matter of supranational criminology. The discussion on this point is therefore still open.

Secondly we need to develop a conceptual and theoretical framework. This new field of research should develop clear definitions and identify, study and analyse the specific characteristics of international crimes as forms of state sponsored or state facilitated crimes with special focus on phenomena such as globalisation, victims of political power, corporations and the role of ideology, perpetrators and organisational structures. Some would prefer to study criminality from the perspective of globalisation and the changed world order and do not like to limit themselves to international crimes whereas others specifically focus on international crimes. The authors of this contribution are as a matter of course of the opinion that criminology needs to study all types and forms of criminality albeit not necessarily under the heading of supranational criminology.

In order to have supranational criminology grow into a fully developed and fully accepted field of study within criminology it is crucial to have conceptual clarity. The terms *state crime, state organised crime, state corporate crime* and *corporate crime* gradually find their way into the criminological discourse but also the terms genocide, crimes against humanity and war crimes need to be defined. For all these terms there are clear legal definitions but these definitions are seldom workable definitions which can be used for empirical research. To find an appropriate and workable definition is not easy however. Among genocide scholars the debate on the definition of genocide for example is far from concluded (Drost 1959b; Dadrian 1975; Horowitz 2002; Kuper 1981; Fein 1984, 1990/1993; Chalk and Jonassohn 1990; Charny 1994; Shaw 2007). Criminologists who study international crimes need to acquaint themselves with this scholarly debate on genocide. Surprisingly enough, far less is written about other forms of international crime: crimes against humanity (such as torture and sexual violence) and war crimes. Genocide scholars have often limited themselves to the 'crime of crimes', namely genocide and have not studied other forms of international crime although there seems to be growing attention for sexual crimes as a form of genocide. Among genocide scholars this discussion has triggered the debate on definitional issues: the *Journal of Genocide Research* published a debate launched by Gerlach on extremely violent societies (8(4) 2006) and the *Journal on Genocide Studies and Prevention* devoted a lot of attention to the difference between the terms genocide and atrocities in a debate triggered by Scheffer (1(4) 2006 and 2(1) 2007).

When focusing on the conceptual and theoretical framework it is important to note in what way international crimes can be distinguished from ordinary crimes. Some very important characteristics are that these crimes are usually committed within a context of structural violence; they are committed on a mass scale and often on behalf of the state. International crimes are furthermore manifestations of collective violence. In some cases only a particular institution within a state, for example the military police, is involved in the crimes: for example they may use torture in order to force suspects to give statements. In other cases many more governmental institutions are involved or even the whole of society gets involved, for instance in cases of a large scale civil war. It is important to note that in all these cases the violence is a clear product of a social process and is committed in a particular social context – a context in which many people become involved in or are complicit in committing international crimes. Gupta (2001) pointed to the fact that individuals no longer act as individuals but as representatives of a collective. They submit their individual identities to a collective identity. This can cause law-abiding citizens to turn into law-abiding criminals. In order to be able to understand the aetiology of international crimes we need to study this context. Especially when the whole state is involved in the crimes, as for example in the case of genocide, the remarkable conclusion is that the context has changed to such an extent that crime has become nothing out of the ordinary. Crime becomes the norm and many law-abiding citizens take part in it thinking that this is the right thing to do. Many of the perpetrators are just ordinary people within extraordinary circumstances. Pathetic little and colourless men who are 'terribly and terrifyingly normal' (Arendt 1963, 276) can come to play a crucial role in a monstrous plan. Individual barbaric acts consequently need to be studied within the broader context of systematic violence. Many social scientists and historians have tried to describe and analyse these circumstances but our knowledge of these situations can be enhanced by testing to what extent criminological theory can be used to explain this phenomenon. When studying mass violence, collective violence or structural violence we need to recognise and be aware of structural and historical dimensions in a changed world. We need to unravel the institutional responsibility of the state and civil institutions; we need to identify useful parameters to study international crimes and structural violence; we need to develop a coherent typology of transnational, international and global crime; we need to study phenomena such as international citizenry and the global community; we need to study both acts of commission and acts of omission; we need to study victims of the abuse of political and economic power and we need to reconceptualise the concept of post-conflict justice in search for social justice.

Since the supranational penal system is still only in its infancy, many concepts, definitions and terms still have to be determined, interpreted and refined (Haveman et al. 2003). We need to find workable definitions for all international crimes. We furthermore need to focus on the particularities of certain crimes, like genocide and torture but also sexual violence.

Sexual violence is usually a widespread phenomenon during armed conflicts (Morris 1996; Chang 1997; Lilly 2003) and genocides (HRW 1996; Zarkov 1997) but is also often found in dictatorial regimes (Graziano 1992). These are not the 'common' rapes and other common forms of sexual violence which can be found in every society; these are rapes and sexual torture, which are used as deliberate and systematic weapons (Brownmiller 1975). It was for example used and applied in a widespread and systematic way during both the Rwandan genocide and the war in the former Yugoslavia (HRW 1996; De Brouwer 2005; Bijleveld and Morssinkhof 2006). The exact number of cases is not clear; quantitative research is urgently needed. It is not always easy to determine whether a particular rape is an 'ordinary' crime or a crime against humanity. Indications are that a disproportionate part of rape victims are members of a specific ethnic group. Many examples can be mentioned, with as many victims: the women and men who had to endure the sexual violence but also those who have witnessed the crimes. Estimates exist that in Rwanda between 250,000 and 500,000 women have been the victims of rape and sexual torture; about 10,000 men have been indicted as offenders. A study of 3,000 children who were between 7 and 18 years old during the genocide shows that 31% of them have witnessed rape or sexual violence (Dyregrov et al. 2000). Another aspect of sexual violence is the spread of HIV/Aids as a method of genocide. An estimated 70% of the women raped during the Rwandan genocide suffer from HIV/Aids, an illness that in Europe and northern America no longer is as deadly as it was about 15 years ago, but in Africa still in many cases leads to a painful death, due to a lack of affordable medicine. Infection with HIV/Aids could also be brought under the heading of genocide – *deliberately inflicting on the group conditions of life calculated to bring about its physical destruction in whole or in part* – but this has not yet been done. The same pertains to crimes as sexual slavery and forced marriages; also sexual violent crimes during genocides (De Brouwer 2005).

We have focused on sexual violence as an illustration of venues of research which can and should be taken in the near future. There are however other forms of violence which need to be scrutinised. Almost every topic that has been and will be studied by criminologists on a national level has its supranational pendant, like for example group crimes versus collective violence, hate crimes versus genocide, youth delinquency versus child soldiers. There are also some particular study objects which require our full attention as for example the role of the media in spreading a genocidal ideology, as for instance *Radio Télévision Libre de Mille Collines* did in Rwanda.

3.   METHODOLOGICAL CLARITY AND SOUNDNESS

In studying international crimes we need to rely on methodological sound empirical research in which we should take the particular methodological issues and difficulties which arise when studying international crimes into account. Scholars need to develop reliable methodological tools and instruments and regularly test these tools. We need to assess the incidence of conflicts and outbreaks of violence and should gauge the damage. We will probably never be able to exactly measure the number of people killed, raped or otherwise mistreated in periods of collective and structural violence but in her contribution Bijleveld stressed that this should not stop us from trying to give accurate estimates. We need to study mortality rates and the death excess figures because only with this data can we test hypotheses, find correlations, study patterns, show temporal and spatial variations and thus understand the underlying processes which lead to genocide. We need to focus on the incidence and prevalence of international crimes, create typologies and test them empirically not only in relation to the victims but also in relation to the economic damage and the perpetrators. Academic debate on these issues is crucial. Especially when confronted with the specific and particular difficulties of studying international crimes for example in relation to estimating the numbers of victims, scholars can learn a lot from each other and by doing so can refine their own methods. Expert meetings, roundtables, symposia, conferences and published research should stimulate this debate.

4. STUDYING INTERNATIONAL CRIMES THROUGH A CRIMINOLOGICAL FRAMEWORK

One of the core domains of criminology should be the aetiology of international crimes. An important element is to develop explanatory theories which can be translated into testable hypotheses. New venues of research should be explored by testing to what extent existing criminological theories can help to explain the aetiology of international crimes. In which criminological traditions should we place the research on international crimes? Which theories from mainstream criminology can provide answers for the prevalence or causes of international crimes? How can the phenomenon of international crimes be explained? To which crimes can we compare international crimes? These are just some of the relevant research questions which need to be studied.

It has already been mentioned in the introduction and stressed by Rothe and Mullins in their contribution that we have to study international crimes at four different levels: the individual, the group, the state and the international community. And that we have to be specifically aware that the role of the state is entirely different: instead of enforcing the law, the state in many cases becomes the transgressor of the rules it needs to uphold. The perpetrators, individuals, groups and organisations who commit the crimes consequently do not commit acts of deviance but rather crimes of obedience. The question is to what extent this changes the applicability of theories from mainstream criminology. In the following subparagraphs we will deal with the relevant research issues relating to the perpetrator (par. 4.1), the groups, organisations and states (par. 4.2) and the international community (par. 4.3) before we discuss how to deal with the past in paragraph 5.

4.1. THE PERPETRATOR

One of the most challenging questions within the field of supranational criminology is how it can be explained that so many otherwise law-abiding citizens get involved in this type of criminality. International crimes are committed in a very specific political, ideological and social context which seems to turn ordinary morality upside down and makes ordinary people believe that committing murder and genocide is a necessary duty. The crimes committed should in most cases be qualified as crimes of obedience rather than crimes of deviance and need to be studied as such. This is not to say that the crimes are only committed on direct orders but that the crimes are committed in an environment in which the authority seems to support and legitimise the crimes. Perpetrators of international crimes are therefore a different type of perpetrator and it would be interesting to see what mainstream criminology has to say about these perpetrators. It seems that theories which focus on either physical or mental deficiencies or a failed socialisation are of limited use in relation to explaining this type of crime because they cannot explain why so many otherwise law-abiding people get involved in a period of collective violence or as Gupta (2001) called it: a period of collective madness. These theories will therefore not be widely applicable although these theories could come in handy as they might help explain the behaviour of certain types of perpetrators, like the criminal mastermind, the fanatic and the sadist. These perpetrators are usually driven by internal drives which are rooted in physical, mental or social deficiencies. Probably far more useful are theories which emphasise the influence of a specific social context on an individual who commits crimes. Theories which are thus very useful are the social-learning theories, theories which focus on differential association and neutralisation techniques. Many scholars nowadays consider criminal behaviour as learned social behaviour. It is learned within a specific social context and in the process of social interaction. An extreme example thereof is the Greek torture school which has already been referred to in this book. Within these institutions torturing and killing is the outcome of an enforced social learning process (Bandura 1973; Haritos-Fatouras 2003) which is continuously reinforced by peer pressure and the pressure to obey. Many ordinary crimes are furthermore committed within groups, and the interaction and dynamics within a group can influence the behaviour of an individual and incite him or her to commit crimes (Warr 2002). These assumptions are particularly true in relation to international crimes and interesting comparative research could be done.

Many international crimes are committed by members of the army, police or other militarised units. It is consequently necessary to study these institutions: their organisational dynamics, the information flow and also the specific subculture within these institutions. An important and crucial aspect thereof is that these institutions train people to kill. These institutions have a monopoly on arms and may legitimately use them under legally well described and defined circumstances. Recruits within these institutions are deliberately trained to make them respond to orders and to make them submit their individual personality to group identities to make them conform to the ruling military culture and to reduce both physical and moral constraints to killing a fellow human being. The used training methods have been successfully refined since the Second World War. Research has shown that during WW II only 15–20 percent of the soldiers were prepared to fire their rifles whereas during the Korean War this figure rose to 50% and to 90% during the Vietnam war (Grossman 1995). Some of the recruits who have gone through these types of training commit horrendous crimes simply because they were trained to do so. A better example of crime committed after a period of social learning can hardly be given. But not only the actual training but also the specific climate and culture within the military can be conducive to violations like Morris (1996) showed in relation to military culture and sexual violence.

Many elements from the control theories might be useful to explain international crimes as the context of mass violence in which most international crimes are committed is marked by on the one hand a lack of social control and on the other excessive social control. Take for example a period of war in which some people get completely out of control. They can eat, drink, steal, kill and commit sexual violence at will without being prosecuted or punished. Perpetrators who can be categorised as profiteers take advantage of this type of situation and commit crimes they might otherwise not have committed. On the other hand many perpetrators are socialised into committing crime on behalf of the state. They commit crimes of obedience precisely because their bonds with society are so strong. The rational choice theories also offer useful insights. In this theory, criminals commit crimes because the benefits outweigh the costs and it is therefore rational to commit crimes or these types of crimes. In a period of collective violence many people can get involved in international crimes simply because it is the most rational thing to do at the time. Other useful theories are strain theories as well as theories which focus on a particular subculture as they see the social context as the main explanatory factor in understanding crime. The particularities of the social context in which these crimes are committed need to be analysed as well as the effects thereof on the individual perpetrators. Especially the neutralisation techniques identified and described by Sykes and Matza (1957) are particularly relevant to understanding international crimes. Sykes and Matza concluded that people who can otherwise be very well adapted and live by the rules can come to see certain types of immoral and illegal behaviour as acceptable. Research on individual perpetrators of international crimes has shown that this is also true for many perpetrators who indeed consider their involvement as something good and important. The very same neutralisation techniques as described by Sykes and Matza are used by perpetrators of international crimes (Alvarez 1997; Neubacher 2006). They are often institutionalised into state rhetoric or feature in the ideology.

The presented typology of perpetrators of international crimes which needs to be tested and refined in future research can be used to take a more balanced approach to the perpetrators. Perpetrators are definitely not all sadists, nor are they mere passive and unwilling products of the environment. Individuals interact with their environment and make many small and seemingly insignificant choices which influence whether they do or do not get involved in international crimes. At a certain point however their involvement seems to become inevitable as they get caught up in violence and feel entrapped in their own psychological defence mechanisms. There are remarkable similarities in the transformation process which turns ordinary people into perpetrators but individuals differ in what drives them. Individual case studies or general case studies can further enhance our knowledge of perpetrators. In future comparative research these case studies should be used to test and refine the proposed typology. The typology can then be used to better understand intergroup dynamics and group processes.

In future research it would furthermore be very interesting to compare perpetrators of international crimes with ordinary perpetrators. Interesting comparisons would be between criminal masterminds of states with leaders of religious and violent sects. Fanatics will probably have a lot in common with people committing hate crimes whereas it will be very unlikely that devoted warriors will be involved in crime under ordinary circumstances. The phenomenon of child soldiers may be considered as the supranational pendant of youth delinquency. This is one of those issues about which there is a dire need for quantification; the media seems to exaggerate the number of child soldiers in the world. When thinking about child soldiers our mental flat screen shows the image of very young boys and girls being abducted, given drugs and being forced to commit atrocious crimes. Without doubt this is true for quite a few child soldiers. But with respect to many others it may be more productive to make a comparison with street gangs, football hooligans or recreational crime.

Another research venue would be to focus on particular groups of perpetrators like for example women. Most physical perpetrators of international crimes are men for the very simple reason that within the ranks of the military and police we still predominantly find men. But Milgram already showed that women are equally prone as men to follow orders and there are various reports of extremely cruel and sadistic women guards in the Nazi concentration camps. Women can be furthermore very much involved in international crimes without physically committing these crimes. The telling title of a report by African Rights on women involved in the Rwandan genocide is *Not so innocent* (African Rights 1995). There are also some well known examples of very influential 'first ladies', like the infamous Jiang Qing but also Mira Markovic the wife of Slobodan Milosevic (Drakulic 2004; Windgassen 2006).

Another phenomenon which needs to be studied is the bystander and especially may be the 'unresponsive bystander'. Research has shown that the greater the number of bystanders the lesser the chance that someone intervenes. The infamous murder of Kitty Genovese is usually cited as the extremely sad but typical example of impassive bystanders. An active stance of bystanders is furthermore hampered by the just world theory (Lerner 1980) which can be particularly strong in bystanders to violence in dictatorial or oppressive regimes. According to this theory people have a strong urge to believe in a fair and just world and will thus generally and instinctively judge violent police actions as justified: they will reason that the targets of these actions must have done something wrong to deserve it. It is a deliberate but also vital and protective lie because individuals do not have to reckon or deal with the fact that the violence is arbitrary and they might be next. The phenomenon of the *unresponsive bystander* can be partially explained by this just world thinking but there might be other phenomena involved. An example of a study in which the author tries to explain passiveness in relation to international crimes is the study by Shorey (2000), writing about the murder of Arone, a Somali citizen, by Canadian peacekeepers in 1993.

> '*Over the course of approximately four hours – and within earshot of other members of the [Canadian Airborne] Regiment – Arone was subjected to an ongoing brutal beating, which included several blows to his head, periodic burning and suffocation eventually killed him*' (Shorey 2000, 19).

None of the other soldiers within earshot intervened. Shorey, linked to the Canadian 'Department of Military Psychology and Leadership at Royal Military College', tried to understand this. In future research it might be interesting to study the role of bystanders not only in various case studies but also in comparison to bystanders to ordinary crimes.

A last suggestion for future research would be to compare the perpetrators of international crimes with those people who refused to commit such crimes. Many recruits of the army or police of a dictatorial country have committed horrendous crimes but did everyone commit crimes? What about those who refused? What happened to them? Why did they refuse? Did they have specific characteristics? What about the deserters and defectors? Comparing these so-called refusers with those who complied might shed more light on the reasons why some comply and others do not.

4.2. GROUPS, ORGANISATIONS AND STATES

Most crimes are committed in groups. This is true for ordinary crimes (Warr, 2002) and international crimes are no exception to this phenomenon. International crimes are manifestations of collective violence (Gupta 2001) and thus a particular form of group crime. Quite a lot of social-psychological research has been done on the influence of groups on individuals and it is known that groups have a profound effect on the acts, ideas and behaviour of the group members, and that ideas can easily get polarised within groups (Baron and Kerr 2003): groups furthermore tend to think in in-group and out-group dimensions. It is also known that the pressure to conform is very strong (Asch 1951). Within large groups people tend to feel less responsible for their individual acts which probably influences their inclination to commit crimes. Unfortunately rather little is known about the precise processes and dynamics within a group which precede crimes even in relation to ordinary crime (Warr 2002) but it would be interesting to conduct more research on the dynamics within groups.

The network-perspective could also lead to interesting findings, for instance concerning the relatively small elite in conflict ridden countries with strong inter-relationships but at the same time consciously inciting and maintaining controversies and conflicts between each other, whilst on the other hand protecting each other, for instance by mutually promising immunity for criminal prosecutions. Also amongst those who actively murder and plunder, an analysis of the network within which they function and their social relations may lead to interesting insights into group dynamics of war criminals or *génocidaires*. How has a network been formed and how does it function? Are there special codes and rules within the network? To what extent does the network exercise power over an individual? What does the network mean for the career opportunities of an individual member of the group? How can the network structure be torn down?

In a period of difficult life conditions groups can be formed by political entrepreneurs who abuse a situation of uncertainty or crisis and manage to motivate people to join the safety of the ranks of a new revolutionary movement which is about to change the world. Such movements attract the masses, and individuals, scared of being left out, join the ranks and submit themselves fully to the group, the ideology or the leader. Individuals submerge their individual identity into a collective identity (Gupta 2001; Tajfel & Turner 1986) and submit their own norms and values to those of the group. They trade their freedom for security and the luxury of feeling part of a self-declared elite. In some cases often when spurred on by charismatic leaders such groups are ultimately prepared to use violence against their neighbours who they suddenly no longer see as their neighbours but as representatives of the enemy. The crimes committed are political crimes and we should thus also study the mechanisms of political mobilisation

(Tilly 1978, 2003). As has been stressed by Alvarez in his contribution for this book, ideology plays an important role in motivating people and thus needs to be studied closely.

An important issue in relation to ordinary crime is the question how and why people get the feeling that they belong to a specific group? In relation to international crimes, the groups are often defined beforehand: soldiers and policeman are assigned to a particular unit, and especially within a war situation bonding occurs almost naturally. Many soldiers have reported that the bondage with their fellow soldiers during combat is even stronger than bondage through friendship or marriage: lives depend on whether each one is prepared to risk his or her life in order to save the other. From criminological research we know that within groups we can often identify a leader and followers. Some of these followers just go along, some will be eager while others will be reluctant captives within a social context. This is also true in relation to international crimes.

Genocide and other international crimes do not occur out of the blue. They are the sometimes logical and inevitable outcomes of a genocidal process. Future studies should try to get more insight into the social dynamics and processes which lead to violence and crime and should compare ordinary crime with situations leading to international crimes. It would surely ameliorate our potential to prevent or stop international crimes from being committed when we understand these dynamics and processes and when we can identify and pinpoint preconditions and even predict when international crimes are likely to be committed. To many scholars the pictures of abuse in Abu Ghraib did not come as a surprise (cf. Huggins in this book). To be a prison warden in Iraq, in a dangerous, sometimes life threatening situation in a war of terror in which the Iraqi people have been described as enemies and have been dehumanised by the harsh and bad prison conditions, is what Lifton would call an *atrocity producing situation*. This becomes even more clear when we take the political rhetoric of the war on terror into account which seemed to give a wide discretion to the prison wardens to use violence in order to break the prisoners and make them confess to terrorism. All these factors contributed to an environment in which the threshold to use violence was lowered and the abuse of violence seemed to be legitimised and even required.

International crimes such as war crimes, crimes against humanity and genocide also need to be studied from a social organisations perspective. What is the organisational culture within these institutions, what are the social and organisational dynamics which control the social processes and how does the information flow function? All these questions can be useful in explaining violent dynamics. The role of corporations also needs to be explored. The model used by Kauzlarich and Kramer (1998) is a useful model which we should fill with empirical data in order to explain the involvement of corporations in international crimes. We should use statistical analyses of country and corporate-based case studies in order to unravel the complex relationship between corporations and human rights. It is furthermore of paramount importance to study corporations which end up committing crimes alongside those who did not. Huisman referred to two Dutch cases in which Dutch businessmen got involved with respectively Charles Taylor from Liberia and Saddam Hussein's Iraq as two interesting cases to be studied, but there are many more. The role of (international) organisations and enterprises in causing and maintaining situations in which atrocities are committed is an important new venue for research. Diamond and weapon trade, oil companies and banks may play a role in causing large scale human rights violations. How can one break through this role of business organisations? Some time ago the UN-Human Rights Commission adopted draft norms for multinational companies entailing obligations regarding human rights. These obligations however faced many objections from the side of multinational concerns. On the other hand there are examples of enterprises that temper tensions in the region where they operate.

Most, albeit not all international crimes are manifestations of state crime. We thus need to study the state as perpetrator rather than merely as the powerful law-enforcer. Cunneen and Welch showed that even democratic states have been or are involved in international crimes. An obvious theoretical exercise is studying the extent to which organisational criminology can be applied to states that commit crimes against humanity and genocide. The organisational structure and dynamics that lay at the basis of the functioning of the state are at least partly comparable to the structure and dynamics of an ordinary organisation. Notwithstanding the similarities, it is expected that theories on organisational criminology have to be adapted to the specific circumstances of international crimes committed by states. After all, states have much more political power, a monopoly on their use of violence and a legislative function. These characteristics have an enormous impact on the options to abuse power.

4.3. THE INTERNATIONAL COMMUNITY

As mentioned before: in studying international crimes we need to take four rather than three levels of analysis into account. The international level, the macro level (i.e. the state), the meso level (the group or organisation) and the micro level (the individual) and the interrelationship between these levels. States can for example get involved in an international armed conflict with each other which sets the stage for many war crimes. On the basis of international law, states need to protect the rights of their citizens and take an active stance therein. The international human rights treaties set the standard to which states need to comply. Contrary to national law there is however no clear enforcer of these rules. The international community and other states can assert diplomatic pressure; other states and individuals can in some cases lodge a complaint and the bodies which look into these complaints can express their views or give judgment but the international community does not have the means to enforce compliance with these rules. Only when a situation becomes a threat to international peace and security can the United Nations Security Council act on the basis of Chapter VII of the UN Charter and enforce binding measures. We can therefore generally state that when a state itself is involved in committing international crimes, social control mechanisms and enforcement is usually lacking.

The 'unresponsive bystander' (Latané & Darley 1970) is thus also on the supranational level an interesting field of study. Can international crimes be prevented by (international) bystanders? What can bystanders do? Does the 'just world theory' (Lemer 1980) also play a role with regard to the international community facing international crimes? What is the influence of bystanders on the behaviour of offenders? Are there examples of effective and active interventions? And what if there is no intervention or even no response whatsoever; to what extent does this contribute to the legitimacy and normalisation of crimes? Cohen, in his book *States of Denial* (2001), demonstrates how to apply the phenomenon of the unresponsive bystander on states which although they know that atrocities are committed, do not actively intervene. In several publications Grünfeld (2000, 2003; together with Huijboom in 2007) writes about the inertia of the international community in view of gross human rights violations. Third states and the international community might for example have prevented the genocide in Rwanda, but instead of sending more troops to Rwanda they retracted many troops around the time the genocide started. What can other states do in cases of gross human rights violations? Are they allowed or even obliged to intervene? Are there examples of effective interventions by other states, and if so, which lessons can be learned thereof? What can be learned from situations where the international community did too little too late as in Rwanda?

It is not disputed that bystanders can influence perpetrators and that their action or inaction affects the perpetrators. On the individual level bystanders can stop the perpetrator by opposing him or her; inactivity on the other hand is often experienced as tacit approval. This is no different on the international level. Violent and oppressive states will also try to assess to what extent their behaviour will be opposed or whether they can get away with it. The international community has the power and resources to force a state to stop committing genocide. Yet we have to conclude that the international community failed miserably twice at the beginning of the 90s. The mass executions at Srebrenica and Potocari in Bosnia-Herzegovina during the war in the former Yugoslavia – which were later qualified as genocide – took place after these areas were declared safe havens protected by the UN. Yet Dutchbat stood by while the Serb army of General Mladic invaded Srebrenica and separated the men from the women and children. The men were brought to places in the vicinity of the safe area and were executed (Honig and Both 1996). In Rwanda too the UN stood by passively. As Grünfeld notes in his contribution to this book, an analysis of the information flow and decision-making in relation to Rwanda in 1993 and 1994 shows that this genocide could and should have been prevented. Dallaire's so-called genocide fax sent to the UN in January 1994 contained sufficient accurate information on the ongoing preparations and plans for the upcoming genocide (Dallaire 2004). The UN bureaucracy however failed to forward this message to the UN Security Council and precluded them from acting upon this information (Barnett 2002; Grünfeld & Huijboom 2007). The UN has learned from its failure and seems to have taken a more active stance but the consensus on the duty to protect is unfortunately one of principle rather than practice, as Theo van Boven concluded in a presentation on a meeting in Utrecht (24 May 2007). The principal agreement on the existence of and need for a duty to protect and the preparedness to actually accept the consequences thereof, are two different things. Especially when the only means to fulfil this duty is to risk and sacrifice the lives of young soldiers from within a particular state's own ranks, the decision to act is sometimes too hard to take. Protecting human rights in far away places is fine but the sinister consequences become clearly visible when planes with body-bags and deceased soldiers start to return home. This is often an enormous setback to the preparedness of a state to continue its involvement and is referred to as the body-bag syndrome.

Third states and the international community have not played a very heroic role so far within history in relation to preventing and stopping gross human rights violations from occurring. It often takes self-interest before states are prepared to take risks and consider the costs acceptable losses. Research can enhance our understanding of the mechanisms and processes which play a role. We need to establish means of identifying early warning mechanisms and develop appropriate responses and mobilise the political will to act at an early stage. This is far less dangerous and costly than trying to stop an ongoing war or genocide. At the same time however we are faced with the dilemma that at an early stage, a legal and legitimate justification for intervening is not present. Research might help to find the means of how to prevent a dangerous situation from escalating.

In the following paragraph we will focus on the various means of dealing with the past and we will focus on the role of the international community in this. It will become clear that the international community has tried to make up for its inactive stance by playing a more active role in prosecuting war criminals.

Alette Smeulers and Roelof Haveman

5.   DEALING WITH THE PAST

International crimes have been considered so horrendous and an affront to humanity and mankind that the crimes carry universal jurisdiction, which means that all states are entitled to prosecute the perpetrators. Jurisdiction is normally limited to the right to prosecute crimes committed on a state territory, by a national of the state, in violation of the specific interests of a state or because the victim of the crime was a national of the state. States can only assert jurisdiction when there is a link between the crime and the state. There is no such link required for jurisdiction based on the universality principle. The rationale behind this is that all states are regarded to have an interest in prosecuting the perpetrators of certain crimes regardless of whether or not these crimes were committed against a particular state or its population. The perpetrators are considered to be enemies of all humankind. Few states however actually prosecute international crimes: either because they do not have the means and resources or because they do not have the will to prosecute the crimes. Prosecution by third states is rare. A brave attempt by Belgium to open its own criminal system to charges against functionaries of other states which committed international crimes ultimately failed. At a certain point in time the Belgian public prosecutor had to look into charges against several heads of states amongst whom Ariel Sharon, prime minister of Israel at the time and president George Bush, the current president of the United States. After a lot of diplomatic pressure and a ruling by the International Court of Justice on 14 February 2002 in the case of the Arrest Warrant against the Congolese minister Yerodia Ndombasi, Belgium had to restrict the applicability of the law.

The last two decades were however nevertheless marked by the emergence of an international criminal law system which was initiated by the international community. After the trials at Nuremberg and Tokyo in 1945 and 1946, the Cold War prevented any further developments in this area for almost fifty years. In 1993 and 1994 two international criminal tribunals were established by the UN Security Council on the basis of its powers on Chapter VII of the UN Charter. The two tribunals had to prosecute those responsible for the atrocious crimes in the former Yugoslavia (since 1991) and for the genocide in Rwanda (1994). Next to these two international criminal tribunals several so-called hybrid courts or mixed tribunals were established like for instance the Special Panels for Serious Crimes in East Timor (2000), the Special Court for Sierra Leone (2002) and the Special Chambers for Cambodia (2003). These courts were all established after an agreement of the ruling regime and the UN. Another important milestone was the signing of the so-called Rome Statute of the International Criminal Court on 17 July 1998 and the entry into force of this statute on 1 July 2002 after the 60th ratification. Cases are under investigation by the ICC regarding the LRA/Lords

Resistance Army in Uganda, the war in east-DRC (Ituri and the Kivus) and the crimes committed in Sudan.

Effectively dealing with the past is important to prevent a relapse into violence. In the short term there might be a dilemma between peace and justice. This is the reason why some of the current ICC activities in relation to Uganda are heavily criticised. The perceived dilemma is that states need peace to ensure justice but that true peace can only be achieved via justice. Warlords who are on the losing side can easily abuse this dilemma by offering peace in exchange for impunity. But is this an acceptable trade-off? The Security Council established the tribunals because it was of the opinion that the prosecution of persons responsible for the extreme crimes committed in the area of the former Yugoslavia and in Rwanda would contribute to the restoration and maintenance of peace. It would indeed be interesting to test whether these tribunals succeeded in their aim. Was peace restored and to what extent can this be attributed to these courts? Do the courts function efficiently? What is their prosecution policy and has this turned out to be the most fair, effective and efficient one? The results thereof might help find proper means to deal with crimes committed in a war which is still ongoing.

Other important areas in which empirical research can ameliorate our understanding is to study why certain types of behaviour are considered an international crime whereas others are not and what the effects thereof are. The ICC has played a very important role in the development of supranational criminal law to the extent that in the statute many sexual crimes have been incorporated as crimes against humanity and war crimes. Some years earlier the ICTR already ruled for the first time in history that rape could in some cases be considered an act of genocide. An interesting question is how these crime definitions can be applied in the interest of the victims of sexual violence. Other relevant questions would be to what extent criminal procedural law and more particularly protective measures, victim participation and reparation should be used in order to successfully prosecute the perpetrators of sexual violence (De Brouwer 2005).

In the next few paragraphs we will specifically focus on the possibly important influence that empirical research can have on international criminal law and international criminal justice.

5.1. INTERNATIONAL CRIMINAL LAW AND INTERNATIONAL CRIMINAL JUSTICE

International criminal law has been developed mainly by the statutes and case law of the international criminal tribunals. The tribunals have combined aspects of common law and civil law. An often debated question is to what extent international criminal law is a law *sui generis* (Haveman et al. 2003). The main principles and concepts on which international criminal law is founded have been derived from principles and concepts prevalent in national jurisdictions dealing with ordinary crime. In her study on individual criminal responsibility van Sliedregt (2003, 361) for example concludes that the international criminal tribunals did not 'generate a concept of international individual criminal responsibility that deviates from individual criminal responsibility as it has taken shape in national criminal law systems.' A crucial question however is whether concepts of national criminal law are appropriate concepts to deal with international crimes as these crimes are manifestations of collective violence often instigated, authorised or at least condoned by states and thus are of a very different nature to ordinary crimes. Perpetrators are held criminally responsible by using the concepts of ordinary criminal law but one may question whether this is appropriate as the perpetrators of international crimes often commit crimes of obedience (Smeulers in this book) and thus 'fundamentally differ from the perpetrator of ordinary crime' (Drumbl 2007, 8). The point is that within international law the perpetrators of these crimes are considered *enemies of all humankind.* Yet we have seen that most perpetrators are just ordinary people in extraordinary circumstances – law-abiding citizens who have turned into devoted warriors and followers and conformists. The question can be posed to what extent these perpetrators do have the necessary *mens rea* or in other words whether they have a guilty mind. Having such a criminal mind is within ordinary criminal law a prerequisite to hold individuals criminally responsible. Many perpetrators of international crimes and especially those perpetrators who can be categorised as devoted warriors genuinely believe that what they do is necessary and good. If they are really genuine, can we blame them? Can we punish them? Can we really say that they have a guilty mind? Or should we change the underlying concepts of individual criminal responsibility within international law and just say that no matter what they believed, they committed crimes and should thus be punished?

In criminal cases so far judges often fail to accept the possibility that the defence of the perpetrators is genuine. Hannah Arendt for example noted that judges in the landmark case against Adolf Eichmann, who can qualify as being the prototype of a law-abiding criminal, have not adequately faced this dilemma, because they couldn't 'admit that an average, "normal" person, neither feeble-minded nor indoctrinated nor cynical, could be perfectly incapable of telling right from wrong. They preferred to conclude from occasional lies that he was a liar (…).' According to Arendt (1963, 26) Eichmann wasn't a liar and the judges should have acknowledged that and by not doing so they 'missed the greatest moral and even legal challenge of the whole case.' It might be an interesting exercise to take each and every type of perpetrator as presented in the typology and judge them on their blameworthiness. This might give judges a theoretical framework to better understand the roles individuals played, their influence on the group dynamics and might be helpful in drafting sentencing guidelines.

When studying and judging these perpetrators it is for example important to distinguish between crimes initiated by the state, a governmental organisation and those initiated by an individual or group of individuals. In theory we can clearly distinguish these two types of crime. In practice it is however not always possible to make such a clear cut distinction. States seldom give direct written and easily retrievable orders to commit genocide, torture or war crimes. Heads of states that do initiate and instigate these types of crimes often only imply what is to be done. In some cases the crimes do not originate from heads of states but from other high-ranking state officials, for example in the army or the police. In other cases it is not possible to get a clear answer on who actually instigated the violence especially because the violence might be a resultant of a continuous interaction between various groups and stakeholders within society. Another problematic aspect is that within organisations the official power structure might not represent the actual power structure. An example thereof was discussed at the ICTR trial of Akayesu. Akayesu was officially the *bourgmestre* of the Taba commune in Gitarama who initially resisted the genocide. He however did not hold actual power: as of a certain time Silas Kubwimana had much more influence and allegedly coerced Akayesu into participating in the genocide (Fletcher 2007, 25). Due to these circumstances it is often very difficult to tell where the ideas and orders originated from. This becomes even more difficult after the facts have been committed, when blame is attributed as everyone will point to someone else. Leaders and superiors will deny that they gave these orders and/or try to put the blame on their subordinates who must have misunderstood, whereas the subordinates will try to avoid responsibility by saying that these were the orders they received. Empirical research and theoretical frameworks might help understand both group and organisational dynamics and thus help to attribute blame in a fairer way.

5.2. SENTENCING AND SANCTIONING

Many topics wait to be studied within the sphere of penology, the theory of punishment, for instance, the effects of prosecuting and punishing international crimes. The international community presupposes that punishing war criminals and offenders of crimes against humanity and genocide has a deterrent effect. However, it may be questioned whether this is the case. Criminological studies reveal that regarding ordinary crime, the perceived chance to be arrested has far more influence than the eventual punishment in deterring an individual from committing a specific crime. If the chance is very small indeed that offenders of international crimes will be prosecuted, the question arises what the function of sentencing and incarceration is in relation to international crimes (Haveman 2006b; Drumbl 2007). Criminologists with their interdisciplinary approach are better equipped to study these issues than lawyers are (Roberts & McMillan 2003; Drumbl 2003–2004).

Knowledge of the true causes and nature of international crimes can help find effective means to deal with these crimes. Drumbl (2007, 2) for example strongly doubts whether international criminal law and especially sentencing on this level is effective. He wonders whether 'the punishments issued [within international criminal law] actually attain the goals they ascribed.' The trouble is that the perpetrators of international crimes have often submitted their individual identity to a collective one. International crimes are by their very nature collective crimes and thus it is not so self-evident to attribute individual criminal responsibility without having the possibility to bring organisations or even states that are much more powerful to justice and to hold them responsible. This point was brought forward by both Huisman and Balint in their contributions to this book. The statement by the Nuremburg Tribunal that *'crimes against international law are committed by men, not by abstract entities, and only by punishing individuals who commit such crimes can the provisions of international law be enforced,'*[1] is well known. However this statement can be challenged, as Harding does: '[S]hould states and governments be on trial in this supranational criminal jurisdiction, either in place or alongside the now more familiar human defendants?' (Harding 2006). Already the concept of joint criminal enterprise is gradually developing in supranational criminal law, through which one person in fact stands for a more complex structure. Prosecuting and judging states or governments would be an interesting next step in the development of supranational criminal law. And it seems right; there is something very dissatisfying in judging individuals without being able to call the actual state to the dock. There always is this feeling that we fail to address the real causes of genocide or crimes against humanity, notably the structure behind the acts.

Punishing the state of course does not relieve individuals of their individual (criminal) responsibility, nor does it mean that all punishments are applicable to states. A state cannot be incarcerated. This is no restraint, but in fact it opens new windows to maybe far more effective punishments or interventions, really aiming at prevention for the future instead of retroactively avenging misdeeds. Together with supranational criminal lawyers, criminologists can for instance search for effective punishments in case of delinquent states, effective in the sense that it has a preventive effect.

---

[1]   Judgment of the Tribunal. See the text in 41 *American Journal of International Law* 172 (1947).

Even on the individual level the standard of punishment causes controversy. On the supranational level the death penalty has been excluded, but almost as controversial is the issue of life imprisonment, whether or not without parole. Whereas some countries say they 'cannot exist' without life sentences, other countries consider life imprisonment to be more inhuman than the death penalty. There is no agreement between countries on 'the' standard of sentencing, not even in the case of grave crimes, as this exists to a certain extent in individual countries. However, it is not only differences in opinion on the standard of sanctioning between individual countries that count, there also seems to be a difference in the standard of sentencing between the supranational tribunals on the one hand and domestic sentencing in general on the other hand. Taking these two differences into account, the question arises as to what, within the range of potential sentences, the proper sanction is for a crime against humanity, an act of genocide or a war crime. Is 25 years imprisonment too much or too little, or maybe just right? A supranational tribunal that sentences a person found guilty of multiple murders as acts of genocide to 25 years in prison has something to explain to people who live in countries in which perpetrators who have committed one single murder are sometimes imprisoned for life or even executed. Apparently the measuring rod behind supranational sentences is different from the ones in domestic jurisdictions. An illustration of this is the article in the ICC-Statute that determines that the maximum penalty is 30 years' imprisonment, and that only a life sentence can be imposed *'when justified by the extreme gravity of the crime'*.[2] Compared to the national contexts however every case that is and will be tried by the ICC and the *ad hoc* tribunals falls within the category of extreme grave cases. When applying the national standard to these cases one could not decide to anything other than maximum penalties: life imprisonment (if not the death penalty). On the supranational level however, within the category of cases that from a national perspective without exception can be regarded as belonging to the most severe cases ever, one has created a new hierarchy between grave and extremely grave cases, with a new hierarchy of sentences. These are interesting issues for instance in the light of the aims and functions of punishing (Haveman & Olusanya 2006).

Also sentencing guidelines are an interesting topic for further research (Haveman 2006a). The typology of perpetrators as presented in this book can in the future be helpful to develop sentencing guidelines, because the typology can be used as a theoretical framework to determine the various roles, ranks and motives the perpetrators had and can thus shed light on their blameworthiness and the function of punishment. Some types of perpetrators such as the criminal masterminds and the fanatics can be considered to deserve more severe sentences than the compromised. For some the punishment will prevent them from committing further crimes (the fanatics and sadists) whereas for others it will be

---

[2]   'and the individual circumstances of the convicted person'; Art. 77(1) ICC Statute.

extremely unlikely that they will get involved in crimes after the fall of the regime such as the devoted warriors.

Studying specific groups of perpetrators might shed some light on whether or not they are actually victims or perpetrators and whether or not they deserve punishment. There, for example, seems to be an emerging consensus that child soldiers should be free of punishment for what they have done, but is it indeed appropriate not to punish child soldiers? Olusanya (2006) challenges this general opinion, more specifically the legal rules regarding immunity for 'child' soldiers for war crimes, crimes against humanity and genocide under supranational criminal law. Indeed the question is whether or not an age limit for immunity for children and young people should be universalised – *supranationalised* – 'rather than customised to fit the particular circumstances of each individual country', as Olusanya states. Age limits for immunity all over the world range from 7 to 15 years old, with exceptions for 'grave crimes' in which cases the child offenders can be tried and sentenced as adults. Also the international tribunals and courts are divergent: from 15 (SCSL) to 18 (ICC) years old or no age limit at all (ICTY and ICTR). In Olusanya's view, in particular a one-size-fits-all approach for children would prove to be unworkable at the international level. Owing to heterogeneous factors like economic inequality and cultural differences, the policy of granting immunity to child soldiers may in some instances serve as a blanket for innocent children, who because of their age, vulnerability and immaturity, are easy to coerce and control; whilst in others, it may be misused as a sword by hardened war criminals posing as children.

5.3. THE ROLE OF THE VICTIMS AND VICTIMOLOGY

An important group which needs to be taken into account when looking for means to deal with the past are the victims. An important venue for research is to study victims of international crimes as a separate group within the research area of victimology. Victimology can be defined as the scientific study of the possible role of victims in the genesis of crimes, the consequences of crimes for victims and the various ways of victim assistance to minimise these consequences (Van Dijk et al. 2002, 266). Victimology expressly includes in its research victims of war crimes, crimes against humanity and genocide. A first question then is how to define 'victim'. The Rules of Procedure and Evidence (RPE) of the ICC, in fact the Code of Criminal Procedure for the supranational penal system of the ICC, contains a definition of victim: *'"Victims" means natural persons who have suffered harm as a result of the commission of any crime within the jurisdiction of the court'*. This is an extremely wide definition with many consequences for the functioning of the penal system.

There may be a need for a specific victimology for victims of state crime. Kauzlarich et al. (2001, 175) for instance state that the study of victimology must be deemed crucial for the development of state crime. One of their conclusions is that victims of state crime in every respect – including reparation and dealing with the aftermath of the crimes – are dependent on the one who stigmatised them and made them into victims, notably the state. This requires a specific kind of study; in particular the necessity to study the needs of this particular group of victims is evident (Rombouts 2004).

Participation in criminal proceedings is one of the ways that some consider being of great importance to victims in terms of being able to cope with the consequences of the crimes committed against them. Participation of victims has gained an important position within the ICC framework (De Brouwer 2005). Victims can make opening and closing statements to tell their story; victims have the right to be informed about the progress of the proceedings and may be present when the court reaches its verdict or, alternatively, are notified thereof when they cannot be there; in case of a guilty plea, victims and their interests are taken into account as well, and the court may decide not to accept the plea if their interest so dictates. Their views may also be sought where the indictment may be amended. It may be an interesting research topic to see to what extent the good intentions of these participatory measures in the ICC rules will be applied in practice. Pretending that the position of the victims of international crimes in general has improved substantially is asking for disillusion amongst victims. The number of the victims in respective conflicts is far too big to indeed be able to fulfil the needs of 'the' victims in this respect. In terms of the ICC the conflict of DR-Congo for instance has produced over 9 million victims. Rwanda knows little less victims: apart from the 800,000 people killed, there are 250,000 direct survivors, but in terms of the ICC also the children who have seen the violence, all those other people who did not actively take part in the genocide and maybe even the (family of the) offenders have to be counted as victims. Taking into account these numbers, direct participation is a fallacy. Management of expectations, one of the buzz-words in the supranational arena, is therefore crucial with respect to victims. Victims might however also prefer alternative or additional means to deal with the past.

5.4.   ALTERNATIVE MEANS TO DEAL WITH THE PAST

Empirical research can play a role in trying to find alternative approaches to international crimes. Criminal prosecution is not the only and in many cases certainly not the most effective approach to international crimes (Bassiouni 2002a; Haveman 2002, 2006; Klip & Smeulers 2004). Many studies have been conducted on *transitional justice* and *post-conflict justice*, in which a broad spectrum of interventions and responses are presented to gross human rights violations, which have been committed by a former regime. Other strategies range from truth finding, lustration and compensation to reconciliation. Many studies have been performed on the possibilities to apply Braithwaite's shaming theory (1989) and the principles of restorative justice to violent political conflicts and genocides, for instance in the form of truth and reconciliation commissions (Hayner 1994; Cohen 1995; Minow 1998; Rotberg & Thompson 2000; Stover & Weinstein 2004).

In line with the research tradition on restorative justice Parmentier, Vanspauwen and Weitekamp developed the so-called TARR model, which identifies the four main needs of a post-conflict society: Truth, Accountability, Reparation and Reconciliation. The developed model which was presented in this book however needs to be tested: empirical research needs to be done on whether the presumptions underlying the model are correct. If they are, we need to find ways how to integrate the mechanisms of restorative justice in post-conflict justice. Many scholars have focused on these issues but the presented model and empirical testing thereof are promising endeavours. Other means and ways of dealing with collective violence have been elaborated by Balint and Haveman in this book. They all show that there are viable alternatives and we need to test these alternatives and search for means to strengthen these initiatives. It however remains to be seen which approach fits a particular situation best and which conditions need to be fulfilled to make either criminal prosecution or an alternative approach a viable option. It is interesting to see that often alternative responses require much more evidence regarding their effect(iveness) than the 'traditional' penal approach, and are rejected far easier than those penal approaches, which are taken for granted without little scientific basis. The development of theories such as by Drumbl (2000), in which he uses a typology of 'post-genocidal social geographies' to distinguish between homogeneous, dualistic and pluralistic societies, are very valuable and open new venues for research as these kinds of theories can give some insight into the various and sometimes opposing effects of certain choices but more research is needed, especially research in which the effects of the chosen methods are measured and the extent to which victims needs are adequately addressed.

6.   EPILOGUE

This book is an attempt to have criminologists break out of the state of denial regarding international crimes. The study of these crimes deserves to grow into a separate and fully fledged specialisation within criminology: *supranational* criminology. Supranational criminology – or the criminology of international crimes – entails the study of war crimes, crimes against humanity and genocide, behaviour that shows affinity with these crimes, the causes and the situations in which they are committed, as well as possible interventions and their effectiveness; these interventions comprise penal systems – domestic, internationalised and supranational – in which the crimes are prosecuted and tried, as well as non-penal interventions. This means that these crimes are studied from a criminological perspective, using the theoretical framework and research methodology of regular criminology. By integrating all the research done in other disciplines, like history, political science, sociology, psychology and many other sciences, criminology might contribute to the prevention of these kinds of extreme violence. The number of topics to be studied is unlimited, as are the sources: research already done in all those other domains. The bibliography to this book, which is longer than any of the individual chapters, may be seen as a reflection of the width and depth of the field.

In this final chapter we propose an agenda for future supranational criminological research. A clear conceptual and theoretical framework has to be developed. 'What exactly entails supranational criminology?' and 'what are international crimes?' are the most obvious questions to be discussed. Should other forms of behaviour also qualify as international crimes? Why are certain types of behaviour considered an international crime whereas others are not and what are the effects thereof? Clear definitions have to be developed. The specific characteristics of international crimes as forms of state sponsored or state facilitated crimes have to be identified, studied and analysed, with special focus on phenomena such as globalisation, victims of political power, corporations and the role of ideology, perpetrators and organisational structures. The particular methodological issues and difficulties which arise when studying international crimes have to be taken into account. Scholars need to develop reliable methodological tools and instruments and regularly test these tools. Explanatory theories have to be developed which can be translated into testable hypotheses. New venues of research should be explored by testing to what extent existing criminological theories can help to explain the aetiology of international crimes. In which criminological traditions should we place the research on international crimes? Which theories from mainstream criminology can provide answers for the prevalence or causes of international crimes? How can the phenomenon of international crimes be explained? Have the international(ised) courts and tribunals succeeded in their aim. Was peace restored and to what extent can this be attributed to these courts? Do these courts and tribunals function efficiently? What is their prosecution policy and has this turned out to be the most fair, effective and efficient one?

These are just some of the multitude of relevant research questions which need to be studied. One thing is clear: a lot of research needs to be done to enhance our knowledge of the prevalence of war crimes, crimes against humanity and genocide, the patterns and causes and the most efficient means to prevent such crimes and effectively deal with them in retrospect. Quoting Friedrichs, with this book we hope to repair the "fundamental and historical neglect of criminology" and to break out of a state of denial by putting international crimes on the criminological agenda.

BIBLIOGRAPHY

Achvarina, V. & Reich, S. (2006).
> No Place to Hide: Refugees, Displaced Persons, and the Recruitment of Child Soldiers, *International Security* 31(1), 127–164.

Aertsen, I., Arsovska, J., Rohne, H-C., Valiñas, M., & Vanspauwen, K. (eds.) (forthcoming).
> *Restoring justice after large-scale violent conflicts. Kosovo, Israel-Palestine and Congo*, Cullompton: Willan Publishing.

Afflitto, F. M. (2000).
> Victimization, survival and the impunity of forced exile: A case study from the Rwandan genocide, *Crime, Law & Social Change* 34(1), 77–97.

African Rights (1994/1995)
> *Rwanda, Death, Despair and Defiance*, London: African Rights.

African Rights (1995).
> *Rwanda – not so innocent – when women become killers*, London: African Rights.

African Rights (1996).
> *Rwanda, Killing the Evidence*, London: African Rights.

Agamben, G. (2005).
> *State of exception*, Chicago: University of Chicago Press (Translated by Kevin Attell).

Akers, R. (1977).
> *Deviant Behavior: A Social Learning Approach*, Belmont CA: Wadsworth.

Akhavan, P. (2006).
> Report on the Work of the Office of the Special Adviser of the United Nations Secretary-General on the Prevention of Genocide, *Human Rights Quarterly* 28, 1043–1070.

Alcock, J. B. (2006).
> *The Social Scientist as Expert and as Witness*, paper presented at the colloquium at the University of Paris, 30 March – 1 April 2006 (unpublished).

Allen, T. (2006).
> *Trial Justice: The International Criminal Court and the Lord's Resistance Army*, Zed Press: London.

Alliance Report (2006).
> *Alliance of Civilizations*, Report of the High-Level Group, 13 November 2006, United Nations, New York.

Allison, G.T. (1999).
> *Essence of Decision, Explaining the Cuba Missile Crisis*, New York: Longman.

Alnasrawi, A. (2001).
> Iraq: Economic sanctions and consequences, 1990–2000, *Third World Quarterly* 22(2), 205–218.

Alston, Ph. (Ed.) (2006).
Non-State Actors and Human Rights, Oxford: Oxford University Press.
Altheide, D.L. (2006).
The Mass Media, Crime and Terrorism, *Journal of International Criminal Justice 4*, 982–997.
Alvarez, A. (1997).
Adjusting to genocide: the techniques of neutralization and the Holocaust, *Social Science History* 21, 39–178.
Alvarez, J.E. (1999)
Crimes of states/crimes of hate: lessons from Rwanda, *Yale Journal of International Law* 24, 365–483.
Alvarez, A. (2001).
Governments, Citizens, and Genocide: A Comparative and Interdisciplinary Analysis, Bloomington, Ind.: Indiana University Press.
Alvarez, A. (2002).
Justifying Genocide: The Role of Professionals in Legitimizing Mass Killing, *Idea: A Journal of Social Issues* 6(1).
Alvarez, A. (2006).
Militias and genocide, War Crimes, Genocide & Crimes against Humanity 2, 1–33.
Amadiume, I., & An-Na'im, A. (eds.) (2000).
The Politics of Memory: truth, healing and social justice, London: Zed Books.
Amann, D. (2004).
Guantanamo Bay, *Columbia Journal of Transnational Law* 42, 263–348.
Ambos, K. (2006).
Nulla Poena Sine Lege in International Criminal Law, in: Haveman, R.H. & Olusanya, O. (eds.). *Sentencing and Sanctioning in Supranational Criminal Law*, Antwerp/Oxford: Intersentia, 17–35.
Ambos, K. and M. Othman (Eds.) (2003).
New approaches in International Criminal justice: Kosovo, East Timor, Sierra Leone and Cambodia, Freiburg i. Br.: Max-Planck Institut für ausländisches und internationales Strafrecht.
American Association for World Health (1997).
Denial of Food and Medicine: The Impact of the U.S. Embargo on Health and Nutrition in Cuba, Washington D.C.: American Association for World Health.
Amnesty International (1977).
Torture in Greece -The first torturer's trial, London: Amnesty International Publications.
Amnesty International (2001a).
Brazil: Commentary on Brazil's first report to the UN Committee against Torture, AMR 19/016/2001.
Amnesty International (2001b).
Universal jurisdiction: The duty of states to enact and implement legislation, (AI Index: IOR 53/002–018/2001), London: Amnesty International.

Amnesty International (2001c).

Amnesty International's appeal to all governments to end impunity for the worst crimes known to humanity, (AI Index: IOR 70/003/2001), London: Amnesty International.

Amnesty International (2004a).

Annual Report.

Amnesty International (2004b).

Rwanda: The Enduring Legacy of the Genocide and War, Retrieved June 18, 2007, http://web.amnesty.org/library/index/engafr470082004.

Amnesty International (2006a).

Annual Report, http://www.amnestyusa.org/annualreport/2006/overview.html

Amnesty International (2006b).

Outsourcing Facilitating Human Rights Violations, http://www.amnestyusa.org/annualreport/2006/overview.html

Andries, A., van den Wyngaert, C., David, E., & Verhaegen, J. (1994).

Commentaire de la loi du 16 juin 1993 relative à la répression des infractions graves au droit international humanitaire, *Revue de Droit Pénal et de Criminologie*, 1114–1184.

Annan, K. (2004).

SG observes international day of reflection on 1994 Rwanda Genocide, Commission on Human Rights, Geneva, April 7, 2004, www.un.org/events/rwanda/ last visited June, 13, 2007.

Annan, K. (2005).

Billions of Promises to Keep, *New York Times*, April 13, 2005, A29.

Anzulovic, B. (1999).

Heavenly Serbia: From Myth to Genocide, New York: New York University Press.

Appiah, K. A. (2006).

Cosmopolitanism: Ethics in a World of Strangers, New York: Norton.

Arat-Koc, S. (2005).

The Disciplinary Boundaries of Canadian Identity After September 11: Civilizational Identity, Multiculturalism, and the Challenge of Anti-Imperialist Feminism, *Social Justice: A Journal of Crime, Conflict, and World Order* 32(4), 32–49.

Arendt, H. (1963).

Eichmann in Jerusalem: A Report on the Banality of Evil, Harmondsworth: Penguin.

Arendt, H. (1973).

Origins of totalitarianism, New York: A Harvest Books/HBJ Book.

Aronson, E. (2004).

The social animal, 9th Ed., New York: Worth Publishers.

Asch, A. (1951).

Effects of group pressure upon the modification and distortion of judgment, in: Guetzkow, M.H. (ed.), *Groups, leadership and men*, Pittsburgh: Carnegie.

Ashworth, A. (2000).

Is the criminal law a lost cause? *Law Quarterly Review* 116, 225–256.

Ashworth, A. (2003).
  Principles of criminal law, Oxford: Oxford University Press.
Ashworth, A. (2004).
  Social control and 'anti-social behaviour': The subversion of human rights? *Law Quarterly Review* 120, 263–291.
Associated Press (2005).
  Survey: Many Thousands Killed in Darfur Attacks, January 20, 2005.
Astourian, S. H. (1992).
  Genocidal Process: Reflections on the Armeno-Turkish Polarization, in: Hovannisian, R.G. (ed.), *The Armenian Genocide: History, Politics, Ethics*, New York: St Martin's Press.
Avocats sans Frontières (2004).
  Vademecum; Le crime de génocide et les crimes contre l'humanité devant les juridictions ordinaires du Rwanda, Kigali/Brussels.
Avocats sans Frontières (2005).
  Monitoring des Juridictions Gacaca; phase de Jugement, Rapport Analytique, Mars Septembre 2005, Kigali
Avocats sans Frontières (2006).
  Monitoring des Juridictions Gacaca; phase de Jugement, Rapport Analytique No 2, Octobre 2005-Septembre 2006, Kigali.
Babiker, M. A. (2007).
  Application of international humanitarian and human rights law to the armed conflicts of the Sudan: complementary or mutually exclusive regimes, Antwerp: Intersentia.
Bagaric, M. & Morss, J. (2006).
  In Search of Coherent Jurisprudence for International Criminal Law: Correlating Universal Human Responsibilities with Universal Human Rights, *Suffolk Transnational Law Review* 29, 157–206.
Balint, J. (1996a).
  The place of law in addressing international regime conflicts, *Law and Contemporary Problems* 59(4), 105–126.
Balint, J. (1996b).
  Conflict, conflict victimization and legal redress 1945–1996, *Law and Contemporary Problems* 59(4), 231–247.
Balint, J. (2001).
  Law's Constitutive Possibilities: Reconstruction and Reconciliation in the Wake of Genocide and State Crime, in: Christodoulidis, E. & Veitch, S. (eds.), *Lethe's Law. Justice, Law and Ethics in Reconciliation*, Oxford: Hart Publishing.
Ball, P. & Asher, J. (2002).
  Statistics and Slobodan: Using Data Analysis and Statistics in the War Crimes Trial of Former President Milosevic, *Chance* 15, 17–24.
Ball, P., Betts, W., Scheuren, F., Dudukovich, J. & Asher, J. (2002).
  Killings and Refugee Flow in Kosovo March-June 1999, Washington: American Association for the Advancement of Science.

Ball, P., Kobrak, P. & Spirer, H.F. (1999).

State violence in Guatemala, 1960-1996: a quantitative reflection, Washington: American Association for the Advancement of Science.

Bandura, A. (1973).

Aggression- a social learning analysis, New Jersey: Prentice-Hall.

Bandura, A. (1999).

Moral disengagement in the perpetration of inhumanities, *Personality and Social Psychology Review* 3(3), 193–209.

Barak, G. (1991a).

Toward a Criminology of State Criminality, in: Barak, G. (ed.), *Crimes by the Capitalist State: An Introduction to State Criminality*, Albany, NY: State University of New York Press, 3–16.

Barak, G. (ed.) (1991b).

Crimes by the Capitalist State: An Introduction to State Criminality, Albany: State University of New York Press.

Barak, G. (1994).

Crime, Criminology, and Human Rights: Toward an Understanding of State Criminality, in: G. Barak (ed.), *Varieties of Criminology. Readings from a Dynamic Discipline*, Westport, Connecticut: Praeger.

Barak, G. (ed.) (2000).

Crime and Crime Control: A Global View, Westport, CN: Greenwood Press.

Barak, G. (2001).

Crime and Crime Control in an Age of Globalization: A Theoretical Dissection, *Critical Criminology: An International Journal* 10(1), 57–72.

Barak, G. (2003).

Violence and Nonviolence: Pathways to Understanding, Thousand Oaks, CA: Sage Publications.

Barak, G. (2005).

A Reciprocal Approach to Peacemaking Criminology: Between Adversarialism and Mutualism, *Theoretical Criminology: An International Journal* 9(2), 132–151.

Barak, G. (2006).

Applying Integrated Theory: A Reciprocal Theory of Violence and Nonviolence, in: Henry S. & Lanier, M. (eds.), *The Essential Criminology Reader*. Boulder, CO: Westview Press.

Barak, G. (2007).

Violence, Conflict, and World Order: Critical Conversations on State-Sanctioned Justice, New York: Rowman and Littlefield Publishers.

Barash, D.P. & Webel, C.P. (2002).

Peace and Conflict Studies, Thousand Oaks, CA: Sage Publications.

Barnett, M. (2002).

Eyewitness to a Genocide: The United Nations and Rwanda, London: Cornell University Press.

Barnett, M. & Duvall, R. (eds.) (2003).

Power in Global Governance, Cambridge, UK: Cambridge University Press.

Barnhizer, D. (2001).
> Trade, Environment and Human Rights: The Paradigm case of industrial Aquaculture and the Exploitation of Traditional Communities, in: Barnhizer, D. (ed.), *Effective Strategies for Protecting Human Rights*, Aldershot: Ashgate Dartmouth.

Baron, R.S. & Kerr, N.L. (2003).
> *Group process, Group decision, Group action*, 2nd ed., Buckingham: Open University Press.

Bass, G. J. (2000).
> *Stay the Hand of Vengeance: The Politics of War Crimes Tribunals*, Princeton: Princeton University Press.

Bassiouni, M.C. (1997).
> From Versailles to Rwanda in seventy-five years. The need to establish a permanent international criminal court, *Harvard Human Rights Journal* 10, 11–62.

Bassiouni, M. C. (1999).
> The Sources and Theory of International Criminal Law: A Theoretical Framework, in: Bassiouni, M.C. (ed.), *International Criminal Law. Volume I. Crimes*, Ardsley, New York: Transnational Publishers, Inc.

Bassiouni, M.C. (2000).
> *Basic Principles and Guidelines on the Right to a Remedy and Reparation for Victims of Violations of International Human Rights and Humanitarian Law* (Report submitted to the UN Commission on Human Rights, UN Doc. E/CN.4/2000).

Bassiouni, M. C. (2002a).
> *Post-Conflict Justice*, New York, Ardsley: Transnational Publishers.

Bassiouni, M. C. (2002b).
> Proposed Guiding Principles for Combating Impunity for International Crimes, in: Bassiouni, M.C. (ed.), *Post-Conflict Justice*, New York, Ardsley: Transnational Publishers Inc.

Bassiouni, M.C. (2006).
> *Crimes of War: The Book*, www.crimesofwar.org/thebook/crimes-against-humanity.html.

Bauman, Z (1989).
> *Modernity and the Holocaust,* Cambridge: Polity Press.

Bazemore, G. & Walgrave, L (1999).
> Restorative juvenile justice: in search for fundamentals and an outline for systematic reform, in: Bazemore, G., & Walgrave, L. (eds.), *Restorative juvenile justice: repairing the harm of youth crime*, Monsey: Criminal Justice Press.

Beaumont, P. (2006).
> Darfur Terror Chief Slips into Britain, *The Observer*, March 12, 2006.

Beccaria, C. [1764] (1995).
> *On Crimes and Punishment and Other Writings* (edited by Richard Bellamy), Cambridge texts in the history of political thought, Cambridge: Cambridge University Press.

Beck, A. (1999).
> *Prisoners of Hate: The Cognitive Basis of Anger, Hostility, and Violence*, New York: Harper Collins.

Becker, H. (1963).
> *Outsiders: Studies in the Sociology of Deviance*, Glencoe, Il.: The Free Press.

Becker, H. (1967).
> Who's side are we on? *Social Problems* 14, 239–247.

Beck, U. & Sznaider, N. (2006).
> Unpacking Cosmopolitanism for the Social Sciences: A Research Agenda, *The British Journal of Sociology* 57, 1–23.

Beirne, P. & South, N. (eds.) (2007).
> *Issues in Green Criminology*, Devon: Willan Publishing.

Bell, L.S., Nathan, A.J., & Peleg, I. (Eds.) (2001).
> *Negotiating Culture and Human Rights,* New York: Columbia University Press.

Bellamy, A.J. (2005).
> Responsibility to Protect or Trojan Horse? The Crisis in Darfur and Humanitarian Intervention after Iraq, *Ethics & International Affairs* 19(2).

Benson, M.L. (1985).
> Denying the guilty mind: Accounting for involvement in white-collar crime, *Criminology* 23, 583–607.

Bentham, J. (1996 [1789]).
> *An introduction to the principles of morals and legislation*, Edited by Hart, H.L.A., & Burns, J.H. Oxford: Clarendon Press.

Berkowitz, B.D. (1994).
> Rules of Engagement for UN peacekeeping forces in Bosnia, *Orbis: A Quarterly Journal of World Affairs,* 38(3), 637–646.

Bernstein, V. H. (1947).
> *Final Judgment: The Story of Nuremberg,* New York: Boni & Gaer.

Berting, J., Baehr, P.R., Burgers, J.H., Flinterman, C., De Klerk, B., Kroes, R. et al. (eds.) (1990).
> *Human Rights in a Pluralist World: Individuals and Collectivities,* Westport, CT: Meckler, 243–244.

Bigagaza, J., Abong, C. et al. (2002).
> Land Scarcity, Distribution and Conflict in Rwanda, in: Lind, J. & Sturman, K. (eds.), *Scarcity and Surfeit: The Ecology of Africa's Conflicts*, South Africa: Institute for Security Studies.

Bijleveld, C.C.J.H. (2005).
> They want the land without the people, *ESC – Criminology in Europe – Newsletter of the European Society of Criminology*, February 2005, 1 & 10–12.

Bijleveld, C.C.J.H. & Haveman, R.H. (2005).
> *On International (Criminal) Law and Human Rights Violations: The case study of Sudan*, conference paper, conference on Sudan, The Hague 8 April 2005, Grotius Centre for International Legal Studies (Leiden University).

Bijleveld, C.C.J.H., Mehlbaum, S. & Degomme, O. (2007).
A Very Dark Figure; Direct and Indirect Mortality in southern Sudan 1983–2003, Paper under preparation.

Bijleveld, C.C.J.H. & Morssinkhof, A. (2006).
Counting the countless. Rape victimisation during the Rwandan genocide, Paper presented at the Annual Meeting of the American Society of Criminology, Los Angeles, November.

Bilton, M. & Sim, K. (1992)
Four hours in My Lai – a war crime and its aftermath, London: Viking.

Black, D. (1983).
Crime as Social Control, *American Sociological Review* 48, 34–45.

Black, E. (2001).
IBM and the Holocaust, New York: Little, Brown.

Blankenship, M.B. (1993).
Understanding Corporate Criminality, New York: Garland Publishing.

Bleiker, R. (2000).
Popular Dissent, Human Agency, and Global Politics, Cambridge: Cambridge University Press.

Bloche, M.G. & Marks, J.H. (2005).
Doctors and Interrogators at Guantanamo Bay, *The New England Journal of Medicine* 353(1), 6–8.

Blom, J.H.C. & Romijn, P. (2002).
Srebrenica, a Safe Area: Reconstruction, Background, Consequences and Analyses of the Fall of a Safe Area, Amsterdam, http://www.niod.nl.

Bloomfield, D., Barnes, T., & Huyse, L. (eds.) (2003).
Reconciliation after violent conflicts. A handbook, Stockholm: International Institute for Democracy and Electoral Assistance.

Bodissey, B. (2006).
Breaking the Rules of Engagement, 21 June 2006,
http://gatesofvienna.blogspot.com/2006/06/breaking-rules-of-engagement.html, last visited: March 2007.

Bohl, K. (2006).
Breaking the Rule of Transitional Justice, *Wisconsin International Law Journal* 24, 557–585.

Bohlander, M. (2007).
International criminal justice: a critical analysis of institutions and procedures, London: Cameron May Ltd.

Bonomy, I. (2007).
The Reality of conducting a War Crimes Trial, *Journal of International Criminal Justice* 5, 348–359.

Borkin, J. (1978).
The Crime and Punishment of IG Farben, New York: Free Press.

Bosch, W. J. (1970).
Judgment on Nuremberg: American Attitudes toward the Major German War-Crime Trials, Chapel Hill, NC: University of North Carolina Press.

Box, S. (1983).
Power, Crime and Mystification, London: Tavistock.
Boyle, F.A. (2004).
Destroying World Order: U.S. Imperialism in the Middle East Before and After September 11, Atlanta: Clarity Press.
Bracher, K.D. (1982).
The Age of Ideologies: A History of Political Thought in the Twentieth Century, London: Weidenfeld and Nicolson.
Bradley, C.A. & Goldsmith, J.L. (2005).
Congressional authorization and the war on terrorism, *Harvard Law Review* 118, 2047–2130.
Braithwaite, J. (1985).
To punish or to persuade, Albany: State University of New York Press.
Braithwaite, J. (1989).
Crime, shame and reintegration, Cambridge: Cambridge University Press.
Braithwaite, J. (2002).
Restorative justice and responsive regulation, Oxford: Oxford University Press.
Braithwaite, F. & Achanfuo-Yeboah, D. (2004).
Victims of Crime in the Criminal Justice System in Barbados, *Journal of Criminal Justice* 32(5), 431–442.
Breitman, R. (2004).
The architect of Genocide – Himmler and the final solution, London: Pimlico.
Breloer, H. & R. Zimmer (2005).
Unterwegs zur Familie Speer – Begegnungen, Gespräche, Dokumente, Berlin: Propyläen.
Brett, R. & I. Specht (2004).
Young soldiers – why they choose to fight, Boulder: Lynne Rienner Publishers.
Breyer, St. G. [1946] (1999).
A Call for Reasoned Justice, in: Cooper, B. (Ed.), *War Crimes. The Legacy of Nuremberg*, New York: TV books, 40–43.
Brinkley, J. (2005).
A Diplomatic Lone Ranger with 3 x 5 Cards, *New York Times*, April 17, 2005, 10.
Brody, R. (2004).
The Road to Abu Ghraib, Washington, D.C.: *Human Rights Watch*, June, 1. http://hrw.org/reports/2004/usa0604/usa0604.pdf.
Brody, R. (2005).
Getting Away with Torture? Command Responsibility for the U.S. Abuse of Detainees, Washington, D.C.: *Human Rights Watch*, April, 24. http://www.hrw.org/reports/2005/us0405/us0405.pdf.
Browning, C. (1992).
Ordinary men: Reserve police battalion 101 and the final solution in Poland, New York: HarperCollins.
Brownmiller, S. (1975).
Against our Will: Men, Women and Rape, New York: Simon and Schuster.

Brysk, A. (1994).
> The Politics of Measurement: The Contested Count of the Disappeared in Argentina, *Human Rights Quarterly* 16, 676–692.

Buergenthal, T. (2006).
> The Evolving International Human Rights System, *The American Journal of International Law* 100, 783–807.

Bulliet, R.W. (2006).
> Civilization: Truth or Tool? *Workshop on "What is 'Civilization'?"* 21 April 2006, UN Initiative for an "Alliance of Civilizations", New York.

Bullock, A. (1991)
> *Hitler and Stalin – parallel lives*, London: HarperCollins.

Bureau of Democracy, Human Rights, and Labor. (2003).
> *Rwanda – Country Reports on Human Rights Practices – 2002*, Retrieved June 18, 2007, http://www.state.gov/g/drl/rls/hrrpt/2002/18221.htm

Bureau of Refugee Programs (1985).
> *Assessment Manual for Refugee Emergencies*, Washington, D.C.: U. S. Department of State.

Burke-White, W. (2006).
> *Double Edged Tribunals: The Political Effects of International Criminal Tribunals*, Guest Lecture Series of the Office of the Prosecutor, The Hague: ICC-CPI.

Burkholder, B.T., & Toole, M.J. (1995).
> Evolution of Complex Disasters, *The Lancet* 346, 1012–1015.

Burleigh, M. (2000).
> *The Third Reich: A New History*, New York: Hill & Wang.

Burleigh, M., & Wippermann, W. (1991).
> *The Racial State: Germany 1933–1945*, Cambridge: Cambridge University Press.

Burnham, G., Lafta, R., Shannon Doocy, S. & Roberts, L. (2006).
> Mortality after the 2003 invasion of Iraq: a cross-sectional cluster sample survey, *The Lancet* 368, 1421–1428.

Bursik, R.J. Jr. & Grasmick, H.G. (1993).
> *Neighborhoods and Crime: Effective Dimensions of Effective Community Control*, New York: Lexington Books.

Burton, F. & Carlen, P. (1979).
> *Official Discourse Analysis, Government Publications, Ideology and the State*, London: Routledge and Kegan Paul.

Burton, J. (1991).
> Development and Cultural Genocide in the Sudan, *Journal of Modern African Studies* 29, 511–520.

Buti, A. (2004).
> *Separated: Aboriginal Childhood Separation and Guardianship Law*, Sydney: Sydney Institute of Criminology Monograph Series.

Butler, J. (2004).
> *Precarious life: The powers of mourning and violence*, London: Verso.

Calhoun, C.J. (1998).
> *Nationalism*, Minneapolis, MN: University of Minnesota Press.

Campbell, R. (2001).
>   *Emotionally Involved: The Impact of Researching Rape*, New York: Routledge.

Campbell, T. & Miller, S. (2004).
>   *Human rights and the moral responsibilities of corporate and public sector organizations*, Dordrecht: Kluwer Academic Publishers.

Campbell, M. (2006).
>   Bombs over Baghdad: Addressing Criminal Liability of a U. S. President for Acts of War, *Washington University Global Studies Law Review* 5, 235–263.

Canely, S. (2006).
>   Cosmopolitan Justice and Institutional Design: An Egalitarian Liberal Conception of Global Governance, *Social Theory & Practice* 32, 725–756.

Carroll, L. (1872).
>   *Through the looking glass*, New York: Macmillan.

Carroll, J. (2001).
>   *Constantine's Sword: The Church and the Jews*, Boston: Houghton Mifflin Company.

Cassese, A. (1998).
>   On the Current Trends toward Criminal Prosecution and Punishment of Breaches of International Humanitarian Law, *European Journal of International Law* 9, 2–17.

Castells, M. (1996).
>   *The Rise of the Network Society*, Cambridge, MA: Blackwell.

Catalano, S. (2006).
>   *Criminal Victimization, 2005*, U.S. Department of Justice: Washington, D.C.

Cavanagh, J. & Mander, J. (2002).
>   *Alternatives to Economic Globalization: A Better World is Possible*, San Francisco: Berrett-Koehler Publishers.

Cesarani, D. (2004).
>   *Eichmann – His life and Crimes*, Chatham: Mackays of Chatham plc.

Chakravarty, A. (2006).
>   Gacaca Courts in Rwanda: explaining divisions within the Human Rights Community, *Yale Journal of International Affairs* winter/spring 2006, 132.

Chalk, F. & K. Jonassohn (Eds.) (1990).
>   *The History and Sociology of Genocide – Analyses and Case Studies*, New Haven: Yale University Press.

Chambliss, W. J. (1989).
>   State-organized Crime, *Criminology* 27, 183 -208.

Chambliss W. J. (1995).
>   Commentary by William J. Chambliss, *Society of Social Problems Newsletter* 26, 1–9.

Chandler, D. (1992).
>   *Brother Number One: A Political Biography of Pol Pot*, Boulder: Westview Press.

Chandler, D. (1997).
>   *Voices from S-21: Terror and History in Pol Pot's Secret Prison*, Berkeley, CA.: University of California Press.

Chang, I. (1997).

The Rape of Nanking: The Forgotten Holocaust of World War Two, New York: Basic Books.

Chang, N. (2002).

Silencing political dissent: How post-September 11 anti-terrorism measures threaten our civil liberties, New York: Seven Stories Press.

Charlesworth, H. (2002).

Author! Author! A Response to David Kennedy, *Harvard Human Rights Journal* 15, 127–132.

Charny, I. (1984).

Toward the understanding and prevention of genocide – proceedings of the international conference on the Holocaust and Genocide, Boulder and London: Westview Press.

Charny, I. (1994).

Toward a generic definition of genocide, in: Andreopoulos, G.J. (ed.), *Genocide – conceptual and historical dimensions*, Philadelphia: University of Pennsylvania Press, 64–94.

Charny, I.W. (1999a).

A Proposed Definitional Matrix for Crimes of Genocide, in: Charny, I.W. (ed.), *Encyclopedia of Genocide*, Santa Barbara, California: ABC-CLIO.

Charny, I. (1999b).

Classification of Genocide in Multiple Categories, in: Charny, I.W. (ed.) *Encyclopedia of Genocide, Vol. 1*, Santa Barbara: ABC-ClIO, 3–7.

Chemerinsky, E. (2005).

Enemy combatants and separation of powers, *Journal of National Security Law and Policy* 1, 73–125.

Chesterman, S. (2005).

You, the People: The United Nations, Transitional Administration, and State-Building, Oxford: Oxford University Press.

Chesterman, J. & Galligan, B. (1997).

Citizens Without Rights, Melbourne: Cambridge University Press.

Chevigny, P. (1987).

Police abuse in Brazil: Summary executions and torture in Sao Paulo and Rio de Janeiro, New York: Human Rights Watch.

Chevigny, P. (1997).

Edge of the Knife: Police Violence in the Americas, New York, N.Y.: The New Press.

Christie, N. (1977).

Conflicts as property, *British Journal of Criminology* 17, 1–15.

Christie, N. (2001).

Answers to Atrocities. Restorative Justice in Extreme Situations, in: Fattah, E. & Parmentier, S. (eds.), *Victim Policies and Criminal Justice on the Road to Restorative Justice. Essays in Honour of Tony Peters*, Leuven: Leuven University Press.

Christie, N. (2004).

Peace or Punishment?, in: Gilligan, G. & Pratt, J. (Eds.), *Crime, Truth and Justice. Official inquiry, discourse, knowledge*, Portland: Willan Publishing, 243–256.

Chua, A. (2003).
World on Fire, New York: Anchor Books.
Churchill, W. (1986).
Genocide: Toward a Functional Definition, *Alternatives* 11(3), 403–430.
Churchill, W. (1997).
A Little Matter of Genocide: Holocaust and Denial in the Americas, 1492 to the Present, San Francisco: City Lights Books.
Cigar, N. (1995).
Genocide in Bosnia: The Policy of Ethnic Cleansing, College Station: Texas A&M University.
Clapham, A. (2006).
Human Rights Obligations of Non-State Actors, Oxford: Oxford University Press.
Clark, I. (2005).
Legitimacy in International Society, New York: Oxford University Press.
Clinard, M.B. & Yeager, P.C. (1980).
Corporate Crime, New York: Free Press.
Cobban, H. (2002).
The legacies of Collective Violence: the Rwandan genocide and the limits of law, *Boston Review* 27(2), 253–281.
Cocker, M. (1998).
Rivers of Blood, Rivers of Gold: Europe's Conquest of Indigenous Peoples, New York: Grove Press.
Coebergh, J. (2005).
Sudan: Genocide Has Killed More than Tsunami, *Parliamentary Brief* 7, 5–6.
Coghlan, R., Brennan, P., Ngoy, D., Dofara, B., Otto, M., Clements, T. & Stewart, B. (2006).
Mortality in the Democratic Republic of Congo: a nationwide survey, *The Lancet* 367, 44–51.
Cohen, A. K. (1955).
Delinquent Boys. The Culture of the Gang, Glencoe, Ill.: The Free Press.
Cohen, D. (2005).
Intended to Fail. The Trials before the ad hoc Human Rights Court in Jakarta, Report, Berkeley: International Centre for Transitional Justice.
Cohen, D.V. (1995).
Ethics and Crime in Business Firms: Organizational Culture and the Impact of Anomie, *Advances in Criminological Theory* 6, 183–206.
Cohen, E.A. (1985).
De negentien treinen naar Sobibor, Amsterdam: Sijthoff.
Cohen, S. (1993).
Human rights and crimes of the state: the culture of denial, *Australian & New Zealand Journal of Criminology* 26, 97–115.
Cohen, S. (1995).
State crimes of previous regimes: knowledge, accountability, and the policing of the past, *Law and social inquiry* 20, 7–50.

Intersentia

525

Cohen, S. (2001).

> *States of Denial: Knowing About Atrocities and Suffering*, Cambridge: Polity Press.

Coicaud, J.M., Heiskanen, V. (Eds.)(2001).

> *The Legitimacy of International Organizations*, New York: United Nations University Press.

Coleman, J.S. (2002).

> Organizational Actors and the Irrelevance of Persons, in: Ermann, M.D. & Lundman R.J. (eds.) *Corporate and Governmental Deviance; Problems of Organizational Behaviour in Contemporary Society*, New York and Oxford: Oxford University Press, 95–104.

Coleman, J.W. (1987).

> Toward an Integrated Theory of White-Collar Crime, *American Journal of Sociology*, 93(2), 406–439.

Coleman, W. & Wayland, S. (2006).

> The Origins of Global Civil Society and Non-Territorial Governance: Some Empirical Reflections, *Global Governance* 12, 241–261.

Colquhoun, P. (1800; 1969).

> *A Treatise on the Police of the Metropolis*, Montclair, NJ: Patterson Smith.

Commissie bestuursrechtelijke en privaatrechtelijke handhaving (1998).

> *Handhaven op niveau*, Deventer: W.E.J. Tjeenk Willink.

Concerned Psychologists (2006).

> Letter To APA On Psychologist Involvement In Torture. Concerned Psychologists to APA President Sharon Brehm, Ph.D. June 6. (http://www.scoop.co.nz/stories/WO0706/S00113.htm).

Conquest, R. (1990).

> *The Great Terror: A Reassessment*, New York: Oxford University Press.

Conroy, J. (2001).

> *Unspeakable Acts; Ordinary People*, Berkeley, CA: University of California press.

Cooper, A.F., English, J., & Thakur, R. (Eds.) (2002).

> *Enhancing Global Governance: Towards a New Diplomacy?* New York: United Nations University Press.

Cooper, B. (1999).

> Introduction, in: Cooper, B. (Ed.), *War Crimes. The Legacy of Nuremberg*, New York: TV books, 11.

Cooper, H. & Sanger, D.E. (2006).

> Rice's Counselor Gives Advice Others May Not Want to Hear, *New York Times*, October 28, EV1–4.

Cortright, D. & Lopez, G. (1999).

> Are Sanctions Just? The Problematic Case of Iraq, *Journal of International Affairs* 52, 735- 756.

Cousins, M. & Hussain, A. (1984).

> *Michel Foucault*, New York: St. Martin's Press.

Crelinsten, R.D. (1993).

> In their own words: the world of the torturer, in: Crelinsten, R.D. & Schmid, A.P. (eds.), *The politics of pain – torturers and their masters*, Leiden: COMT, 39–72.

Crelinsten, R.D. (2003).
The world of torture: a constructed reality, *Theoretical Criminology* 7(3), 293- 318.
Crelinsten, R & Schmidt, A. (1995).
The Politics of Pain: Torturers and their masters, Boulder, CO.: Westview.
Cressey, D.R. (1989).
The poverty of theory in corporate crime research, in: Adler F., Laufer, W.S. (eds.), *Advances in criminological theory,* New Brunswick: Transaction.
Croes, M. & Tammes, P. (2004).
'Gif laten wij niet voortbestaan' [We will not let poison live'], Amsterdam: Aksant.
Crossland, J. (2006).
Churchill: execute Hitler without trial; Nazi justice, *The Sunday Times,* January 1, 2006.
CRS Issue Brief for Congress (2006).
Sudan: Humanitarian Crisis, Peace Talks, Terrorism, and U.S. Policy, Congressional Research Service, Library of Congress, April 12, 2006, 11.
Cunneen, C. (1999).
Criminology, genocide and the forced removal of indigenous children and their families, *Australian and New Zealand Journal of Criminology* 32(2), 124–138.
Cunneen, C. (2001).
Conflict, Politics and Crime. Aboriginal Communities and the Police, St. Leonards: Allen and Unwin.
Cunneen, C. (2005).
Consensus and Sovereignty: Rethinking Policing in the Light of Indigenous Self-determination, in: Hocking, B.A. (ed.), *Unfinished Constitutional Business. Rethinking Indigenous Self-determination,* Canberra: Aboriginal Studies Press.
D'Aspremont, J. (2006).
Legitimacy of Governments in the Age of Democracy, *NYU Journal of International Law and Politics* 38, 877–917.
Dadrian, V.N. (1975).
A Typology of Genocide, *International Review of Modern Sociology* 5(2), 201–212.
Dadrian, V.N. (1976).
A Theoretical Model of Genocide. With Particular Reference to the Armenian Case, *Sociologia Internationalis* 14(1–2), 99–126.
Dadrian, V.N. (1986).
The Role of Turkish Physicians in the World War I Genocide of Ottoman Armenians, *Holocaust and Genocide Studies* 1(2), 10–46.
Dadrian, V.N. (1994).
The Documentation of the World War I Armenian Massacres in the Proceedings of the Turkish Military Tribunal, *Journal of Political and Military Sociology* 22(1), 97–131.
Dadrian, V.N. (1997).
The Turkish Military Tribunal's Prosecution of the Authors of the Armenian Genocide: Four Major Court-Martial Series, *Holocaust and Genocide Studies* 11(1), 28–59.

Dallaire, R. (2004).
Shake Hands with the Devil, The Failure of Humanity in Rwanda, London: Arrow Books.

Daly, E. (2002).
Between punitive and reconstructive justice: the gacaca courts in Rwanda, *International Law and Politics* 34, 355.

David, R. & Yuk-Ping, S.C. (2005).
Victims on Transitional Justice: Lessons from the Reparation of Human Rights Abuses in the Czech Republic, *Human Rights Quarterly* 27(2), 392–435.

Day, L.E. & Vandiver, M. (2000).
Criminology and Genocide Studies: Notes on What Might Have Been and What Still Could Be, *Crime, Law & Social Change* 34, 43–59.

Deacon, R.A. (2003).
Fabricating Foucault: Rationalising the Management of Individuals, Milwaukee: Marquette University Press.

de Brouwer, A-M. (2005).
Supranational Criminal Prosecution of Sexual Violence, The ICC and the Practice of the ICTY and the ICTR, Antwerp: Intersentia.

de Brouwer, A. (2007).
Reparation to Victims of Sexual Violence: Possibilities at the International Criminal Court and at the Trust Fund for Victims and Their Families, *Leiden Journal of International Law* 20, 207–237.

De Feyter, K., Parmentier, S., Bossuyt, M., & Lemmens, P. (2005) (eds.)
Out of the Ashes. Reparation for Victims of Gross and Systematic Human Rights Violations, Antwerp: Intersentia.

De Gaay Fortman, B. (1990).
The Dialectics of Western Law in a Non-Western World, in: Burting, J., & Baehr, P.R. (eds), *Human Rights in a Pluralist World: Individuals and Collectivities*, The Hague: UNESCO.

De Greiff, P. (2004).
Reparation efforts in international perspective: What compensation contributes to the achievement of imperfect justice, in: Doxtader, E., & Villa-Vicencio, C. (eds.), *Repairing the irreparable. Dealing with the double-binds of making reparations for crimes in the past*, Claremont: David Philip.

De Greiff, P. & Wierda, M. (2005).
The Trust Fund for Victims of the International Criminal Court: Between Possibilities and Constraints, in: De Feyter, K., Parmentier, S., Bossuyt, M., & Lemmens, P. (eds.), *Out of the Ashes. Reparation for Victims of Gross and Systematic Human Rights Violations*, Antwerp: Intersentia.

de Hullu, J. (2005).
Enkele opmerkingen over het strafrechtelijk daderschap van rechtspersonen, in: Harteveld, A.E. et al (red), *Systeem in ontwikkeling, liber amicorum G. Knigge*, Nijmegen: Wolf Legal Publishers.

Delanty, G. (2006).

The Cosmopolitan Imagination: Critical Cosmopolitanism and Social Theory, *The British Journal of Criminology* 56, 25–47.

Del Ponte, C. (2006a).

Interview with Sylvie Matton in *Paris Match. Carla del Ponte: Seule contre Tous*, 1 November 2006, http://www.domovina.net/archive/2006/20061104_telegraaf. php last visited: March 2007; http://www.domovina.net/fokus/argos.php.

Del Ponte, C. (2006b).

Srebrenica plan was known to Internationals, Caroline Fletscher, Der Tagesspiegel, 2 November 2006, http://www.domovina.net/archive/2006/20061102_tagesspiegel. php, last visited: March 2007.

Del Ponte, C. (2007a).

Die Schweiz überlebt nur in einer Welt, in der das Recht und nicht die Macht regiert. *Baseler Zeitung*, 26 March 2007, 1–2.

Del Ponte, C. (2007b).

Address of Carla Del Ponte at the Policy Briefing, European Policy Centre, Brussels, The Hague, 3 July 2007.

Del Ponte, C. (2007c)

Address by chief prosecutor Carla Del Ponte at the conference on Establishing the Truth about War Crimes and Conflicts, Zagreb, Croatia, 8–9 February, http://www. un.org/icty/pressreal/2007/cadelst-070215.htm.

de Mildt, D. (1997).

Exemplaren van de soort, *Tijdschrift voor Criminologie* 39(2), 117–127.

Depoortere, E., et al. (2004).

Violence and Mortality in West Darfur, Sudan (2003–04): Epidemiological Evidence from four Surveys, *The Lancet* 364, 1315–1320.

Derber, C. (1998).

Corporation Nation: How Corporations are Taking Over Our Lives and What We Can Do About It, New York: St. Martins Press.

Derluyn, I., Broekaert, E., Schuyten, G. & Temmerman, E. (2006).

Post-traumatic Stress in Former Ugandan Child Soldiers, *The Lancet*, 363(13), 861–863.

de Schutter, O. (2005).

The Accountability of Multinationals for Human Rights Violations in European Law, in: Alston, Ph. (ed.), *Non-State Actors and Human* Rights, Oxford: Oxford University Press, 227–314.

Des Forges, A. (1995).

The Ideology of Genocide, *Issue: A Journal of Opinion* 23(2), 44–47.

Des Forges, A. (1999).

Leave None to Tell the Story: Genocide in Rwanda, New York: Human Rights Watch.

de Waal, A. (1997).

Famine Crimes: Politics and the Disaster Relief Industry in Africa, Oxford: Currey.

De Waal, A. (2002).

> *Famine Crimes, politics & the disaster relief industry in Africa,* London: African Rights.

de Waal, A. (2003).

> Human rights organisations and the political imagination: how the West and Africa have diverged, *Journal of Human Rights* 2(4), 475–494.

de Waal, A. (2004).

> Tragedy in Darfur, *Boston Review: A Political and Literary Forum,* retrieved from: Http://www.bostonreview.net/BR29.5/dewaal.html.

Dickason, O.P. (1997).

> *The Myth of the Savage and the Beginnings of French Colonialism in the Americas,* Edmonton: University of Alberta Press.

Dicks, H.V. (1972).

> *Licensed mass murder – a sociopsychology study of some SS-killers,* London: Chatto.

Dillon, M. (2004).

> The Security of Governance, in: Larner, W. & Walters, W. (Eds.), *Global Governmentality: Governing International Spaces,* New York: Routledge, 76–94.

Dingwerth, K. & Pattberg, P. (2006).

> Global Governance as a Perspective on World Politics, *Global Governance* 12, 185–203.

Dolot, M. (1985).

> *Execution by Hunger: The Hidden Holocaust,* New York: W.W. Norton & Company.

Dongala, E. (2003).

> *Johnny, valse hond,* Breda: De Geus/Novib

Donnelly, J. (2003).

> *Universal Human Rights in Theory and Practice* (Second edition), Ithaca, NY: Cornell University Press.

Donoho, D. (2006).

> Human Rights Enforcement in the Twenty-First Century, *Georgia Journal of International and Comparative Law* 35, 1–52.

Dorn, W. (2002).

> *Early Warning of Armed Conflict: An Introduction,* Pearson Peacekeeping Centre, http://www.rmc.ca/academic/gradrech/dorn26_e.html

Douglas, L. (1995).

> Film as Witness: Screening 'Nazi Concentration Camps' before the Nuremberg Tribunal, *Yale Law Journal* 105(2), 449–481.

Douglas. T. (1995).

> *Scapegoats: Transferring Blame,* New York: Routledge.

Doxtader, E. (2004).

> The matter of words in the midst of beginnings: unravelling the 'relationship' between reparation and reconciliation, in: Doxtader, E., & Villa-Vicencio, C. (eds.), *Repairing the irreparable. Dealing with the double-binds of making reparations for crimes in the past,* Claremont: David Philip.

Drahms, A. (1900) [1971].

> *The Criminal – His Personnel and Environment,* Montclair, NJ: Patterson Smith.

Drakulic, S. (2004).

They would never hurt a fly – war criminals on trial in The Hague, London: Penguin Books.

Dreyfus, H.L., & Rabinow, P. (1983).

Michel Foucault: Beyond Structuralism and Hermeneutics, Chicago: University of Chicago Press.

Drost, P. N. (1959a).

The Crime of State: Penal Protection for Fundamental Freedoms of Persons and Peoples – Book I: Humanicide: International Governmental Crime against Individual Human Rights, Leyden: A. W. Sythoff.

Drost, P. N. (1959b).

The Crime of State: Penal Protection for Fundamental Freedoms of Persons and Peoples – Book II: Genocide: United Nations Legislation on International Criminal Law, Leyden: A. W. Sythoff.

Drumbl, M.A. (2000).

Punishment, Postgenocide: From Guilt to Shame to *Civis* in Rwanda, *New York University Law Review* 75(5), 1221–1326.

Drumbl, M.A. (2002).

Sclerosis: retributive justice and the Rwandan genocide, *Punishment & Society* 2, 287.

Drumbl, M.A. (2003).

Toward a Criminology of International Crime, *Ohio State Journal of Dispute Resolution* 19, 263–282.

Drumbl, M.A. (2007).

Atrocity, Punishment and International Law, Cambridge: Cambridge University Press; with book review by Parmentier, S., *Journal of International Criminal Justice* 5, 1215–1218.

Du Plessis, M., & Peté, S. (2007) (eds.).

Repairing the Past? International Perspectives on Reparations for Gross Human Rights Abuses, volume 1 of the Series on Transitional Justice, under the direction of general editors Parmentier, S., Sarkin, J., & Weitekamp, E., Antwerp: Intersentia.

Dunning, J.D. (1993).

Multinational Enterprises and the Global Economy, Reading: Addison-Wesley Publishing Company.

Durkheim, E. (1951).

Suicide, Glencoe, Ill.: The Free Press.

Dyer, G. (1985).

War, London: The Bodley Head.

Dyregrov, A., Gupta, L., Gjestad, R., Mukanoheli, E. (2000).

Trauma Exposure and Psychological Reactions to Genocide among Rwandan Children, *Journal of Traumatic Stress* 13(1), 3–21.

Dyson, M. (2006).

Come Hell or High Water, New York: Basic Books.

Dyzenhaus, D. (1998).

Truth, Reconciliation and the Apartheid Legal Order, Cape Town: Juta & Co.

Eckstein, S.E. & Wickham-Crowley, T.P. (eds.) (2003).
What Justice? Whose Justice? Fighting for Fairness in Latin America, Berkeley: University of California Press.

Edelheit, A., & Edelheit, H. (1994).
History of the Holocaust: A Handbook and Dictionary, Boulder: Westview Press.

Ehrenberg, J. (1999).
Civil Society: The Critical History of an Idea, New York: New York University Press.

Ericson, R.V. (2007).
Crime in an insecure world, Cambridge: Polity Press.

Erikson, E.H. (1966).
Ontogeny of Ritualization, in: Lowenstein, R.M., Newman, L.M., Schur, M., & Solnit, A.J. (eds.), *Psychoanalysis: A General Psychology*, New York: International Universities Press.

Eriksson, M., & Wallensteen, P. (2004).
Armed Conflict, 1989–2003, *Journal of Peace Research* 41, 625–31.

Ermann, M.D. & Lundman, R.J. (eds.) (2002).
Corporate and Governmental Deviance; Problems of Organizational Behaviour in Contemporary Society, New York and Oxford: Oxford University Press.

Esty, D.C. (2006).
Good Governance at the Supranational Scale: Globalizing Administrative Law, *The Yale Law Journal* 125, 1490–1561.

Evans, R.J. (1999).
Fakten und Fiktionen. Über die Grundlagen historischer Erkenntnis, Campus Verlag. Frankfurt/M., New York (Orig. title: In Defence of History, London: Granta Books, 1997).

Ewald, U. (2006).
Large-Scale Victimization and the Jurisprudence of the ICTY: Victimological Research Issues, in: Ewald, U. & Turkovic, K. (eds.), *Large-Scale Victimization as a Potential Source of Terrorist Activities: Importance of Regaining Security in Post-Conflict Societies*, Amsterdam: IOS Press.

Ewald, U. & Turkovic, K. (eds.) (2006).
Large-Scale Victimization as a Potential Source of Terrorist Activities: Importance of Regaining Security in Post-Conflict Societies, Amsterdam: IOS Press.

Expert Report (2005).
Summary of the Report to the Secretary-General of the Commission of Experts to Review the Prosecution of Serious Violations of Human Rights in Timor-Leste (then East Timor) in 1999 (S/2005/458).

Falk, R.A. (2006).
The Declining World Order: America's Imperial Geopolitics, New York: Routledge.

Farge, A. & Foucault, M. (1982).
Le désordre des familles : Lettres de cachet des archives de la Bastille au XVIIIe siècle, Paris: Gallimard.

Farina, C. (2001–2002).
A Review of 'Torture through the Ages', *Journal of Criminal Justice and Popular Culture*, 9(1), 31–32.

Faust, K. & D. Kauzlarich (unpublished).

Victims of Government, Natural Disaster, or Both? Hurricane Katrina Survivors' Perceptions of the Sources of their Victimization, Unpublished paper.

Fay, Major General George. (2004).

Major General George Fay, see: "Executive Summary: Investigation of Intelligence Activities At Abu Ghraib," 8/25 *(http://fl1.findlaw.com/news.findlaw.com/hdocs/ docs/dod/fay82504rpt.pdf)*

Fein, H. (1984)

Scenarios of Genocide: models of genocide and critical responses, in: Charny, I.W. (1984), *Toward the understanding and prevention of genocide – proceedings of the international conference on the Holocaust an Genocide*, Boulder and London: Westview Press, 3–31.

Fein, H. (1990).

Genocide: A Sociological Perspective, *Current Sociology* 38(1), 1–101.

Fein, H. (ed.) (1992).

Genocide watch, New Haven: Yale University Press.

Fein, H. (1993).

Genocide: A Sociological Perspective, London: Sage Publications.

Feitlowitz, M. (1998).

A Lexicon of Terror: Argentina and the Legacies of Torture, New York: Oxford University Press.

Fellman, G. (1998).

Rambo and the Dalai Lama: The Compulsion to Win and the Threat to Human Survival, Albany, NY: State University of New York Press.

Felson, M. (1998).

Crime and Everyday Life, 2nd edition, Thousand Oaks, Ca: Pine Forge Press.

Ferguson, N. (2004).

Colossus: The Price of American Empire, New York: Penguin.

Fest, J.C. (1980).

Das Gesicht des Dritten Reiches – profile einer totalitären Herrschaft, München: Piper.

Fest, J.C. (1987).

Speer – eine Biographie, Frankfurt am Main: Fischer Taschenbuch Verlag 2001.

Fest. J.C. (2005).

Die unbeantwortbaren Fragen, Reinbek: Rohwolt.

Festinger, L. (1957).

A theory on cognitive dissonance, Evanston: Row Peterson.

Festinger, L. & Carlsmith, J.M. (1959).

Cognitive consequences of forced compliance, *Journal of abnormal and social psychology* 47, 203–210.

Fichtelberg, A. (2006).

Democratic Legitimacy and the International Criminal Court. A Liberal Defence, *Journal of International Criminal Justice* 4, 765–785.

Fierens, J. (2005).
 Gacaca Courts: Between Fantasy and Reality, *Journal of International Criminal Justice* 3, 896–919.
Fijnaut, C. (2005).
 Onwetendheid en wetenschap in de criminologie, WODC-lezing.
Findley, T. (2002).
 The use of force in UN peace operations, Oxford: Oxford University Press.
Findlay, M., & Henham, R. (2005).
 Transforming International Criminal Justice. Retributive and restorative justice in the trial process, Cullompton: Willan Publishing.
Finer, S.E. (1988).
 The man on horseback: the role of the military in politics, London: Pinter.
Fisher, B., Daigle, L. & Cullen, F. (2003).
 Reporting Sexual Victimization to the Police and Others: Results from a National-level Study of College Women, *Criminal Justice and Behavior* 30(1), 6–38.
Fischer, C. (2002).
 The Rise of the Nazis, 2nd ed., Manchester: Manchester University Press.
Fisher, L. (2005).
 Military tribunals and presidential power, Lawrence: University of Kansas Press.
Fisher, W. & Ponniah, J. (2003).
 Another World is Possible: Popular Alternatives to Globalization at the World Social Forum, London: Zed Books.
Fisse, B. & J. Braithwaite (1993).
 Corporations, Crime and Accountability, Cambridge and Melbourne: Cambridge University Press.
Flint, J. & Waal, A. de (2005).
 Darfur: A Short History of a Long War, London: Zed Books.
Fokwa, T.J.B. (2004).
 In search for direct corporate responsibility for human rights violations in Africa: Which way forward?, Thesis at the Centre for Human Rights, University of Pretoria.
Foucault, M. (1977).
 Discipline and punish: The birth of the prison, Translated by Alan Sheridan, New York: Vintage.
Foucault, M. (1980).
 Power/Knowledge. Selected Interviews and Other Writings 1972–1977, ed. by C. Gordon, Brighton: Harvester Wheatsheaf.
Foucault, M. (1991).
 Questions of method, in: Burchell, G., Gordon, C. & Miller, P., *The Foucault effect: Studies of governmentality*, Chicago: University of Chicago Press, 73–86.
Franck, T.M. (2006).
 The Power of Legitimacy and the Legitimacy of Power: International Law in an Age of Power Disequilibrium, *American Journal of International Law* 100, 88-106.
Franklin, J.H. (1985).
 George Washington Williams: A Biography, Chicago: University of Chicago Press.

French, P.A. (ed.) (1972), *Individual and Collective Responsibility: The massacre at My Lai*, Cambridge, Massachusetts: Schenkman Publishing Company.

French Parliament (1998).
Assemblée Nationale, Rapport d'information, Mission d'information sur le Rwanda, No. 1271, December 15, 1998.

Friedlander, H. (1995).
The Origins of Nazi Genocide: From Euthanasia to the Final Solution, Chapel Hill, N.C.: University of North Carolina Press.

Friedman, J. (1999).
Indigenous Movements and the Discrete Charm of the Bourgeoisie, *Taja: Australian Journal of Anthropology* 10, 1.

Friedman, J. (ed.) (2003).
Introduction, in: Friedman, J. (ed.), *Globalization, the State, and Violence*, Walnut Creek, CA: Alta Mira Press, 7–15.

Friedman, M. (1962).
Capitalism and Freedom, Chicago: University of Chicago Press.

Friedrichs, D.O. (ed.) (1998).
State Crime, Volumes I & II, Aldershot: Ashgate.

Friedrichs, D.O. (2000a).
The Crime of the Century? The Case for the Holocaust, *Crime, Law & Social Change* 34(1), 21–41.

Friedrichs, D.O. (2000b).
Crime in High Places: A Criminological Perspective on the Clinton Case, in: Jeffery T. Ulmer (ed.), *Sociology of Crime, Law and Deviance*, Volume II, Amsterdam: JAI, 281–300,

Friedrichs, D.O. (2004a).
Trusted Criminals, New York: Wadsworth.

Friedrichs, D.O. (2004b).
White-Collar Crime in a Globalized World, Presentation at Western Michigan University.

Friedrichs, D.O. (2007a).
Trusted Criminals: White Collar Crime in Contemporary Society, 3rd edition, Belmont, CA: Thomson/Wadsworth.

Friedrichs, D.O. (2007b).
White-Collar Crime in a Postmodern, Globalized World, in: Pontell, H.N. & Geis, G. (eds.), *International Handbook of White-Collar and Corporate Crime*, New York: Springer, 163–184.

Friedrichs, D.O. (forthcoming).
Transnational Crime and Global Criminology: Definitional, Typological and Contextual Conundrums, *Social Justice*.

Friedrichs, D.O. & Friedrichs, J. (2002).
The World Bank and Crimes of Globalization: A Case Study, *Social Justice* 29, 13–36.

Friedrichs, D.O. & D. Rothe (2006).
The State of the Criminology of Crimes of the State, *Social Justice* 33(1), 147–161.

Fromm, E. (1942).
   The fear of freedom, London: Kegan Paul, Trench, Trubner.
Fromm, E. (1973).
   The anatomy of human destructiveness, London: Penguin Books.
Frynas, J.G. & Pegg, S. (2003).
   Transnational corporations and human rights, New York: Palgrave MacMillan.
Gabisirege, S., & Babalola, S. (2001).
   Perceptions about the Gacaca law in Rwanda: Evidence from a multi-method study,
   Baltimore: Johns Hopkins University.
Garfinkel, H. (1991).
   Conditions of successful status degradation ceremonies, New York: Irvington
   Publishers (reprints).
Garkawe, S. (2003).
   Victims and the International Criminal Court: Three Major Issues, *International
   Criminal Law Review* 3(4), 345–367.
Garland, D. (1990).
   Punishment and modern society: A study in social theory, Chicago: University of
   Chicago Press.
Gaston, E.L. (2005).
   Review of The Dark Side of Virtue, *Harvard International Law Journal* 46,
   547–559.
Geltman, P.L., Grant-Knight, W., Mehta, S.D., Lloyd-Travaglini, C., Lustig, S., Landgraf,
   J.M., Wise, P.H. (2005).
   The "Lost Boys of Sudan". Functional and Behavioral Health of Unaccompanied
   Refugee Minors Resettled in the United States, *Archives of Pediatrics* 159, 585–591.
Gellately, R. & Kiernan, B. (eds.) (2003).
   The Spectre of Genocide. Mass Murder in Historical Perspective, Cambridge:
   Cambridge University Press.
Gerlach, Ch. (2006).
   Extremely violent societies: an alternative to the concept of genocide, *Journal of
   Genocide Research* 8(4), 455–471.
Gerson, J. (1995).
   With Hiroshima Eyes: Atomic War, Nuclear Extortion, and Moral Imagination, New
   York: New Society Publishers.
Ghemawat, P. (2007).
   Why the World Isn't Flat, *Foreign Policy* (March/April), 54–61.
Ghezzi, S. & Mingione, E. (2003).
   Beyond the Informal Economy: New Trends in the Post-Fordist Transition, in:
   Friedman, J. (ed.), *Globalization, the State, and Violence*, Walnut Creek, CA: Alta
   Mira Press, 87–106.
Gibson, J.L. (2004)
   Overcoming Apartheid: Can Truth Reconcile a Divided Nation?, *Politikon: South
   African Journal of Political Studies* 31, 129–155.

Gibson, J.L., & Gouws, A. (1999).
> Truth and reconciliation in South Africa. Attributions of blame and the struggle over Apartheid, *American Social Science Review* 93, 501–517.

Gibson, J.T. & Haritos-Fatouras, M. (1986).
> The education of a torturer, *Psychology Today* 20(11), 50–58.

Giddens, A. (2000).
> *The Third Way and Its Critics*, Oxford, U.K.: Polity Press.

Gilbert, G.M. (1948).
> *Nuremberg Diary*, London: Eyre & Spottiswoode.

Gillroy, J.M. (2006).
> Adjudication Norms, Dispute Settlement Regimes and International Tribunals: The Status of 'Environmental Sustainability' in International Jurisprudence, *Stanford Journal of International Law* (Winter), 1–52.

Gilpin, R. (1987).
> *The Political Economy of International Relations*, New Jersey: Princeton University Press.

Gingerich, T. & Leaning, J. (2004).
> *The Use of Rape as a Weapon of War in the Conflict in Darfur, Sudan*, Boston, MA: Harvard School of Public Health.

Ginzburg, C. (1999).
> *The judge and the historian: marginal notes on a late-twentieth-century miscarriage of justice*, London/New York: Verso.

Glueck, S. (1966).
> *War Criminals: Their Prosecution and Punishment*, New York: Kraus Reprint Corporation.

Gobert, J. & Punch, M. (2003).
> *Rethinking corporate crime*, Cambridge: Cambridge University Press.

Gobodo-Madikizela, P. (2003).
> *A human being died that night. A story of forgiveness*, Claremont: David Philip Publishers.

Gold, H. (1996).
> *Unit 731 Testimony*, Singapore: Yen Books.

Goldberg, M. (2005).
> Zoellick's Appeasement Tour, *The American Prospect Online*, April 29, 2005.

Goldenberg, S.L. (1972).
> Crimes against Humanity – 1945–1970, *The Western Ontario Law Review* 11, 1–55.

Goldhagen, D.J. (1997).
> *Hitler's willing executioners: ordinary Germans and the Holocaust*, London: Abacus.

Goldstein, R.J. (1986).
> The limitations of using quantitative data studying human rights abuses, *Human Rights Quarterly* 8, 607–627.

Goleman, D. (1996).
> *Vital lies, simple truths: The Psychology of Self Deception*, New York: Simon & Schuster.

Goma Epidemiological Group (1995).
Public Health Impact of Rwandan Refugee Crisis: What Happened in Goma, Zaire in July 1994, *The Lancet* 345, 339–344.
Goodall, H. (1996).
Invasion to Embassy. Land in Aboriginal Politics, 1770–1972, St Leonards: Allen and Unwin.
Gordon, D. (2004).
Poverty, Death and Disease, in: Hillyard, P., Pantazis, C., Tombs, S. & Gordon, D. (eds.), *Beyond Criminology: Taking Harm Seriously*, London: Pluto Press, 251–266.
Gosine, A. (2005).
Dying Planet, Deadly People: 'Race'-Sex Anxieties and Alternative Globalizations, *Social Justice: A Journal of Crime, Conflict, and World Order* 32(4), 69–86.
Gourevitch, P. (1998).
We Wish to Inform You That Tomorrow We Will Be Killed With Our Families: Stories From Rwanda, New York: Farrar, Straus, & Giroux.
Graybill, L. (2002).
Truth and reconciliation in South Africa miracle or model? Boulder: Lynne Rienner Publishers.
Graybill, L. & Lanegran, K. (2004).
Truth, Justice, and Reconciliation in Africa: Issues and Cases, *African Studies Quarterly* 8(1), 1
Graziano, F. (1992).
Divine violence: spectacle, psychosexuality & radical Christianity in the "Dirty War", Boulder Col.: Westview Press.
Gready, P. (ed.) (2004).
Fighting for Human Rights, New York: Routledge.
Green, P. (2005).
Disaster by Design, *British Journal of Criminology* 45(4), 528–546.
Green, P., & Ward, T. (2000).
State Crime, Human Rights, and the Limits of Criminology, *Social Justice* 27, 101–120.
Green, P., & Ward, T. (2004).
State Crime: Governments, Violence, and Corruption, London: Pluto Press.
Greenhouse, L. (2004).
Justices affirm legal rights of enemy combatants, *New York Times*, June 29, A1, A14.
Groen, K. (1994).
Als slachtoffers daders worden: de zaak van joodse verraadster Ans van Dijk, Baarn: Ambo.
Grossman, D. (1995).
On Killing – The Psychological Cost of Learning to Kill in War and Society, Boston: Little, Brown and Company.
Grissett, S. (2004).
Shifting Federal Budget erodes Protection from Levees, *Times-Pacayune*, 6/4/2006.

Grünfeld, F. (2000).

The Role of the Bystanders in Human Rights Violations, in: Coomans, F., Grünfeld, F., Westendorp, I. & Willems, J. (eds.), *Rendering Justice to the Vulnerable. Liber Amicorum in Honour of Theo van Boven*, The Hague, London, Boston: Kluwer Law International, 131–143.

Grünfeld, F. (2003).

Vroegtijdig optreden van omstanders ter voorkoming van oorlogen en schendingen van de rechten van de mens, oratie, (*Early action of bystanders to prevent wars and gross human rights violations*, inaugural lecture) December 10, 2003, Universiteit Utrecht.

Grünfeld, F. & Huijboom, A. (2007).

The Failure to Prevent Genocide in Rwanda: The Role of Bystanders, Leiden/Boston: Transnational Publishers, Nijhoff/Brill.

Guha-Sapir, D., Degomme, O. & Phelan, M. (2005).

Darfur: Counting the Deaths: Mortality Estimates from Multiple Survey Data, Centre for Research on the Epidemiology of Disasters, University of Louvain, School of Public Health, Brussels. Http://www.cred@esp.uci.ac.be.

Guha-Sapir, D. & Panhuis, W.G. van (2003).

The importance of conflict-related mortality in civilian populations, *The Lancet* 361, 2126–1402.

Guichaoua, A. (2005)

Rwanda 1994; les politiques du génocide à Butare, Paris: Karthala.

Gupta, D.K. (2001).

Path to Collective Madness- A study in social order and political pathology, Westport: Preager.

Gurr, T.R. (1970)

Why men rebel, Princeton: University Press.

Gustafson, D. (1997).

Facilitating communication between victims and offenders in cases of serious and violent crime, *The ICCA Journal* 3, 44–49.

Hacking, I. (1986).

Making people up, in: Heller, T.C., et al. (eds.), *Reconstructing individualism*, Stanford: Stanford University Press.

Haebich, A. (1992).

For their Own Good: Aborigines and Government in the South West of Western Australia 1900-1940, Perth: University of Western Australia Press.

Hagan, J. (2003).

Justice in the Balkans: Prosecuting Crimes of War in The Hague Tribunal, Chicago: University of Chicago Press.

Hagan, J. & Greer, S. (2002).

Making War Criminal, *Criminology* 40, 231–264.

Hagan, J. & Levi, R. (2004).

Social Skill, the Milosevic Indictment, and the Rebirth of International Criminal Justice, *European Journal of Criminology* 1, 445–475.

Hagan, J., Rymond-Richmond, W. & Parker, P. (2005).
   The Criminology of Genocide: The Death and Rape of Darfur, *Criminology* 43(3), 525–562.
Hagan, J., Schoenfeld, H. & Palloni, A. (2006).
   The Science of Human Rights, War Crimes, and Humanitarian Emergencies, *Annual Review of Sociology* 32, 329–349.
Hagenaars, J. (1993).
   Loglinear Models with Latent Variables, London: Sage.
Halter, R. (2007).
   Statement, http://www.hmd.org.uk/files/1149791888-12.pdf
Hamber, B., Nageng, D. & O'Malley, G. (2000).
   Telling it Like it is: Understanding the Truth and Reconciliation Commission from the Perspective of Survivors, *Psychology in Society* 26, 18–42.
Haney, C. & Zimbardo, P.G. (1977).
   The socialization into criminality: On becoming a prisoner and a guard, in: Tapp, J.L. & Levine, F.J. (eds.), *Law, justice and the individual in society: Psychological and legal issues*, New York: Holt, Rinehart & Winston.
Hansen, O.K. (unknown).
   Operation 'Hooligan-bashing' – Danish Tanks at War: http://www.milhist.dk/post45/boellebank/boellebank_uk.htm, last visited: March 2007.
Harbom, L., & Wallensteen, P. (2005).
   Armed Conflict, 1989–2006, *Journal of Peace Research* 44, 623–634.
Harding, C. (2006).
   Human Action or State Action. Locating the Site of Supranational Criminality, in: Haveman, R. & Olusanya, O. (eds), *Sanctioning and Sentencing in Supranational Criminal Law*, Antwerp, Oxford: Intersentia.
Hardt, M. & Negri, A. (2000).
   Empire, Cambridge: Harvard University Press.
Harff, B. (1986).
   Genocide as State Terrorism, in: Stohl, M. & Lopez, G.A. (eds.), *Government Violence and Repression: An Agenda for Research*, London: Greenwood Press.
Harff, B. (2003).
   No Lessons Learned from the Holocaust? Assessing Risks of Genocide and Political Mass Murder since 1995, *American Political Science Review* 97(1), 57–73.
Harff, B. & Gurr, T.R. (1988).
   Toward Empirical Theory of Genocides and Politicides: Identification and Measurement of Cases Since 1945, *International Studies Quarterly* 32(3), 359–371.
Harff, B. & Gurr, T.R. (1989).
   Victims of the State: Genocides, Politicides and Group Repression since 1945, *International Review of Victimology* 1, 23–41.
Haritos-Fatouras, M. (1993)
   The official torturer: a learning model for obedience to the authority of violence, in: Crelinsten, R.D. & Schmid, A.P., *The politics of pain: torturers and their masters*, Leiden: COMT, 141–159.

Haritos-Fatouros, M. (2002).
The Psychological Origins of Institutionalized Torture, New York: Routledge.
Harper, A. & Israel, M. (1999).
The Killing of the Fly: State-corporate victimization in Papua New Guinea, *Resource Management in Asia Pacific Working Paper*, nr. 22, Research School of Pacific and Asian Studies, Canberra: The Australian National University.
Harvey, D. (1989).
The Condition of Postmodernity, Oxford: Basil Blackwell.
Hashemian, F., Khoshnood, K., Desai, M., Falahati, F., Kasl, S. & Southwick, S. (2006).
Anxiety, Depression, and Posttraumatic Stress in Iranian Survivors of Chemical Warfare, *Journal of the American Medical Association* 296(5), 56—566.
Hatzfeld, J. (2005).
A time for machetes – the Rwandan genocide: the killers speak, New York: Ferrar, Strauss and Giroux (transl. from French).
Haveman, R.H. (2002).
Nut, noodzaak en nadelen van supranationaal straffen, *Internationale Spectator* 56(5), 252–257.
Haveman, R.H. (2004).
De rationaliteit van het supranationale straffen, *Justitiële Verkenningen* 5, 67–78.
Haveman, R.H. (2005a).
De supranationale grens van de overspannen verwachting, in: Haveman, R.H. & Wiersinga, H. (red.), *Langs de randen van het strafrecht*, Nijmegen: Wolf Legal Publishers.
Haveman, R.H. (2005b).
Supranationale criminology, in: Jordaans, A.H.E.C., Mevis, P.A.M. & Wöretshofer, J. (red.), *Praktisch strafrecht – liber amicorum J.M. Reijntjes*, Nijmegen: Wolf Legal Publishers.
Haveman, R. (2006a)
Sentencing and Sanctioning in Supranational Criminal Law, in: Haveman, R.H. & Olusanya, O. (eds.), *Sentencing and Sanctioning in Supranational Criminal Law*, Antwerp, Oxford: Intersentia, 1–15.
Haveman, R. (2006b).
Supranational Expectations of a Punitive Approach, in: Haveman, R.H. & Olusanya, O. (eds.), *Sentencing and Sanctioning in Supranational Criminal Law*, Antwerp, Oxford: Intersentia, 145–160.
Haveman, R.H., Kavran, O. & Nicholls, J. (eds.) (2003).
Supranational Criminal Law, a System Sui Generis, Vol. I in the series 'Supranational Criminal Law: Capita Selecta', Antwerp: Intersentia.
Haveman, R.H. & Olusanya, O. (eds.) (2006).
Sentencing and Sanctioning in Supranational Criminal Law, Vol. IV in the series 'Supranational Criminal Law: Capita Selecta', Antwerp, Oxford: Intersentia.
Hayner, P.B. (1994).
Fifteen Truth Commissions-1974–1994: A Comparative Study, *Human Rights Quarterly* 16, 597–655.

Hayner, P.B. (2001).
Unspeakable truths. Confronting state terror and atrocity. Preface by Timothy Ash, New York: Routledge.

Hayner, P.B. (2002).
Unspeakable Truths: Facing the Challenge of Truth Commissions, New York: Routledge.

Hayner, P.B. (2006).
Truth Commissions: A Schematic Overview, International Review of the Red Cross 862, 295–310.

Heinz, W.S. (1993).
The military, torture and human rights: experiences from Argentina, Brazil, Chili and Uruguay, in: Crelinsten, R.D. & Schmid, A.P. (eds.), The politics of pain – Torturers and their masters, Leiden: COMT, 73–108.

Hemptinne, J. (2007).
The Creation of Investigating Chambers at the International Criminal Court. An Option Worth Pursuing?, Journal of International Criminal Justice 5, 402–418.

Henry, S. & Lanier, M. (eds.) (2001).
The Nature of Crime: Controversies over the Content and Definition of Crime, Boulder, CO: Rowman & Littlefield.

Henry, V. (2004).
Death work: Police trauma and the psychology of survival, New York: Oxford University Press.

Herszenhorn, D. (2007).
Democrats, Promising to Force Change in War Strategy, Aim to Reframe Iraq Debate, New York Times, September 5, 2007, A10.

Hilberg, R. (1992)
Perpetrators, victims, bystanders – the Jewish catastrophe 1933–1945, New York: Aaron Asher Books.

Hillyard, P., Pantazis, C., Tombs, S. & Gordon, D. (2004).
Beyond Criminology: Taking Harm Seriously, London: Pluto Press.

Hillyard, P., Sims, J., Tombs, S. & Whyte, D. (2004).
Leaving a 'Stain Upon the Silence,' British Journal of Criminology 44, 369–390.

Hillyard, P. & Tombs, S. (2005).
Beyond Criminology?, in: Hillyard, P., Pantazis, C., Tombs, S., Gordon, D. & Dorling, D. (eds.), Criminal Obsessions: Why Harm Matters More than Crime, London: Crime and Society Foundation.

Hinton, A.L. (2005).
Why Did They Kill?: Cambodia in the Shadow of Genocide, Berkeley: University of California Press.

Hirsch, H. (1995).
Genocide and the Politics of Memory: Studying Death to Preserve Life, Chapel Hill: University of North Carolina Press.

Hirsch, H. (2002).
Anti-Genocide: Building an American Movement to Prevent Genocide, Westport, Ct.: Praeger.

Hirsch, S. (2004).
  Annals of National Security: 'Torture at Abu Ghraib', The *New Yorker,* May 10, http://www.newyorker.com/archive/2004/05/10/040510fa_fact
Hirsch, S. (2007).
  Annals of National Security, 'The General's Report: How Antonio Taguba, who investigated the Abu Ghraib scandal, became one of its casualties,' *The New Yorker Magazine,*6/20/2007.(http://www.newyorker.com/reporting/2007/06/25/070625fa_fact_hersh.)
Hitchcock, R.K. & Twedt, T.M. (1997).
  Physical and Cultural Genocide of Various Indigenous Peoples, in: Totten, S., Parsons, W.S. & Charny, I.W. (eds.), *Century of Genocide: Eyewitness Accounts and Critical Views,* New York: Garland Publishing.
Hochschild, A. (1998).
  King Leopold's Ghost, Boston: Houghton Mifflin Company.
Hoess, R. (1959).
  Commandant of Auschwitz, New York: World.
Hoffer, E. (1951).
  The true believer: thoughts on the nature of mass movements, New York: HarperCollins Publishers.
Hofman, J. (1981).
  De Collaborateur – een sociaal-psychologisch onderzoek naar misdadig gedrag in dienst van de Duitse bezetter, Meppel: Boom.
Hoffman, S. (2003).
  World Governance: Beyond Utopia, *Daedalus* (Winter), 27–35.
Hoge, W. (2005).
  International War-Crimes Prosecutor Gets List of 51 Sudan Suspects, *New York Times,* April 6, 2005, A6.
Hoge, W. (2006).
  UN Council Imposes Sanctions on 4 Men in Darfur War Crimes, *New York Times,* April 26, 2006, A10.
Hogg, R. (2002).
  Criminology beyond the nation state: global conflicts, human rights and the new world disorder, *Critical criminology,* 185–217.
Hoig, S. (1961).
  The Sand Creek Massacre, Norman, Okl.: University of Oklahoma Press.
Holmes, R. (1985).
  Acts of War: Behavior of Men in Battle, New York: Simon & Schuster Inc.
Holtzman, E. (2006).
  The Impeachment of George W. Bush, *The Nation* (January 30), 11–18.
Honig, J.W. & Both, N. (1996).
  Srebrenica: record of a war crime, London: Penguin.
Honwana, A. (2006).
  Child soldiers in Africa, Philadelphia: University Press of Pennsylvania.

House of Commons International Development Committee, Darfur, Sudan (2005).
   The Responsibility to Protect, Fifth Report of the Session 2004–2005, Vol. II, Oral and Written Evidence, London: Station Office Limited.
Horowitz, I.L. (2002).
   Taking Lives – Genocide and State Power, 5th revised edition, New Jersey: Transaction Publishers.
Höss, A. (1992).
   The Trial of Perpetrators by the Turkish Military Tribunals: The Case of Yozgat, in: Hovannisian, R.G. (ed.), *The Armenian Genocide: History, Politics, Ethics*, New York: St Martin's Press.
Huberts, L.W.J.C. & Nelen, J.M. (2005).
   Corruptie in het Nederlandse openbaar bestuur. Omvang, aard en afdoening, Amsterdam: Vrije Universiteit.
Huff, C.R., Killias, M. (Eds.)(forthcoming).
   International Perspectives on Miscarriages of Justice, Philadelphia: Temple University Press.
Huggins, M. (1998).
   Political policing: The United States and Latin America, Durham, NC: Duke University Press.
Huggins, M. (1999).
   Policia e politica: Relacoes Estados Unidos/America Latina, Sao Paulo: Cortez Editora.
Huggins, M. (2002).
   Treat prisoners like human beings, *The Albany Times Union*, March 26, 2002.
Huggins, M.K. (2003).
   Moral Universes of Torturers and Murderers, *Albany Law Review* 67(2), 527–535.
Huggins, M.K., Haritos-Fatouros, M. & Zimbardo, P. (2002).
   Violence Workers: Torturers and Murderers Reconstruct Brazilian Atrocities, San Francisco: University of California Press.
Huggins, M.K., Haritos-Fatouros, M. & Zimbardo, P. (2006).
   Operarios da violencia, Brasilia: Editora Universidade da Brasilia.
Huisman, W. (2001).
   Tussen winst en moraal. Achtergronden van regelnaleving en regelovertreding door ondernemingen, (Between profit and morality. Background factors of regulatory compliance and violation by corporations), The Hague: Boom Juridische uitgevers.
Human Rights Watch (1997).
   The scars of death: Children abducted by the Lord's Resistance Army in Uganda, New York: Human Rights Watch.
Human Rights Watch (1999a).
   Leave none to tell the story: Genocide in Rwanda, New York: Human Rights Watch (report by Alison Des Forges).
Human Rights Watch (1999b).
   The Enron Corporation: Corporate Complicity in Human Rights Violations, New York: Human Rights Watch.

Human Rights Watch (2000).
 Rwanda: The Search for Security and Human Rights Abuses, New York: Human Rights Watch.
Human Rights Watch (2003a).
 Rwanda Lasting Wounds: Consequences of Genocide and War for Rwanda's Children, New York: Human Rights Watch
Human Rights Watch (2003b).
 Ituri: 'Covered in Blood.': Ethnically Targeted Violence in Northeastern Democratic Republic of Congo, New York: Human Rights Watch.
Human Rights Watch. (2003c).
 Sudan, Oil, and Human Rights, New York: Human Rights Watch.
Human Rights Watch (2004a).
 Child Solider Use 2003: Uganda, New York: Human Rights Watch.
Human Rights Watch (2004b).
 How to fight, How to kill: Child soldiers in Liberia, New York: Human Rights Watch.
Human Rights Watch (2006a).
 What Future? Street Children in the Democratic Republic of Congo, New York: Human Rights Watch.
Human Rights Watch (2006b).
 Q and A: Military Commissions Act of 2006, New York: Human Rights Watch.
Human Rights Watch (2007).
 US mark five years of Guantanamo by closing it: Congress should restore detainees' access to courts, New York: Human Rights Watch.
Hume, D. (1948).
 Moral and Political Philosophy, New York: Hafner Press.
Humphrey, M. (2003).
 From Victim to Victimhood: Truth Commissions and Trials as Rituals of Political Transition and Individual Healing, *Journal of Anthropology* 14(2), 171–188.
Huntington, S.P. (1997).
 The Clash of Civilizations and the Remaking of World Order, New York: Touchstone Press.
Huyse, L. (1996).
 Justice after Transition: On The Choices Successor Elites, Make in Dealing with the Past, in: Jongman, A. (ed.), *Contemporary Genocides*, Leiden: PIOOM.
Huyse, L. (1998).
 Young democracies and the choice between amnesty, truth commissions and prosecution, Brussels: Directorate-General Development Aid, 13–21.
Huyse, L. (2003).
 Justice, in: Bloomfield, D., Barnes, T., & Huyse, L. (eds.) *Reconciliation After Violent Conflicts. A Handbook*, Stockholm: International Institute for Democracy and Electoral Assistance.
Huyse, L. (2007).
 Reconciliation and Traditional Justice: Learning from African Experiences (preliminary findings), Strömsborg.

Huyse, L., & Dhondt, S. (1991).
Onverwerkt verleden, Leuven: Kritak.
ICG (International Crisis Group) (1999).
ICG report Rwanda n° 1, 7 April 1999, *'Five years after the genocide in Rwanda: Justice in question'*.
Ignatieff, M. (1978).
A just measure of pain: The penitentiary in the industrial revolution, London: Penguin Books.
Ignatieff, M. (1993).
Blood and Belonging: Journeys into the New Nationalism, New York: The Noonday Press.
Ingelaere, B. (2007).
Does the Truth Pass across the Fire without Burning? Tradition justice and its discontents in Rwanda's Gacaca Courts, Discussion Paper, Antwerp: Institute of Development Policy and Management.
Integrated Regional Information Network for Central and Eastern Africa (1999).
IRIN CEA Update No. 645 (April 8, 1999). Nairobi: United Nations Office for the Coordination of Humanitarian Affairs.
International Council on Human Rights Policy (2002).
Beyond Voluntarism: human rights and the developing international legal obligations of companies, retrieved from www.ichrp.org/paper_files/107_p_01.pdf.
International Monetary Fund (1999).
The IMF's Enhanced Structural Adjustment Facility (ESAF): Is It Working? Retrieved from mf.org/external/pubs/ft/esaf/exr/index.htm.
International Rescue Committee (2004).
Mortality in the Democratic Republic of the Congo: Results from a Nationwide Survey, New York: International Rescue Committee.
Isenberg, D. (2004).
A Fistful of contractors: The case for a pragmatic assessment of private military companies in Iraq, British-American Security Information Council, Basic Report 2004.2, http://www.basicint.org/pubs/Research/2004PMC.htm].
Jackson, K.D. (1989).
Ideology of Total Revolution, in: Jackson, K.D. (ed.), *Cambodia: 1975–1978, Rendezvous with Death*, Princeton: Princeton University Press, 37–78.
Jäger, H. (1989).
Makrokriminalität Studien zur Kriminologie kollektiver Gewalt, Frankfurt am Main: Suhrkamp.
Jamieson, R. (1998).
Towards a Criminology of War in Europe, in: Ruggiero, V., Smith, N. & Taylor, I. (eds.), *The New European Criminology*, London: Routledge, 480–506.
Jamieson, R. & McEvoy, K. (2005).
State Crime by Proxy and Juridical Othering, *The British Journal of Criminology*, 45(4), 504–527.

Jankowski, M S. (1991).

Islands in the Street: Gangs and American Urban Society, Berkeley: University of California Press.

Jaspers, K. & Augstein, R. (1966).

The Criminal State and German Responsibility: A Dialogue, trans. Werner J. Dannhauser, *Commentary* 41(2), 33–39.

Jaukovic, J. (2002).

The Forms of Victimization in the Territory of the Former Yugoslavia, *European Journal of Crime, Criminal Law, and Criminal Justice*, 10(2–3), 109–116.

Jenkins, B. (2000).

Elite units troublesome but useful, *Los Angeles Times*, March 27.

Jinks, D. & Sloss, D. (2004).

Is the president bound by the Geneva Conventions? *Cornell Law Review* 90, 97–202.

Johnson, C. (2004).

The Sorrows of Empire: Militarism, Secrecy and the End of the Republic, London: Verso.

Johnson, R. (1997).

Death work: A study of the modern execution process, Belmont, CA: Wadsworth.

Jonassohn, K. & Björnson, K.S. (1998).

Genocide and Gross Human Rights Violations, New Brunswick/London: Transaction Publishers.

Jones, A. (2006).

Genocide: A Comprehensive Introduction, London: Routledge.

Jorgensen, N. (2000).

The Responsibility of States for International Crimes, Oxford: Oxford University Press.

Judah, T. (1997).

The Serbs: History, Myth & the Destruction of Yugoslavia, New Haven: Yale University Press.

Judt, T. (2007).

Is the UN Doomed? *The New York Review of Books*, 45–48.

Junge, T. & Müller, M. (2002).

Bis zur ltezten Stunde – Hitlers Sekretärin erzählt ihr Leben, München: List Taschenbuch Verlag.

Kacprowski, N. (2004).

'Stacking the deck' against suspected terrorists, *Seattle University Law Review* 26, 651–697.

Kaiser, G. (1988).

Kriminologie. Ein Lehrbuch, Heidelberg: Müller Juristischer Verlag.

Kaitesi, U. (2006).

Evaluation of the functioning of gacaca courts by Rwandans as of January 2006, National University of Rwanda.

Kaldor, M. (2003).

Global Civil Society: An Answer to War, Cambridge: Cambridge University Press.

Karadjis, M. (2006).
>   Atrocities: evidence of the US complicity, Green Left Week Online, 17 November 2006, found at: http://www.domovina.net/archive/2006/20061117_gleft.php

Karekezi, U.A., Nsimiyimana, A., & Mutamba, B. (2004).
>   Localizing justice: gacaca courts in post-genocide Rwanda, in: Stover, E., & Weinstein, H.M. (eds), *My Neighbor, My Enemy; Justice and Community in the Aftermath of Mass Atrocity*, Cambridge: Cambridge University Press, 69–84.

Karpinski J. with S. Strasser (2005).
>   *One woman's army – the commanding general of Abu Ghraib tells her story*, New York: Miramax Books.

Karskens, A. (2007).
>   *Geen cent spijt. De jacht op oorlogsmisdadiger Frans van Anraat*, Amsterdam: Meulenhoff.

Kater, M. (1989).
>   *Doctors under Hitler*, Chapel Hill: University of North Carolina at Chapel Hill Press.

Katyal, N. & Tribe, L.H. (2002).
>   Waging war, deciding guilt: Trying the military tribunals, *Yale Law Journal* 111, 1259–1310.

Katz, F.E. (1993).
>   *Ordinary people and extraordinary evil – a report on the beguildings of evil*, Albany: State University of New York Press.

Katz, J. (1988).
>   *Seductions of Crime: Moral and Sensual Attractions in Doing Evil*, New York: Basic Books.

Katz, M. (2006).
>   A Very Long Engagement: Bush Channels Neville Chamberlain, *The New Republic*, May 15, 2006, 24.

Kauzlarich, D. (1995).
>   A Criminology of the Nuclear State, *Humanity and Society* 19, 37–57.

Kauzlarich, D. (1998).
>   *Crimes of the American Nuclear State: At Home and Abroad*, Boston: Northeastern University Press.

Kauzlarich, D. (2007).
>   Seeing War as Criminal: Peace Activist Views and Critical Criminology, *Contemporary Justice Review* 10(1), 67–85.

Kauzlarich, D. & Friedrichs, D. (2005).
>   Crime, Definitions of, in: Wright, R.A. & Miller, J.M. (eds.), *Encyclopedia of Criminology*, Volume I, New York: Routledge, 273–275.

Kauzlarich, D. & Kramer, R.C. (1993).
>   State-Corporate Crime in the U.S. Nuclear Weapons Production Complex, *The Journal of Human Justice* 5(1), 1–26.

Kauzlarich, D. & Kramer, R.C. (1998).
>   *Crimes of the American Nuclear State*, Boston: Northeastern University Press.

Kauzlarich, D., Kramer, R.C. & Smith, B. (1992).

> Toward the Study of Governmental Crime: Nuclear Weapons, Foreign Intervention, and International Law, *Humanity and Society* 16(4), 543–563.

Kauzlarich D, Matthews, R.A. and Miller, W.J. (2001).

> Toward A Victimology of State Crime, *Critical Criminology: An International Journal* 10(3), 173–194.

Kauzlarich, D., Mullins, C.W. & Matthews, R.A. (2003).

> A Complicity Continuum of State Crime, *Contemporary Justice Review* 6(3), 241–254.

Kaysen, C. & Rathjens, G. (2003).

> The Case for a Volunteer UN Military Force, *Daedalus* (Winter), 91–103.

Kazarian, H.K. (1971).

> Turkey Tries its Chief Criminals: Indictment and Sentence Passed Down By Military Court of 1919, *The Armenian Review* 24, 3–26.

Keely, C.B., Reed, H.E. & Waldman, R.J. (2001).

> *Understanding Mortality Patterns in Complex Humanitarian Emergencies*, in: Reed, H.E. & Keely, C.B. (eds.), *Forced Migration and Mortality*, Washington D.C.: National Academy Press, 1–37.

Keller (2006).

> *Seeking Justice at the International Criminal Court: Victims' Reparations*, Thomas Jefferson School of Law, San Diego, CA.

Kelman, H.C. (2005).

> The policy context of torture: a social-psychological analysis, *International Review of the Red Cross* 87, 123–134.

Kelman, H.C., & Hamilton, V.L. (1989).

> *Crimes of Obedience: Toward a Social Psychology of Authority and Responsibility*, New Haven: Yale University Press.

Kennedy, D. (2004).

> *The Dark Side of Virtue: Reassessing International Humanitarianism*, Princeton: Princeton University Press.

Kennedy, L.W. (1988).

> Going It Alone: Unreported Crime and Individual Self-Help, *Journal of Criminal Justice* 16, 403–412.

Kennedy, P. (2006).

> *The Parliament of Man – The Past, Present, and Future of the United Nations*, New York: Random House.

Kent, L. (2004).

> *Unfulfilled Expectations: Community Views of CAVR's Community Reconciliation Process*. Retrieved June 18, 2007, the Judicial System Monitoring Programme website: http://www.jsmp.minihub.org/new/otherreports.htm

Kercher, B. (1995).

> *An Unruly Child*, St. Leonards: Allen and Unwin.

Kershaw, I. (1991).

> *Hitler*, London: Longman.

Kessler, G. (2005).
  State Department Defends Estimate of Deaths in Darfur Conflict, *Washington Post* April 27, 2005, A17.
Khagram, S. (2006).
  Possible Future Architectures of Global Governance: A Transnational Perspective/ Prospective, *Global Governance* 12, 97–117.
Kidd, R. (1997).
  The Way We Civilise, Brisbane: University of Queensland Press.
Kidd, R. (2000).
  Black Lives, Government Lies, Sydney: University of New South Wales Press Ltd.
Kiernan, B. (1996).
  The Pol Pot Regime: Race, Power, and Genocide in Cambodia under the Khmer Rouge, 1975–1979, New Haven: Yale University Press.
Kimball, C. (2002).
  When Religion Becomes Evil, San Francisco: Harper San Francisco.
Kirkby, C. (2006).
  Rwanda's Gacaca Courts: a Preliminary Critique, *Journal of African Law* 50(2), 94–117.
Kittichaisaree, K. (2001).
  International Criminal Law, Oxford: Oxford University Press.
Kiza, E. (2006).
  Victimization in Wars: A Framework for Further Inquiry, in: Ewald, U. & Turkovic, K. (eds.), *Large-Scale Victimization as a Potential Source of Terrorist Activities: Importance of Regaining Security in Post-Conflict Societies*, Amsterdam: IOS Press.
Kiza, E., Rathbgeber, C. & Rohn, H.C. (2006).
  Victims of War: An Empirical Study on War-Victimization and Victims' Attitudes towards Addressing Atrocities, Hamburg: Hamburger Institut fur Sozialforschung.
Klee, E., Dressen, W. & Riess, V. (eds.) (1988).
  The Good Old Days: The Holocaust as Seen By Its Perpetrators and Bystanders, New York: The Free Press.
Klemperer, V. (1995).
  Ich will Zeugnis ablegen bis zum letzten, Berlin: Aufbau Verlag.
Klemperer, V. (2000).
  LTI; de taal van het Derde Rijk, Amsterdam/Antwerpen: Uitgeverij Atlas, (*LTI, Notizbuch eines Philologen*, 1975).
Klip, A.H. & Smeulers, A.L. (2004).
  Afrekenen met het verleden: de afdoening van internationale misdrijven, in: Klip, A.H., Smeulers, A.L. & Wolleswinkel, M.W. (red.), *Krities – Liber amicorum et amicarum voor prof. mr. E. Prakken*, Deventer: Kluwer, 313- 330.
Kluge, J., Stein, W., Licht, T., Bendler, A., Elzenheimer, J., Hauschild, S., et al. (2001).
  Knowledge Unplugged: The Mckinsey & Company Global Survey on Knowledge Management, New York: Palgrave.
Knoke, D. & Burke, P.J. (1980).
  Log-linear models, London: Sage.

Knoops, G.-J. A. (2006).
> Redressing miscarriages of justice: practice and procedure in (international) criminal cases, in: Bassiouni, M.C. (ed.), *International and comparative criminal law series*, Ardsley, NY: Transnational Publishers.

Knopp, G. (1996).
> *Hitlers Helfer*, München: Bertelsmann.

Köchler, H. (2003).
> *Global Justice or Global Revenge? International Criminal Justice at the Crossroads*, Springer: Wien.

Kok, A. (1995).
> *De Verrader – Leven en dood van Anton van der Waals*, Epe: De Arbeidspers.

Korten, D.C. (2006).
> *The Great Turning: From Empire to Earth Community*, San Francisco/Bloomfield: Berrett-Koehler Publishers/Kumarian Press.

Kramer, R.C. (1990).
> *State-Corporate Crime*, Paper presented at the North Central sociological Association and the Southern Sociological Association, Louisville, KY.

Kramer, R.J. (1992).
> The Space Shuttle Challenger Explosion: A Case Study of State-Corporate Crime, in: Schlegel, K. & Weisburd, D. (ed.), *White-Collar Crime Reconsidered*, Boston: Northeastern University Press, 214–243.

Kramer, R.C. (1995).
> Exploring State Criminality: The Invasion of Panama, *Journal of Criminal Justice and Popular Culture* 3(2), 43–52.

Kramer, R.C., & Kauzlarich, D. (1999).
> The International Court of Justice Opinion on the Illegality of the Threat and Use of Nuclear Weapons: Implications for Criminology, *Contemporary Justice Review*, 4(2), 395–413.

Kramer, R.C. & Michalowski, R.J. (1990).
> *Toward an Integrated Theory of State-corporate Crime*, Presented at the American Society of Criminology, Baltimore, MD.

Kramer, R.C. & Michalowski, R.J. (Eds.) (2006).
> *State-corporate crime: wrongdoing at the intersection of business and government*, Pisacway: Rutgers University Press.

Kramer, R.C. & Michalowski, R.J. (2005).
> War, Aggression, and State Crime: A Criminological Analysis of the Invasion and Occupation of Iraq, *British Journal of Criminology* 45, 446–469.

Kramer, R.C., Michalowski, R.J. & Kauzlarich, D. (2002).
> The Origins and Development of the Concept and Theory of State-corporate Crime, *Crime and Delinquency* 48(2), 263–282.

Kramer, R.C., Michalowski, R.J. & Rothe, D. (2005).
> The Supreme International Crime: How the U.S. War in Iraq Threatens the Rule of Law, *Social Justice* 32(2), 52–81.

Kreft, I.G.C. & De Leeuw, J. (1998).
> *Introducing Multilevel Modeling*, London: Sage.

Kren, G.M. & Rappaport, L. (1980).
The Holocaust and the crises of human behavior, New York: Holmes and Meier.
Kressel, N.J. (2002).
Mass Hate: The Global Rise of Genocide and Terror, New York: Plenum Press.
Kriger, N. (2000).
Traditional Justice as Socioeconomic Rights, *Peace Review* 12(1), 59–65.
Kristof, N. (2005).
Day 141 of Bush's Silence, *New York Times,* May 31, 2005, A19.
Kritz, N. (ed) (1995).
Transitional justice. How emerging democracies reckon with former regimes, 3 Vols. Washington D.C: United States Institute of Peace Press.
Kritz, N. (1996).
Coming to Terms with Mass Atrocities: A Review of Accountability Mechanisms for Mass Violations of Human Rights, *Law and Contemporary Problems* 59, 127–152.
Krog, A. (1999).
Country of my Skull, London: Vintage.
Krugman, P (2007).
Snow Job in the Desert, *New York Times,* September 3, 2007, A17.
Kuper, A. (2004).
Democracy beyond Borders: Justice and Representation in Global Institutions, New York: Oxford University Press.
Kuper, L. (1981)
Genocide, New Haven: Yale University Press.
Labaton, S. (2007).
Court endorses law's curbs on detainees, *New York Times,* February 21, 2007, E1–2.
Lacey, M. (2005).
Nobody Danced. No Drus. Just Fear. Some Holiday! *New York Times,* April 22, 2005, A4.
Lacina, B., & Gleditsch, N.P. (2005).
Monitoring Trends in Global Combat: A New Dataset of Battle Deaths, *European Journal of Population* 21, 145–166.
Lambert, E., Hall, D., Clarke, A., Ventura, L.A. & Oko, O. (2005).
The War on Terrorism: The Views of Criminal Justice and Non-Criminal Justice Majors on Terrorism and the Punishment of Terrorists, *Electronic Journal of Sociology,* http://www.sociology.org/archive.html.
Lambourne, W. (2004).
Post-Conflict Peacebuilding: Meeting Human Needs for Justice and Reconciliation, *Peace, Conflict and Development* 4, 1–22.
Langman, L. (2005).
From Virtual Public Spheres to Global Justice: A Critical Theory of Inter-networked, Social Movements, *Sociological Theory* 23, 42–74.
Lanotte, O. (2007).
La France au Rwanda (1990-1994): Entre abstention impossible et engagement ambivalent, Brussel: P.I.E. Peter Lang.

Laplante, L. & Theidon, K. (2007).
> Truth with Consequences: Justice and Reparations in Post-Truth Commission Peru, *Human Rights Quarterly* 29, 228–250.

Latané, B. & Darley, J.M. (1970).
> *The Unresponsive Bystander: Why doesn't he help?*, New York: Meredith Corp.

Laufer, W.S. (1999).
> The forgotten criminology of genocide, in: Laufer, W.S. & Adler, F. (eds.), *The Criminology of criminal law*, London: Transaction Publishers.

Lautsch, E. (1995).
> *Methoden und Anwendungen der Konfigurationsfrequenzanalyse (KFA)*, Weinheim: Beltz, Psychologie-Verl.-Union.

Lea, J. (1992).
> The Analysis of Crime, in: Young, J., & Matthews, R. (eds.), *Rethinking Criminology, the Realist Debate*, London: Sage.

Lea, J. (1999).
> Social crime revisited, *Theoretical Criminology* 3, 307–326.

Lederach, J.P. (1999).
> The Challenge of the 21st Century: Just peace, in *People Building Peace: 35 Inspiring Stories from Around the World*, Utrecht: European Centre for Conflict Resolution.

Leitenberg, M. (2006).
> *Death and Wars in Conflicts in the 20th Century*, Peace Studies Program Occasional Paper #29, Ithaca: Cornell University.

Lemarchand, R. (1995).
> Rwanda: The Rationality of Genocide, *Issue: A Journal of Opinion* 23(2), 8–11.

Leopold, E. (2005).
> UN Envoy Says Deaths in Darfur Underestimated, *Reuters*, March 10, 2005.

Lemkin, R. (1944).
> *Axis Rule in Occupied Europe. Laws of Occupation. Analysis of Government. Proposals for Redress*, Washington: Carnegie Endowment for International Peace.

Lerner, M.J. (1977–1978).
> The Effectiveness of a Definite Sentence Parole Program, *Criminology* 15, 211–224.

Lerner, M.J. (1980).
> *The belief in a just world: a fundamental delusion,* New York: Plenum Press.

Letner, B. (2004).
> Transnational Corporations and Human Rights: Silencing the Ontological Controversy, *Public Organization Review: A Global Journal* 4, 259–277.

Leurdijk, D. (1996).
> *The United Nations and NATO in Former Yugoslavia, 1991–1996; Limits to Diplomacy and Force*, The Hague: Netherlands Atlantic Commission.

Leurdijk, B.A. (1997).
> *Humanitarian Action and Peace-keeping Operations: Debriefing and Lessons*, Report of the 1997 Singapore Conference, February 1997, Kluwer Law International.

Levi, B. & Sidel, V. (1967).
> *War and Public Health*, New York and Oxford: Oxford University Press.

Lewis, N.A. (2004).

Fate of Guantanamo Bay detainees is debated in federal court, *New York Times*, December 2, A36.

Lewy, G. (1964).

Pius XII, the Jews, and the German Catholic Church, *Commentary* 37(2), 23–35.

Lichtenberg, I., Lune, H. & McManimon, P. Jr. (2004).

Darker than any prison, hotter than any human flame: Punishment, choice, and culpability in A Clockwork Orange, *Journal of Criminal Justice Education* 15(2), 429–450.

Lifton, R. (1986).

The Nazi doctors: Medical killing and the psychology of genocide, New York: Basic Books.

Lifton, R.J. & E. Markusen (1990).

The genocidal mentality – Nazi Holocaust and Nuclear Threat, New York: Basic Books.

Lilly, J. (2007).

Taken by force – rape and American GIs in Europe during World War II, Palgrave Macmillan (org. French).

Lobwein, W. (2006).

Experiences of the Victims and Witnesses Section at the I.C.T.Y., in: Ewald, U. & Turkovic, K. (eds.), *Large-Scale Victimization as a Potential Source of Terrorist Activities: Importance of Regaining Security in Post-Conflict Societies*, Amsterdam: IOS Press.

Long, W.J., & Brecke, P. (2003).

War and Reconciliation: Reason and Emotion in Conflict Resolution, Cambridge: MIT Press.

Longman, T. (2004).

Placing genocide in context: research priorities for the Rwandan genocide, *Journal of Genocide Research* 6(1), 29.

Lopez, G.A. (1984).

A Scheme for the Analysis of Government as Terrorist, in: Stohl, M. & Lopez, G.A. (eds.), *The State as Terrorist. The Dynamics of Governmental Violence and Repression*, Westport, Connecticut: Greenwood Press.

Los, C.J. (1976).

Dr. Eduard Wirths-SS arts in Auschwitz, Baarn: Uitgeverij in den Toren.

Los, M. & Zybertowicz, A. (2000).

Privatizing the Police State: The Case of Poland, Basingstoke: Macmillan.

Love, N.S. (ed.) (1991).

Dogmas and Dreams: Political Ideologies in the Modern World, Chatham, N.J.: Chatham House Publishers.

Lozowick, Y. (2000)

Hitlers Bürokraten – Eichmann, seine willigen Vollstrecker und die Banalität des Bösen, Zürich: Pendo.

Lynch. M.J. & Michalowski, R.J. (2006).
The New Primer in Radical Criminology: Critical Perspectives on Crime, Power, and Identity (4th ed.), Monsey: Criminal Justice Press.

Lyon, D. (2006).
Theorizing surveillance: The panopticon and beyond, Collompton: Willan Publishing.

Macdonald, D. (1957).
The Responsibility of Peoples and Other Essays in Political Criticism, London: Victor Gollancz Ltd.

Mackenzie, S. (2004).
Systematic Crimes of the Powerful: Criminal Aspects of the Global Economy, Social Justice 33, 162–182.

MacManners, H. (1993).
The scars of war, London: HarperCollins Publishers.

Maier-Katkin, D. (n.d.).
Course syllabus: Human Rights and Crimes against Humanity, Florida State University (www.criminology.fsu.edu/syllabus/dmkatkin/ccj4938.pdf).

Malkin, P.Z. & Stein, H. (1990).
Eichmann in my hands – a first person account by the Israeli agent who captured Hitler's chief executioner, New York: Warner Books.

Malmvig, H. (2007).
Humanitarian Intervention and State Sovereignty: A Social Constructionist Analysis, in: Lagoutte, S., Sano, H-O. & Smith, P.S., Human Rights in Turmoil: Facing Threats, Consolidating Achievements, Leiden: Martinus Nijhoff Publishers, 163–180.

Mamdani, M. (1996).
Reconciliation without Justice, Southern African Review of Books 46, 3–5.

Mamdani, M. (1997).
Reconciliation without justice, Southern African Review of Books 10(6), 22–25.

Mamdani, M. (2000a).
A Diminished Truth, in: James, W., & Vijver, L. van de (eds.), After the TRC. Reflections on truth and reconciliation in South Africa, Claremont: David Philip Publishers.

Mamdani, M. (2000b).
The Truth According to the TRC, in: Amadiume, I. & An-Naim, A. (eds.), The Politics of Memory: Truth, Healing and Social Justice, London: Zed Books.

Mamdani, M. (2001).
When Victims become Killers. Colonialism, Nativism and the Genocide in Rwanda, Princeton: University Press.

Mani, R. (2002).
Beyond Retribution. Seeking Justice in the Shadows of War, Cambridge: Polity Press.

Mann, M. (2000).
Were the perpetrators of genocide 'ordinary men' or 'real nazis'? Results from fifteen hundred biographies, Holocaust and Genocide Studies 14(3), 331–360.

Mann, M. (2004).

 Incoherent Empire, London: Verso.

Mann, M. (2005).

 The Dark Side of Democracy: Explaining Ethnic Cleansing, New York: Cambridge University Press.

Manuel, F.E., & Manuel, F.P. (1979).

 Utopian Thought in the Western World, New York: Belknap Press.

Margulies, P. (2004).

 Judging terror in the 'zone of twilight', *Boston University Law Review* 84, 383–443.

Mark, M. (1973).

 Modern Ideologies, New York: St. Martin's Press.

Marshall, T.F. (1999).

 Restorative Justice. An overview, London: Home Office: Research Development and Statistics Directorate.

Martin, J. (2006).

 The Meaning of the 21ˢᵗ Century, New York: Riverhead Books.

Mathiesen, T. (1997).

 The viewer society: Michel Foucault's 'panopticon' revisited, *Theoretical Criminology* 1(2), 215–234.

Matthews, R.A. (2006).

 Ordinary Business in Nazi Germany, in: Michalowski, R.J. & Kramer, R.C. (eds.), *State-Corporate Crime; Wrongdoing at the Intersection of Business & Government*, New Brunswick, New Jersey and London: University Press.

Matthews, R.A. & Kauzlarich, D. (2000).

 The Crash of ValuJet flight 592: A Case Study in State-Corporate Crime, *Sociological Focus* 3, 281–298.

Mason, T. (1981).

 Intention and Explanation: A Current Controversy about the Interpretation of National Socialism, in: Hirschfeld, G. and Kettenacker, L. (eds.), *"The Führer State", Myth and Reality: Studies on the Structure and Politics of the Third Reich*, Stuttgart: Klett-Cotta.

May, R. & Wierda, M. (2002).

 International criminal evidence, Ardsley: Transnational Publ.

McCoy, A. (2006).

 A Question of Torture: CIA Interrogation, from the Cold War to the War on Terror, New York: Metropolitan Books.

McDonald, K. (2006).

 Global Movements: Action and Culture, Malden, MA: Blackwell Publishing.

McGoldrick, D. (2003).

 War crimes trials before international tribunals: legality and legitimacy, in: Melikan, R.A. (ed.), *Domestic and International Trials, 1700-2000*, Manchester: Manchester University Press.

McGrath, A. (1993).

 Colonialism, Crime and Civilisation, *Australian Cultural History* 12, 100–114.

McKelvey, T. (2007a).
   Monstering: Inside America's Policy of Secret Interrogations and Torture in the Terror War, New York: Carroll & Graf Publishers.
McKelvey, T. (2007b).
   One of the Guys: Women as Aggressors and Torturers, New York: Transition
McNeil, D. (2006).
   The Worrier: At the UN: This Virus Has an Expert 'Quite Scared, *New York Times,* March 28, 2006, D4.
Meershoek, G. (1999).
   Dienaren van het gezag – de Amsterdamse politie tijdens de bezetting, Amsterdam: Van Gennep.
Melossi, D. & Pavarini, M. (1981).
   The prison and the factory: Origins of the penitentiary system, London: Macmillan.
Melson, R.F. (1992).
   Revolution and Genocide: on the Origins of the Armenian Genocide and the Holocaust, Chicago: University of Chicago Press.
Melvern, L. (2000).
   A People Betrayed. The Role of the West in Rwanda's Genocide, London: Zed Books.
Melvern, L. (2004).
   Conspiracy to Murder: The Rwandan Genocide, London: Verso.
Mendes, E., & Mehmet, O. (2003).
   Global Governance, Economy and Law: Waiting for Justice, London: Routledge.
Meredith, M. (2002)
   Our votes, our guns – Robert Mugabe and the tragedy of Zimbabwe, New York: Public Affairs.
Meyer, W.H. (1998).
   Human Rights and International Political Economy in Third world Nations: Multinational Corporations, Foreign Aid and Repression, Westport: Praeger Publishers.
Michalowski, R.J. (1985).
   Order, Law, and Crime, New York: Random House.
Michalowski, R.J. & Kramer, R.C. (eds.) (2006).
   State-Corporate Crime: Wrongdoing at the Intersection of Business and Government, New Brunswick, NJ: Rutgers University Press.
Miles, S. (2004).
   Abu Ghraib: Its legacy for military medicine, *The Lancet,* 364.
Milgram, S. (1974).
   Obedience to Authority, New York: Harper and Row.
Miller, G. & Meyer, J. (2007).
   U.S. Relies on Sudan Despite Condemning It, *Los Angeles Times,* June 11, 2007.
Milloy, J. (1999).
   A National Crime. The Canadian Government and the Residential School System 1879 to 1986, Winnipeg: The University of Manitoba Press.

Milovanovic, D. & Henry, S. (2001).
    Constitutive Definition of Crime: Power as Harm, in: Henry, S. & Lanier, M. (eds.),
    What is Crime? Controversies about the Nature of Crime and What to do about it,
    Lanham, Maryland: Rowman and Littlefield.
Minear, R.H. (1971).
    Victors' Justice: The Tokyo War Crimes Trial, Princeton, New Jersey: Princeton
    University Press.
Minow, M. (1998).
    *Between Vengeance and Forgiveness: Facing History after Genocide and Mass
    Violence*, Boston: Beacon Press.
Mitchell K.J. & Finkelhor, D. (2001).
    Risk of Crime Victimization among Youth Exposed to Domestic Violence, *Journal
    of Interpersonal Violence* 16(9), 944–964.
Mohammad, F. (2000).
    Torture, Murders, Confessions & Hegemony—A Case Study of Pakistan, *Injustice
    Studies*, published on-line by Illinois State University, 2.
Mohawk, J.C. (2000).
    Utopian Legacies: A History of Conquest and Oppression in the Western World, Santa
    Fe: Clear Light Press.
Mokhiber, R. (1989).
    Corporate crime and violence; Big business power and the abuse of public trust, San
    Francisco: Sierra Club Books.
Molenaar, A. (2005).
    Gacaca: Grassroots justice after genocide, African Studies Centre, Research Report
    77/2005, Leiden.
Molier, G. (2006).
    Humanitarian Intervention and the Responsibility to Protect after 9/11, *Netherlands
    International Law Review LIII*, 37–62.
Morales, F. (1999).
    The militarization of the police, *Covert Action Quarterly* 67 (Spring-Summer).
Morrice, D. (1996).
    Philosophy, Science and Ideology in Political Thought, New York: St. Martin's Press.
Morris, B. (1992).
    Frontier Colonialism as a Culture of Terror, in: Attwood, B. & Arnold, A. (eds.),
    Power, Knowledge and Aborigines, Bundorra: La Trobe University Press.
Morris, M. (1996).
    By force of arms: rape, war and military culture, *Duke Law Journal* 45, 651- 781.
Morrison, W. (2004).
    Criminology, Genocide, and Modernity: Remarks on the Companion that
    Criminology Ignored, in: Sumner, C. (ed.), *The Blackwell Companion to Criminology*,
    Malden, MA: Blackwell Publishers, 68–88.
Moses, D. (2000).
    An Antipodean Genocide? The Origins of the Genocidal Moment in the Colonisation
    of Australia, *Journal of Genocide Research* 2(1), 89–106.

Muchlinski, P.T. (2001).

Human rights and Multinationals: Is There a Problem?, *International Affairs* 77(1), 31–47.

Mueller, G.O.W. (2001).

Transnational Crime: Definitions and Concepts, in: Williams, Ph. & Vlassis, D. (eds.), *Combating Transnational Crime. Concepts, Activities and Responses*, London: Frank Cass, 13–21.

Mulisch, H. (1962).

De zaak 40/61 – een reportage, Amsterdam: De Bezige Bij.

Müller-Hill, B. (1988).

Murderous Science: Elimination by Scientific Selection of Jews, Gypsies, and Others, Germany 1933–1945, Oxford: Oxford University Press.

Mullins, C.W. (2006).

Bridgestone-Firestone, Ford and the NHTSA, in: Michalowski, R.J. & Kramer, R.C. (eds.), *State-Corporate Crime; Wrongdoing at the Intersection of Business & Government*, New Brunswick, New Jersey and London: University Press.

Mullins, C.W. & Kauzlarich, D. (2000).

The Ghost Dance: A Criminological Examination, *Social Pathology* 6(4), 264–283.

Mullins C.W. & Rothe, D.L. (2006).

On the Legitimacy of International Law: Reflections on Toronto, *The Critical Criminologist* 15, 135–158.

Mullins C.W. & Rothe, D.L. (2007).

The Forgotten Ones, *Critical Criminology: An International Journal* 15, 2.

Murphy, C.F. Jr. (1999).

Theories of World Governance: A Study in the History of Ideas, Washington, D.C.: The Catholic University Press of America.

Murphy, R. (2006).

Gravity issues and the International Criminal Court, *Criminal Law Forum* 17, 281–315.

Mutanguha, F. (2006).

Statement, http://www.hmd.org.uk/files/1152280458-77.pdf.

Mythen, G. & Walklate, S. (2006).

Criminology and terrorism: Which thesis? Risk Society or Governmentality, *British Journal of Criminology* 46, 379–389.

Nabarro, D. (2004).

Media Briefing Notes, UN Palais press corps, Geneva, 'Mortality Projections for Darfur, 15 October 2004.' Presented by David Nabarro, Representative of the World Health Organization Director-General.

Nadelson, Th. (2005).

Trained to kill – soldiers at war, Baltimore and London: The Johns Hopkins University Press.

Nagataki, S., Shibata, Y., Inoue, S., Yokoyama, N., Izumi, M. & Shimaoka, K. (1994).

Thyroid Diseases among Atomic Bomb Survivors in Nagasaki, *Journal of the American Medical Association* 272, 5.

Natsios, A.S. (1997).

U.S. Foreign Policy and the Four Horsemen of the Apocalypse: Humanitarian Relief in Complex Humanitarian Emergencies, Westport, Connecticut: Praeger Centre for Strategies of International Studies.

National Criminal Justice Reference Service (NCJ) (1999a).

Cruelty in control? The stun belt and other electro-shock equipment in law enforcement.

National Criminal Justice Reference Service (NCJ) (1999b).

Survivors of Politically Motivated Torture: A Large, Growing, and Invisible Population of Crime Victims.

National Criminal Justice Reference Service (NCJ) (2005).

"Making their own rules:" Police beatings, rape, and torture of children in Papua New Guinea.

National Inquiry into the Separation of Aboriginal and Torres Strait Islander Children from Their Families (NISATSIC) (1997).

Bringing Them Home, Report of the National Inquiry into the Separation of Aboriginal and Torres Strait Islander Children from Their Families, Sydney: Human Rights and Equal Opportunity Commission.

Ndiaye, B.W. (1993).

Extrajudicial, summary or arbitrary executions, report by the Special Rapporteur, Bacré Waly Ndiaye, submitted pursuant to Commission on Human Rights resolution 1993/71, E/CN4/1994/7.

Nelken, D. (2002).

White-Collar Crime, in: Maguire, M., Morgan, R. & Reiner, R. (eds.), *The Oxford Handbook of Criminology*, Oxford: Clarendon Press.

Neubacher, F. (2006).

How can it happen that horrendous state crimes are perpetrated? An overview of criminological theories, *Journal of International Criminal Justice* 4(4), 787–799.

Newman, D.M. (1997).

Sociology: Exploring the Architecture of Everyday Life, Thousand Oaks, Ca.: Pine Forge Press.

Newman, G. & Marongiu, P. (1990).

Penological Reform and the Myth of Beccaria, *Criminology* 28(2), 325.

Nietzsche, F. [1888](2005).

Fragmente XII, Umwertungsheft Frühjahr – Sommer 1888, Gondrom Verlag, Bindlach.

Nobles, R. (2000).

Understanding miscarriages of justice: law, the media, and the inevitability of crisis, New York: Oxford University Press.

Noji, E. (1997).

The Public Health Consequences of Disasters, New York: Oxford University Press.

Noji, E. & Toole, M. (1997).

The Historical Development of Public Health Responses of Disasters, *Disasters* 21, 366–376.

Nordland, R. (1994).

The Mouse ate the Cat, *Newsweek*, http://hem.passagen.se/bankel/nordbat.htm, last visited: March 2007.

Ntaganda F. (2003).

La Justice Participative Gacaca et la Justice Internationale: Opposition ou complémentarité?, thèse de maitrise, l'Institut des Droits de l'Homme, Université Catholique de Lyon.

(NYT) New York Times (2004a).

Photos of dead show the horrors of abuse, *May 7, A-11.*

(NYT) New York Times (2004b).

'My deepest apology' from Rumsfeld; 'nothing less than tragic,' says top General, May 8, A-6.

(NYT) New York Times (2005).

CIA empowered to send suspects abroad to jails, March, 5, A-1, A-11.

O'Connell, M.E. (2005).

Enhancing the status of non-state actors through a global war on terror, *Columbia Journal of Transnational Law* 43, 435–458.

O'Keefe, R. (2004).

Universal Jurisdiction: Clarifying the Basic Concept, *International Journal of Criminal Justice* 2, 735–760.

O'Shea, A. (2002).

Amnesty for Crime in International Law and Practice, New York: Kluwer Law International.

Omaar, R. & Waal, A. de (1995).

Rwanda, Death, Despair and Defiance, London: African Rights.

Olusanya, O. (2006).

Granting immunity to child combatants supranationally, in: Haveman, R.H. & Olusanya, O. (eds.), *Sentencing and Sanctioning in Supranational Criminal Law,* Antwerp, Oxford: Intersentia, 87–108.

Oomen, B. (2005).

Donor-Driven Justice and its Discontents: The Case of Rwanda, *Development and Change* 36(5), 887–910.

Oomen, B. (2006).

Rwanda's Gacaca: Objectives, Merits and their Relation to Supranational Criminal Law, in: Haveman, R.H. & Olusanya, O. (eds.), *Sentencing and Sanctioning in Supranational Criminal Law,* Antwerp/Oxford, Intersentia, 161–184.

Orentlicher, D. (1991).

Settling Accounts: The Duty to Prosecute Human Rights Violations of a Prior Regime, *Yale Law Journal* 100, 2537–2615.

Orentlicher, D. (2005).

Report of the Independent Expert to Update the Set of Principles to Combat Impunity (UN Doc. E/CN.4/2005/102 Feb. 18, 2005).

Organization of African Unity (OAU), (2000).
The Preventable Genocide of the International Panel of Eminent Personalities to Investigate the 1994 Genocide in Rwanda and Surrounding Events, at: http://www.visiontv.ca/RememberRwanda/Report.pdf.

Osiel, M. (2001).
Mass Atrocity, Ordinary Evil, and Hannah Arendt: Criminal Consciousness in Argentina's Dirty War, New Haven: Yale University Press.

Otterman, M. (2007).
American torture: from the Cold War to Abu Ghraib and beyond, Melbourne Australia: Melbourne University Publishing.

Overy, R. (2001).
Interrogations: The Nazi Elite in Allied Hands, 1945, New York: Viking Books.

Overy, R. (2004).
The dictators – Hitler's Germany, Stalin's Russia, London: Penguin Books.

Padfield, P. (2001).
Himmler – Reichs Führer-SS, London: Cassel and Co.

Parlevliet, M. (1998).
Considering truth. Dealing with a legacy of gross human rights violations, *Netherlands Quarterly of Human Rights* 16, 141–174.

Parliamentary Report (1994).
Netherlands Parliamentary Reports on Rwanda, 1993–1994, 23727, nrs. 1–7 and 13.

Parliamentary Report (2003).
Parlementaire Enquête Srebrenica, (Netherlands Parliamentary Inquiry Report on Srebrenica) Tweede Kamer, vergaderjaar 2002–2003, 28 506, nrs.2–3.

Parmentier, S. (2001).
The South African Truth and Reconciliation Commission. Towards Restorative Justice in the Field of Human Rights, in: Fattah, E., & Parmentier, S. (eds.), *Victim Policies and Criminal Justice on the Road to Restorative Justice. Essays in Honour of Tony Peters*, Leuven: Leuven University Press.

Parmentier, S. (2003).
Global Justice in the Aftermath of Mass Violence. The Role of the International Criminal Court in Dealing with Political Crimes, *International Annals of Criminology* 41(1–2), 203–224.

Parmentier, S. (2007).
Compensation for victims of genocide, in: De Lange, R. (ed.), *Aspects of Transitional Justice and Human Rights*, Proceedings of the 2006 Annual Conference of the Netherlands School of Human Rights Research, Nijmegen: Wolf Publishers.

Parmentier, S., & Weitekamp, E. (2007).
Political Crimes and Serious Violations of Human Rights. Towards a Criminology of International Crimes, in: Parmentier, S., & Weitekamp, E. (eds.), *Crime and Human Rights*, Amsterdam/Oxford: Elsevier/JAI Press.

Passas, N. (1990).
Anomie and corporate deviance, *Contemporary Crises* 14, 157–178.

Passas, N. (1999).

Globalization, Criminogenic Asymmetries and Economic Crime, *European Journal of Law Reform* 1, 399–423.

Passas, N. (ed.) (2003).

International Crimes, Aldergate, UK: Ashgate.

Passavant, P.A., Dean, J. (Eds.) (2004).

Empire's New Clothes: Reading Hardt and Negri, New York/London: Routledge.

Paust, J. (2005).

Executive plans and authorizations to violate international law concerning the treatment and interrogation of detainees, *Columbia Journal of Transnational Law* 43, 811–863.

Payne, L. (2003).

Perpetrators' Confessions – truth, reconciliation, and justice in Argentina, in: Eckstein, S.E. & Wickham-Crowley, T.P. (Eds.), (2003), *What Justice? Whose Justice? Fighting for fairness in Latin America*, Berkeley: University of California Press, 158–183.

Pearce, F. (2003).

Foreword: Holy Wars and Spiritual Revitalization, in: Tombs, S. & Whyte, D. (eds.), *Unmasking the Crimes of the Powerful: Scrutinizing States and Corporations*, New York: Peter Lang Publishing, 9–14.

Peladeau, N. (2005).

WordStat. Content Analysis Module for SIMSTAT & QDA Miner. User's Guide, Montreal: Provalis Research.

Pemberton, S. (2004).

A Theory of Moral Indifference: Understanding the Production of Harm by Capitalist Society, in: Hillyard, P., Pantazis, C., Gordon, D. & Tombs, S. (eds.), *Beyond Criminology: Taking Harm Seriously*, London: Pluto Press.

Penal Reform International (2002).

Interim report on research on Gacaca jurisdictions and its preparations (July-December 2001). London: Penal Reform International.

Perdue, W.D. (1989).

Terrorism and the State: A Critique of Domination through Fear, Westport: Praeger Publishers.

Persaud, R.B. (2002).

Situating Race in international Relations. The dialectics of civilizational security in American immigration, in: Chowdhry, G. & Nair, S. (eds.), *Postcolonialism, and International Relations: Reading Race, Gender, and Class*, London: Routledge.

Pham, P., Vinck, P., Wierda, M., Stover, E. & di Giovanni, A.(2005).

Forgotten Voices: A Population-Based Survey of Attitudes about Peace and Justice in Northern Uganda, Berkeley: University of California press.

Phytian, M. (2000).

The Politics of British Arms Sales Since 1964: 'To secure our rightful share', Manchester: Manchester University Press.

Pious, R.M. (2006).

The war on terrorism and the rule of law, Los Angeles: Roxbury.

Pleming, S. (2005).
  Aid Group Criticizes U.S. Policy on Sudan, *Reuters*, April 26, 2005.
Pocock, J.G.A. (2006).
  Western historiography and the problem of "Western" history, Workshop on "What is 'Civilization'?" 21 April 2006. UN Initiative for an "Alliance of Civilizations", New York.
Poe, S.C., Carey, S.C. & Vazquez, T.C. (2001).
  How are these pictures different? A quantitative comparison of the US state Department and Amnesty International Human Rights Reports 1976–1995, *Human Rights Quarterly* 23, 650–677.
Pogge, T. (2005).
  World Poverty and Human Rights, *Ethics and International Affairs* 19, 1–7.
Porter, B. (1994).
  War and the Rise of the State: The Military Foundations of Modern Politics, New York: Free Press.
Posner, R. (1976).
  Antitrust Law, Chicago: University of Chicago Press.
Post, J.M. (2004).
  Leaders and their followers in a dangerous world – the psychology of political behavior, Ithaca: Cornell University Press.
Pottier, J. (2002).
  Re-Imagining Rwanda; Conflict, Survival and Disinformation in the Late Twentieth Century, Cambridge: Cambridge University Press.
Power, S. (2001).
  Bystanders to Genocide – Why the United States let the Rwandan tragedy happen, *The Atlantic Monthly*, September.
Power, S. (2002).
  A problem from hell: America and the age of genocide, New York: basic books.
Powles, S. (2004).
  Joint Criminal Enterprise: Criminal Liability by Prosecutorial Ingenuity and Judicial Creativity?, *Journal of International Criminal Justice* 2(2), 606–619.
Prager, D., & Telushkin, J. (1983).
  Why the Jews: The Reason for Antisemitism, New York: Touchstone Books.
Pratt, J., & Gilligan, G. (2004).
  Introduction: crime, truth and justice – official inquiry and the production of knowledge, in: Gilligan, G. & Pratt, J. (Eds.), *Crime, Truth and Justice. Official inquiry, discourse, knowledge*, Oxford: Oxford University Press, 1–7.
Presser, J. (1965).
  Ondergang. De vervolging en verdelging van het Nederlandse Jodendom 1940–1945, Den Haag: Staatsuitgeverij/Martinus Nijhoff.
Presser, L. (2004).
  Violent Offenders, Moral Selves: Constructing Identities and Accounts in the Research Interview, *Social Problems* 51(1), 82–101.
Princeton University, Program in Law and Public Affairs (2001).
  The Princeton Principles on Universal Jurisdiction, New York: Princeton University.

Provisional Verbatim Record (1993).
  Statement by the Representative of the United States, 3217th Meeting of the Security Council, 25 May 1993.
Prunier, G. (1995).
  The Rwanda Crisis: History of a Genocide, New York: Columbia University Press.
Prunier, P. (2005).
  Darfur: The Ambiguous Genocide, Ithaca: Cornell University Press.
Pugh, D. (2006).
  Documentary Review, Torture: America's Brutal Prisons, *Journal of Criminal Justice and Popular Culture* 13, 1.
Punch, M.E. (1996).
  Dirty Business. Exploring corporate misconduct: analysis and case, London: Sage.
Punch, M.E. (2000).
  Suite Violence: Why managers murder and corporations kill, *Crime, law and social change* 33, 243–280.
Quinny, R. (1973).
  Critique of Legal Order, Boston: Little, Brown.
Ramasastry, A. & Thompson, R.C. (2006).
  Commerce, Crime and Conflict. Legal Remedies for Private Sector Liability for Grave Breaches of International Law. A Survey of Sixteen Countries, FAFO-report 535, Fafo institute for Applied International Studies, Norway.
Rasmussen, M.V. (2005).
  'What's the Use of it?': Danish Strategic Culture and the Utility of Armed Force, Cooperation and Conflict, 40, 67, found at: http://cac.sagepub.com/cgi/content/abstract/40/1/67, last visited: March 2007
Razack, N. (2005).
  'Bodies on the Move': Spatialized Locations, Identities, and Nationality in International Work, *Social Justice: A Journal of Crime, Conflict, and World Order* 32(4), 87–104.
Reeves, E. (2005).
  Darfur Mortality Update: June 30, 2005, *Sudan Tribune,* July 1, 2005.
Rejali, D.(1994).
  Torture and Modernity: Self, Society, and State in Modern Iran, Denver: Westview.
Rense, J. (2005).
  De rechtspersoon in het strafrecht, *Delikt en Delinkwent* 17, 272–298.
Reuters (2005).
  Over 180,000 Darfur Deaths in 18 Months – UN Envoy, March 15, 2005.
Reynolds, H. (1993).
  The Unrecorded Battlefields of Queensland, in: Reynolds, H. (ed.), *Race Relations in North Queensland,* Townsville: Department of History and Politics, James Cook University.
Reynolds, H. (1995).
  Fate of a Free People, Ringwood: Penguin.
Reyntjens, F. (1990).
  Le gacaca ou la justice du gazon au Rwanda, *Politique Africaine,* 31–41.

Richardson, P. (2003).
  Corporate Crime in a Globalized Economy. An Examination of the Corporate Legal Conundrum and Positive Prospects for Peace, Ottawa: NPSIA/CIFP Carleton University.
Rieff, D. (1995).
  Slaughterhouse: Bosnia and the Failure of the West, New York: Touchstone Books.
Riley, J. (2005).
  Teaching on terrorism: Problems of interdisciplinary integration in introductory level texts, *Journal of Criminal Justice Education* 16(1).
Roberts, P. & McMillan, N. (2003).
  For Criminology in International Criminal Justice, *Journal of International Criminal Justice* 1, 321–338.
Robertson, R. (1992).
  Globalization: Social Theory and Global Culture, London: Sage.
Robertson, G. (2002).
  Crimes Against Humanity: The Struggle for Global Justice, New York: Penguin books.
Robinson, W.C., Lee, M., Hill, K. & Burnham, G. (1999).
  Mortality in North Korean Migrant Households, *The Lancet* 354, 291–295.
Robinson, A. & Stroshine, M. (2005).
  The Importance of Expectation Fulfillment on Domestic Violence Victims' Satisfaction with the Police in the UK, *Policing* 28(2), 301–321.
Robinson, P. L. (2005).
  Rough Edges in the Alignment of Legal Systems in the Proceedings at the ICTY, *Journal of International Criminal Justice* 3, 1037–1058.
Roche, D. (2003).
  Accountability in Restorative Justice, Oxford: Oxford University Press.
Roef, D. & de Roos, Th.A. (1998).
  De strafrechtelijke aansprakelijkheid van de rechtspersoon in Nederland: Rechtstheoretische beschouwingen bij enkele praktische knelpunten, in: Faure, M.G. & Schwarz, C.A. (eds.), *De strafrechtelijke en de civielrechtelijke aansprakelijkheid van de rechtspersoon en zijn bestuurders*, Antwerpen: Intersentia, 87–94.
Rogers, R. & Copeland, E. (1993).
  Forced Migration: Policy Issues in the Post-Cold War World, Medford, Massachusetts: Tufts University Press.
Rogovin, V.Z. (1998).
  1937: Stalin's Year of Terror, Oak Park: Mehring Books.
Rohde, D. (1997).
  Endgame: The Betrayal and Fall of Srebrenica, Europe's Worst Massacre Since World War II, New York: Farrar, Straus and Giroux.
Roht-Arriaza, N. (2005).
  The Pinochet Effect: Transnational Justice in the Age of Human Rights, Philadelphia: University of Pennsylvania.

Roht-Arriaza, N., & Gibson, J. (1998).
  The Developing Jurisprudence on Amnesty, *Human Rights Quarterly* 20, 841–885.
Roht-Arriaza, N. & Mariezcurrena, J. (eds.) (2006).
  Transitional Justice in the Twenty-First Century, New York: Cambridge University Press.
Romano, C.P.R., Nollkaemper, A. & Kleffner, J.K. (eds.) (2004).
  Internationalized Criminal Courts, Oxford: Oxford University Press.
Rombouts, H. (2004).
  Victim Organisations and the Politics of Reparation: a case study on Rwanda, Antwerp: Intersentia.
Rosenberg, T. (1991).
  Children of Cain: violence and the violent in Latin America, New York: William Morrow and comp.
Rosett, C. (2006).
  How Corrupt is the United Nations? *Commentary* (April), 29–36.
Ross, J.I. (1995).
  Controlling State Crime: An Introduction, New York: Garland.
Ross, J.I. (1998).
  Situating the Academic Study of Controlling State Crime, *Crime, Law and Social Change* 29, 331–340.
Ross, J.I. (2000a).
  Controlling State Crime, New Brunswick: Transaction Publishers.
Ross, J.I. (2000b).
  Introduction: Protecting Democracy by Controlling State Crime in Advanced Industrialized Countries, in: Ross, J. (ed.), *Varieties of State Crime and Its Control*, Monsey, New York: Criminal Justice Press, 1–10.
Ross, J.I. (ed.) (2000c).
  Varieties of State Crime and its Control, Monsey, New York: Criminal Justice Press.
Ross, J., Barak, G., Ferrell, J., Kauzlarich, D., Hamm, M., Friedrichs, D., Matthews, R., Pickering S., Presdee, M., Kraska, P. and Kappeler, V. (1999).
  The State of State Crime Research: A Commentary, *Humanity & Society* 23(3), 273–281.
Ross, W. (2003).
  Uganda's atrocious war, Online: <news.bbc.co.uk/1/hi/world/africa/2982818.stm>
Rotberg, R., & Thompson, D. (2000).
  Truth v. justice. The morality of truth commissions, Princeton, N.J: Princeton University Press.
Rothe, D. (2006).
  Iraq and Halliburton, in: Michalowski, R.J. & Kramer, R.C. (eds.), *State-Corporate Crime; Wrongdoing at the Intersection of Business & Government*, New Brunswick, New Jersey & London: University Press.
Rothe, D. & Friedrichs, D.O. (2001).
  The State of the Criminology of Crimes of the State, *Social Justice* 33, 162–182.
Rothe, D. & Friedrichs, D.O. (2006).
  The state of the criminology of state crime, *Social Justice* 33(1), 147–161.

Rothe, D. & Mullins, C.W. (2006a).

The International Criminal Court: Symbolic Gestures and the Generation of Global Social Control, Lanham, MD: Lexington Books.

Rothe, D. & Mullins, C.W. (2006b).

The International Criminal Court and United States Opposition, *Crime, Law, and Social Change* 45(3), 201–226.

Rothe, D. & Mullins, C.W. (2006c)

International Community: Legitimizing a Moral Consciousness, *Humanity and Society* (forthcoming).

Rothe, D., Muzzatti, S. & Mullins, C.W. (2006).

Crime on the High Seas: Crimes of Globalization and the Sinking of the Senegalese Ferry Le Joola, *Critical Criminology* 14(2), 159–180.

Rothman, D. (1971).

The discovery of the asylum in the new republic, Boston: Little Brown.

Royal Commission on Aboriginal Peoples (RCAP) (1996).

Report of the Royal Commission on Aboriginal Peoples, Ottawa: Canada Communication Group.

Rummell, R.J. (1994).

Death by Government, New Brunswick: Transaction Publishers.

Rumsey, M. (2006).

Bibliography, in: Alston, Ph. (Ed.), *Non-State Actors and Human Rights*, Oxford: Oxford University Press, 351–368.

Russell, S. (2005).

Since September 11, All Roads Lead to Rome, *Critical Criminology* 13(1), 37–53.

Sabini, J.P. & M. Silver (1993).

Destroying the innocent with a clear conscience: a sociopsychology of the Holocaust, in: Dimsdale, J.E. (Ed.), *Survivors, victims, and perpetrators – essay on the Nazi Holocaust*, New York: Hemisphere Publishing corporation, 329–358.

Sallah, M. & Weis, M. (2006)

Tiger Force – a true story of men and war, New York: Little Brown.

Salter, M. & Charlesworth, L. (2006).

Ribbentrop and the Ciano Diaries at the Nuremberg Trial, *Journal of International Criminal Justice* 4, 103–127.

Sands, P. (2005).

Lawless World: Making and Breaking Global Rules, London: Penguin.

Sarkin, J. (2000).

Promoting Justice, Truth and Reconciliation in Transitional Societies, *International Law Forum* 2, 112–121.

Sarkin, J. (2001).

The tension between justice and reconciliation in Rwanda: politics, human rights, due process and the role of the gacaca courts in dealing with the genocide, *Journal of African Law* 45(2), 143–172.

Sarkin, J. (2004a).

Pursuing private actors for reparations for human rights abuses committed in Africa in the Courts of the United States of America, in: Doxtader, E., & Villa-

Vicencio, C. (eds.), *Repairing the irreparable. Dealing with the double-binds of making reparations for crimes in the past,* Claremont: David Philip.

Sarkin, J. (2004b).
Carrots and Sticks: The TRC and the South African Amnesty Process, Antwerp: Intersentia.

Sassen, S. (2003).
Economic Globalization and the Redrawing of Citizenship, in: Friedman, J. (ed.), *Globalization, the State, and Violence,* Walnut Creek, CA: Alta Mira Press, 67–86.

Savelsberg, J. & Flood, S.M. (2004).
Criminological Knowledge: Period and Cohort Effect in Scholarship, *Criminology* 42, 1009–1041.

Scarbrough, E. (1984).
Political Ideology and Voting: An Exploratory Study, Oxford: Clarendon Press.

Schabas, W.A. (1996).
The Death Penalty As Cruel Treatment And Torture: Capital Punishment Challenged in the World's Courts, Boston: Northeastern University Press.

Schabas, W.A. (2000).
Hate Speech in Rwanda: the Road to Genocide, *McGill Law Journal* 46, 141.

Schabas, W.A. (2002).
The Rwanda Case: Sometimes It's Impossible, in: Bassiouni, M.C. (ed.), *Post-Conflict Justice,* New York, Ardsley: Transnational Publishers Inc.

Schabas, W.A. (2005a).
Genocide Trials and Gacaca Courts, *Journal of International Criminal Justice* 3, 879–895.

Schabas, W.A. (2005b).
Reparation Practices in Sierra Leone and the Truth and Reconciliation Commission, in: De Feyter, K., Parmentier, S., Bossuyt, M., & Lemmens, P. (eds.), *Out of the Ashes. Reparation for Victims of Gross and Systematic Human Rights Violations,* Antwerp: Intersentia.

Scharf, M.P. (2007).
Saddam Hussein on Trial: What went awry? The Iraqi High Tribunal. A Viable Experiment in International Justice, *Journal of International Criminal Justice* 5, 258–263.

Scheffer, D. (2007).
Genocide and atrocity crimes, *Genocide Studies and Prevention* 1(3), 229–250.

Schivelbusch, W. (2001).
The Culture of Defeat: On National Trauma, Mourning, and Recovery, New York: Metropolitan Books.

Schwartzmantel, J. (1998).
The Age of Ideology: Political Ideologies from the American Revolution to Post-modern Times, New York: New York University Press.

Schwelb, E. (1946).
Crimes Against Humanity, *The British Year Book of International Law* 23, 178–226.

Schwendinger, H. & Schwendinger, J. (1970).
> Defenders of Order or Guardians of Human Rights?, *Issues in Criminology* 5(2), 123–157.

Scully, D. & Marolla, J. (1985).
> Riding the Bull at Gilley's: Convicted Rapists Describe the Rewards of Rape, *Social Problems* 32(3), 251–263.

Segev, T. (2000).
> *Soldiers of evil – the commandants of the Nazi concentration camps*, London: diamond books (orig. publ. 1987).

Selengut, C. (2003).
> *Sacred Fury: Understanding Religious Violence*, Walnut Creek: AltaMira Press.

Sell, L. (2002).
> *Slobodan Milosevic and the Destruction of Yugoslavia*, Durham: Duke University Press.

Sénat de Belgique (1997).
> Commission d'Enquête parlementaire concernant les événements au Rwanda, (Commission of parliamentary enquiry concerning the events in Rwanda), session de 1997–1998, 6 décembre 1997, Rapport fait au nom de la commission d'enquête par MM Mahoux et Verhofstadt.

Senate Standing Committee on Legal and Constitutional Affairs (2006).
> *Unfinished Business: Indigenous Stolen Wages*, Canberra: Commonwealth of Australia.

Serbin, K. (2000).
> *Secret Dialogues: Church-State Relations, Torture, and Social Justice in Authoritarian Brazil*, Pittsburgh: University of Pittsburgh Press.

Serbrock, F. (2006).
> *The role of the Bystander*, University College Maastricht, December 20, 2006 (unpublished master thesis).

Sereny, G. (1974).
> *Into that darkness: from mercy killing to mass murder*, London: McGraw-Hill.

Sereny, G. (1995).
> *Albert Speer: His battle with truth*, London: Picador.

Serrano, R.A. (2005).
> Civil-Liberties Report Spotlights U.S. Use of Rendition, *Los Angeles Times*, April 25, 2005.

Service National des Juridictions Gacaca (2005).
> *Le Guide Simplifie de la Procédure de Jugement*, Kigali, Avril 2005.

Sevastopulo, D. (2005).
> Activists condemn Abu Ghraib verdict, *Financial Times* (London), April, 25.

Seymour, A. (2000).
> Providing Victim Service with a Restorative Justice Paradigm, *Corrections Management Quarterly* 4(3), 21–29.

Shamir, R. (2004).
> Between self-regulation and the alien Tort Claims Act: On the Contested Concept of Corporate Social Responsibility, *Law & Society Review* 38(4), 635- 663.

Shane, S. (2005).
> C.I.A. Role in Visit of Sudan Intelligence Chief Causes Dispute Within Administration, *New York Times*, June 18, 2005, A7.

Shattuck, J. (2003).
> *Freedom on Fire: Human Rights Wars and America's Response*, Cambridge: Harvard University Press.

Shaw, C.R. & McKay, H.D. (1942).
> *Juvenile Delinquency and Urban Areas*, Chicago: University of Chicago Press.

Shaw, M. (2007).
> *What is genocide?*, Cambridge: Polity.

Shelden, R., Tracy, S. & Brown, W. (2004).
> *Youth Gangs in American Society*, 3rd edition, Belmont: Wadsworth.

Sheleff, L.S. (1987).
> *Ultimate penalties: capital punishment, life imprisonment, physical torture*, Columbus: Ohio State University Press.

Sheridan, A. (1990).
> *Michel Foucault: The Will to Truth*, London: Routledge.

Sherman, M.A. (2000).
> Some Thoughts on Restoration, Reintegration and Justice in the Transnational Context, *Fordham International Law Journal* 23(5), 1397–1402.

Shorey, G. (2000).
> Bystander non-intervention and the Somali incident, *Canadian Military Journal* 1(4), 19–28.

Short, P. (2004)
> *Pol Pot – The History of a Nightmare*, London: John Murray.

Shover, N. & Bryant, K.M. (1993).
> Theoretical Explanations of Corporate Crime, in: Blankenship, M.B. (ed.), *Understanding Corporate Criminality*, New York: Garland Publishing.

Siegel, R.L. (1998).
> Transitional Justice. A Decade of Debate and Experience, *Human Rights Quarterly* 20, 431–454.

Siklová, J. (1999).
> Lustration or the Czech Way of Screening, in: Krygier, M. & Czarnota, A. (eds.), *The Rule of Law after Communism*, Ashgate, Dartmouth: Aldershot.

Silva, R. & Ball, P. (2006).
> *The Profile of Human Rights Violations in Timor-Leste, 1974–1999*, Palo Alto: The Benetech Initiative.

Silverstein, K. (2005a).
> Official Pariah Sudan Valuable to American War on Terror, *Los Angeles Times*, April 29, 2005, A1.

Silverstein, K. (2005b).
> Sudanese Visitor Split U.S. Officials, *Los Angeles Times*, June 17, 2005.

Simeant, J. (2005).
> What is Going Global? The Internationalization of French NGOs 'Without Borders', *Review of International Political Economy* 12, 851–883.

Simon, D.R. (2006).
> *Elite Deviance*, 8th edition, Boston: Allyn & Bacon.

Simon, J. (1998).
> Refugees in a carceral age: The rebirth of immigration prisons in the United States, *Public Culture* 10(3), 577–607.

Simon, J. (2007).
> *Governing through crime: How the war on crime transformed American democracy and created a culture of fear*, New York: Oxford University Press.

Singer, P.W. (2006).
> *Children at war*, Berkeley: University of California Press.

Skinnider, E. (2005).
> *International Norms, Gender and the Law of Evidence*, paper, part of the Canadian International Development Agency funded Implementing International Standard Criminal Justice China Project, International Centre for Criminal Law Reform and Criminal Justice Policy, Vancouver BC.

Skogan, W.G. (1984).
> Reporting Crimes to the Police: The Status of World Research, *Journal of Research in Crime and Delinquency* 21, 113–137.

Skolnick, J. (1966).
> *Justice without trial*, New York: John Wiley & Sons.

Skolnick, J. & Fyfe, J. (1993).
> *Above the law: Police and the excessive use of force*, New York: The Free Press.

Slapper, G. & Tombs, S. (1999).
> *Corporate crime*, Harlow: Longman.

Slaughter, A.-M. (2003).
> *A New World Order*, Princeton: Princeton University Press.

Smeulers, A. (1996).
> Auschwitz and the Holocaust through the eyes of the perpetrators, *Driemaandelijks Tijdschrift van de Stichting Auschwitz* 50(1), 23–55.

Smeulers, A. (2004).
> What transforms ordinary people into gross human rights violators? in: Carey, S.C. & Poe, S.C. (ed.), *Understanding Human Rights Violations: New Systematic Studies*, London: Ashgate, 239–156.

Smeulers, A. (2006).
> Criminologie in een 'state of denial'?, *Tijdschrift voor Criminologie* 48(3), 275–289.

Smith, C. (2006).
> What is the Role of Criminologists in Informing United Nations Public Policy? *The Criminologist* 31(1), 3–5.

Smith, J.M. & Walker, B. (2004).
> *Darfur: Blueprint for Genocide,* Retford: The Aegis Institute, Report # R01/04.

Snider, L. (2000).
> The Sociology of corporate Crime: An Obituary. (Or: Whose Knowledge Claims have Legs?), *Theoretical Criminology* 4(2), 169–206.

Solzhenitsyn, A. (1975).
> *The Gulag Archipelago, vol. 2*, New York: Harper & Row.

Sooka, Y. (2006).
> Dealing with the Past and Transitional Justice: Building Peace through Accountability, *International Review of the Red Cross* 862, 311–325.

Speer, A. (1975).
> *Spandauer Tagebücher*, Frankfurt am Mein: Verlag Ullstein GmbH.

Spencer, P. & Wollmann, H. (2002).
> *Nationalism: A Critical Introduction*, Thousand Oaks: Sage.

Spiegel, P. & Salama, P. (2000).
> War and Mortality in Kosovo, 1998–1999: An Epidemiological Testimony, *Lancet* 355, 2204–2209.

Spierenburg, P. (1984).
> *The spectacle of the suffering: Executions and the evolution of repression*, Cambridge: Cambridge University Press.

Spinedi, M. (1989).
> International Crimes of State: The Legislative History, in: Weiler, J.H.H., Cassese, A. & Spinedi, M. (eds.), *International Crimes of State. A Critical Analysis of the ILC's Draft Article 19 on State Responsibility*, Berlin and New York: Walter de Gruyter.

Stanley, E. (2005a).
> *Torture and Transitional Justice in Timor Leste: A Report for the Judicial System Monitoring Project*, Dili: JSMP (www.jsmp.minihub.org/reports.htm).

Stanley, E. (2005b).
> Truth Commissions and the Recognition of State Crime, *The British Journal of Criminology* 45(4), 582–597.

Stanley, E. (2006).
> Towards a Criminology of Human Rights, in: Barton, A., Corteen, K., Scott, D. & Whyte, D. (eds.), *The Criminological Imagination: Readings in Critical Criminologies*, Cullompton: Willan.

Stannard, D. (1993).
> *American Holocaust*, New York: Oxford University Press.

Staub, E. (1989).
> *The Roots of Evil: The Origins of Genocide and Other Group Violence*, New York: Cambridge University Press.

Staub, E. (2002).
> The Psychology of Bystanders, Perpetrators, and Heroic Helpers, in: Newman, L.S. & Erber, R. (eds.), *Understanding Genocide: The Social Psychology of the Holocaust*, New York: Oxford University Press, 11–42.

Staub, E. (2003).
> *The Psychology of Good and Evil: Why Children, Adults, and Groups Help and Harm Others*, Cambridge: Cambridge University Press.

Steiner, J.M. (1980)
> The SS yesterday and today: a sociopsychological view, in: Dimsdale, J.E. (1980), *Survivors, victims, and perpetrators – essays on the Nazi Holocaust*, Washington: Hemisphere Publishing Corporation, 405–445.

Stohl, M. & Lopez, G.A. (Eds.) (1984).
The state as terrorist: the dynamics of governmental violence and repression, London: Aldwych.

Stohl, M., Carleton, D., Lopez, G. & Samuels, S. (1986).
State violation of human rights: issues and problems of measurement, *Human Rights Quarterly* 8, 592–606.

Stohl, R. (2005).
Fighting the Illicit Trafficking of Small Arms, Center for Defense Information, May 13: 1, http://www.cdi.org/program/document.cfm?DocumentID= 2996.

Stolberg, S.G. (2006a).
Bush Signs Bill Setting Detainee Rules, *New York Times*, October 17, E1–2.

Stolberg, S.G. (2006b).
Bush Signs New Rules to Prosecute Terror Suspects, *New York Times*, October 18, E1–2.

Stover, E. (2005).
The Witnesses: War Crimes and the Promise of Justice in The Hague, Philadelphia: University of Pennsylvania Press.

Stover, E. & Nightingale, E.O. (1985).
The Breaking of bodies and minds: torture, psychiatric abuse, and the health professions, Washington, D.C.: AAAS Science and Human Rights Program.

Stover, E. & Weinstein, H.M. (eds.) (2004).
My Neighbor, My Enemy; Justice and Community in the Aftermath of Mass Atrocity, Cambridge: Cambridge University Press.

Sutherland, E.H. (1939; 1940).
White-collar Criminality, *American Sociological Review* 5, 1–12.

Sutherland, E.H. (1949).
White Collar Crime, New York: Holt, Rinehart & Winston.

Sutherland, E. (1947)
Principles of Criminology, Philadelphia: J.B. Lippincott.

Sutherland, E.H. (1983).
White collar crime. The Uncut Version, New Haven: Yale University Press.

Svaldi, D. (1989).
Sand Creek and the Rhetoric of Extermination: A Case Study in Indian-White Relations, Lanham: University Press of America.

Swanson, S. (2004).
Enemy combatants and the writ of habeas corpus, *Arizona State Law Journal* 35, 939–1022.

Sykes, G.M. & Matza, D. (1957).
Techniques of neutralization: A theory of delinquency, *American Sociological Review* 22, 664–70.

Tabachnik, B.G. & Fidell, L.S. (1989).
Using multivariate statistics, New York: Harper Collins.

Tajfel, H. & Turner, J. (1986).
The Social identity Theory of Intergroup Behaviour, *Annual Review of Psychology* 33, 1–39.

Tanner, L.E. (1994).

Intimate violence: reading rape and torture in twentieth century fiction, Bloomington: Indiana University Press.

Tappan, P. (1947).

Who is the Criminal? American sociological review, 96–102.

Tarrow, S. (2005).

The New Transnational Activism, New York: Cambridge University Press.

Taylor, C.C. (1999).

Sacrifice as Terror: The Rwandan Genocide of 1994, Oxford: Berg.

Taylor, I. (1999a).

Criminology, Post-Maastricht, Crime, Law & Social Change 30, 333–346.

Taylor, I. (1999b).

Crime in Context: A Critical Criminology of Market Societies, Cambridge: Polity Press.

Teitel, R. (2000).

Transitional Justice, New York: Oxford University Press.

Telford, T. (1970).

Nuremberg and Vietnam: an American Tragedy, Chicago: Quadrangle Books.

Telford, T. (1992).

The anatomy of the Nuremberg trials: A personal memoir, New York: Knopf.

Terreblanche, S. (2000).

Dealing with systematic economic injustice, in: Villa-Vicencio, C., & Verwoerd, W. (eds.), Looking Back Reaching Forward. Reflections on the Truth and Reconciliation Commission of South Africa, Cape Town: University of Cape Town Press.

Thakur, R., Weiss, Th.G. (2007).

The UN and Global Governance: An Idea and its Prospects, Bloomington: Indiana University Press.

Therborn, G. (1980).

The Ideology of Power and the Power of Ideology, London: NLB.

Thieren, M. (2007).

Medicine and public health in dark times, retrieved from International Relations and Security Network (http://www.isn.ethz.ch/news/sw/details.cfm?ID=17544).

Thompson, J.B. (1990).

Ideology and Modern Culture, Stanford: Stanford University Press.

Thys, P. (2004).

Contribution á l'étude des violences extremes: le criminal de guerre actuel, Revue internationale de criminology et de police technique et scientifique 4, 480–503.

Tieger, A., Shin, M. (2005).

Plea Agreements in the ICTY. Purpose, Effects, Propriety, Journal of International Criminal Justice 3, 1–14.

Tiemessen, A.E. (2004).

After Arusha, Gacaca Justice in Post-Genocide Rwanda, African Studies Quarterly 8(1), 1.

Tifft, L. & Sullivan, D. (1980).

The Struggle to be Human: Crime, Criminology, and Anarchism, Sanday, Orkney, UK: Cienfuegos Press

Tifft, L. & Sullivan, D. (2001).

A Needs-Based, Social Harms Definition of Crime, in: Henry, S. & Lanier, M. (eds.), *What is Crime? Controversies about the Nature of Crime and what to do about it*, Lanham, Maryland: Rowman and Littlefield.

Tifft, L. & Sullivan, D. (2006).

Needs-Based Anarchist Criminology, in: Henry, S. & Lanier, M. (eds.), *The Essential Criminology Reader*, Boston: Roman and Littlefield.

Tilly, C. (1978).

From mobilization to revolution, New York: McGraw-Hill.

Tilly, C. (2003).

The politics of collective violence, Cambridge: Cambridge University Press.

Timaeus, I. & Jasseh, M. (2004).

Adult Mortality in Sub-Saharan Africa: Evidence from Demographic and Health Surveys, *Demography* 41, 757–772.

Toch, H. (1969).

Violent men: An inquiry into the psychology of violence, Chicago: Aldine.

Toch, H. (1996).

The violence-prone police officer, in: Geller, W.A. & Toch, H. (eds.), *Police violence: Understanding and controlling police abuse of force*, New Haven: Yale University Press.

Tochilovsky, V. (2005).

Charges, Evidence, and Legal Assistance in International Jurisdictions, Nijmegen: Wolf Legal Publishers.

Tochilovsky, V. (2006).

Jurisprudence of the international criminal courts: procedure and evidence, Nijmegen: Wolf Legal Publishers

Todorov, T. (1996).

Facing the Extreme: Moral Life in the Concentration Camps, New York: Metropolitan Books.

Todorov, T. (1999).

Facing the Extreme – Moral Life in the Concentration Camps, London: Phoenix paperback.

Todorov, T. (2001).

In search of lost crime. Tribunals, apologies, reparations, and the search for justice, *The New Republic*, January 29, 2001, 29–36.

Tombs, S., & Whyte, D. (eds.) (2003).

Unmasking the Crimes of the Powerful: Scrutinizing States and Corporations, New York: Peter Land Publishing.

Tonry, M., & Reiss, A.J. (1993).

Beyond the Law; Crime in Complex Organizations, Chicago and London: The University of Chicago Press.

Toole, M., & Waldman, R. (1990).
Prevention of Excess Mortality in Refugee and Displaced Populations in Developing Countries, *Journal of the American Medical Association* 263, 3296–3302.
Toole, M., & Waldman, R. (1993).
Refugees and Displaced Persons: War, Hunger, and Public Health, *Journal of the American Medical Association* 270, 600–605.
Torpey, J. (2001).
Making Whole What Has Been Smashed: Reflections on Reparations, *The Journal of Modern History* 73(2), 333–358.
Totten, S. (2005).
The United Nations and Genocide, *Society*, 6–13.
Toussaint, S. (1995).
Western Australia, in: McGrath, A. (ed.), *Contested Ground*, Sydney: Allen and Unwin.
Transparency International (2007).
Global Corruption Report 2007, Cambridge: Cambridge University Press.
Trial of the Major War Criminals (1947).
Vol 1, Nuremberg: International Military Tribunal.
Trials of War Criminals Before the Nuremberg Military Tribunals under Control Council Law No. 10. (1949–1953).
Trials of War Criminals Before the Nuremberg Military Tribunals under Control Council Law No. 10. Vols 1–15, Washington D.C.: U.S. Government Printing Office.
Truth and Reconciliation Commission of South Africa (1998).
Truth and Reconciliation Commission of South Africa Report. Cape Town: Juta Publishers (interim report).
Truth and Reconciliation Commission of South Africa (1999a).
Truth and Reconciliation Commission of South Africa Report, Vol. 1, London: MacMillan Reference.
Truth and Reconciliation Commission of South Africa (1999b).
Truth and Reconciliation Commission of South Africa Report, Vol. 4, London: MacMillan Reference.
Truth and Reconciliation Commission of South Africa (1999c).
Truth and Reconciliation Commission of South Africa Report, Vol. 5, London: MacMillan Reference.
Tsosie, R. (2004).
Acknowledging the Past to Heal the Future: The Role of Reparations for Native Nations, *Reparations: An Interdisciplinary Examination of Some Philosophical Issues Conference*, Queens University Kingston Ontario Canada 6–8 Feb 2004.
Tunnell, K. (1993).
Political Crime in Contemporary America: A Critical Approach, New York: Garland.

Turner, T. (2003).

Class Projects, Social Consciousness, and the Contradictions of 'Globalization', in: Friedman, J. (ed.), Globalization, *the State, and Violence*, Walnut Creek, CA: Alta Mira Press, 35–66.

UBC Report (2007).

Human security Report, Liu Institute for Global justice, Vancouver: University of British Columbia.

Ubutabera (1998).

Independent Newsletter on the International Criminal Tribunal for Rwanda, April 13, 1998, No 34.

Umbreit, M., Bradshaw, W., & Coates, R. (2003).

Victims of severe violence in dialogue with the offender. Key principles, practices, outcomes and implications, in: Weitekamp, E., & Kerner, H-J. (eds.), *Restorative Justice in context. International practice and directions*, Cullompton: Willan Publishing.

United Nations (1999a).

Report of the Independent Inquiry into the Actions of the United Nations during the 1994 Genocide in Rwanda, S/1999/1257, New York: United Nations, 1999.

United Nations (1999b).

Srebrenica Report of the Secretary-General Pursuant to General Assembly Resolution 53/35 (1998), A/54/549, New York: United Nations, 1999.

United Nations (2005).

2005 World Summit Outcome, October 24, 2005. UNDoc. A/RES/60/1; Resolution adopted by the General assembly 60/1 found at: http://www.un.org/Depts/dhl/res-guide/r60.htm

United Nations (2006a).

Children and Armed Conflict, Report of the Secretary General, 26 October.

United Nations (2006b).

The United Nations Charter, Retrieved May 25, 2006, http://www.un.org/aboutun/charter/

United States Department of State (2004).

Documenting Atrocities in Darfur, Human Rights and Labor and Bureau of Intelligence and Research, Washington, D.C.: Bureau of Democracy.

United States Department of State (2005).

Sudan: Death Toll in Darfur. Fact Sheet. Bureau of Intelligence and Research. March 25, 2005. Http://www.state.gov/s/inr/rls/fs/2005/45105.htm (accessed April 26, 2005).

United States National Weather Service (2005).

The Eight Days of Katrina, Washington, D.C.: U.S. Government Printing Office.

Urusaro Karekezi, A., Nshimiyimana, A.& Mutamba, B. (2004).

Localizing justice: gacaca courts in post-genocide Rwanda, in: Stover, E. & Weinstein, H.M., *My Neighbor, My Enemy*, Cambridge: Cambridge University Press.

Uvin, P. (2003).

The Gacaca Tribunals in Rwanda, in: Bloomfield, D., Barnes, T., & Huyse, L. (eds.), *Reconciliation After Violent Conflict. A Handbook*, Stockholm: International Idea.

Uvin, P. & Mironko, C. (2003).

Western and local approaches to justice in Rwanda, *Global Governance* 9, 219.

van Boven, T. (1993).

Study Concerning the Right to Restitution, Compensation and Rehabilitation for Victims of Gross Violations of Human Rights and Fundamental Freedoms, Final report, United Nations Commission on Human Rights.

van de Bunt, H.G. & Huisman, W. (2007).

Corporate Crime in The Netherlands, in: Tonry, M. & Bijleveld, C. (eds.) *Crime and Justice in the Netherlands, Crime & Justice. A Review of Research* 35, 217–260.

Vandeginste, S. (1999).

Justice, Reconciliation and Reparation after Genocide and Crimes against Humanity: the Proposed Establishment of Popular Gacaca Tribunals in Rwanda, paper for the All-Africa Conference on African Principles of Conflict Resolution and Reconciliation, Addis Ababa.

Vandeginste, S. (2004a).

Justice for Rwanda, ten years after: some lessons learned for transitional justice, paper, (unpublished).

Vandeginste, S. (2004b).

Legal norms, moral imperative, and pragmatic duties: reparation as a dilemma of transitional governance, in: Doxtader, E. & Villa-Vicencio, C. (eds.), *To Repair the Irreparable. Reparation and Reconstruction in South Africa*, Claremont, South Africa: David Philip.

van den Berg, J. (1995).

Het verloren volk. Een geschiedenis van de Banda-eilanden, Amsterdam: BZZTôH.

van den Bosch, H.H. (1994).

Medisch programma van Memisa in Mugunga-kamp, Goma, Zaïre, augustus-oktober 1994, *Nederlands Tijdschrift voor Geneeskunde*, 139(14), 1246–1249.

van den Herik, L.J. (2005).

The Contribution of the Rwanda Tribunal to the Development of International Law, Leiden: Martinus Nijhoff.

van den Heuvel, G.A.A.J. (1998).

Collusie tussen Overheid en Bedrijf; een vergeten hoofdstuk uit de organisatiecriminologie, Maastricht: Universiteit Maastricht.

van der Merwe, H. (2001).

National and Community Reconciliation: Competing Agendas in South African Truth and Reconciliation Commission, in: Biggar, N. (ed.), *Burying the past: making peace and doing justice after civil conflict*, Washington, DC: Georgetown University Press.

Vande Walle G. (2002).

The collar makes the difference – Masculine criminology and its refusal to recognise markets as criminogenic, *Crime, Law & Social Change* 37(3), 277–291.

Vande Walle, G. (2005).

Conflictafhandeling of risicomanagement? Een studie van conflicten tussen slachtoffers en ondernemingen in de farmaceutische industrie, Brussel: VUBPress.

van Dijk, T.A. (1998).

Ideology: A Multidisciplinary Approach, London: Sage Publications.

van Dijk, J.J.M., H.I. Sagel-Grande & L.G. Toornvliet (2002).

Actuele Criminologie, 4[de] herziene druk, Den Haag: Sdu Uitgevers.

van Krieken, R. (2004).

Rethinking Cultural Genocide: Aboriginal Child Removal and Settler-Colonial State Formation, *Oceania* 75(2), 125–151.

van Liempt, A. (2002).

Kopgeld – Nederlandse premiejagers op zoek naar joden 1943, Amsterdam: Uitgeverij Balans.

van Ruller, S. (1999).

Over fietsendiefstal en de Tweede Wereldoorlog, (rede uitgesproken op het jubileumcongres van de Nederlandse Vereniging voor Kriminologie).

van Sliedregt, E. (2003).

The criminal responsibility of individuals for violations of international humanitarian law, The Hague: T.M.C. Asser Institute.

van Zyl Smit, D. (2004).

Responding to offences against International Criminal Law, Paper presented at the 4th Annual Meeting of the European Society of Criminology, Amsterdam.

Verbitsky, H. (1996).

The Flight: Confessions of an Argentine Dirty Warrior, New York: The New Press.

Verdoolaege, A. (2002).

The debate on truth and reconciliation: A survey of literature on the South African Truth and Reconciliation Commission, Ghent: University of Ghent (unpublished paper).

Verwimp, P. (2001).

A quantative analysis of genocide in Kibuye prefecture, Rwanda, Leuven: University of Leuven.

Verwimp, P. (2003).

Testing the Double-Genocide Thesis for Central and Southern Rwanda, *Journal of Conflict Resolutions* 47(4), 423–442.

Verwimp, P. (2004).

Death and Survival during the 1994 Genocide in Rwanda, *Population Studies* 58, 233–245.

Viano, E.C. (2000).

Victimology today: Major issues in research and public policy, in: Tobolowsky, P.M. (ed.), *Understanding victimology*, Cincinnati, OH: Anderson Publishing.

Villa-Vicencio, C. (2000).

Why Perpetrators Should not Always be Prosecuted: Where the International Criminal Court and Truth Commissions Meet, *Emory Law Journal* 49, 101–118.

Villa-Vicencio, C. (2001).
Restorative Justice in Social Context: The South African Truth and Reconciliation Commission, in: Biggar, N. (ed.), *Burying the past: making peace and doing justice after civil conflict*, Washington, DC: Georgetown University Press.

Villa-Vicencio, C. (2003).
Restorative Justice: Ambiguities and Limitations of a Theory, in: Villa-Vicencio, C. & Doxtader, E. (eds.) *The Provocations of Amnesty. Memory, Justice and Impunity*, Claremont: David Philip Publishers.

Villa-Vicencio, C., & Doxtader, E. (eds.) (2003).
The Provocations of Amnesty. Memory, Justice and Impunity, Claremont: David Philip Publishers.

Vincent, A. (1995).
Modern Political Ideologies, 2nd ed., Oxford: Blackwell.

Volkan, V. (1997).
Bloodlines: From Ethnic Pride to Ethnic Terrorism, New York: Farrar, Straus and Giroux.

von Lang, J. (1991).
Das Eichmann-Protokoll – Tonbandaufzeichnungen der Israelischen Verhöre, München: Propyläen Taschenbuch.

Voorhoeve, J. (2005).
Televisie interview: Spraakmakende Zaken, aflevering 2: Srebrenica, 10 jaar later, 9 July 2005; http://www.nos.nl/nosjournaal/artikelen/2005/7/9/090705_voorhoeve_srebrenica.html, last visited: March 2007

Voorhoeve, J. (2007)
radio interview, Former Dutch Minister: US Deliberately Held Off on Srebrenica, from NIS New Bulletin, January 5, 2007, http://www.domovina.net/archive/2007/20070105_argos_pb.php, last visited: March 2007; Argos uitzending, 22 December 2006

Wæver, O. (2003).
Securization: Taking Stock of a research programme in Security Studies, Copenhagen Peace Research Institute, Working Papers.

Waldman, R. & Martone, G. (1999).
Public Health and Complex Emergencies: New Issues, New Conditions, *American Journal of Public Health* 89, 1483–1485.

Waller, J. (2002/ 2007).
Becoming Evil: How Ordinary People Commit Genocide and Mass Killing, Oxford: Oxford University Press.

Waller, J. (2007)
Becoming evil: perpetrators of ethnic cleansing in the former Yugoslavia, Paper IAGS Conference, Sarajevo Tuesday July, 10th 2007.

Wallerstein, I. (2006).
The Curve of American Power, *New Left Review* 40, 77–94.

Warden, E. (1996).

The causes of police brutality: Theory and evidence on police use of force, in: Geller, W.A., & Toch, H., *Police violence: Understanding and controlling police abuse of force*, New Haven, CN.: Yale University Press.

Warr, M. (1996).

Organization and instigation in delinquent groups, *Criminology* 34, 11–37.

Warr, M. (2002).

Companions in crime – the social aspects of criminal conduct, Cambridge: University Press.

Washington Post (2004).

Bush administration documents on interrogation, June 23, 2004.

Washington Post (2005).

Darfur's Real Death Toll, Editorial Page, April 24, 2005. Http://www.washingtonpost. com/ac2/wp-dyn/admin (Accessed April 24, 2005).

Washington Technology Online (2004).

Top 100 federal prime contractors: Companies by ranking, May 2.

Watkins, F.M. (1964).

The Age of Ideology – Political Thought, 1750 to the Present, New York: Prentice Hall.

Watson, J. (1973).

Deindividuation and changing appearance before battle, *Journal of Abnormal and Social Psychology* 25, 342–345.

Watson, F., Kulenovic, I., & Vespa, J. (1993–1994).

Nutritional Status and Food Security: Winter Nutrition Monitoring in Sarajevo, *European Journal of Clinical Nutrition* 49, 23–32.

Weindling, P. (2000).

Epidemics and Genocide in Eastern Europe 1890–1945, Oxford: Oxford University Press.

Weiss, J. (1996).

Ideology of Death: Why the Holocaust Happened in Germany, Chicago: Elephant Paperbacks.

Weitekamp, E., Parmentier, S., Vanspauwen, K., Valiñas, M., & Gerits, R. (2006).

How to Deal with Mass Victimization and Gross Human Rights Violations. A Restorative Justice Approach, in: Ewald, U., & Turkovic, K. (eds.), *Large-Scale Victimization as a Potential Source of Terrorist Activities. Importance of Regaining Security in Post-Conflict Societies*, Amsterdam: IOS Press.

Weitz, E.D. (2003).

A Century of Genocide: Utopias of Race and Nation, Princeton, New York: Princeton University Press.

Welch, M. (2002a).

The Truth about Sanctions against Iraq, *Policy* 18(2), 8–16.

Welch, M. (2002b).

Detained: Immigration laws and the expanding I.N.S. jail complex, Philadelphia: Temple University Press.

Welch, M. (2006a).

Scapegoats of September 11th: Hate crimes and state crimes in the war on terror, New Brunswick, New Jersey: Rutgers University Press.

Welch, M. (2006b).

Immigration, Criminalization, and Counter-Law: A Foucauldian Analysis of Laws Against Law, Merging Immigration and Crime Control: An Interdisciplinary Workshop, Baldy Center for Law and Social Policy, University at Buffalo Law School, Buffalo, New York, April 28–29, 2006.

Welch, M. (2007).

Sovereign Impunity in America's War on Terror: Examining Reconfigured Power and the Absence of Accountability, Crime, Law, and Social Change 47(3), 135–150.

Welzer, H. (2005).

Täter – wie aus ganz normalen Menschen Massenmörder werden, Frankfurt am Main: Fischer Verlag.

Wemmers, J. & Cyr, K. (2005).

Can Mediation Be Therapeutic for Crime Victims? An Evaluation of Victims' Experiences in Mediation with Young Offenders, Canadian Journal of Criminology and Criminal Justice 47(3), 527–544.

Wessells, M. (2006).

Child soldiers – from violence to protection, Cambridge: Harvard University Press.

Whyte, D. (2003).

Lethal Regulation: State-Corporate Crime and the United Kingdom Government's New Mercenaries, Journal of Law and Society 30(4), 575–600.

Wiebes, C. (2002).

NIOD – Intelligence and the war in Bosnia 1992–1995: The Role of the intelligence and security services, New Brunswick: Transaction Publishers.

Wierzynska, A. (2004).

Consolidating democracy through transitional justice: Rwanda's gacaca courts, New York University Law Review 79, 1934.

Wiesel, E. (1995).

The Town Beyond the Wall, New York: Schocken Books, Random House [original from 1962 by Seuil in Paris: La ville de la Chance].

Wieviorka, M.(2003).

The New Paradigm of Violence, in: Friedman, J. (ed.), Globalization, the State, and Violence, Walnut Creek, CA: Alta Mira Press, 107–140.

Willetts, P. (Ed.). (1996).

The Conscience of the World: The Influence of Non-Governmental Organisations in the UN System, Washington, DC: Brookings Institution Press.

Williams, I. (2005).

U.S. Opposition to International Criminal Court May Preclude a Hearing on Darfur, Washington Report on Middle East Affairs 24, 28.

Wilson, R.A. (2001).

The politics of truth and reconciliation in South Africa. Legitimizing the Post-Apartheid State, Cambridge: Cambridge University Press.

Wilson, R.A. & Mitchell, J.P. (Eds.). (2003).

Human Rights in Global Perspective: Anthropological Studies of Rights, Claims and Entitlements, New York: Routledge.

Windgassen, A. (2006).

Vrouwen van dictators – heulen met de macht, 's Graveland: Fontaine Uitgevers.

Winslow, D. (1999).

Rites of Passage and group bonding in the Canadian Airborne, *Armed Forces and Society* 25(3), 429–457.

Withopf, E. (2005).

Presentation at Seminar on Counsel Issues, Transcript of Proceedings, 23rd May 2005, 80–83.

Wojak, I. (2001)

Eichmanns Memoiren – Ein kritischer essay, Frankfurt: Campus Verlag.

Wood, J. & Shearing, C. (2007).

Imagining security, Cullompton: Willan.

Woolford, A. (2006).

Making Genocide Unthinkable: Three Guidelines for a Critical Criminology of Genocide, *Critical Criminology* 14, 87–106.

Working for Change (2001).

Help end child slave labor, 2001, August 2, Retrieved October 9, 2002, from http://209.15.12.20/csny/action.htm.

World Health Organisation (2002).

World report on violence and health: summary, Retrieved 29 March 2006 from: www.who.int/whr/wn.

World Health Organisation (2004a).

Retrospective Mortality Survey Among the Internally Displaced Population, Greater Darfur, Sudan, Retrieved 29 March 2006 from: www.who.int/disasters/repo/14656.pdf.

World Health Organization (2004b).

Darfur: One Year On, WHO's Work to Save Lives and Reduce Suffering, Geneva: WHO Press.

Wouters, J., & Panken, H. (2002) (eds.)

De Belgische genocidewet in internationaalrechtelijk perspectief, Brussel: Larcier.

X. (2002).

Combatting Impunity. Proceedings of the symposium held in Brussels from 11 to 13 March, followed by The Brussels Principles against impunity and for international justice, Brussels: Bruylant.

Yacoubian, G.S. (1997)

Underestimating the Magnitude of International Crime: Implications of Genocidal Behavior for the Discipline of Criminology, *Injustice Studies* 1(1).

Yacoubian, G. (2000).

The (in)significance of genocidal behavior to the discipline of criminology, *Crime, Law and Social Change* 34, 7–19.

Yacoubian, G.S. (2003)
Evaluating the efficacy of the international criminal tribunals for Rwanda and the former Yugoslavia: implications for criminology and international criminal law, *World Affairs* 165(3), 133–142.

Yasushi, A. (1998).
Newspaper interview by Robert van de Roer of Yashusi Akashi on April 25, 1998, article found at http://www.nrc.nl/W2/Nieuws/1998/04/25/Vp/bijvoegsel.html.

Young, A. (2006).
The Self-Traumatized Perpetrator: From Vietnam to Abu Ghraib, in: Ewald, U. & Turkovic, K. (eds.), *Large-Scale Victimization as a Potential Source of Terrorist Activities: Importance of Regaining Security in Post-Conflict Societies*, Amsterdam: IOS Press.

Zalaquett, J. (1995).
Chile, in: A. Boraine and J. Levy (eds.), *The Healing of a Nation?*, Cape Town: Justice in Transition.

Zappala, S. (2003).
Human Rights in International Criminal Proceedings, London: Oxford University press.

Zarkov, D. (1997).
War rapes in Bosnia – on masculinity, feminity and power of the rape victim identity, *Tijdschrift voor Criminologie* 39(2), 140–151.

Zehr, H. (1991).
Changing Lenses: A New Focus for Crime and Justice, Scottdale: Herald Press.

Zehr, H. (2003).
Retributive justice, restorative justice, in: Johnstone, G. (ed.), *A Restorative Justice Reader. Texts, sources, context*, Cullompton: Willan Publishing.

Zimbardo, P.G. (1970).
The human choice: Individuation, reason, and order versus deindividuation, impulse, and chaos, in: Arnold, W.J. & Levine, D. (ed.), *1969 Nebraska symposium on motivation*, Lincoln: University of Nebraska Press.

Zimbardo, P.G., Haney, C., Banks, W.C. & Jaffe, D. (1973).
The mind is a formidable jailer: A Pirandellian prison, *New York Times Magazine*, April 8, 38.

Zimbardo, P.G., Haney, C. Curtis Banks, W. and Jaffe, D. (1974).
The psychology of imprisonment: privation, power, and pathology, in: Zick, R. (ed.), *Doing unto others*, London: Englewood Cliffs, 61–73.

Zimbardo, P.G., Maslach, C. & Haney, C. (2000).
Reflections on the Stanford Prison Experiment: Genesis, transformations, consequences, in: Blass, T. (ed.), *Obedience to authority: Current perspectives on the Milgram paradigm*, Mahwah, New York: Erlbaum.

Zoellick, R. (2005).
On Darfur, A Call for the Wrong Action, *Washington Post*, Letter to Editor, April 27, 2005.

Zumach, A. (1995a).

US Intelligence knew Serbs were planning an assault on Srebrenica, Basic Reports, Newsletter on International Security Policy, British American Security Information Council, 16 October 1995, Number 47.

Zumach, A. (1995b).

Intelligence Agencies fail to supply information to war crimes tribunal, Basic Reports, Newsletter on International Security Policy, British American Security Information Council, 20 November 1995, Number 48.

Zumach, A. (1997).

Basic Reports, New Evidence further implicates France in fall of Srebrenica, in Newsletter on International Security Policy, 11 February 1997, 56, 1, article found at: http://www.basicint.org/pubs/BReports/BR56us.pdf, last visited: March 2007.

Zumach, A. (2002).

Keine Rettung für Srebrenica, *Die Tageszeitung,* 4 November 2002, article found at: http://www.taz.de/pt/2002/04/11/a0064.1/text last visited: March 2007.

CONTRIBUTORS AND EDITORS

Alex Alvarez earned his Ph.D. in Sociology from the University of New Hampshire in 1991 and is a Professor in the Department of Criminal Justice at Northern Arizona University. From 2001 until 2003 he was the founding Director of the Martin-Springer Institute for Teaching the Holocaust, Tolerance and Humanitarian Values. His main areas of study are in the areas of collective and interpersonal violence, including homicide and genocide. His first book, *Governments, Citizens, and Genocide* was published by Indiana University Press in 2001 and was a nominee for the Academy of Criminal Justice Sciences book of the year award in 2002, as well as a Raphael Lemkin book award nominee from the International Association of Genocide Scholars in 2003. His other books include *Murder American Style* (2002) and *Violence: the Enduring Problem* (2007). He has also served as an editor for the journal *Violence and Victims*, was a founding co-editor of the journal *Genocide Studies and Prevention*, was a co-editor of the H-Genocide List Serve and is an editorial board member for the journals *War Crimes, Genocide, and Crimes Against Humanity: An International Journal*, and *Idea: A Journal of Social Issues*. He has been invited to present his research in various countries such as Austria, Bosnia, Canada, Germany, the Netherlands and Sweden. Dr. Alvarez also gives presentations and workshops on various issues such as fatality review, violence, genocide and bullying.

Jennifer Balint is Director of the Socio-Legal Studies Programme in the School of Political Science, Criminology and Sociology at the University of Melbourne, Australia. Her research has been in the area of State crime and genocide and post-conflict reconciliation and reconstruction. It has taken her to Rwanda, the former Yugoslavia, Ethiopia, South Africa and to the international criminal tribunals in The Hague and in Arusha. She is currently working on a book manuscript titled *In the Name of the State. Genocide, State Crime and the Law.*

Gregg Barak is a Professor of Criminology and Criminal Justice at Eastern Michigan University, a Visiting Distinguished Professor and Scholar at the College of Justice and Safety, Eastern Kentucky University, and the editor and/or author of more than a dozen books including the recently published *Violence, Conflict, and World Order: Critical Conversations on State-Sanctioned Justice* (2007).

Catrien Bijleveld is professor of Research Methods in Criminology at the VU University Amsterdam as well as senior researcher at the NSCR Institute for the Study of Crime and Law Enforcement, in Leiden, the Netherlands. Catrien Bijleveld obtained her PhD from Leiden University on categorical state space analysis. Apart from working at Leiden University and the Netherlands Ministry of Justice before moving to her current positions, she carried out numerous missions for the Netherlands ministry of Foreign Affairs to Yemen and Sudan. Next to gross human rights violations, her research interests extend to criminal careers, the intergenerational transmission of criminality and sex offending.

Chris Cunneen is the NewSouth Global Professor of Criminology at the University of New South Wales, Sydney, Australia. He has published widely in the area of restorative justice and Indigenous legal issues. His books include *Juvenile Justice. Youth and Crime in Australia* (Oxford University Press, 2002), *Conflict, Politics and Crime* (Allen and Unwin, 2001), *Faces of Hate* (Federation Press, 1997) and *Indigenous People and the Law in Australia* (Butterworths, 1995).

Uwe Ewald is currently working as Strategic Crime Analyst at the International Criminal Tribunal for the former Yugoslavia in The Hague, the Netherlands. He is affiliated with the Max Planck Institute for International and Foreign Criminal Law in Freiburg, i.Br. (MPI), Germany as senior researcher and lecturer for Supranational Criminology at the University of Bochum, Germany. Teaching positions and research since 1983 at the Humboldt-University Berlin, Free University Berlin, MPI (Germany), Simon Fraser University Burnaby/Vancouver (Canada) focussed on various criminological and victimological topics. Beside his academic positions he worked as defence counsel between 1996 and 2002 primarily representing juvenile offenders, former functionaries of the GDR, but also victims of State crime. Current research activities refer to the construction of war crimes, the analytical-evidentiary process of the emerging international criminal justice system and international sentencing. His recent publications includes a book and contribution on large-scale victimisation (Amsterdam, 2006).

David O. Friedrichs is Professor of Sociology/Criminal Justice and Distinguished University Fellow at the University of Scranton (Pennsylvania, USA). He is author of *Trusted Criminals: White Collar Crime in Contemporary Society* (Thomson/ Wadsworth, 1996, 2004, 2007) and *Law in Our Lives: An Introduction* (Oxford University Press, 2001, 2006), and editor of *State Crime, Volumes I and II* (Ashgate/ Dartmouth, 1998). He has published over 100 journal articles, book chapters, encyclopaedia entries and essays, and over 300 book reviews. He has been a visiting professor or guest lecturer at many colleges and universities, including the University of South Africa and Flinders University in Australia. He served as Editor of Legal Studies Forum (1985–1989) and President of the White Collar Crime Research Consortium (2002–2004). In November, 2005, he received a Lifetime Achievement Award from the Division on Critical Criminology of the American Society of Criminology.

Fred Grünfeld (1949, the Netherlands) studied Political Science at the VU University in Amsterdam. He is now extraordinary professor in the causes of gross human rights violations at the Faculty of Law and the Human Rights Institute of the Utrecht University and associate professor of International Relations and of the Law of International Organizations at the University of Maastricht at the Maastricht Centre for Human Rights. He wrote his Ph. D. *The Netherlands and the Near East: the international political role of the Netherlands in the Arab-Israeli conflict* in 1991. His inaugural lecture in 2003 was on *Early action of bystanders to prevent wars and gross human rights violations*. He has published in 2007 with A. Huijboom *The failure to Prevent Genocide in Rwanda; The Role of Bystanders* (Brill/Nijhoff, Leiden/Boston). He has written moreover in books on *Human Rights Violations: A Threat to International Peace and Security* (1998), *The Role of the Bystanders in Human Rights Violations* (2000), *Human Rights in the Foreign Policy of the Netherlands* (2002), *Srebrenica and restitution to returning Jews after the Holocaust in the Netherlands* (2004), *The relationship between the increasing Palestinian-Israeli conflict and the deterioration of the rights of the child* (2006).

John Hagan is John D. MacArthur Professor of Sociology and Law at Northwestern University and Co-Director of the Center on Law and Globalization at the American Bar Foundation in Chicago. He is the recent author of *Justice in the Balkans: Prosecuting War Crimes at The Hague Tribunal* (University of Chicago Press, 2003) and *Northern Passage: American Vietnam War Resisters in Canada* (Harvard University Press, 2001), which received the Albert J. Reiss Distinguished Scholar Award. He recently co-authored with Alberto Palloni *Death in Darfur* in Science (September, 2006).

Roelof H. Haveman is the vice-dean in charge of academic affairs and research of the ILPD/Institute of Legal Practice and Development in Rwanda. He has lived and worked in Rwanda since 2005, initially managing a project supporting two law faculties in raising the quality of legal education. Since its establishment in 2002 and until 2005, Roelof Haveman was the founding programme-director of the *Grotius Centre for International Legal Studies* at Leiden University's Campus in The Hague, the Netherlands. Until the summer of 2005 he has been an associate professor of (international) criminal law and criminal procedure at Leiden

University and fellow of the E.M. Meijers Institute of Legal Studies of the Faculty of Law, Leiden University. In 1998 he defended his PhD-dissertation on *Conditions for Criminalizing Trafficking in Women* (Utrecht University). Over the past 20 years he has published many articles and a number of books on gender-related crimes, trafficking in persons and prostitution, the principle of legality and supranational criminal law. He is an expert on international and supranational criminal law and criminal procedure; his scholarship currently concentrates on the law of the ICTY, ICTR and ICC, covering such topics as Rwandan *gacaca*, prosecutorial discretion, gender crimes, legality, evidence, fair trial, comparative criminal law and the sui generis character of the supranational penal system. He is the editor-in-chief of the series: *Supranational Criminal Law, Capita Selecta*, Intersentia, Antwerp. Roelof Haveman participates in many teaching and training activities for scholars and practitioners in the field of supranational criminal law (defence lawyers, diplomats and others), in Africa, Europe and North America.

Martha K. Huggins (Tulane University, Department of Sociology, Newcomb Hall, 220, New Orleans, LA 70116 [mhuggins@tulane.edu]) is Charles A. and Leo M. Favrot Professor of Human Relations at Tulane University. Author of over 30 articles and six books about State violence, including torture, Huggins has won two national prizes for each of two of her books: *Political Policing* (Duke University, 1998) and *Violence Workers* (University of California Press, 2002 [with Philip Zimbardo and Mika Haritos-Fatouros]). Huggins is currently involved in two research projects: Studying Sao Paulo, Brazil's largest gang – from street '*larangas*' to money laundering businesses and to banking institutions – and research on police responses to 'physical' and 'socially-defined' emergencies in Sao Paulo, Brazil and New Orleans, Louisiana.

Wim Huisman is an associate professor of criminology and vice-dean of the Faculty of Law of the VU University of Amsterdam. His main fields of study are organisational crime and regulatory enforcement. He has published several books and articles on corporate crime in the Netherlands, governmental deviance, forensic accountancy, regulatory compliance and regulation of business. Currently, Wim Huisman is conducting a research project on corporate complicity in committing international crimes. Huisman is also an editor of the Dutch Journal of Criminology.

David Kauzlarich, Ph.D., is Associate Professor and Chair of the Department of Sociology and Criminal Justice Studies at Southern Illinois University Edwardsville. He has published several books and articles in the areas of State crime, State-corporate crime, international law and the victimology of elite crime.

Christopher W. Mullins is an Assistant Professor of criminal justice at the University of Southern Illinois. His research focuses on violence, especially interconnections between street culture, gender and street violence, and violence by nation-states and paramilitary groups. His work has appeared in *Criminology*, *The British Journal of Criminology*, *The Australian and New Zealand Journal of Criminology*, *Critical Criminology* and *Criminal Justice Review*, and several edited research volumes. He is the author of *Holding Your Square: Masculinities, Streetlife and Violence*, with Willan Press, *The International Criminal Court: Symbolic Gestures and the Generation of Global Social Control*, with Lexington Books and *Blood, Power and Bedlam: Crimes of the State in Post-Colonial Africa* forthcoming from Peter Lang.

Stephan Parmentier (1960) studied law (Lic., 1983; Ph.D., 1997), political science (Cand., 1982) and sociology (Lic., 1987) at the K.U.Leuven (Belgium), and sociology and conflict resolution (M.A.,1987) at the Humphrey Institute for Public Affairs of the University of Minnesota-Twin Cities (U.S.A.). He currently teaches sociology of crime, law and human rights at the Faculty of Law of the K.U.Leuven, and serves as the Chairperson of the Department of Criminal Law and Criminology. Stephan Parmentier has been a visiting professor at the International Institute for Sociology of Law in Oñati (Spain), and a visiting scholar at the University of Stellenbosch, the University of Oxford and the University of New South Wales (Sydney). He was the editor-in-chief of the Flemish Yearbook on Human Rights between 1998 and 2003, and has served as an advisor to the European Committee for the Prevention of Torture, the Belgian Minister of the Interior, the King Baudouin Foundation and Amnesty International. His research interests include political crimes, transitional justice and human rights, and the administration of criminal justice. Between 1999 and 2002, he served as the vice-chairman of the Flemish section of Amnesty International.

Dawn L. Rothe is an Assistant Professor of Criminology at old Dominion University. She is the author of over nearly three dozen articles and book chapters as well as two co-authored books: *Symbolic Gestures and the Generation of Global Social Control: The International Criminal Court* and *Power* (2006); and *Bedlam, and Bloodshed: State Crime in Africa* (2008) and is active in several national and international professional organisations.

Alette Smeulers is associate professor at the Department of Criminal Law and Criminology of the VU University Amsterdam. Her research focuses on the criminology of international crimes and more in particular on the perpetrators thereof. She is the initiator and coordinator of the Amsterdam Centre for Interdisciplinary Research on International Crimes (ACIC) which was established at the VU University Amsterdam (www.rechten.vu.nl/ACIC) in December 2007. She is one of the initiators of the scientific platform on supranational criminology and launched the website of this international research network in August 2005: www.supranationalcriminology.org and is chief editor of the newsletter of the platform. In 2005 she was awarded a VENI Scholarship by the Netherlands Science Organisation (NWO) for a post-doctoral research project entitled a criminological approach to individual criminal responsibility for international crimes.

Theo van Boven is honorary professor of public international law, University of Maastricht (the Netherlands). In earlier years he carried out a series of functions in relation to the United Nations. Thus, he served as the Netherlands representative on the UN Commission on Human Rights, he was the Director of Human Rights of the United Nations, he was the Special Rapporteur on the right to reparation for victims of gross violations of human rights, he was a member of the UN Committee on the Elimination of Racial Discrimination (CERD) and more recently he was the UN Special Rapporteur on Torture. Theo van Boven was also the first Registrar of the UN Criminal Tribunal for the Former Yugoslavia. He holds honorary doctorats of the Catholic University of Louvain-la Neuve (Belgium), the Erasmus University of Rotterdam (the Netherlands) and the University of New York at Buffalo (United States). He was a holder of the Cleveringa Chair at the University of Leiden (the Netherlands). Theo van Boven has written extensively on issues relating to international human rights law and international humanitarian law.

Kris Vanspauwen is a researcher at the Leuven Institute for Criminology, Catholic University of Leuven. He holds a Candidate (1999) and Licentiate Degree (2001) in Criminology from the Catholic University of Leuven. He has studied at the University of Regina (2000–1) and obtained an accredited training in conflict resolution from the Justice Department of Saskatchewan (2000). He is currently working as a victim-offender mediator at Suggnome, the Forum for Victim-Offender Mediation and Restorative Justice in Flanders. As of 2003 he was the chief researcher in a four-year project funded by the Research Foundation – Flanders on mass victimisation and restorative justice, with a case study in South Africa. In the framework of this project he has been visiting the School of Government, University of Western Cape (2003), the Department of Social Work and Criminology, University of Pretoria (2004) and the Institute for Criminology, University of Cape Town (2005). He has published on restorative justice and post-conflict justice. His latest publication will be the forthcoming co-edited reader *Restoring Justice after Large-scale Violent Conflicts. Kosovo, DR Congo and the Israeli-Palestinian case*, published by Willan.

Elmar G.M. Weitekamp studied Social Work at the Fachhochschule Niederrhein in Mönchengladbach, Germany and received his Diploma (M:S:W) in 1980. After working for a short period of time as a Juvenile Court Aid in Mönchengladbach he studied Criminology at the University of Pennsilvania in Philadelphia, USA where he received his M.A.in Criminology in 1982 and his Ph.D. in Criminology for the Graduate Group of Managerial Sciences and Applied Economics in 1989. He was a lecturer at the University of Pennsylvania before he started as a Senior Research Associate at the University of Tuebingen, Germany. He was a visiting professor at the University of Melbourne. He is currently a special guest professor of Criminology, Victimology and Restorative Justice at the University of Leuven, Belgium; Distinguished Adjunct Professor of Sociology at the Central China Normal University in Wuhan, the People's Republic of China and Senior Research Associate at the Institute of Criminology at the University of Tuebingen, Germany. He is responsible together with Professor Gordon Bazemore (Florida Atlantic University) for the International Network for Research on Restorative Justice for Juveniles and serves as the coordinator for the Eurogang Research Group. He is the organiser and a co-director of the annual Postgraduate Course in Victimology, Victim Assistance and Criminal Justice in Dubrovnik, Croatia. He was the co-chair together with Professor Parmentier (K.U.Leuven) of the Europe-Canada Exchange Programme on Social Justice and Human Rights in an area of Globalisation. He received in 2006 the Gerhard O.W. Mueller Award for Outstanding Contributions to International Criminal Justice by the International Section of the Academy of Criminal Justice Sciences. His research interests include Social and Justice Services for Young people in Transition; Gangs; Chronic and Habitual Offenders in Longitudinal Perspective, Youth and Criminal Justice Policy, Victimology and Mass Victimisations of Human Rights and Restorative Justice.

Michael Welch is a Professor in the Criminal Justice Program at Rutgers University, New Brunswick, New Jersey (USA). He is author of several books including *Scapegoats of September 11th: Hate Crimes and State Crimes in the War on Terror* (Rutgers University Press, 2006) and currently completing a book *Crimes of Power: Responses to Terror and the Culture of Impunity*. In 2006–2007 and 2005, Welch was a Visiting Fellow at the Centre for the Study of Human Rights at the London School of Economics. His website is www. professormichaelwelch.com and email is retrowelch@aol.com.